The Psychosomatic Approach:
Contemporary Practice of
Whole-person Care

The Psychosomatic Approach:
Contemporary Practice of Whole-person Care

Edited by

Margaret J. Christie

Royal Holloway and Bedford New College
University of London

and

Peter G. Mellett

Horton Hospital, Epsom, Surrey

JOHN WILEY & SONS LIMITED

Chichester · New York · Brisbane · Toronto · Singapore

Library of Congress Cataloging-in-Publication Data:
Main entry under title:

The Psychosomatic approach: contemporary practice
of whole-person care.
    Includes index.
    1. Medicine and psychology.   2. Holistic medicine.
    I. Christie, Margaret J.   II. Mellett, Peter G.
    [DNLM: 1. Holistic Health.   2. Psychophysiology.
    3. Psychosomatic Medicine.   WM 90 P9724]
    R726.5.P796   1986   616.08   85-15554

ISBN 0 471 90370 1

British Library Cataloguing in Publication Data:

The Psychosomatic approach: contemporary practice
of whole-person care.
    1. Medicine, Psychosomatic
    I. Christie, Margaret J.   II. Mellett, Peter
    616.08   RC49

ISBN 0 471 90370 1

Printed and Bound in Great Britain

CONTRIBUTORS

MARK R. BAKER

Bradford Health Authority, 109 Duckworth Lane, Bradford BD9 6RL, West Yorkshire, UK
and
Clinical Epidemiology Research Unit, University of Bradford, UK

RUTH BERKOWITZ

MRC Social Psychiatry Unit, Friern Hospital, Friern Barnet Road, London N11 3DP, UK

M. RÖÖSHMIÈ BHAGAT

Department of Clinical Psychology, Airedale Health Authority, Airedale General Hospital, Keighley, West Yorkshire, BD 20 6TD, UK
and
Postgraduate School of Studies in Psychology, University of Bradford, UK

SANDRA A. BIRTCHNELL

Academic Department of Psychiatry, Jenner Wing, St George's Hospital Medical School, Granmer Terrace, Tooting, London SW17 0RE, UK

JOHN E. BLUNDELL

Biopsychology Group, Department of Psychology, University of Leeds, UK

MARGARET J. CHRISTIE

Royal Holloway and Bedford New College, Egham Hill, Egham, Surrey TW20 0EX, UK
and
Applied Psychobiology Research Unit, University of Bradford, UK

SUE M. COPSTICK

Department of Psychology, North East London Polytechnic, Romford Road, West Ham, London E15 4LZ, UK

MICHAEL J. F. COURTENAY

Department of General Practice, St Thomas' Hospital Medical School, London SE1 7EH, UK

HUGH DUDLEY   *Academic Surgical Unit, St Mary's Hospital*
                      Medical School, London W2 1NY, UK

ALAN E. H. EMERY   *Medical School, The University of Edinburgh,*
                      Teviot Place, Edinburgh EH8 9AG, UK

MEYER FRIEDMAN   *Harold Brunn Institute, Mount Zion Hospital*
                      and Medical Center, San Francisco, USA

ANDREW J. HILL   *Biopsychology   Group,   Department   of*
                      Psychology, University of Leeds, UK

J. HUBERT LACEY   *Academic Department of Psychiatry, Jenner*
                      Wing, St George's Hospital Medical School,
                      Cranmer Terrace, Tooting, London SW17
                      0RE, UK

JULIAN LEFF   *MRC Social Psychiatry Unit, Friern Hospital,*
                      Friern Barnet Road, London N11 3DP, UK

ANTHONY P. LEWIS   *The Health Centre, Codriggy, Hayle, Cornwall,*
                      UK

ZBIGNIEW J. LIPOWSKI *The Clarke Institute of Psychiatry, University*
                      of Toronto, Toronto M5T 1R8, Canada

GRAHAM LUCAS   *Medical Division, Health and Safety Executive,*
                      Baynards House, 1 Chepstow Place, London
                      W2 4TF, UK
                      and
                      King's College Hospital, Denmark Hill,
                      London SE5 9RS, UK

COLIN MACKAY   *Medical Division, Health and Safety Executive,*
                      Magdalen House, Stanley Precinct, Bootle L20
                      3QZ, Merseyside, UK

PETER G. MELLETT   *Horton Hospital, Epsom, Surrey, UK*

NORMAN MORRIS   *Department of Obstetrics and Gynaecology,*
                      Charing Cross Medical School Department of
                      Obstetrics, West London Hospital, London
                      W6, UK

DAVID A. MRAZEK — *Department of Child Psychiatry and Pediatrics, School of Medicine, University of Colorado, USA*
and
Pediatric Psychiatry Unit, National Jewish Hospital and Research Centre, Colorado, USA

SHIRLEY PEARCE — *Department of Psychology, University College London, Gower Street, London WC1E 6BT, UK*

LYNDA H. POWELL — *Department of Epidemiology and Public Health, School of Medicine, Yale University, USA*

ROBERT G. PRIEST — *Academic Department of Psychiatry, St Mary's Hospital Medical School, Praed Street, London W2 1NY, UK*

IAN M. PULLEN — *Andrew Duncan Clinic, Royal Edinburgh Hospital, Morningside Terrace, Edinburgh EH10 5HF, UK*

CICELY SAUNDERS — *St Christopher's Hospice, 51–53 Lawrie Park Road, Sydenham, London SE26 6DZ, UK*

RICHARD W. SHILLITOE — *Department of Clinical Psychology, Airedale Health Authority, Airedale General Hospital, Keighley, West Yorkshire, BD20 6TD, UK*
and
Undergraduate School of Studies in Psychology, University of Bradford, UK

ANDREW STEPTOE — *Department of Psychology, St George's Hospital Medical School, Jenner Wing, Cranmer Terrace, Tooting, London SW17, UK*

BASIL A. STOLL — *Department of Oncology, St Thomas' Hospital, London SE1 7EH, UK*
and
Royal Free Hospital, Pond Street, London, NW3 2QG, UK

ANNE T. STOTTER — *Academic Surgical Unit, St Mary's Hospital Medical School, London W2 1NY, UK*

KATHY E. TAYLOR   *Department of Psychology, North East London Polytechnic, Romford Road, West Ham, London E15 4LZ, UK*

CONTENTS

PREFACE

This volume complements our earlier book *Foundations of Psychosomatics* which was published in 1981. We hope that readers may be encouraged to look at the earlier material alongside the chapters of this second selection from contemporary psychosomatics.

Contemporary psychosomatics has been described as 'an inseparable blend of psychophysiology and the holistic approach'. This volume of selected essays reflects the latter aspect while the earlier book focused on the psychobiological foundations of psychosomatics. Contributions to the present volume reflect each author's individual approach to whole-person care, in such medical specialties as obstetrics, surgery, general practice, etc. Most of the authors have university affiliations in North America or the UK, and are actively involved in teaching and research, having links with the behavioural and life sciences. The readership is envisaged as being in medical and paramedical fields, clinical psychology and health science, while authors have been chosen for their ability to communicate across disciplinary and specialty boundaries.

Both books have been published by John Wiley & Sons, and Michael Coombs has been associated with their preparation since the late 1970s. Wendy Hudlass also has had a major role in facilitating their production: we have enjoyed significant amounts of pleasant and productive interaction!

We are grateful for the secretarial assistance which was provided by Louise Rhodes in the first phase of preparation, while Catrina Ure and Christine Hibbert coped cheerfully with the demands of the final stages. Funding for Christine's activities as secretary of an Applied Psychobiology Research Unit was provided by Eli Lilly & Company, whose support of the unit's activities is greatly appreciated.

Our thanks are due to all of these and to our authors who, despite the demands of their busy lives, found time to write for us. We have enjoyed and learnt from their chapters: we hope that our readers will also.

Margaret J. Christie
Peter G. Mellett

SECTION 1

Contemporary Psychosomatics

The Psychosomatic Approach: Contemporary Practice
  of Whole-person Care
Edited by M. J. Christie and P. G. Mellett
© 1986 John Wiley & Sons Ltd

1

BUILDING ON PSYCHOSOMATIC FOUNDATIONS: COMMUNICATION AND THE HOLISTIC CONCEPTION IN CLINICAL PRACTICE

MARGARET J. CHRISTIE

Royal Holloway and Bedford New College, University of London, UK
and
Applied Psychobiology Research Unit, University of Bradford, UK

AIMS AND INTENTIONS

This is the second of two complementary volumes which were planned a decade ago and originated from ideas generated during the London Conferences of the Society for Psychosomatic Research. The opening chapter (Christie, 1981a) of our first book (Christie and Mellett, 1981) outlined the development of these volumes and reviewed the contents of the first one, which had as its theme the *scientific foundations of psychosomatics*. Its authors had proven ability to communicate across disciplinary boundaries and it was hoped that their contributions would facilitate the '. . . interactions of epidemiologists, neurologists, psychologists, sociologists . . . with representatives of psychiatry and general medicine'. Such interactions were a feature of the Psychosomatic Conferences and subsequent reviewers of the 'foundations' book seemed to suggest that interdisciplinary interaction had been successfully achieved in its pages. Further, some of our reviewers encouraged us to plan this second volume, which is similarly designed to communicate across boundaries, but with the theme of the *psychosomatic approach in medical practice*. This second volume attempts to respond to our reviewers' invitation. We have again selected authors with the capacity to communicate, and with the ability to provide material which reflects their own experience of 'whole-person care'—their own interpretation of the psychosomatic approach in medical practice.

The decade between our early planning and the present volume has been one in which several terms additional to 'psychosomatic' have been fashioned as descriptions of the attempt to develop a holistic approach in medicine. Labels such as 'behavioural medicine' (Schwartz and Weiss, 1978) and 'health psychology' (Krantz, Grunberg and Baum, 1985) serve to emphasize the contribution of behavioural science to the holistic approach. Krantz, Grunberg and Baum (1985), for example, describe behavioural medicine as an 'interdisciplinary field bringing together biomedical and behavioural knowledge relevant to health and disease' while 'health psychology refers to psychology's role in this domain'.

Our own preference is for Lipowski's (1976) description of the holistic approach in terms of a tripartite endeavour:

> — a science of the relations between biological, psychological and social variables as they pertain to human health and disease
> — an approach to the practice of medicine that advocates the inclusion of psychosocial factors in the study, prevention, diagnosis and management of all disease
> — clinical activities at the interface of medicine and the behavioural sciences.

Most of this volume's material is concerned with the second and third aspects of psychosomatic endeavour, while the earlier book offered material from the first, from the scientific foundations of psychosomatics. Contributors to both volumes have university affiliations and are concerned with the education of those who, in their various and complementary ways, will be responsible for the future practice of whole-person care. We envisage a readership in medical and paramedical contexts, and as some may feel more comfortable with the label 'behavioural medicine' an exploration of relations between this and 'psychosomatic' may be helpful at this point.

THE TERM 'PSYCHOSOMATIC'

One reviewer of the 'foundations' volume (Philips, 1982) wrote:

> The growth of behavioural medicine has extended the scope and preoccupation of psychosomatics, but it has also undermined its previous significance. All contemporary medical problems are in one sense psychosomatic. Consequently there is no further purpose in describing a narrow set of disorders as 'psychosomatic'. Perhaps the spirit of this change, acknowledged by the editors in their eclectic selection of papers, should also be demonstrated in the title. *There seems no further use in retaining the term 'psychosomatic'.* (Emphasis added.)

The term certainly does generate ambiguity and controversy, as Chapter 2, by Lipowski, indicates. He also argues, however, that the term is deeply entrenched and resists attempts at elimination. This being so, one must live with, but obviously must define, psychosomatic.

Chapter 2 offers as a definition '. . . a term referring or related to the inseparability and interdependence of psychosocial and biological (physiological, somatic) aspects of humankind', and Lipowski expands on this in his review. Looking back at the past two decades he sees psychosomatic endeavour as 'an inseparable blend of psychophysiology and the holistic approach'. He also envisages behavioural medicine as reflecting, in part, those 'clinical activities at the interface of medicine and the behavioural sciences' which were noted on page 4.

Returning to Philips, however, one senses another source of ambiguity and controversy—in the term 'behavioural medicine'. Clarification of this is invited and seems appropriate at this point.

BEHAVIOURAL MEDICINE

A recent editorial review (Eiser, 1983), written from within the field of behavioural medicine, brings to our notice several of the important issues addressed by subsequent chapters of the present volume. Eiser notes, for example, the illness caused by overeating—which has been examined in the chapters by Blundell and Hill and by Lacey and Birtchnell. Baker's forthright analysis of governmental response to the effects of smoking on the public's health resonates with Eiser's view that an urgent priority 'seems to be to understand the wide variety of social, economic and political factors that create and even legitimate an environment in which smoking is widespread, as well as understanding the personal and interpersonal factors that predict differential responses to such environmental factors'. Eiser is concerned about the threats to health associated with industrial environments; similar concern has been recently expressed from within psychosomatics (Christie and Cullen, 1983) and is reflected in the present volume's chapter from Mackay and Lucas. Further, the issue of medical technology in obstetrics, which Eiser raises, is addressed by Morris and his colleagues in Chapter 4, while the concern of Eiser that medical and paramedical staff 'improve their own behaviour, in such contexts as communicating with patients', is met with contributions from London medical school departments of general practice and surgery in Chapters 13 and 17, by Courtenay and by Stotter and Dudley respectively.

So 'psychosomatics', as defined by Lipowski, might be 'behavioural medicine' as envisaged by Eiser (1983), but we should attempt a historical and semantic inquiry into the latter and lay the results of this alongside that offered on behalf of psychosomatics in our second chapter.

What is behavioural medicine?

Eiser's (1983) article alerts us to the possibility the 'confusion nowadays about the subject matter and scope of psychosomatic medicine' (Lipowski, 1977) is matched in behavioural medicine by 'an unresolved debate over how the field is to be defined'. He offers a brief description of its development, but a more comprehensive account can be found in Gentry (1982), who reviews its short history and attempts 'to eliminate some of the confusion that has already arisen with respect to this newly emerging concept'.

Gentry views 1973 as the year which saw the first public use of the term 'behavioural medicine', by Birk (1973). Given that (according to Weiner (1986) citing Margetts (1954)) the first public use of the term 'psycho-somatic' was in 1818, one can only marvel that in little more than a decade this North American endeavour has managed to generate semantic confusion matching that which developed from European origins, but took nearly 140 years to do so! Birk's (1973) view of behavioural medicine was of an application of 'behaviourism' to medicine, perhaps more familiar as it is reflected in the biofeedback techniques described by McCroskery and Engel (1981) in our earlier volume. Gentry (1982) associates with Birk's view of behavioural medicine the broader one of Pomerleau and Brady (1979) which includes behaviour modification for the treatment of physical disease of physiological dysfunction, as exemplified by some aspects of Steptoe's chapter with its account of psychophysiological contributions to the understanding and management of essential hypertension.

Gentry's description of behavioural medicine, however, includes aspects of two viewpoints in addition to the above: one exemplified by Asken (1979) and by Wright (1979) is, he suggests, limited to medical psychology and health education activities, while the other appears to be inclusive of 'all persons and disciplines which might ultimately shed some light on the complexities of health and disease in humans, regardless of whether one was interested primarily in diagnostic or therapeutic issues'. This all-inclusive view of behavioural medicine was presented in the definition of Schwartz and Weiss (1978) which emerged as a revised statement after a conference sponsored by Yale University in 1977. Gentry (1982) quotes Weiss's (1979) view that behavioural medicine is 'an idea whose time had to come' and emphasizes the 'integration of ideas and technologu'.

Returning now to Philips (1982) and her suggestion that the term 'psycho-somatic' has no further use, it would seem evident that substitution of 'behavioural medicine' is no solution. Nor, it can be argued, is there value in attempting to decide who pulled the rug from under whom—who undermined whose activities. Rather than waste time on these somewhat arid pursuits it is preferable to pursue what Leigh (1981), in a paper on behavioural medicine, called 'a comprehensive psychosomatic approach' and to opt for an exploration of commonality. We can follow paths from key words or phrases such as interdependence, psychophysiology, the 'integration of ideas and technology' and 'the complexities of health and disease in humans' in our pursuit of a comprehensive psychosomatic approach to whole-person care.

INTERDEPENDENCE, INTEGRATION AND INTERACTIONS

Our opening paragraph introduced the theme of interdisciplinary interaction and of the attempt to foster communication across boundaries. In an earlier decade Hebb (1958) warned of the demands and difficulties inherent in such an attempt, of the need to acquire at least a smattering of one's colleagues' languages and an understanding of their concepts. This was in the context of biological science, in the foundational region of psychosomatics, where one's major concern is for the *horizontal* integration of sciences basic to medicine, for the crossing of disciplinary boundaries and the attenuation of fragmentation. Even more demanding is an attempt at *vertical* integration, an attempt to perceive the contribution of foundational sciences to the development of the clinical skills needed for whole-person care. Lipowski presents his view that there is an inseparable blend of psychophysiology and the holistic approach in contempory psychosomatics. This vertical integration of foundational science and clinical skill may become clearer, however, after some account of contemporary psychophysiology.

Psychophysiology and psychosomatics

A dozen chapters in our first book included significant amounts of psychophysiological material, and one (Siddle and Trasler, 1981) included a brief orientation to psychophysiological measurements. Another swift summary is available in Christie (1983) together with some indication of introductory reading, while Christie, Little and Gordon (1980) review its use within biological psychiatry. Venables and Christie (1975) edited a collection of contributions from psychophysiological research—some of it foundational for psychosomatics—while Martin and Venables (1980) have edited a major overview of measurement techniques. From sources such as these one may discern that psychophysiology is an aspect of psychobiological endeavour concerned with relations between psychological, biological and behavioural phenomena. Moreover, its concern is with human rather than infra-human subjects, and in relation to this it has developed the wide range of non-invasive methods for intact subjects which are described in sources such as Martin and Venables (1980).

Another aspect of psychobiological activity is often designated as physiological psychology, and here the independent variable, manipulated in experimental work, is the biological. Thus brain lesioning or stimulation, drug injection and similar 'invasive' manipulations of the biological state are characteristic of physiological psychology. Psychophysiologists, however, in their experimental activities, typically manipulate the psychological and examine the effects on dependent variables which are physiological or behavioural. Examples of the latter activity were evident in our first volume: Dixon (1981) described changes in the electroencephalogram (EEG) following the visual presentation, at thresholds below the level of awareness, of emotionally arousing material; Carruthers (1981), with electrocardiogram (ECG) recording from subjects who watched filmed violence, reported slowing of the heart rate, despite the high level of sympathetic activity evidenced by increased catecholamine excretion; findings reported in a chapter by Cook *et al.* (1981) indicated the value of electrodermal recording in laboratory examination of physiological responses to an executive role.

Two of these psychophysiological indices—EEG and ECG—are familiar as everyday clinical tools. But their use within psychophysiology, where one is often examining individual differences within the normal range, demands more sophisticated refinement than is usually required to distinguish frank abnormality. The recording of electrodermal activity (EDA) is less familiar: introductory accounts of this are available in Christie (1976, 1981b) while more detailed material is offered in Venables and Christie (1973, 1980). In addition to electrophysiological techniques, such as those above, biochemical analyses of body fluids have been added to the psychophysiologists' battery of methods. A simplified schematic presentation of some psychophysiological indices and their interrelations can be found in Christie, Little and Gordon (1980), with a more complex view of these being available in Christie and Woodman (1980) which surveys the range of biochemical methods having particular relevance for psychophysiology.

These dependent variables of psychophysiology can reflect the consequences of variation in the associated independent variables—the psychological states of human subjects. Such psychological states can be roughly classed as affective and cognitive, as involving emotion and information processing. The latter aspect has, in recent years, assumed greater importance within academic psychophysiology, but earlier work was largely concerned with physiological correlates of emotional state. One example is the attempt to delineate specific patterns of physiological change accompanying the emotions of fear and anger. The early work of Ax (1953) and Funkenstein (1956) led to the suggestion that body fluid levels of noradrenaline are increased in angry, hostile, aggressive states while subsequent investigations of such subjects as Dutch adolescent males (Ekkers, 1975) and UK patients in a maximum security hospital (Woodman, Hinton and O'Neill, 1977, 1978a, 1978b; Woodman and Hinton, 1978) have maintained interest in the suggestion. It has, of course, obvious relevance for those concerned with cardiovascular disorder and psychosocial risk factors: the Type A Behaviour Pattern described in Chapter 9 includes a significant amount of aggressive hostility.

Thus affective states and the correlates of emotion are enduring themes in psychophysiology, as they are in psychosomatics. Psychophysiology, also, is characterized by a comprehensive approach—its development of holistic methods for assessment of physiological, psychological and behavioural phenomena offers scope for work in the scientific foundations of psychosomatics. Some work on individual differences in vulnerability and stress, for example, is reviewed in Christie (1983) whose chapter includes a brief discussion, written by Bennett, of the need for multivariate statistics and for the 'multivariate thinking' which 'involves conceptualizing relationships between families or patterns of elements, and inhibiting the tendency to go back to thinking of elements in isolation'. A similar theme is offered by the psychophysiologist Johnson (1977) who alerts us to the need for a systems approach to psychosomatics, reminding us that in addition to appropriate data analysis one needs sophisticated monitoring of those complex feedback mechanisms which underpin a psychophysiological response. There is, he suggests, a need to 'take a multivariate look' at the total organism—at work, at play, in sleep—with 'special emphasis on how the living organism maintains itself at optimal levels in the midst of an onslaught of exogenous and endogenous disturbances'.

Thus one sees evidence of Lipowski's 'inseparable blend of psychophysiology and the holistic approach' in the *foundations* of contemporary psychosomatics, while its *clinical* aspects, reflected in the subsequent chapters of this volume, include evidence of contributions to the understanding and management of the two major Western medical problems of malignancy and cardiovascular disorder. Stoll in an objective appraisal examines the possible role for psychosomatic influences in the modulation of cancer growth activity: there would appear to be, at present, a particular need for such objectivity.

Much of the material in both our volumes might sit happily under the headings of either 'behavioural medicine' or 'psychosomatics': each adopts a holistic approach and each involves psychophysiological activity in its scientific foundations and its clinical practice. Both strive for horizontal and vertical integration of foundational science and clinical practice but, one might argue, the notion that behavioural medicine is in some way innovative requires further appraisal: *is* it, as Weiss (1979) suggests, 'and idea whose time had to come' or a unique 'integration of ideas and technology'? One might usefully look backward through the history of medical practice and medical education to examine these statements. Our backward view is limited to the UK, and even more constrained by its focus on London, its hospitals and its medical schools. Even so, they are sufficient to make the point that one might reasonably regard both psychosomatics and behavioural medicine, of the Yale 1977 variety, as contemporary reflections of an enduring attempt to integrate ideas and technology into medical education and practice, as is suggested below.

THE INTEGRATION OF IDEAS AND TECHNOLOGY

Before 1858

The Medical Act of 1858 was intended to bring about the formal registration of medical practitioners and the supervision of their education. As a result, the General Council of Medical Education and Registration of the United Kingdom was set up; an event which might also be seen as something which 'had to come'. The time scale for this achievement was the seven centuries between the establishment of St Bartholomew's hospital in 1123 (Medvei and Thornton, 1974) and the Act of 1858. St Bartholomew's and St Thomas' hospitals—the latter founded in 1173—were established by religious orders to care for the poor, homeless, needy. But in the eighteenth century five hospitals—Westminster, Guy's, St George's, the London and the Middlesex—were established within the space of less than three decades. Porter's (1982) excellent account of Georgian England gives us the flavour of this time—the growing wealth and the buoyant optimism. Porter sees the expansion of hospitals in this period as a reflection of the optimistic assumption that mankind could tackle, and solve, virtually any problem. At this time of expansion, medical activity included, as Porter (1985; in press) describes, physic practised as a liberal science, surgery as a craft, the apothecary keeping a shop, and a fringe of respectable and tolerated irregulars. Four medical schools were established within this period in association with Guy's, the London, St Bartholomew's and St Thomas' hospitals, but these reflected more of a cooperative entrepreneurial attempt to manage the financial arrangements of the consultants and their pupils than a purely educational endeavour. There was, however, the possibility of a 'holistic' approach towards patients: maybe there was little more than that on offer at the time as effective treatment! And despite the division between physician, surgeon and apothecary, according to Porter there was not the 'fragmentation' of medicine until the 1858 Act which, he states, 'marked the beginning of the modern medical profession'. Immediately before this, however, six more medical schools—University College, King's College, St George's, Charing Cross, Westminster and the Middlesex—had been established within the space of 6 years, together with hospitals at Charing Cross (1818), University College (1834) and King's College (1839). These developments reflect a response to the problems engendered by a population increase which, in the UK, had probably exceeded 50 per cent in the course of the eighteenth century, though, an increase in the number of hospitals was not necessarily beneficial, since the appalling risk of infection made them lethal institutions.

The Medical Act, however, followed several major developments in the sciences basic to medicine which eventually led to improvements in this situation: Jenner had established the practice of vaccination for smallpox, Gordon had attributed puerperal fever to contagion, Brettoneau had stimulated ideas about aetiological specificity in relation to diphtheria, Bassi had introduced sterilization by flame, Snow pinpointed the source of Soho cholera, Pasteur opened up the world of micro-organisms and fermentation—followed in 1867 by Lister's paper on antisepsis. Additionally, work on inhalation anaesthesia had culminated in Simpson's mid-century introduction of chloroform and dissection had been legalized by the Anatomy Act in 1832.

Thus there was in the nineteenth century a tremendous surge of scientific knowledge foundational for medicine, and what became the 'preclinical' courses of study were indeed pressed into integrating technological developments into ideas of clinical management.

1858–1968

The development of fragmentation and specialization within this period of significant scientific expansion, together with the mechanistic approach to patients and their management, is evident in sources such as those cited in the next chapter and the recent review of Weiner (1986). One must, however, bear in mind the fact that the holistic attitude in medicine—the psychosomatic approach to whole-person care—remained evident even then, as it has been since Plato. Weiner's (1986) review of 'a medicine of living persons' takes his reader through centuries of holistic attitude, and a relatively recent (Coplans, 1946) paper—a medical student's essay entitled 'The importance of psychological factors in organic disease' which won the Guy's Hospital Treasurer's Prize—serves to indicate its existence in the later years of this period. In 1957, the General Medical Council (GMC), as part of its enduring concern with the integration into medical education of appropriate foundational science, recommended that 'instruction should be given in the elements of normal psychology'. Then in 1967 the council recommended that 'the study of human structure and function should be combined with the study of human behaviour . . . the Council considers that instruction should be given in those aspects of the behavioural sciences which are relevant to the study of man as an organism adapting to his social and psychological no less than to his physical environment'. One can discern in statements such as these the encouragement of holistic attitudes and perhaps the hope that horizontal integration would develop in the teaching offered during the so-called preclinical years. The opportunity for psychology to have an integrating role was grasped in some of the London medical schools—particularly in the third phase of their development, from 1968 to the present day.

The Royal Commission on Medical Education: The Todd Report (1968)

Around 1968 one may find, in addition to the encouragement of integration, a growing awareness of the importance of psychological and social factors in health and disease. In our earlier volume Marmot (1981) reviewed the epidemiological evidence for cultural influences on the development of cardiovascular disorder, while Wadsworth and Ingham (1981) looked at psychosocial aspects of the early stages in which dysfunction becomes evident and what is regarded as 'health' then becomes viewed as 'illness'.

There was, additionally in this period, a growth of pressure groups concerned to 'humanize' the treatment of patients, and in the Todd Report one finds indications of all three aspects: integration, psychosocial factors, more sensitive awareness that patients are people. The report indicates, for example, the 'increasing interest in the circumstances in which patients live and work', the need for students to have 'an appreciation of the biological, environmental and personal factors which underlie structural disease and disturbances of function' and to 'be aware of the important influence which a patient's mental and emotional state may have on his physical well-being and practical abilities'. Todd found it necessary to state that medical students require to 'learn how to treat human beings in trouble' as well as reporting a need for human biology to be presented in much broader terms.

After the Todd Report there was, in London medical schools, a rapid expansion of the behavioural science teaching which had already been informally undertaken in some of them, and by the middle of the next decade the subject was taught and formally assessed in the first and second year professional examinations. Psychologists were appointed to develop the 'Psychology as Applied to Medicine' courses. These individuals tended to fall into two general classes: clinical psychologists (such as the author of an early chapter in our first book—Winefield, 1981) and psychobiologists such as Steptoe who has provided for this volume the review of psychophysiological contributions to the understanding and management of essential hypertension. Where psychobiologists were in post it probably facilitated the horizontal integration of foundational science teaching while clinical psychologists have, perhaps, contributed more to vertical integration.

If one turns from teaching to practice, as reflected in our authors' contributions, one sees the collaborative activities of psychologists in specialties such as obstetrics (Chapter 4), general practice (Chapter 13) and occupational health (Chapter 15), while other chapters review collaborative work in relation to obesity, coronary heart disease, oncology, the management of chronic pain and of schizophrenia. One would like to think that some at least of this collaborative activity is a consequence of the developments in medical education, evident in recent decades in the many parts of the world, which Winefield (1981) reviewed. There have been, as she notes, 'unprecedented efforts to provide formal training for medical students in the behavioural sciences'. For instance Weinman's introductory textbook (1986) gives an indication of his excellent teaching at Guy's, and there has been steady progress in many medical schools.

An anonymous reviewer of our first volume wrote in 1982 that 'the honeymoon period between behavioural science and the medical profession is over and it is up to the former to prove that they have something to add to the well established medical procedures and practice'. Our present volume's contributors suggest that there *is* something to add, to be integrated into contemporary practice, just as nineteenth-century developments in foundational science became integrated in subsequent decades. The anonymous reviewer also indicated the plethora of labels associated with the endeavour to develop an interface between the behavioural sciences and medicine—medical psychology, behavioural medicine, medical behavioural science and so on—bringing us full circle to the problems associated with the terms 'psychosomatic' and 'holistic' which Lipowski's chapter notes. It appears evident that the Todd report (1968) eschews both labels, yet all the while, in the report's consideration of undergraduate medical education, the language and concepts of whole-person care are used. Similarly, it is unfortunate, as Lipowski also indicates, that the term 'holistic' has been adopted by some enthusiasts for esoteric and largely unscientific approaches to what are viewed as health promoting practices. Other labels are in evidence within this present period of reappraisal, labels such as 'alternative', 'complementary', 'fringe' and so on. It has never been easy to generalize about such 'alternative' approaches—as Cooter (in press) suggests—and it may be useful at this point to examine the nature of some activities subsumed under these various titles in the UK, several of which are becoming integrated into traditional medical practice.

'Respectable and tolerated irregulars' in the 1980s

Porter (1985) has recently reviewed the history of alternative and complementary medicine. There was evident, he suggests, in the middle of the nineteenth century, a 'philosophy of holism' which declined in its later decades, but which has been revived in recent years: contemporary interest is centred on the evaluation and possible integration of several 'respectable and tolerated irregulars' such as osteopaths, homeopaths, chiropractors, etc., by the medical establishment. In the UK the Royal Society of Medicine has recently established a series of symposia which involve representatives from osteopathy, homeopathy and the like; the British Medical Association has a committee involved in the examination of such; there is a Research Council for Complementary Medicine, and the British Holistic Medical Association has been formed.

The Times has on a number of occasions in recent years (e.g. West and Inglis, 1983a, 1983b, 1983c, 1985) offered articles relating to various alternative and complementary therapies, but it is particularly unfortunate that the leader of 13 March 1985, while headed 'Holistic healing', discussed *alternatives* to 'conventional medicine'.

The subsequent chapters of this volume bear witness to the fact that one need not look *beyond* the medicine now being taught and practised to find holistic healing and holistic care. Mrazek's account of paediatric hospitalization, for example, offers a broad perspective and a comprehensive view while Priest's review of benzodiazepines includes an account of non-pharmaceutical paths to tranquillity. And holistic care is undoubtedly evident in the book's concluding pages: the hospice philosophy reflected in them takes account of body, mind and spirit, of the needs of patient, family and the care-givers.

There is surely a clear reflection of Lipowski's 'inseparability and interdependence of psychosocial and biological aspects' in the following chapters. We trust that they provide interest, and even inform some who may be unaware of the whole-person care provided by those such as our authors. Whatever label is chosen to describe holistic care and whatever term is used to designate the incorporation of—and benefit from—advances in its scientific foundations, this care remains an enduring feature of much medical practice.

Adequate communication is vital for optimal interaction, not least within the field of medicine; our authors have contributed significantly toward improved communication of the message from contemporary psychosomatics.

ACKNOWLEDGEMENT

I am grateful to David Christie, Mathijs Muijen and Mark Pitkethly who read and commented helpfully on early versions of this chapter.

REFERENCES

Anonymous (1982). Review. *Behavioural Psychotherapy*, **10**, 370–371.

Asken, M. J. (1979). Medical psychology: toward definition, clarification and organization. *Professional Psychology*, **10**, 66–73.

Ax, A. (1953). The physiological differentiation between fear and anger in humans. *Psychosomatic Medicine*, **5**, 433–442.

Birk, L. (ed.) (1973). *Biofeedback: Behavioral Medicine*. New York: Grune & Stratton.

Carruthers, M. (1981). 'Field studies': emotion and β-blockade. In M. J. Christie and P. G. Mellett (eds), *Foundations of Psychosomatics*. Chichester: Wiley.

Christie, M. J. (1976). Electrodermal activity. In O. W. Hill (ed.), *Modern Trends in Psychosomatic Medicine*. London: Butterworths.

Christie, M. J. (1981a). Foundations of psychosomatics. In M. J. Christie and P. G. Mellett (eds), *Foundations of Psychosomatics*. Chichester: Wiley.

Christie, M. J. (1981b). Electrodermal activity in the 1980's: a review. *Journal of the Royal Society of Medicine*, **74**, 616–622.

Christie, M. J. (1983). Contemporary psychosomatics. In J. Nicholson and B. Foss (eds), *Psychology Survey*, no. 4. Leicester: British Psychological Society.

Christie, M. J., and Cullen, J. H. (1983). European industrial psychosomatics: recent perspectives. In A. J. Krakowski and C. P. Kimball (eds), *Psychosomatic Medicine*. New York: Plenum.

Christie, M. J., Little, B. C., and Gordon, A. M. (1980). Psychophysiology of depressive state. In H. M. Van Praag, H. M. Lader, O. J. Rafaelsen and J. Sachar (eds), *Handbook of Biological Psychiatry*, vol. III: *Brain Mechanisms and Abnormal Behavior*. New York: Dekker.

Christie, M. J., and Mellett, P. G. (eds) (1981). *Foundations of Psychosomatics*. Chichester: Wiley.

Christie, M. J., and Woodman, D. D. (1980). Biochemical methods. In I. Martin and P. H. Venables (eds), *Psychophysiological Techniques*. London: Wiley.

Cook, E., Christie, M. J., Gartshore, S., Stern, R. M., and Venables, P. H. (1981). After the 'Executive Monkey'. In M. J. Christie and P. G. Mellett (eds), *Foundations of Psychosomatics*. Chichester: Wiley.

Cooter, R. (1985). On interpreting the fringe. In R. Cooter (ed.), *Alternatives: Essays in the Social History of Irregular Medicine*. London: Macmillan.

Coplans, M. P. (1946). The importance of psychological factors in organic disease. *Guy's Hospital Gazette*, 325–327.

Dixon, N. F. (1981). Psychosomatic disorder: a special case of subliminal perception. In M. J. Christie and P. G. Mellett (eds), *Foundations of Psychosomatics*. Chichester: Wiley.

Eiser, R. J. (1983). Behavioural medicine: What kind of medicine? What kind of behaviour? *Journal of the Royal Society of Medicine*, **76**, 629–632.

Ekkers, C. L. (1975). Catecholamine excretion, conscience function and aggressive behaviour. *Biological Psychology*, **3**, 15–30.

Funkenstein, D. H. (1956). Norepinephrine-like and epinephrine-like substances in relation to human behaviour. *Journal of Nervous and Mental Diseases*, **124**, 58–65.

Gentry, W. D. (1982). What is behavioural medicine? In J. R. Eiser (ed.), *Social Psychology and Behavioural Medicine*. Chichester: Wiley.

Hebb, D. O. (1958). Alice in Wonderland, or psychology among the biological sciences. In H. F. Harlow and C. N. Woolsey (eds), *Biological and Biochemical Base of Behaviour*. Madison: University of Wisconsin Press.

Johnson, L. C. (1977). Psychophysiological research: aims and methods. In Z. J. Lipowski, D. R. Lipsitt and P. C. Whybrow (eds), *Psychosomatic Medicine: Current Trends and Clinical Applications*. New York: Oxford University Press.

Krantz, D. S., Grunberg, N. E., and Baum, A. (1985). Health psychology. *Annual Review of Psychology*, **36**, 349–383.

Leigh, H. (1981). Behavioral medicine: toward a comprehensive psychosomatic approach. *Psychotherapy and Psychosomatics*, **36**, 151–158.

Lipowski, Z. J. (1976). Psychosomatic medicine: an overview. In O. W. Hill (ed.), *Modern Trends in Psychosomatic Medicine*, no. 3. London: Butterworths.

Lipowski, Z. J. (1977). Psychosomatic medicine: a science, movement, or point of view? In Z. J. Lipowski, D. R. Lipsitt and P. C. Whybrow (eds), *Psychosomatic Medicine: Current Trends and Clinical Applications*. New York: Oxford University Press.

McCroskery, J. H., and Engel, B. T. (1981). Biofeedback and emotional behaviour. In M. J. Christie and P. G. Mellett (eds), *Foundations of Psychosomatics*. Chichester: Wiley.

Margetts, E. L. (1954). Historical notes on psychosomatic medicine. In E. D. Wittkower and R. A. Cleghorn (eds), *Recent Developments in Psychosomatic Medicine*. Philadelphia: Lippincott.

Marmot, M. (1981). Culture and illness: epidemiological evidence. In M. J. Christie and P. G. Mellett (eds), *Foundations of Psychosomatics*. Chichester: Wiley.

Martin, I., and Venables, P. H. (eds) (1980). *Techniques in Psychophysiology*. Chichester: Wiley.

Medvei, V. C., and Thornton, J. (1974). *The Royal Hospital of Saint Bartholomew 1123–1973*. London: Royal Hospital of Saint Bartholomew.

Merrington, W. R. (1976). *University College Hospital and its Medical School: A History*. London: Heinemann.

Philips, C. (1982). Review. *Behaviour Research and Therapy*, **20**,

Pomerleau, O. F., and Brady, J. P. (1979). *Behavioural Medicine. Theory and Practice*. Baltimore, Md: Williams & Wilkins.

Porter, R. (1982). *English Society in the Eighteenth Century*. Harmondsworth, Middx: Penguin.

Porter, R. (1985b). Before the fringe. *History Today*.

Porter, R. (in press). Before the fringe. *History Today*.

Royal Commission on Medical Education (1968). 1965–68 Report. London: HMSO.

Schwartz, G. E., and Weiss, S. M. (1978). Behavioral medicine revisited: an amended definition. *Journal of Behaviural Medicine*, **1**, 249–252.

Siddle, D. A. T., and Trasler, G. B. (1981). The psychophysiology of psychopathic behaviour. In M. J. Christie and P. G. Mellett (eds), *Foundations of Psychosomatics*. Chichester: Wiley.

Times The, (1985). Holistic healing. 13 March leader.

Venables, P. H., and Christie, M. J. (1973). Mechanisms, instrumentation, recording techniques and quantification of responses. In W. F. Prokasy and D. C. Raskin (eds), *Electrodermal Activity in Psychological Research*. New York: Academic Press.

Venables, P. H., and Christie, M. J. (eds) (1975). *Research in Psychophysiology.* London: Wiley.

Venables, P. H., and Christie, M. J. (1980). Electrodermal activity. In I. Martin and P. H. Venables (eds), *Psychophysiological Techniques.* London: Wiley.

Wadsworth, M., and Ingham, J. (1981). How society defines sickness: illness behaviour and consultation. In M. J. Christie and P. G. Mellett (eds), *Foundations of Psychosomatics.* Chichester: Wiley.

Weiner, H. (1986). Psychosomatic medicine and the mind–body problem in psychiatry. In E. Wallace and J. Gach (eds), *Handbook of the History of Psychiatry.* New Haven, Conn.: Yale University Press.

Weinman, J. (1986). *An Outline of Psychology as Applied to Medicine,* 2nd ed. Bristol: Wright.

Weiss, S. M. (1979). Behavioral medicine: an idea. . . . In J. R. McNamara (ed.), *Behavioral Approaches to Medical Treatment.* Cambridge, Mass.: Ballinger.

West, R., and Inglis, B. (1983a). If the mind is fit, the body will cure itself. *The Times,* 8 August, p. 6.

West, R., and Inglis, B. (1983b). New path to the roots of illness. *The Times,* 9 August, p. 6.

West, R., and Inglis, B. (1983c). Time to shake the medicine. *The Times,* 10 August, p. 6.

West, R., and Inglis, B. (1985). Taking the alternative road to health. *The Times,* 13 March, p. 10.

Winefield, H. R. (1981). Behavioural science in the medical curriculum: why and how. In M. J. Christie and P. G. Mellett (eds), *Foundations of Psychosomatics.* Chichester: Wiley.

Woodman, D. D., and Hinton, J. W. (1978). Catecholamine balance during stress anticipation. *Journal of Psychosomatic Research,* **22,** 477–483.

Woodman, D. D., Hinton, J. W., and O'Neill, M. T. (1977). Abnormality of catecholamine balance relating to social deviance. *Perceptual and Motor Skills,* **45,** 493–494.

Woodman, D. D., Hinton, J. W., and O'Neill, M. T. (1978a). Plasma catecholamines, stress and aggression in maximum security patients. *Biological Psychology,* **6,** 147–154.

Woodman, D. D., Hinton, J. W., and O'Neill, M. T. (1978b). Cortisol secretion and stress in maximum security hospital patients. *Journal of Psychosomatic Research,* **22,** 133–136.

Wright, L. (1979). A comprehensive program for mental health and behavioral medicine in a large children's hospital. *Professional Psychology,* **10,** 458–466.

The Psychosomatic Approach: Contemporary Practice
of Whole-person Care
Edited by M. J. Christie and P. G. Mellett
© 1986 John Wiley & Sons Ltd

2

WHAT DOES THE WORD 'PSYCHOSOMATIC' REALLY MEAN? A HISTORICAL AND SEMANTIC INQUIRY

ZBIGNIEW J. LIPOWSKI

The Clarke Institute of Psychiatry, University of Toronto, Canada

INTRODUCTION

Students, colleagues and lay people have often asked me: 'What is psychosomatic medicine? What does the word "psychosomatic" really mean?' To try and answer these questions with reasonable clarity I have reviewed the literature and given the matter a good deal of thought. The literature, however, reveals a lack of consensus with regard to the meaning of these terms, and it actually addresses the issue infrequently. Journals and societies calling themselves 'psychosomatic' exist in various countries and are presumably based on the assumption that their professed field of interest is a distinct and clearly delimited one. Discussions with concerned colleagues reveal, however, that ambiguity and controversy persist, and that some individuals would gladly bury the word 'psychosomatic' altogether, and replace it by some other, hopefully less ambiguous, term such as 'biopsychosocial', for example. Yet, as a historian of psychosomatic medicine shrewdly observed years ago, even though the word 'psychosomatic' is unsatisfactory, it is 'so deeply entrenched in the literature that it will never be eradicated' (Margetts, 1950). Indeed, it has so far resisted all attempts to eliminate it. This being so, another attempt to trace the roots of, and to define, the terms in question is called for so as to provide a basis for a wider discussion.

Having proposed a definition of psychosomatic medicine in the past (Lipowski, 1968, 1982), I was challenged to return to this subject by a recently published account of the history of this field written by Ackerknecht (Ackerknecht, 1982), a medical historian. He argues that if one defines psychosomatic medicine in terms which convey the 'recognition of a partial, or sometimes total, *psychogenesis of disease*' (emphasis added), then its origins reach back to ancient Greece. Ackerknecht ends his article with a conclusion that 'the basic element of psychosomatic medicine represents a dialogue between doctor and patient, their cooperation. . . . The psychosomaticist seems above all to be the physician who specializes in listening to the patient . . . we may be glad to have retained a specialist of this type' (Ackerknecht, 1982, p. 23).

17

Thus, in the eyes of the historian just quoted, psychosomatic medicine constitutes an ill-defined area, one concerned with demonstrating psychogenesis of disease, and a medical specialty distinguished by listening to patients. If this view of the field is correct, then the contents of the current psychosomatic journals, for example, are largely irrelevant to its proper scope. If it is not, then a rebuttal and clarification are called for in order to put the matter straight and to avoid the spread of misleading conceptions. It appears that a disturbing gulf exists between a historian's conception of what psychosomatic medicine is about and the interpretation endorsed by most workers who are active in this field and identify themselves with it. This discrepancy may well have arisen because of the historical development of psychosomatic concepts and the coexistence of several connotations of the word 'psychosomatic' in the literature. In an attempt to clarify this issue I propose to review some of the representative dictionary definitions as well as the historical development and roots of the terms 'psychosomatic' and 'psychosomatic medicine'. I will also formulate a set of definitions which hopefully, will prove acceptable to the majority of the workers in this field.

DICTIONARY MEANING OF 'PSYCHOSOMATIC'

The *Oxford English Dictionary* lists the word 'psychosomatic' for the first time in a supplement published in 1982, and offers a set of definitions. It defines the adjective 'psychosomatic' as one 'involving or depending on both the mind and the body as mutually dependent entities' (Burchfield, 1982, p. 888). The term has been used to refer to the following: (1) *physical disorders*, those caused or aggravated by psychological factors, and, less often, to mental disorders caused or aggravated by physical factors; (2) the *branch of medicine* concerned with the mind–body relations; and (3) the *field of study*, one sometimes designated 'psychosomatics', concerned with the relationship between mind and body.

It is noteworthy that the above definitions highlight two distinct connotations of the word 'psychosomatic', viz. concern with *mind–body relationship* and the *psychogenesis* of physical disorders. By emphasizing the mind–body issue the dictionary gives the term 'psychosomatic' a strong philosophic stamp, one that workers in psychosomatic medicine have tried to stay away from, as I will show later on. Moreover, to speak of mind and body as 'entities' implies dualism and hence invites controversy. Psychosomatic writers have traditionally, if not always logically and consistently, affirmed their antidualistic stance and tended to opt for some form of monism, arguing that mind and body are one or are merely separate aspects of a person, or of the organism as a whole. Nevertheless, this connotation of the word 'psychosomatic' may be referred to as the *holistic* one, in the sense that it presupposes the inseparability of mind and body as well as their mutual dependence. Yet to state, as the dictionary does, that the chief concern and the object of study of psychosomatic medicine is the relationship between mind and body strikes me as a misleading assertion, because it is too abstract and too far removed from what workers in this field actually try to accomplish. Thus, the dictionary definitions highlight and compound the ambiguity of the word 'psychosomatic' (Hinsie and Campbell, 1960).

A representative psychiatric dictionary offers an even narrower and more contentious definition of the word 'psychosomatic' (Hinsie and Campbell, 1960). It states that the word may be used only in a 'methodological sense', to refer to 'a type of approach in the study and treatment of certain disturbances of body function' (p. 613). Furthermore, it deplores the tendency to use the word 'psychosomatic' to refer to a class of disorders whose causation is believed to implicate emotional factors, and thus to imply a dualism that does not really exist, since no disease is free from the influence of psychological factors. Such a criticism of this particular connotation and usage of the term has been voiced by many authors (Lipowski, 1968). An Expert Committee of the World Health Organization, for instance, has deplored the common use of the term 'psychosomatic disorders' as one reaffirming mind–body dichotomy and undermining a much-needed holistic approach to the practice of medicine (World Health Organization, 1964). The committee wisely recommended that efforts should be made to work out generally acceptable terms and definitions which would be useful for teaching and research.

One may conclude that representative dictionary definitions of the terms 'psychosomatic' and 'psychosomatic medicine' are unsatisfactory, since they fail to reflect adequately the connotations of these words contained in psychosomatic literature. The sources of this semantic confusion might become clearer as one traces the historical development of these terms.

HISTORY OF THE WORD 'PSYCHOSOMATIC'

Margetts (1950, 1954) is, to my knowledge, the only writer to make a serious effort to trace the historical development of the term 'psychosomatic'. He asserts that the word was first used in 1818 by the German psychiatrist Heinroth, in a rather cryptic sentence: 'As a general rule, the origin of insomnia is psycho-somatic, but it is possible that every phase of life can itself provide the complete reason for insomnia' (Margetts, 1950, p. 403). Margetts points out that Heinroth regarded the body and soul as one, but the quoted passage gives little indication of what he really implied by the word 'psychosomatic', one that appears to reflect a fashion, common in the German literature of the early nineteenth century, to use combined terms such as psycho-physical or somato-psychic (Margetts, 1950). That tendency was adopted by some English writers, such as the eminent psychiatrist Bucknill, who in 1857 argued that one could distinguish three theories of insanity, i.e. the somatic, the psychic and the somato-psychic (Bucknill, 1857). Bucknill went on to say: 'The psychosomaticists find in the liability of the cerebral instrument to disease, a reasonable basis for the irresponsibility of the insane'

(Bucknill, 1857, p. 15). Gray (1868–1869), editor of the *American Journal of Insanity*, misquoted Bucknill to say that one of his three proposed theories was 'psycho-somatic'. This may have been the first time when that term appeared in America. In the same article, Gray asserts: 'The reciprocal influence of body and mind is a fact constantly before the physician' (p. 155).

A curious early example of the use of the word 'psychosomatic' turns up unexpectedly in the novel *Hard Cash*, written in 1863 by a prolific English writer, Charles Reade (Reade, no date). The main theme of that novel is the abuse of psychiatric commitment in England for the purpose of getting rid of offensive relatives. A devious asylum doctor tries to persuade a father to commit his son by extolling the virtues of the asylum under his directorship, and promises to provide 'the nocturnal and diurnal attendance of a psycho-physical physician, who knows the psycho-somatic relation of body and mind . . .' (Reade, no date, p. 405).

Apart from the above scattered examples, the word 'psychosomatic' was used infrequently in the literature of the nineteenth century and prior to the 1930s (Margetts, 1954). It is absent from the unusually comprehensive *Dictionary of Psychological Medicine* edited by Tuke (1892) which lists only the term 'psychosomatiatria', one defined as 'a medicine for mind and body' (p. 1034). Nor does it appear in Tuke's (1884) classic compilation of works illustrating the influence of the mind on the body, first published in 1872, in which he uses related terms such as 'psychophysical phenomena' and 'psycho-physiology' (p. 455).

Felix Deutsch, in 1922, was probably the first author to introduce the term 'psychosomatic medicine' (Stokvis, 1959). The 1920s may be generally viewed as a period during which the ground was prepared for the emergence of psychosomatic medicine in the following decade. In 1925, a book was published in Vienna which presented philosophical arguments as well as clinical observations from several areas of medicine supporting the notion that medicine had neglected to consider the role of psychological factors in the aetiology of disease and in the treatment of patients (Schwarz, 1925). The several contributors, including Paul Schilder, cited the work of Gestalt psychologists, Freud, Pavlov, and Cannon to bolster their contention that the proper subject of medicine should be the organism as a structural and functional unity, one that includes the psyche. The publication of that comprehensive treatise paved the way for an encyclopaedic compilation of the relevant literature to appear 10 years later (Dunbar, 1935).

The heyday of the term 'psychosomatic' and the true beginning of psychosomatic medicine were both launched by the publication in 1935 of Dunbar's (1935) *Emotions and Bodily Changes: A Survey of Literature on Psychosomatic Interrelationships: 1910–1933*. Dunbar seemed to have some misgivings about her choice of the term 'psychosomatic interrelationships', which, she remarked, was 'inadequate to express the conviction that psyche and soma are . . . two aspects of a fundamental unity' (Dunbar, 1935, p. 427). She could not think of a better term, however, and her legacy is, for better or worse, still with us today. However one might regret Dunbar's choice of the word 'psychosomatic', which she helped to popularize, the appearance of her book marked the emergence of psychosomatic medicine as an *organized* field of scientific inquiry and a movement aimed at propagating a holistic approach to medical practice. Until then, psychosomatic conceptions had been sustained by conviction and clinical anecdotes, rather than based on systematic observations applying scientific methodology to demonstrate their empirical validity.

An event of singular importance for the development of psychosomatic conceptions and medicine was the appearance, in 1939, of the first issue of the journal *Psychosomatic Medicine*. It was inaugurated by an 'Introductory statement' (*Psychosomatic Medicine*, 1939), in which its editors tried to come to grips with the definition of the new field and offered the following: 'Its object is to study in their interrelation the psychological and physiological aspects of all normal and abnormal bodily functions and thus to integrate somatic therapy and psychotherapy' (p. 3). The editors took pains to spell out what psychosomatic medicine was *not*: '(1) equivalent with psychiatry; (2) restricted to any specific area of pathology; (3) a medical specialty; (4) concerned with the 'metaphysics' of the mind–body problem. On the positive side, they emphasized that the new field was (1) concerned with the psychological approach to general medicine and all of its subspecialties; (2) interested in the interrelationships between emotional life and all bodily processes; (3) based on the premise that there is no 'logical distinction' between mind and body; (4) involving research on correlation of psychological and physiological processes in man; and (5) both a special field and an integral part of every medical specialty.

In so far as the statement represents the views of the early leaders of psychosomatic medicine, it is in a sense authoritative, and since, to my knowledge, it has never been formally repealed, it presumably expresses the 'official' position of the current editors of *Psychosomatic Medicine*. For these reasons alone it deserves critical scrutiny. The proposed definition of the field rightly encompasses both its scientific and clinical aspects. The editors define the scope of psychosomatic medicine, and hence the object of its scientific interests, as the interrelation of psychological and physiological aspects of the functions of the body rather than of the person. Moreover, by stressing that psychosomatic medicine is distinct from psychiatry which, as they put it, is concerned with the 'diseased mind', they appear unwittingly to affirm mind–body dualism, a position which they explicitly disavow. By emphasizing the distinction between the two disciplines, the editors convey the impression that psychosomatic conceptions do not apply to psychiatry. This is an unfortunate implication, one that contradicts the holistic viewpoint and deepens the deplorable gap between medicine and psychiatry. Had the editors referred in their definition to the dual functions or aspects of the person rather than the body, they would have reaffirmed their otherwise implied holistic stance.

Another major flaw of the statement is the absence of any mention of the environmental, and especially the social, factors. Thus the impression is conveyed that psychosomatic medicine is concerned exclusively with psychophysiological phenomena occurring, as it were, in a social vacuum. This is a serious omission which may have resulted from a strong psychoanalytic orientation of some of the editors and their consequent preoccupation with intrapersonal rather than interpersonal issues. In view of that bias, it is remarkable that the statement makes no direct reference to the concept of psychogenesis, one that plays a prominent role in the writings of such psychosomatic pioneers and editors as Alexander (Alexander, 1950). That concept has attracted considerable criticism over the years and will not be missed.

The editors emphatically dissociate themselves from philosophical ('metaphysical') concerns, yet by asserting lack of logical distinction between mind and body they betray their distinct monistic, i.e. metaphysical, bias. It cannot be gainsaid that many psychosomatic writers have concerned themselves, explicitly or not, with the mind–body problem and have taken a strongly antidualistic position (Alexander, 1950). To deny this fact would be intellectually dishonest. One can, however, understand the reluctance of researchers and clinicians to define their area of interest in terms of highly abstract and perennially controversial philosophical concepts. Yet the latter lurk in the background of many psychosomatic theoretical statements and are often implicit in them. This may be the reason behind the *Oxford English Dictionary*'s definitions quoted earlier which put the emphasis squarely on the mind–body problem as the main concern of psychosomatic medicine. Historical roots of psychosomatic conceptions, to be discussed later, may help clarify this contentious issue.

On the clinical side, the statement stresses that psychosomatic medicine designates a *method of approach* to the problems of aetiology and therapy, one applicable to all medical specialties, but fails to specify what this should imply in practice. They only allude vaguely to the understanding of the 'psychic component of disease process', call for integration of somatic therapy and psychotherapy without saying how this can be done, and mention the doctor–patient relationship. Equally vague are the references to emotional 'tensions' and 'life', which appear to reflect the one-sided emphasis on emotions as the main psychological factors influencing and correlating with physiological changes (Schwarz, 1925; Alexander, 1950).

All in all, the 'Introductory statement' represents an important historical landmark in the development of psychosomatic conceptions and medicine. It may be viewed as a bench-mark and starting point for the more recent attempts to define the field. Looked at from the perspective of over 40 years, it was a bold effort to launch and delimit the scope of a new field, yet one with ancient antecedents. The editors' statement may be criticized for its errors of omission and commission touched on above, and should be revised and reformulated to reflect recent developments in the field and to serve as a point of reference for historians, teachers and investigators.

It would be neither feasible nor profitable to try and review all the variants of the definition of psychosomatic medicine which have appeared in the literature since 1939. It must suffice to say that the authors who have bothered to define the field at all have on the whole tended to stress its holistic or biopsychosocial connotation (Alexander, 1950; Mirsky, 1957; Lipowski, 1968). Some writers have insisted that the term 'psychosomatic' should be used only to designate a method of approach to both research and clinical work, one that features concurrent and integrated use of biological and psychosocial methods, concepts and languages (Alexander, 1950; Mirsky, 1957). The writers holding this latter view object to the notion that psychosomatic medicine be considered a distinct scientific discipline with a defined object of study.

There is an inherent problem with the link-up of the words 'psychosomatic' and 'medicine', since they belong, at least in part, to two distinct levels of abstraction and discourse. Medicine is concerned with issues of health and disease. 'Psychosomatic', however, has a broader and more abstract connotation, one that touches on the problem of mind and body, and hence pertains to views on the nature of man. When by somebody's whim those two words became linked up, confusion and ambiguity resulted that perplex us to this day. What has come to be designated 'psychosomatic medicine' constitutes a recent phase in the long history of efforts to apply a set of premises and precepts, which may be called 'psychosomatic', to the issues of health and disease, and to the care of patients. At the same time, however, the word 'psychosomatic' may be used to refer to certain philosophical conceptions which are part of the Western intellectual history, one that has a broader scope than, and encompasses, the history of Western medicine. I will try to develop this thesis further by a brief outline of the history of psychosomatic conceptions. My discussion is not to be viewed as an aborted attempt to present a comprehensive history of the subject, a task for which I possess neither requisite competence nor space; it is a task for a historian. To my knowledge, no such history has ever been published and it is badly needed. What follows is merely a selective historical sketch germane to my thesis.

PSYCHOSOMATIC CONCEPTIONS: HISTORICAL PERSPECTIVE

Historians tell us that what we call 'psychosomatic medicine' represents, in part, continuation in modern dress of conceptions whose origins go back to the beginning of Western thought and medicine (Dunbar, 1935; Margetts, 1950; Drabkin, 1955; Rather, 1965; Ackerknecht, 1982). In other words, these ideas antedate the coining of the word 'psychosomatic' and the emergence of psychosomatic medicine as a discipline by over 2,000 years. A brief review of some of those historical antecedents may help us to appreciate not only a remarkable continuity of the conceptions under discussion, but also the roots of the contemporary connotations of the word 'psychosomatic' and its puzzling ambiguity. I submit that the modern meaning of that term incorporates two old conceptions, namely the *holistic* and the *psychogenic*, which are not usually clearly distinguished and thus contribute to its ambiguity. I will try to support this contention with selected historical references and quotations.

The holistic conception

The word 'holistic' is derived from the Greek *holos*, or whole, and was introduced into the literature by Smuts (1926). Though of recent vintage, this term may be applied to postulates about the nature of man and to precepts about medical care that can be found in the writings of Greek philosophers such as Plato and Aristotle. The core postulate of the holistic viewpoint is that the notions of mind and body refer to inseparable and mutually dependent aspects of man. As Drabkin (1955) observes, 'A sense of inseparability of the psychic and the somatic life grows out of basic human experience, and ancient literature, medical and non-medical, has no end of examples of the somatic effects of emotional changes and the emotional effects of somatic changes' (p. 227). Applied to the practice of medicine, the holistic conception affirms the need for physicians to take into account both the mental or psychological and the physical or physiological aspects in the study of disease and the treatment of patients. In his much quoted passage in the dialogue Charmides, Plato (1942) argues; 'The cure of many diseases is unknown to the physicians of Hellas, because they disregard the whole, which ought to be studied also, for the part can never be well unless the whole is well.' Plato seems to imply that attention to the person as a whole, a mind–body complex, is the best approach a physician can adopt in treating patients.

Plato's observation suggests that a holistic attitude was by no means predominant in medicine of his time, and it is an open question if it has ever dominated the medical scene since. Western medicine from Hippocrates on has tended to be staunchly naturalistic and somatic or physiological, although this has not prevented many medical writers from emphasizing the need to treat the whole person. Regardless of what philosophical views, if any, a physician may hold about the mind–body problem, he or she can apply a holistic approach in clinical work. Many medical writers from the Greek times on have explicitly or implicitly advocated such an approach. Even the formulation of a radical dualism by Descartes in his *Discourse on Method* in 1637 did not result in the disappearance of the holistic conceptions from the medical literature. This is especially well exemplified by the work of the eighteenth-century Dutch physician Gaub, who wrote that 'the reason why a sound body becomes ill, or an ailing body recovers, very often lies in the mind. Contrariwise, the body can frequently both beget mental illness and heal its offspring' (Rather, 1965, p. 21). Hence, argues Gaub, 'should the physician devote all of his efforts to the body alone, and take no account of the mind, his curative endeavors will pretty often be less than happy and his purpose either wholly missed or part of what pertains to it neglected' (Rather, 1965, p. 70). As Rather, the translator of Gaub's remarkable Essays, published in 1747 and 1763 respectively, comments, the Dutch writer's views were neither original nor isolated, as they had been expressed by many medical authors before him. For that reason Rather argues that Gaub cannot be regarded as a true forerunner of psychosomatic medicine. It was only the advent of cellular pathology, founded by Virchow in the 1850s, that largely resulted in 'wiping out recollection of the attention traditionally accorded to mind–body relationships. Hence psychosomatic medicine in our time has appeared to many as a new and almost unprecedented movement in medical thought' (Rather, 1965, p. 15).

Another eighteenth-century medical writer, Benjamin Rush (1745–1813), the most prominent American physician of his time and the man officially declared the father of American psychiatry, expressed holistic conceptions no less clearly than Gaub (Lipowski, 1981). As a professor of medicine at the College of Philadelphia and later at the University of Pennsylvania, Rush taught the importance of viewing the patient as a whole and was concerned with psychosomatic relations (Shryock, 1966). In one of his lectures, for example, he spelled out the holistic approach to medicine in these memorable words: 'Man is said to be a compound of soul and body. However proper this language may be in religion, it is not so in medicine. He is, in the eye of a physician, a single and indivisible being, for so intimately united are his soul and body, that one cannot be moved, without the other' (Rush, 1811, p. 256). It is justifiable to consider Rush as a true forerunner of American psychosomatic medicine, as Binger (1966), his biographer, has suggested.

In the nineteenth century, the holistic conceptions in medicine suffered considerable decline but did not vanish (Stainbrook, 1952). Outstanding examples of their survival are provided by the writings of Henry Holland (1852), Physician Extraordinary to Queen Victoria, and of Daniel Hack Tuke (1884), who in 1872 published an extraordinary compilation of anecdotal clinical evidence illustrating the influence of psychological factors on bodily functions. Tuke, however, was not just a compiler. He tried to provide a theoretical framework for his anecdotal illustrations, one based on physiological principles, and to offer physicians an empirical justification to use 'psycho-therapeutics' in a deliberate, methodical manner in the treatment of physical illness. At the end of the nineteenth century, Sir William Osler (1928) reviewed the holistic statements of Plato as they pertain to medical practice, and saw in them a foreboding that 'in the medicine of the future the interdependence of mind and body will be more fully recognized, and that the influence of the one over the other may be exerted in a manner which is not now thought possible' (p. 58).

Osler made the above prediction in a talk given in 1893. Within only one year an article by Hughes appeared in which he not only spelled out the holistic conception with clarity, but also offered a remarkable corollary to Osler's forecast (Hughes, 1894). Hughes, editor of the journal *Alienist and Neurologist*, foresaw, perhaps too optimistically, that 'we are approaching an era when the whole patient is to be treated, no more only a part or organ solely' (Hughes, 1894, p. 901). He asserted: 'In estimating the causal concomitants and sequences of his diseases, we consider the whole man in his psycho-neuro-physical relations.' Hughes proposed that all bodily functions are influenced by emotions, both in health and disease, through the mediation of the central and vegetative nervous systems. For example, he asserted that a 'breakdown in the central nervous system by which trophic and resisting powers are greatly lessened, makes possible and precedes all cases of cancer' (Hughes, 1894, p. 901). He argued that if the mind has, through the agency of the neural mechanisms, such a widespread influence on bodily processes, then this fact provides the 'physiologic basis of all forms of psychotherapy', and the latter should be employed by physicians as a powerful therapeutic tool. Hughes's article may be considered a landmark in the development of the holistic approach to medicine, even though it is seldom quoted (Lipowski, 1981).

In the first 30 years of this century the holistic conceptions became elaborated and propagated by the psychobiological school of psychiatry, notably by Meyer and White (Lipowski, 1981; Powell, 1977). The basic premise of the psychobiologists was that mind and body are not separate entities acting on one another, but only two distinct yet integral aspects of the human organism, a psychobiologic unit, as a whole interacting with the environment. Disease should be viewed as a product of this interaction, and it always encompasses both somatic and psychological aspects. Powell (1977), in one of the few scholarly recent papers on the history of psychosomatic medicine, points out that the holistic conceptions of the psychobiologists were adopted by Dunbar, and through her writings became one of the three main theoretical positions in psychosomatic medicine. The other two viewpoints were the psychoanalytic and the psychophysiological (Powell, 1977). The holistic approach was also prominently represented by Goldstein, in his book *The Organism* published in 1939, and many other writers, not necessarily identified with psychosomatic medicine, since then.

In my view, the holistic conception has been most concisely stated by Woodger, a British biologist and philosopher of science, in his book *Biology and Language*:

the notions of body and mind are both reached by abstraction from something more concrete. For these more concrete objects we have the convenient and familiar word *persons*. But even the notion of person is abstract in the sense that every person is a member of some *community* of persons, upon which the *kind* of person he is, and even his continued existence *as* a person, depends. (Woodger, 1952, p. 257)

This statement may be regarded as an expression of a *methodological* and *linguistic* approach to the mind–body problem rather than a metaphysical one, hence it appears to be most appropriate for psychosomatic medicine and for clinical work generally. For Woodger, the person, a member of a social group, is the starting point and indivisible unit, one from which the notions of mind and body are abstracted for the purpose of study, and hence as a methodological strategy. These two abstractions require separate languages in which to formulate descriptive and theoretical statements about the functioning and behaviour of persons, both in health and disease. This type of formulation eschews the concept of mind and body as *entities*, whose mutual relationship is the subject of philosophical speculation and is expressed in terms of competing metaphysical viewpoints, be they dualistic or monistic.

I have tried to present in this section some of the historical antecedents as well as the core meaning of that connotation of the word 'psychosomatic' which I propose to call 'holistic'. This connotation lies at the heart of what many writers have referred to as the 'psychosomatic approach' to issues of health and disease, and to the treatment of patients. As Dubos puts it, 'The understanding and control of disease requires that the body–mind complex be studied in its relations to external environment' (Dubos, 1968, p. 83). He points out, however, that the holistic (or psychosomatic) approach refers to an abstract ideal which cannot be fully attained in actual practice and which does not lend itself to the acquisition of exact knowledge. Other critics have asserted that adoption of the holistic approach is not a necessary condition for humane patient care (Zucker, 1981). Be that as it may, it is not the purpose of this chapter to defend the merits of holistic conceptions or approach, but merely to bring out their semantic and historical relation to the word 'psychosomatic'. In the next section, I propose to discuss the second main connotation of that term, i.e. the psychogenic one.

The psychogenic conception

The second core connotation of the term 'psychosomatic' may be referred to as equivalent to 'psychogenic', in the sense that it implies an aetiologic hypothesis about the role of psychological factors in human disease. In other words, the psychogenic conception asserts that certain attributes or functions of the organism, those which may be called 'psychological' or 'mental', constitute a class of causative agents in morbidity. This conception, as I propose to illustrate by selected examples, has a lineage as old as the holistic one.

According to Lewis, the word 'psychogenic' was introduced into psychiatry by Sommer, a German psychiatrist, in 1894, to refer to hysteria (Lewis,

1972). The term has been variously defined and applied since. Originally, authors used it only in reference to certain mental disorders which were thus implied to be of psychological origin (Lewis, 1972). In the 1920s, however, the words 'psychogenic' and 'psychogenesis' came to be applied by some writers to bodily disorders in which psychological factors were believed to play a major causal role (Schwarz, 1925). Lewis concluded his review of the term 'psychogenic' with the wry comment that this vague word touched on unresolved issues of causality and dualism, and should best be buried (Lewis, 1972). In the following discussion I will use 'psychogenic' to imply psychological causation.

From Hippocrates on, countless medical writers have postulated that *emotions* influence body functions and may cause disease. He himself is quoted as saying: 'Fear, shame, pleasure, passion . . . to each of these the appropriate member of the body responds by its action. Instances are sweats, palpitations of the heart . . .' (Hippocrates, 1886, p. 143). A similar statement can be found in Aristotle's work 'On the soul' (Dunbar, 1935). For centuries after Hippocrates, emotions, or rather 'passions' as they used to be called then, were viewed not only as having an effect on the functions of the body but also as causative, pathogenic factors (Dunbar, 1935; Rorty, 1982; Solomon, 1976). Galen (1963), one of the most influential medical writers of all times, included the passions among the causes of bodily disease. He referred to grief, anger, lust and fear as 'diseases of the soul' to be diagnosed and cured. Rather (1965) asserts that as a result of Galen's influence on European medicine down to the nineteenth century, physicians had devoted a great deal of attention to the psychological causation of disease, and especially to the role of emotions as aetiologic factors in a wide range of diseases, including some of the contagious and epidemic ones. A typical illustration of this statement is provided by this passage from Archer's *Every Man His Own Doctor*, published in 1673: 'The observation I have made in practice of physick these several years, hath confirmed me in this opinion, that the original, or cause of most men and womens sickness, disease, and death is, first, some great discontent, which brings a habit of sadness of mind . . .' (p. 120). As Ackerknecht comments, 'It is not clear why it has never been fully realized that for 1700 years there has been in existence a continuous tradition of psychosomatics under the label of "passions" ' (Ackerknecht, 1982, p. 18).

In 1637, a book appeared which was to have a profound influence on Western thought, i.e. Descartes' *Discourse on Method*, in which the problem and antithesis of mind and body were formulated more explicitly and radically than ever before (Lindeboom, 1979; Rather, 1965; Wilson, 1978). Descartes separated mind (*res cogitans*), the thinking entity, from the non-thinking, machine-like body. This was a turning point in the development of modern medicine and in the ancient debate on the mind–body issues. While Cartesian dualism dealt a blow to the holistic conceptions in medicine, it did not, paradoxically, prove detrimental to psychogenic conceptions. On the contrary, the latter flourished in the seventeenth and eighteenth centuries. Descartes himself regarded the passions as bodily phenomena which could influence other somatic functions, and even have a pathogenic effect (Lindeboom, 1979).

Despite the spread of a mechanistic approach to medicine in the seventeenth century, the greatest physicians of that age and the true founders of modern medicine, Harvey, Willis and Sydenham, paid considerable attention to emotional factors in disease. Of particular interest in view of the recent concern with the role of psychological factors in the development and course of cancer is the following comment by a German physician, Pechlin, made in 1691, and quoted by Rather: 'Indeed, I have never seen a cancer of the breast so thoroughly removed, even after extirpation, that would not, in consequence of fear and sorrow, rather suddenly once again slowly recrudesce and, after long difficulties, at length put an end to life' (Rather, 1978, p. 182).

In the eighteenth century, a systematic account of the influence of emotions on bodily function and disease appeared in Gaub's Essay of 1763 (Rather, 1965). He speaks of the harmful effects on the body of overt as well as suppressed anger, grief, terror, unrequited love and excessive joy. His comments have a remarkably modern ring, as when he says of grief, for example, that when it is not 'discharged in lamentation and wailing, but instead remains seated firmly within and is for a long time repressed and fostered, the body no less than the mind is eaten up and destroyed' (Rather, 1965, p. 140).

Other eighteenth-century medical writers, notably Stahl, developed elaborate, philosophically based, psychogenic conceptions (Rather, 1961, 1965). Two works which appeared at the end of that century offer a systematic presentation of contemporary views of the influence of the mind on the body (Corp, 1791; Falconer, 1796). Corp discusses in his monograph both the pathogenetic and the beneficial effects of the 'mental faculties', including thoughts, attention and emotions, such as hope, joy, anger, fear, grief and anxiety, and proclaims 'the dependence of mind and body on each other'. Speaking of anger, for example, Corp lists among its potential harmful effects 'palsy, apoplexy, and sudden death' (p. 56). He asserts that prolonged anxiety may injure the brain, resulting in failure of memory. Of grief, he says that it can lead to any bodily disorder. Persons who are afflicted with fear or dread of disease, claims Corp, have long been known to be the first to fall victim to plague during an epidemic of it. Hope, by contrast, may help protect against plague, and has generally curative powers which physicians ought to promote.

The above selected examples, to which many others could readily be added, have to suffice as illustrations of the widespread interest in the influence of emotions on bodily functions and the occurrence of disease among seventeenth- and eighteenth-century medical writers. Friedreich (1830), an early historian of psychiatry, wrote that one of the dominant themes in the eighteenth-century medical literature was the reciprocal relationship between body and soul, including the influence of passions and affects on the former. He quotes numerous authors who dealt with that topic. In America, Rush (1811) wrote at length about how useful the knowledge of the actions of the mind on the body should be to physicians, since those actions 'influence many of the functions of the body in health. They are the causes of many diseases; and if properly directed, they may easily be made to afford many useful remedies' (p. 256).

It is notable that those psychogenic conceptions were not held by mavericks but, on the contrary, were presented as a matter of fact by the leaders of the medical profession and by the most influential medical writers of the seventeenth and eighteenth centuries. Furthermore, those views were expressed by authors who held opposed opinions on the nature of the mind and its relationship to the body. Dualists and monists, materialists and idealists all seemed to find such views congenial irrespective of their own philosophical positions. That trend waned to some extent during the nineteenth century, not so much because of a major shift in philosophical views, but rather because medicine was becoming more technological, specialized, and focused on the body to the exclusion of mental factors. Virchow's theory of cellular pathology, followed by the discoveries of Pasteur and Koch in bacteriology, propelled medicine in the direction of the Cartesian mechanistic approach to the body and towards the doctrine that for every disease there is a single specific cause (Freymann, 1981). It was that very trend which provoked in this century the rise of a counterreformation which came to be labelled 'psychosomatic medicine'.

During the nineteenth century, the psychogenic conceptions still continued to be represented in the medical literature, if on a lesser scale than previously (Stainbrook, 1952). An event of especial importance was the appearance, in 1833, of Beaumont's study of a man with exposed gastric mucosa (Beaumont, 1833). That work was a landmark, as it reported the first *systematic* and prolonged observations of the influence of emotional states on the functions of an internal organ. The study of psychophysiological relations was becoming scientific in the hands of Beaumont, a 'backwood physiologist', as Osler called him (Osler, 1902). Almost a whole century had passed before such studies, having been given impetus by the work of Pavlov (1902) and Cannon (1915), became in the 1930s an integral component of psychosomatic medicine (Powell, 1977). Psychophysiological studies have focused on mechanisms mediating between psychological variables on the one hand and the normal and abnormal body functions on the other. As such, they have been concerned with processes and correlations rather than with issues of disease aetiology which are implied by the word 'psychogenesis'. Psychophysiology may be viewed as that outgrowth of the ancient concern with the impact of emotions on the working of the body which has been most consistently 'scientific' in its approach to that subject, in the sense of relying on the experimental method and eschewing sweeping generalizations. Today, psychophysiological research continues to be one of the most vital and indispensable divisions of psychosomatic studies (Lipowski, 1982), but it would be incorrect to equate *all* of psychosomatic medicine with psychophysiology; a part is not identical with the whole.

A very different approach to the study of the influence of emotions on the body, one concerned with their precise nature and role in the aetiology of disease, took its inspiration from psychoanalysis (Alexander and Selesnick, 1966). Freud's technique of free association afforded access to unconscious mental processes, while his concepts of unconscious conflict, repression and conversion provided conceptual tools which could be applied to hypotheses about psychosomatic relationships. For Freud, hysterical symptoms appeared when affect associated with an idea strongly conflicting with the ego, and consequently repressed, became discharged in somatic innervation and symptoms. Freud used the term 'conversion' to refer to the process whereby psychic excitation was transmuted into somatic symptoms, but he confined this hypothesis to hysteria and did not extend it to organic disease. By contrast, some followers of Freud, such as Groddeck, Deutsch and Jelliffe, advanced propositions about the aetiology of organic disease which were modelled after his formulations about the origin of hysterical symptoms (Alexander and Selesnick, 1966). Groddeck, for example, asserted that every illness served the purpose of symbolically representing an inner conflict and aimed at resolving it, repressing it, or preventing that which was already repressed from becoming conscious (Groddeck, 1961, p. 101). His was the most radical formulation of psychogenesis to emerge as an offshoot of psychoanalytic theory and drew sharp critique from some of his psychoanalytic colleagues, such as Alexander, who advanced his own, more moderate, conception of psychogenesis.

Alexander, one of the pioneers of psychosomatic medicine, embarked in 1932 on a series of studies designed to elucidate the putative causal role of emotional factors in several chronic diseases of unknown aetiology. His was an attempt to apply psychoanalytic technique and concepts to the ancient ideas about psychogenesis (Alexander, 1950). He distinguished sharply between conversion symptoms as symbolic expressions of psychological issues in the form of somatic symptoms on the one hand, and organic diseases which he viewed as vegetative responses to chronic emotional states, and hence devoid of any symbolic meaning, on the other. He called the latter disorders 'vegetative' or 'organ' neuroses, and referred to them as psychogenic organic disorders. Alexander postulated that every emotional state had its own physiological syndrome, and both could be induced together by appropriate emotional stimuli. He maintained that fear, aggression, guilt and frustrated wishes, if repressed, would result in chronic 'emotional tensions' and consequent dysfunction of body organs (Alexander, 1950). The repression of wishes and emotions would occur if they gave rise to inner conflicts. Such conflicts, believed Alexander, displayed a predilection for, and hence tended to disturb the function of, *specific* internal organs, by analogy to the affinity of certain micro-organisms for specific body parts. He named his hypothesis 'specificity theory', one which asserted that a specific 'dynamic constellation' consisting of a nuclear conflict, the defences against it, and the emotions engendered by it, tended to correlate with a specific 'vegetative' response. Alexander applied these conceptions to such diseases as essential hypertension, rheumatoid arthritis, thyrotoxisosis and peptic ulcer, and formulated complex psychogenic hypotheses to account for their occurrence.

Alexander took pains to stipulate that his theory of psychogenesis implied no more than that those physiological processes in the brain which could preferably be studied by psychological methods because they were subjectively experienced as emotions, ideas or wishes, could, in some cases, constitute the first links in a causal chain leading initially to disturbance of function and ultimately to structural organic disease. Psychogenesis could not, however, fully account for the development of any such disease, since available evidence on the whole pointed to multicausality of all diseases. It was only the coexistence of specific emotional *and* somatic factors that could result in disease such as peptic ulcer, for example. Alexander explicitly disavowed the concept of 'psychosomatic disease' as one incompatible with the doctrine of multifactorial aetiology (Alexander, 1950, p. 52), but nevertheless he spoke of 'psychogenic organic disorder' (1950, p. 44) as an acceptable concept.

Alexander's hypotheses represent the most elaborate formulation of psychogenesis of organic disease ever advanced. They constitute, therefore, an important landmark in the history of the development of that conception, and of psychosomatic medicine generally. His views exerted, for better or worse, widespread influence for some 25 years, between about 1935 and 1960, and were clearly much more moderate than Groddeck's extreme panpsychologism. Despite their relative moderation, however, his theory of specific psychogenesis of selected diseases, those which many writers have referred to as 'psychosomatic', encountered growing criticism and suffered gradual eclipse (Galdston, 1955; Grinker, 1973; Lewis, 1967; Lipowski, 1968; Lipowski, 1977). The very notion of psychogenesis has come under attack as one which seemed to imply that psychosomatic medicine was concerned with the role of the psyche as a 'morbific agent' and promoted a simplistic notion of a linear causal chain leading from emotions to disease (Gladston, 1955). Such linear causality has come to be regarded as inadequate to account for the development of most of human morbidity.

Alexander's hypotheses may be seen as a sophisticated modern reformulation of the idea expressed in a rudimentary form by Galen in the second century AD, that passions can have a harmful effect on the body and may actually cause disease. Over the centuries, it was mostly the passions or emotions which were for some reason singled out from the whole repertoire of psychological variables as potential aetiologic agents. The most recent variation on this theme is represented by the concept of alexithymia, one proposed in 1972 to refer to persons having difficulty in describing their emotions and exhibiting stunted fantasy life (Lesser, 1981). This ill-defined clinical construct has been misapplied by some writers as an explanatory concept in hypotheses about the origin of the so-called psychosomatic disorders.

The proposition that emotions 'cause' disease is largely viewed today as arbitrary and invalid. Rather, they are considered to be intervening variables interposed between the meaning for the individual of the information impinging upon him or her on the one hand, and somatic responses that follow on the other (Lipowski, 1977). Indeed, the whole notion of psychogenesis, one incompatible with the currently prevailing doctrine of multicausality of disease, is no longer tenable, and hence the psychogenic connotation of the word 'psychosomatic' should be explicitly discarded. The word 'psychosomatic' should not be used to imply causality in any sense or context, but only to refer to the reciprocal relationships between psychosocial and biological factors in health and disease (Engel, 1967). Concern with the nature and role of the interplay of those factors in the development, course and outcome of all diseases remains one of the central issues in psychosomatic medicine, but it can be adequately subsumed under the holistic or biopsychosocial connotation of the word 'psychosomatic' (Engel, 1967). I propose that the latter connotation is the only one acceptable today (Lipowski, 1982; Weiner, 1982).

PROPOSED DEFINITIONS

Ackerknecht's (1982) article as well as the *Oxford English Dictionary*'s definition of the word 'psychosomatic' quoted earlier in this chapter attest to the need to define once more the core terms relevant to psychosomatic medicine, and to delineate this field. A recent comment by a psychologist highlights this need: 'The field of psychosomatic medicine suffers from definitions and concepts that have emerged, over time, without the adequate forethought and structure to remove ambiguity and ensure that the field is properly delineated' (Wright, 1977, p. 625). The ambiguity to which that author alludes appears to have two main sources: (1) the dual connotation of the term 'psychosomatic' which I have tried to bring out in this article from a historical perspective; and (2) the fact that psychosomatic medicine has focused on the study of relationships among phenomena which cut across several branches of science and make sharp delineation of the field difficult if not actually undesirable. The problem of the complex relationships among psychological, social and biological aspects of health and disease has puzzled interested observers for over 2000 years and remains a riddle. No wonder that a relatively recently organized scientific discipline which has concerned itself with that tangled knot has been beset by semantic confusion, false starts and ambiguity. These obstacles related to the very subject matter of psychosomatic medicine should not, however, discourage periodic efforts to define it with reasonable clarity. Having tried to do so several times over the past 18 years (Lipowski, 1968, 1977, 1982), I propose to try once more in the hope that my effort will stimulate discussion and facilitate teaching.

Psychosomatic is a term referring or related to the inseparability and interdependence of psychosocial and biological (physiological, somatic) aspects of man. (This connotation may be called 'holistic' as it implies the view of man as a whole, a mind–body complex embedded in a social environment.)

Psychosomatic medicine (psychosomatics) refers to a discipline concerned with (1) the study of the correlations of psychological and social phenomena with physiological functions, normal or pathological, and of the interplay of biological and psychosocial factors in the development, course and outcome of diseases; and (2) advocacy of a holistic (or biopsychosocial) approach to patient care and application of methods derived from behavioural sciences to the prevention and treatment of human morbidity. (This aspect of the field is currently represented by liaison psychiatry and behavioural medicine.)

As a field of study, or scientific discipline, psychosomatic medicine is concerned with observation and description of the phenomena which are its object of interest, and with the formulation of testable hypotheses and theories about biopsychosocial relationships, both in health and disease. While all this activity may be regarded as being highly relevant to the debate about the mind–body problem, the latter cannot be viewed as the subject matter of psychosomatic medicine, which is an empirical and not a philosophic discipline. As an operational working approach, mind and body may be regarded as abstractions derived for methodological purposes for the study of person. *Mind*, in this view, refers to those aspects of man which are most conveniently studied using methods of the behavioural sciences and described in the language of psychology. *Body*, by contrast, is that aspect to which the investigative methods, concepts and language of biology are applied.

As organized advocacy of a holistic approach to health care, psychosomatic medicine propagates the following premises and precepts:

(1) Man is a biopsychosocial organism, one that receives, stores processes, creates and transmits information, and assigns meaning to it which in turn elicits emotional responses. The latter, by virtue of their physiological concomitants, may affect all body functions, both in health and disease.

(2) Health and disease are more or less arbitrarily defined states of the organism which are codetermined by psychological, social and biological factors, and always possess biopsychosocial aspects.

(3) Study, prevention, diagnosis and treatment of disease should take into account the varying contribution of all of the above three classes of variables.

(4) Aetiology is as a rule *multifactorial*. The relative weight of each class of causative factors, however, varies from disease to disease and from case to case; some are necessary and some only contributory.

(5) Optimal patient care requires that the above postulates be applied in actual clinical practice.

'Psychosomatic disorder' (or illness or symptom) is a term still unfortunately used by some writers to refer to any somatic disease or dysfunction in which psychological factors are postulated to play a necessary or sufficient causal role. This term has given rise to pointless and misleading polemics as to whether a given disease or disorder was or was not eligible for inclusion in the 'psychosomatic' class. The continued use of this term should be discouraged, as it tends to perpetuate the obsolete notion of psychogenesis, one incompatible with the doctrine of multicausality which constitutes a core assumption of psychosomatic medicine. Like many other writers, I have repeatedly urged that this term be discarded (Lipowski, 1968, 1982).

SUMMARY AND CONCLUSIONS

Semantics and history of psychosomatic medicine are not popular topics nowadays, if they ever were, yet both of them constitute indispensable facets of any discipline which lays claim to a separate identity, as psychosomatics does. The latter, being an inchoate and inherently complex field of study, is especially in need of repeated efforts to clarify the meaning of its key terms, to delineate its scope and to chart its development over time. Such efforts should pay off in improved teaching of this subject and in more effective communication with workers in other disciplines and with the general public.

I have tried in this chapter to sketch the historical development of psychosomatic conceptions and address some relevant semantic issues. It appears that the convergence of two ancient conceptions, the holistic and the psychogenic, early in this century, prepared the ground for the emergence in the 1930s of psychosomatic medicine as an organized scientific discipline and a counterreformation against the mechanistic view of man and medicine. Those two conceptions came to be subsumed by the word 'psychosomatic' and thus contributed its two distinct connotations. The latter have not usually been clearly distinguished, hence the ambiguity of the term. I have argued that only the holistic connotation should be retained as it properly conveys the contemporary viewpoint.

It is unfortunate that the word 'holistic' has been appropriated recently by an antiscientific and anti-intellectual so-called 'holistic health movement' with resulting increment in semantic confusion and, in the eyes of many, loss of credibility for the misappropriated term (Kopelman and Moskop, 1981). To retain it, however, has merit as it is short, simple and derived from Greek just like the very conceptions which it has come to connote. Moreover, 'holistic' has been part of the basic vocabulary of psychosomatic medicine from the beginning and conveys its core premises and purpose faithfully. As a historian aptly put it, the historical function of the psychosomatic movement has been to 'vitalize the whole of medicine, psychiatry no less . . . with the holistic and ecological viewpoint' (Galdston, 1955, p. 9).

Eric Wittkower, one of the earliest psychosomatic investigators and my recently deceased former teacher, predicted in 1960 that in the future psychosomatic medicine would likely follow one of three directions: (1) become a narrow speciality dominated by psychoanalysis; (2) confine itself to psychophysiological research; or (3) develop into a holistic approach to medical problems (Wittkower, 1960). Looking back at the past two decades I would argue that the field has become an inseparable blend of psychophysiology and the holistic approach (Lipowski, 1977; Weiner, 1982).

ACKNOWLEDGEMENT

Reprinted, with minor amendments, by permission of the publisher from *Psychosomatic Medicine*, **26**, 153–171. Copyright 1984 by the American Psychosomatic Society, Inc.

REFERENCES

Ackerknecht, E. H. (1982). The history of psychosomatic medicine. *Psychological Medicine*, **12**, 17–24.

Alexander, F. (1950). *Psychosomatic Medicine*. New York: Norton.

Alexander, F. G., and Selesnick, S. T. (1966). *The History of Psychiatry*. New York: Harper & Row.

Archer, J. (1673). *Every Man His Own Doctor*. London.

Beaumont, W. (1833). *Experiments and Observations on the Gastric Juice and the Physiology of Digestion*. Plattsburgh, New York: F. P. Allen.

Binger, C. (1966). *Revolutionary Doctor. Benjamin Rush, 1746–1813*. New York: Norton.

Bucknill, J. C. (1857). *Unsoundness of Mind in Relation to Criminal Acts*. London: Longmans, Brown, Green, Longmans & Roberts.

Burchfield, R. W. (ed.) (1982). *A Supplement to the Oxford English Dictionary*, vol. III. Oxford: Clarendon Press.

Cannon, W. B. (1915). *Bodily Changes in Pain, Hunger, Fear and Rage*. New York: Appleton.

Corp (1791). *An Essay on the Changes Produced in the Body by Operations of the Mind*. London: Ridgway.

Drabkin, I. E. (1955). Remarks on ancient psychopathology. *Isis*, **46**, 223–234.

Dubos, R. (1968). *Man, Medicine, and Environment*. New York: New American Library.

Dunbar, H. (1935). *Emotions and Bodily Changes: A Survey of Literature on Psychosomatic Interrelationships: 1910–1933*. New York: Columbia University Press.

Engel, G. L. (1967). The concept of psychosomatic disorder. *Journal of Psychosomatic Research*, **11**, 3–9.

Falconer, W. (1796). *A Dissertation on the Influence of the Passions upon Disorders of the Body*. London: Dilly.

Freyman, J. G. (1981). The origins of disease orientation in American medical education. *Preventive Medicine*, **10**, 663–673.

Friedreich, J. B. (1830). *Versuch einer Literaergeschichte der Pathologie und Therapie der psychischen Krankheiten*. Würzburg: Carl Strecker.

Galdston, I. (1955). Psychosomatic medicine. *American Medical Association Archives of Neurology and Psychiatry*, **74**, 441–450.

Galen (1963). *On the Passions and Errors of the Soul* (P. W. Harkins, trans.). Ohio State University Press.

Goldstein, K. (1939). *The Organism*. New York: American Book.

Gray, J. P. (1868–1869). Insanity and its relations to medicine. *American Journal of Insanity*, **25**, 145–172.

Grinker, R. R. (1973). *Psychosomatic Concepts*, (revised edn). New York: Jason Aronson.

Groddeck, G. (1961). *The Book of the It*. New York: Vintage.

Hinsie, L. E., Campbell, R. J. (eds) (1960). *Psychiatric Dictionary*, 3rd edn. New York: Oxford University Press.

Hippocrates (1886). *Aphorisms* (F. Adams, trans.). London: William Wood.

Holland, H. (1852). *Mental Physiology*. London: Longmans, Brown, Green & Longmans.

Hughes. C. W. (1894). The nervous system in disease and the practice of medicine from a neurologic standpoint. *Journal of the American Medical Association*, **22**, 897–908.

Kopelman, L., and Moskop, J. (1981). The holistic health movement: a survey and critique. *Journal of Medicine and Philosophy*, **6**, 209–235.

Lesser, I. M. (1981). A review of the alexithymia concept. *Psychosomatic Medicine*, **43**, 531–543.

Lewis, A. (1967). *Inquiries in Psychiatry*. New York: Science House Inc.

Lewis, A. (1972). 'Psychogenic': a word and its mutations. *Psychological Medicine*, **2**, 209–215.

Lindeboom, G. A. (1979). *Descartes and Medicine*. Amsterdam: Radopi.

Lipowski, Z. J. (1968). Review of consultation psychiatry and psychosomatic medicine. III. Theoretical issues. *Psychosomatic Medicine*, **30**, 395–422.

Lipowski, Z. J. (1977). Psychosomatic medicine in the seventies: an overview. *American Journal of Psychiatry*, **134**, 233–244.

Lipowski, Z. J. (1981). Holistic-medical foundations of American psychiatry: a bicentennial. *American Journal of Psychiatry*, **138**, 888–895.

Lipowski, Z. J. (1982). Modern meaning of the terms 'psychosomatic' and 'liaison psychiatry'. In F. Creed and J. M. Pfeffer (eds), *Medicine and Psychiatry: A Practical Approach*. London: Pitman.

Margetts, E. L. (1950). The early history of the word 'psychosomatic'. *Canadian Medical Association Journal*, **63**, 402–404.

Margetts, E. L. (1954). Historical notes on psychosomatic medicine. In E. D. Wittkower and R. A. Cleghorn (eds), *Recent Developments in Psychosomatic Medicine*. London: Pitman, pp. 41–68.

Mirsky, I. A. (1957). The psychosomatic approach to the etiology of clinical disorders. *Psychosomatic Medicine*, **19**, 424–430.

Osler, W. (1902). William Beaumont. A backwood physiologist. *Journal of the American Medical Association*, **39**, 1223–1231.

Osler, W. (1928). *Aequanimitas*, 2nd edn. London: H. K. Lewis & Company.

Pavlov, I. P. (1902). *The Work of the Digestive Glands* (W. H. Thompson, trans.). Philadelphia: Lippincott.

Plato (1942). Charmides. In B. Jowett (trans.), *The Best Known Works of Plato*. Garden City, New York: Blue Ribbon Books.

Powell, R. C. (1977). Helen Flanders Dunbar (1902–1959) and a holistic approach to psychosomatic problems. I. The rise and fall of a medical philosophy. *Psychiatric Quarterly*, **49**, 133–152.

Psychosomatic Disorders (1964). *World Health Organization Technical Reports* (serial no. 275).

Psychosomatic Medicine (1939). Introductory Statement. *Psychosomatic Medicine*, **1**, 3–5.

Rather, L. J. (1961). G. E. Stahl's psychological physiology. *Bulletin of the History of Medicine*, **35**, 37–49.

Rather, L. J. (1965). *Mind and Body in Eighteenth Century Medicine*. Berkeley: University of California Press.

Rather, L. J. (1978). *The Genesis of Cancer*. Baltimore, Md: Johns Hopkins University Press.

Reade, C. (no date). *Hard Cash*, vol. I. Boston: Dana Estes & Company.

Rorty, A. O. (1982). From passions to emotions and sentiments. *Philosophy*, **57**, 159–172.

Rush, B. (1811). *Sixteen Introductory Lectures*. Philadelphia: Bradford & Innskeep.

Schwartz, O. (ed.) (1925). *Psychogenese und Psychotherapie Körperlicher Symptome*. Wien: Julius Springer.

Shryock, R. H. (1966). *Medicine in America. Historical Essays*. Baltimore, Md: Johns Hopkins Press.

Smuts, J. C. (1926). *Holism and Evolution*. New York: Macmillan.

Solomon, R. C. (1976). *The Passions*. Garden City, NY: Anchor Press.

Stainbrook, E. (1952). Psychosomatic medicine in the nineteenth century. *Psychosomatic Medicine*, **14**, 211–227.

Stokvis, B. (1959). Psychosomatik. In V. E. Frankl, V. E. Gebsattel and J. H. Schultz (eds), *Handbuch der Neurosenlehre and Psychotherapie*, vol. 3. München: Urban & Schwarzenberg, pp. 435–506.

Tuke, D. H. (1884). *Illustrations of the Influence of the Mind Upon the Body in Health and Disease* (2nd edn). Philadelphia: Henry C. Lea's Son & Company.

Tuke, D. H. (ed.) (1892). *A Dictionary of Psychological Medicine*, vol. II. Philadelphia: Blakiston.

Weiner, H. (1982). The prospects for psychosomatic medicine: selected topics. *Psychosomatic Medicine*, **44**, 491–517.

Wilson, M. D. (1978). *Descartes*. London: Routledge & Kegan Paul.

Wittkower, E. D. (1960). Twenty years of North American psychosomatic medicine. *Psychosomatic Medicine*, **22**, 308–316.

Woodger, J. H. (1952). *Biology and Language*. Cambridge: Cambridge University Press.

World Health Organization (1964). *Psychosomatic Disorders*. World Health Organization Technical Report Service No. 275.

Wright, L. (1977). Conceptualizing and defining psychosomatic disorders. *American Psychologist*, **32**, 625–628.

Zucker, A. (1981). Holism and reductionism: a view from genetics. *Journal of Medicine and Philosophy*.

SECTION 2

The Beginnings of Life

*The Psychosomatic Approach: Contemporary Practice
   of Whole-person Care*
Edited by M. J. Christie and P. G. Mellett
© 1986 John Wiley & Sons Ltd

3

A CONTEMPORARY APPROACH TO GENETIC COUNSELLING

ALAN E. H. EMERY

Medical School, The University of Edinburgh, UK

and

IAN M. PULLEN

Royal Edinburgh Hospital, UK

INTRODUCTION

Over the last few decades, the patterns of morbidity and mortality in childhood have changed considerably. These changes have been due to several factors, medical and social, which have led to a gradual decline in the incidence of infectious diseases and nutritional deficiencies. As these disorders have declined, others have been uncovered which are largely or even entirely genetically determined. The latter include single gene, or unifactorial, disorders and various cytogenetic abnormalities in which there is an inherent abnormality of chromosome number or structure. So far, some 3000 unifactorial disorders and more than 50 cytogenetic disorders have been recognized though most are individually rare. Many common disorders also have a genetic component but here environmental factors are involved as well and, for this reason, they are referred to as being multifactorial. These include many of the common congenital malformations (such as spina bifida, cleft lip and palate), certain diseases of modern society (coronary artery disease, essential hypertension, diabetes mellitus), various psychiatric disorders (such as schizophrenia) and probably many common cancers. In most multifactorial disorders, the risks to relatives are usually low (less than 1 in 20) and some at least are treatable. Further, it seems likely that within the not-too-distant future the precipitating environmental factors in many of these disorders may be identified which should then make primary prevention possible. For example, there is increasing evidence that a vitamin supplementation as well as general dietary improvement may significantly reduce the incidence of spina bifida and the related condition of anencephaly. But in the case of unifactorial and cytogenetic abnormalities, the situation is quite different. In unifactorial disorders, and certain inherited chromosome abnormalities, the risks to relatives are often high. These disorders are also serious and very few are treatable. Parents who are at risk of having a child affected with one of these disorders are therefore faced with a serious

41

dilemma, and it is in this situation that genetic counselling has an important role to play.

GENETIC COUNSELLING

Genetic counselling is essentially a process of communication between the counsellor and those who seek genetic counselling, and the information communicated falls roughly into two main areas. First, information about the disorder itself: its severity and prognosis, and whether or not there is any effective therapy; what the genetic mechanism is that caused the disease and what are the risks of its recurring in the family. Second, information on the available options open to a couple who find that the risk of having an affected child is unacceptably high. These options may include contraception (including sterilization), adoption, artificial insemination by donor (AID), and prenatal diagnosis with selective abortion. But there are very serious problems in attempting to communicate information of such a personal and delicate nature in a situation where the parents may be grieving over the loss of a child, and which may also be emotionally charged with feelings of guilt and recrimination frequently associated with a loss of self-esteem. Information about genetic disease is rarely emotionally neutral and often has profound psychological effects. These effects may have long-term consequences and extend throughout the family to other relatives. If the genetic counsellor is to be an effective communicator, the psychological impact on the family has to be appreciated and taken into account. As a prelude to genetic counselling it is, therefore, essential to divine a couple's attitudes to a particular genetic disorder, their interpretation of its implications, and how they see it affecting their lives and family relationships.

What is quite clear is that all individuals presenting for genetic counselling are under considerable stress. The psychological sequence of events that evolves from the time when the diagnosis of a genetic disease in a child is first made is referred to as the *coping process* and is similar to that which follows any stressful event such as the death of a child, spouse or other close relative. The particular stage in the coping process which a couple has reached has to be recognized so that the approach to counselling can be tailored accordingly.

THE COPING PROCESS

Five sequential stages have been recognized in the coping process (Falek, 1977, 1984). The duration of each stage varies considerably. In some circumstances, a particular stage may be very short or may not even occur at all, while some individuals may never progress beyond one of the early stages. For example, in exceptional cases, a parent may never progress beyond the first stage and, therefore, never accept the diagnosis and its implications.

Shock and denial

This is the initial stage of the coping process and is an attempt to maintain the *status quo*. The individual will not accept the situation, insists there is a mistake in the diagnosis and may seek other medical opinions. During this stage, little new information will be absorbed and any attempt at genetic counselling will be rejected. It may well account for the poor recall of genetic information in some individuals when followed up subsequently. When the diagnosis of a genetic disease or serious congenital malformation is first made is therefore not the time to embark on lengthy discussions and genetic counselling. The counsellor needs to be very tactful, sympathetic and patient at this stage.

Anxiety

This second stage of the coping process is when the individual first begins to accept the reality of the situation. But as Falek (1984) has pointed out, the new situation is beginning to be accepted only at the intellectual level and not at the emotional level. Since there has been no psychological adjustment, the individual begins to experience fear which generates anxiety. This manifests itself as various somatic complaints such as insomnia, poor appetite, irritability and fatigue. It is important that the counsellor recognizes these manifestations and so provides appropriate support. For those in whom anxiety is high, clearly any information which might threaten the individual's self-esteem needs to be presented in a low key and every effort made to avoid generating more anxiety.

Anger and guilt

As the individual is still unable completely to accept the situation, unsuccessful attempts to explain events to his or her own satisfaction lead to frustration and feelings of hostility which may be directed towards friends, relatives or medical personnel. Thus, the individual may challenge the counsellor by asking 'Why was the diagnosis not made earlier?', 'Why was nothing more done?' and so on. This anger may also be directed inwardly, resulting in feelings of guilt and recrimination. In both the angry and the guilt-ridden, the individual is attempting to resolve conflicts and frustrations by trying to find a responsible agent. The counsellor should be prepared for anger to be directed towards him and to accept the irrationality of this. He has to be empathic and show that he is aware of the full extent of these angry feelings and this will require considerable time and patience.

Depression

The repeated and frustrated attempts to resolve the problem lead to depression. The individual is faced with the emotional burden of the situation and becomes depressed. This manifests itself as withdrawal with lack of interest in home and family. Appropriate medication may be useful by helping the individual to deal with the events of everyday life until the final stage of the coping process is reached.

Psychological homeostasis

At this final stage, the individual begins to accept the situation both intellectually and emotionally, and so becomes receptive to new ideas. It is at this stage that genetic counselling is most usefully given and detailed discussions of various options can now be entertained. But cycling between the various coping phases may still continue and the counsellor has to be prepared for this. Thus, the counsellor may feel that a couple have reached a stage when prenatal diagnosis may be discussed, only to discover that this generates anger because they were not offered this in a previous pregnancy. Or, by emphasizing the increased risk of Down's syndrome in older mothers, this may reawaken and potentiate guilt feelings in a mother of an affected child. But usually with time, the situation at both the intellectual and emotional levels is accepted and the duration and intensity of each of the coping phases gradually diminishes.

Many of the problems which may arise in counselling result from the counsellor not recognizing and appreciating the various stages of the coping process and not providing clear and straightforward help right from the beginning. Thus, in one recent extensive study of parents with boys with Duchenne muscular dystrophy, most stress was produced by delays in making the correct diagnosis and the inadequate and insensitive way in which this information was then communicated (Firth, 1983). It is essential in all cases of genetic disease that a firm and precise diagnosis is established as soon as possible, and only then should counselling be considered. A further point is that the more the counsellor becomes involved in establishing the diagnosis and in communicating information, the more likely he or she is to be held responsible by the parents. This responsibility has to be accepted and it often makes considerable demands on those who have to 'break the bad news' (Buckman, 1984).

The role of the genetic counsellor is not easy, and the particular qualities which make for a really sensitive and effective counsellor may well be largely a reflection of personality and be at least partly inherent. Nevertheless, basic skills of genetic counselling can be acquired by formal training (Emery, 1982; Maguire, 1984). One of us (AEHE) has found role-play a useful means of teaching counselling techniques to graduate students. Those who are to play the role of would-be parents adopt one of the stages of the coping process and those who are to play the role of the counsellor have to divine the stage and deal with the situation accordingly. Role-play has also been found to be a useful means of teaching communicating skills in other stressful situations such as in terminal cancer (Anderson and Kvan, 1983).

EFFECTS OF GENETIC DISEASE ON VARIOUS FAMILY MEMBERS

So far, the emphasis has been on the effects of a parent realizing that he or she is at risk of having a child with a serious genetic disease. Such individuals may themselves be healthy, as in the case of parents who carry an autosomal recessive trait or a mother who is a carrier of an X-linked trait. But in some situations one of the parents may be affected, as in the case of an autosomal dominant disorder, and this introduces another and separate problem. Here, the counsellor can be faced with a dilemma: on the one hand, to present an optimistic picture to the affected parent and avoid emphasizing the serious aspects of the disease, yet on the other hand perhaps having to embark upon discussions of preventive measures such as prenatal diagnosis and abortion which may exacerbate the individual's loss of self-esteem.

When the disease is progressive and incapacitating, then marital relationships may also be strained. Despite the genetic risks, the couple may also still want children and special counselling on sex techniques may be indicated. Thus, a husband physically incapacitated by one of the adult forms of X-linked muscular dystrophy may have considerable difficulties in having intercourse and getting his wife to conceive. In some instances, fathering children may seem to the affected individual the only way of redeeming some of his self-respect, for in X-linked disorders, though all his daughters will be carriers, none of his children will be affected.

Nor should the possible psychological effects of an incapacitating genetic disease on an affected child be ignored since these can be quite significant and have repercussions throughout the family. However, they may not be obvious and may have to be specifically looked for. This can be achieved through careful questioning regarding the child's relationships with other members of the family and with peers and with performance at school. In young children these questions can be addressed to the parents, but older children can be asked directly. There are also a number of specific tests available for assessing psychosocial functioning in such children (Pless, 1984).

A chronic incapacitating genetic disease may have serious psychosocial effects on various other family members—the mother, the father, as well as the unaffected siblings (Sabbeth, 1984). Mothers may be particularly affected, often becoming depressed and physically as well as emotionally exhausted through caring for the affected child (Siegel et al., 1983). By adopting an overprotective attitude and by giving the affected child excessive attention, she may ignore her husband and any unaffected siblings, who may then develop feelings of resentment.

The impression in many studies seems to be that fathers may be less affected than mothers. But fathers may well have special problems in adjusting to an affected child. In general, the exclusion of the father from much of the detail of child care may exacerbate his feelings of helplessness and sense of isolation, made worse by the societal stereotype which prohibits men from expressing feelings or demonstrating vulnerability (Sabbeth, 1984).

But it would seem that as parental roles in future become more closely aligned, the effects on both spouses may become more similar.

Unaffected siblings have very special problems. In early childhood they may fear that they might develop the disease, and may even envy the attention paid to the affected child. Later, they may become increasingly concerned about having affected children themselves as well as perhaps having to care for the affected sibling when, through age, the parents can no longer cope.

There seems little doubt that the occurrence of a serious genetic disease in a family is likely to have significant psychosocial effects, not only on the affected individual but also on parents and any unaffected siblings, and in this way affect the family unit as a whole. All this will add to any problems the parents already have concerning the possibility of transmitting the disease to any future children and should be taken into account when genetic counselling is being given.

HOLISTIC APPROACH TO COUNSELLING

In the past, much emphasis in genetic counselling has been given to the medical aspects and risks of recurrence. The widespread existence of genetic heterogeneity—that clinically similar disorders can be inherited differently and have different prognoses—means that the establishment of a precise genetic diagnosis is an essential first step in counselling. The determination of a risk figure for the recurrence of a disorder in a family is also very important. But neither of these matters should obscure the essential function of genetic counselling which is to help couples come to terms with the problem and reach a decision which is the right one for themselves. Thus, rather than being *content-oriented*, genetic counselling should be *person-oriented* where the emphasis is more on the psychological aspects of the problem (Kessler, 1979). The need for this approach has been emphasized by the realization that couples given genetic counselling may opt for a course of action which may be at variance with what the counsellor might have considered 'reasonable' or 'responsible'. This was highlighted, for example, in a 2-year follow-up study of 200 consecutive couples seen in a genetic counselling clinic in which over one third of those who were told they were at high risk planned further pregnancies (Emery *et al.*, 1979). In the past, such behaviour might have been considered 'irresponsible' and the results an indictment of counselling in general. But when the couples in this study were carefully questioned, their reasons for planning further children were often very understandable. Further pregnancies were planned in some cases because, after seeing the effects of a disorder in a previous child or in one of the parents, it was not considered sufficiently serious (congenital deafness, peroneal muscular atrophy), or because prenatal diagnosis was available, or in other cases because if a subsequent child were affected, it would not survive (renal agenesis) or would be likely to succumb within a year or so

(Werdnig-Hoffmann disease). There was also a small but lamentable group of couples who had no living children and dearly wanted a family at whatever cost. Thus, a course of action which may seem unreasonable to the counsellor may well be eminently reasonable to the couple. In a free society, the choice must be the individual's prerogative provided it is made in the full knowledge of all the available facts and appreciation of the possible consequences.

A particularly difficult problem has arisen recently with new tests which make it possible by DNA studies to detect, in affected families, healthy individuals who have inherited the gene for Huntington's chorea and who may therefore transmit the disease to their children (see review in Emery, 1984). Those who are tested and found to be negative can be reassured and they will present no problem. But those who prove positive may well find the knowledge that they will inevitably develop an extremely distressing and incurable disease quite intolerable. *Prediagnostic* counselling is therefore essential in this and any other late-onset serious dominant disorders for which similar tests will become available in future. Perhaps only when the counsellor is convinced the individual could accept the results if positive, and the individual clearly appreciates all the consequences, should the test be carried out. The hope is that eventually a treatment will be found when the problem will then be that much less.

Finally, it has to be appreciated that each of the options available to a couple who consider that the risks of having an affected child are unacceptably high, can also be associated with particular psychological problems and these too have to be considered.

PSYCHOLOGICAL PROBLEMS ASSOCIATED WITH VARIOUS OPTIONS

Until a few years ago, the only option available to a couple who considered that the risk of having an affected child was unacceptably high was family limitation with perhaps adoption of a healthy child. But with recent developments, a couple faced with this problem can consider several alternatives, including sterilization, artificial insemination by donor, prenatal diagnosis with selective abortion, and perhaps even *in vitro* fertilization with embryo transfer. Each of these procedures is likely to be associated with different psychological effects on the couple concerned.

Sterilization

Sterilization is indicated when a definitive means of contraception is indicated, as when the parents find the risk of having an affected child unacceptably high and more usual forms of contraception are considered aesthetically displeasing, unsafe in the long-term or insufficiently reliable. The very deep fear of having an affected child may well generate serious psychosexual problems which can often be prevented only by resort to sterilization.

Nowadays, the available techniques for sterilization carry either little risk (female sterilization by tubal ligation) or virtually no risk (male sterilization by vasectomy) when carried out by a competent and experienced surgeon and are associated with very few side-effects. Apart from rare (tubal ligation) or very rare (vasectomy) exceptions the procedure cannot be reversed and sterilization is permanent.

Female sterilization is the most frequently chosen means of sterilization for genetic reasons, though male sterilization is increasingly being requested, perhaps because it is a simpler procedure and is becoming generally more acceptable among the male population. Psychological sequelae following sterilization are especially likely when prenatal diagnosis has not been possible or the parents have previously failed to have a normal child through prenatal diagnosis. In such circumstances, couples may decide upon sterilization to avoid further abnormal pregnancies but may still desire children. Such couples need to be identified and given special counselling. In cases where prenatal diagnosis and selective abortion has been carried out, the couple will require time to separate their feelings of disappointment in not achieving a normal baby from the desire to terminate childbearing (Hollerbach and Nortman, 1984).

After sterilization, a couple may wish to consider adoption but in the last few years this has become increasingly difficult. This is partly because some adoption agencies have become reluctant to place children in families where a parent may have a disabling disorder, but mainly because fewer children are now available for adoption. Therefore, even before raising this option, the counsellor should first determine whether or not, in a particular case, this is a realistic possibility, otherwise there can be considerable frustration and disappointment.

Artificial insemination by donor (AID)

AID can be offered when both parents carry the same *rare* recessive gene, or the father has an autosomal dominant disorder, or he carries a chromosome translocation which in the unbalanced state is likely to result in an affected child as, for example, in some cases of Down's syndrome. In recent years, many centres have been established which can offer this service. However, the success rate, even in expert hands, is not always high and several attempts may be necessary before success is achieved. This can generate considerable frustration and disappointment unless the couple are warned about these problems beforehand. Many couples also find this an unacceptable option for personal and aesthetic reasons, and if the counsellor senses that this is so, the subject should not, of course, be pursued. Nevertheless, increasing numbers of couples are beginning to choose AID, though these are still mainly from the upper socioeconomic classes. In general, the responses of couples to the procedure are largely favourable (Kremer, Frijling and Nass, 1984). But it would be unrealistic to expect that the birth of a child by AID will immediately alleviate feelings of loss by either parent and full and open discussion with a couple on this point is very important.

Prenatal diagnosis

In the last few years, prenatal diagnosis has been a major development which has removed much of the uncertainty in genetic counselling. The technique usually involves withdrawing a small amount of amniotic fluid by the procedure of transabdominal amniocentesis. From studying alphafetoprotein levels in the fluid, it is possible to diagnose neural tube defects (anencephaly and spina bifida) in the foetus. Or the contained amniotic fluid cells can be cultured and the cultured cells then used for cytogenetic and biochemical studies. In this way, disorders such as Down's syndrome and various inborn errors of metabolism can be diagnosed prenatally. The sex of the foetus can also be determined so that if a mother is at risk of having a son with a serious X-linked disorder which cannot yet be diagnosed *in utero*, she can be offered an abortion if the foetus is a male; if the foetus proves to be a female, the pregnancy can be allowed to continue to term since females are not affected. Some of the main indications for prenatal diagnosis are summarized in Table 3.1.

TABLE 3.1   Main indications for prenatal diagnois

---

(1) *Cytogenetic abnormalities*
Mainly Down's syndrome with a previously affected child or maternal age >35–40.
(2) *Inborn errors of metabolism*
Over 60 can now be diagnosed *in utero*. Most are rare recessive disorders.
(3) *Foetal sexing*
X-linked disorders which cannot yet be diagnosed *in utero* (e.g. Duchenne muscular dystrophy).
(4) *Congenital abnormalities*
Mainly neural tube defects with a previously affected child or raised maternal serum alphafetoprotein.

Amniocentesis cannot be carried out much before 14 weeks gestation because, prior to this, there is little amniotic fluid and the uterus is also below the pelvic brim which makes the procedure impossible. In fact, for various reasons, amniocentesis is usually performed at about 16 weeks gestation. This means, at least in the case of biochemical disorders where cells may have to be cultured for several weeks, the pregnancy may have progressed perhaps as far as 20 weeks before a positive prenatal diagnosis can be made. By this stage of pregnancy, the mother may have experienced foetal movements and if termination is indicated this may therefore be especially psychologically traumatic. Recently, however, a new technique of chorion biopsy has been introduced for prenatal diagnosis. This can be carried out as early as 8–10 weeks gestation and coupled with the new DNA tests, which do not require tissue to be cultured, will make prenatal diagnosis possible at a much earlier stage of pregnancy and the procedure, therefore, more acceptable to many couples.

Much has been written about the possible psychological problems associated with prenatal diagnosis, and many of the more important studies have been reviewed by Blumberg (1984). It is useful to consider the problems which may arise in sequence: before the pregnancy, from conception to the time prenatal diagnosis is made, at pregnancy termination when this is indicated, and during the period following termination. When a couple has been told that in their case prenatal diagnosis is possible, this is likely to generate contrasting feelings. On the one hand, the relief that an abnormal child can be avoided in a subsequent pregnancy, while on the other, anxiety that if the test is positive then there is the prospect of abortion. Some couples, especially those who have been fortunate to have a normal child already as well as those whose religious beliefs preclude abortion, may decide against the procedure. But those mothers who opt for prenatal diagnosis may actually suspend recognition of the pregnancy until a test result reveals that the foetus is indeed a potential child (Blumberg, 1984). In these circumstances, the mother may well postpone pregnancy-related behaviour till a normal diagnostic result assures continuation of the pregnancy (Beeson and Golbus, 1979). Almost all mothers questioned experienced considerable anxiety and depression during this waiting period which in most cases disappeared dramatically when the foetus proves to be normal. However, in some mothers there may well linger fears of abnormality in the foetus and they require to be reassured and convinced that their fears are groundless. The communication of the positive result of a prediagnostic test, of course, requires considerable sensitivity.

The actual medical procedure employed for pregnancy termination may exacerbate the psychological problems (Kaltreider, Goldsmith and Margolis, 1979). The vaginal delivery of a dead foetus following a 'mini-labour' induced by prostaglandin, for example, is much more traumatic than dilatation and curettage under general anaesthesia. If the aborted foetus is clearly abnormal (on the basis of its morphology, cytogenetics or biochemistry) then the couple should be assured of this in order to help reduce any feelings of guilt they may have. Such feelings of guilt are likely to be compounded when the mother knows there is a chance the foetus could have been normal. For example, at least a half of the male foetuses of a mother at risk of being a carrier of an X-linked disease will be normal. In these cases, however, there is no way of knowing whether the foetus would or would not have been affected and perhaps it is, therefore, best for the counsellor in this situation to give more emphasis to the negative possibility.

After pregnancy termination, there will follow a period of loss comparable to the grief response to a perinatal death. During this period, the mother may well experience some of the stages of the coping process. Some degree of depression is almost inevitable. A further contributing factor to the emotional burden at this time is the realization that the experience may have to be repeated in any subsequent pregnancy. As mentioned earlier, a couple will require time to separate feelings of disappointment from the desire to terminate childbearing altogether. A few families do experience the misfortune of abnormal prenatal diagnostic results in successive pregnancies and this may well be followed by chronic depression and an unwillingness to risk any further pregnancies (Blumberg, 1984). In this situation, some definitive form of contraception is certainly indicated.

From this brief discussion of some of the psychological problems associated with prenatal diagnosis, it will be clear that prediagnostic counselling is essential. Many of the problems which could arise can then be discussed beforehand so that couples are more prepared. But it is also important that reassuring discussions continue throughout the pregnancy as well as during the post-abortion period. Even then, it seems likely that after a therapeutic abortion most mothers will continue to harbour at least some residual feelings of guilt and loss which in a few cases may never disappear completely.

In Vitro fertilization with embryo transfer

This procedure has already been successfully performed in several centres for certain cases of female infertility. The genetic indications would be where the wife is a carrier of a chromosome translocation or a serious X-linked recessive disorder or she has an autosomal dominant disorder. Here an ovum is donated by an unrelated woman which is then fertilized *in vitro* by sperm from the husband of the carrier in whose uterus it is then implanted. Thus, the wife can carry a baby which at least has been fathered by her husband but to which she herself has made no genetic contribution. There are a number of ethical and legal issues concerned with this technique (Brahams, 1983), but in time it may find a place among the options available to some couples. Doubtless many of the psychological problems associated with AID will also beset couples who select *in vitro* fertilization and embryo transfer. But speculation about these problems seems futile until research provides some hard data. Nevertheless, sensitive counselling, both before and after the procedure, would certainly be necessary.

SUMMARY AND CONCLUSIONS

In recent decades, as environmentally determined disorders as causes of morbidity and mortality have declined, so their place has been taken by genetic disorders. Most of these are serious and few are treatable and so the only approach is through genetic counselling. This is essentially a process of communication between the counsellor and those who seek counselling. The information to be communicated concerns the disease itself (its prognosis, genetics, risks of recurrence) and the options open to a couple who find the risks of having an affected child unacceptably high (sterilization, artificial insemination by donor, prenatal diagnosis with selective abortion, and *in vitro* fertilization with embryo transfer). The profound psychological effects which genetic disease may have on parents, as well as on other family members, have to be appreciated by the counsellor if communication is to be meaningful and helpful.

The occurrence of a genetic disorder in a family frequently generates considerable stress, and the psychological sequence of events which follows is referred to as the 'coping process'. The particular stage in this process reached by a couple has to be recognized so that counselling can be tailored accordingly. Further, each of the options available to a couple at risk can be associated with psychological problems and these also have to be taken into account. For these various reasons, a holistic approach to genetic counselling is essential if this is really to help couples reach decisions which are the right ones for themselves.

REFERENCES

Anderson, J. L., and Kvan, E. (1983). The effect of introducing role-play in a practical on communicating with terminal cancer patients. *Medical Teacher*, **5**, 144–145.

Beeson, D., and Golbus, M. S. (1979). Anxiety engendered by amniocentesis. *Birth Defects*, **15**, 191–197.

Blumberg, B. (1984). The emotional implications of prenatal diagnosis. In A. E. H. Emery and I. M. Pullen (eds), *Psychological Aspects of Genetic Counselling*. London and New York: Academic Press, pp. 201–217.

Brahams, D. (1983). In vitro fertilisation and related research. *Lancet*, **ii**, 726–729.

Buckman, R. (1984). Breaking bad news: why is it still so difficult? *British Medical Journal*, **288**, 1597–1599.

Emery, A. E. H. (1982). Postgraduate training in medical genetics. In B. Bonné-Tamir (ed.), *Human Genetics—The Unfolding Genome. Proceedings of the VI International Congress of Human Genetics*. New York: Alan Liss, pp. 491–497.

Emery, A. E. H. (1984). *An Introduction to Recombinant DNA*. Chichester and New York: John Wiley.

Emery, A. E. H., Raeburn, J. A., Skinner, R., Holloway, S., and Lewis, P. (1979). Prospective study of genetic counselling. *British Medical Journal*, **1**, 1253–1256.

Falek, A. (1977). Use of the coping process to achieve psychological homeostasis in genetic conditions. In H. A. Lubs and F. de la Cruz (eds), *Genetic Counseling*. New York: Raven Press, pp. 179–191.

Falek, A. (1984). Sequential aspects of coping and other issues in decision making in genetic counselling. In A. E. H. Emery and I. M. Pullen (eds), *Psychological Aspects of Genetic Counselling*. London and New York: Academic Press, pp. 23–36.

Firth. M. A. (1983). Diagnosis of Duchenne muscular dystrophy: experiences of parents of sufferers. *British Medical Journal*, **286**, 700–701.

Hollerbach, P. E., and Nortman, D. L. (1984). Sterilization. In A. E. H. Emery and I. M. Pullen (eds), *Psychological Aspects of Genetic Counselling*. London and New York: Academic Press, pp. 169–186.

Kaltreider, N., Goldsmith, S., and Margolis, A. (1979). The impact of midtrimester abortion techniques on patients and staff. *American Journal of Obstetrics and Gynecology*, **135**, 235–238.

Kessler, S. (1979). The psychological foundations of genetic counseling. In S. Kessler (ed.), *Genetic Counseling: Psychological Dimensions*. New York: Academic Press, pp. 17–33.

Kremer, J., Frijling, B. W., and Nass, J. L. M. (1984). Psychological aspects of parenthood by artificial insemination donor. *Lancet*, **i**, 628.

Maguire, P. (1984). Training in genetic counselling. In A. E. H. Emery and I. M. Pullen (eds), *Psychological Aspects of Genetic Counselling*. London and New York: Academic Press, pp. 219–228.

Pless, I. B. (1984). Clinical assessment: physical and psychological functioning. *Pediatric Clinics of North America*, **31**, 33–45.

Sabbeth, B. (1984). Understanding the impact of chronic childhood illness on families. *Pediatric Clinics of North America*, **31**, 47–57.

Siegel, I. M., Davidson, H., Kornfeld, M., and McCready, W. C. (1983). Coping with muscular dystrophy: psychosocial correlates of adaptation. *Muscle and Nerve*, **6**, 607–609.

The Psychosomatic Approach: Contemporary Practice
of Whole-person Care
Edited by M. J. Christie and P. G. Mellett
© 1986 John Wiley & Sons Ltd

4

CONTEMPORARY ATTITUDES TO CARE IN LABOUR

NORMAN MORRIS

Charing Cross Hospital Medical School, University of London and
Department of Obstetrics, West London Hospital, London, UK

SUE M. COPSTICK

and

KATHY E. TAYLOR

Department of Psychology, North East London Polytechnic and Department
of Obstetrics, Charing Cross Hospital Medical School, University of
London, UK

INTRODUCTION

There is no doubt that obstetrics has become one of the most controversial areas of medicine, since hospital deliveries replaced home confinements around the 1960s. The main issues centre on what has been called the 'medicalization' of the 'natural' act of childbirth, where modern obstetrics is frequently viewed as intervening or interfering with the process of labour and delivery rather than aiding it. Indeed, obstetrics has been accused of transforming the act of childbirth into a pseudo-illness which it must 'cure', and many women's movements have sought to reemphasize childbirth as a positive and natural act in which women must actively participate rather than to which they must passively submit.

Unfortunately, many obstetricians and obstetric researchers dismiss the claims and aims of such women's movements almost as quickly as some women dismiss the claims of obstetricians! However, for more than 26 years, the Charing Cross maternity department has prided itself on listening to the opinions and hopes of women, and traditionally has attempted to understand the process of 'natural' childbirth. Underlying this tradition has been the common aim of obstetrics—to produce a healthy child (at the culmination of labour), at the least physical and psychological cost to the mother. Not only have we questioned and examined, for example, the routine use of episiotomy in labour, and the most useful position for delivery of the child, we have also looked at the quality of relationships present throughout labour, and their contribution to obstetric outcome. Ironically, although we have grave doubts about some of the accusations made regarding maternity care by various women's groups, it does seem that the quality of the experience of childbirth can be improved if women are respected, and cared for in much the same way as they would be at home by their friends and family.

At the West London Hospital, we have actively attempted to create a 'new obstetrics' where women can have babies in a secure, caring atmosphere which encourages them to participate actively in their labours with the minimum 'interference' and the maximum help and encouragement. At the same time they are secure in the knowledge that they are in safe hands should any major medical intervention be necessary. We are not alone in this quest, and this chapter will outline some of the newest advances in obstetrics and midwifery which endeavour to improve the quality of the labour experience for the mother and her child. Before presenting and discussing these ideas and techniques, it is important to turn to the history of care in labour in order to understand how ideas have developed as a result of social and environmental influences.

APPROACHES TO LABOUR IN PAST CENTURIES

The story of how midwifery began is well recorded by Flack (1946–1947). It seems that every present-day primitive tribe has the same kind of story to tell but they differ greatly in detail across the world.

In the beginning when the women gave birth to children they might or might not receive any help and encouragement. Whether they were helped by men or by women or not at all depended on the degree of social development of the particular community. Apparently, in the most primitive communities, the woman remained alone and helped herself as best she could. Her menfolk would welcome the child, especially if it was a boy, but were quite indifferent to the process of bringing him into the world. Intuition, for want of a better word, would lead the primitive woman, as it does animals, to bear her young and sever with her teeth the umbilical cord.

Later, and this represented an important cultural advance, the husband no longer forsook the woman in labour but remained with her and helped her as best he could. This apparently still happens among the natives of the Brazilian interior. As soon as the woman feels the birth beginning, she lies on the ground, her husband stays with her and when the child is delivered he ties the umbilical cord, he then bites through it, leaving the placenta to be delivered in the usual way. He paints the child red before laying it ceremonially in a specially prepared cot. Indian women of the Caraya tribe in Brazil deliver in the squatting position, grasping a post with their hands. The husband takes up the same position immediately behind and with both hands presses down on the contracting woman. Apparently, a similar procedure is followed by husbands of the women of Gorngay and Tungu on the Malayan island of Kola and Kobroor.

In a later phase of cultural development, the husband was no longer actively engaged in assisting in the labour, but had a symbolic role to play. In Guyana and among certain Caribbean tribes the husband takes to his bed and groans terribly to inform everyone of the pain he is sharing. Apparently Marco Polo observed the same custom in China 600 years ago.

The next stage of cultural development excluded the husband and came to regard parturition as an exclusively female concern. This was not so much from modesty as for mixed magical and social reasons. Birth became a purely female business and an event to be kept from profane male eyes. Almost certainly at this stage of development help was given by all the women who had themselves experienced childbirth. In certain groups, especially among the Maori, there was strict order of precedence; assistance was given by the maternal grandmother, or if she no longer existed the paternal grandmother presided; failing that, the mother-in-law came next. Among the Trobriand islanders, society is matrilineal and patrilocal and the pregnant woman goes to her father's house, for there she can be looked after by her mother and her mother's kinsmen; all males leave the house but keep guard to prevent the approach of sorcerers. The husband helps in this duty, but plays a very minor role.

Another step forward in the care of women during labour came when the women of the family gave way to 'experienced women', and these experienced women must be regarded as the forerunners of modern midwives. Formal payment of these wise women was later developed, but it has always been customary among the wives of Borneo headhunters to give them presents of some kind as a reward for their assistance. Among the Sudanese, the Abyssinians, the Bedouin and the Kabyle, experienced women were always present at a birth and usually made arrangements well beforehand for their attendance. The wives of Hottentots, and bushmen, ordered their wise women well in advance and were delivered lying on the left side. Three or four women would take it in turns to exert pressure on the uterus at each pain.

From 'experienced women' to the first midwives proper is a rather long step. It is not unreasonable to assume that this step has been taken when we find that a tribe has a special word for these women, and one that can mean much more than 'experienced'. In the Temimber and Timrlaut islands *wata siting* is the word; on the island of Ceram *ahinatukaan*; in Fiji *alewa vuku* and in the Philippines *mabutingilot*. There is good evidence that primitive birth was associated with various forms of positions involving sitting, squatting or kneeling and possibly standing. Elaborations of these positions involved the setting up of posts or crossbars to which the woman could cling. It seems that the development of a recumbent position came very much later and the first reference is towards the end of the seventeenth century. At about the same time male accoucheurs became more involved with labour. It seems that recumbent posture must to some extent be related to their appearance on the scene, and in recent years a new interest has developed regarding the importance of posture in labour (Dunn, 1976; Caldeyro-Barcia, 1979; Odent, 1980).

It seems that a primitive form of birth chair has also been used for countless centuries. For example, the bas-reliefs of the royal birth rooms at Luxor and in other temples confirm this conclusion. One of the best known shows a

queen of the eighteenth dynasty; she is in labour on an obstetric chair and
has four midwives in attendance. Another is a bas-relief in the temple of
Esneh which is believed to show the labour of Cleopatra. The queen is in a
squatting position and is assisted by a group of five women, one of whom
holds two ankhs or tau crosses, royal symbols of generation. The child that
is illustrated is almost full grown at delivery which is another symbolic
recording of royal power (Ploss, Bartles and Bartles, 1935). The Westcar
papyrus mentions the special birth chair. In its simplest form this consists of
two stones, one to support each buttock of the bearing-down woman.

In Roman times the practice of obstetrics was considerably influenced by
Soranus of Ephesus, who flourished about AD 200. He lived for some time
in Alexandria and then practised as a Physician in Rome during the reigns
of Trajan and Hadrian. On coming to Rome, Soranus immediately undertook
a crusade against the superstitious practices of the midwives and advocated
management of the pregnant woman based upon knowledge rather than
superstition. In reading his life one is struck by the similarity to that of
Smellie who appeared in London 15 centuries later and who was certainly a
kindred spirit. Soranus' knowledge of female anatomy, unique in his time,
gave him a foundation upon which he could base a rational technique for
the management of the parturient women. His work *De utero et pudendo
muliebri* was later translated and published in London in 1545 by William
Raynalde as *The Byrth of Mankynde*. This little book had a very profound
influence on the practice of obstetrics in the sixteenth century—much more
than that of the contemporary and more scientific workers.

The midwife was advised to 'instruct and comfort the party with sweet
words giving her good hope of a speedful deliverance, encouraging and
enstomaching her to patience and tolerance, bidding her to hold her breath
insomuch as she may, and stroking with her hands her belly above the navel
for that helpeth to depress the birth downward'.

The use of forceps came relatively late in the development of obstetric
practice and probably was first used during the early to mid seventeenth
century by Peter Chamerlain working in London. Caesarean section,
although probably practised in relation to women who died just before or
during childbirth, was not used for delivery in a live woman until the end of
the nineteenth century.

Inevitably, it is difficult to obtain reliable records of the results of primitive
birth; neither is there any evidence that women usually had a relatively
straightforward and natural experience. Almost certainly, serious problems
did arise during labour which resulted in the death of the baby and frequently
the mother. It seems, therefore, that it is quite unjustified to blame civiliz-
ation for the development of pain in labour as well as other problems such
as ineffective uterine action and postpartum haemorrhage. The whole question of natural labour is explored more fully later in the chapter. However,
the evidence from previous centuries does not support the concept that
labour, even in healthy women, has ever been completely straightforward,
uncomplicated and painless, i.e. natural.

The experience of childbirth

Around the 1940s, male obstetricians forwarded the notion that childbirth was a painless experience (Dick-Read, 1933; Velvosky, Platonov and Ploticher 1960), and the idea that the psychological state of women before and during labour were paramount in determining obstetric outcome. With this in mind, Dick-Read in England, and Velvosky in Russia, set out to produce a formal set of techniques to be used in labour to affect the mother's psychological state and therefore her experience of labour. This was one of the first attempts to improve care in labour and, as we shall see, it also introduced the idea that antenatal preparation or education was an essential part of obstetric practice. In the following section we shall examine the various theories and techniques of Dick-Read and Velvosky, and discuss the efficacy of these in reducing anxiety and pain in labour.

PSYCHOLOGICAL ASPECTS OF LABOUR

The psychological state of women in labour can affect their experiences of childbirth and their ability to cope with the considerable pain of contractions. Although this has been known for some time, the relation between psychological factors and obstetric outcome remains poorly understood. For example, a study carried out at the West London Hospital found that highly anxious women (anxiety was assessed on the state index of the State-Trait Anxiety Inventory (Spielberger, 1966) required anaesthetics (epidural block) more frequently than non-anxious women (Haddad and Morris, 1982). Even though this result was extremely significant, the processes and mechanisms relating anxiety to the extent of need for the epidural block are still being isolated and examined.

Research in psychology, however, suggests that anxious women in labour are less able to tolerate, or to cope with, painful contractions than are non-anxious, fairly relaxed women. The obvious clinical implication of this is the need to devise methods of helping women in labour to relax and overcome their anxiety—which was one of the aims of the antenatal training programmes devised by Dick-Read (1933) and Velvosky, Platonov and Ploticher, (1960).

Grantley Dick-Read

Throughout the history of obstetrics, there have been many attempts to explain and understand the role of psychological factors in childbirth. For example, Dick-Read (1933, 1944) proposed what he called the 'fear–tension–pain syndrome' to explain why many of his anxious patients reported having distressing and painful labours. Dick-Read felt that 'natural' childbirth should be relatively painless, and that labour pain was created by 'socially induced expectations' and 'cultural misconceptions' about labour: specifically the belief that labour is painful. He claimed that anxiety and tension in labour gave 'rise to resistance at the outlet of the womb', which produced the experience of pain because 'the uterus was supplied with organs which record pain set up by excessive tension' (Dick-Read, 1944). Thus Dick-Read's theory postulated a causal relationship between anxiety and labour pain, where worry and fear created perceptions of pain during contractions. It followed that a reduction of anxiety and fear would lead to a reduction in pain throughout labour, and to this end Dick-Read proposed a series of techniques to reduce or abolish labour pain.

It was proposed that the 'fear–tension–pain syndrome' could be reversed if mothers were adequately prepared for labour. First, pregnant mothers attended a series of lectures concerning developmental and procedural details of their pregnancy and labour. Mothers were educated to expect painless, uncomplicated labour and delivery and were reassured that labour was not a distressing experience. Second, any tension or anxiety which occurred in labour was to be reduced by the use of muscle relaxation and slow, regular deep breathing. These techniques were introduced and rehearsed in the antenatal period, but were used during contractions in labour.

Velvosky

Another theory attempting to understand and explain the role of psychological factors in labour was proposed by Velvosky and his team in Russia around the 1940s. Velvosky (Velvosky, Platonov and Ploticher, 1960) introduced 'psychoprophylaxis', or the Pavlov method of childbirth, to obstetrics, which conceptualized labour pain as a conditioned response produced by an imbalance or disruption of the excitatory–inhibitory processes in the cortex and subcortex. This disruption of equilibrium which created the sensation of pain was catalysed by 'negative emotions' such as anxiety, insecurity and lack of confidence. Thus, the less negative emotion was apparent throughout labour the less pain would be experienced. The term 'psychoprophylaxis' referred to a series of techniques aimed to prevent or reduce anxiety and pain in labour, and the five basic components of the techniques were that mothers should be

(1) provided with a rational framework in which to comprehend pain control techniques, pregnancy and delivery by attending lectures on anatomy and physiology; in other words, the neurophysiology of pain was considered in some detail;
(2) taught deep breathing which they were to use throughout labour;
(3) taught how and where to stroke the abdomen during contractions to ease discomfort and pain;
(4) trained in how pressure applied to certain 'pressure points' (these were located along the small of the back and the medial surface of the anterior superior ilia) could reduce pain when contractions occurred;
(5) encouraged to manage their own labour by timing contractions, and the intervals between contractions, and applying their training accordingly.

Subsequent techniques evolved from psychoprophylaxis, such as physiop-sychoprophylaxis (Petrov-Mascolov, 1972), where mothers participated in antenatal gymnastic training and were given hydrotherapy. Lamaze (1958) integrated Soviet techniques into his notion of 'controlled neuromuscular relaxation', which involved relaxing and controlling specific muscle groups, and using deep breathing during the first stage of labour, rapid breathing during the second stage, and panting during crowning and delivery.

Both these theories claimed that an anxious, ignorant woman lacking in confidence was likely to have a painful and distressing labour because anxiety produces an increase in pain for a variety of theoretical reasons. Although interesting, such theories remain mere opinions unless substantiated by reliable evidence, and the initial support for these theories was the clinical observations of the theorists themselves. Their clinical reports are largely anecdotal, and totally devoid of adequate scientific control, and do not prove any theories or validate any claims made by theorists concerning the role of anxiety and its relation to labour pain.

Typical research into the efficiency of antenatal training

There are no studies to our knowledge that directly test the validity of the theories of Velvosky and Dick-Read. Indeed, the most common approach has been to accept or reject theories on the basis of the efficiency of the techniques suggested. In accordance with this line of thinking, many studies have now been conducted attempting to assess the efficiency of psychopro-phylaxis in preparation for labour in reducing pain and anxiety in labour itself, and generally have reported significant results. Unfortunately, it is the authors' opinion that little can be concluded from such studies regarding the status of antenatal training and the role of psychological factors in labour, due to the limited designs, methodological errors and inadequate controls of studies.

As pointed out previously by Beck and Hall (1978), Beck, Geden and Brouder (1979) and Beck and Seigel (1980), many studies fail to allocate subjects randomly to different experimental conditions (Bergström-Walan, 1963; Davis and Morrone, 1975; Enkin, Smith and Dermer, 1972; Huttel, Mitchell and Fischer, 1972; Klusman, 1975; Scott and Rose, 1976; Zax, Sameroff and Farnum, 1975) and also fail to include appropriate control groups. In addition, many studies make a fundamental error in their design by including a range of measures which may or may not directly assess the efficiency of antenatal training. Most studies involve two groups of primip-arous women, a group who attend antenatal classes and a group who do not. Differences in the labours of these groups are then assessed in a number of ways, most of which comprise details of medical procedures which occurred during the labour such as forceps, anaesthesia, analgesia, length of labour and rate of cervical dilatation. Although a minority of studies have assessed subjective indices throughout labour such as pain or anxiety (Beck and

Seigel, 1980; Davids and DeVault, 1962), the majority fail to assess the subjective experiences of women in any way; a serious example of negligence in research which claims to assess the efficiency of techniques specifically aimed at modifying subjective experience in labour.

The only way to assess the extent to which antenatal training reduces pain and anxiety in labour is directly to measure such variables throughout labour. As it is, many studies have to assume that pain is indexed by, for example, epidural administration as results typically show that fewer women who have attended antenatal classes require epidural blocks than women who have not (Bergström-Walan, 1963; Davis and Morrone, 1975; Enkin, Smith and Dermer 1972; Huttel, Mitchell and Fischer, 1972; Klusman, 1975; Scott and Rose, 1976; Zax, Sameroff and Farnum, 1975; Charles et al., 1978). However, it is unclear whether this assumption can be made in the light of research which illustrates the potency of sociocognitive variables in determining illness and pain behaviour. For example, it may be that women, who have attended antenatal classes, and who complete labour without anaesthesia, feel less inclined to verbalize their pain and discomfort openly because of social pressure and expectations generated from classes. If so, then it is possible that class attenders simply complained less about their discomfort and distress (Skevington, 1983).

A second study carried out in the Charing Cross unit emphasized another oversight of many studies examining the efficiency of antenatal training (Copstick et al., in press). This study examined the extent to which women could use their antenatal training throughout labour, as it seemed many studies assumed that women who attended antenatal classes automatically used their training during their labour to good effect. We assessed women on three occasions: at the onset of contractions, when they were newly established on the labour ward and at the onset of the second stage of labour. We found there was a very significant inverse relationship between use of antenatal techniques such as breathing, relaxation and postural techniques and progression through labour: the further labour had progressed the less likely the women were to be using their pain control techniques. This relationship held regardless of whether the women were anaesthetized or not, although those women who had an epidural block tended to use their coping skills—pain control techniques—less than non-anaesthetized women at all stages of labour. These results are consistent with previous coincidental observations in clinical populations, which noted that the use of antenatal training or pain control techniques was both difficult and ineffectual in the later stages of labour (Wardle, 1975; Perfrement, 1982; St James Roberts et al., 1983). Thus it cannot be assumed that all women use their antenatal training throughout labour.

This finding could be interpreted in two ways. First, it could be suggested that the theories of Grantley Dick-Read and Velvosky require modification as their antenatal programmes do not automatically produce a decrease in pain and anxiety in labour. Alternatively, the basic theories may remain untested and unrefuted if it could be argued that there were discrepancies between the antenatal programmes suggested by Dick-Read and Velvosky and the programmes operated by studies. Unfortunately, most published studies do not provide details of their antenatal training programmes; even so, one large discrepancy between the original version and the modernized counterpart of psychoprophylaxis became clear. Velvosky and his team emphasized the importance of the nurse, friend or obstetrician present with the woman throughout her labour, encouraging her to use her breathing and postural techniques as well as providing pain relief by massage. Although some antenatal programmes do involve a labour partner (usually the father of the child: Vellay, 1959; Davenport-Slacks and Boylan, 1975), the majority do not. The significance of our study must be to reemphasize the importance of those present throughout labour in encouraging the use of pain control techniques, and in supporting and reassuring the woman in labour, as was suggested originally by Soviet research and more recently by others (Morris, 1983; Vellay, 1983). Until the pain control techniques taught in the antenatal period are actually used in labour during painful contractions, then the status of the theories of Dick-Read and Velvosky regarding the role of certain psychological variables in labour remain obscure and uncertain.

Support and encouragement during labour

Although there is no direct evidence to confirm the suggestion that the successful use of pain control techniques depends largely on the presence of supportive attendants who encourage their use, studies exist which have examined the effects of the presence of a partner in labour (usually the father of the child). Some studies report that the mere presence of a partner in labour produces a reduction in the length of labour, medication levels and reported pain (Davenport-Slacks and Boylan, 1974; Henneborn and Cogan, 1975) while others claim the effectiveness of fathers, who have been trained to prevent anxiety occurring, in reducing pain and anxiety in labour (Worthington and Martin, 1980). These studies also report a reduced frequency of anaesthesia (Davenport-Slacks, 1974; Bright and Wallan, 1963; Henneborn and Cogan, 1963) and of forceps deliveries when a partner has been present. Such findings may be further validated in the light of psychological research, showing that the supported use of pain control techniques (as taught in antenatal classes) can effectively reduce reported pain (Worthington and Martin, 1980; Stone, Demchik-Stone and Horan, 1977), and such results have been shown to have predictive value in obstetric populations (Worthington, 1982). We feel that the influence of encouragement and support from staff in labour has in recent years been understated, and suggest that the effects of various types of psychological intervention in labour would be a fruitful and important area of investigation for future research into 'natural childbirth'. For although there is no direct evidence that the use of antenatal training reduces difficulties and distress in labour, it does seem that support and encouragement in labour are as important as preparation for labour in the antenatal period.

Anxiety and pain reduction

Whether the use of antenatal training does restore the excitatory–inhibitory equilibrium in the brain as Velvosky suggested, or it reduces pain via relaxation as Dick-Read suggested, is as yet unknown, but recent research confirms that one aspect of their theories may be accurate. Many observers found that highly anxious women reported more pain in labour than non-anxious women and it is probable that such complaints from patients promoted the administration of anaesthetics and analgesics, thus producing the increased incidence of pain medication in anxious women (Crandon, 1975; Beck *et al.*, 1980; Cogan, Henneborn and Klopfer, 1976; Klusman, 1975). The theories of Dick-Read and Lamaze claimed that anxiety *produced* pain, and while their concept of anxiety was one which encompassed worry and apprehension, their conceptualization of pain was as a quasi-mechanistic physiological process. Indeed, it is only recently that medical psychology has begun to understand pain as having an emotional or cognitive component, which may be as important in determining the quality and intensity of pain as physiological and biochemical factors.

Essentially, we feel that the relationship between anxiety and pain is not such that anxiety directly modifies the sensory experiences of women in labour; we suggest that anxiety does directly relate to the way in which women *react* to their sensory experiences, which are mainly the uterine contractions. Psychological theorists have hypothesized that maternal anxiety may make mothers intolerant of their bodily experiences, leading them readily to label sensations as 'awful', 'excruciating' or 'intolerable', whereas non-anxious of women experience much the same physical sensations but do not 'catastrophize' or panic about them in the same way (Wardle, in press; Gracely, Dubner and McGrath, 1979). The implication is that the use of antenatal training enables mothers to tolerate or cope with painful contractions, rather than reducing the total physical discomfort of these contractions as, for example, an epidural block would (Pearce, 1983). Thus, rather than claim that the use of antenatal training 'reduces pain', it should be more appropriately claimed that the use of relaxation and breathing techniques in labour enables women to *tolerate* their labour pain, and non-anxious women may be better equipped to tolerate labour pain because they are not at the outset beset by fears and worries of pain and labour. The derogatory and incapacitating effects of anxiety on pain tolerance have also been observed in other clinical populations, such as those recovering from major surgery (Ridgway and Mathews, 1982).

Thus, Dick-Read and Velvosky both appear accurate in their claims that the non-anxious woman will tolerate her pain better than anxious women rather than actually experience less pain than anxious women. However, the question still remains of the validity of their claims for the efficacy of their various techniques in reducing pain and anxiety in labour.

The efficacy of pain control in labour

Dick-Read claimed that women in labour experienced pain because they had approached the whole experience of labour with the expectation that it was going to be distressing, unpleasant and painful. Expectations of pain led to fear and anxiety, which in turn created somatic conditions likely to enhance pain and discomfort in labour. He theorized that pain would be tolerated better if mothers were led to expect a painless labour, and to expect that, although uncomfortable, labour was a positive and potentially fulfilling event. Mothers were also to be well informed of procedural details in labour, so as to understand events around them. However, at least one study has shown that information about obstetric procedures given to unprepared women in labour can actually increase their anxiety rather than decrease it (Astbury, 1980), and generally it has been suggested that psychological characteristics of the mother concerning expectations or attitudes towards labour and motherhood are unrelated to obstetric outcome in labour (Zajicek, 1981). At the moment there is little evidence to support the notion that expectations of pain in labour induce painful contractions and multiple obstetric complications in labour.

Psychoprophylaxis, on the other hand, puts much more emphasis on the correct use of breathing, posture, muscle control and relaxation in labour to reduce anxiety and increase pain tolerance. In practice it does appear that the use of appropriate pain control techniques in labour effectively modifies experiences of pain in relation to various alternative treatments. Relaxation, for example, has been found to reduce labour pain (Cogan, 1978; Clum, Luscomb and Scott, 1982) and ischemic pain to a greater extent than no treatment at all. Others have found that women who did not 'catastrophize' their pain, and who were able to distract themselves by singing or praying, were better able to tolerate contractions (Booth, 1983; Niven, 1983), perhaps suggesting that relaxation techniques and the coping statements rehearsed by mothers simply act as distractors (McCarl and Malott, 1984). In Lamaze training, for example, the woman is asked to select an object on which to focus her attention, and this may distract her from her sensations (Leventhal et al., 1981), so lessening her awareness of pain. Indeed, not only do individuals seem to prefer distraction techniques in comparison with other techniques (Hackett and Horan, 1980) but it may be that the effectiveness of a partner in labour is due to the distracting effects of having a familiar person to attend to. Women may be able to cope with the labour pain when they do not exclusively attend to it, and the presence of a partner who encourages a woman to rehearse relaxation and breathing techniques, engage in conversation and change bodily position must to some extent offer alternative stimuli with which to occupy her (Bobey and Davidson, 1976). A partner in labour would also encourage the mother to be active throughout her labour, rather than passively to submit to medical management and pain relief, and the inverse relation between physical and/or psychological activity and levels of pain have been documented in chronic pain management (Folkard, 1976) and in back pain (Slade *et al.*, 1983; Rosenstiel and Keefe, 1983). Thus, regardless of whether psychoprophylaxis is effective by operating as a distractor or whether its efficacy is due to some other mechanism, evidence suggests that it can be effective and therefore should be encouraged in labour.

The clinical implications of research

It is known that anxious women are less likely to cope with, or tolerate, their labour pain, and it is known that rehearsal of breathing and relaxation techniques reduces anxiety. It would follow that women who rehearse their pain control techniques *in labour* will increase their pain tolerance, and thereby stand a better chance of completing labour without epidural anaesthesia which in turn often appears to increase the need for forceps application. Antenatal preparation for labour may prime the woman to use her pain control techniques in labour, but as we have shown, it does not guarantee that she will. Therefore, we regard it as one of the duties of staff on the labour ward to encourage and support the use of breathing, relaxation and postural techniques through labour. A mother should not only be encouraged to rehearse her 'coping' techniques in the antenatal period, but should also be instructed to recruit a labour partner to distract her from concentrating solely on her painful contractions, and encourage her to use her breathing, relaxation and postural skills. The labour partner is often the father of the child and an intimate of the mother's, which has the advantage that the couple already have a trusting relationship established, and the disadvantage of the professional inexperience of the partner (birth will often be frightening novelty for him also). Obstetricians such as Vellay (1983) have suggested that a midwife or experienced woman (monitress) specially trained to be supportive and encouraging in labour, should be present with the couple. Our recommendations are, of course, conjectures until research assesses the efficacy of various types of pain control techniques in labour, and assesses the importance of support in labour, but research in the psychology of pain cited earlier would tend to support our hypothesis.

OTHER CONTEMPORARY VIEWS

Not all innovations in labour care have exclusively involved psychology. Indeed, obstetricians have examined a whole range of factors which may contribute to the quality of labour, and the following sections will present the ideas of three obstetricians who have richly contributed to the study of childbirth and who have attempted to improve care in labour.

Frederic Leboyer

Frederic Leboyer, in his book *Pour une naissance sans violence* (1974), drew our attention to the circumstances which surround the birth of the baby in a hospital environment. He suggests that the neonate is often subject to violent exposure to noise and other stimuli. In addition he emphasizes that frequently the baby is not handled with very great gentleness. Whilst there is no immediate proof that this kind of birth does produce problems later in life, it has been the view of many psychoanalysts that violence at birth may be a factor which is not unrelated to psychological problems later in life. There is still uncertainty and controversy about the factors that influence the early development of the baby, both from a physical and a physhological point of view. It has been naïvely assumed that the foetus *in utero*, both during pregnancy and labour, as well as the neonate immediately after birth, is relatively immune to the trauma that Leboyer describes, though this needs to be viewed against the background of Barratt (1981) and Mills (1981) in the earlier companion volume. Leboyer admits that the scientific proof of his theory has yet to be established, but he emphasizes that in the present state of our ignorance it may be unwise to perpetuate a system of violent birth, particularly in an age when technological interference is more frequent than ever before.

Leboyer is concerned with every aspect of perception that may influence the newborn's reaction to birth. For this reason he considers that both the noise level and the method of illumination in the labour ward should receive consideration. In other words, he believes that babies should be born in an environment where all external stimuli are reduced to a minimum, and wherever practical subdued lighting should be provided. Leboyer is not suggesting that the accoucheur should be encouraged to work without sufficient light, but merely pleads for dim lights as opposed to the hard, violent lighting which is commonplace in many labour wards today. Frederic Leboyer produced a film to illustrate his ideas, which stimulated many contemporary obstetricians to rethink their attitudes to the management of the second stage of labour and more particularly the actual moment of birth.

Leboyer also advanced the proposition that the baby may derive comfort from being immersed in a warm bath immediately following delivery and his film demonstrates this in the most dramatic way by recording the early neonate's reaction to this experience, ending with a smile. Certainly it does suggest that at least in this particular instance the young child received considerable comfort and confidence from immersion in a warm bath. The views of Leboyer have made an impact on the contemporary obstetric scene, but evidence that this approach has any ultimate value is still awaited. Most labour wards remain rather noisy, insensitive places where the needs of the medical and nursing staff sometimes seem to be of more importance than those of the mother, father and child.

Frederic Leboyer's main contribution has probably been to encourage the modern midwife and obstetrician to treat the moment of birth as something rather more important than a mere physical event. There is evidence that women are now treated with greater understanding at the moment of birth and that babies are no longer handled in such a rough and ready manner. In our own labour ward at the West London Hospital, where we have largely adopted the views of Leboyer, we find that the mother and father very much appreciate the tranquil atmosphere that we try to create. Within this atmosphere the mother, and in particular her baby, seem to receive more consideration and respect.

Michel Odent

Michel Odent works in a small maternity unit in Pithiviers, a large village 60 kilometres to the south of Paris. Although this department delivers only just over 1000 babies a year it has become a centre which is now well known in obstetric circles. Odent's approach is similar to that of Leboyer, and he claims that he was much influenced by Leboyer's philosophy. Essentially, Odent tries to create an accommodating atmosphere in which the mother is encouraged to follow her own instincts. Odent does not believe in formal childbirth education classes; he thinks they are rigid and inflexible because they lay down a series of instructions which involve complicated exercises which cannot always be carried out in labour by the average mother. In his department women meet together during the antenatal period but these sessions are mainly for discussion amongst themselves. Frequently they also join in singing accompanied by a piano in the room where they meet.

This philosophy is followed through to the labour ward itself where he provides both conventional and unconventional labour rooms. The unconventional room is a very simple room indeed in which he provides the minimum of facilities and there is a complete absence of medical equipment. The room is painted brown, the curtains are orange, a rafia shade covers the light bulb, there is a low, spacious platform with many brightly coloured cushions; there is a wooden armchair which can also be used as an obstetric chair. In addition, there is a record player and records are available as required. In this *salle sauvage*, Odent encourages his mothers to adopt whatever position they feel is best for them. No instructions of any kind are given to them, either antenatally or in labour, regarding the posture that others (midwives or doctors) think they should adopt. For this reason women in Odent's department adopt a wide range of different postures when in labour and Odent claims he has observed that women adopt 'a boundless variety of positions'. Odent emphasizes that there is a need to search for alternative positions because of the frequent asymetric position of the pelvis. He also claims that by adopting this permissive approach to posture in the first and second stages of labour we are encouraging 'the woman's body to find again what she has forgotten during the last millennia'.

Baths

More recently, Odent has encouraged his mothers to immerse themselves in a bath during labour and sometimes the midwife gets into the bath with the patient. He considers the effect of the bath very relaxing and reassuring and the women often stay in the bath for very long periods of time and occasionally actually deliver the baby in the bath without apparent ill-effect. Here again, this seems a very unconventional approach to the management of labour. But our preliminary observations of the use of a bath during labour support Odent's claims. This is an area where very much more research is required in order to establish whether in fact immersion in a bath has any real effect upon the progress of labour, and also whether it does effectively reduce the woman's need for analgesics and anaesthesia. Michel Odent (1983) has in fact reported 100 deliveries under water and only two of these required suction and a short period of manual ventilatory support. Our preliminary studies with the baths available in our unit suggest that women do often obtain a considerable sense of comfort and pain relief by being immersed in a bath for varying periods of time. We therefore intend to increase the provision of baths and our ultimate objective is to have a bath attached to each individual delivery room. The present intention is not to deliver the baby in the bath, but merely to immerse the woman during the first and second stage in order to provide additional pain relief. More information is required in relation to this new development, but our preliminary observations are encouraging.

Roberto Caldeyro-Barcia

It is interesting that another distinguished obstetrician who has been well known for many years for his scientific investigation of uterine action has reached similar conclusions to those of Odent. He believes that women should be encouraged to ambulate during the first stage of labour as freely as they wish (Caldeyro-Barcia, 1960). Caldeyro-Barcia (1979) has, however, also raised another issue. He thinks that women should not be encouraged to push with a closed glottis during the second stage. This, of course, has been the conventional way for women to assist their delivery during the second stage of labour and obviously it will take some time for midwives and mothers to adjust their approach to a more gentle way of pushing. Caldeyro-Barcia has shown that with the closed glottis there is a slow but very definite fall in P_{O_2} and pH accompanied by a rise in P_{CO_2}.

If, on the other hand, the woman is encouraged to push in a gentle manner without closure of the glottis, although the second stage will often last longer, there is in fact no reduction in P_{O_2}, even if labour goes on for 3 hours. Obstetricians generally have so far been reluctant to accept the evidence that Caldeyro-Barcia has presented and there are few reports of studies being undertaken that will confirm his results. Obviously, the conventional way of pushing with a closed glottis has become so deeply entrenched within modern obstetric practice that it will take some time to eradicate.

Caldeyro-Barcia suggests that during the second stage we should also try to ensure that the woman adopts a vertical position, squatting or otherwise, and any voluntary effort on her part should be limited to very gentle pushing with an open glottis, associated with different styles of squatting. It is an accepted fact that in the majority of childbirth education classes carried out in the UK the mother is actually encouraged during the antenatal period to rehearse pushing in the second stage with a closed glottis.

Ambulation

In recent years there has been increasing emphasis on the value of ambulation in labour. Here again the evidence has not been conclusive.

On the whole, however, there does seem to be general agreement that ambulation is desirable and that in the 'normal' case it may well have a beneficial effect on the course of labour. First, if women are free to walk around they are often better able to cope with labour pains by adopting a variety of positions. Second, it does seem that at least in some women, ambulation encourages the development of more effective uterine action and may therefore shorten the labour. It has to be admitted, however, that more studies are required in order to clarify the situation one way or another. When an epidural anaesthetic is administered, the woman is no longer able to ambulate and in this sense an epidural can be seen as a disadvantage.

Humphrey et al., (1974), Flynn et al., (1978) and more recently Stewart and Calder (1984) have shown that an upright position and ambulation are associated with a shorter and easier labour. Stewart and Calder, however, claim that it is because labour is easier for some women that they can manage to ambulate.

Other observers—McManus and Calder (1978), and Calvert, Newcombe and Hubbard (1982)—have not agreed with these findings. In other words, it seems that at least for the time being this must remain an open issue.

Squatting

It is interesting that Ingleman's book *Labour Among Primitive Peoples* published in 1882 states that

> a vast and important fund of knowledge may be derived from a study of the various positions occupied by women of different peoples in their labours. The recumbent position is rarely assumed among those who live naturally and have escaped the influence of civilisation and modern obstetrics. According to their build, to the shape of their pelvis, they stand, squat, kneel or lie on the belly. So also they vary their positions

in the various stages of labour according to the position of the child's head in the pelvis.

He continues

I deem it a great mistake that we should follow custom or fashion so completely to the exclusion of reason and instinct. In a mechanical act which so nearly concerns our animal nature, instinct will guide the woman more correctly than the varying customs of the times. For the moment it seems that the instinct of many centuries has been modified and inhibited by the accepted conventions of the past few centuries. It will be interesting to see how far this movement towards squatting in labour does assume the significant proportion.

As we have seen earlier, squatting was usually the position adopted by primitive women during the second stage of labour in order to deliver the baby. Some women, indeed, delivered standing up. There has been a recent reawakening of interest in the squatting position and this is now adopted in some departments. In our own department, we carried out a preliminary study on 50 primiparous patients who volunteered to attempt squatting. Indeed, they came to us asking to have this form of delivery. The results of this study are shown in Table 4.1. The data suggest that at least in this particular series squatting was an advantage as there were no Caesarean sections and there was a forceps delivery rate of about 50 per cent below the average. In addition it can be seen, however, that these initial volunteers were an unusually extravert and tough group. It can also be seen by comparison of the two Apgar scores that the babies appeared to be in just as satisfactory a condition as those delivered by the conventional form of position in the second stage (Figures 4.1 and 4.2). Following this study, we then introduced squatting generally into our department; mothers are now free to chose which position they would like during the second stage. A recent review (Tables 4.2 and 4.3) showed that 24 per cent of nulliparae were adopting squatting in the second stage compared with 13 per cent of multiparae. At this time we cannot claim that squatting offers a distinct advantage either to the mother or to the baby. On the other hand, we do believe that we have sufficient evidence and experience to claim that mothers

TABLE 4.1   Results of first 50 primiparous women who volunteered to squat in labour

Spontaneous deliveries	Forceps deliveries	Caesarean sections
40	10	0

Note: Eysenck Personality Questionnaire showed significance for toughness, extraversion and low social desirability.

TABLE 4.2 Recent series of 598 nulliparous women who were allowed to choose squatting or usual position in labour	
Squat	Non-squat
143	455
(23.9%)	(76.1%)

TABLE 4.3 Recent series of 490 multiparous women who were allowed to choose squatting or usual position in labour	
Squat	Non-squat
63	427
(12.86%)	(87.14%)

often benefit psychologically from being free to choose the position they would like to adopt during labour, rather than being forced to adopt the position of our choice. We intend to investigate this method of delivery more fully and to produce further data.

To summarize, it seems that the natural instinct of many centuries has been considerably modified and inhibited by the accepted but doubtful conventions of the past two centuries. It will be interesting to see whether squatting in labour does once again become the standard accepted position—an issue which we consider again later in this chapter.

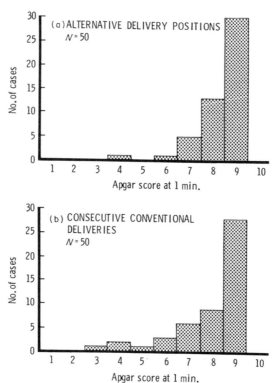

Figure 4.1   Apgar score at 1 minute, comparing babies delivered from (a) mothers who squatted with (b) mothers who adopted conventional positions

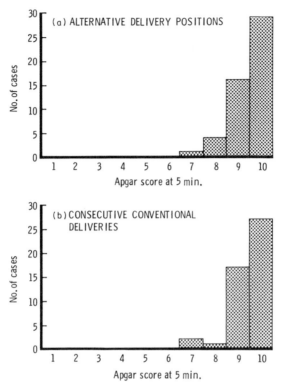

Figure 4.2 Apgar score at 5 minutes, comparing babies delivered from (a) mothers who squatted with (b) mothers who adopted conventional positions

MEDICAL INTERVENTION AND 'NATURAL CHILDBIRTH'

The techniques outlined have emphasized facilitating labour and delivery without 'interfering' with progress by the use of chemicals and machines. The increasing popularity of antenatal preparation for childbirth and of the 'Leboyer birth' reflect the growing antagonism towards medical intervention in labour; the following sections will outline common techniques and methods used by obstetrics today to aid labour and delivery. As will be seen, the use of various interventions in obstetric practice has generally increased, but although we at the West London Hospital, for example, encourage 'natural childbirth' we do not and would not propagate 'natural childbirth' at the expense of the mother or her child. Obstetric care should emphasize intervening in the labour process only when absolutely necessary, but we do believe that medical aid *is* sometimes necessary. Perhaps obstetrics has been guilty of over-using certain techniques such as induction, but modern obstetrics is generally more conservative in its intervention than it is given credit for. Different types of medical procedures will be presented and discussed before we finally go on to consider whether today's women who expect and insist on 'natural childbirth' have an unrealistic and oversimplistic conception of what labour and obstetrics are about.

In the last two decades, there has been a significant increase in the rate of interference in labour. This interference involves the following procedures: induction, augmentation, electronic monitoring, Caesarean section, epidural anaesthesia, forceps delivery and the use of episiotomy.

During recent years, there has been increasing objection from many women, as well as from the media, that obstetricians and midwives are interfering unnecessarily in the course of labour and that as a consequence the labour experience for many women is no longer as rewarding and satisfying as they have the right to expect.

We have therefore witnessed a marked increase in the demand for 'natural' labour. Such a development was inevitable, but it is worrying that the quest for 'natural' labour has led some women to assume that labour can be reasonably uncomplicated if they are left to deliver on their own with a minimum of interference. It is of importance, therefore, to analyse the reasons why the 'interference rate' has increased so much recently in order to judge whether this interference is really justified and also whether it has produced worthwhile results.

Induction

About 10 years ago there was a massive increase in the use of induction of labour. The reason for this was that it was thought that if induction was carried out just after a woman had reached her expected date of delivery, then it was likely that the baby would be in a better state for delivery and less subject to the uncommon but possible risk of 'post-maturity'. There was a general view that after 40 weeks the placenta becomes less efficient and the transfer of oxygen and other nutrients become less effective. Admittedly, this reduction in efficiency develops, but very slowly. In fact, only a relatively small number of babies suffer from brain damage or die *in utero* from this cause. However, it was assumed that a radical induction policy would virtually eliminate these deaths. Unfortunately, induction of labour has its own hazards and, as with many procedures in medical practice, the gain is often matched by the loss resultant upon the complications of the particular procedure adopted. This proved to be the case in relation to induction of labour.

Using modern techniques, it is still not always possible to ensure that women go into labour. Failure to go into labour may in turn result in prolonged labour and foetal distress, which may necessitate Caesarean section. It soon became obvious that this new approach had little to offer and induction rates all over the country have fallen precipitously. In most departments they are now between about 10 and 15 per cent which is the level they were at about 20 years ago. This is yet another example of how medical treatment may sometimes go in circles without any apparent benefit being achieved. Naturally, there was an outcry from mothers when the induction policy was introduced and certainly in regard to this particular procedure they were more than justified in their protest. It can also be claimed that their protest did stimulate a number of research studies which helped to resolve this important issue.

Augmentation

Unfortunately, particularly in the first stage of labour, the uterine muscle function can be inadequate, resulting in a prolonged labour which may go on for more than 20 hours and in some instances may even last up to 48 hours. There is little question that prolonged labour is a very unfortunate complication and imposes severe stress on the mother as well as on the baby and the attendant staff. The use of 'augmentation', which means stimulating the uterus with an oxytocic agent, was pioneered at a hospital in Dublin. The National Maternity Hospital has an intake of more than 8000 deliveries per year and their present policy, which they have pursued now for more than 10 years, promises women that they will deliver within 12 hours of coming into hospital. Indeed, they claim that in 1983 they had only 11 cases of prolonged labour (Annual Report for 1983). The Dublin workers also claim that they have a very low incidence of Caesarean section, as well as a relatively low incidence of forceps delivery (8.9 per cent and 14.6 per cent respectively), and they believe that this style of management reduces the need for analgesis or anaesthesia. Epidural anaesthesia was used in 20 per cent of cases. This compares with an overall rate of around 40 per cent in the West London Hospital.

O'Driscoll and Meagher (1980) who developed this approach to labour claim that if women know that labour will be over within 12 hours then they are far better able to withstand the stress and the pain that is involved. They feel that one of the major problems in labour which makes the use of analgesia and anaesthetics so necessary is its length. If this can be reduced then they consider the outlook generally is very much improved. In this Dublin unit 'augmentation' is required in just over 30 per cent of all patients in order to achieve this result.

Other units in different parts of the UK have tried to achieve these results, but on the whole have not been as successful as their Irish colleagues. There are several possible reasons for this. First, the National Maternity Hospital has a unique system of organization based on the 'Master' as overall director of the hospital. Almost certainly this organizational pattern has a great deal to do with the results that are obtained. Second, the mothers who go into this hospital, who are mostly Roman Catholics, have enormous confidence in the doctors and the midwives who will be looking after them. Third—and this requires emphasis—usually one midwife or one pupil midwife sits with the mother in close eye-to-eye contact through the whole length of her labour. There is no question that this particular psychological approach is extremely important in the successful conduct of labour within this department. It seems probable that it is almost as valuable as the application of 'augmentation'. If one visits this department one observes the relative tranquillity in the labour ward, and certainly there is rarely evidence of women being in severe distress.

Electronic monitoring

During the last decade the electronic monitor has been introduced into most departments of obstetrics in the UK. This is a relatively simple device for recording the baby's heart rate, and the strength of the uterine contraction. It has been shown that in general the pattern of the baby's heart rate is a relatively reliable index of the condition of the baby *in utero*. If an abnormal pattern is identified then this allows the obstetrician to make further investigations which may determine that the baby is in distress. The main additional procedure is to obtain a sample of blood from the scalp of the baby. Even with a very small sample of blood it is possible to measure the pH and sometimes the P_{O_2} and P_{CO_2} of the baby's blood. A pH of below 7.25 is usually cause for serious concern.

There has been a very intense debate about the use of electronic monitoring because in most instances it requires the mother to be strapped to an apparatus which means that she is in bed whilst the recordings are taking place. Although Birmingham workers have developed a monitor which allows the woman to ambulate it seems that it does not always provide satisfactory response in some departments because of electrical interference. Because monitoring is regarded by mothers as interference, the debate regarding its use continues unabated. However, probably the most significant study that has been recently produced is that published by the National Maternity Hospital in Dublin with the cooperation of the Obstetric Perinatal Unit in Oxford (MacDonald *et al.*, awaiting publication). This study of 12 960 patients was divided into 6474 who were subject to electronic monitoring (EM) and 6486 who had intermittent monitoring with the Pinard stethoscope (IM). This study revealed a convulsion rate of only 9 in the EM group compared with 21 in the IM group. The 1-year follow-up, however, showed only that infants in each group were suffering from cerebral palsy. These results suggest that monitoring does have a slight edge over more old-fashioned methods, but the difference was not as striking as many would have expected.

These workers emphasize that it is essential to back up electronic monitoring with the use of foetal scalp sampling.

The Dublin study cannot be regarded as the last word in this ongoing debate but it raises an important issue. Further studies should be carried out as soon as possible in order that this question can be resolved one way or another. Meanwhile, most units are carrying out continuous electronic monitoring of women who are known to have 'high-risk' pregnancies—that is, where there have been established complications during the pregnancy or where there is a high risk of complications developing during labour. Unfortunately, distress in the foetus does develop in women who have 'low-risk' pregnancies, although the incidence is inevitably not so great as in 'high-risk' pregnancies.

Caesarean section

With the use of electronic monitoring the incidence of Caesarean section has also risen substantially and now in many units the level is approximately 12 per cent or more. Certainly, when electronic monitoring is first introduced it does seem to lead to an increase in the use of Caesarean section. Of course, in the pre-penicillin era it was extremely unwise to carry out Caesarean section for foetal distress because the risk of the woman contracting puerperal fever was very great indeed. In fact, in 1948 Mackintosh Marshall reporting on a study from Liverpool recorded a mortality rate of over 30 per cent among women who were in labour when this operation was carried out! With the introduction of penicillin and other antibiotics we can now interfere by means of Caesarean section with relative impunity. On the other hand, it has to be accepted that the mortality rate, although still very low, is much higher than in women who have a natural spontaneous delivery.

Epidural anaesthesia

Another form of interference which has increased substantially over the past decade is the use of epidural anaesthesia. This is a form of anaesthetic that has been popular for many decades in the USA. An epidural anaesthetic nearly always provides substantial relief from pain, but here again 'epidurals' do have their problems from time to time. One of the least serious complications is the dural tap which results in persistent headaches during the postpartum phase. At the other end of the complication spectrum is the risk of sudden collapse, hypotension and meningitis. Death may result following any of these setbacks. When the rare mortality occurs, there is always the heart-searching doubt about whether the 'epidural' was really necessary.

Forceps delivery

During recent years, it has become the general principle that it is probably unwise to allow the second stage of labour to continue for longer than 1 hour. After this time, there is some evidence that the foetus may show signs of distress. As a consequence, forceps delivery is usually carried out in order to relieve the foetus and the mother of unnecessary stress. Generally, this can be done under a local pudendal block or epidural anaesthesia; hence the mother is not deprived of the experience of being conscious when the baby is born. Women's reactions to forceps delivery vary as they do with other procedures, and now there is increased desire on the part of some women to be allowed to go on pushing for as long as possible in the second stage. Here again, it is difficult in any individual case to define what is the permissible limit, and it seems highly probable that if we reverse our present policy and allow labour to go on for 2 hours or more we may see a slow but definite rise in the perinatal death rate and in neonatal brain damage due to the foetus becoming asphyxiated during the second stage.

Syntometrine

The use of oxytocics to reduce the level of postpartum haemorrhage was introduced at University College Hospital, London, in 1952–1953. The incidence of postpartum haemorrhage at that time was between 6.0 and 6.5 per cent. With oxytocic injections this haemorrhage rate was reduced to just over 2 per cent and most people have regarded this as a major step forward. However, here again in recent years women have been pressing obstetricians and midwives to delay the administration of syntometrine until it is absolutely necessary, namely until there are signs that haemorrhage is occurring.

There is no evidence that women are less likely to develop haemorrhage than they were 30 years ago. If another study were to be carried out today it might well confirm that without this form of therapy the incidence of haemorrhage would be even greater than 6 per cent because midwives and obstetricians today are much less experienced at handling the third stage of labour than those of 30 years ago. On the face of it, therefore, it seems that this demand by women not to have oxytocic therapy is not justified and may well put the clock back.

Episiotomy

The use of episiotomy has almost certainly been excessive, and in many units it had almost become routine for a woman having her first baby. It has now been shown that a much lower episiotomy rate is desirable and that whilst a tear may occur in a higher percentage of cases, often this tear is of less consequence than an episiotomy. Episiotomies in association with forceps have been shown to be extremely painful and do result in pain being present for several weeks afterwards. In most hospitals there is now a general trend towards reducing the incidence of episiotomy but a recent study in our department has shown that the episiotomy rate varies dramatically from one unit to another (House, Cario and Jones, awaiting publication). Some 100 departments reported an incidence of episiotomy that varied between 14 and 98 per cent (average 57 per cent) in nulliparae and 16 and 71 per cent (average 33 per cent) in multiparae.

Summary of medical intervention

The main reasons for interference have been discussed. Most of these aim to reduce the effect of stress and especially of hypoxia upon the baby—in particular, the risk of cerebral or neurological injury, which might result in death or, if the baby survives, in lifelong handicap. It can be seen that it is not always easy to be absolutely certain when the baby is in trouble. The decision when to intervene calls for fine judgement based upon considerable experience.

It is indeed possible that we intervene too frequently, but that has to be set against the overall success or failure of our methods. One of the most acceptable measures of our efforts is surely revealed in the perinatal mortality rates.

Figure 4.3 shows the overall rate for England and Wales and this reveals a steady decline during recent years. In 1983 it fell from 11.3 to 10.4 per thousand total births.

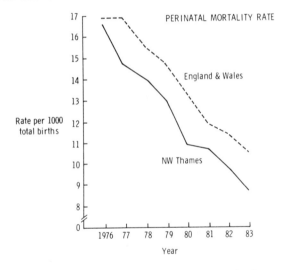

Figure 4.3   The steady decline in perinatal mortality in recent years

The best results were in the NW Thames Region with a rate of 8.6. In our own department, the rate in 1983 was 8.2 per cent. This satisfactory figure was achieved by careful obstetric care but also with the aid of superb neonatal care provided by a team of extremely dedicated neonatologists.

It is well established that a multitude of complex factors—environmental, social and nutritional—contribute to a reduction in perinatal loss. Nevertheless, surely it would be naïve to assume that maternity care does not play a major part in achieving this encouraging result? And could it be that the NW Thames area has the best results because it has some of the best obstetric units in the country within its boundaries?

NATURAL LABOUR—IS IT A REASONABLE EXPECTATION?

As we have seen, the debate about natural labour really began just over 50 years ago with the publication of Grantly Dick-Read's (1933) book devoted to that subject. The topic creates as much interest today as it did then, and there are still widely divergent views on certain basic issues. The previous section outlined some of the problems that can arise during labour: two of these are of major significance, and in many senses they interrelate. The length of labour and the degree of pain that women experience are both impossible to predict. The factors that influence them both are also not very well understood. Some women have fast, relatively painless labours, others have slower and more painful labours. On the whole, the painful labours are in the majority.

The main debate hinges on how far education and training programmes outlined in an earlier section can improve a woman's individual performance in labour. As we have seen, there are many factors that appear to influence a woman's response to labour and her ability to tolerate labour pain. Several women's groups are now suggesting that the atmosphere of the modern labour unit with its intensive care and frequent resort to electronic monitoring and to interference increases the stress and anxiety that is inherent to some degree in every woman. This in turn, they suggest, impairs uterine action, making labour longer and also more painful, increasing the risk of foetal distress. Furthermore, these groups claim that if women are allowed to labour in an atmosphere that has less background tension and where interference is kept to a minimum, then the confinement would be much more straightforward. It is difficult to know whether this hypothesis in regard to stress, interference and the general atmosphere of the labour ward is really acceptable.

Obviously, for many women the atmosphere in their own home is more pleasant and reassuring than that of the hospital labour ward. Therefore, from a purely emotional point of view there is much to commend in a domiciliary confinement.

As recently as 1964, over 30 per cent of women were having their babies at home in England and Wales. This picture has changed dramatically in the last two decades, and now under 1 per cent of women are having domiciliary confinements. Just recently, it seems, there is once again an increasing demand for home confinements in certain parts of the country. In view of the dramatic reduction in home confinements, inevitably it has been difficult to carry out up-to-date studies in relation to maternal and perinatal morbidity and mortality associated with this form of maternity care. However, there are some studies that suggest that if a 'low-risk' woman can deliver safely at home then the results are perhaps rather better than if the confinement had taken place in hospital (Tew, 1978, 1979a, b). On the other hand, these studies do not take into account those women who have to be transferred to hospital either during or just after delivery of their baby.

The sudden transfer of a woman and her baby into hospital raises considerable difficulties and it is not surprising that morbidity and mortality in this group were relatively high. However, even when these figures are added to the results of women who deliver without any problems at home, the difference between these results and those of women delivering in hospital seems to be very small indeed. In other words, there does seem to be a suggestion that if a woman has her baby in an unsympathetic atmosphere, particularly in a highly stressed modern labour ward, there may be some deleterious effect upon her performance.

Two interesting studies in relation to hospital care were published recently (Klein *et al.*, 1983). These studies from the John Radcliffe Hospital in Oxford analysed just over 5000 births where delivery took place in two different types of unit located within the same hospital. These were respectively (1) an integrated general practitioner unit (GPU) and (2) a consultant (shared care) system. Perinatal mortality in the two units was the same, but the incidence of interference was much higher in the consultant, shared care, unit than in the general practice unit. Some 3 per cent of infants of multiparous women were intubated in the shared care unit whereas none was intubated in the general unit. This report does suggest an association between a hospital where women can be delivered in a less stressed atmosphere and the need for a lower incidence of interference. On the other hand, there does not seem to be any definitive proof yet that either home delivery or delivery in a lower-stress unit results in a lower overall perinatal morbidity and mortality rate. Quite clearly, more carefully controlled comparative studies are urgently required.

One of the particular problems that has to be emphasized in regard to the increased quest for home confinement is that with the rundown of domiciliary practice the back-up services in most districts are now inadequate. Indeed, even in the past these services were relatively inefficient. The common conditions which require urgent transfer of the mother from home to hospital are

(1) foetal distress developing in the first or second stage,
(2) delay in the second stage,
(3) intrapartum haemorrhage,
(4) severe postpartum haemorrhage,
(5) neonatal asphyxia.

All of these complications demand speedy transport. Unfortunately, in spite of the theoretical availability of 'flying squads', these squads usually take quite a long time to get into action and during the lengthy period of transport the condition of the baby and/or mother may deteriorate significantly. This means that there is an inevitable delay in putting into effect the measures already described that will reduce morbidity and mortality.

We consider that it should be possible to devise a system in which this particular 'delay' problem could be overcome, or at least reduced to a minimum. If every woman in labour at home and her attendants could communicate by means of short-wave radio with the nearest hospital maternity unit, this would have the very positive advantage of enabling the midwife and the doctor to consult the hospital staff, and advice could be obtained during the course of labour. If it became obvious that additional support or transfer to hospital were required, then a flying squad could be sent out in good time.

In order for the flying squad to go out rapidly, new arrangements would be required to ensure that a fully equipped maternity ambulance were immediately available. Unfortunately, in the present system ambulances in general use have to be diverted from the general pool. Clearly, a stand-by ambulance available for a flying squad which may only be called out once every 2 or 3 weeks is not an acceptable provision at the present time. This problem illustrates one facet of the overall difficulty of providing for an adequate domiciliary service.

In addition to a satisfactory means of transferring the mother from home to hospital, it also seems essential that both the midwife and the doctor in the home should have the ability and the facilities with which to cope with any emergency. This would involve the capability of giving an intravenous transfusion as well as the ability to intubate the baby so that pulmonary ventilation could be achieved with an oxygen supply. Here again, it should not prove an insuperable administrative obstacle to ensure that both the midwife and the doctor are competent to carry out these procedures and that they also have the necessary equipment.

Given that these facilities are available—namely direct radio communication with the hospital, rapid transfer in the suitably equipped ambulance, and the midwife and the general practitioner having the ability and facilities to resuscitate mother and baby—it would be reasonable to assume that the present high morbidity and mortality rate associated directly with transfer would be substantially reduced. In these circumstances, it would probably follow that the perinatal morbidity and mortality rates associated with home delivery would then prove very favourable in relation to hospital perinatal morbidity and mortality rates. However, until these provisions are available it is probable that domiciliary confinements will not be associated with reduced perinatal morbidity and mortality. In other words, babies will die and others will suffer lifelong handicap, consequent upon intrapartum hypoxia, as a direct result of inadequate flying squad and other simple but vital facilities.

FATHERS IN THE LABOUR WARD

The Charing Cross maternity department was one of the first units to advocate that husbands being present during labour had no overall deleterious effect upon them or their wives. Indeed, we have shown that husbands can provide support for their wives, although admittedly this varies from one couple to another (Pawson and Morris, 1972). It was previously supposed that if husbands were allowed to be present during labour they would faint, or generally prove to be a nuisance, both to their wives and to the attendant nursing staff. Whilst it is true that in a small percentage of cases a husband can prove obstructive to the provision of adequate care to his wife, in general this is certainly not the case. During the last decade, other maternity units in the UK have followed our example and now it is very rare for men not to be allowed to be with their wives in labour.

When an instrumental delivery is required and when the mother is conscious, it is now also the custom in our department for the husband to be present. We have shown that Caesarean section under an epidural anaesthetic allows the husband and wife to maintain a very satisfactory rapport during the course of labour and few problems, if any, seem to arise.

If an emergency occurs at a delivery, then the husband becomes involved in the stress associated with that development. However, here again husbands do not necessarily express the view that they would have preferred to be elsewhere when the setback occurred. Most of them feel that they should be prepared to share the experience with their wife, even if this does involve being in a situation which can sometimes threaten the life of the mother and baby. Whilst they get caught up in the inevitable tension that such a problem creates in the medical and nursing staff, at the same time they are usually able to observe and be reassured by the efficient way in which this problem is dealt with.

In his latest book, *Birth Reborn*, Michel Odent (1984) seems to have changed his mind to some extent about the value of husbands in the labour ward. He claims that 'in all traditional civilizations, women giving birth were assisted by their mothers and aunts and female neighbours, and not their menfolk'. He suggests that the presence of a man does not seem compatible with the intimacy a woman needs when giving birth, and that if such a habit has been avoided till now, perhaps there is a good reason for it. He does not discourage partners from participating and he does not deny that it can be beneficial. On the other hand, he claims that labour may be slowed up when a father is present, and he believes that many fathers are so chronically nervous that they transmit this anxiety to their wives and this in turn inhibits the uterine contractions.

An over-anxious father may talk too much and a possessive father may intrude too much, caressing and encouraging his labouring wife when really she wants to be calm. A pushy father may interfere too much, offering well-intentioned but unwelcome advice both to his wife and to the nursing staff.

Sometimes there is a conflict in a couple's relationship which gets in the way, but few women dare say they would rather their partner weren't there and also few men dare leave because it is almost a rule now to be present.

Michel Odent also worries that the intimacy needed during childbirth is not necessarily the kind that a woman has with a sexual partner. 'For instance, there may come a point when a woman in her labour empties her rectum. She would not normally do that in front of her partner. We just don't know what effect such things can have on a couple's future sex life.' Michel Odent suggests that sexual attraction needs mystery to make it last and a woman must keep something of herself unknown to a man. 'If I were a woman in the feminist movement I would fear that the participation of men in birth was just another stage in the control of childbirth by men.' He considers that the support may better be given by midwives and other mothers or women than by fathers. Michel Odent's views will obviously cause a wide range of reaction.

In the UK, most midwives and obstetricians would accept that fathers usually fit well into the labour ward situation. There are some fathers who fall into the categories outlined by Michel Odent. It is unfortunate if some fathers feel that they must now be present in the labour ward against their own instincts. We should take care to explain to both the father and the mother that this is very much a problem for them to work out beforehand, taking into account their own particular relationship and sensitivity. In other words, what may be perfectly acceptable for one couple may be intolerable for another. This decision should be accepted without implying that it reflects in any way on the integrity of the relationship.

Our work have shown that many men are upset by the amount of pain and some of the other problems that women have to contend with during labour (Pawson and Morris, 1972). However, the couple admitted in our study that sharing this experience and observation of the stress involved usually meant a deepening of their respect and an enhancement of their mutual rapport and understanding. If doctors and midwives feel a particular father is proving an embarrassment, they should summon up enough courage to ask him to leave the ward. Inevitably, they need to present their views unemotionally and this is not always easy.

THE FUTURE

Coping with pain in labour

We have demonstrated that the various antenatal preparation procedures currently in use in this country have a limited effect in regard to enabling women to cope with their pain in labour. However, a recent study (Copstick et al., 1984) suggests that where antenatal preparation is followed by continuous active support during labour then this results in a success rate of about 80 per cent. In other words, even with effective support, 20 per cent of women still require pain relief, usually in the form of an epidural anaesthetic. When intermittent and relatively inadequate support is available, then the success rate of coping falls to 60 per cent. This study confirms the importance of adequate support during labour, which if possible should be provided by more than one individual.

Antenatal preparation, therefore, does not ensure that a woman can go through labour without requiring support from those present in the labour unit. This observation is not surprising, but it is worthy of receiving more consideration when care in labour is discussed. Inevitably, midwives and doctors vary in their ability to provide professional and physical support. It is possible that in the selection of midwives and obstetricians more attention should be paid to their personality and their ability to provide empathy and understanding. Unfortunately, the present training programmes of midwives, undergraduate medical students and obstetricians still contain very little content in relation to the psychology of the pregnant and parturient woman. This is a deficiency which is slowly being rectified, but it has not yet attracted sufficiently widespread interest. We all need to learn more about our own reactions in order that we may understand the feelings and reactions of our patients.

In our department, we have found that the provision of regular seminars devoted to the psychological problems of patients and staff, conducted by a psychiatrist (who is in a sense detached from the immediate clinical decisions involved in the department), has proved to be immensely helpful in enabling medical and nursing staff to have a better awareness of their own feelings and capabilities as well as those of the mothers who are under their care.

Women's vulnerability

One of the main observations that requires far greater emphasis is that many pregnant women experience a special vulnerability, which is probably not present at any other time in their lives. This means that an unfortunate word can reactivate latent anxieties and fears and result in a great deal of unnecessary misery and anxiety. Here again, our ability to communicate satisfactorily with our patients and with our fellow members of staff is a matter that requires constant evaluation. We believe that it is our inability to understand and deal with these psychological stresses that results in the present widespread criticism expressed by mothers and fathers in regard to the care that we provide. It is indeed a sad reflection on our present care that at the time when we are achieving better results than ever before (as demonstrated by low perinatal morbidity and mortality), mothers and fathers are expressing more discontent than ever before.

If this discontent is to be brought under control, we must achieve an effective balance between our understanding of the physical and technical developments on the one hand and the need to provide sensitive understanding of the emotional needs of mothers and fathers on the other. It is not enough to be highly skilled in one or other of these, and one can never compensate for the deficiency of the other.

Labour wards

The design and atmosphere of labour wards should receive much more critical consideration. Currently, many labour wards have more in common with an operating theatre than with meeting the needs of a maternity department. As we have seen, it is possible, but not yet proven, that the austerity, bleakness, tension and noise of the average labour ward may so undermine a woman's confidence and tranquillity that it may in turn inhibit the normal progress of labour. New ideas should be deployed in the design and in the practice of our labour units that are directed essentially towards reinforcing confidence and reducing any sense of stress and anxiety. This may also mean some degree of separation of those women regarded as being at 'high risk' from those who are at 'low risk'. Inevitably, the care of women in labour is always set against a background of anxiety on the part of labour attendants. Disasters happen and sometimes with amazing suddenness. Constant vigilance is essential, but at the same time this vigilance must be sustained without transmitting anxiety to the mothers in labour. This is a difficult skill to master but it should not prove impossible.

In every medical condition there is a complex interplay between mind and body—in a sense every disease process is psychosomatic or somato-psychic, depending on the respective contribution of psyche and soma. Labour is a classic illustration of a psychosomatic situation where both the psyche and the soma have a vital role to play.

Unfortunately, our knowledge of brain function and our understanding of the mind is far more primitive and less developed than is our awareness of the various organic changes that are involved in health and disease of the body.

The body is far easier to study with the aid of modern technology than the brain. Because we tend to play down the importance of things which are difficult to understand and quantify, many clinicians have been led to ignore or even denigrate the importance of the psyche. Inevitably, during the next century this imbalance of knowledge will be corrected and progress in psychology and psycho-neuro-endocrinology will almost certainly accelerate dramatically.

Just as we look back on the apparent barbaric physical conditions existing in society and in hospitals of a century ago, so our successors 100 years hence will almost certainly look back on our present practice of medicine as demonstrating a singular degree of barbarism because of its lack of interest in the importance of emotions and the role of the psyche.

This presupposes that we will have successors 100 years from now and that the world will not be destroyed, either by a nuclear holocaust or by overpopulation—or by both!

However, we ourselves are optimists because, after all, man has shown himself through countless centuries to have a unique capacity for survival.

REFERENCES

Astbury, J. (1980). The crises of childbirth: can information and childbirth education help? *Journal of Psychosomatic Research*, **24**, 9–13.

Barrett, J. H. W. (1981). Intra-uterine experience and its long-term outcome. In M. J. Christie and P. G. Mellett (eds), *Foundations of Psychomatics*. Chichester: Wiley, pp. 41–64.

Beck, N. C., Geden, E. A., and Brouder, G. T. (1979). Preparation for labour: a historical perspective. *Psychosomatic Medicine*, **41**, 243.

Beck, N. C., and Hall, D. G. (1978). Natural childbirth. *Obstetrics and Gynaecology*, **52**, 373–379.

Beck, N. C., and Seigel, L. J. (1980). Preparation for childbirth and contemprary research on pain, anxiety and stress reduction: a review critique. *Psychosomatic Medicine*, **42**, 429.

Beck, N. C., Seigel, L. J., Davidson, P. N., Kormeier, S. K., Breitenstein, A., and Hall, D. G. (1980). The rediction of pregnancy outcome: maternal preparation, anxiety and attitudinal sets. *Journal of Psychosomatic Research*, **24**, 343–351.

Bobey, M. J., and Davidson, P. O. (1976). Psychological factors affecting pain tolerance. *Journal of Psychosomatic Research*, **14**, 371–376.

Booth, A. (1983). The importance of coping strategies in women's experiences of childbirth. Paper presented at the Society for Reproductive and Infant Psychology. Annual Conference, 1983.

Bergström-Walan, M-B. (1963). Efficacy of education for childbirth. *Journal of Psychosomatic Research*, **7**, 131–146.

Caldeyro-Barcia, R. (1979). Scientific Publication No. 858 of Latin American Centre of Perinatology and Development, Montevideo, Uruguay. Pan American Health Organization and WHO.

Caldeyro-Barcia, R., Noriega-Guerra, L., Cibils, L. A., Alvarey, H., Poseiro, J. J., Rose, S. V., Sica-Blanco, Y. (1960). The effect of position changes on the intensity and frequency of uterine contractions in labour. *American Journal of Obstetrics and Gynecology*, **80**, 284–290.

Calvert, J. P., Newcombe, R. G., and Hubbard, R. M. (1982). An assessment of radiotelemetry in the monitoring of labour. *British Journal of Obstetrics and Gynaecology*, **89**, 285–291.

Charles, G. A., Norr, L. K., Block, C. R., Meyering, S., and Meyers, M. A. (1978). Obstetric and psychological effects of psychoprophylactic preparation for childbirth. *American Journal of Obstetrics and Gynecology*, **131**, 44–52.

Clinical Report (1983). Rotunda Hospital, Dublin.

Clum, C. A., Luscomb, R. L., and Scott, L. (1982). Relaxation training and cognitive redirection strategies in the treatment of acute pain. *Pain*, **12**, 175–183.

Cogan, R. (1978). Practice time on prepared childbirth. *Journal of Obstetrics, Gynaecology and Neonatal Nursing*, **7**, 33.

Cogan, R., Henneborn, W., and Klopfer, F. (1976). Predictors of pain during prepared childbirth. *Journal of Psychosomatic Research*, **20**, 523–533.

Cogan, R., and Kluthe, K. H. (1981). The role of learning in pain reduction associated with relaxation and patterned breathing. *Journal of Psychosomatic Research*, **25**, 535–541.

Copstick, S. M., Hayes, R. J., Taylor, K. E., and Morris, N. (in press). A test of common assumptions regarding the use of antenatal training during labour. *Journal of Psychosomatic Research*.

Copstick, S. M., Hayes, R. J., Taylor, K. E., and Morris, N. (1984). The importance of support in labour in determining obstetric outcome. Unpublished study.

Crandon, A. J. (1979). Maternal anxiety and obstetric complications. *Journal of Psychosomatic Research*, **23**, 109–111.

Davenport-Slacks, B., and Boylan, C. H. (1974). Psychological correlates of child-birth pain. *Psychosomatic Medicine*, **36**, 215.

Davids, A., and DeVault, S. (1962). Maternal anxiety during pregnancy and child-birth abnormalities. *Psychosomatic Medicine*, **24**, 464–470.

Davis, C. D., and Morrone, F. A. (1975). An objective evaluation of a prepared childbirth program. *American Journal of Obstetrics and Gynecology*, **123**, 185–191.

Dick-Read, G. (1933). *Natural Childbirth*. London: Heinemann.

Dick-Read, G. (1944). *Childbirth Without Fear*. New York: Harper Brothers.

Dunn, P. H. (1976). Obstetric delivery today for better or worse? *Lancet*, **i**, 790.

Englemann, G. J. (1882). *Labour Among Primitive Peoples*. St Louis: J. H. Chambers & Company.

Enkin, M. W., Smith, S. L., and Dermer, S. W. (1972). An adequately controlled study of the effectiveness of PPM training. In N. Morris (ed.), *Proceedings of the Third International Congress of Psychosomatic Medicine in Obstetrics and Gynaecology*. London: Karger, pp. 62, 67.

Flack, I. H. (1946–1947). The pre-history of midwifery. *Proceedings of the Royal Society of Medicine*, **40**, 713–722.

Flynn, A. M., Kelly, J., Hollins, G., and Lynch, P. F. (1978). Ambulation in labour. *British Medical Journal*, **ii**, 591–593.

Folkard, S. (1976). Diurnal variation and individual differences in the perception of intractable pain. *Journal of Psychosomatic Research*, **20**, 289–301.

Gracely, R. H., Dubner, R., and McGrath, P. (1979). Narcotic analgesia; Fentanyl reduces the intensity but not the unpleasantness of painful tooth-pulp sensations. *Science*, New York, **203**, 126.

Hackett, G., and Horan, J. J. (1980). Stress innoculation for pain: what's really going on? *Journal of Counselling Psychology*, **27**, 107–362.

Haddad, P. F., and Morris N. (1982). Relationship of maternal anxiety and events in labour. *Journal of Obstetrics and Gynaecology*, **3**, 94–97.

Henneborn, N. J., and Cogan, R. (1975). The effect of husband participation on reported pain and probability of medication during labour and birth. *Journal of Psychosomatic Research*, **19**, 215–222.

House, M. J., Cario, G., and Jones, M. H. (awaiting publication). Episiotomy and the perineum: to tear or not to tear? A randomised controlled trial.

Humphrey, M. D., Chang, A., Wood, E. C., Morgan, S., and Honslow, D. (1974). A decrease in the foetal pH during the second stage of labour and the conduct in the dorsal position. *Journal of Obstetrics and Gynaecology of the British Commonwealth*, **81**, 600–602.

Huttel, F. A., Mitchell, I., and Fischer, M. W. (1972). A quantitative evaluation of psychoprophylaxis in childbirth. *Journal of Psychosomatic Research*, **16**, 81–92.

Klein, M., Lloyd, F., Redman, C., Bull, M., and Turnbull, A. C. (1983). A comparison of low risk pregnant women booked for delivery in two systems of care: shared care (consultant) and integrated general practice unit and obstetrical procedures and neonatal outcome. *British Journal of Obstetrics and Gynaecology*, **90**, 118–122.

Klusman, E. L. (1975). Reduction of pain in childbirth by the alleviation of anxiety during pregnancy. *Journal of Consulting and Clinical Psychology*, **43**, 162–165.

Lamaze, F. (1958). *Painless Childbirth* (L. B. Celestin, trans.). London: Burke Publishing Company.

Leboyer, F. (1974). *Pour une naissance sans violence*. Paris: Seuil.

Levanthal, H., Shacham, S., Boothe, L. S., and Levanthal, E. (1981). The role of attention in distress and control during childbirth. Unpublished manuscript, University of Wisconsin—Madison.

McCarl, K. D., and Havgvedt, C. (1982). Attention, distraction and cold pressor pain. *Journal of Personality and Social Psychology*, **43**, 154–162.

McCarl, K. D., and Malott, J. M. (1984). Distraction and coping with pain. *Psychological Bulletin*, **95**, 516–533.

MacDonald, D., Grant, A., Sheridan-Pereira, Boylan, and Chalmers, I. (awaiting publication). The Dublin randomised controlled trial of intrapartum foetal heart rate monitoring.

McManus, T. J., and Calder, A. A. (1978). Upright posture and the efficiency of labour. *Lancet*, **i**, 72–74.

Mills, M. (1981). Individual differences in the first week of life. In M. J. Christie and P. G. Mellett (eds), *Foundations of Psychosomatics*. Chichester: Wiley.

Morris, N. (1983). Labour. In L. Dennerstein and G. D. Burrows (eds), *Handbook of Psychosomatic Obstetrics and Gynaecology*. Oxford: Elsevier Biomedical Press.

Niven, K. (1983). A study of labour pain: the relationship between the intensity of labour pain and the experience of pain unrelated to childbirth. Paper presented at Society for Reproductive and Infant Psychology Annual Conference.

Odent, M. (1980). Obstetric positions, consciousness and maternity practice. Energy and character. *Journal of Bioenergy Research*, **11**, 9–14.

Odent, M. (1983). Birth under water. *Lancet*, **ii**, 1476–1477.

Odent, M. (1984). *Birth Reborn*. London: Souvenir Press.

O'Driscoll, K., and Meagher, D. (1980). *Active Management of Labour*. London: W. B. Saunders.

Pawson, M., and Morris, N. (1972). The role of the father in pregnancy and labour. In N. Morris (ed.), *Psychosomatic Medicine in Obstetrics and Gynaecology*. Basel: S. Karger, pp. 273–276.

Pearce, S. (1983). A review of cognitive-behavioural methods for treatment of chronic pain. *Journal of Psychosomatic Research*, **27**, 431–434.

Petrov-Mascolov, M. A. (1972). Physiopsycho-prophylactic preparation for labour in pathology of pregnancy. In N. Morris (ed.), *Psychosomatic Medicine in Obstetrics and Gynaecology*. Basel: Karger, pp. 59–61.

Ploss, H. H., Bartles, M., and Bartles, P. (1935). *Woman*. London: William Heinemann (Medical Books).

Pefrement, S. (1982). Women's information on pregnancy, childbirth and baby care. Unpublished report by the Centre for Medical Research, University of Sussex.

Raynalde, W. (1545). *The Byrth of Mankynde*, London.

Ridgway, V., and Mathews, A. (1982). Psychological preparation for surgery: a comparison of methods. *British Journal of Clinical Psychology*, **21**, 271–280.

Rosenstiel, A. K., and Keefe, F. J. (1983). Use of coping strategies in chronic low back pain patients: relationship to patient characteristics and current adjustment. *Pain*, **17**, 33–44.

Scott, J. R., and Rose, N. B. (1976). Effect of psychoprophylaxis (Lamaze Preparation) on labour and delivery in primiparas. *New England Journal of Medicine*, **294**, 1205–1207.

Skevington, S. M. (1983). Social conditions, personality and chronic pain. *Journal of Psychosomatic Research*, **27**, 431–444.

Slade, P. D., Trour, J. D. G., Lethem, J., and Bentley, G. (1983). The fear-avoidance model of exaggerated pain perception—II. *Behaviour Therapy and Research*, **21**, 409–416.

Soranus (200). *De utero et pudendo meliebri*. Rome.

Spielberger, C. D. (ed.) (1966). *Anxiety and Behaviour*. New York: Academic Press.

Stewart, P., and Calder, A. A. (1984). Posture in labour; patients' choice and its effect on performance. *British Journal of Obstetrics and Gynaecology*, **91**, 1091–1095.

St James Roberts, L., Hutchinson, C., Horan, F. J., and Chamberlain, G. (1983). Can biofeed back-based relaxation training be used to help women in childbirth? *Journal of Reproductive and Infant Psychology*, **1**, 5–10.

Stone, C. L., Demchik-Stone, D. A., and Horan, J. J. (1977). A component analysis of Lamaze and cognitive-behavioural procedures. *Journal of Psychosomatic Research*, **21**, 451–456.

Tew, M. (1978). The case against hospital deliveries: the statistical evidence. In S. Kitzinger and J. Davis (eds), *The Place of Birth*. Oxford: Oxford University Press, pp. 55–56.

Tew, M. (1979a). Home versus hospital confinement: the statistics. *Update*, **18**, 1317–1322.

Tew, M. (1979b). The safest place of birth—further evidence. *Lancet*, **i**, 1388.

Vellay, P. (1959). *Childbirth Without Pain*. London: Hutchinson with George Unwin.

Vellay, P. (1983). Environmental stress and its psychosomatic consequences during pregnancy and delivery. In Lorraine Dennerstein and Myriam de Senarclens (eds): *Proceedings: 7th International Congress of Psychosomatic Obstetrics and Gynaecology*, Amsterdam, Oxford, Princeton: Exerpta Medica, pp. 276–282.

Velvosky, I. Z., Platonov, K., and Ploticher, V. (1960). *Painless Childbirth through Psychoprophylaxis* (D. A. Myshne, trans.). Moscow: Foreign Language Publishing House.

Wardle, J. (1975). An investigation into some characteristics of pain. Master's thesis, University of London.

Wardle, J. (in press). Dental pessimism: negative cognitions in fearful dental patients. *Behaviour Research and Therapy*.

Worthington, E. L., Jr, (1982). Labour room and laboratory; clinical validation of the cold pressor as a means of testing preparation for childbirth strategies. *Journal of Psychosomatic Research*, **26**, 223–230.

Worthington, E. L., Jr, and Martin, G. A. (1980). A laboratory analysis of response to pain after training in three Lamaze techniques. *Journal of Psychosomatic Research*, **24**, 109–116.

Zajicek, E. (1981). Labour. In S. Wolkind and E. Zajicek (eds), *Pregnancy: A Psychological and Social Study*. London: Academic Press.

Zax, M., Sameroff, A. F., and Farnum, J. E. (1975). Childbirth education maternal attitudes and delivery. *American Journal of Obstetrics and Gynecology*, **123**, 185–190.

The Psychosomatic Approach: Contemporary Practice of Whole-person Care
Edited by M. J. Christie and P. G. Mellett
© 1986 John Wiley & Sons Ltd

5

PAEDIATRIC HOSPITALIZATION: UNDERSTANDING THE STRESS FROM A DEVELOPMENTAL PERSPECTIVE

DAVID A. MRAZEK

Department of Child Psychiatry and Pediatrics, School of Medicine, University of Colorado, USA
and
Pediatric Psychiatry Unit, National Jewish Hospital and Research Centre, Colorado, USA

Our understanding of the effects of hospitalization on children's development as well as the impact of hospitalization on subsequent family interactions has become increasingly sophisticated over the past 50 years. Of particular importance has been recent progress in the conceptualization of stress, coping and human interactions within the framework of transactional and systems models as opposed to more simplified cause and effect mechanisms (Garmezy and Rutter, 1983). Thus, it has become apparent that answering what appears to be a simple question—'What will be the emotional reaction of a child on entering the hospital?'—is actually a quite complex problem. To be able to predict accurately, a great deal of information about the entire family and medical system is needed. However, it is perhaps most important to understand the developmental capacities of the child in question. This variable alone can provide a good deal of guidance in making decisions related to how to prepare a child for hospitalization, and how he should be supported throughout the process.

The paediatric medical centres of today only minimally resemble the children's institutions at the beginning of the twentieth century. Those unhappy hospitals were clearly to be avoided at all costs, as evidenced by the staggering infant mortality rate (Chapin, 1915). Progress was slow, and infant mortality still stood at 10 per cent at Belleview Hospital in New York City in the years preceding World War II (Bakwin, 1942). In part because of the devastating effects of epidemics in these institutional settings, protocols were developed that led to isolation and stimulus deprivation for hospitalized infants. The consequence of this was the development of severe psychological reactions in these infants and young children. While the famous observations of Spitz (1945) were actually made in residential homes for infants as opposed to medical settings, the aseptic approach to the care of these infants without regard for its effect on their emotional development resulted in mortality rates of greater than 50 per cent in a population of healthy infants. An appreciation for the condition Spitz called 'hospitalism' and the films that he made illustrating the lethargic marasmic state of these children made a strong impact on both paediatric and child psychiatric practices.

A series of empirical studies were completed in the 1950s focusing on psychological effects of hospitalization. Prugh and his colleagues described key characteristics of hospitalizations that affect the child's emotional response (Prugh et al., 1953), and Illingworth and Holt (1955) demonstrated that behavioural problems during or following hospitalization were most likely to result in children 4 years of age or younger. Schaffer and Callender (1959) further supported these observations and additionally pointed out that infants younger than 6 months of age showed few behavioural effects following hospitalization.

The work of Bowlby (Bowlby, Robertson and Rosenbluth, 1952) and the Robertsons (Robertson and Robertson, 1971) also played an important role in sensitizing paediatricians to the emotional effects of hospitalization on young children. Robertson's film A Two Year Old Goes to Hospital (1952) has become a teaching classic. The key factor that was identified in these studies was the separation from the maternal attachment figure, although the influence of five other variables was discussed. These were (1) 'ego maturity', (2) previous parent–child relationship, (3) length of separation, (4) adequacy of mothering substitute and (5) degree of strangeness of environment. These variables were a natural focus given the observations of clinicians in paediatric hospital units who cared for these children. However, these studies did not systematically consider individual differences in children's abilities to cope with such experiences, variations in the nature of the parent–child relationships prior to hospitalization, or effects of different hospital environments.

The goal of this chapter is to discuss the specific experiences of young children and adolescents on being admitted to a paediatric hospital unit, with one objective being a demonstration of the wide range of possible positive and negative outcomes. After reviewing the primary issues that may affect the child's reaction and some of the empirical evidence justifying the inclusion of these variables in a conceptual model, four case examples illustrating major developmental shifts in childhood will be discussed. This will be followed by the presentation of a proposed conceptual framework for understanding the interplay of the multiple factors. Finally, new directions for research that can better demonstrate the respective effects of these variables will be suggested.

CRITICAL VARIABLES

The presentation of this particular set of factors is influenced by Engel's biopsychosocial conceptual model (Engel, 1977). Following his hierarchical schema, variables will be reviewed in the order of their increasing complexity: (1) the effects of the disease on the child's experience, (2) the child's ability to cope with disease stressors, (3) the importance of the family as a mediating influence, (4) the family's role within the more complex perspective of the paediatric unit, and (5) the effects of the more extensive sociocultural milieu on the medical system.

The disease level

When considering the child's ability to cope, an assessment of the child's and the family's perceptions of the disease is a natural starting place. In addition, consideration must be given to the nature of the disease. For example, in the presence of central nervous system disease the child's capacity to cope may be directly affected by cognitive difficulties. While there is relatively little evidence that different physical illnesses are the result of specific stressors, there is clinical support for the concept that the nature of children's illnesses often has a specific meaning for them. In this regard, a disease such as asthma, although intermittent in its expression, can be extremely frightening during an acute exacerbation. Young asthmatic children with quite severe symptoms have been shown to have a higher incidence of behavioural difficulties (Mrazek, Anderson and Strunk, 1985) while young children with mild disease are less likely to have emotional problems (Gauthier et al., 1978). This pattern of illness experience is in contrast to that of a disease such as juvenile rheumatoid arthritis, which is more unremitting in its persistent negative effects but less likely to result in the fear of a sudden fatal episode.

For any physical illness, it is important to consider the severity of the disease as a key variable. The effect of severity has been clearly demonstrated in some chronic diseases such as cystic fibrosis, in which considerable variability exists in the degree of disability as well as individual prognosis (Steinhausen, Schindler and Stephan, 1983). A related characteristic is the patient's and the family's perceptions of the severity of the illness. Frydman (1980) considered this issue with parents of cystic fibrosis patients and found that overestimation of severity by parents as compared with the child's physician's estimation was related to a high incidence of parental psychopathology.

Some hospitalizations are not the consequence of a disease process, but rather the result of extreme dysfunction within the family. Probable child neglect, physical abuse or sexual abuse may all lead to paediatric hospitalization, not only to assess the child's physical status, but also to provide a safe environment for the child until an appropriate disposition can be made. Such an admission can easily be described as a family crisis and often results in a mixture of confusing emotions for the child ranging from relief in temporary safety to fear that the family may not remain intact because of exposure of their abusive behaviour.

Physical limitations of the patient brought on by the disease is another important variable to be considered in understanding the child's responses. Some relatively serious problems, including many malignancies, may result in relatively mild limitations in a child's capacity to interact normally until late in the course of the illness. Other diseases, such as exercise induced asthma or haemophilia, may result in the need to restrict the child's activity in only specific circumstances. Still other more pervasive problems such as severe juvenile rheumatoid arthritis may result in inability on the part of the child to engage in many otherwise developmentally appropriate activities. A related concern is the degree of physical deformity. Taking into consideration only the severity of the illness may be deceiving in that children with problems of a primarily cosmetic nature, such as facial scarring, may still be emotionally very vulnerable. Yet another related issue is the amount of pain associated with the disease. This is a major problem for children with burns as they are often unable to escape the stressor of recurring painful dressing changes, which can become a psychological strain on the entire family.

A final consideration is the lethality of the illness. It is one thing for a child to be admitted to the hospital for a relatively routine and safe procedure, but quite another if the outcome is uncertain. Helping children to cope with the more lethal malignancies requires considerable sensitivity on the part of the caretaking staff to the anticipated grief of both the child and the parents. This capacity to facilitate mourning is quite independent of whether the child is an inpatient or not. Furthermore, the cumulative impact on medical staff of treating dying children is difficult to overestimate, particularly if they are dealing with quite young children who may be very frightened and quite difficult to reassure verbally (Stedeford, 1984). With the increasing effectiveness of medical treatments, the uncertainty of medical prognosis in what were previously thought to be fatal illnesses has created a dilemma for families and medical staff. Nevertheless, despite the dramatically increased survival rate in both childhood leukaemia and cystic fibrosis, premature death is probable for most patients, and a childhood death still occurs in approximately half of these populations. Koocher and O'Malley (1981) described the uncertainties of such a child's future in their choice of the term the 'Damocles Syndrome', which brings to mind the degree of anxiety that must be associated with the chronic threat of death.

The individual level of the child

Clearly, there are large individual differences in children's capacities to deal with stressors. The concept of the invulnerable child (Garmezy and Neuchterlein, 1972; Anthony, 1974; Rutter, 1979; Werner and Smith, 1982) has highlighted the perception that some children have the capacity to 'make the best of' severely distressing circumstances. The concept of temperament has also been helpful in defining individual children's differences, but it has been difficult to define empirically. Thomas and Chess (1977) focused on early patterns of adaptability but used the generic divisions of 'easy', 'slow to warm up' and 'difficult' to describe the children they studied. These concepts have more recently been considered in chronically ill groups (Kim et al., 1981) and may provide the basis for the development of different approaches to individual patient's hospital care. However, methodologies for the assessment of temperament that do not rely on parental report will be a critical development in the validation of these important early findings (Campos *et al.*, 1983).

The developmental stage of the child is one of the most critical variables in the entire interactive system. Empirical evidence initially supported the view that children younger than 4 are at increased risk for behavioural problems during and after paediatric hospitalization (Prugh *et al.*, 1953; Illingworth and Holt, 1955; Schaffer and Callender, 1959). Douglas (1975) found that a single short period of hospitalization did not have a major effect even within the first 4 years of life. However, he did find increased emotional problems in this age group after multiple hospitalizations. Furthermore, he suggested that enuresis in adolescence may be a delayed response to multiple hospitalizations in the preschool years (Douglas, 1973). Quinton and Rutter (1976) noted that early multiple hospitalizations were associated with both emotional and conduct disorders later in childhood. They stressed that the cumulative effect of repeated hospitalizations was at least additive. Rutter (1979) considered the possibility that chronic family problems could account for these findings, but found that children with the risk factor of multiple early hospitalizations even without the risk factor of chronic family difficulties were more likely to develop later psychopathology. However, those children who had both risk factors were most likely to develop later psychiatric difficulties. One way to conceptualize this is to consider that increased family tension may potentiate the negative effects of multiple hospitalizations. An alternative view would be that a child may become sensitized during a first hospitalization, which could lead to an increased vulnerability during subsequent admissions.

These issues were examined in a population of severely asthmatic preschool children (Mrazek, 1984). Both maternal report data and direct observational data were collected during an inpatient hospital stay. By both of these measures, children with multiple hospitalizations during the period between 2 and 4 years showed a high frequency of behavioural difficulties. Comparisons were made between three groups: (1) severely ill asthmatic children with multiple hospitalizations within this time frame, (2) chronically ill asthmatics without multiple hospitalizations during this time period, and (3) a healthy comparison sample. Based on parental report data, statistically significant differences were shown between all three groups, with the most dramatic difference being between the multiply hospitalized sample and the healthy comparison sample. This increased behavioural difficulty was directly correlated with more frequent admissions and included problems related to dependency and peer interaction, as well as more oppositional behaviour, particularly at bedtime. However, a high frequency of oppositionality during direct observation was demonstrated predominantly in the asthmatic sample with multiple hospitalizations, suggesting that this intense oppositionality may be particularly associated with the hospital experience.

These data suggest that during the period when children are developing an initial sense of independence and autonomy many of the experiences associated with illness and hospitalization may have a disorganizing short-term effect on the child's ability to cope. Clearly, the child is cognitively at a phase of development where preoperational thinking predominates. Thus the child's attempts to understand the experiences around him centre on idiosyncratic and egocentric explanations. Additionally, the concepts related to causality are poorly established, often with distortions in the child's ability to perceive quantitative relationships. Furthermore, the child's concept of the finality of death as well as a perspective on the life-span are relatively primitive. While clinicians have been impressed by the 'precocious' appreciation of some children's perceptions of impending death, this appears to be at least in part due to the centrality of the issue for their families and the medical staff who have been involved in their care.

The cognitive awareness of the child in the sensorimotor period of development as described by Piaget (1952) bears little resemblance to adult thinking. Clearly, a child who is just beginning to form increasingly complex sets of ideational associations through the processes of assimilation and accommodation can not be expected to comprehend any part of the rationale for hospitalization. Parents and adults in the medical system must provide the child with a secure base that consequently allows him the opportunity to cope with novel experiences. How the child at this early age actually manages to adjust to intrusive, painful stimuli is poorly understood, although speculations about intrapsychic defences suggest that various forms of dissociation are important. Babies of less than 6 months of age appear to show relatively little behavioural disturbance if treated sensitively throughout a medical hospitalization, particularly if the mother is present. This may reflect the fact that if a primary secure base is maintained, other environmental factors have less influence.

Older children in the concrete operational stage, or adolescents who have developed abstract thinking, have many more coping strategies available to them with which to manage the stresses related to medical illness and hospitalization. An appreciation of the child's level of understanding regarding his disease has direct bearing on how best to communicate with him, as described by Eiser (1984). Specifically, if children are able to understand the basic pathophysiology of their illness and the rationale for their treatment, they can become a partner in their own therapy instead of victims who may be confused and frightened by events out of their control. Many of the current strategies directed towards minimizing negative effects of hospitalization take into consideration the greater abilities of children in this age range to know what is happening and incorporate methods to give them more control over their own treatment regimes.

An awareness of the emotional level of development of paediatric patients is no less critical for understanding how they adapt to medical stressors. Specifically, preschool children may be at some increased vulnerability because central developmental tasks at that age include the establishment of a sense of autonomy and independence. On entering the hospital they find themselves in a confusing and dependent position and suddenly lose control of many of the aspects of their environment they had previously learned to manage. Furthermore, as a consequence of their more egocentric cognitive view of reality, any misconceptions they may have related to guilt and responsibility may be inadvertently reinforced by the negative medical experience. A classic concern for children at this stage of development is that they may misconstrue necessary medical treatments as punishment or retaliation for some unstated, unacceptable impulse or behaviour.

Other key developmental issues include the establishment of appropriate interactive peer relationships, the evolution of more complex communications through cooperative play, and early mastery of athletic skills. These activities may be severely curtailed by physical limitations that result from illnesses. Taken in total, specific concerns related to the development of self, over and above the identity of being physically imperfect, are magnified by these specific developmental failures.

During infancy, milestones of emotional development include the establishment of affect regulation in the context of a predictable and sensitive interpersonal environment. This process is dependent upon the parenting figures' abilities to respond reciprocally in an affective manner to their child's cues. This clearly requires an empathetic sensitivity on the part of the parents and the ability to communicate their awareness of the child's signals in an affective context that is comprehensible to the child. This delicate system can be disrupted by the poorly modulated events that often occur during hospitalization. However, when the parents of young children can remain with them and provide a sense of emotional stability throughout the course of the medical treatment, much of the disruptive quality of the experience may be mediated. This may be a partial explanation of why some children seem to have a less immediate response during this developmental period.

Most adolescents have established a sense of competence, but this identity may be vulnerable during periods of stress. Probably as a consequence of more sophisticated coping strategies, acute hospitalization is usually a more manageable life event for teenagers. This theory is supported by empirical evidence that a single hospitalization is minimally disruptive for older children and can have a positive effect (Brown *et al.*, 1981). Determining the effect of a chronic illness that necessitates the additive stressful effects of multiple hospitalizations is more complex and requires taking into consideration the child's compensatory modes of interaction.

An overall consequence of greater emotional maturity is that the child develops a greater range of adaptive skills. However, there are large environmentally mediated individual differences between children that must be clinically considered. A more 'invulnerable' 10-year-old child may be able to conceptualize an explanation for his medical predicament and use a wide variety of problem-solving skills to adapt to his illness. In contrast, a less skilful 15-year-old patient may have relatively few coping strategies because of poor cognitive abilities or disruptive and unregulated emotional experiences. Such a child may find the stresses of a single acute hospitalization overwhelming and may become dysfunctional as a consequence. Further conceptualization of the complete range of adaptive strategies and the developmental origins of each should be the goal of future empirical studies.

The belief system of the child is also an important variable. It is widely appreciated that adults utilize their religious or personal beliefs to provide an explanatory frame of reference when they must face serious stressors such as the death of a loved one. The same principle is true for children, although they are more likely to develop an idiosyncratic explanatory system. This is particularly true for young children who used preoperational thinking and are prone to develop elaborate fantasies that may be discounted by adults. An appreciation of how children use play and story telling to communicate their feelings and deal with anxiety can often guide the sensitive clinician in his/her approach to paediatric patients.

Parent variables

Individual differences between parents and within family systems are among the most important mediating variables in determining children's responses to stressors. While examining children's responses to separations and reunions during the hospitalization experience, it has been difficult to demonstrate how the quality of the parent–child relationship prior to the separation subsequently affects the child's reaction. Hinde and McGinnis (1977) examined aspects of this issue using a primate model and demonstrated that primate responses were consistently related to the quality of the preseparation relationship as defined by observational criteria. Dunn and Kendrick (1980) similarly demonstrated that a first child's response to the emotional stress of the birth of a sibling was consistently associated with the quality of the prenatal mother–child relationship. Fagin (1966) made observations of children's reactions to hospitalization and suggested that there may be a relationship between their reactions and the quality of the family support system.

A parent's response may actually be quite complicated as it often is mediated by competing dyadic relationships between both parents and other siblings. In order to conceptualize the manner in which these interactions affect the child's ability to cope with the stressors related to medical admission, the emotional strengths and personality characteristics of both the parents must be considered. A basic clinical objective is for the parents to provide their child with a sense of stability throughout the admission. Parents who have developed certain personality disturbances may have a paradoxical effect on their children that interferes with their attempts to cope. This is particularly true of excessively anxious parents as their fears are easily transmitted to their child who turns to them for reassurance. Similarly, depressed parents may be unable to respond affectively to their children at critical moments, which can be perceived as an emotional abandonment. Perhaps one of the greatest problems is a parent with an intense paranoid orientation who develops an overt distrust of hospital staff. Such a parent can create an intense fear and shared paranoid ideation in his child.

The parents' abilities to understand the needs of their child is a necessary step in their being able to provide appropriate support. Young parents with little experience with children often do not understand how to create a stable environment for their hospitalized child. This may lead to their making insensitive decisions that evoke strong medical staff reaction. Perhaps most important for the provision of emotional support is the parents' realization that they must be present when a child has to undergo a particularly painful or frightening procedure.

Another common problem is a parent's inability to communicate clearly to the child regarding the necessity of specific medical treatment. If a parent is unable to support firmly the implementation of a medical procedure when faced with resistance on the part of the child, a pattern of non-compliance may be initiated that may potentially exacerbate the condition that precipitated the hospitalization. Medical staff may be quick to perceive the parent's difficulty in securing the child's compliance as a reflection of more generalized problems in parenting. Some anxious parents will find such criticism intolerable, and there is a risk that they will subsequently avoid further contact with doctors and nurses.

The parents' ability to maintain their own emotional equilibrium is essential. If anxiety related to the wellbeing of their child becomes overwhelming, some parents may experience an acute or delayed stress reaction that could inhibit their ability to provide appropriate medical care. Making an assessment of the parents' abilities to deal with the stressors associated with their child's illness and providing them with specific support must be an important part of maximizing the benefits of a hospitalization.

The financial and emotional resources of the family must also be considered. The expenses related to medical care can be devastating and often include loss of wages and salary in addition to direct medical costs. Negative patterns of interaction may arise if a large proportion of the family's resources must be expended to care for the ill child, resulting in overt hardship for other children in the family. This situation may be further aggravated if the parents' emotional energies are also dominated by their concern for their chronically ill child. This may leave children who are in good health feeling angry at perceived emotional abandonment, but guilty about such feelings towards a hospitalized sibling. In this regard, mobilizing an extended familial or community system to give tangible help to the parents and siblings should be considered vital.

The religious or philosophical belief system of the family can be a powerful influence on the child's reactions to hospitalization. In deeply religious families who ascribe a divine meaning to the negative stressors in their lives, there is at least a potential mechanism for them to understand their unhappiness. The converse is true for families with uncertain philosophical foundations who may find their child's illness incomprehensible and particularly disorganizing. However, it would be wrong to minimize the complexity of this factor. The belief that a great hardship is the will of God can lead to tremendous bitterness instead of a greater acceptance and resignation. Similarly, a paradox can occur for a family with few spiritual beliefs who find that their attempts to understand their child's illness provide them with a sense of purpose that helps them to cope with these stressors. Parents' organizations that support the care for children with specific illnesses as well as research into the aetiology and new treatments of the illness owe much to parents of all philosophical persuasions who have chosen this active response to their own adversity, thus helping others in the process.

Hospital variables

Much has been written about the importance of the doctor–patient relationship, but this concept has only slowly been expanded to include the doctor–family interactions. However, the basic principles are still cogent. The paediatrician must demonstrate a high level of competence if the family is to develop a sense of reassurance and trust in him. Additionally, he must have an empathetic appreciation of the needs of the child if he is to be effective in minimizing the stressful components of the hospital experience. Nurses have increasingly taken an assertive position in identifying coping problems that families may have on a child's entry into the hospital. Also, nursing staff often provide specific orientation on hospital admission with the goal of decreasing the anxiety of families and organize educational programmes to facilitate understanding of the pathophysiology of the illness and its treatment.

One of the goals of the child psychiatric consultation/liaison team to paediatrics is to mediate positively the hospital experience for the child and family. Paediatric liaison diagnostic skills and interventions can be conceptualized as representing a subspecialty of child psychiatry (Mrazek, in press). However, one of the basic expectations of the liaison clinician is that he make an assessment of the level of coping within the family system and the degree of sensitivity of the medical team to the family's psychological needs. A classic role of the liaison psychiatrist is to evaluate the family's understanding of the rationale and necessity of specific medical procedures and to help them overcome any emotional responses that distort their perceptions. Additional functions include development of a differential diagnosis of psychiatric illness, exploration of the family's feelings about the prognosis of their child's illness, identification of appropriate crisis intervention when stressors become overwhelming, and coordination of the efforts of the psychiatric team. The effectiveness of such comprehensive family approaches on improving the long-term outcome of paediatric patients has begun to be demonstrated (Bingley *et al.*, 1980).

Hospitalizations are often associated with acute discomfort that can be difficult for children to tolerate. Coming to the hospital for a period of observation following head trauma that results in no specific medical intervention, and the agonizing rehabilitation following extensive burns, must be conceptualized as being two very different stressors. Naturally, there is an interaction between the severity of the illness and the duration and discomfort of the procedures. These two variables have been combined in a 'Morbidity Scale' that Minde and his coworkers have developed to monitor the impact of persistent severe illness on the psychological response of infants in an intensive care nursery and the subsequent relationship between the infants and their mothers (Minde, Perrotta and Orter, 1982; Minde *et al.*, 1983). Similar methods for the quantification of the degree of distress experienced by older children in the course of hospitalization, particularly related to pain and loss of control, will lead to a better understanding of some of the large variations in children's responses to hospitalization.

Finally, the physical design of the hospital unit and its policies regarding the provision of medical treatment are additional important variables, as reviewed by Gordon (1981) in the earlier volume, complementary to this one. The amount of attention that is paid to the creation of an environment in which the family is able to be with their child over the course of the hospital stay varies widely. For younger children the presence of their families is particularly important. Appropriate opportunities must also be offered to allow older children to continue to master normal developmental tasks. These include opportunities to (1) continue to advance educationally either through the use of specific tutorial arrangements or in a hospital school; (2) maintain contact with friends, classmates and supportive adults; and (3) develop a supportive peer network within the hospital if a long hospital stay is required. For children who have chronic illnesses and require prolonged hospitalizations, failure to provide such services is likely to have negative effects on both their cognitive and emotional development.

Sociocultural variables

While it is appropriate to consider these widely differing influences on the child's response to hospitalization, it is difficult to address their interaction empirically. Common approaches include the review of historical changes in clinical practice, such as shifts in perinatal practice, on child development (Klaus and Kennell, 1982). Cross-cultural studies have demonstrated societal differences in the appreciation and definition of children's needs. Furthermore, societal 'rules' regarding emotional expression play a role in the child's experience during hospitalization. Where close physical proximity between parents and children and open expression of affect is encouraged, one would expect fewer disruptive behavioural responses during hospitalization than in societies that require a very stoic acceptance of the stressors associated with medical care.

Perhaps most overwhelming in cross-cultural comparisons are the differences in resources between societies. Wealthy countries may be in a position to provide supportive services for families to help them deal with emotional stressors, while Third World countries with insufficient resources for even maintaining basic physical survival are often disinclined to address issues of emotional development, which they may assess as being comparatively irrelevant. Even within societies with high standards of living, different systems of health care vary in the comprehensiveness of the medical services they provide. Good health care is increasingly becoming a basic expectation in Western societies. However, with a concurrent demand for greater equity in the availability of medical services, it is not always possible to afford the highest level of medical technology. Clearly, careful consideration of what care can be afforded is crucial. When families have good insurance coverage, whether through a national or a private insurance scheme, the immediate cost of medical services is less of an issue. However, when the cost of recommended medical care must be met by the family, a number of difficult decisions must be faced. In these cases, a relatively straightforward but prolonged hospitalization may have minimally negative emotional consequences for the child's development, but may result in financial disaster for the family.

Certainly, a society's predominant value system plays a role in how limited resources are allocated. Religious orders have often placed a high priority on providing compassionate medical services. This fact is evidenced by the historic evolution of hospitals and the current large number of medical institutions supported by religious bodies. However, this sense of compassion is not restricted to cultures characterized by a predominant formal religious creed; for instance, non-denominational philanthropic organizations also make major contributions towards the provision of care for children.

CASE ILLUSTRATIONS

The following case vignettes illustrate interactions between the previously described subsystems. They have been chosen to demonstrate the importance of developmental considerations and the interplay between the specific components of the family and the medical care system.

Donald—a preschool child's use of physical symptoms for secondary gain

Donald was a 4-year-old boy who had developed eczema and severe asthma in his first year of life. Because of the severity of these problems and their reactive nature, he had required multiple hospitalizations and intensive home care which had created conflicts between his parents. His father in particular had begun to find the demands being placed upon him to be excessive and had responded by withdrawing from his family responsibilities and becoming more involved in his work. Donald's mother had become progressively more frustrated, exhausted and lonely. Her solution to this dilemma was to turn to Donald to meet her emotional needs.

For Donald, the effects of previous paediatric hospitalization have to be understood within this context. The objective of this current hospitalization was to explore thoroughly the triggering stimuli for his asthmatic attacks. This more extended hospital stay exaggerated and clarified the problems that had developed in the family's interactions but had been less evident during outpatient treatment. His father rarely visited. Donald began to demonstrate regressed and immature behaviour, which included intense protest on separation from his mother and clever attempts to manipulate his mother's behaviour through the use of his asthmatic symptoms. When she tried to set appropriate limits, he became increasingly defiant. This oppositional behaviour became a problem for the nurses on the unit, and his mother often capitulated because of her embarassment about his tantrums. Unfortunately, this only reinforced his maladaptive behaviour.

Donald was seen individually by the liaison child psychiatrist to assess the nature of these reactions. It became clear that he very much valued his special relationship with his mother and appeared content with his successful exclusion of his father from the nuclear family. He responded intensely to any threat to his exclusive hold on his mother and boasted in the diagnostic session of his ability to 'get what he wanted'. His fantasies were dominated by hostile themes including aggressive impulses directed towards adult men and a sense of his own omnipotence demonstrated by a strong identification with a series of 'superheroes'.

Night-time problems became more severe when his mother would not remain overnight in the hospital. This included secondary enuresis and disturbing nightmares. However, throughout the hospitalization Donald remained very talkative and when left alone with ward staff was often a charming and likeable child. In contrast, on short afternoon outings away from the hospital with his mother he often became unmanageable and had severe temper tantrums.

The primary therapeutic approach for Donald and his family was to focus on the difficulties within the marriage and to try to re-ally the parents to assume mutually supportive positions in their efforts to deal with Donald's unreasonable demands. This was accomplished through a short series of marital sessions as well as a meeting with the three of them together to help the parents reinforce their newly developed alliance in managing Donald's behaviour. Donald was at some points quite enraged by this shift, but he was gradually able to begin to identify with his father. Specific interventions designed to increase father's involvement included designating certain illness-related responsibilities to him and arranging outings for father and son together. Individual sessions with Donald helped him to cope with his resistance to these changes and allowed him to verbalize some of his sadness related to his perception of losing a special and exclusive relationship with his mother. His night-time problems were quickly resolved, and his behavioural confrontations were gradually modified with no concurrent exacerbation of his asthmatic attacks.

In considering Donald's hospitalization, was there a negative effect? His behaviour became disturbed and there was no doubt that he experienced intense separation reactions. Yet, in the balance, a much better family approach to his illnesses emerged. On follow-up a year later, Donald was doing well.

Donna—a school-aged girl faces a malignancy

Donna was a 9-year-old- girl who was admitted to an acute paediatric unit with symptoms of headache and disequilibrium. Her parents were in late middle-age, and her mother had some cognitive impairments. The family's first language was not English, and communication between the family and the many consultants involved in Donna's medical care was often strained.

As days passed, it was determined that Donna was suffering from a malignant tumour of the cerebellum. Donna had been a popular girl in school and an active member of the gymnastics team. It was inconceivable to her family that she could have a fatal illness, and her mother would not accept the terminal prognosis. Subsequently, a variety of questions arose related to the degree to which her mother was able to understand the well-meaning explanations of the paediatric neurologist and neurosurgeon. As a result of the anxiety and confusion regarding prognosis, considerable conflict arose between family members regarding how much Donna should be told about her own future. As some medical staff were also uncomfortable when having to deal openly with Donna about her impending death, their anxieties increased her parents' ambivalence about discussing the implications of her tumour with her. What followed were several days during which Donna became progressively more withdrawn and depressed while her mother became virtually noncommunicative with medical staff.

A large family meeting was held, and a plan for helping the extended family to support Donna's mother was developed. Also, the liaison child psychiatrist met with Donna's mother and established a plan to allow Donna to be told about her disease in a way that her mother could accept. This was followed by a joint discussion, which included the neurosurgeon, the child psychiatrist, Donna and her mother, to address the nature of Donna's neurologic illness and her serious prognosis in a developmentally comprehensible manner.

The consequences of this meeting were a dramatic improvement in Donna's affective state and a mobilization of both the medical staff and the family in a joint attempt to normalize her remaining months. This effort was coupled with strong community support, which included a fund-raising drive to raise money to pay for Donna's care, and considerable emotional support from her classmates, their families and the family's church. Donna met with the child psychiatrist who was able to help her to continue to cope with the intense affects that she experienced over the course of her last months.

In Donna's case, the effect of hospitalization was small in comparison to the impact of her prognosis. The liaison psychiatrist was able to use the resources available within the hospital to work through the family's initial intense denial. In this case, both the family's religious belief system and the community's support were important mediating variables in the outcome.

John—a teenager's adaptation to amputation

John was 16 and a member of his high school football team. He came from an active and supportive upper-middle-class family. John developed leg pain subsequent to a football injury and was admitted to a large medical centre. After an initial medical examination it was suggested that he had developed an osteosarcoma. This diagnosis was confirmed, and his leg was amputated above the knee. Medical staff immediately bonded with John and his family and were able to share affectively the family's initial disbelief and anger while continuing to be supportive and available to them throughout his rehabilitation. An appreciation of the impact that this surgery would have on John's body image and peer relationships was helpful in guiding his treatment. Other adolescents who had had amputations and who were still active in a variety of sports were contacted and visited John while he was still in the hospital. In addition, his school classmates were encouraged to maintain communication with John throughout his hospitalization and rehabilitation so that he had a minimal sense of alienation throughout this process. John was able to take a philosophical view of the future that would not have been possible for a younger child. Demonstrating a very adaptive response, he began making plans that would allow him to compensate for his disability. This resulted in his designing an active physical rehabilitation programme and setting ambitious goals for himself, which he subsequently was able to meet through a very aggressive exercise programme. An important consideration was that his parents were able to grieve over the loss of their son's leg and sporting career, with the support of hospital staff, while still helping him develop plans for the future in a realistic, competent manner.

John's hospitalization was an acute crisis, but the main issue was the tragic loss of his leg. His family's steady emotional support and his own outstanding coping ability dominated the events related to his hospitalization.

Tom—an illustration of hospitalization positively mediating other life stressors

Tom was a 12-year-old boy who was admitted to hospital for an extended stay after recurrent episodes of severe persistent asthma. His attacks were associated with periods of high family stress, and he had a recent history of exacerbations of his behavioural disturbance. Tom was being treated with multiple anti-asthmatic medications but was still losing several days of schooling each week.

Tom's medical management was complicated by the disruptive quality of his family situation. His father had a long history of bipolar depressive illness that had been successfully treated in the past with lithium. Unfortunately, he had discontinued taking this medication. Father was working long hours but was unpredictable in his support for the family. Tom's mother had a history of multiple major depressive episodes and had been successfully treated with antidepressant medication in the past. Also, she had repeatedly abused amphetamines but had stopped by the time of this admission and was undergoing psychotherapeutic treatment.

Tom's family lived some distance from the hospital. His father was unavailable during the hospitalization and remained very critical of his wife and son. Tom's mother, in contrast, was initially very actively involved with Tom's medical care but then suddenly left the hospital and Tom to return home to her husband. She stated that she was going to use the period of Tom's hospitalization as an opportunity to 'work on her marriage', and that this plan was supported by her psychotherapist. Tom was initially angry at what he perceived as an abandonment, but he dealt with his feelings in what appeared to be an adaptive manner. He developed increasingly high spirits and seemed full of energy. A psychiatric evaluation was requested for him based both on his past history of behaviour problems and the perception that his asthmatic symptoms were frequently exacerbated by emotional conflict within the family. During the evaluation, Tom presented in a very grandiose and euphoric manner, acknowledging no difficulties. He did well both medically and behaviourally during the initial weeks of his hospitalization.

Tom's course took a dramatic turn for the worse when his mother returned for an extended visit. He became acutely depressed after her arrival, refused to eat, remained in bed, and became hostile and agitated when confronted. He soon developed tangential associations and became acutely suicidal. Given his father's bipolar diagnosis, he was treated with lithium and showed a dramatic improvement in his psychotic thinking.

After several more weeks of stable functioning, a trial discharge was planned at the time of his sister's wedding. After 1 week away from the hospital he developed a severe asthmatic attack and became intensely depressed. He was readmitted, and it was found that his theophylline and lithium levels were both zero. These drugs were started once again, and both his respiratory symptoms and his mental status improved rapidly. Given the clarity of the relationship of these symptoms, the degree of his family's disorganization, and the absence of any extrafamilial support system, his discharge planning focused on enacting change in the family situation. Tom's discharge was contingent on the entire family engaging in ongoing supportive family treatment as well as Tom continuing to receive individual psychiatric treatment. Tom began to feel more self-confident and was able to distance himself effectively from his parents' affective lability. These strivings for autonomy were strongly reinforced by his therapist and in family treatment so that he was eventually able to make a good independent adjustment.

The psychological benefits of this hospitalization clearly outweighed any negative emotional effects. This paradoxical response must be considered whenever the relative degree of disruption within the family system is sufficiently high for a hospital environment to be perceived as a sanctuary. While this phenomenon is well known in psychiatric facilities, it is not always appreciated in paediatric settings. A lack of an awareness of this reality can result in making decisions that on the surface seem logical but can actually exacerbate the child's psychological difficulties.

A MULTIVARIATE INTERACTIVE CONCEPTUALIZATION

The preceding case histories illustrate the complexity of children's responses to hospitalization. Simply to suggest that an exacerbation of a physical illness and the subsequent separation from the familiarity of the home environment are going to have a specified behavioural effect ignores the complexities of the hospitalization process as well as individual differences in family and

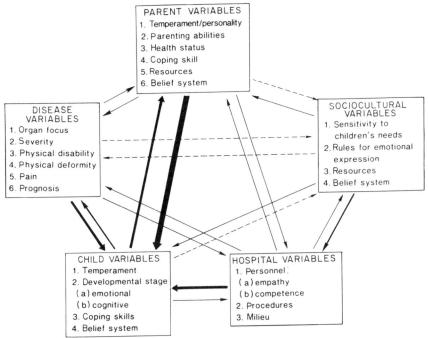

Figure 5.1   The biopsychosocial model applied to pediatric hospitalization (width of arrow reflects hypothesized strength of relationship)

community support. For families with a strong nuclear structure and with a history of relatively minimal stress, the experience of hospitalization may be perceived as a new and very potent stressor. For multiple-problem families where stressors are chronic, admission to the hospital may actually be seen as a peaceful interlude and a positive mediating factor. This is particularly true if the hospital staff are sensitive to this family's emotional needs and can formulate an appropriate intervention that extends beyond a reflex medical response.

Given an appreciation of the complexities of these interactions, simply talking about the 'stress of hospitalization' in the generic sense is relatively unhelpful. Rather, each component of the critical variables discussed previously must be assessed. Figure 5.1 illustrates how these interactions may be viewed. In this representation, the width of the arrows reflects the hypothesized degree of influence. For example, the reciprocal interactions between the child and the family preceding admission, during hospitalization, and following discharge are probably the most influential aspects of this complex system. However, the specific implications of the illness for both the child and the family as well as the response of the medical staff to the child's illness are also critical. Certainly, the tone and quality of these interactions will be affected by pervasive social and cultural expectations within the community.

FUTURE RESEARCH

Clearly what are not needed are more studies that look at two variables and that hope to find a correlation. It is pointless at this stage in our understanding of this complex process to investigate whether school-age children are going to have a negative or positive response to hospitalization of a certain duration for any of a wide variety of possible reasons. What is needed is an understanding of how children with a specific set of risk factors are likely to respond given comparable stressors and, perhaps most importantly, how specific mediating factors can influence this response. To do this requires careful estimation and quantification of the various factors under study and statistical analyses that take into account their reciprocal effects. Recent studies such as those by Steinhausen, Schindler and Stephan (1983) and Venters (1981) reflect promising new techniques in examining stressors by using multivariate analyses. However, further expansion of these models is necessary if we are to continue to increase our understanding of these complex interactions.

Given a formulation of the relative risks of specific variables, prospective studies of children with particular characteristics could use discriminant analyses to differentiate outcomes with respect to mediating factors. Further definition of important mediating factors may well lead to a better awareness of appropriate interventions that are disease-specific and targeted for a variety of family constellations. An example is new family therapy techniques that are being advocated for the manipulation of family systems when either a child or a parent is physically ill (Minuchin, Rosman and Baker, 1978). Other strategies look beyond the nuclear family in an attempt to mobilize extrafamilial support.

A series of steps towards understanding must be achieved by the clinician. First, the rationale for the medical treatment of the child must be understood as well as the psychological meaning of his illness. This must include an assessment of the child's coping skills and past successes in adaptation to similar stressors. The next step is an evaluation of the parents' abilities to understand their child's emotional reactions and to take developmentally appropriate effective action. Finally, there must be a sensitization of the medical system to think beyond the pathophysiology of the illness and to appreciate the impact of emotional interactions on the final expression of symptoms. Using this context, the experience of paediatric hospitalization can be effectively restructured. Instead of admission to hospital acting as a traditional and potent stressor for a young child, it can be perceived as a potential opportunity for positively mediating negative influences on the child's emotional and physical adaptation.

REFERENCES

Anthony, E. J. (1974). The syndrome of the psychologically invulnerable child. In E. J. Anthony and C. Koupernik (eds), *The Child in his Family: Children at Psychiatric Risk*, vol. 3. New York: John Wiley & Sons.

Bakwin, H. (1942). Loneliness in infants. *American Journal of Diseases of Childhood*, **63**, 30–40.

Bingley, L., Leonard, J., Hensman, S., Lask, B., and Wolff, O. (1980). Comprehensive management of children on a paediatric ward: a family approach. *Archives of Disease in Childhood*, **55**, 555–561.

Bowlby, J., Robertson, J., and Rosenbluth, D. (1952). A two-year-old goes to hospital. *Psychoanalytic Study of the Child*, **7**, 82–94.

Brown, G., Chadwick, O., Shaffer, D., Rutter, M., and Traub, M. (1981). A prospective study of children with head injuries. III Psychiatric sequelae. *Psychological Medicine*, **11**, 63–78.

Campos, J. J., Barrett, K. C., Lamb, M. E., Goldsmith, H. H., and Stenberg, C. (1983). Socioemotional development. In P. H. Mussen (ed.), *Handbook of Child Psychology*. New York: John Wiley & Sons.

Chapin, H. D. (1915). Are institutions for infants necessary? *Journal of the American Medical Association*, **64**, 1–3.

Douglas, J. W. B. (1973). Early disturbing events and later enuresis. In I. Kolvin, R. C. MacKeith and S. R. Meadow (eds), *Bladder Control and Enuresis* (Clinics in Developmental Medicine No. 48/49). London: William Heinemann Medical Books.

Douglas, J. W. B. (1975). Early hospital admissions and later disturbances of behaviour and learning. *Developmental Medicine and Child Neurology*, **17**, 456–480.

Dunn, J., and Kendrick, C. (1980). The arrival of a sibling. *Journal of Child Psychology and Psychiatry*, **21**, 119–132.

Eiser, C. (1984). Communicating with sick and hospitalized children. *Journal of Child Psychology and Psychiatry*, **25**, 181–189.

Engel, G. L. (1977). The need for a new medical model: a challenge for biomedicine. *Science*, **196**, 129–136.

Fagin, C. M. R. N. (1966). *The Effects of Maternal Attendance During Hospitalization on the Post-hospital Behavior of Young Children*. Philadelphia: F. A. Davis.

Frydman, M. I. (1980). Perception of illness severity and psychiatric symptoms in parents of chronically ill children. *Journal of Psychosomatic Research*, **24**, 361–369.

Garmezy, N., and Neuchterlein, K. (1972). Invulnerable children: the fact and fiction of competence and disadvantage. *American Journal of Orthopsychiatry*, **42**, 328–329.

Garmezy, N., and Rutter, M. (eds) (1983). *Stress, Coping, and Development in Children*. New York: McGraw-Hill.

Gauthier, Y., Fortin, C., Drapeau, P., Breton, J., Gosselin, J., Quintal, L., Weisnagel, J., and Lamarre, A. (1978). Follow-up study of 35 asthmatic preschool children. *Journal of the American Academy of Child Psychiatry*, **17**, 679–694.

Gordon, A. M. (1981). The treatment environment. In M. J. Christie and P. G. Mellett (eds), *Foundations of Psychosomatics*. New York: John Wiley & Sons.

Hinde, R. A., and McGinnis, L. (1977). Some factors influencing the effect of temporary mother–infant separation: some experiments with rhesus monkeys. *Psychological Medicine*, **7**, 197–212.

Illingworth, R. S., and Holt, K. S. (1955). Children in hospital: some observations on their reactions with special reference to daily visiting. *Lancet*, **ii**, 1257–1262.

Kim, S. P., Ferrara, A., Mattsson, A., and Chess, S. (1981). Comparative temperament profiles of children with chronic diseases. Paper presented at the 28th annual meeting of the American Academy of Child Psychiatry.

Klaus, M. H., and Kennell, J. H. (1982). *Parent–Infant Bonding*, 2nd edn. St Louis: C. V. Mosby.

Koocher, G. P., and O'Malley, J. E. (1981). *The Damocles Syndrome: Psychosocial Consequences of Surviving Childhood Cancer*. New York: McGraw-Hill.

Minde, K., Perrotta, M., and Orter, C. (1982). The effect of neonatal complications in same-sexed premature twins on their mother's preference. *Journal of the American Academy of Child Psychiatry*, **21**, 446–452.

Minde, K., Whitelaw, A., Brown, J., and Fitzhardinge, P. (1983). The effects of neonatal complications in premature infants on early parent–infant interactions. *Developmental Medicine and Child Neurology*, **25**, 763–777.

Minuchin, S., Rosman, R., and Baker, L. (1978). *Psychosomatic Families: Anorexia Nervosa in Context*. Cambridge, Mass.: Harvard University Press.

Mrazek, D. A. (1984). Effects of hospitalization on early child development. In R. N. Emde and R. J. Harmon (eds), *Continuities and Discontinuities in Development*. New York: Plenum.

Mrazek, D. A. (in press). Child psychiatry consultation and liaison with paediatrics. In M. Rutter and L. Herzov (eds), *Child Psychiatry: Modern Approaches*, 2nd edn. London: Blackwell.

Mrazek, D. A., Anderson, I. S., and Strunk, R. C. (1958). Disturbed emotional development in severely asthmatic preschool children. In J. E. Stevenson (ed.), *Recent Research in Developmental Psychopathology*. Oxford: Pergamon Press.

Piaget, J. (1952). *The Origins of Intelligence in Children*. New York: International Universities Press.

Prugh, D. G., Straub, E. M., Sands, H. H., Kirschbaum, R. M., and Lenihan, E. A. (1953). A study of the emotional reactions of children and families to hospitalization and illness. *American Journal of Orthopsychiatry*, **23**, 70–106.

Quinton, D., and Rutter, M. (1976). Early hospital admissions and later disturbances of behaviour: an attempted replication of Douglas' findings. *Developmental Medicine and Child Neurology*, **18**, 447–459.

Robertson, J. (1952). Film: *A Two Year Old Goes to Hospital*. London: Tavistock Child Development Research Unit; New York: New York University Film Library.

Robertson, J., and Robertson, J. (1971). Young children in brief separation. *Psychoanalytic Study of the Child*, **26**, 264–315.

Rutter, M. (1979). Protective factors in children's responses to stress and disadvantage. In M. W. Kent and J. E. Rolf (eds), *Primary Prevention of Psychopathology*, vol. 3, *Social Competence in Children*. Hanover, NJ: University Press of New England.

Schaffer, H. R., and Callender, W. M. (1959). Psychologic effects of hospitalization in infancy. *Pediatrics*, **24**, 528–539.

Spitz, R. A. (1945). Hospitalism: an inquiry into the genesis of psychiatric conditions in early childhood. *Psychoanalytic Study of the Child* (New York: International University Press), **1**, 53–74.

Stedeford, A. (1984). *Facing Death: Patients, Families and Professionals*. London: William Heinemann.

Steinhausen, H., Schindler, H., and Stephan, H. (1983). Correlates of psychopathology in sick children: an empirical model. *Journal of the American Academy of Child Psychiatry*, **22**, 559–564.

Thomas, A., and Chess, S. (1977). *Temperament and Development*. New York: Brunner/Mazel.

Venters, M. (1981). Familial coping with chronic and severe childhood illness: the case of cystic fibrosis. *Social Science in Medicine*, **15A**, 289–297.

Werner, E. E., and Smith, R. S. (1982). *Vulnerable but Invincible: A Study of Resilient Children*. New York: McGraw-Hill.

SECTION 3

Eating Behaviours

The Psychosomatic Approach: Contemporary Practice
 of Whole-person Care
Edited by M. J. Christie and P. G. Mellett
© 1986 John Wiley & Sons Ltd

6

BIOPSYCHOLOGICAL INTERACTIONS UNDERLYING THE STUDY AND TREATMENT OF OBESITY

JOHN E. BLUNDELL

and ANDREW J. HILL

Biopsychology Group, Department of Psychology, University of Leeds, UK

EVOLUTION OF A PSYCHOSOMATIC APPROACH

Obesity is now recognized as one of the major health hazards of modern civilized societies, yet it has no agreed cause and there is no agreed manner of treatment. Obesity is one of the most perplexing and refractory of all disorders. Over the years a variety of extreme treatments have been employed including metabolic starvation, ileojejunum bypass, brain surgery, jaw wiring, vagotomy and chemical agents such as thyroxin or chorionic gonadotrophin. These treatments are largely ineffective, unsafe or both. Of course, it is recognized that the major problem is not weight loss itself but the maintenance of a lowered level of body weight. But why should this be such a formidable problem?

The word 'obesity' is constructed from *ob* meaning over, and *edere*, to eat, and this derivation has for centuries carried with it the belief that obesity is due to overeating. Indeed, some 40 years ago certain authorities had reached the conclusion that in the overwhelming majority of cases obesity was not caused by any organic disorder of metabolism, but was simply a result of overeating (e.g. Newburgh, 1942). Subsequently, Kaplan and Kaplan (1957) suggested that in at least 97 per cent of cases the accumulation of adipose tissue was due to the consumption of an 'excessive amount of food over and above the bodily need' (p. 189). Moreover, these authors, capitalizing on the work of Hilde Bruch, set the pattern for a psychosomatic approach to the study of obesity by specifying that the most important aspect of the relationship between psychological factors and excessive food intake was the mechanism by which any emotional conflict resulted in the symptom of overeating. Central to this approach was the belief that overeating was functional since eating reduced anxiety.

A decade ago, an influential paper by Stunkard (1975a) revised and advanced psychosomatic thinking about obesity. Instead of searching for premature *explanations* of obesity which could be used in psychodynamic treatment methods, Stunkard advocated the employment of experimental procedures and positive behavioural interventions. The directive was to reduce concentration on the emotional determinants of obesity and firmly to identify the social, psychological and physiological parameters which characterize the condition.

This chapter can be seen as a continuation of the movement instigated by Stunkard. Within the last 10 years scientific thinking about obesity has markedly changed and there has been a greater degree of collaboration between the disciplines of physiology, biochemistry, psychology and nutrition. There is no longer the insistence that obesity arises from, or is maintained by, frank hyperphagia; consequently the importance of emotional disturbance in generating overeating (and therefore obesity) is lessened. Indeed, convincing experimental evidence for the causal relationship between anxiety and eating has been extremely difficult to obtain (e.g. Abramson and Wunderlich, 1972). Currently, there is even a strong call to regard obesity as a disorder of underactivity rather than overeating (e.g. Gwinup, 1975; Stern, 1984), but it seems unnecessary to insist on the universal operation of a single principle of this type (see Blundell, 1984).

In recent years the philosopher Waddington has exhorted scientists to give up the strategy of seeking cause–effect relationships and to make interpretations in terms of interacting systems (Waddington, 1977). Adapting this approach, the control of food consumption can be viewed as resulting from complex interactions between the biological, psychological and social domains (Blundell, 1982a). This is the conceptual framework which now characterizes the psychosomatic approach to obesity. However, the evolution of the approach from emotional determinants to interacting processes does not entail the abandonment of emotional factors to a matrix of impersonal variables. It is clear from an examination of the meaning of obesity in our present society that a dynamic state of tension embraces the condition of fat people. It is this element which makes obesity such an appropriate target of study by means of the psychosomatic approach.

THE ISSUE OF OBESITY

Any approach to the study of obesity must be based on certain characteristics of the condition and of the circumstances which have led to it becoming a cause for concern. An analysis of this type suggests that the present era can be regarded as a time of crisis. This proposition is based on five observations. First, the incidence of obesity is extremely high in modern industrialized societies such as those in North America and on the European continent. Van Itallie (1983) has reported that more than 36 million people in America can be regarded as being statistically overweight, whilst Garrow (1982) has estimated that between one third and one quarter of the adult population of the UK may be defined as mildly obese. Clearly, a slight degree of plumpness does not carry medical risks but the condition creates hazards due to other circumstances. Second, the cultural ethos is antagonistic to obesity and this disapproval is propagated by the media—particularly the daily tabloids and women's magazines. An obese person is widely regarded as being unhealthy, unfit, aesthetically displeasing, or all of these. This hostility is directed largely towards women for whom an arbitrarily defined ideal body shape (models, athletes, etc.) is depicted as being the norm which all should strive to achieve. Consequently, many people, and women in particular, are exhorted to attempt to attain a body shape which, on morphological grounds alone, is unrealistic and unattainable for the majority. The body shape currently preferred by European and American cultures is a transient phenomenon, and one which bears little relationship to the natural body contours of womanhood. Elsewhere in the world, e.g. in parts of North Africa, obesity is regarded as aesthetically pleasing (Adadevoh, 1974; Verngiaud, Englebert and Bruggman, 1977).

Third, this negative cultural view of obesity means that great psychological pressure is exerted on fat people (in the mild, moderate and severe categories of obesity—Stunkard, 1984) to lose weight. It seems beyond dispute that almost all fat or plump individuals are coerced into feeling concern for their condition and into adopting measures to avoid cultural disapproval. Fourth, there is no truly effective treatment for obesity that does not carry risks and which is being made available to the vast number of people who seek help. Some 25 years ago Stunkard and McLaren-Hume (1959) reached a gloomy conclusion about the possibilities of effectively treating fat people and it may be argued that the situation is the same today. Consequently, although many hundreds of thousands of people actively seek treatment for fatness, evidence shows that the large majority of attempts to become permanently slimmer are unsuccessful.

Fifth, the circumstances set out above have led to a crisis in which people concerned about their body weight (or more probably body shape) have adopted desperate measures including unregulated fasting, vomiting and the use of purges and laxatives. In certain places vomiting has reached almost epidemic proportions (Wooley and Wooley, 1984). Accordingly, the excessive concern about body shape coupled with the lack of effective treatment has led to the massive increase in a class of eating disorders (see Chapter 7, by Lacey and Birtchnell), including conditions known as bulimarexia (Boskind-Lodahl, 1976) or bulimia nervosa (Russell, 1979) which are far more prevalent than previously believed (Cooper and Fairburn, 1983). Moreover, these eating disorders appear not only in fat people, but in individuals (usually women) of normal or subnormal body weight. Clinical experience suggests that eating disorders (including vomiting) occur in non-obese women as an attempt to prevent the development of a condition (obesity) which meets with strong cultural hostility. Consequently, although obesity may not necessarily arise as a result of an eating disorder, the condition itself may provoke feeding disturbances. For this reason it is appropriate to consider obesity within a system which embraces biological, psychological and social factors.

THE NATURE OF OBESITY

The above section illustrates why obesity constitutes such a formidable scientific and social problem. Owing to the cultural circumstances, the objective definition of obesity is often irrelevant (the psychological appraisal of obesity and the fear of developing the condition may themselves be sufficient to generate disorders of mental state and behaviour). Moreover, a comprehensive description of the nature of obesity is beyond the scope of this chapter. It is useful, however, to set out certain significant features of the condition.

First, how should obesity be defined? Often the terms 'fat' and 'overweight' are used synonymously although they are not identical. The degree of fatness is usually based on triceps skinfold measurements made by calipers, and obesity is defined as measures falling above the sex-specific 85th percentile for persons 20–29 years of age (see Bray, 1979a). Overweight is defined by the deviation (usually 10–19 per cent or greater than 20 per cent) above the desirable weight for age and height obtained from norms established by the Metropolitan Life Insurance Company and adapted by the Fogerty Centre Conference on Obesity (Bray, 1979b). However, it is now recommended that investigators use the body mass index (BMI) as a method for measuring obesity. This index relates weight to height and is computed by the formula:

$$\frac{\text{Weight (kg)}}{\text{Height}^2 \text{ (m)}}$$

Using this index the severity of obesity can be graded into the following categories: mild (BMI 25–30), moderate (30–40), severe (40+). Since the physiological and psychosocial circumstances differ markedly according to the severity of obesity, this grading system has implications for the investigation and treatment of obesity.

Although the definition (and grading) of obesity poses problems for investigators, the most important methodological issue concerns the difference between the development and the maintenance of obesity—or the distinction between getting fat and being fat. Experimental obesity in animals has demonstrated that the attainment of obesity can be divided into the dynamic and static phases: the first of these characterized by notable shifts in energy balance and the rapid deposition of body fat and the second by the maintenance of a stable level of adipose tissue (Sclafani, 1981). Human obesity can be similarly classified and it is clear that there will be marked physiological and behavioural differences between the accumulation of fat tissue (through hypertrophy or hyperplasia of adipocytes) and the maintenance of a particular level of body fat. Of course, the difficulty facing investigators is how to establish criteria to distinguish between dynamic and static phases, given that many fat people will be artificially maintained at a stable level due to self-imposed dieting. It follows that many studies on obesity will be undermined by the selection of heterogeneous samples containing individuals at various stages of the development of obesity. The issue is further compli-cated by physiological and biochemical differences characteristic of the android and gynoid morphological types (Björntörp, 1983).

This problem for investigators is mirrored in treatment by the distinction between weight loss and weight maintenance. The major problem in obesity therapy, known for years (Stunkard and McLaren-Hume, 1959), is the main-taining of body weight at a lower level once weight has been initially lost (Bistrian, 1981). Most people who adopt some technique for slimming or who offer themselves for invasive treatments are able to lose substantial amounts of fat; the problem experienced in almost every individual case and clinical trial is how to prevent the replacement of the lost kilograms of weight. The problem has both physiological and psychological aspects. The picture which emerges from a brief consideration of the nature of obesity is that changes occurring internally have implications for external (public) events and vice versa. These interrelationships lend themselves to an approach which emphasizes interactions between different elements of a biopsycholog-ical system.

SYSTEMS AND INTERACTIONS—A MODEL

The field of obesity has been the subject of research for numerous scientists including geneticists, biochemists, physiologists, psychologists, nutritionists, endocrinologists and others. Despite a tremendous amount of research effort over 60 years, there is still no known mechanism for the cause of obesity nor is there any safe and effective treatment. Why have sophisticated biological techniques and procedures so far failed to provide a real understanding of the nature of obesity? One reason is surely the insularity of the separate research fields. As Bruch (1974) has pointed out,

Though it is now common to speak of the multiple factors that are involved in the development of obesity, with the exception of a few reports coming from the basic sciences, the majority of papers continue to focus on one or other aspects as the 'cause' of the condition. The more an investigator is convinced of the importance of his own theory the more he is inclined to use his particular findings as explanation for the whole picture. (p. 6)

She continues, 'The obesity literature abounds with examples of [researchers] ignoring well-documented findings of workers from different disciplines' (p. 7). Despite this general picture, in psychosomatic medicine one can recognize a shift from the linear model of causality towards a cyclic model in which illness is viewed as resulting from interrelated factors in the physiological, psychological and environmental domains. As Bruch argues from her own work, it is clear that early influences in an individual's life have profound and lasting effects not only on mental and emotional characteristics but also

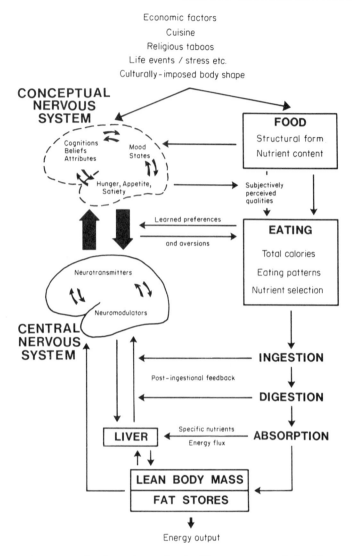

Figure 6.1   Conceptualization of certain significant aspects of the biopsychological system underlying the control of feeding behaviour

upon the anatomic, physiologic and metabolic characteristics of the adult.

The strategy we have followed is one of attempting to understand obesity as a condition arising out of, and maintained by, a complex sequence of interactions among elements forming part of a biopsychological system which controls body weight. A simplified model of the system is set out in Figure 6.1. This conceptualization draws attention to the interrelationships between particular spheres of interest including the external environment (cultural and physical), the behavioural act of eating (quantitative and qualitative dimensions), processes of ingestion and assimilation of foods, the storage and utilization of energy, brain mechanisms implicated in the control system, and mediating subjective states such as attributions and cognitions.

It is, of course, easy for a systems approach to give the impression of accommodating complex interactions at a variety of levels. The strength of such an approach lies in the capacity to demonstrate links between different levels of the system. Central to this view is the proposal that alterations in any one domain will provoke changes elsewhere. For example, links exist between the biochemistry of adipose tissue and eating behaviour, subjective states and physiological responses, intestinal function and taste perception. This section will be concerned with illustrations of these interrelationships.

Eating behaviour and metabolism

Food consumption is one of the classic stimuli which provoke an increase in energy expenditure or heat production. This utilization of calories is known as diet-induced thermogenesis and is believed to be an adaptive response of the regulatory system, although the size of the effect is widely disputed. However, this phenomenon indicates that increasing the flow of calories into the body does not simply result in more calories being stored; the system acts in a compensatory manner. Individual variation in the degree of the thermogenic response to food has been suggested as a causal factor in obesity (Rothwell and Stock, 1979) though the experimental evidence for such a hypothesis is still extremely weak (Hervey and Tobin, 1983). The converse relationship between food intake and metabolic rate also occurs and is an important factor to be considered in the treatment of obesity. Caloric restriction leads to a depression of metabolic rate, the diminution being severe when there is a marked and abrupt reduction in intake (Bray, 1969). Moreover, it appears that these changes are not restricted to subjects in whom caloric restriction leads to weight loss (Buskirk et al., 1963), for they appear to be most marked in subjects whose initial metabolic rate is low (see Garrow, 1974). This means that reducing food intake (through behavioural control of eating, dietary management or various types of fasting) does not simply deny calories to the body, but also leads to an adjustment in metabolism. This lowering of metabolic rate is generally seen as an adaptive response to food restriction: a form of biological defence in the face of scarce commodities. It is also an example of the principle that interventions in one domain (behavioural) do not simply induce changes in that domain but provoke consequences in other systems. The relationship between behaviour (eating) and metabolism (in particular, oxygen consumption) is a fundamental link in the system.

Adiposity and eating behaviour

There is a strong interest in the eating styles of obese people together with a belief that differences in eating patterns between obese and lean subjects may be responsible for increased caloric consumption. For example, it has been suggested that a pattern of infrequent eating may be a significant factor in the aetiology of human obesity (Fábry and Tepperman, 1970). Indeed, there are a number of reports of decreased meal frequency associated with human obesity (Beaudoin and Mayer, 1953; Monello, Seltzer and Mayer, 1965; Huenemann, 1972; Kulesza, 1982), with breakfast being the meal most often missed by the overweight person. Kulesza's study was a comprehensive survey of the eating habits of 150 women living in Warsaw. Of the 100 obese subjects, 70 per cent ate only two or three meals a day, whilst over 80 per cent of the lean women reported eating four meals deaily. According to Fábry, this pattern should favour the development of adiposity. Contrary to this idea is the proposal that a reduction in meal frequency arises as a *consequence* of the development of obesity. Of course, it could be argued that obese people eat fewer meals as a deliberate strategy to reduce caloric intake in response to social pressure. However, the results from animal studies suggest a more intimate link between adiposity and meal taking.

The simple procedure of offering rats a varied and tasty diet of human foods provides a powerful means of inducing a dietary form of experimental obesity (Sclafani and Springer, 1976). The development of obesity proceeds through dynamic and plateau phases and is accompanied by changes in feeding parameters such as meal size and meal frequency (Rogers and Blundell, 1980). In the early stages, animals display a strong hyperphagia characterized by an increase in meal size and meal frequency. However, as body weight rises meal size remains high but meal frequency drops to a low level (Rogers and Blundell, in press). Clearly, these rats are not being subjected to social pressure to slim and the palatable diet is still active as indicated by the persistence of large meal sizes. It appears that fatness is suppressing the frequency of meal taking in these animals. Consequently, in the biopsychological system, eating behaviour is not only influenced by external factors or by cognitive strategies; the pattern of feeding (as well as total food intake) is influenced by the level of adiposity. In turn, it may yet be revealed that fatness, depending primarily upon the hypertrophy or hyperplasia of adipocytes, may exert differing behavioural tendencies.

Sensory stimuli, behaviour and physiological response

The complex interrelationships between internal and external stimuli, behavioural actions and physiological responses can best be considered within the context of a biopsychological system. Three phenomena are particularly important. First, it is clear that the act of eating is prompted and modulated by the perception of two general classes of stimuli: food-related stimuli in the external environment and physiological stimuli (mainly visceral sensations) in the internal environment. It may be deduced that if either of these sets of stimuli exerts an unusually dominant effect on behaviour, then the eating pattern will be distorted. There is some evidence that this occurs in obesity. Some years ago it was reported that obese people were unlikely to report feelings of hunger in the presence of gastric motility (Stunkard and Koch, 1964), and from this it was argued that obese people were less responsive to internal regulatory cues (visceral stimuli) than normals. Moreover, the observed absence of the 'satiety curve'—slowing of the rate of intake towards the end of a meal—when subjects were denied visual information and required to rely solely on internal signals (Pudel and Oetting, 1977) supported this view. Indeed, there is a considerable body of evidence indicating that obese people fail to respond to internal feedback cues for satiation (Blundell, 1977a). In addition, experimental evidence from laboratory studies suggested that obese people behaved as if they were 'stimulus-bound'—that is, they responded in an exaggerated way to salient cues in the external environment (Schachter and Rodin, 1974). How should all of this evidence be interpreted? On methodological grounds, it is now clear that the neat separation in responsiveness between obese and normal weight individuals cannot be sustained. Highly responsive individuals can be detected in all weight categories; therefore, this tendency is probably related to rate of weight change or to the distance between 'natural' and 'actual' body weight, rather than to absolute body weight. However, an imbalance in the relative strength of internal and external stimuli does influence food consumption and eating patterns.

The second but related phenomenon concerns the range of internal physiological changes which are instigated by the perception of food stimuli (sight, smell and taste of food) and which serve to prepare the system for ingestion (Sjöström et al., 1980). These anticipatory reactions are referred to as cephalic phase responses (Powley, 1977). Consequently, it can be argued that the greater a person's susceptibility to external sensory stimuli, then the more intense will be the cephalic phase responses. Some human research suggests that this is true (e.g. Rodin, 1978; Wooley and Wooley, 1973). Moreover, strong evidence has also been provided by animal research. In experiments on rats, the strength of cephalic phase responses can be assessed by measuring the amplitude of the rapid release of insulin to a sweet-tasting solution placed on the tongue. When subsequently given the opportunity to eat a highly palatable diet, the high-insulin responders ate more and gained more weight than the low responders (Jeanrenaud et al., 1981). Consequently, strong cephalic phase responses confer a susceptibility to overconsumption.

The third phenomenon indicating relationships in this domain is called 'alliesthesia'—a hybrid word derived from *esthesia* (meaning sensation) and *allios* (meaning changed). In its most simple form, the phenomenon describes the decline in pleasantness of a sweet-tasting substance following the consumption of a glucose meal (Cabanac, 1971). In more natural circumstances it represents that diminution in the attractiveness of food after a meal has been eaten. A change in hedonic appreciation of this type reflects the operation of the process of satiation and serves the biological purpose of limiting consumption (Blundell, 1975). One significant study indicated that obese individuals failed to display strong alliesthesia (Cabanac and Duclaux, 1970), and it was therefore argued that obese people lack an important mechanism serving to curtail eating. These data form part of the evidence which suggests a weak satiation process in obesity. The principle illustrates how the metabolic state of the body (depleted or well nourished) can modify the perception (perceived pleasantness) of food-related stimuli. As in other areas of research, it is now clear that the presence or absence of a strong alliesthesia reaction is not related to absolute body weight, but to some parameter associated with body weight change. Moreover, processes of conditioning are known to play a role in this perceptual phenomenon (see, for example, Stunkard, 1975b; Booth, 1977). The decline in perceived pleasantness of a particular food may occur within minutes of its consumption (Rolls, Rowe and Rolls, 1980), well in advance of any metabolic change following digestion and absorption of the product.

The phenomena set out above indicate the complexity of the relationships between sensory stimuli, metabolism and physiological and behavioural responses. These events form a set of cycles within the biopsychological system controlling food consumption. Are these events important in the development or maintenance of obesity? It is clear that the disposition to eat may be enhanced in three ways—the intensification of cephalic phase responses, the imbalance in influence between external and internal sensory stimuli, and a weak feedback of metabolic information (conditioned or unconditioned) to modulate perception. If these occurred simultaneously, then there would be a marked lack of control over eating and a pronounced susceptibility to overconsume. A deficiency in these processes would render individuals particularly vulnerable in the face of plentiful and highly attractive food items.

Eating, taste preference and intestinal function

A simplified view of intestinal function is that these organs provide the means of transferring digested food into the body's circulatory system. This view of a passive role for the intestines has had to be markedly revised following the advent of a radical surgical treatment for massive obesity. The jejunoileal bypass operation was based on the rationale that obesity could be treated by allowing patients to eat freely but weight would be lost if the absorptive capacity could be reduced by removing or isolating a portion of the small intestine. The loss of malabsorbed calories pouring out of the body in faeces would create a negative energy balance. After undergoing the operation patients do indeed lose significant amounts of body weight, but it quickly became apparent that the loss of weight was due mainly to a reduction in food consumption rather than to an increased loss of non-absorbed material. Bray (1980) has reported that for a group of 45 patients, caloric intake declined from 6300 kcal per day preoperatively to a low of 1200 kcal postoperatively. The loss of calories in the stool rises from 131 kcal preoperatively to 593 kcal postoperatively. Consequently, the measured reductions in food intake can account for 60–75 per cent of the weight loss observed in patients who have had intestinal by-pass.

This finding was counterintuitive and could not have been predicted as a consequence of the operation. Indeed, any prediction based on the regulation of weight would have been that food intake would increase after the by-pass as a compensatory response for the loss of calories. It therefore seems that there is some link between the control of food intake and the absorption of certain digested products across the intestine. Moreover, alterations occur not only in total caloric content but in eating patterns (Mills and Stunkard, 1976; Bray et al., 1978) and in taste preference (there is a marked reduction in the preference for sucrose solutions—Bray et al., 1976), suggesting that the reduced intake is not simply a strategy to avoid the period of severe diarrhoea which follows the by-pass operation. Both the quantitative and qualitative changes extend beyond the period of rectal irritation.

In addition, similar changes have been observed in animals subjected to the bypass operation. Rats made obese by knife cuts in the ventromedial hypothalamus showed a marked weight loss after jejunoileal bypass surgery and reduced intake of a sucrose solution (Sclafani et al., 1978). A similar effect has been demonstrated in the Zucker (fa/fa) obese rat together with a permanent change in meal patterns (Kissileff, Nakashima and Stunkard, 1979). Accordingly, in obese animals as well as in humans, jejunoileostomy significantly reduces food consumption and this appears to be the major cause of weight loss. Interestingly, the effect also occurs following transposition of a segment of the ileum to the duodenum (Koopmans et al., 1982). This may be due to hormonal or neural signals arising from an overstimulated lower ileum. Indeed, there is evidence that the factor with anorectic activity is present in plasma after intestinal by-pass surgery (Atkinson and Brent, 1982). Taken together, these studies indicate that the intestine is not a passive recipient of digested food. An intact intestine is essential for the normal control of quantitative and qualitative aspects of eating. One possible interpretation of the repercussions in eating following disturbance of the intestine is that there exists significant feedback of information directly (via humoral or neural pathways) to the mechanisms controlling eating and food preferences.

Nutrients, brain chemistry and behaviour

One traditional concept in research on the control of food intake is that some consequence of ingested food is ultimately detected by the brain which uses this signal to modulate the behaviour of eating. The glucostatic and aminostatic hypotheses are based on this principle. Specialized receptors in the brain (e.g. glucoreceptors) are usually invoked for the operation of this putative mechanism. Clearly, feeding behaviour must be adapted in some way to the consequences of ingestion.

Recently it has been proposed that the operative mechanism is sensitive to the macronutrient content of ingested food. The proposal that the intake of each particular nutrient (such as protein or carbohydrate) is controlled separately is an alternative to the view that total food intake (energy/calories) is the regulated factor. Moreover, the nutrient control hypothesis embodies an original mechanism for the involvement of brain processes in feeding. The mechanism depends on the fact that the neurotransmitter serotonin is synthesized from the amino acid precursor tryptophan. The concentration of serotonin in the brain is dependent upon the amount of tryptophan in the brain, which is in turn dependent upon the ratio of tryptophan to other large neutral amino acids in the plasma (Fernstrom and Wurtman, 1974). The nutrient content of the diet exerts a major influence over this plasma ratio and paradoxically a high carbohydrate meal can lead to increases in brain tryptophan and serotonin (Fernstrom and Wurtman, 1972). Tryptophan cannot be synthesized at all by mammalian cells and is truly an essential amino acid. Although it is ingested in proteins, a high carbohydrate intake, which causes the rapid release of insulin, increases the ratio of tryptophan to large neutral amino acids in the plasma. This occurs because insulin strips non-esterified fatty acid molecules from circulating albumen to which they are bound, thereby allowing tryptophan molecules to become bound. The ratio of total tryptophan in plasma (free plus bound) to large neutral amino acids therefore increases and the uptake of tryptophan into the brain is favoured. It has been proposed that serotonin-containing brain neurons may function as 'ratio-sensors'—the rate of neurotransmitter synthesis in these neurons varying with the nutrient composition of the diet. Also, that the serotonin neurons could discriminate between the metabolic effects of various diets (Fernstrom and Wurtman, 1973). The extension of this argument is that brain serotonin activity will influence the choice of nutrients and it has been proposed that serotonin neurons participate in feeding not by regulating total caloric intake but by adjusting protein intake (Anderson, 1979) or by controlling the balance of protein and carbohydrate in the diet (Wurtman, Heftl and Melamed, 1981).

This hypothesis can be tested in animal and human studies by experimentally manipulating the activity of serotonin with drugs or precursors (see Blundell, 1977b; 1979a; 1983 for reviews). In man, the drug fenfluramine, which causes a release of, and blocks the re-uptake of, serotonin, creates a tendency to suppress preference for carbohydrates in normal subjects (Blundell and Rogers, 1980a) and results in a reduction of carbohydrate snacking in obese subjects (Wurtman and Wurtman, 1981). The proposed mechanism therefore has functional properties.

One important aspect of this link between nutrient intake and brain neur-otransmitters is the demonstration that ingested food cannot simply be regarded as fuel for the maintenance and repair of body tissues. The nutrient content of the diet provokes adjustments in neurochemistry which serve as a feedback device for the control of nutrient intake and which also influence a wide variety of activities in addition to eating. Obese people who attempt to slim by restricting intake of fats and carbohydrates may therefore create quite unexpected subjective experiences and behavioural dispositions. More-over, the overall restriction of calorie intake during dieting not only deprives the body of fuel, but is also likely to produce certain psychological changes mediated by the adjustments in brain neurochemistry. Consequently, the manipulation of the behavioural portion of the system (nutritional input) has far-reaching implications.

Cognitions, physiology and behaviour

It is often proposed that a homeostatic system for regulating body weight need only incorporate some specified relationships between body weight itself, certain physiological signals reflecting the state of the system and a behavioural output (see, for example, Brobeck, 1981). Such systems may vary in complexity, but the basic principle is that any departure of the body weight from a specified set value will, via negative feedback, drive the system in a self-correcting manner. Such models may offer an account of the behaviour of animals, but they cannot describe human behaviour in which any regulation involves the participation of cognitions (see, for example, Booth, 1980). It is obvious that deliberate and voluntary actions by humans constitute interventions in their own 'natural' regulatory processes. These actions are driven by certain cognitions which have been described and measured. Consequently, in addition to purely mechanical regulatory systems, it is necessary to consider self-regulation brought about by cognitive dispositions.

Some years ago it was recognized that attempts to detect differences between groups of obese and of normal weight individuals contained a metho-dological flaw. Nisbett (1972) argued that owing to cultural pressure of adverse opinion, most fat people would be attempting to reduce weight and therefore could be considered to be below their 'natural' weight or 'set-point'. It followed from this that many normal weight individuals who were rigorously restricting their intake, could be regarded as latent obese. Conse-quently, the important factor distinguishing between individuals was not their absolute body weight, but the distance from their natural set-point. This proposal was extended by Herman (see Herman and Polivy, 1980, for review), who described the nature of the cognitive element which kept people below their hypothesized set-point. The cognitive factor was termed 'restraint' and a scale was produced to provide a workable measure (Herman and Mack, 1975; Stunkard and Messick, 1985). Individuals who scored high on the restraint scale were preoccupied with their own weight and strictly controlled their food intake: they were dieters. Moreover, highly restrained individuals were observed at all weight levels and the presence of restrained eaters of normal weight provides an operational measure of latent obesity.

Significantly, it is the severity of restraint rather than body weight *per se* which predicts food consumption in a variety of circumstances. For example, in experimental circumstances in which subjects are somewhat coerced into eating, highly restrained individuals will go on to consume much more than low restrainers. It is argued that this occurs through a process of disinhibition or inhibition of inhibition. Once the restraint or dietary restriction has been broken, then the underlying drive to eat is released and this results in so-called 'counterregulatory' eating. Interestingly, when subjects are coerced into eating a preload, it is the perceived rather than the actual caloric value which determines the extent of subsequent counterregulatory eating (Polivy, 1976; Spencer and Fremouw, 1979). Other factors which lead to a breakdown of restraint and counterregulatory eating are consumption of alcohol (Polivy and Herman, 1976), and the presence of another subject (actually a confederate of the experimenter) who overeats (Polivy *et al.*, 1979). Of particular significance for psychosomatic theory is the demonstrated effect of anxiety. In contrast to the traditional psychosomatic view that anxiety provokes eating through the role of food as a tranquillizing reinforcer, it has been demonstrated that mild experimentally induced anxiety leads to overeating only in restrained individuals (Herman and Polivy, 1975). Accordingly, it must be considered that anxiety provokes food intake by interfering with restraint thereby leading to counterregulatory eating.

The significance of restraint in the lifestyle of people who manifest this phenomenon, is the induction of a cyclic pattern of fasting (imposition of restraint) and binge-eating (breakdown of restraint and counterregulatory eating). This oscillating style of eating behaviour has been frequently described (e.g. Mitchell and Pyle, 1982; Palmer, 1979). Moreover, Hibscher and Herman (1977) have demonstrated that elevated plasma free fatty acid levels are typical of restrained subjects, regardless of the degree of underweight or overweight. Consequently, there is an intimate relationship between measured cognitions (restraint), behaviour (counterregulatory eating pattern) and physiology. The biopsychological perspective indicates how any proposed homeostatic machinery is subjected to manipulations from the non-somatic (psychological) domain under impositions from the cultural scene.

THE ANALYSIS OF HUNGER—A MULTIDIMENSIONAL CONSTRUCT

The notion of hunger is widely regarded as playing a central role in the control of eating and thereby constituting an important factor in weight regulation. For example, Bruch (1974) has argued that in the child, feelings arising from various somatic sensations may become labelled as hunger if they are followed by the presentation and consumption of food. In time this leads to a number of physical sensations, unrelated to physiological need, generating hunger and thereby stimulating the tendency to eat. Underlying the use of this term is the recognition that 'normal' hunger is dependent upon a state of need or energy depletion. In most dictionaries, 'hunger' is generally described as an uneasy or painful sensation caused by the want of food, a compelling need or craving, or a state of weakness caused by the want of food. More technically, Silverstone (1976) has suggested that the term 'hunger' should be reserved for somatic sensations experienced as a result of significant food deprivation, whilst Sclafani (1976) considers hunger to be stimulated when body weight falls below a particular set-point. Consequently, both real hunger and pseudo-hunger are regarded as depending upon the arousal of internal physical sensations registering a state of physiological disturbance.

In turn this notion of hunger as a unitary physiological dimension forms the base for the subjective experience of hunger, which in clinical and experimental situations is usually assessed by ratings made on a visual analogue scale. Consequently, in the common use of the term 'hunger' there is a chain of suppositions relating the ratings of hunger as quantitative expressions of subjective experience to the strength of physical sensations which depend upon a physiological state of need. Are these assumptions consistent with the meanings which underly a person's subjective experience of hunger? When someone declares a feeling of hunger he may be referring to local sensations in the body, the passage of time since the last meal or the presence of salient cues associated with eating; or he may be making an attribution to justify the imminent act of eating (Blundell, 1979b). Consequently, the way in which the term 'hunger' is used by experimental subjects or patients may be quite unrelated to the generally accepted view of hunger as the subjective reflection of a unitary physiological need. One indication that hunger is not a simple response to need, is the observation that strength of hunger is not necessarily related to the amount of food eaten. The correlation between hunger ratings and food consumption is often low (Siverstone and Stunkard, 1968; Blundell and Rogers, 1980a), and in certain cases these two measures can be completely dissociated (Trenchard and Silverstone, 1983).

If hunger is a more complicated and elusive entity than is generally conceived, how can the conceptualization of hunger be modified to provide a more realistic understanding for experimental work and clinical practice? Initially, hunger may be regarded as a state which is related to a number of elements in the biopsychological system. Hunger may be instigated and modulated by information coming from a number of sources both within and outside of the body. Figure 6.2 illustrates one way of describing the compound structure of hunger. It has been demonstrated in several cases (Monello and Mayer, 1967; Garfinkel, 1974; Blundell and Rogers, 1980a) that feelings of hunger are associated with a particular constellation of

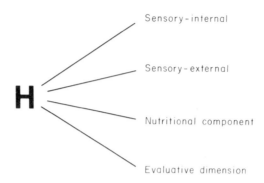

Figure 6.2   The different inputs contributing to the experience of hunger

physical sensations in the body. This profile of sensations is replaced by a different one after eating has taken place (Monello and Mayer, 1967; Mather, 1977). It seems reasonable to suggest that the perception of these physical sensations (and their change over time) constitutes one source of information contributing to the experience of hunger. However, hunger is modulated not only by the calorific value of food but also by its palatability (Hill, Magson and Blundell, 1984). Good-tasting food, which is highly preferred, augments the experience of hunger once eating begins. In addition, hunger also appears to be related to the macronutrient composition of foods (Blundell and Hill, 1983). When subjects reported feelings of hunger these were associated with a relative preference for protein rather than carbohydrate food items. This finding indicates that the feeling of hunger embodies not only a quantitative dimension of the willingness to eat food in general, but also a directional (qualitative) component to eat certain foods (high protein) rather than others.

Other researchers have shown how beliefs or attributions about foods can influence hunger. For example, when subjects consumed high- or low-calorie milkshakes the consistency of which was manipulated to give an apparent calorific value (high or low) contrary to their actual energy value, then hunger ratings were influenced by the apparent rather than the real values (Wooley, Wooley and Dunham, 1972). Moreover, the strength of a belief or commitment to a particular policy has been reported to adjust feelings of hunger arising from food deprivation (Brehm, Back and Bogdonoff, 1964). Consequently, hunger is dependent upon cognitions about food as well as its actual physical (sensory or nutritional) properties.

Taken together, these findings indicate that hunger is not merely a reflection of an internal need. Far from being a unitary dimension, hunger appears to have a compound structure in which the expressed level of hunger results from the presence of physical sensations reflecting an energy deficit, the nutrient and sensory qualities of food together with cognitions concerning the energy value of food. Consideration of this compound structure suggests why reported hunger and the amount of food consumed may only be weakly related. However, this revision does not mean that the importance of hunger in the control of feeding is diminished. Hunger can be seen to be related to various portions of the biopsychological system and the role of hunger therefore remains central. This interactive approach suggests that a more considered interpretation of subjective reports of hunger will lead to a more realistic understanding of its role in the control of food intake and weight regulation.

IMPLICATIONS FOR TREATMENT

From the foregoing passages it is clear that obesity is not a disorder that conforms to the traditional medical model of illness, involving a causal link between some source of a putative disease and a cluster of symptoms. However, it is clear that this concept has guided the development of treatments which have sought to correct specific failings in those parts of the body critical for the control of food intake, absorption of nutrients or the expenditure of energy. Equally, obesity is not a condition that can be explained purely in psychological terms. Probably more than any other disorder, obesity can be regarded as a condition that stands at the interface of the internal physiological domain and the external environmental domain. Eating is a form of behaviour which bridges these domains in a unique way. Indeed, with the exception of breathing there is no more intimate way in which organisms come into contact with their environments. For this reason, eating has been regarded as a transaction (Blundell, 1982a; Blundell and Rogers, 1980b). Even if overeating is not the cause of obesity, food consumption certainly contributes to the maintenance of the condition and affects the patterning of symptoms. The simultaneous, powerful influences of internal and external environments means that obesity, therefore, cannot be treated as a simple illness.

Equally important, the term 'treating obesity' suggests that there is a definable condition (fatness, weight, body mass index) which can be dealt with directly. Obviously, this parameter must ultimately be adjusted, but initially the interactions outlined above indicate that treatment should be directed not to a condition (objectively defined symptom), but to a whole person within a biopsychological system. Evidence set out in this chapter illustrates the strength of interrelationships between cognitions, behaviour, physical sensations, physiological responses and metabolic events. Interventions aimed at particular components of this system provoke readjustments elsewhere—often in a way which may be counterproductive to the progress of treatment. Therefore, one implication of the biopsychological approach is that rational treatment should take cognizance of the interactions of the system.

Some form of dieting, involving a diminution in total caloric intake or a reduction in the proportion of fats and carbohydrates in the food, is one of the most common forms of treatment—either self-imposed or supervised. Such a procedure is the most obvious and seemingly innocuous form of therapy. Indeed, it would be highly effective if dieting took place whilst all the other parts of the system remained stable. However, evidence indicates that the withholding of food consumption incorporates a number of changes including a lowering of the metabolic rate, the cultivation of a form of psychological inhibition (restraint), the possible induction of periodic hypoglycaemia, and the avoidance of certain nutrients leading to particular neurochemical profiles and the development of 'cravings'. Consequently, dieting (a form of behaviour), considered to be the most mild of treatments, can lead to serious and enduring consequences owing to various components of the biopsychological system. These readjustments probably explain why dieting alone is not an effective form of management, why dieters are prone to relapse and why such a treatment can only bring about permanent weight loss at tremendous personal cost to the individual.

Obesity is not an acute condition, nor is the pathology one in which the person remains passive. Most people who seek treatment for obesity have been fat for some time and they have probably made repeated attempts to treat their own condition. Indeed, many patients have a history of periods of weight loss followed by regain. Unlike a broken leg or a viral infection, some form of self-therapy is possible, but usually ineffective. However, the cultural pressure which obliges fat people to attempt to remedy their condition means that the dynamics of the system will have been altered by the time serious treatment is undertaken. Repeated bouts of dieting may have had a depressive effect on basal metabolic rate, avoidance of particular nutrients may have provoked aberrant neurochemical profiles and periodic failure may have created negative expectations. In addition, during the period for which the person has been obese certain roles and patterns of behaviour, consistent with the lifestyle of a fat person, may have become habitual. Consequently, prior to treatment, a range of adjustments—metabolic, neurochemical, mental and behavioural—can have produced an unusual picture, with an enhanced resistance to weight loss. Knowledge of the biopsychological system and its temporal history can provide a realistic basis for the initiation of a treatment programme.

Two other points can be made. First, although there is no overwhelming evidence that an eating disorder is responsible for the inducement of obesity, having the condition and attempting to treat it may provoke such a disorder. It is clear that self-imposed eating regimes and the adoption of eccentric diets (see Dwyer, 1980) can lead to highly idiosyncratic styles of food consumption and aberrant eating patterns. More significantly, there is evidence that the cycles of bingeing and fasting or bingeing and vomiting can arise as strategies to control body weight (Cooper and Fairburn, 1983). Therefore, obesity itself, or the fear of becoming obese, can lead to other disorders with behavioural pathology and physiological consequences.

A second issue concerns the widespread use of psychotropic medication. Every year, hundreds of thousands of people are prescribed tranquillizers or antidepressant drugs for mild psychological disturbances. There is now evidence that three of the major classes of psychotropic drugs—benzodiazepines, phenothiazines and tri-cyclic antidepressants—give rise to increases in appetite or alter food preferences (Blundell, 1981). Indeed, the benzodiazepines have been referred to as hunger-mimetic agents (Cooper, 1980), and in animal studies the administration of diazepam represents a most powerful stimulus for the instigation of eating. The mechanism of action of these agents on eating is presumably through the complex interplay of neurotransmitter systems in the basal forebrain (Blundell, 1982b; Hoebel and Leibowitz, 1981). Consequently, a subclass of obese people may be made up of people with pharmacologically induced eating disorders, and it follows that the administration of any such compounds will obviously work against any treatment regime.

Following these comments, it may be asked: How should obesity be treated? Given the dynamics of the biopsychological system, any treatment should be multimodal. For example, knowing that dietary restriction will provoke metabolic slowing, any adjustment of energy intake should be accompanied by a strategy (such as programmed physical activity) designed to augment metabolic rate and to counter any suppression. One piece of documented evidence indicates that this is possible (Schultz et al., 1980). This formula has already been adopted in behavioural approaches to treatment (see, for example, Stuart, 1971; Blundell, 1984). As noted previously, the intensity of the psychological restraint involved in voluntary forms of dietary control leaves the individual susceptible to agencies provoking counterregulation. Consequently, any behavioural or physiological intervention should be accompanied by cognitive interventions designed to provide coping strategies for particular circumstances of vulnerability.

In general, the major implication from the biopsychological approach is that treatment should be holistic. It is extremely unlikely that a 'magic bullet' principle will be unearthed to solve the problem of obesity. The millions of people who at present suffer the moralizing recommendations of society can only find relief through the application of nutritional, behavioural, physiological and psychological adjustments. In other words, the system must be treated rather than the primary symptom of body weight. Obesity is maintained not by some internal biochemical error (although aberrant processes in lipogenesis and thermogenesis may exist), but by the prevailing cultural attitudes and expectations. These attitudes encourage the acquisition and consumption of high-calorie, highly palatable foods (through advertising) and then condemn the consequences of this promoted extravagance. Recognizing this cultural duplicity, one may ask: Should obesity be treated? Perhaps the only permanent and secure solution resides in the adjustment of those cultural forces which form part of the biopsychological system. Whatever treatment is adopted, people will always have to eat, and eating is an activity which links the biological domain of energy transactions with the psychological domain of knowledge. Accordingly, treatment can become an arena in which people can enhance awareness of the way bodies and minds interact. This will allow a better understanding of the forces—biological and psychological—which control our lives.

REFERENCES

Abramson, E. E., and Wunderlich, R. A. (1972). Anxiety, fear and eating: a test of the psychosomatic concept of obesity. *Journal of Abnormal Psychology*, **79**, 317–321.

Adadevoh, B. K. (1974). Obesity in the African. In W. Burland, P. Samuel and J. Yudkin (eds), *Obesity*. London: Churchill Livingstone.

Anderson, G. H. (1979). Control of protein and energy intake: role of plasma amino acids and brain neurotransmitters. *Canadian Journal of Physiology*, **57**, 1043–1057.

Atkinson, R. L., and Brent, E. (1982). Appetite suppressant activity in plasma of rats after intestinal bypass surgery. *American Journal of Physiology*, **243**, R60–R64.

Beaudoin, R., and Mayer, J. (1953). Food intakes of obese and non-obese women. *Journal of the American Dietetic Association*, **29**, 29–33.

Bistrian, B. R. (1981). The medical treatment of obesity. *Archives of Internal Medicine*. **141**, 429–430.

Björntörp, P. (1983). Adipose tissue in obesity. *Proceedings of the 4th International Congress on Obesity*, New York.

Blundell, J. E. (1975). *Physiological Psychology*. London: Methuen.

Blundell, J. E. (1977a). Hunger and satiety in the control of food intake: implications for the treatment of obesity. *Clinical Dietology*, **23**, 257–272.

Blundell, J. E. (1977b). Is there a role for serotonin (5–hydroxytryptamine) in feeding? *International Journal of Obesity*, **1**, 15–42.

Blundell, J. E. (1979a). Serotonin and feeding. In W. B. Essman (ed.), *Serotonin in Health and Disease*, vol. 5, *Clinical Applications*. New York: Spectrum, pp. 403–450.

Blundell, J. E. (1979b). Hunger, appetite and satiety—constructs in search of identities. In M. Turner (ed.), *Nutrition and Lifestyles*. London: Applied Science Publishers, pp. 21–42.

Blundell, J. E. (1980). Pharmacological adjustments of the mechanisms underlying feeding and obesity. In A. J. Stunkard (ed.), *Obesity*. Philadelphia: Saunders, pp. 182–207.

Blundell, J. E. (1981). Biogrammar of feeding: pharmacological manipulations and their interpretations. In S. J. Cooper (ed.), *Progress in Theory in Psychopharmacology*. London: Academic Press, pp. 233–276.

Blundell, J. E. (1982a). Factors regulating food intake: from causes to interactions. *Alimentazione, Nutrizione, Metabolismo*, **3**, 7–19.

Blundell, J. E. (1982b). Neuroregulators and feeding: implications for the pharmacological manipulation of hunger and appetite. *Reviews in Pure and Applied Pharmacological Sciences*, **3**, 381–462.

Blundell, J. E. (1983). Processes and problems underlying the control of food selection and nutrient intake. In R. J. Wurtman and J. J. Wurtman (eds), *Nutrition and the Brain*, vol. 6. New York: Raven Press, pp. 163–221.

Blundell, J. E. (1984). Behaviour modification and exercise in the treatment of obesity. *Postgraduate Medical Journal*, **60**, (Suppl. 3), 36–48.

Blundell, J. E., and Hill, A. J. (1983). Analysis of hunger: inter-relationships with palatability, nutrient composition and eating. Paper presented at a conference entitled 'Obesity and Behaviour', a satellite symposium of the 4th International Congress on Obesity, Philadelphia.

Blundell, J. E., and Rogers, P. J. (1978). Pharmacologic approaches to the understanding of obesity. *Psychiatric Clinics of North America*, **1**, 629–650.

Blundell, J. E., and Rogers, P. J. (1980a). Effects of anorectic drugs on food intake, food selection and preferences and hunger motivation and subjective experiences. *Appetite*, **1**, 151–165.

Blundell, J. E., and Rogers, P. J. (1980b). Fame e appetito—una prospettiva biopsicologica. In M. Cairella and A. Jacobelli (eds), *Obesita*. Roma: Societa Editrice Universo, pp. 99–119.

Booth, D. A. (1977). Satiety and appetite are conditioned reactions. *Psychosomatic Medicine*, **39**, 76–81.

Booth, D. A. (1980). Acquired behaviour controlling energy intake and output. In A. J. Stunkard (ed.), *Obesity*. Philadelphia: Saunders, pp. 101–143.

Boskind-Lodahl, M. (1976). Cinderella's stepsisters: a feminist perspective on anorexia nervosa and bulimia. *Signs: Journal of Women in Culture and Society*, **2**, 342–356.

Bray, G. A. (1969). Effect of caloric restriction on energy expenditure in obese patients. *Lancet*, **ii**, 397–398.

Bray, G. A. (1979a). *Obesity in America*. NIH Publication No. 79–359.

Bray, G. A. (1979b). Obesity in America. An overview of the Second Fogarty International Center Conference on Obesity. *International Journal of Obesity*, **3**, 363–375.

Bray, G. A. (1980). Jejunoileal bypass, jaw wiring and vagotomy for massive obesity. In A. J. Stunkard (ed.), *Obesity*. Philadelphia: Saunders, pp. 369–387.

Bray, G. A., Barry, R. E., Benfield, J., Castelnuovo-Tedesco, P., and Rodin, J. (1976). Food intake and taste preferences for glucose and sucrose after intestinal bypass surgery. In D. Novin, W. Wyrwicka and G. A. Bray (eds), *Hunger: Basic Mechanisms and Clinical Implications*. New York: Raven Press, pp. 431–439.

Bray, G. A., Zachary, B., Dahans, W. T., Atkinson, R. L., and Oddie, T. H. (1978). Eating patterns of massively obese individuals. *Journal of the American Dietetic Association*, **72**, 24–27.

Brehm, M. L., Back, K. W., and Bogdonoff, M. D. (1964). A physiological effect of cognitive dissonance under stress and deprivation. *Journal of Abnormal and Social Psychology*, **69**, 303–310.

Brobeck, J. R. (1981). Models for analysing energy balance in body weight regulation. In L. A. Cioffi, W. P. T. James and T. B. Van Itallie (eds), *The Body Weight Regulatory System: Normal and Disturbed Mechanisms*. New York: Raven Press, pp. 1–9.

Bruch, H. (1974). *Eating Disorders: Obesity, Anorexia Nervosa and the Person Within*. London: Routledge & Kegan Paul.

Buskirk, E. R., Thompson, R. H., Lutwak, L., and Whedon, G. D. (1963). Energy balance of obese patients during weight reduction: influence of diet restriction and exercise. *Annals of the New York Academy of Science*, **110**, 918–940.

Cabanac, M. (1971). Physiological role of pleasure. *Science*, **173**, 1103–1107.

Cabanac, M., and Duclaux, R. (1970). Obesity: absence of satiety aversion to sucrose. *Science*, **168**, 497–499.

Cooper, P. J., and Fairburn, C. G. (1983). Binge-eating and self-induced vomiting in the community: a preliminary study. *British Journal of Psychiatry*, **142**, 139–144.

Cooper, S. J. (1980). Benzodiazepines as appetite-enhancing compounds. *Appetite*, **1**, 7–19.

Dwyer, J. (1980). Sixteen popular diets: brief nutritional analyses. In A. J. Stunkard (ed.), *Obesity*. Philadelphia: Saunders, pp. 276–291.

Fábry, P., and Tepperman, J. (1970). Meal frequency—a possible factor in human pathology. *American Journal of Clinical Nutrition*, **23**, 1059–1069.

Fernstrom, J. D., and Wurtman, R. J. (1972). Brain serotonin content: physiological regulation by plasma neutral amino acids. *Science*, **178**, 414–416.

Fernstrom, J. D., and Wurtman, R. J. (1973). Control of brain 5-HT content by dietary carbohydrates. In J. Barchas and E. Usdin (eds), *Serotonin and Behaviour*. New York: Academic Press, pp. 121–128.

Fernstrom, J. D., and Wurtman, R. J. (1974). Nutrition and the brain. *Scientific American*, **230**, 84–91.

Garfinkel, P. E. (1974). Perception of hunger and satiety in anorexia nervosa. *Psychological Medicine*, **4**, 309–315.

Garrow, J. (1974). *Energy Balance and Obesity in Man*. New York: Elsevier.

Garrow, J. (1982). Does plumpness matter? *Nutrition Bulletin*, **7**, 49–53.

Gwinup, G. (1975). Effects of exercise alone on the weight of obese women. *Archives of Internal Medicine*, **135**, 676–680.

Herman, C. P., and Mack, D. (1975). Restrained and unrestrained eating. *Journal of Personality*, **43**, 647–660.

Herman, C. P., and Polivy, J. (1975). Anxiety, restraint and eating behaviour. *Journal of Abnormal Psychology*, **84**, 666–672.

Herman, C. P., and Polivy, J. (1980). Restrained eating. In A. J. Stunkard (ed.), *Obesity*. Philadelphia: Saunders, pp. 208–225.

Hervey, G. R., and Tobin, G. (1983). Luxuskonsumption, diet-induced thermogenesis and brown fat: a critical review. *Clinical Science*, **64**, 7–18.

Hibscher, J. A., and Herman, C. P. (1977). Obesity, dieting, and the expression of 'obese' characteristics. *Journal of Comparative and Physiological Psychology*, **91**, 374–380.

Hill, A. J., Magson, L. D., and Blundell, J. E. (1984). Hunger and palatability: tracking ratings of subjective experience before, during and after the consumption of preferred and less preferred food. *Appetite*, **5**, 361–371.

Hoebel, B. G., and Leibowitz, S. F. (1981). Brain monoamines in the modulation of self-stimulation, feeding and body weight. In H. A. Weiner, M. A. Hofer and A. J. Stunkard (eds), *Brain, Behaviour and Bodily Disease*. New York: Raven Press, pp. 103–142.

Huenemann, R. L. (1972). Food habits of obese and non-obese adolescents. *Postgraduate Medicine*, **51**, 99–105.

Jeanrenaud, B., Assimacopoulos-Jeannet, P., Crettaz, M., Berthoud, H. R., Bereiter, D. A., and Rohner-Jeanrenaud, F. (1981). Experimental obesities: a progressive pathology with reference to the potential importance of the CNS in hyperinsulinaemia. In P. Björntörp, M. Cairella and A. N. Howard (eds), *Recent Advances in Obesity Research*. London: Libby, pp. 159–171.

Kaplan, H. I., and Kaplan, H. S. (1957). The psychosomatic concept of obesity. *Journal of Nervous and Mental Disease*, **125**, 181–201.

Kissileff, H. R., Nakashima, R. K., and Stunkard, A. J. (1979). Effects of jejunoileal bypass on meal patterns in genetically obese and lean rats. *American Journal of Physiology*, **237**, R217–R224.

Koopmans, H. S., Sclafani, A., Fitchner, P., and Aravich, P. F. (1982). Ileal transection reduces food intake and causes substantial weight loss in hypothalamic obese rats. *American Journal of Clinical Nutrition*, **35**, 284–293.

Kulesza, W. (1982). Dietary intake in obese women. *Appetite*, **3**, 61–68.

Mather, P. (1977). Covert nutrient supplementation and normal feeding in man and rat: experimentation and simulation. Unpublished MSc thesis, University of Birmingham, UK.

Mills, M. J., and Stunkard, A. J. (1976). Behavioural changes following surgery for obesity. *American Journal of Psychiatry*, **133**, 527–531.

Mitchell, J. E., and Pyle, R. L. (1982). The bulimic syndrome in normal weight individuals: a review. *International Journal of Eating Disorders*, **1**, 61–73.

Monello, L. F., and Mayer, J. (1967). Hunger and satiety sensations in men, women, boys and girls. *American Journal of Clinical Nutrition*, **20**, 253–261.

Monello, L. F., Seltzer, C. C., and Mayer, J. (1965). Hunger and satiety sensations in men, women, boys and girls: a preliminary report. *Annals of the New York Academy of Science*, **131**, 593–602.

Newburgh, L. H. (1942). Obesity. *Archives of Internal Medicine*, **70**, 1033–1047.

Nisbett, R. (1972). Taste, deprivation, and weight determinants of eating behaviour. *Psychological Review*, **79**, 433–453.

Palmer, R. L. (1979). The dietary chaos syndrome: a useful new term? *British Journal of Medical Psychology*, **52**, 187–190.

Polivy, J. (1976). Perception of calories and regulation of intake in restrained and unrestrained subjects. *Addictive Behaviours*, **1**, 237–243.

Policy, J., and Herman, C. P. (1976). Effects of alcohol on eating behaviour: influence of mood and perceived intoxication. *Journal of Abnormal Psychology*, **85**, 601–606.

Polivy, J., Herman, C. P., Younger, J. C., and Erskine, B. (1979). Effects of a model on eating behaviour: the induction of a restrained eating style. *Journal of Personality*, **47**, 100–114.

Powley, T. L. (1977). The ventromedial hypothalamic syndrome, satiety, and a cephalic phase hypothesis. *Psychological Review*, **84**, 89–126.

Pudel, V. E., and Oetting, M. (1977). Eating in the laboratory: behavioural aspects of the positive energy balance. *International Journal of Obesity*, **1**, 369–386.

Rodin, J. (1978). Has the distinction between internal and external control of eating outlived its usefulness? In G. Bray (ed.), *Recent Advances in Obesity Research*, vol. 2. London: Newman, pp. 75–85.

Rogers, P. J., and Blundell, J. E. (1980). Investigation of food selection and meal parameters during the development of dietary-induced obesity. *Appetite*, **1**, 85.

Rogers, P. J., and Blundell, J. E. (1984). Meal patterns and food selection during the development of cafeteria-induced obesity. *Neuroscience and Biobehavioural Reviews*, **8**, 441–453.

Rolls, B. J., Rowe, E. A., and Rolls, E. (1980). Appetite and obesity: influences of sensory stimuli and external cues. In M. Turner (ed.), *Nutrition and Lifestyles*. London: Applied Science Publishers, pp. 11–20.

Rothwell, N. J., and Stock, M. J. (1979). A role for brown adipose tissue in diet-induced thermogenesis. *Nature*, **281**, 31–35.

Russell, G. (1979). Bulimia nervosa: an ominous variant of anorexia nervosa. *Psychological Medicine*, **9**, 429–448.

Schachter, S., and Rodin, J. (1974). *Obese Humans and Rats*. New York: Wiley.

Schultz, C. K., Bernauer, E., Mole, P. A., Superko, H. R., and Stern, J. S. (1980). Effects of severe caloric restriction and moderate exercise on basal metabolic rate and hormonal status in adult humans. *Federation Proceedings*, **39**, 783.

Sclafani, A. (1976). Appetite and hunger in experimental obesity syndromes. In D. Novin, W. Wyrwicka and G. Bray (eds), *Hunger: Basic Mechanisms and Clinical Implications*. New York: Raven Press, pp. 281–295.

Sclafani, A. (1981). Extremes in body weight in experimental animal preparations. In L. A. Cioffi, W. P. T. James and T. B. Van Itallie (eds), *The Body Weight Regulatory System: Normal and Disturbed Mechanisms*. New York: Raven Press, pp. 153–160.

Sclafani, A., Koopmans, H. S., Vasselli, J. R., and Reichman, M. (1978). Effects of intestinal bypass surgery on appetite, food intake, and body weight in obese and lean rats. *American Journal of Physiology*, **234**, E389–E398.

Sclafani, A., and Springer, D. (1976). Dietary obesity in adult rats: similarities to hypothalamic and human obesity syndromes. *Physiology and Behaviour*, **17**, 461–466.

Siverstone, J. T. (1976). *Appetite and Food Intake*. Berlin: Abakon.

Silverstone, J. T., and Stunkard, A. J. (1968). The anorectic effect of dexamphetamine sulphate. *British Journal of Pharmacology and Chemotherapy*, **33**, 513–522.

Sjöström, L., Garellick, G., Krotkiewski, M., and Luyckx, A. (1980). Peripheral insulin in response to the sight and smell of food. *Metabolism*, **29**, 901–909.

Spencer, J. A., and Fremouw, W. J. (1979). Binge eating as a function of restraint and weight classification. *Journal of Abnormal Psychology*, **88**, 262–267.

Stern, J. S. (1984). Is obesity a disease of inactivity? In A. J. Stunkard and E. Stellar (eds), *Eating and its Disorders*. New York: Raven Press, pp. 131–140.

Stuart, R. B. (1971). A three-dimensional program for the treatment of obesity. *Behaviour Research and Therapy*, **9**, 177–186.

Stunkard, A. J. (1975a). From explanation to action in psychosomatic medicine: the case of obesity. *Psychosomatic Medicine*, **37**, 195–236.

Stunkard, A. J. (1975b). Satiety is a conditioned reflex. *Psychosomatic Medicine*, **37**, 383–387.

Stunkard, A. J. (1984). The current status of treatment for obesity in adults. In A. J. Stunkard and E. Stellar (eds), *Eating and its Disorders*. New York: Raven Press, pp. 157–173.

Stunkard, A. J., and Koch, C. (1964). The interpretation of gastric motility. *Archives of General Psychiatry*, **11**, 74–82.

Stunkard, A. J., and McClaren-Hume, M. (1959). The results of treatment for obesity: a review of the literature and a report of a series. *Archives of Internal Medicine*, **103**, 79–85.

Stunkard, A. J., and Messick, S. (1985). The three-factor eating questionnaire to measure dietary restraint, disinhibition and hunger. *Journal of Psychosomatic Research*, **29**, 71–83.

Trenchard, E., and Silverstone, J. T. (1983). Naloxone reduces the food intake of normal human volunteers. *Appetite*, **4**, 43–50.

Van Itallie, T. B. (1983). Hazards of obesity and hazards of treatment. *Proceedings of the 4th International Congress on Obesity*, New York.

Verngiaud, F., Englebert, V., and Bruggman, M. (1977). *Sahara*. Paris: Robert Laffont.

Waddington, C. H. (1977). *Tools for Thought*. St Albans: Paladin.

Wooley, O. W., Wooley, S. C., and Dunham, R. B. (1972). Can calories be perceived and do they affect hunger in obese and non obese humans? *Journal of Comparative and Physiological Psychology*, **80**, 250–258.

Wooley, S. C., and Wooley, O. W. (1973). Salivation to the sight and thought of food: a new measure of appetite. *Psychosomatic Medicine*, **35**, 136–142.

Wooley, S. C., and Wooley, O. W. (1984). Should obesity be treated at all? In A. J. Stunkard and E. Stellar (eds), *Eating and its Disorders*. New York: Raven Press, pp. 185–192.

Wurtman, J. J., and Wurtman, R. J. (1981). Suppression of carbohydrate consumption as snacks and at mealtime by DL-fenfluramine or tryptophan. In S. Garattini and R. Samanin (eds), *Anorectic Agents—Mechanisms of Action and Tolerance*. New York: Raven Press, pp. 169–182.

Wurtman, R. J., Heftl, F., and Melamed, E. (1981). Precursor control of neurotransmitter synthesis. *Pharmacology Reviews*, **32**, 315–335.

The Psychosomatic Approach: Contemporary Practice
of Whole-person Care
Edited by M. J. Christie and P. G. Mellett
© 1986 John Wiley & Sons Ltd

7

ABNORMAL EATING BEHAVIOUR

J. HUBERT LACEY

and SANDRA A. BIRTCHNELL

Academic Department of Psychiatry, St George's Hospital Medical School,
University of London, UK

INTRODUCTION

Attitudes to food are rarely simple. Although such attitudes are biological at root, the processes of evolutional and social change have led to food being associated with bizarre behaviours and emotions. Various psychological and psychopathological patterns have developed which have been given the generic title of the 'eating disorders'. This term has replaced the previous 'weight disorders' because symptoms which used to be associated with the extremes of emaciation or massive obesity are now commonly reported within a normal range of body weight. New terms—such as bulimia—have been introduced and diagnostic criteria have become confused and lack standardization. This chapter will restrict its compass to those patients who have a markedly disordered eating pattern at a low or normal weight: it will examine the aetiological and clinical features of the syndromes and compare diagnostic criteria and outline treatment approaches.

DIAGNOSTIC CRITERIA FOR ANOREXIA NERVOSA AND BULIMIA

Although both anorexia nervosa and bulimia are not difficult to diagnose, there is no consensus of clinical opinion regarding the criteria necessary for their diagnosis. For reasons which will be explained, the diagnosis of bulimia can usually only be made after the absence of anorexia nervosa has been established. Therefore it would seem appropriate to clarify the diagnostic issues involved in anorexia nervosa, before moving on to bulimia.

Most clinicians agree that the diagnosis of anorexia nervosa must be made on psychological grounds; that is to say, that there is a core psychological disturbance, such as a pursuit of thinness, and consequent secondary behaviour and physical sequelae, e.g. starvation, vomiting or amenorrhoea. The problem of diagnosis is that the psychological disturbance lacks objectivity, particularly for research purposes, whilst the secondary phenomena are just that: secondary and occurring widely in illness. The reader must therefore accept that there are layers of diagnosis and that if the diagnostic formulation is approached this way, the clinician will find few problems.

139

Crisp (1967) stated that the pathognomonic feature of anorexia nervosa is a phobia—that is, an irrational fear—of normal body weight. He explains this as 'the preoccupation of the anorectic with maintaining a low subpubertal body weight and of avoiding any weight gain'. This central feature of the disorder has been repeatedly described by other clinicans, usually using slightly different words. Thus Bruch (1973) referred to the 'relentless pursuit of thinness' whilst Selvini Palazzoli (1974) described a 'deliberate wish to slim' and Russell (1970) emphasized that the patient manifests the 'characteristic psychopathology of a morbid fear of becoming fat'. It will be appreciated that these are similar concepts, though differently expressed and reflecting the different approaches to the illness pursued by the above authors.

Attempts have been made to determine objective diagnostic criteria, particularly for use in clinical research. These criteria usually require evidence of metabolic disturbance in addition to the pathological fear of weight gain. Dally and Gomez (1979) state that the patient must lose at least 10 per cent of her previous body weight, that amenorrhoea must be of at least 3 months' duration and that the age at onset should be between 11 and 35 years. They also specifically exclude preexisting psychotic or organic illness. Similarly, Feighner (Feighner et al., 1972) devised strict criteria. These, however, can be criticized for they include that the age of onset must be prior to 25 years (although there have been many reports of patients developing the illness in their thirties and forties); that weight loss must exceed 25 per cent of original body weight (without making reference to whether the patient was premorbidly massively obese or slim); and that the patient must express anorexia (whilst it is common clinical knowledge that most anorectics are ravenously hungry).

Russell's (1970) definition of anorexia nervosa is useful and is based on the following criteria:

(1) That the patient resorts to a variety of devices aimed at achieving weight loss, such as starvation, vomiting or laxative abuse.
(2) That there is evidence of an endocrine disorder, amenorrhoea in the female and loss of sexual interest in the male.
(3) That the patient manifests the characteristic psychopathology of a morbid fear of becoming fat.

It should be noted that a specified degree of weight loss is not required and thus criteria are not arbitrarily restrictive. Further, the requirement of an endocrine dysfunction eliminates women who are taking their dieting to an excessive extreme yet remain within a 'normal' range. The *Diagnostic and Statistical Manual of Mental Disorders* (DSM III, 1980) no longer specifies age of onset but still requires that the patient should have lost a quarter of her premorbid weight. It is possible that this will change in subsequent editions.

Whilst the diagnosis of anorexia nervosa hinges, as Theander (1970) said, on the totally preoccupying pursuit of thinness, the biological changes, age of onset and weight loss cannot be ignored for otherwise the anorectic label would be applied widely and to relatively minor aberrations from the norm.

In 1979 Russell described an 'ominous variant of anorexia nervosa' which he called bulimia nervosa. The disorder he described had been reported earlier and during its relatively brief life has been given many names. The core symptom is the presence of binge-eating, yet such eating has never been defined nor is the symptom pathognomonic of the syndrome. Binge-eating (often called 'bingeing', though in its strictest sense this refers to drinking alcohol) is the consumption of a large amount of food in a brief period of time. It is different from overeating for binge-eating is more variable in frequency and in the amount consumed, and is associated with more distress. Unlike overeating, which tends to occur at established meal times, bingeing displaces meals, leading to an increasingly chaotic pattern of eating. It is closely associated with the desire to lose a small amount of weight—'dieting'. There is carbohydrate starvation leading to a compensatory carbohydrate craving at the root of binge-eating.

However, the symptom occurs widely in psychiatric disorders, being a feature of depression, personality disorder and, of course, the eating disorders themselves. As a symptom it is present in a subgroup of massively obese patients and anorexia nervosa patients. It is important for the clinician to be aware of this, for the binge-eating in bulimia nervosa is comparatively easy to disperse but when it occurs in association with a weight disorder it tends to indicate a poorer prognosis (Lacey, 1983a).

In Russell's original description (Russell, 1979), he proposed that there were three necessary diagnostic criteria.

(1) That the patients suffer from powerful and intractable urges to overeat.
(2) That they seek to avoid 'fattening' effects of food by inducing vomiting or using purgatives or both.
(3) That they have a morbid fear of becoming fat.

All these features could occur in anorexia nervosa and, as originally defined by Russell, bulimia nervosa and anorexia nervosa are not mutually exclusive categories. However, we believe that where the psychopathology of anorexia nervosa remains, it is best to regard the patient as still suffering from anorexia nervosa of a bulimic type; little in clinical reality has changed other than a few kilograms in weight! In particular, the true bulimic—whether having a previous history of anorexia nervosa or not—does not declare a phobia of normal body weight. She may demonstrate the normal female preoccupation with shape and weight (Nylander, 1971; Heunemann et al., 1966) and perhaps express it more forcibly than most. Whilst she is terrified of getting fat, she is not averse to normal body weight to the extent of being phobic of it. It is, if you like, the difference between a phobia and an extreme dislike and it is this lack of entrenchment in the repudiation of normal body weight as an issue that is the probable reason why bulimia is more responsive to treatment than Anorexia nervosa.

The American Psychiatric Association, in their *Diagnostic and Statistical Manual of Mental Disorders* (DSM III, 1980), have established diagnostic criteria for the syndrome of 'bulimia'. These are:

(1) Recurrent episodes of binge-eating.
(2) At least three of the following:
   (a) consumption of high-calorie food;
   (b) termination of such eating episodes by abdominal pain, sleep, social interaction or self-induced vomiting;
   (c) repeated attempts to lose weight by severely restricted diets, self-induced vomiting or the use of cathartics and/or diuretics;
   (d) frequent weight fluctuation.
(3) Awareness that the eating pattern is abnormal and fear of not being able to stop eating voluntarily.
(4) Depressed mood and self-deprecating thoughts following eating binges.
(5) Bulimic episodes not caused by anorexia nervosa or any known physical disorder.

Thus, according to DSM III (1980), a history of anorexia nervosa precludes a primary diagnosis of bulimia. We would take issue with this as some patients with normal body weight bulimia give a previous history of anorexia nervosa, some even a previous history of massive obesity. This led us (Lacey, 1984a) to emphasize the need to categorize bulimia into three aetiological types which appear to be important for treatment outcome. These are:

(a) Type I bulimia. In this neither the patient nor her family describe a history of previous anorexia nervosa, weight phobia or massive weight loss although weight fluctuation is common. This has been referred to as the bulimic syndrome (Lacey, 1984a).
(2) Type II bulimia. In this the previous anorexia nervosa has 'recovered' to normal body weight. The patient no longer expresses a phobia of normal body weight. (If she did, then she would remain within anorexia nervosa—see above—and in practice such a patient is usually at a low normal weight and frequently returns to classical anorexia nervosa.)
(3) Type III bulimia. These patients enter bulimia from massive obesity and, as such, have a history of being at least 60 per cent above mean matched population weight in the past and are usually in excess of 10 per cent above mean matched population weight on presentation.

The responses of these groups to treatment are discussed later.

Although Russell (1979) did not exclude Type I bulimics from his original description of bulimia nervosa, he has recently stated (Russell, 1985) that bulimia nervosa is a form of anorexia nervosa at normal body weight.

We would suggest that the term 'bulimia' be used as the general diagnostic term where binge-eating is the principal symptom. Where a phobia of normal body weight is still expressed, the diagnosis should be anorexia nervosa, bulimic variant.

Whilst 'bulimic syndrome' has been reserved for those with no previous history of anorexia nervosa and bulimia nervosa has mainly included those with such a history, we would suggest that allocation into Types I, II and III, as designated above, in preference to the plethora of alternative diagnostic terms, would greatly facilitate and clarify clinical and research thinking.

INCIDENCE AND PREVALENCE

Anorexia nervosa

The incidence of anorexia nervosa derived from psychiatric case register studies is approximately 0.8 per 100 000 population per year (Kendell et al., 1973). Allowing for the possible effects of greater awareness and reporting of this condition, there is growing evidence that the incidence is increasing (Halmi, Falk and Schwartz, 1974; Crisp, Palmer and Kalucy, 1976). Epidemiologically, anorexia nervosa is commoner in females with a ratio of 10:1 female to male cases in clinic populations. It tends to develop during adolescence and is overrepresented in the upper social classes. In a community survey of a population that would therefore be considered at risk, Crisp, Palmer and Kalucy (1976) found a prevalence of 1 in 100 for 16–18-year-old girls in a private school with a decreased prevalence of 1 in 300 in a comprehensive school. In those professions with a particular stress on slimness, an increased prevalence has also been reported; Garner and Garfinkel (1980) report a prevalence of 5 per cent in ballet dancers.

Apart from these severe cases that fully meet the diagnostic criteria, a number of reports have described the existence of mild or 'forme-fruste' anorexia nervosa, and some would view anorexia nervosa as the extreme end of a dieting spectrum, with that dieting almost universally observed in young women at the other end. In Nylander's (1971) study of female Swedish high school students many had 'felt fat' at some time and almost 10 per cent reported at least three anorexic symptoms in connection with weight loss. Fries (1977) has also reported on a group of women who, whilst not fulfilling the diagnostic criteria for anorexia nervosa, have amenorrhoea associated with weight loss, body size misperception and 'anorexic' attitudes. Garner and Garfinkel (1980) and Button and Whitehouse (1981) have also described 'sub-clinical' anorexia nervosa.

Bulimia

Bulimia occurs overwhelmingly in women. Its social spread within the population is more general than anorexia nervosa or massive obesity. Whilst anorexia nervosa predominantly occurs in Social Class I and obesity in Social Class V, the median social class of bulimia is Social Class III. The reasons for this are unclear but a possible explanation has been given by Lacey (1983a, p. 48).

The prevalence of the syndrome 'bulimia' in the general population is not known, but reports from clinics and surveys of groups at risk, as well as clinical experience, tend to lead to the conclusion that the disorder is reaching 'epidemic proportions', although the effect of media coverage of this relatively recently delineated condition must be acknowledged. As with anorexia nervosa, milder forms of dietary abuse, not meeting the criteria for bulimia nervosa, or the syndrome 'bulimia', have been described.

Binge-eating is a common response to emotional distress and has been described in the general population, especially amongst teenage girls (Lacey *et al.*, 1978). Hawkins and Clement (1980) reported that 79 per cent of female and 49 per cent of male American college students had episodes of uncontrolled excessive eating but only 4 per cent practised self-induced vomiting. In a similar population Halmi, Falk and Schwartz (1981) state that whilst 65 per cent of their sample acknowledged having had a 'binge', 13 per cent experienced all the major symptoms of the syndrome 'bulimia' and under 10 per cent self-induced vomiting. In a middle-class Canadian surburban population 5 per cent vomited to control weight (Cleghorn and Brown, 1964). Cooper and Fairburn (1983), examining attenders at a family planning clinic, found 2 per cent who fulfilled the criteria for a diagnosis of bulimia nervosa, whilst 21 per cent reported binge-eating. The same team (Fairburn and Cooper, 1984), studying the women who responded to a request for subjects following a television documentary on bulimia, stress that of those who fulfilled the criteria for bulimia nervosa, three quarters thought they needed help, but only a third have been referred for treatment, and that bulimia nervosa represents a largely undetected source of psychiatric morbidity.

AETIOLOGY—ANOREXIA NERVOSA

The aetiology of anorexia nervosa is not known but a number of premorbid factors have been delineated as associated with the disease; placing the emphasis on different areas of concern, a number of theories have been advanced. These are not necessarily mutually exclusive and can largely be accommodated in a multifactorial interactional model such as that proposed by Garner and Garfinkel (1980). Such variables as cultural influences, individual and family factors such as early life experiences, a premorbid personality and later family psychodynamics can be viewed as predisposing and rendering the individual vulnerable to the development of anorexia nervosa if relevant precipitants occur with the subsequent generation of maintenance factors.

Predisposing factors

Cultural

In Western society, thinness is promoted as a cultural idea, identified with self-control, asceticism and stereotypic feminine attractiveness. In spite of the feminine protest, it is upon their shape and weight that many women base their assessment of their attractiveness, desirability and self-worth. Dissatisfaction with weight and shape is widespread in Western women (Berscheid, Walster and Hohrnstedt, 1973). Young women commonly report wishing to be lighter (Heunemann *et al.*, 1966) and many feel fat irrespective of actual weight (Crisp, 1967). Whilst this does not account for the onset of anorexia nervosa it may well be a precondition.

Boskind-Lodahl (1976) sees anorectics as desperately striving to copy a female stereotype of thinness and passivity where personal effectiveness is defined in terms of shape and dietary restraint. In addition there is increased pressure to achieve academically and in a career, and these young women sometimes appear to be caught up in a conflict between their desire to achieve and be academically 'ideal' and their desire to be what they perceive as ideally and incompatibly feminine. Palazolli (1974) feels that these new and often contradictory roles for women may in part account for the increase in anorexia nervosa.

Individual: genetic/biochemical vulnerability

Much discussion has concerned the position of anorexia nervosa along the spectrum of psychosomatic disorders and some workers place emphasis on a biological vulnerability with the possibility that hypothalamic control abnormalities are present before the illness. Support for the concept of an underlying hypothalamic dysfunction can be derived from anorexia-like conditions caused by hypothalamic structural abnormalities, and animal studies where feeding and menstrual disorders were consequent upon lesions in the ventromedial hypothalamus. Russell (1977) notes that the endocrine disturbances which result in the amenorrhoea accompanying anorexia nervosa are not resolved when normal body weight is restored. However, it is not refuted that weight loss might secondarily and irreversibly damage some hypothalamic functions, or that restoration of normal body weight is necessarily accompanied by emotional equilibrium or even 'normal' eating habits—which might in themselves affect endocrine function. Menstrual irregularities are commonly reported by bulimics at normal body weight.

In a large study of twins (34 pairs and 1 set of triplets) 55 per cent of the female monozygotic (MZ) pairs and 7 per cent of the female dizygotic pairs were concordant for anorexia nervosa (Holland *et al.*, 1984). This may indicate a genetic predisposition to develop anorexia nervosa, but the authors also suggest an alternative hypothesis emphasizing the greater similarity and identification between MZ pairs and the greater stress they may be subjected to at adolescence. Crisp (1966) has reported on three pairs of MZ twins who were discordant for the illness, and also (Crisp, 1967), emphasizing environmental factors, two unrelated anorectics brought up at different times in the same household, by a diet-preoccupied couple. Some writers have postulated that anorexia nervosa may be an atypical affective disorder. Cantwell *et al.* (1977) found an increased incidence of affective disorder in the family and found anorectics at follow-up more likely to develop affective disorder than a relapse of the eating disorder, although problems of methodology have been raised (Hsu, 1980). Similarly Winokur, March and Mendels (1980) found 22 per cent of the relatives of anorectics to have a history of primary affective disorder, similar to that of the relatives of patients with affective disorder. Although certain biological markers of primary affective disorder such as high plasma cortisol and dexamethasone non-suppression have also been found in some anorectics, they appear to be reversible with weight gain (Halmi *et al.*, 1978; Walsh, 1982) and the complex relationship between affective disorder and anorexia nervosa remains to be further elucidated.

Premorbid nutrition

Considerable attention has been paid to the childhood feeding and nutrition patterns of patients with anorexia nervosa and the frequent occurrence of food fads, overeating and obesity has been emphasized (Kay and Leigh, 1954; King, 1963; Nemiah, 1950). Crisp (1965a) has commented that many of his series of patients were said to have been plump in childhood whilst few were faddish about food. In the more recent past many investigators have reported a phase of obesity or overeating prior to the onset of the illness (Nemiah, 1950).

Personality

Difficulties arise when discussing the personality of anorectics in that it is not always clear whether the described characteristics are after the onset of the illness or are premorbid. In addition, precise dating of the onset of the illness may be difficult and 'premorbid' may be dated as pubertal or prepubertal, in which case it is misleading to talk of established personality.

Anorectics are generally typified by somewhat above average intelligence, compliance, perfectionism and externally bound self-esteem. They have been described as having obsessional personality traits (King, 1963) and an additional group has been described with hysterical traits (Kay and Leigh, 1954). Dally and Gomez (1979) described the premorbid personality of anorectics in similar groups 'O' and 'H' together with their 'mixed' group. King also described postpubertal traits of egocentricity, sensitivity, shyness, introspection, irritability and a hostile/dependent attitude to the mother. In childhood most of Kay and Leigh's patients were said to demonstrate neurotic traits but Crisp (1965a) has commented on the absence of childhood neurotic traits in his patients. Similarly, Bruch (1973) describes the patient as a child as characteristically obedient, helpful and dependable but feels that this reflects a denial of family interpersonal difficulties and illness.

It is, of course, artificial to separate individual personality from early family influences, especially those concerning mother/child interaction. Bruch (1973) has advanced a theory that the relentless pursuit of thinness is a desperate struggle for identity against powerful and controlling parents, where the child's personal experiences and sensations have been invalidated by the superimposition of the parent's attitudes and wishes. Family interaction and rearing practices, such as proffering food as a response to any signal of distress whatever the origin, preclude the child from learning the significance of her own bodily feelings because these have been anticipated or negated with resultant associated disturbances of body image, misinterpretations of proprioceptive stimuli and a paralysing sense of personal ineffectiveness. In adolescence the tasks of individuation and the development of autonomy arouse serious psychic conflict and the control of weight becomes an overwhelmingly important metaphor by which personal worth is evaluated. Bruch's formulations are consistent with observations on the self-system of narcissistically disturbed patients as described by Kohut (1972), and with Mahler, Pine and Bergman's (1975) developmental theory of separation–individuation, and with the traits observed by King (1963). The 'robot-like' obedience in childhood has affinities with Winnicott's 'false self'. It may be that it is this personality organization that distinguishes the potential anorectic from other equally stressed and weight-conscious contemporaries. Garner et al. (1984), comparing psychological traits of patients with anorexia nervosa to those of weight-preoccupied and non weight-preoccupied controls, showed that although some weight-preoccupied women displayed psychopathology quite similar to that of patients with anorexia nervosa, others only superficially resembled them and were differentiated by the EDI subscales Ineffectiveness, Interoceptive awareness and Interpersonal distrust.

Family

Anorectics tend to come from the upper social classes (Bruch, 1978; Crisp, 1965b). Bruch has described the mothers of anorectics as being conscientious mothers but frustrated in their need to follow a career, and the fathers as prosperous but having with feelings of being only 'second best'. King (1963) describes mothers as typically dominant and restrictive and fathers as characteristically passive. Nemiah (1950) has reported families as overprotective with excessive dependancy of the patient on the parent, usually the mother. In Kay and Leigh's (1954) study maternal oversolicitude was reported in 30 per cent of the patients and in 24 per cent the mother was a strict disciplinarian, or the relationship between mother and patient was intensely hostile.

It must, of course, be borne in mind that assessment of parents and their interaction with their anorectic child at the time of presentation, may be affected by illness and not representative of the earlier situation. Crisp emphasizes that he has found no characteristic personality traits in the parents of his series of anorectics. The psychosomatic family theory of Minuchin, Rosman and Baker (1978) proposes that in overprotective, conflict-avoiding and enmeshed families it is the family interaction, viewed as a system, that produces and maintains the anorectic's symptoms, which play a role in maintaining the *status quo*.

Precipitants

Puberty

Adolescence, as described by Erikson (1981), brings the task of identity versus role confusion. This is a period of rapid body growth, fat deposition and genital maturation, with the necessity of coming to terms with both the physiological revolution within and the with adult tasks ahead. The mean menarchal age is dropping (Tanner, 1962) and for anorectics a number of factors associated with anorexia have also been shown to be associated with earlier puberty, including higher social class, high birth weight, greater height and weight in childhood (Shuttleworth, 1937). These factors are interrelated. For example, the differences in menarchal ages between social classes corre- spond to the differences in height and body size found between social classes around the time of puberty and adolescence (Tanner, 1962). In addition, Shuttleworth mentions that 'early' maturing girls had greater chest and hip breadth at all ages and that the earlier the adolescent growth spurt the more intense it was and the sooner after it did the menarche occur. Crisp (1970) has reported early menarche in anorectics and it may thus be that the challenge of puberty is greater for girls destined to be anorectic; they are already vulner- able in their personality structure and will have to deal with body changes and tasks of maturation at an earlier age than, and when physically distinguished from, their peers. A psychobiological regression model has been proposed by Crisp (1980) where the central symptom of anorexia nervosa, the phobia of normal weight, follows the growth changes of puberty. Dieting, initially in response to the dislike of being 'fat', becomes the pursuit of security in physiological childhood with freedom from the demands of adolescence, particularly those concerned with sexuality and related family turmoil.

Life events

In common with the model for many diseases, life events may be the final precipitant to the frank manifestation of the illness, although difficulty in accurately dating the onset of anorexia nervosa impedes scientific verification of this. Such events as bereavement or other loss, the pressure of examinations, move to new circumstances—e.g. leaving home to go to university—and events involving sexual conflict may trigger the development of pathological dieting in a girl already vulnerable. Of course, such events are common in this adolescent age group many members of which will also be dieting, and it is perhaps the vulnerability of the personality and family structure which mark out those destined for anorexia nervosa.

Maintenance factors

Dieting becomes overdetermined once around 20 per cent of normal body weight is lost and the effects of starvation may serve to perpetuate the condition. An altered sense of satiety and gastric emptying and disturbed temperature regulation lead to eating less. Psychologically the distorted body image and the accentuation of depression, anxiety and obsessionality may strengthen the resolve to 'keep control' by starvation. Carbohydrate craving and a preoccupation with food may strengthen the resolve 'not to give in' or bulimia may result.

In addition, in line with the various aetiological hypotheses, the condition may be perpetuated by weight loss being felt as equivalent to personal effectiveness, and its assumption of a functional role in a disturbed family setting. Relief from the distress of pubertal weight changes, exemption or withdrawal from academic pressure and other secondary gain may maintain and reinforce the condition.

AETIOLOGY—BULIMIA

There is considerable overlap and interrelationship between the eating disorders. In patients still suffering from anorexia nervosa, bingeing and vomiting occur in between 16 and 50 per cent (bulimic variant). Anorectics restored to, and no longer expressing a phobia of, normal body weight may continue to binge and vomit and account for around a third of the patients suffering from the syndrome 'bulimia'; recently Russell (1985) has suggested that the term 'bulimia nervosa' be reserved for those cases where there is a previous history of anorexia nervosa. For those patients currently suffering from bulimia with no previous history of anorexia nervosa Lacey (1980) has suggested the term 'bulimic syndrome'; all these patients will have engaged in less severe carbohydrate-restricted dieting. Much then of what has been said regarding the aetiology of anorexia nervosa will also apply to bulimia. Lacey, Coker and Birtchnell (1986) have reported on the aetiology of bulimia using a multifactorial model of underlying and precipitant factors. The sample was divided into two groups on the basis of a previous history of anorexia nervosa; the underlying factors were common to both groups and the reported precipitants to both severe dieting and first episode of binge-eating very similar.

Predisposing factors

Individual—premorbid obesity

In the study Lacey, Coker and Birtchnell (1986) all patients had initially dieted; around half the sample were 6 kg or more above mean matched population weight at this time and the remainder dieted because of concern about shape.

Personality

Lacey (1983a) has described bulimics as mainly falling into two groups: the 'neurotics' are striving and perfectionist with high achievement paradoxically coupled to low self-esteem, whilst the 'personality disordered' are shallow and histrionic with problems of impulse control manifest not only with food but also with alcohol, drugs and sexual activity. In the Lacey, Coker and Birtchnell (1986) study, doubts concerning femininity, intense academic striving and poor peer group relationships were reported.

Family

Patients with bulimia tend to have moved social class by education (Lacey, 1980). Their family backgrounds are similar to those of the massively obese, and a family history of obesity has been reported that may carry implications for a genetic factor as well as early experience of the attitude of the family towards food. Conflicts over food and the use of sweets as reward and demonstration of affection are often described. A poor relationship with their parents is often reported by bulimic women as well as a poor relationship between the parents Lacey, Coker and Burtchnell (1986), often related to issues of sexuality.

Precipitants

Just as life events may precipitate the initial dieting, they may also result in bulimia in the already dieting woman. Under the stress of events which threaten the identity of an already fragile and vulnerable woman, and in the presence of carbohydrate craving, bingeing occurs. In the Lacey, Coker and Birtchnell (1986) study the commonest type of event involved sexual conflicts—the beginning or termination of a first major heterosexual relationship, often that in which first intercourse occurred. Also reported were 'moves' with a change in location or occupation leaving the patient rootless and insecure, and 'loss' involving bereavement or estrangement from a significant family member. A majority of patients reported more than one of these factors concurrently.

Maintenance

Once bulimia occurs there may be a pendulum of guilt, shame and resolve leading to severe compensatory dieting, leading back via carbohydrate craving to more bingeing. In addition, self-induced vomiting may contribute via metabolic disturbance to a dysphoria from which temporary relief is sought in a binge. Food may be used as a sedative or comfort at times of distress or unhappiness, but in turn bingeing provokes a reaction of further distress and disgust. The patient may thus become trapped in a pattern of chaotic eating.

CLINICAL FEATURES

Anorexia nervosa

Anorexia nervosa patients can be divided into two groups clinically. The most common group contain those anorectics who maintain their low body weight by avoidance of carbohydrate, whilst about a third of the clinic population remain within their weight limit by purgation and self-induced vomiting.

The carbohydrate abstainers are younger and lighter than the vomiters. Clinically, they appear emaciated, being usually below 43 kg. Many patients have dieted in the past along with their friends and, like them, have given up after 3 or 4 days. However, the future anorectic gradually develops the control necessary to stick to a diet such that she can diet alone and not as a member of a group. This leads to a sense of identity and autonomy and reinforces her determination to make her body 'perfect'. Dally and Gomez (1979) point out that dieting can become the focus of adolescent idealism such that the drive to lose weight becomes compelling, overcoming pangs of hunger. Certainly the patient becomes preoccupied with food, reading anything on the subject and taking over many aspects of the family cooking! She attempts to 'feed up' other siblings, particularly a younger sister (thereby attempting, as it were, to change places with her!).

The patient will eat slowly, 'playing' with her food, such behaviour becoming the focus of family resentment. The diet becomes increasingly bizarre. Strange fads develop which often become rationalized in terms of the need to eat 'healthy' food. However, the most obvious development is the avoidance of carbohydrate foods and their replacement by fruit and vegetables. Some take excess fruits for their laxative effect and, for similar reasons, will eat All-Bran. The result is a diet of about 800 kcal with resultant precipitant weight loss. Later, the patient will increase her caloric intake to about 1500 kcal and her body weight will then become stable. (This is much less than the 2200 kcal needed each day by an adult woman but the anorectic appears to reset her metabolic demand.)

Almost always, the patient is amenorrhoeic. Weight loss commonly occurs before or simultaneously with the onset of amenorrhoea. In the series studied by Crisp and Stonehill (1971) the mean amount of weight loss between the onset of dieting and the last menstrual period was 9 kg, although the mean weight at the time of the last menstrual period was only 3 kg above normal weight. With refeeding, menstruation is unlikely to return until the patient is about 80 per cent of normal weight. The majority, however, do not begin menstruating until they have been at a normal weight for a number of months. Crisp believes that the critical weight for any patient is related to her weight at menarche; in other words, patients who are overweight at menarche require to be relatively heavier before menstruation will return. Dally and Gomez (1979) disagree with this. The general clinical consensus is that menstruation is most likely to return when a patient is within a normal range of weight, her body having a reasonable fat cover, and that this has been stable for a number of months without food abuse.

The abstaining anorectic has a 'prepubertal' hormone pattern (Russell and Beardwood, 1968) and is sexually quiescent. The majority have had little or no sexual experiences and tend to discuss such matters with the interviewer in a naïve and childlike way. The normal adolescent interest in sexual matters is replaced by the preoccupation with food.

The anorectic has high ethical standards and is distressed that she is forced by her phobia to lie to her parents (and teachers) about her food intake. It is not unusual for the patient to tell her mother that she is having a large lunch at school and her teachers that she has a heavy meal in the evening with her family. Both Bruch and Selvini have emphasized the patient's untruthfulness about the amount of food that she eats. Dally and Gomez (1979) have emphasized that the patient is not simply lying but that the apparent untruthfulness reflects what she is feeling and perceiving: a tiny slice of bread can become magnified into half a loaf. This characteristic, hated by the patient herself, becomes the basis of the deviousness which so irritates her medical and nursing attendants.

The patient's characteristic emotional immaturity is mirrored by an 'immature' carpal radiograph. The patient's radiological age bears no statistical relationship to her chronological age but is arrested at the age of onset of the anorexia and can be calculated as the sum of that age, plus any periods of refeeding (Lacey et al., 1979).

At low body weight, anorectics describe sleep disturbance marked by early morning waking, although, unlike the depressed, they rarely complain of it. In a study examining anorectics refeeding in hospital (Lacey et al., 1975) initial weight gain was associated with an increase in slow wave sleep (SWS) which tended to decrease as the weight was finally restored to normal. It has been suggested that SWS is associated with general bodily synthetic processes, and such processes characterized these patients at this stage of treatment. As weight gain approaches there is a dramatic increase in rapid eye movement sleep to normal levels. This stage of sleep, which may perhaps be associated with cerebral synthetic activity, occurred during a period of psychotherapy and restoration of reproductive physiology and presumably, therefore, a related increase in cerebral activity.

Characteristically, the patient has fine lanugo hair over her body which presumably develops as a means of heat conservation as fat insulation is depleted. The lanugo hair grows particularly on the back, arms, legs and side of the face, and has given rise to the suggestion (Lacey, 1982a) that this was the basis of the descriptions made by the early Church of bearded female saints. Certainly, the clinical description of these saints is remarkably like that of the anorectic of today!

The anorectic will also describe severe acrocyanosis which during cold weather can become painful. Dally and Gomez (1979) state that patients with a poor circulation prior to anorexia nervosa are likely to have had irregular menstruation.

The anorectic is hyperactive and occasionally frenetic. Below 43 kg a reversed temperature rhythm is noted which rights itself when weight is regained. Anorectics claim not to get colds and virus infections and this may be due either to an altered immune response (Armstrong-Esther et al., 1978) or to social isolation.

Bulimia

The bulimic and vomiting anorectic presents a slightly different clinical picture. She is heavier, usually being about 48 kg, and presents to the clinic when she is slightly older. She often gives a history of being unable to maintain her anorexia by carbohydrate avoidance and most authorities see bulimic anorexia as a malignant extension of the more characteristic avoidance pattern. Because she is heavier, above the 43 kg threshold of sexual awareness, the bulimic anorectic tends to have sexual feelings but is terrified of them. Characteristically, there may be quite marked swings of body weight. Lanugo hair is rare. Teeth, particularly the palatal surfaces, may be eroded from persistent vomiting (Hurst, Lacey and Crisp, 1977). The patient appears more disturbed psychologically and the prognosis seems poorer (Crisp, 1967; Crisp, 1980).

Bulimics at normal body weight are attractive, if not in personality then in appearance, and the possibility that this is related to the pathogenesis of the disorder cannot be discounted. They present in their twenties and thirties; the average of presentation in a consecutive series of 112 patients seen in our clinic was 24.8 years. Although many will initially claim that it is the disordered eating that has finally brought them to a doctor, this is rarely the whole story. Nearly half the patients report interpersonal difficulties with men and over a third claim to be 'depressed'. Some patients describe persistent and ongoing emotional difficulties with a man friend, or series of men, which leads to a deterioration in the eating pattern with consequent gain in weight and associated depression. Others describe being 'fed up'(!) with their chaotic eating and deciding to come to the clinic because they have heard of the treatment programme; alternatively, some desire a baby but are fearful that the bulimia would damage its development.

The physical state will depend on whether or not vomiting has recently occurred. If the patient has had a substantial binge within an hour of presenting at the clinic she will appear distressed, sweaty and, occasionally, with a mild pyrexia. Her neck will appear swollen and perhaps she will wear a kerchief to mask it. Salivary glands will be swollen but painless, and if the parotid are affected she may complain of tinnitus or facial ache. The abdomen will be swollen and painful and the patient will lie still in the foetal position holding her stomach. Borborygmi will be heard. Examination will show stretch marks in the lower abdomen and on the lower outer quadrant of the breasts. The breasts may be tense and swollen and benign breast dysplasia is not infrequent. If vomiting occurs metabolic disturbances such as hypokala-emia may result. Cardiac arrhythmias, renal damage, tetany and peripheral paraesthesae, epileptic seisures and dehydration have been reported. Persistent vomiting may also give rise to chronic hoarseness and erosion of dental enamel (Hurst, Lacey and Crisp, 1977), particularly on the palatal surfaces.

The binge-eating

The mean age of onset of binge-eating is 18½ years which is some 1–2 years later than the onset of symptoms reported in anorexia nervosa. Bulimia reaches is maximum severity at an average age of 23½ years. Patients suffer their symptoms for an average of 6 years before seeking medical help.

Two thirds of the women seeking help report bingeing attacks at least daily. In some the episodes of binge-eating may run into one other, often disrupting the patient's life. More typically, the patient will binge two or three times in the day and consider herself out of control; 'good' days will follow—these being days not when she is eating normally but when caloric intake is severely reduced. In other words control can only be obtained by near starvation, which, because it runs counter to metabolic demand, must in the end be ineffective: hunger and carbohydrate craving leading to yet another binge.

The patients report three main triggers to their attacks which maintain the cycle of the disorder. Carbohydrate craving is the most commonly reported, but in those patients where the bulimia occurs less than daily the episodes are often triggered by emotional stress. Patients use starchy and sugary foods like a tranquillizer to squash and repress feelings; alternatively, they may use the food to fill the hollowness of their existence, almost like a stimulant.

Later, with frequent daily bingeing, such triggers are less evident and the behaviour becomes a habit, behaviourally learned.

Before the attack there is usually excitement and a sense of expectancy followed by a compulsion to 'stuff something into the mouth'. Hunger is usually absent. The patients are adamant that it is the oral cavity that must be satisfied, not the stomach. Afterwards, the patient feels guilt-ridden and degraded, feelings which can only be expunged by vomiting and by a transiently held decision never to do it again.

Caloric intake

The caloric intake of vomiting bulimics is markedly different from that of purgers. In a recent study (Lacey and Gibson, 1985) the mean caloric intake of vomiting bulimics was 6024 kcal per day which is nearly three times that needed to maintain weight and metabolism (2100 kcal/day). There was marked daily variation and vomiters can eat huge amounts of good—up to nearly 30 000 kcal in a day. The mean caloric intake of those patients who solely purged to control their weight was within a normal range (2220 kcal in a day).

Body weight

Bulimic patients are just slightly heavier than the norm, the mean being 5 per cent above mean matched population weight which was 61 kg in our clinic group. Nearly all describe marked weight fluctuation, highest weight being, on average, 22 per cent above the norm and the lowest weight, on average, being 15 per cent below.

Vomiting is a highly effective way of preventing weight gain. The mean weights of vomiting bulimics in our clinic group being very close (98 per cent) to matched population mean weight in spite of greatly elevated caloric intake. Daily variations of 3 kg are common and the vomiters describe feeling puffy after a binge and oedema may be detected. Purgation alone seems to be a relatively ineffective means of preventing weight gain for, despite the smaller caloric intake described above, purgers are, unlike the vomiters, above mean matched population weight (average 14 per cent above). Weight fluctuation is more marked in purging bulimics where long-term swings are of the order of 6–12 kg.

Self-induced vomiting

Just less than 90 per cent of the clinic population describe a history of vomiting and over three quarters regularly use it for weight control. Vomiting begins on average 18 months after the onset of the bulimia, that is at about 20 years, which is some 2 years later than the average age of onset of vomiting in vomiting anorectics. Its discovery, whether learned or spontaneous after a massive binge, is greeted at first as welcome relief. Unfortunately, the knowledge that it is available if bingeing occurs encourages the development of a vicious circle whereby excess eating may be facilitated.

Initially, vomiting occurs only after bingeing, but later it follows normal meals as well. Typically, therefore, the daily frequency of vomiting is about a third higher than the bulimia. To begin with, emetics (4 per cent) or irritating the back of the throat (77 per cent) are used to induce vomiting, but some 27 per cent of patients develop an ability to vomit at will, without mechanical aids. A number (15 per cent) start vomiting before they binge-eat.

Purgative abuse

Some 60 per cent of the clinic population describe using laxatives and nearly 40 per cent describe using them daily at some point in the course of their illness. The dose is variable but massive dosages have been reported, up to 70 times the recommended dose on the package. However, on average, just less than 13 times the recommended dose is used. Abdominal pain and violent watery stools commonly result. Patients claim that purgative abuse prevents weight gain although the pharmacological mechanism is unsure. Certainly, there is little evidence that laxatives interfere significantly with intestinal absorption. In a recent study Lacey and Gibson (1985) showed that purgation was relatively ineffective as a means of preventing weight gain and that purging bulimics persisted with their abuse for two reasons: first, to induce intestinal hurry (and thereby reduce their abdominal distention), and second, they appreciated the 'diuretic' effect of the laxative (and thereby its tendency to reduce oedema and body overperception).

Over 20 per cent of bulimics take 'slimming' pills such as bran tablets, cellulose or even amphetamines, and nearly a third have a history of diuretic abuse.

The menstrual disorder

Some 70 per cent of the population describe a menstrual dysfunction during the course of their illness. Irregularity of menstruation is mainly associated with binge-eating whilst amenorrhoea is associated with both weight loss and initial binge-eating. There was no association between the presence or absence of vomiting and the general pattern of menstrual activity. Just less than three quarters report menstrual dysfunction within the first 6 months following the onset of the initial diet manipulation and 70 per cent reported a dysfunction at the time of first interview, 36 per cent being amenorrhoeic.

It is interesting to speculate on the reasons for the high incidence of menstrual dysfunction in bulimia. It is noteworthy that those women in the Third World whose food intake is high in carbohydrate, yet in overall calorie deficit, maintain menstruation whilst bulimics who selectively avoid or manipulate carbohydrate, yet have adequate energy intake, do not. Could it be that a constant and adequate supply of carbohydrate is a necessary criterion for continuing ovulation? Whilst this hypothesis is contentious it would make sense in evolutionary terms. The diet of primitive woman as evolved from higher apes was carbohydrate. If, therefore, carbohydrate was the major source of energy, a sensitive switch, possibly hormonal, linking carbohydrate ingestion to ovulation would be essential if pregnancy and lactation were not to deplete fat stores dangerously at times of reduced availability. Such a 'switch' would have evolutionary survival value.

Mood disturbance

Initial reports of bulimia commented on the significant level of depression among the population. There is a tendency to helplessness, pessimism and self-criticism and a general instability of affect. There is a high incidence of primary affective disorder amongst first-degree relatives and Hudson (Hudson *et al.*, 1983) has argued that bulimia may simply be a form of affective disorder. However, response to antidepressant medication is poor.

Lacey (1982b) has attempted to categorize the mental state and has divided the population into three groups.

The largest group, the *neurotic* group, tend to be hardworking and ambitious. Superficially they appear to be little disturbed in personality in the sense that they give every impression to their friends and relatives of being stable, generally coping and resourceful. On deeper examination, they declare low self-esteem and a feeling of being a failure, particularly in relationship terms. They declare their difficulties with impulse control, show an exaggerated sense of guilt and recurrent anxiety. They find the expression of anger difficult, often denying its presence, preferring instead to be sad or depressed. It is often difficult to disentangle whether the eating disorder develops in the context of the depression, bingeing relieving the dysphoria temporarily, but setting an 'addictive' vicious cycle; or whether, as many patients described, the depression is secondary to the feelings of guilt and shame in suffering the bulimia. Following treatment, when the eating symptoms are given up, depression commonly ensues. This group does particularly well in treatment.

The *personality disordered* group is smaller, less than 20 per cent of the clinic population, and is much more difficult to treat. In this group manipulation of food is associated with intolerance of frustration and a lack of impulse control which is not limited to food but includes also the abuse of alcohol or street drugs. Appetitive behaviour is out of control and impulsiveness manifests as periods of sexual disinhibition. The patients commonly present as emotionally shallow or histrionic. A fear of going out of control leads some into 'safe' relationships with men unable or unwilling to be committed. Stealing may also occur.

The smallest group in the psychiatric clinic is *secondary bulimia*. In this the syndrome is secondary to physical illness such as epilepsy or diabetes. A constant feature within the history of such patients is of a difficult illness which began in the context of puberty, the normal insecurities of that time being heightened by the lack of control intrinsic within the symptoms of the primary disorder. Asthma and other allergic phenomena may also provide the background for a secondary bulimic syndrome which can then generalize into a psychological food intolerance (Joint Committee Report, 1984).

BODY IMAGE DISTURBANCE IN ANOREXIA NERVOSA AND BULIMIA

In recent years there has been considerable interest in the issue of body image in relation to the eating disorders and, fuelled by clinical observations, a large number of studies have attempted to objectify and measure different aspects of body image distortion. Body image is a complex construct. Described by Schilder (1935) as 'the picture of our own body which we form in our minds, that is to say, the way in which our body appears to ourselves', its evolution can be traced back to observations on patients with neurological impairment. Head (1920) delineated the brain's ability to detect weight/shape/size and to form and incorporate these into schemata, and Gerstmann (1958) has described the syndrome associated with right-sided parietal lesions. That body image is not necessarily consistent with actual physical appearance is supported by observations on patients with phantom limb phenomena. As well as that 'perceptual' aspect of body image, the accurate assessment of body size, several writers have stressed the inclusion into this concept of cognitive and affective aspects—the feelings and attitudes of the individual towards his body (Secord and Jourard, 1953). Operating independently, but not to the exclusion of body size misperception, an extreme loathing for all or part of the body may be described, or an exaggerated pleasure in extreme emaciation. In addition, body image has been conceptualized as a personality construct (Schilder, 1935; Fisher and Cleveland, 1958; Kolb, 1975). Schontz (1974) has discussed the different levels at which the body image construct may function and has reviewed the wide range of techniques that have been developed to measure different aspects of body image. These include size estimation of body widths by movable calipers or lights (Reitman and Cleveland, 1964; modified by Slade and Russell, 1973), image marking (Askevold, 1975) and total body size estimation (distorting photograph-Glucksman and Hirsch, 1969), as well as projective instruments, figure drawings, questionnaires and clinical interviews.

Body image disturbance was first recognized as an essential characteristic of anorexia nervosa by Bruch (1962) who stressed the patient's apparent inability to recognize her emaciation. Disturbance of body image is now included in the DMS III (1980) diagnostic criteria for anorexia nervosa with as an example 'claiming to "feel fat" even when emaciated', and it should be noted that this does not necessarily imply misperception of actual body size. Some patients may correctly assess their physical dimensions but be disgusted by their shape—well beyond that dislike common in Western women (Berscheid, Walster and Hohrnstedt, 1973); alternatively, the emaciation may be recognized but overvalued as an exceptional achievement and proof of the transcendence of 'oral asceticism' over self-indulgence (Thoma, 1967). It has also been noted (Garner and Garfinkel, 1981–1982) that patients with anorexia nervosa may restrict body image distortion to particular parts of their body; for example, overall emaciation may be acknowledged but a 'protruding stomach' or 'fat thighs' be bitterly complained of. Perhaps reflecting a mistrust of subjective evaluation of size, bizarre objective measures may be employed such as being able to rest a ruler across the hip bones without it touching the abdomen. The misperceived part may have special psychological significance, perhaps concerning aspects of sexuality. Although included in the diagnostic criteria for anorexia nervosa, distortion of body image is not peculiar to anorexia nervosa, nor even to the eating disorders, but has been described also in schizophrenics (Fries, 1977), thin, neurotic and obese women (Garner et al., 1976), pregnant women (Slade, 1977) and normal young female controls in a number of studies.

The results of studies directed at the objective measurement of that aspect of body image distortion manifest in faulty estimation of actual body size has been reviewed in detail by Garfinkel and Garner (1982). Using the movable light technique to measure subjects' estimation of body width, Slade and Russell (1973) demonstrated that anorectics overperceived face, chest, waist and hip widths compared to normal controls and that this overperception decreased as normal weight was restored, and weight loss after discharge was related to inpatient overestimation. Fries (1977) and Pierloot and Houben (1978) similarly reported overestimation by anorectics compared to controls. However, although Crisp and Kalucy (1974), using similar apparatus, confirmed that anorectics overperceive body widths, particularly after a high carbohydrate meal, their controls overperceived to a similar degree and they suggested that overestimation may be age related, the controls in the earlier studies being older than the anorectics. The replication of Slade and Russell's study by Button, Fransella and Slade (1977) with carefully age-matched controls found no difference in the overestimation of body widths between the two groups although in the anorectics overestimation was related to vomiting and early relapse. Similarly, Casper et al. (1979), whilst finding that both anorectics and age-matched controls overestimated, for the anorectics this was associated with poorer prognosis and psychopathology. Garner et al. (1976) confirmed that overestimation of body width using a visual size estimation apparatus did not distinguish anorectic or obese subjects from controls, but found that these groups were differentiated using a measure of general body size, by the distorting photograph technique. For the eating disorder groups, body size estimates were significantly correlated with personality features and, on follow-up (Garfinkel, Moldofsky and Garner, 1977) of anorectics, predictive of poor prognosis. Studies using the image-marking method (Askevold, 1975) have generated similar results, with some studies (Pierloot and Houben, 1978; Wingate and Christie, 1978) differentiating anorectics from controls on body width estimation whilst others (Strober et al., 1979) find that controls overestimate to a similar degree.

Not all anorectics overestimate body size; comparing marked overestimators to other anorectics, using the distorting photograph technique, Garner and Garfinkel (1981–1982) report overestimation as related to higher scores on the Eating Attitudes Test, increased depression and anxiety and more body image disturbance on an attitudinal measure of body satisfaction. Overall, it would appear that whilst anorectics do not overperceive more than controls using body width estimation apparatus, a difference may be revealed by the distorting photograph technique, which confronts the subject with a whole body representation, and that within the anorectic group marked overestimation is associated with psychopathological features and poorer prognosis.

Following Bruch's (1973) statement that she considered the correction of distorted body image a 'precondition to recovery', attempts have been made to incorporate this directly into the therapeutic approach. Gottheil, Backup and Cornelison (1969) report the successful treatment of an anorectic by confronting her with motion pictures of herself, but a more general assumption seems to be that once more fundamental psychological issues have been resolved, body image distortion will 'self-correct', and Garner and Garfinkel (1981–1982) state that they have found direct modification of the patient's unrealistic self-perceptions to be unproductive. Crisp and Kalucy (1974) found that on restoration to normal weight overestimation persisted, and that this was related to premorbid weight; they suggested that overestimation may reflect 'surviving perception of maximum ever weight and size'.

The association in anorectics of vomiting with overestimation has been noted (Button, Fransella and Slade, 1977) but at present little data are available on body image perception in the patients with the syndrome 'bulimia'. Touyz et al., (1984) measured ten bulimics' perceived size and ideal size using a video monitor with a distorting control knob, and found that they overperceived and desired to be slimmer by a factor of 18.5 per cent. In a study of 50 women with bulimia nervosa (Birtchnell, Lacey and Harte, 1985) it was found that although they consistently overestimated body width, this did not differ significantly from that of normal age-matched controls. However, overestimation was significantly decreased in those patients who completed a ten-session outpatient treatment programme. Examining the bulimics by weight index group, it was found that those closest to the mean matched population weight distorted body image least, with the most marked, and significantly different, distortion occurring in the heavier groups. The controls showed a similar though non-significant trend. It may be that greater distortion of body image is associated with greater dissatisfaction with body size. The discrepancies between actual weight and mean matched population weight, and actual and desired weight, were significantly different for the different weight index groups. The bulimics who were slightly below normal weight wished to be 7 kg or so below average weight, the start, perhaps, of 'anorectic' thinking, whereas in the bulimics who were most above average weight, whilst they wished to be considerably lighter (by around 18 kg), this represented a wish to be at average weight rather than below it.

TREATMENT

Anorexia nervosa can be difficult to treat. The difficulty lies in the need to restore the patient to normal body weight, which means that the underlying phobia must be overcome. On the other hand, bulimia is comparatively easy to treat, despite the pessimistic views first expressed (Russell, 1979).

Many treatment programmes have been described for anorexia nervosa, but all successful ones have two main components: first, a nursing programme aimed at the restoration of normal body weight, and second, a psychological programme aimed at getting the patient to accept this weight. Hsu, in a review of outcome studies (Hsu, 1980), found that the initial in-hospital phase of treatment is 'relatively simple and usually successful', but that whatever subsequent psychological treatment method is used, long-term improvement does not necessarily ensue. He reports that disturbed eating patterns are very common amongst treated anorectic patients. Similarly, Dally and Gomez (1979) have concluded that abnormal attitudes towards shape, weight and food are 'likely to continue or to recur in situations of crisis'. Clearly, therefore, treatment for anorexia nervosa and for Type II bulimia should be looked on as a long-term programme which begins with an initial consultation aimed at getting the patient's full cooperation. This in turn should encourage the patient to agree to a hospital admission with the aim of weight restoration and the recognition that there are other ways of dealing with the problems than by abusing food. Finally, long-term psych-otherapeutic support is needed.

In the various descriptions of treatment, the nursing programme is comparatively consistent. Most authorities recommend inpatient admission and this is certainly the case if the disorder has been present for more than a year and if vomiting coexists. The consensus is that the patient should go to bed (Crisp, 1965a; Russell, 1973) and be given a prescribed diet aimed at achieving a target weight. Recommendations for determining an appropriate body weight differ. Most advise setting a target weight based upon average weight, or 90 per cent of average weight as derived from population norm; others argue, based upon the concept of 'set-point', that target weights must be highly individualized, reflecting personal and family weight histories

(Garner and Garfinkel, 1984). We believe that the target weight should be got from standard tables based on the weight for height at the time the patient developed her illness. This weight should never be negotiable. If the patient is unable to accept her target weight, she is, in a way, defining the severity of her anorexia and is not yet ready for treatment.

Views on prescribed diet also vary. We believe that as anorectics particularly avoid carbohydrates, their diet in hospital should be a 'normal' one containing carbohydrate with each meal. Weight gain may be achieved by giving large helpings of food, but the danger of this is that binge-eating can learned behaviourally. Rather, Crisp's idea of giving a supplement of, say, cheese sandwiches, sufficient to create a weight gain of between 1 and 2 kg per week, is preferred. Other treatment programmes recommend a faster rate of weight increase but, again, the danger of binge-eating, or even obesity, must be considered. Latter stages of hospitalization must prepare the patient for discharge. Shopping for new clothes and food, the preparation of food for the patient and for others without anorectic behaviour or ritual, the capacity to eat in restaurants and in the company of others, all must be successfully achieved.

The psychological side of any treatment programme is, for the reasons indicated above, vital. Behavioural methods have been suveyed by Halmi (1984). Most methods have used positive reinforcement contingent on weight gain. Behavioural techniques have also been used as an adjunct to other treatments, particularly medication (Eckert et al., 1979; Lacey and Crisp, 1980). Cognitive therapy for anorexia nervosa has been used successfully by Garner and his colleagues (Garner and Bemis, 1984). They report that their results are encouraging. Multitreatment programmes have been described by Strober (Strober and Yager, 1984) and psychoanalytic approaches by Goodsit (1984) and Orbach (1984).

There have been fewer reports of treatment for bulimia. However, certain general decisions about the treatment required can be made. The clinic population is not homogeneous and the treatment needs of the neurotic group of bulimics are different from the needs of those who are personality disordered. Therefore, at least two treatment programmes would appear to be needed. A large number of patients are affected. Any treatment developed must therefore be cost-effective. For a disorder marked by such chaos, control and structure would appear to be vital.

Lacey has developed a series of treatment programmes, the aim of which has been to remove all eating symptoms without allowing the development of a weight disorder. The principles of treatment are:

(1) that the overt eating symptoms are dealt with by behavioural therapy and counselling, whilst the emotional conflicts, released when the eating is brought under control, are dealt with by insight-directed therapy;
(2) that the behavioural and insight-directed therapy are undertaken by the same therapist;

(3) that the treatment should be time-limited because open-ended treatments tend to lead to a return of symptoms, perhaps as a way of holding on to the therapy or therapist.

Two forms of programme have been successfully developed, one using individual therapy and the other using a mixture of individual and group sessions; the latter have been evaluated in a controlled treatment study and outcome monitored over 2 years (Lacey, 1983b). Subsequent work has shown that alcohol abuse (within the personality disordered group) and a history of previous anorexia nervosa (Type II bulimics) were associated with poorer outcome. Married patients experienced marital difficulties at the end of treatment and illness in the spouse was common. Full details of the programme are published elsewhere (Lacey, 1984b).

Other attempts at treating bulimia have been reported. Antidepressants and appetite suppressants do not influence the course of the disorder (Sabine, Yonace and Farrington, 1983). Anticonvulsants may benefit some (Green and Rau, 1974; Wermuth, Davis and Hollister, 1977), although electroencephalogram (EEG) abnormalities did not correlate with treatment response and abnormal EEG's are infrequent. Such results are perhaps understandable, for any attempt at modification of the disorder must be able to handle the underlying and precipitating factors of the disorder. Other treatments have been reported by Fairburn (1984), who used a cognitive–behavioural method, and Rosen (Rosen and Leitenberg, 1984), who used exposure plus response prevention. Wooley and Wooley (1984) have described both an intensive outpatient treatment and a residential treatment for bulimia although most workers believe that these patients are best treated in an outpatient setting. The initial results of Fairburn suggest that the cognitive–behavioural approach may be effective but no control study has yet been published. Fairburn states that it is 'quite conceivable that its effects are non-specific and that similar results would be obtained by any credible treatment that provides active support and structure'.

Recently, Lacey has shown that dropout from treatment, long assumed to be a feature of treatment of bulimics, can be contained by use of group techniques. Further, long-term success can be maintained by infrequent supportive appointments.

The eating disorders have, at present, an epidemic prevalence, particularly amongst women. Both anorexia nervosa and bulimia stem from an interreaction of individual, family and social factors such that these disorders can fairly be said to be a paradigm of psychosomatic medicine. Their aetiology and clinical presentation have been clarified and they respond well to tested treatment programmes. So long as the debate concerning the role of women in our society continues so the prominence and importance of these disorders will continue.

REFERENCES

Armstrong-Esther, C. A., Lacey, J. H., Crisp, A. H., and Bryant, T. N. (1978). An investigation of the immune response of patients suffering from anorexia nervosa. *Postgraduate Medical Journal*, **54**, 395–399.

Askevold, F. (1975). Measuring body image. *Psychotherapy and Psychosomatics*, **26**, 71–77.

Berscheid, E., Walster, E., and Hohrnstedt, G. (1973). The happy American body: a survey report. *Psychology Today*, **November**, 119–131.

Birtchnell, S. A., Lacey, J. H., and Harte, A., (1985). Body image distortion in bulimia nervosa. *British Journal of Psychiatry*, **147**, 408–412.

Birtchnell, S., and Lacey, J. H. (1984). The bulimic syndrome: a new variant of eating disorder. *Maternal and Child Health—the Journal of Family Medicine*, **9** **August**, no. 8, 247–250.

Boskind-Lodahl, M. (1976). Cinderella's stepsisters: a feminist perspective on anorexia nervosa and bulimia. *Journal of Women in Culture and Society*, **2**, 342–356.

Bruch, H. (1962). Perceptual and conceptual disturbances in anorexia nervosa. *Psychosomatic Medicine*, **24**, 187–194.

Bruch, H. (1973). *Eating Disorders: Obesity, Anorexia Nervosa and the Person Within*. New York: Basic Books.

Bruch, H. (1978). *The Golden Cage—The Enigma of Anorexia Nervosa*. Shepton Mallett: Open Books.

Button, E. J., Fransella, A. F., and Slade, P. D. (1977). A reappraisal of body perception disturbance in anorexia nervosa. *Psychological Medicine*, **7**, 235–245.

Button, E. J., and Whitehouse, A. (1981). Sub-clinical anorexia nervosa. *Psychological Medicine*, **11**, 509–516.

Cantwell, D. P., Sturzenberger, S., Burroughs, J., Salkin, B., and Green, J. K. (1977) Anorexia nervosa—an affective disorder? *Archives of General Psychiatry*, **34**, 1087–1093.

Casper, R. C., Halmi, K. A., Goldberg, S. C., Eckert, E. D., and Davis, J. M. (1979). Disturbances in body image estimated as related to other characteristics and outcome in anorexia nervosa. *British Journal of Psychiatry*, **134**, 60–66.

Cleghorn, R. H., and Brown, W. T. (1964). Eating patterns and nutritional adaptation. *Canadian Psychiatric Association Journal*, **9**, 299–312.

Cooper, P. J., and Fairburn, C. G. (1983). Binge-eating and self-induced vomiting in the community: a preliminary study. *British Journal of Psychiatry*, **142**, 139–144.

Crisp, A. H. (1965a). Clinical and therapeutic aspects of anorexia nervosa: a study of 30 cases. *Journal of Psychosomatic Research*, **9**, 67–78.

Crisp, A. H. (1965b). Some aspects of the evolution, presentation and follow-up of anorexia nervosa. *Proceedings—Royal Society of Medicine*, **58**, 814–820.

Crisp, A. H. (1966). Anorexia nervosa in an identical twin. *Postgraduate Medical Journal*, **42**, 86–92.

Crisp, A. H. (1967). The possible significance of some behavioural correlates of weight and carbohydrate intake. *Journal of Psychosomatic Research*, **11**, 117–131.

Crisp, A. H. (1970). Reported birth weights and growth rates in a group of patients with primary anorexia (weight phobia). *Journal of Psychosomatic Research*, **14**, 25–50.

Crisp, A. H. (1980). *Anorexia Nervosa: Let Me Be*. London: Academic Press.

Crisp, A. H., and Kalucy, R. S. (1974). Aspects of the perceptual disorder in anorexia nervosa. *British Journal of Medical Psychology*, **47**, 349–361.

Crisp, A. H., Palmer, R. L., and Kalucy, K. S. (1976). How common is anorexia nervosa? A prevalence study. *British Journal of Psychiatry*, **128**, 549–554.

Crisp, A. H., and Stonehill, E. (1971). Relationship between aspects of nutritional disturbance and menstrual activity in primary anorexia nervosa. *British Medical Journal*, **3**, 149–151.

Dally, P. J., and Gomez, J. (1979). *Anorexia Nervosa*. London: William Heinemann.

DSM III (1980) (*Diagnostic and Statistical Manual of Mental Disorders 1980*, 3rd edn). Washington, DC: American Psychiatric Association.

Eckert, E. D., Goldberg, S. C., Halmi, K. A., Casper, R. C., and Davis, J. M. (1979). Behaviour therapy and anorexia nervosa. *British Journal of Psychiatry*, **134**, 55–59.

Erikson, E. H. (1981). *Childhood and Society*. London: Imago Publishing Co.

Fairburn, C. G. (1984). Cognitive–behavioural treatment for bulimia. In D. M. Garner and P. E. Garfinkel (eds), *Handbook of Psychotherapy for Anorexia Nervosa and Bulimia*. New York: Guildford Press.

Fairburn, C. G., and Cooper, P. J. (1984). Binge-eating, self-induced vomiting and laxative abuse: a community study. *Psychological Medicine*, **14**, 401–410.

Feighner, J. P., Robins, E., Guze, S. B., Woodruff, R. A., Winokur, A., and Munoz, R. (1972). Diagnostic criteria for use in psychiatric research. *Archives of General Psychiatry*, **26**, 57–63.

Fisher, S., and Cleveland, S. E. (1958). *Body Image and Personality*. New York: Dover Publications.

Fries, H. (1977). Studies on secondary amenorrhoea, anorectic behaviour and body image perception: importance for early recognition of anorexia nervosa. In S. Vigersky (ed.), *Anorexia Nervosa*. New York: Raven Press, pp. 163–176.

Garfinkel, P. E., and Garner, D. M. (1982). *Anorexia Nervosa: A Multi-dimensional Perspective*. New York: Brunner Mazel.

Garfinkel, P. E., Moldofsky, H., and Garner D. M. (1977). Prognosis in anorexia nervosa as influenced by clinical features: treatment and self perception. *Canadian Medical Association Journal*, **117**, 1041–1045.

Garner, D. M., and Bemis, K. M. (1984). Cognitive therapy for anorexia nervosa. In D. M. Garner and P. E. Garfinkel (eds). *Handbook of Psychotherapy for Anorexia Nervosa and Bulimia*. New York: Guildford Press.

Garner, D. M., and Garfinkel, P. E. (1980). Sociocultural factors in the development of anorexia nervosa. *Psychological Medicine*, **10**, 647–656.

Garner, D. M., and Garfinkel, P. E. (1981–1982). Body image in anorexia nervosa measurement, theory and clinical implications. *International Journal of Psychiatry in Medicine*, **11**, 263–284.

Garner, D. M., and Garfinkel, P. E. (1984). Introduction. In D. M. Garner and P. E. Garfinkel (eds), *Handbook of Psychotherapy for Anorexia Nervosa and Bulimia*. New York: Guildford Press.

Garner, D. M., Garfinkel, P. E., Stancer, H., and Moldofsky, H. (1976). Body image disturbances in anorexia nervosa and obesity. *Psychosomatic Medicine*, **38**, 327–336.

Garner, D. M., Olmsted, M. P., Polivy, J., and Garfinkel, P. E. (1984). Comparison between weight-pre-occupied women and anorexia nervosa. *Psychosomatic Medicine*, **46**, 255–266.

Gerstmann, J. (1958). Psychological and phenomenological aspects of disorders of the body image. *Journal of Nervous and Mental Diseases*, **126**, 499–512.

Glucksman, M. L., and Hirsch, J. (1969). The response of obese patients to weight reduction. *Psychosomatic Medicine*, **31**, 1–7.

Goodsitt, A. (1984). Self-psychology and the treatment of anorexia nervosa. In D. M. Garner and P. E. Garfinkel (eds). *Handbook of Psychotherapy for Anorexia Nervosa and Bulimia*. New York: Guilford Press.

Gottheil, E., Backup, C. E., and Cornelison, F. C., Jr (1969). Denial and self image confrontation in a case of anorexia nervosa. *Journal of Nervous Mental Diseases*, **148**, 238–250.

Green, R. S., and Rau, J. H. (1974). The treatment of compulsive eating disturbances with anti-convulsant medication. *American Journal of Psychiatry*, **13**, 428–432.

Halmi, K. A. (1974). Anorexia nervosa demographic and clinical features in 94 cases. *Psychosomatic Medicine*, **36**, 18–25.

Halmi, K. A. (1984). Behavioural management of anorexia nervosa. In D. M. Garner and P. E. Garfinkel (eds), *Handbook of Psychotherapy for Anorexia Nervosa and Bulimia*. New York: Guildford Press.

Halmi, K. A., Dekirmenjian, H., Davis, J. M., Casper, R., and Goldberg, S. C. (1978). Catecholamine metabolism in anorexia nervosa. *Archives of General Psychiatry*, **35**, 459–460.

Halmi K. A., Falk, J. R., and Schwartz, E. (1974). Binge-eating and vomiting: a survey of a college population. *Psychosomatic Medicine*, **11**, 697–706.

Hawkins, R. C., and Clement, P. F. (1980). Development and construct validation of a self-report measure of binge-eating tendencies. *Addictive Behaviour*, **5**, 219–226.

Head, H. (1920). *Studies in Neurology*, vol II. London: Oxford University Press.

Heunemann, R. L., Shapiro, L. R., Hampton, M. C., and Mitchell, B. W. (1966). A longitudinal study of gross body composition and body conformation and their association with food and activity in a teenage population. *American Journal of Clinical Nutrition*, **18**, 325–338.

Holland, A. J., Hall, A., Murray, R., Russell, G. F. M., and Crisp, A. H. (1984). Anorexia nervosa: a study of 34 twin pairs. *British Journal of Psychiatry*, **145**, 414–419.

Hsu, L. K. G. (1980). Outcome of Anorexia nervosa. *Archives of General Psychiatry*, **37**, 1041–1046.

Hudson, J. I., Pope, H. G., Jr, Jonas, J. M., Iurgelun-Todd, D. (1983). Family history study of anorexia nervosa and bulimia. *British Journal of Psychiatry*, **142**, 133–138.

Hurst, P. S., Lacey, J. H., and Crisp, A. H. (1977). Teeth, vomiting and diet: a study of the dental characteristics of seventeen anorexia nervosa patients. *Postgraduate Medical Journal*, **53**, 298–305.

Joint Committee Report (1984) (Royal College of Physicians/BNF). Food Intolerance and Food Aversion. *Journal of the Royal College of Physicians* (London), **18**(2), 3–41.

Kay, D., and Leigh, D. (1954). The natural history, treatment and prognosis of anorexia nervosa based on a study of 38 patients. *Journal of Mental Science*, **100**, 411–431.

Kendall, R. E., Hall, D. J., Hailey, A., and Babigian, H. M. (1973). The epidemiology of anorexia nervosa. *Psychological Medicine*, **3**, 200–203.

Kernberg, O. (1980). Foreword. In J. S. Sours (ed.), *Starging to Death in a Sea of Objects*. New York: Jason Aronson.

King, A. (1963). Primary and secondary anorexia nervosa syndromes. *British Journal of Psychiatry*, **109**, 470–479.

Kohut, H. (1972). Thoughts on narcissism and narcissistic rage. *Psychoanalytic Study*, **27**, 360–400.

Kolb, L. C. (1975). Disturbances of the body image. In S. Arieti (ed.), *American Handbook of Psychiatry*. New York: Basic Books.

Lacey, J. H. (1980). The bulimic syndrome. *Proceedings of 13th European Conference on Psychosomatic Research, Istanbul*.

Lacey, J. H. (1982a). Anorexia nervosa and a bearded female saint. *British Medical Journal*, **285**, 1816–1817.

Lacey, J. H. (1982b). The bulimic syndrome at normal body weight: reflections on pathogenesis and clinical features. *International Journal of Eating Disorders*, **11**, 59–66.

Lacey, J. H. (1983a). The patient's attitude to food. In M. H. Lessof (ed.), *Clinical Reactions to Food*. Chichester: John Wiley & Sons.

Lacey, J. H. (1983b). Bulimia nervosa, binge-eating and psychogenic vomiting: a controlled study and long-term outcome. *British Medical Journal*, **286**, 1609–1613.

Lacey, J. H. (1984a). Moderation of bulimia. *Journal of Psychosomatic Research*, **285**, 355–360.

Lacey, J. H. (1984b). Time-limited individual and group treatment for bulimia. In D. M. Garner and P. E. Garfinkel (eds), *Handbook of Psychotherapy for Anorexia Nervosa and Bulimia*. New York: Guildford Press.

Lacey, J. H., Chadbund, C., Crisp, A. H., and Whitehead, J. (1978). Variations in energy intake of adolescent girls. *Journal of Human Nutrition*, **32**, 419–426.

Lacey, J. H., Coker, S., and Birtchnell, S. A. (1986). *International Journal of Eating Disorders* (in press).

Lacey, J. H., Coker, S., Birtchnell, S. A. (1986). Bulimia: Factors associated with aetology & maintenance. *Inter. J. of Eating Disorders*.

Lacey, J. H., and Crisp, A. H. (1980). Hunger, food intake and weight: the impact of Clomipramine on a re-feeding anorexia nervosa population. *Postgraduate Medical Journal*, **56**, 79–85.

Lacey, J. H., Crisp, A. H., Kalucy, R. S., Hartman, M., and Glen, C. N. (1975). Weight gain and the sleeping electroencephalogram. *British Medical Journal*, **4**, 556–558.

Lacey, J. H., and Gibson, E. (1985). Does laxative abuse control body weight. A comparative study of purging and vomiting bulimics. *Human Nutrition: Applied Nutrition*, 39a, 36–42.

Lacey, J. H., Hart, G., Crisp, A. H., and Kirkwood, B. A. (1979). Weight and skeletal maturation—a study of radiological and chronological age in an anorexia nervosa population. *Postgraduate Medical Journal*, **55**, 381–385.

Mahler, M., Pine, F., and Bergman, A. (1975). *The Psychological Birth of the Human Infant*. New York: Basic Books.

Minuchin, S., Rosman, B. L., and Baker, L. (1978). *Psychosomatic Families. Anorexia Nervosa in Context*. Cambridge, Mass: Harvard University Press.

Nemiah, J. C. (1950). Anorexia nervosa—a clinical psychiatric study. *Medicine*, **29**, 225–230.

Nylander, I. (1971). The feeling of being fat and dieting in a school population: epidemiologic interview investigation. *Acta Socio-Medica Scandinavica*, **3**, 17–26.

Orbach, S. (1984). Accepting the symptom: a feminist psychoanalytic treatment of anorexia nervosa. In D. M. Garner and P. E. Garfinkel (eds), *Handbook of Psychotherapy for Anorexia Nervosa and Bulimia*. New York: Guildford Press.

Palazolli, M. P. (1974). *Anorexia Nervosa*. London: Chaucer.

Peirloot, R. A., and Houben, M. E. (1978). Estimation of body dimensions in anorexia nervosa. *Psychological Medicine*, **8**, 317–324.

Reitman, E. E., and Cleveland, S. E. (1964). Changes in body image following a sensory deprivation in schizophrenia and control groups. *Journal of Abnormal and Social Psychology*, **68**, 168–176.

Rosen, J. C., and Leitenburg, H. (1984). Exposure plus response prevention treatment for bulimia. In D. M. Garner and P. E. Garfinkel, *Handbook of Psychotherapy for Anorexia Nervosa and Bulimia*. New York: Guildford Press.

Russell, G. F. M. (1970). Anorexia nervosa—its identity as an illness and its treatment. In J. M. Price (ed.), *Modern Trends in Psychological Medicine*, vol. 2. London: Butterworths, pp. 131–164.

Russell, G. F. M. (1973). The Management of anorexia nervosa. In T. A. Constable (ed.), *Proceedings of the Symposium on Anorexia Nervosa and Obesity*. Edinburgh: Royal College of Physicians, p. 43.

Russell, G. F. M. (1977). The present status of anorexia nervosa. *Psychological Medicine*, **7**, 363–367.

Russell, G. F. M. (1979). Bulimia nervosa—an ominous variation of anorexia nervosa. *British Journal of Medical Psychology*, **52**, 187–190.

Russell, G. F. M. (1985). *Proceedings—European Conference Psychosomatic Medicine*, London.

Russell, G. F. M., and Beardwood, C. J. (1968). The feeding disorders with particular reference to anorexia nervosa and its associated gonadotrophin changes. In R. P. Michael (ed.), *Endocrinology and Human Behaviour*. London: Oxford University Press, pp. 310–329.

Sabine, E. J., Yonace, A., and Farrington, A. J. (1983). Bulimia nervosa: a placebo controlled double blind therapeutic trial of Mianserin. *British Journal of Clinical Pharmacology*, **15**, 195S–202S.

Schilder, P. (1935). *Image and Appearance of the Human Body*. London: Kegan, Paul, Trench, Trubner & Co.

Schontz, F. C. (1974). Body image and its disorders. *International Journal of Psychiatry in Medicine*, **5**, 150–161.

Secord, P. F., and Jourard, S. M. (1953). The appraisal of body cathexis and the self. *Journal of Consulting Psychology*, **17**, 343–347.

Selvini Palazolli, M. (1974). *Self-starvation*. London: Chaucer.

Shuttleworth, F. C. (1937). Sexual maturation and the physical growth of girls age 6 to 19. *Monograph Society for the Research of Child Development 2–No. 5*, Serial No. 12.

Slade, P. D. (1977). Awareness of body dimensions during pregnancy. An analogue study. *Psychological Medicine*, **7**, 245–252.

Slade, P. D., and Russell, G. F. M. (1973). Experimental investigations of bodily perception in anorexia nervosa and obesity. *Psychotherapy and Psychosomatics*, **22**, 359–363.

Strober, M., Goldenburg, I., Green, J., and Saxon, J. (1979). Body image disturbance in anorexia nervosa during the acute and recuperative phase. *Psychological Medicine*, **9**, 695–701.

Strober, M., and Yager, J. (1984). A developmental perspective on the treatment of anorexia nervosa in adolescents. In D. M. Garner and P. E. Garfinkel (eds), *Handbook of Psychotherapy for Anorexia Nervosa and Bulimia*. New York: Guildford Press.

Tanner, J. M. (1962). *Growth at Adolescence*. Oxford: Blackwell.

Theander, G. K. (1970). Anorexia nervosa. *Acta Psychiatrica Scandinavica* (Supp), 1–194.

Thoma, H. (1967). *Anorexia Nervosa* (G. Brydone, trans.). New York: International University Press.

Thompson, M., and Schwartz, D. (1982). Life and adjustment of women with anorexia nervosa and anorectic like behaviour. *International Journal of Eating Disorders*, **1**, 47–60.

Touyz, S. W., Beaumont, P. J. V., Cowie, I., and Collins, J. K. (1984). Do patients with bulimia distort their body image? *Proceedings of the 15th European Conference on Psychosomatic Research, London*.

Walsh, B. T. (1982). Endocrine disturbance in anorexia nervosa and depression. *Psychosomatic Medicine*, **44**, 85–91.

Wermuth, B. M., Davis, K., and Hollister, L. E. (1977). Phenytoin treatment of the binge-eating syndrome. *American Journal of Psychiatry*, **134**, 1249–1252.

Wingate, B. A., and Christie, M. J. (1978). Ego strength and body image in anorexia nervosa. *Journal of Psychosomatic Research*, **22**, 201–204.

Winokur, A., March, V., and Mendels, J. (1980). Primary affective disorder in relatives of patients with anorexia nervosa. *American Journal of Psychiatry*, **137**, 695–698.

Wooley, S. C., and Wooley, O. W. (1984). Intensive outpatient and residential treatment for bulimia. In D. M. Garner and P. E. Garfinkel (eds), *Handbook of Psychotherapy for Anorexia Nervosa and Bulimia*. New York: Guildford Press.

SECTION 4

Cardiovascular Disorder

The Psychosomatic Approach: Contemporary Practice
of Whole-person Care
Edited by M. J. Christie and P. G. Mellett
© 1986 John Wiley & Sons Ltd

8

PSYCHOPHYSIOLOGICAL CONTRIBUTIONS TO THE UNDERSTANDING AND MANAGEMENT OF ESSENTIAL HYPERTENSION

ANDREW STEPTOE

Department of Psychology, St George's Hospital Medical School, University of London, UK

INTRODUCTION

Physicians sympathetic to the psychosomatic approach have long suspected that essential hypertension has important behavioural and emotional components. Until recently, however, the role of psychological factors has not been acknowledged by the medical profession at large. This position may now be changing. In 1980 the World Health Organization listed its recommendations for hypertension research. These included studies of 'life styles and of attitudes designed to modify them', and of 'the socioeconomic and psychosocial factors' related to hypertension. The problems of the detection, aetiology and treatment of essential hypertension are of such staggering magnitude that professional demarcation and rivalries must be submerged in the common effort to alleviate suffering.

The present chapter outlines psychophysiological contributions to this enterprise. Psychophysiological techniques have yet to be incorporated into clinical practice. They do, however, provide valuable insights on individual differences in aetiology and response to treatment. It is argued in this chapter that an understanding of the psychosomatic components in hypertensive aetiology is vital to the development of behavioural interventions. The emphasis is therefore on foundational research in this area, rather than on specific treatment strategies. The first section outlines the origins and course of essential hypertension, highlighting the role of the autonomic nervous system. In the second section, it is argued that experimental investigations of cardiovascular and neuroendocrine responses to behavioural challenge are central to our understanding of the problem. It is possible that they may aid the prediction of future hypertension, before the disorder has developed to a clinically significant extent. Finally, the implications for the management of essential hypertension are discussed, together with behavioural aspects of treatment.

AUTONOMIC FACTORS AND THE MECHANISMS OF ESSENTIAL HYPERTENSION

It is generally accepted that essential hypertension is multifactorial in origin, and that the pathogenic mechanisms differ not only between cases, but over the course of the disorder. The complications and risks associated with elevated blood pressure (including ischaemic heart disease and cerebrovascular stroke) increase in a broadly linear fashion with pressure level, rather than depending on an absolute criterion defining the presence or absence of hypertension. Analysis of the problem is, however, complicated by the fact that blood pressure is not a stable parameter, but fluctuates continuously over the day and night. The blood pressure criteria for diagnosis of essential hypertension are somewhat arbitrary, and do not rely on the presence of pathognomonic features. It is currently recommended that mild hypertension should be defined by a diastolic pressure of 90 mmHg (Phase V) persisting on three separate occasions spread over a period of 4 weeks (World Health Organization/International Society of Hypertension, 1983).

Blood pressure tends to increase with age in industrialized societies, although not in traditional rural cultures (see Marmot, 1981). Genetic factors account for much of the variation between individuals, although environmental factors are also significant (Pickering, 1968). Salt intake and body weight may have an important influence on blood pressure in adult life. However, the most reliable predictor of essential hypertension is blood pressure level early in life. A number of prospective studies indicate that people with higher than average systolic or diastolic pressure in youth are more likely to develop essential hypertension (Julius and Schork, 1978). Similarly, a state of mild hypertension greatly increases the risk of progression towards seriously elevated blood pressure. This implies that the search for aetiological factors must begin long before the emergence of any diagnosed problem or clinical manifestations.

The role of the sympathetic nervous system

Discussion of the psychosomatic components of essential hypertension must be prefaced by a brief analysis of pathophysiology and the involvement of the autonomic nervous system in the early stages of the disorder. Elevations in blood pressure arise from an imbalance between cardiac output and total peripheral resistance. In cases of sustained, well-established hypertension, vascular resistance is increased in most tissues of the body. The position in mild hypertension is somewhat different. Haemodynamic studies indicate that in a substantial proportion of mild hypertensives, increased cardiac output accounts for the elevated blood pressure (Lund-Johanson, 1980). As the disease progresses, there may be a switch from cardiac to vascular mechanisms, although not all cases of mild hypertension progress to higher blood pressure. Disturbances in autonomic regulation may account for the elevated cardiac output seen in mild hypertension, with augmented activity in the sympathetic branch (Julius and Esler, 1975; Birkenhäger and Schalekamp, 1976).

Perhaps the commonest method of assessing sympathetic nervous tone in essential hypertension is to monitor plasma catecholamine levels. The results must be treated with caution, since there are instances in which alterations in sympathetic activity are not paralleled by changes in catecholamine concentration (Folkow et al., 1983). Many studies in this area have been methodologically weak, failing to take into account age and familiarity with blood sampling. Some investigators have argued that adrenaline, rather than the more commonly assessed noradrenaline, is the critical variable (Brown and MacQuin, 1981). Despite these reservations, a number of studies have shown plasma noradrenaline to be elevated in hypertensives, in comparison with age-matched controls. An extensive review of some 78 comparisons was published by Goldstein in 1983. This indicated that studies of young mild hypertensives are relatively consistent in reporting elevated plasma noradrenaline. In contrast, less reliable effects are observed in older people with hypertension of long duration. It is interesting that elevated catecholamine levels may be present before the appearance of clinically significant blood pressure rises. One study followed up 13–23-year-olds with casual blood pressures above 140/90 mmHg (Hofman et al., 1979). The plasma noradrenaline level in those whose pressure remained high after 2–4 years was significantly greater than in age-matched controls, and was closely correlated with systolic pressure. More recently, Bellin and coworkers (1983) compared young men with blood pressures at the 'low' (average 111/67.3) and 'high' (133/83) ends of the normal blood pressure distribution. In all but one of the nine carefully matched pairs, free adrenaline and noradrenaline sulphate were significantly higher in the 'high' blood pressure subject.

These data suggest that autonomic disturbances may be particularly important in early or mild hypertension, and possibly in the prehypertensive stage. Once increases in blood pressure have emerged, other factors may become more salient and help sustain elevated pressure. Amongst these influences are structural changes in the vasculature (the 'structural autoregulation' described by Folkow and Neil, 1971), renin-angiotensin disturbances, and resetting of the baroreceptor reflex. Renal control of volume and salt balance also comes into play. Guyton (1978) has argued that sustained alterations in haemodynamics ultimately depend on the regulation of fluid volume by the kidney, and plasma volume expansion may itself lead to increased vascular resistance and higher blood pressure. This autoregulation theory is not, however, accepted by some authorities (Korner, 1982).

The implications of these arguments are crucial to psychosomatic hypotheses. If behavioural and emotional factors influence hypertension through autonomic and neuroendocrine pathways, their effects will be most apparent at early stages of the disorder. Investigations should thus be focused upon young or mild hypertensives, or upon people thought to be at risk of developing the disorder. Conversely, any effects found in sustained hypertension may well be secondary to the disease state, rather than aetiologically significant.

Behavioural influences on cardiovascular regulation

There is a substantial literature concerning behavioural factors in the aetiology of hypertension (see Steptoe, 1981, for a detailed discussion). A number of behavioural models have been devised in animals in order to assess the development of 'neurogenic' hypertension (Greenwood, Marshall and Allott, 1984). Sustained elevations in blood pressure may emerge in response to approach/avoidance conflict or aggressive social exchanges in rats and mice, unsignalled shock avoidance in rhesus monkeys, and other manipulations. The possibility has been raised that even animal models of non-neurogenic hypertension (such as renal artery stenosis and salt-sensitive genetic strains) may also function in part through sympathetic nervous disturbances (Mancia et al., 1984).

A clearer picture of the way in which behavioural stimulation influences the haemodynamic mechanisms regulating arterial pressure is beginning to emerge. Short-term maintenance of a stable haemodynamic state is achieved in part by the baroreceptor reflex. The baroreceptors are stretch-sensitive, and are found in the walls of the carotid sinuses and aortic arch. They are integrated centrally into a feedback loop, so that an increase in arterial pressure is compensated for by bradycardia and a reduction in vasoconstrictor tone. The sensitivity of the reflex (reflecting the extent to which changes in pressure induce compensatory cardiac responses) is reduced in essential hypertension (Gribbin et al., 1971). Stephenson, Smith and Scher (1981) have demonstrated that baroreceptor reflex sensitivity is also modified by behavioural stimulation in normotensive baboons. Reflex sensitivity was greatest in sleep, intermediate during lever pressing for reward, and lowest in a shock avoidance task. Somewhat similar patterns have been observed in humans, although the data are not entirely consistent (Forsman and Lindblad, 1983). Conway et al. (1983) tested reflex sensitivity during sleep, reading and mental arithmetic performance. As in the baboon studies, the reflex was most sensitive during sleep, but was inhibited by mental arithmetic. These studies suggest that acute behavioural challenges may mimic the effects of hypertension on haemodynamic regulatory processes. The inhibition of the reflex implies that pressure responses to behavioural stimuli may continue unchecked by compensatory cardiac and vascular adjustments. The way in which these processes may contribute to the disease can best be understood through studies in which physiological responses to behavioural stressors are delineated in detail. Such investigations suggest that people may be at risk of developing essential hypertension only when engaging in specific types of interaction with the environment.

PSYCHOPHYSIOLOGICAL REACTIVITY IN ESSENTIAL HYPERTENSION

Blood pressure varies enormously as people go about their everyday lives. Early investigations with portable sphygmomanometers showed that systolic and diastolic pressures fluctuated by as much as 50–60 per cent during a normal day, and this effect was confirmed with ambulatory intra-arterial pressure monitoring (Bevan, Honour and Stott, 1969). Many of these variations are related to the behavioural state of the organism: sleep, exercise, eating and resting (during sleep, for example, pressures fall by more than 25 per cent). The extent to which they reflect the psychological environment is not at all clear. One well-known phenomenon that may arise from a psychological conditioning process is the 'clinic' effect. Blood pressures recorded in the clinic by medical staff are frequently higher than those measured elsewhere. Laughlin, Sherrard and Fisher (1980) reported that clinic readings from 60 hypertensives averaged 149.4/96.1, compared with 138.1/91.4 for pressures recorded at home. The effect is unlikely to result from patients misreading or falsely recording their own pressures, since similar patterns have been observed with directly measured intra-arterial pressure (Floras et al., 1981). The physical posture and other circumstances surrounding measurement in the clinic and at home are similar; it is probable, therefore, that the psychological significance of the occasion is responsible. It is relevant to note that when patients are at ease and familiar with the clinical setting, home–clinic differences in pressure tend to disappear (Welin, Svardsudd and Tibblin, 1982).

Such effects are interesting. They cannot, however, be used for the refined analysis of psychological influences. Fortunately, laboratory studies of reactivity patterns are beginning to show important differences between hypertensives and normotensives that may have implications for aetiology.

Hypertensives and normotensives in the laboratory

The psychophysiological approach to hypertension is based on the notion that acute cardiovascular and neuroendocrine reactions in the laboratory mimic the processes operating over a longer time-span in the clinical development of the disorder. The theory underlying such experiments is based on the stress-diathesis formulation of disease, in which a disorder is envisaged as arising out of an interaction between psychosocial stimulation and a 'vulnerable' biological system. Some people may be biologically predisposed to develop hypertension, while others may be constitutionally robust, or prone to gastrointestinal or other somatic responses (Steptoe, 1984). One prediction emanating from this formulation is that essential hypertensives will show exaggerated reactions to psychological stressors in blood pressure and related cardiovascular and neuroendocrine parameters. A corollary is that hyperreactivity will be confined to relevant cardiovascular parameters, rather than being a manifestation of general autonomic lability. 'Hyperreactivity' is used here simply to denote heightened responsiveness, and not in the technical sense of metabolically or haemodynamically inappropriate responses.

The simple notion that hypertensives react with greater haemodynamic disturbances than normotensives when confronted with psychological stressors of any type cannot be sustained. A number of careful studies have failed to show heightened blood pressure reactivity from hypertensives exposed to a variety of conditions, including personal interviews, intellectually demanding tasks, isometrics and the cold pressor (see Steptoe, Melville and Ross, 1984, for a review). Even when hypertensive groups do show hyperreactivity, this may be apparent only in absolute but not proportional or percentage terms. In these circumstances, the hypertensive reactions cannot be considered disproportionate.

These data should not be taken to undermine psychophysiological hypotheses; rather, they permit more precise hypotheses to be generated. Three considerations seem to be particularly relevant. The first is that the magnitude of pressor response is not the only critical variable; the pattern of haemodynamic adjustment and the duration of responses following the termination of the stressor are also important. In the classic studies by Brod and his colleagues (1959), marked differences between hypertensives and normotensives in vasomotor responses in muscle and renal beds were observed during taxing mental arithmetic. The duration of reactions was also prolonged in hypertensives (Brod, 1960). Similarly, Hollenberg, Williams and Adams (1981) showed that performance of a cognitive task produced greater decreases in renal blood flow among hypertensives than normotensives, even though arterial pressure responses did not differ. Changes in plasma renin activity were observed as well. Baumann and his associates (1973) found that plasma noradrenaline was still elevated some 2 hours after a stress test in hypertensives, while normotensives adapted rapidly. A decrease in venous compliance has also been discovered in response to emotional stress (Bahlmann, Brod and Cachovan, 1982).

The second important parameter is the stage of hypertension at which patients are tested. The arguments outlined earlier indicate that autonomic disturbances are more likely to be observed in mild or moderate hypertension. Although some investigators have reported greater reactions in severe hypertension (Schulte and Neus, 1979), many have shown more striking effects in mild cases (Nestel, 1969; Jern, 1982). Recently, Eliasson, Hjemdahl and Kahan (1983) compared established hypertensives (tonic pressure above 160/95) with borderline hypertensives and normotensives during performance of a complex colour-word interference task. The largest diastolic pressure responses were observed in the borderline group, while both hypertensive groups showed increases in plasma adrenaline.

The most significant factor governing variations in response pattern is the type of task or psychological stressor imposed. When the range of studies is considered, those which have involved challenging tasks in which the subject is required to make some difficult active response, are more likely to have shown differences between hypertensives and normotensives. For example, consistent effects have been observed with a serial mental arithmetic task, performed during exposure to a distracting sound-track played at 90 dB (Eiff, 1981). Complex visual puzzles, and a task involving the sorting of steel balls by size in the presence of disturbing noise, have also distinguished the responses of normotensives from hypertensives (Nestel, 1969; Lorimer *et al.*, 1971). On the other hand, conditions that are passively stressful or aversive, but do not require effortful behavioural responses, do not tend to elicit differences. The most striking example is the cold pressor test, which provokes substantial increases in blood pressure and heart rate. Voudoukis (1978) showed that hypertensives and normotensives did not differ in the magnitude of their blood pressure responses to the test (see also Eliasson, Hjemdahl and Kahan, 1983; Drummond, 1983). The haemodynamic response patterns in active and passive stress conditions are quite different (Schulte and Neus, 1983). Similarly, when tasks such as mental arithmetic are presented in a mild and unchallenging fashion (with no overt monitoring of performance), differences between hypertensives and normotensives disappear (Fredrikson *et al.*, 1982).

A recent study in our laboratory tested the notion that hypertensives will only display cardiovascular hyperreactivity when performing tasks involving active behavioural responses (Steptoe, Melville and Ross, 1984). Mild hypertensive and normotensive factory workers were administered two active coping tasks (a Stroop colour-word interference task and a video game), and one passive stressor (an anxiety-provoking film). The video game was not a 'stressor' in the conventional sense, since it was pleasurable rather than aversive. Nevertheless, it shared the property of requiring alert decision making and responding with the Stroop task. The results of this comparison are illustrated in Table 8.1. Hypertensives produced significantly greater systolic and diastolic blood pressure (BP) responses to the Stroop and video tasks than normotensives. The two groups were not, however, distinguished on watching the film. The absence of differences in the film condition was not due to the small size of reactions, since the range of reactions between individuals was similar for all three task conditions. Rather, the reactions to the film were inconsistent and unrelated to clinical status.

The precise nature of the behavioural challenge that may be relevant to essential hypertension will be examined in the next section. Before this, some further problems require consideration. One is the prediction that physiological hyperreactivity in essential hypertension is restricted to the cardiovascular system. If hypertensives do not show specific, but rather general heightening of autonomic lability, the relevance of the studies outlined in this section may be undermined; for it would imply that reaction patterns are products of general autonomic disturbance with no specific implications for essential hypertension. Although data concerning this issue

TABLE 8.1   Cardiovascular reactions to three experimental stressors in mild hypertensives ($N = 12$) and age-matched normotensives ($N = 12$). Mean ($\pm$ sd) change from baseline. From Steptoe, Melville and Ross (1984)

	Baseline	Stroop $\triangle$	Film $\triangle$	Video game $\triangle$
Systolic BP				
Hypertensive	146.7 (*12.9*)	22.4 (*11.3*)	7.17 (*7.9*)	22.6 (*11.0*)
Normotensive	131.3 (*12.8*)	17.8 (*7.7*)	5.01 (*4.9*)	12.0 (*6.4*)
Diastolic BP				
Hypertensive	95.3 (*11.9*)	9.82 (*5.7*)	3.74 (*4.8*)	16.6 (*6.1*)
Normotensive	83.8 (*7.7*)	6.96 (*5.5*)	3.07 (*2.7*)	6.52 (*6.0*)
Heart rate				
Hypertensive	74.9 (*12.3*)	10.6 (*6.0*)	0.49 (*3.2*)	5.81 (*5.3*)
Normotensive	77.5 (*14.8*)	11.4 (*5.8*)	0.28 (*3.1*)	3.29 (*5.3*)

are somewhat limited at present, they do suggest that hyperreactivity is confined to cardiovascular parameters. In the study detailed in Table 8.1, hypertensives and normotensives differed in their reactions only on cardiovascular variables (systolic and diastolic pressure, and pulse transit time). No significant differences were seen in electrodermal or respiratory measures. This conclusion is supported by another recent experiment comparing established and borderline hypertensives with normotensives (Fredrikson and Engel, 1985).

A second important issue concerning the reactivity of essential hypertensives in the laboratory is the relation between these effects and fluctuations of pressure in ordinary life. In order to show that these response patterns are not merely isolated laboratory phenomena, it must be demonstrated that similar effects are manifest under natural conditions. Empirical studies are sparse at present, in part because the methodology of unobtrusive ambulatory cardiovascular monitoring is not well established. It is difficult to distinguish variations in ambulatory records that are related to behaviour or psychological state from those emerging as a result of physical activity. A clearer picture is likely to emerge in the next few years as techniques are refined. Another problem that needs further investigation is psychophysiological adaptation, and the reduction in the magnitude of responses on repeated testing (Manuck and Garland, 1980). In order to test prospectively the strength of psychophysiological hypotheses, it is necessary to develop tests in which reactions are maintained across occasions.

Cardiovascular reactions and behavioural demands

The evidence presented in the last section suggests that hypertensives display exaggerated cardiovascular responses when exposed to appropriate behavioural challenges. However, not all experimental conditions produce reactions that are related to clinical status. What types of behavioural demand are, then, most relevant to the progression of essential hypertension?

Our understanding of this issue has been greatly advanced by the work of Obrist and his colleagues (1978). Using pharmacological blockade and multichannel cardiovascular monitoring of normotensive subjects, it was shown that, in comparison with passive stressors (the cold pressor and a pornographic film), a shock avoidance reaction time task provoked much greater modifications in systolic pressure, heart rate and indices of cardiac contractility. This reaction pattern was blunted by β-blockade with propranolol, confirming the involvement of cardiac sympathetic pathways. In further studies, it was found that this pattern of cardiovascular adjustment accompanied active or effortful coping behaviour, elicited under conditions when alert behavioural responses with uncertain outcome were required in order to master the environment.

The concept of active behavioural coping is similar to the notion of behavioural control. It is well established that psychophysiological responses differ according to the degree of control or lack of control over the environment that is available (Henry and Stephens, 1977). For many conditions, lack of control and helplessness in the face of environmental stress appear damaging. However, sympathetically mediated cardiovascular and catecholamine reactions may be enhanced when control over the environment is available (Frankenhaeuser, Lundberg and Forsman, 1980; Steptoe, 1983). None the less, active coping behaviour differs from control over aversive stimulation in two important respects. First, heightened cardiovascular responses are only seen when control over the environment is difficult to achieve. This has been demonstrated in a number of studies (Obrist *et al.*, 1978; Manuck *et al.*, 1978). For instance, Pittner, Houston and Spiridigliozzi (1983) compared different degrees of task-dependent control over electric shocks. Subjects in the condition in which shock administration was always contingent on task performance produced greater systolic and diastolic pressure responses than those without control, or subjects with only intermittent control, over shock.

The second important characteristic of active coping behaviour is that it may be elicited not only under aversive or stressful conditions, but also when rewards and positive stimulation are available (as in the video game tested in Table 8.1). Light and Obrist (1983) studied a reaction time task for monetary bonuses, in which the performance criterion was manipulated. As in the aversive situation, performing to a difficult criterion led to the most persistent blood pressure, pulse transit time and cardiac preejection period responses.

Some difficulties concerning the notion of active behavioural coping have yet to be resolved. Few studies have actually investigated the dimension of behavioural coping in a parametric fashion. The mechanisms underlying the cardiovascular reactions are also uncertain. It appears that stimulation of the cardiac sympathetic pathways is important, since blood pressure reactions tend to be accompanied not only by increased catecholamine output, but by changes in cardiac contractility (McCubbin *et al.*, 1983). Obrist (1981) has argued that the neural stimulation is out of proportion with the metabolic demands placed on the heart, leading to an excessively high cardiac output that may initiate the progression towards essential hypertension. Cardiac responses have been recorded in the absence of parallel changes in oxygen consumption during active behavioural coping in some studies (Turner, Carroll and Courtenay, 1983; Langer *et al.*, in press). None the less, more research is required before this 'overperfusion' hypothesis can be accepted.

Interactions with personality factors

Psychosomatic research into hypertension was dominated for many years by personality theories (see Weiner, 1979); however, the contribution of this work to our understanding of the disorder is limited. Not only have results been inconsistent, but the research has suffered from serious methodological flaws, with the use of unstandardized ratings of subjective measures, and non-blind assessment of subjects. Moreover, hypertensives identified through the conventional medical channels must be studied cautiously, as they may not be typical of the hypertensive population at large (Steptoe, Melville and Ross, 1982). There have been attempts to explore more precisely the manner in which hypertensives deal with their emotional experiences; notable in this respect is the work of Harburg, Blakelock and Roeper (1979) on individual styles of coping with authority in high-stress urban environments. Interactions within the families of hypertensives are beginning to be studied using sociopsychological techniques (Baer *et al.*, 1983).

The possibility that personality factors are important in modulating cardiovascular reactions to behavioural challenge should also be considered. Certainly, Type A behaviour has an important influence on reactivity, and there is also some evidence that hostility measures are relevant. Rüddel and coworkers (1983) found that pressor responses to mental arithmetic were positively related to aggression, but negatively to anxiety and dominance. Holroyd and Gorkin (1983) reported that students who habitually inhibited anger showed higher heart rate responses than others during assertive role-play (similar patterns were not, however, seen in blood pressure). Our own studies have also provided limited support for an interactive process (Steptoe, Melville and Ross, 1984). Participants in the experiment outlined in Table 8.1 completed the Hostility and Direction of Hostility Questionnaire, and total scores were positively correlated with both systolic and diastolic reactions to the two tasks that demanded active coping. This effect was independent of resting pressure level, and seems to have been unrelated to clinical status. Nevertheless, it appears that the personality factors studied thus far make only a minor contribution to the variance in cardiovascular reactivity. The effects of Type A behaviour are more marked, but this characteristic is best seen as a behaviour pattern rather than a personality factor (see Chapter 9).

The prediction of future hypertension

Laboratory studies fall into a relatively consistent pattern in showing that hypertensive patients are especially sensitive to tasks involving active behavioural coping with the environment. In order to maintain that these reactions are of aetiological significance, a vital link in the chain of reasoning must be forged. The fact that hypertensives display aberrant reactions may be an effect rather than a cause, since haemodynamic regulation is (by definition) disturbed. A longitudinal approach is required to establish that hyperreactivity is antecedent and predictive. This strategy has already been used to show that exaggerated blood pressure responses to physical exercise in normotensives are predictive of future pressure elevations (Dlin *et al.*, 1983), but prospective data on responses to behavioural challenges are not yet available. Meanwhile, an alternative paradigm has proved useful: the investigation of individuals who are at high risk of hypertension, but who have not yet developed the disorder. Given the involvement of genetic factors, the problem lends itself to a familial approach.

More than a dozen studies have been published, comparing the cardiovascular or neuroendocrine responses of people with and without a parental history of hypertension (see Steptoe, 1984, for a review). The investigations show a good deal of variation in the thoroughness with which hypertensive history has been collected and confirmed. Nevertheless, experiments using demanding behavioural or cognitive tasks have generally produced greater cardiovascular reactions from people with a positive parental history. Differences have been seen in response to concept formation tests, assertive role-play and other tasks. As an illustration, the results of a study monitoring reactions during mental arithmetic performance are detailed in Table 8.2 (Schulte, Neus and Rüddel, 1981). In contrast to these data, no differences between groups with and without a hypertensive family history have been recorded in studies using only mildly challenging tasks or passive stressors such as the cold pressor test (Ohlsson and Henningsen, 1982).

TABLE 8.2   Cardiovascular reactions to experimental stress in men (mean age 34) with (+, $N = 13$) and without (−, $N = 33$) a family history of hypertension. Mean (± *sd*). From Schulte, Neus and Rüddel (1981)

	Baseline	Stress reaction (Change from baseline)
Systolic history BP	117.0 (*8.9*) 117.6 (*8.7*)	+22.8 (*16.1*) +15.6 (*7.4*)
Diastolic BP	72.2 (*6.2*) 73.0 (*6.1*)	+12.8 (*5.8*) +9.2 (*4.3*)
Heart rate	70.3 (*7.4*) 67.9 (*9.3*)	+21.0 (*13.2*) +16.6 (*7.7*)

An important development in recent years has been the extension of this laboratory strategy to the analysis of neuroendocrine and renal components of the hypertensive process. Light and her colleagues (1983) assessed urinary flow and sodium concentration following a 1-hour competitive task period in male students with and without borderline hypertension or a parental history. Subjects were further divided into low and high heart rate reactors on the basis of their cardiac responses to the task. Despite the small size of the resulting groups, differences in sodium excretion were observed. In particular, the high-risk subjects who displayed high cardiac reactivity showed significant reductions in sodium excretion (averaging 27 per cent) and in fluid excretion (mean 35 per cent), compared with the other subgroups. This effect was probably due to β-adrenergically mediated influences on glomerular filtration rather than the release of vasopressin or aldosterone. It indicates that behavioural stress affects not only systemic haemodynamics, but the vascular beds and renal processes that may be especially important in hypertension. Other investigations have shown that young adults with a family history of hypertension manifest excessive cardiovascular responses to a change in dietary sodium. The results presented by Light et al. (1983) suggest that psychophysiological investigations may allow us to predict risk with greater refinement. It was only those individuals who possessed both a genetic risk and high heart rate reactivity who showed disturbed sodium metabolism.

Studies on risk groups raise the possibility that psychophysiological procedures may be used to identify potential hypertensives before the disease process has reached clinical proportions. Normotensives who display heightened pressor reactions to tasks involving active behavioural coping may be at high risk. Accentuated heart rate reactions may represent an even earlier stage of the process. If future hypertension could be identified at an early stage, it might be possible to introduce preventive strategies so as to avoid the progression to established disease.

BEHAVIOURAL INTERVENTIONS IN ESSENTIAL HYPERTENSION

The growth of behavioural medicine over the last few years has stimulated vigorous attempts to treat many medical conditions with psychological techniques. Essential hypertension has been a focus of great interest, and a substantial literature has accumulated (reviewed by Johnston, 1984). Procedures employing relaxation techniques, either alone or accompanied by electrodermal biofeedback, have been relatively successful (Patel and North, 1975; Agras, Southam and Taylor, 1983). Blood pressure biofeedback has proved less effective, probably because the feedback methods have been cumbersome and obtrusive. Relaxation has been found superior to non-specific attentional control conditions in several studies, and long-term responses enduring for more than 12 months have been reported. It has been used in large-scale studies of hypertensives, who were not specially selected on the basis of their interest in voluntary control, to good effect (Patel,

Marmot and Terry, 1981). Moreover, the modifications in blood pressure persist throughout the day. Southam and coworkers (1982) compared a relaxation programme with a control condition in 42 hypertensive outpatients (mean initial pressures 143/98 and 140/93 respectively). The reductions in blood pressure measured in the clinic were greater in the relaxation condition (averaging 11.7/12.6 against 3.6/2.5), and were maintained when pressures were recorded with a semi-automated ambulatory monitoring device, operating while patients went about their everyday work. The differences in diastolic pressure persisted at 15 months follow-up (Agras, Southam and Taylor, 1983).

These effects notwithstanding, the arguments presented in this chapter suggest that conventionally administered relaxation or biofeedback may not be optimal. If the hypotheses relating cardiovascular reactivity to hypertension are correct, then training might be focused more appropriately on the modification of autonomically mediated reactivity. A number of the more successful behavioural interventions have placed relaxation and other skills within the context of stress management. The technique developed by Chandra Patel involves both meditative relaxation (accompanied by electrodermal biofeedback), and extensions of these skills to stressful situations in everyday life (Patel and North, 1975; Patel, Marmot and Terry, 1981). Patel (1975) showed that after training, blood pressure responses to a step-up test and the cold pressor were attenuated, and recovery to baseline was more rapid.

Direct attempts to use anxiety management or cognitive stress management techniques have also been reported (Jorgensen, Houston and Zurawski, 1981; Wadden, 1984). Crowther (1983) found that stress management training (involving relaxation, rehearsal of stress-provoking situations, modelling and homework assignments) equalled relaxation training in its effect on the blood pressures of established, medicated hypertensives. Kallinke, Kulick and Heim (1982) developed a cognitive stress management procedure based on identifying those situations in ordinary life in which large blood pressure reactions occur. They reported substantial pressure reductions persisting at 12 months after treatment.

Other methods of helping people to control stress-induced cardiovascular reactions have been explored in the laboratory, but not yet evaluated in clinical trials (English and Baker, 1983). Promising results are emerging with biofeedback of heart rate or pulse transit time (Benthem and Glaros, 1982; McCanne, 1983). Steptoe and Ross (1982) compared pulse transit time, biofeedback and relaxation in the modification of cardiovascular reactions to active coping tasks in normotensives. While reductions in reactivity were observed in both conditions (in comparison with no-treatment controls), the biofeedback procedure apparently promoted more rapid modifications. These methods have been extended to the management of unmedicated mild hypertensives in a pilot study with beneficial results, but a full clinical evaluation has not yet proved feasible. Perhaps an even more valuable service would be provided by testing these behavioural techniques prospectively in people at risk of hypertension, in order to determine whether the progression towards established disease might be halted at an early stage.

An approach to the management of hypertensives

Behavioural techniques will only make a substantial impact on general care if they are integrated within conventional medical services. Although direct comparisons of behavioural and pharmacological methods have some value, the two approaches should not be seen as mutually exclusive (Goldstein *et al.*, 1982). Rather, behavioural methods might have a place as supplementary therapeutic modes, to be employed in early or mild hypertension, or when pharmacological procedures prove inappropriate.

The difficulties surrounding drug treatment for essential hypertension should not be underestimated. The problem of adherence of patients to medication regimens has been the object of intense investigation (Haynes, Mattson and Engebretson, 1980). Hypertensives have exceptionally poor compliance rates; one in three hypertensives fails to take medication regularly, and when the proportion dropping out of treatment is considered, only 20–30 per cent of known hypertensives have their blood pressure under adequate control. It may seem paradoxical, but increasing the involvement of patients in their treatment (rather than making treatment easier and less obtrusive) seems the best approach to difficulties with adherence. Adverse reactions to antihypertensive medications may also lead patients to seek alternatives. However, perhaps the strongest reason for considering behavioural approaches is that the decision to treat hypertension is being based on ever lower criteria; while diastolic pressures of 100–110 mmHg went untreated 20 years ago, interventions are now starting when pressure rises above 90 mmHg. Large proportions of the population are confronted with the prospect of long-term medication, commencing in early middle age, and continuing for 30–40 years. Faced with such a possibility, the health care system must develop a range of methods for helping patients.

The process through which psychological techniques might be incorporated into clinical practice has not yet been articulated precisely. It may, however, be helpful to consider a stepped care approach, based on the level of presenting blood pressure. Behavioural techniques do not operate rapidly, nor are their overall effects as great as drugs. If a patient presents with serious hypertension, the aim must be to bring the elevated pressure under rapid control pharmacologically. But when blood pressures are mildly elevated, behavioural techniques can be explored as a first step in suitable patients. Apart from the psychophysiological procedures already outlined, interventions based on salt restriction and weight reduction may also be considered. Salt restriction, in particular, is relatively easy to administer (it does not require extended training with voluntary control techniques), and has produced favourable effects in mild hypertension (Beard *et al.*, 1982).

Weight reduction may be valuable in overweight hypertensives, and has been applied in general practice settings with promising results (Basler *et al.*, 1982).

Psychophysiological methods will have their greatest impact when more evidence on individual differences in response has accumulated. This will permit greater accuracy in the identification of those patients most likely to respond. An understanding of the psychosomatic components of aetiology is central to this programme. New ways of incorporating psychological methods into treatment involve the constant interplay between aetiological and intervention research. The manner in which both aspects are developing in the analysis of essential hypertension perhaps provides a paradigm for the psychophysiological approach to psychosomatic medicine.

ACKNOWLEDGEMENT

The author is grateful to Dr Donald Melville of the Department of Psychiatry, University of Southampton, for his comments on an earlier draft of this chapter.

REFERENCES

Agras, W. S., Southam, M. A., and Taylor, C. B. (1983). Long-term persistence of relaxation-induced blood pressure lowering during the working day. *Journal of Consulting and Clinical Psychology*, **51**, 792–794.

Baer, P. E., Reed, J., Bartlett, P. C., Vincent, J. P., Williams, B. J., and Bourianoff, G. G. (1983). Studies of gaze during induced conflict in families with a hypertensive father. *Psychosomatic Medicine*, **45**, 233–242.

Bahlmann, J., Brod, J., and Cachovan, M. (1982). Stress-induced changes of the venous circulation. *Contributions to Nephrology*, **30**, 43–48.

Basler, H.-D., Brinkmeier, U., Buser, K., Haehn, K.-D., and Mölders-Kober, R. (1982). Psychological group treatment of essential hypertension in general practice. *British Journal of Clinical Psychology*, **21**, 295–302.

Baumann, R., Ziprian, H., Godicke, W., Hartrodt, W., Naumann, E., and Lauter, J. (1973). The influence of acute psychic stress situations on biochemical and vegetative parameters of essential hypertensives at the early stages of the disease. *Psychotherapy and Psychosomatics*, **22**, 131–140.

Beard, C., Cooke, H., Gray, W., and Barge, R. (1982). Randomised controlled trial of a no-added-sodium diet for mild hypertension. *Lancet*, **ii**, 455–458.

Bellin, L. J., Vandongen, R., Arkwright, P. D., and Davidson, L. (1983). Adrenal and sympathetic nervous activity in subjects with 'low' and 'high' normal blood pressure. *Journal of Hypertension*, **1**, 13–18.

Benthem, J. A., and Glaros, A. G. (1982). Self control of stress-induced cardiovascular change using transit time feedback. *Psychophysiology*, **19**, 502–505.

Bevan, A. T., Honour, J., and Stott, F. H. (1969). Direct arterial pressure recording in unrestricted man. *Clinical Science*, **36**, 329–344.

Birkenhäger, W. H., and Schalekamp, M. A. D. H. (1976). *Control Mechanisms in Essential Hypertension*. Amsterdam: Elsevier.

Brod, J. (1960). Essential hypertension. Haemodynamic observations with a bearing on its pathogenesis. *Lancet*, **ii**, 773–778.

Brod, J., Fencl, V., Hejl, Z., and Jirka, J. (1959). Circulatory changes underlying blood pressure elevation during acute emotional stress in normotensive and hypertensive subjects. *Clinical Science*, **18**, 269–279.

Brown, M. J., and MacQuin, I. (1981). Is adrenaline the cause of essential hypertension? *Lancet*, **ii**, 1079–1081.

Conway, J., Boon, N., Vann Jones, J., and Sleight, P. (1983). Involvement of the baroreceptor reflexes in the changes in blood pressure with sleep and mental arousal. *Hypertension*, **5**, 746–748.

Crowther, J. H. (1983). Stress management training and relaxation imagery in the treatment of essential hypertension. *Journal of Behavioral Medicine*, **6**, 169–188.

Dlin, R. A., Hanne, N., Silverberg, D. S., and Bar-Or, O. (1983). Follow-up of normotensive men with exaggerated blood pressure response to exercise. *American Heart Journal*, **106**, 316–320.

Drummond, P. D. (1983). Cardiovascular reactivity in mild hypertension. *Journal of Psychosomatic Research*, **27**, 291–297.

Eiff, A. W. von (1981). Neurogenic hypertension. *Das Medizinische Prisma*, **4**, 1–22.

Eliasson, K., Hjemdahl, P., and Kahan, T. (1983). Circulatory and sympatho-adrenal responses to stress in borderline and established hypertension. *Journal of Hypertension*, **1**, 131–139.

English, E. H., and Baker, T. B. (1983). Relaxation training and cardiovascular response to experimental stressors. *Health Psychology*, **2**, 239–259.

Floras, J. S., Jones, J. V., Hassan, M. O., Osikowska, B., Sever, P. S., and Sleight, P. (1981). Cuff and ambulatory blood pressure in subjects with essential hypertension. *Lancet*, **ii**, 107–109.

Folkow, B., Di Bona, G. F., Hjemdahl, P., Torén, P. H., and Wallin, B. G. (1983). Measurements of plasma norepinephrine concentrations in human primary hypertension. *Hypertension*, **5**, 399–403.

Folkow, B., and Neil, E. (1971). *Circulation*. Oxford: Oxford University Press.

Forsman, L., and Lindblad, L. E. (1983). Effects of mental stress on baroreceptor-mediated changes in blood pressure and heart rate, and on plasma catecholamines and subjective responses in healthy men and women. *Psychosomatic Medicine*, **45**, 435–445.

Frankenhaeuser, M., Lundberg, U., and Forsman, L. (1980). Dissociation between sympathetic-adrenal and pituitary-adrenal responses to an achievement situation characterised by high uncontrollability; comparison between Type A and Type B males and females. *Biological Psychology*, **10**, 79–91.

Fredrikson, M., Dimberg, U., Frisk-Holmberg, M., and Ström, G. (1982). Haemodynamic and electrodermal correlates of psychogenic stimuli in hypertensive and normotensive subjects. *Biological Psychology*, **15**, 63–73.

Fredrikson, M., and Engel, B. T. (in press). Cardiovascular and electrodermal adjustments during a vigilance task in patients with borderline and established hypertension. *Journal of Psychosomatic Research*.

Goldstein, D. S. (1983). Plasma catecholamines and essential hypertension. An analytical review. *Hypertension*, **5**, 86–99.

Goldstein, I. B., Shapiro, D., Thananopavarn, C., and Sambhi, M. P. (1982). Comparison of drug and behavioral treatments of essential hypertension. *Health Psychology*, **1**, 7–26.

Greenwood, D. T., Marshall, P. W., and Allott, C. P. (1984). Animal models for the assessment of stress on arterial blood pressure. In R. E. Ballieux, J. F. Fielding and A. L'Abbate (eds), *Breakdown in Human Adaptation to 'Stress'*, vol. 2. The Hague: Martinus Nijhoff, pp. 1026–1035.

Gribbin, B., Pickering, T. G., Sleight, P., and Peto, R. (1971). Effect of age and high blood pressure on baroreflex sensitivity in man. *Circulation Research*, **29**, 424–431.

Guyton, A. C. (1978). Essential cardiovascular regulation—the control linkages between bodily needs and circulatory function. In C. J. Dickinson and J. Marks (eds), *Developments in Cardiovascular Medicine*. Lancaster: MTP, pp. 265–302.

Harburg, E., Blakelock, E. H., and Roeper, P. J. (1979). Resentful and reflective coping with arbitrary authority and blood pressure: Detroit. *Psychosomatic Medicine*, **41**, 189–202.

Haynes, R. B., Mattson, M. E., and Engebretson, T. O. (eds) (1980). *Patient Compliance to Prescribed Antihypertensive Medication Regimens*. Washington: NIH Publication, pp. 81–102.

Henry, J. P., and Stephens, P. M. (1977). *Stress, Health and the Social Environment*. New York: Springer-Verlag.

Hofman, A., Boomsma, F., Schalekamp, M. A. D. H., and Valkenburg, H. A. (1979). Raised blood pressure and plasma noradrenaline concentrations in teenagers and young adults selected from an open population. *British Medical Journal*, **I**, 1536–1538.

Hollenberg, N. K., Williams, G. H., and Adams, D. F. (1981). Essential hypertension: abnormal renal, vascular and endocrine responses to a mild psychological stimulus. *Hypertension*, **3**, 11–17.

Holroyd, K. A., and Gorkin, L. (1983). Young adults at risk for hypertension: effects of family history and anger management in determining responses to interpersonal conflict. *Journal of Psychosomatic Research*, **27**, 131–138.

Jern, S. (1982]. Psychological and haemodynamic factors in borderline hypertension. *Acta Medica Scandinavica*, Suppl., 662.

Johnston, D. W. (1984). Biofeedback, relaxation and related procedures in the treatment of psychophysiological disorders. In A. Steptoe and A. Mathews (eds), *Health Care and Human Behaviour*. London: Academic Press, pp. 267–300.

Jorgensen, R. S., Houston, B. K., and Zurawski, R. M. (1981). Anxiety management training in the treatment of essential hypertension. *Behaviour Research and Therapy*, **19**, 467–474.

Julius, S., and Esler, M. D. (1975). Autonomic nervous cardiovascular regulation in borderline hypertension. *American Journal of Cardiology*, **36**, 685–696.

Julius, S., and Schork, M. A. (1978). Predictors of hypertension. *Annals of the New York Academy of Science*, **304**, 38–52.

Kallinke, D., Kulick, B., and Heim, P. (1982). Behaviour analysis and treatment of essential hypertensives. *Journal of Psychosomatic Research*, **26**, 541–550.

Keane, T. M., Martin, J. E., Berler, E. S., Wooten, L. S., Fleece, L., and Williams, J. G. (1982). Are hypertensives less assertive? A controlled evaluation. *Journal of Consulting and Clinical Psychology*, **50**, 499–508.

Korner, P. I. (1982). Causal and Homeostatic factors in hypertension. *Clinical Science*, **63**, 5s–26s.

Langer, A. W., Stoney, C. M., McCubbin, J. A., Hutcheson, J. S., Charlton, J. D., and Obrist, P. A. (in press). Cardiopulmonary adjustments during exercise and an aversive reaction time task: effect of β-adrenoceptor blockade. *Psychophysiology*.

Laughlin, K. D., Sherrard, D. J., and Fisher, L. (1980). Comparison of clinic and home blood pressure levels in essential hypertension and variables associated with clinic–home differences. *Journal of Chronic Disease*, **33**, 197–206.

Light, K. C., Koepke, J. P., Obrist, P. A., and Willis, P. W. (1983). Psychological stress induces sodium and fluid retention in men at high risk for hypertension. *Science*, **220**, 429–431.

Light, K. C., and Obrist, P. A. (1983). Task difficulty, heart rate reactivity and cardiovascular responses to an appetitive reaction time task. *Psychophysiology*, **20**, 301–312.

Lorimer, A. R., MacFarlane, P. W., Provan, G., Duffy, T., and Lawrie, T. D. V. (1971). Blood pressure and catecholamine response to 'stress' in normotensive and hypertensive subjects. *Cardiovascular Research*, **5**, 169–173.

Lund-Johansen, P. (1980). State of the art review. Haemodynamics in essential hypertension. *Clinical Science*, **59**, 343s–354s.

McCanne, T. R. (1983). Changes in autonomic responding to stress after practice at controlling heart rate. *Biofeedback and Self-Regulation*, **8**, 9–24.

McCubbin, J. A. Richardson, J. E., Langer, A. W., Kizer, J. S., and Obrist, P. A. (1983). Sympathetic neuronal function and left ventricular performance during behavioral stress in humans: the relationship between plasma catecholamines and systolic time intervals. *Psychophysiology*, **20**, 102–110.

Mancia, G., Ramirez, A., Bertinieri, G., Parati, G., and Zanchetti, A. (1984). Results of experimental studies favouring the hypothesis of the influence of stress on the genesis of hypertension. In R. E. Ballieux, R. F. Fielding and A. L'Abbate (eds), *Breakdown in Human Adaptation to 'Stress'*, vol. 2. The Hague: Martinus Nijhoff, pp. 1013–1025.

Manuck, S. B., and Garland, F. N. (1980). Stability of individual differences in cardiovascular reactivity: a 13–month follow-up. *Physiology and Behavior*, **24**, 621–624.

Manuck, S. B., Harvey, A. H., Lechleiter, S. L., and Neal, K. S. (1978). Effects of coping on blood pressure responses to threat of aversive stimulation. *Psychophysiology*, **15**, 544–549.

Marmot, M. (1981). Culture and illness: epidemiological evidence. In M. J. Christie and P. G. Mellett (eds), *Foundations of Psychosomatics*. Chichester: John Wiley & Sons, pp. 323–340.

Nestel, P. J. (1969). Blood pressure and catecholamine excretion after mental stress in labile hypertension. *Lancet*, **i**, 692–694.

Obrist, P. A. (1981). *Cardiovascular Psychophysiology*. New York: Plenum Press.

Obrist, P. A., Gaebelein, C. T., Teller, E. S., Langer, A. W., Grignolo, A., Light, K. C., and McCubbin, J. A. (1978). The relationship among heart rate, carotid dp/dt and blood pressure in humans as a function of the type of stress. *Psychophysiology*, **15**, 102–115.

Ohlsson, O., and Henningsen, N. C. (1982). Blood pressure, cardiac output and systemic vascular resistance during stress, muscle work, cold pressor test and psychological stress. *Acta Medica Scandinavica*, **212**, 329–336.

Patel, C. (1975). Yoga and biofeedback in the management of 'stress' in hypertensive patients. *Clinical Science and Molecular Medicine*, **48**, 141–154.

Patel, C. H., Marmot, M. G., and Terry, D. J. (1981). Controlled trial of biofeedback-aided behavioural methods in reducing mild hypertension. *British Medical Journal*, **282**, 2005–2008.

Patel, C. H., and North, W. R. S. (1975). Randomised controlled trial of yoga and biofeedback in management of hypertension. *Lancet*, **ii**, 93–99.

Pickering, G. W. (1968). *High Blood Pressure*, 2nd edn. London: Churchill.

Pittner, M. S., Houston, B. K., and Spiridigliozzi, G. (1983). Control over stress, Type A behaviour pattern and response to stress. *Journal of Personality and Social Psychology*, **44**, 627–637.

Rüddel, H., Gogolin, E., Friedrich, G., Neus, H., and Schulte, W. (1983). Coronary-prone behavior and blood pressure reactivity in laboratory and life stress. In T. M. Dembroski, T. H. Schmidt and G. Blümchen (eds), *Biobehavioral Bases of Coronary Heart Disease*, Basle: Karger, pp. 185–196.

Schulte, W., and Neus, H. (1979). Bedeutung von Stressreaktion in der Hypertoniediagnostik. *Herz Kreislauf*, **11**, 541–546.

Schulte, W., and Neus, H. (1983). Haemodynamics during emotional stress in borderline and mild hypertension. *European Heart Journal*, **4**, 803–809.

Schulte, W., Neus, H., and Rüddel, H. (1981). Zum blutdruckverhalten unter emotionalen Stress bei Normotonikern mit familiärer Hypertonieanamnese. *Medizinische Welt*, **32**, 1135–1137.

Southam, M. A., Agras, W. S., Taylor, C. B., and Kraemer, H. C. (1982). Relaxation training: blood pressure lowering during the working day. *Archives of General Psychiatry*, **39**, 715–717.

Stephenson, R. B., Smith, O. A., and Scher, A. M. (1981). Baroreceptor regulation of heart rate in baboons during different behavioral states. *American Journal of Physiology*, **241**, R277–R285.

Steptoe, A. (1981). *Psychological Factors in Cardiovascular Disorders*. London: Academic Press.

Steptoe, A. (1983). Stress, helplessness and control: the implications of laboratory studies. *Journal of Psychosomatic Research*, **27**, 361–368.

Steptoe, A. (1984). Psychophysiological processes in disease. In A. Steptoe and A. Mathews (eds), *Health Care and Human Behaviour*. London and New York: Academic Press, pp. 77–112.

Steptoe, A., Melville, D., and Ross, A. (1982). Essential hypertension and psychological functioning: a study of factory workers. *British Journal of Clinical Psychology*, **21**, 303–311.

Steptoe, A., Melville, D., and Ross, A. (1984). Behavioral response demands, cardiovascular reactivity and essential hypertension. *Psychosomatic Medicine*, **45**, 33–48.

Steptoe, A., and Ross, A. (1982). Voluntary control of cardiovascular reactions to demanding tasks. *Biofeedback and Self-Regulation*, **7**, 149–166.

Turner, J. R., Carroll, D., and Courtenay, H. (1983). Cardiac and metabolic responses to 'space invaders': an instance of metabolically-exaggerated cardiac adjustment? *Psychophysiology*, **20**, 544–549.

Voudoukis, I. J. (1978). Cold pressor test and hypertension. *Angiology*, **29**, 429–439.

Wadden, T A. (1984). Relaxation therapy for essential hypertension: specific or nonspecific effects? *Journal of Psychosomatic Research*, **28**, 53–62.

Weiner, H. (1979). *The Psychobiology of Essential Hypertension*. New York: Elsevier.

Welin, L., Svardsudd, K., and Tibblin, G. (1982). Home blood pressure measurements—feasibility and results compared to office measurements. *Acta Medica Scandinavica*, **211**, 275–279.

World Health Organization (1980). *Hypertension related to health care—research priorities*. EURO Reports and Studies, 32. Copenhagen: World Health Organization.

World Health Organization/International Society of Hypertension (1983). Guidelines for the treatment of mild hypertension. *Lancet*, **i**, 457–458.

The Psychosomatic Approach: Contemporary Practice
  of Whole-person Care
Edited by M. J. Christie and P. G. Mellett
© 1986 John Wiley & Sons Ltd

9

ALTERATION OF TYPE A BEHAVIOUR IN CORONARY PATIENTS

LYNDA H. POWELL

*Department of Epidemiology and Public Health, School of Medicine,
Yale University, USA*

and

MEYER FRIEDMAN

*Harold Brunn Institute, Mount Zion Hospital and Medical Center,
San Francisco, USA*

INTRODUCTION

Individuals engaged in a *chronic* struggle against time and other people have been labelled Type A (Friedman and Rosenman, 1974) and observed to be at increased risk of coronary heart disease (CHD) (Rosenman *et al.*, 1975; Haynes, Feinleib and Kannel, 1980). In contrast Type B men and women described by Friedman and Ulmer (1985) 'do not find it necessary, as do Type A's, to engage in a ceaseless struggle. . .'. In reviewing the evidence for this association in epidemiological, laboratory, clinical and pathological studies, a review panel, sponsored by the National Heart, Lung and Blood Institute in the USA, concluded that Type A behaviour is associated with an increased risk of CHD and that this risk is independent of, but of the same order of magnitude as, that of other standard risk factors including elevated blood pressure, hypercholesterolaemia and smoking (Review Panel on Coronary-prone Behavior and Coronary Heart Disease, 1981). This same review panel reported that no proof had, at that time, been presented to indicate that Type A behaviour can be altered, or that, even if it could, such alteration would result in a significant reduction in CHD incidence.

Few Type A behaviour intervention studies have been conducted (Suinn, 1975; Suinn and Bloom, 1978; Roskies *et al.*, 1978; Roskies *et al.*, 1979; Levenkron *et al.*, 1983; Jenni and Wollersheim, 1979). Those which have been undertaken shared common features. They were short-term (ranging from 5 to 14 hours of treatment), small-scale (from 14 to 42 subjects) attempts to alter indices of physiological, cognitive and/or behavioural hyperreactivity. Since they did not evaluate treatment effectiveness using hard CHD endpoints, it is difficult to determine the clinical significance of observed behavioural change.

The Recurrent Coronary Prevention Project (RCPP) was a unique Type A intervention trial for two reasons. First, it was a large-scale, long-term lifestyle intervention. We studied approximately 1000 post-myocardial infarction subjects over 4.5 years to assess the extent to which a reduction in the intensity of a Type A style of life could be produced. Second, its success was evaluated using a hard CHD end-point. Because we chose to work with post-infarction patients who have a relatively high rate of recurrence, we had enough statistical power to evaluate treatment effectiveness using recurrent cardiac events in 4.5 years' time.

The purpose of this chapter is to describe briefly the major findings of the RCPP and to describe in more detail the clinical aspects of the treatment programme. We hope that by providing details about clinical technique and therapeutic process, we will encourage further research and clinical practice in Type A behaviour alteration to reduce CHD risk.

THE RECURRENT CORONARY PREVENTION PROJECT STUDY

In August 1977, funding was awarded to the RCPP from the National Heart, Lung and Blood Institute for the purpose of exploring the question of the feasibility of altering Type A behaviour as a vehicle for the secondary prevention of CHD. A sample of 1012 post-infarction patients in the San Francisco Bay area were recruited, of whom 862 were allocated at random into either an experimental section receiving a combined treatment of Type A behavioural counselling plus cardiac counselling ($N = 592$), or a control section receiving cardiologic counselling only ($N = 270$). The remaining 150 subjects were assembled to serve as a no-treatment, non-equivalent 'comparison' group (Friedman et al., 1982).

On average, RCPP subjects were 53 years old, male (91 per cent), non-smokers, with a serum cholesterol of 259.6 mg/dL, and a family history of CHD (55 per cent). One third were hypertensive and experienced angina symptoms, and a quarter had undergone coronary bypass surgery. *Over 95 per cent demonstrated some evidence of Type A behaviour as measured by a videotaped structured interview.*

A problem with earlier intervention studies has been the insensitivity of instruments to assess type and magnitude of change in Type A behaviour. Thus, in the RCPP we developed a sensitive and dependable measure of change in Type A behaviour. This measure, called the videotaped structured interview (VSI), permits the *clinical* observation of signs and symptoms indicative of the presence of Type A behaviour. The essential features of this diagnostic procedure have been described earlier (Friedman and Powell, 1984).

After the presence and severity of signs and symptoms of Type A behaviour were assessed by the VSI, questionnaires were filled in by each subject, the subject's spouse and a coworker (i.e. a 'monitor').

The questionnaires were repeated yearly for the duration of the study and the VSI was administered after 3 years, and at the final 4.5 year evaluation.

All four Type A measurements were found to be valid and reliable measures of change in Type A behaviour (Powell *et al.*, 1984).

The results after 3 years of treatment revealed that subjects allocated to the experimental treatment reduced the intensity of their Type A behaviour significantly more than subjects in either control or comparison conditions, as judged by all Type A measures. These differences in Type A behaviour were apparent even after 1 year. No differences between groups were observed on the risk factors of weight, blood pressure, exercise activity or smoking recidivism, or on cardiac treatments including β-blocker drug therapy or new bypass surgery. Both the experimental groups and the control group underwent a significant reduction in serum cholesterol, possibly due to the fact that reports of cholesterol levels were provided for both groups every 6 months for the duration of the study. Experimental subjects were found to have half the incidence of recurrent cardiac events (7.2 per cent) compared with control subjects (13.2 per cent). Figure 9.1 presents the

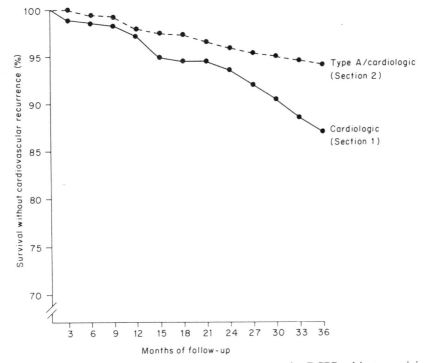

Figure 9.1 'Survival without cardiac recurrence' curves for RCPP subjects receiving Type A and cardiologic counselling and cardiologic counselling alone. The subjects receiving Type A and cardiologic counselling had a significantly greater survival rate (94 per cent) than subjects receiving cardiologic counselling alone (87 per cent) ($p < 0.01$)

(Reproduced with permission from Friedman et al. *(1984), Alteration of Type A behavior and reduction in cardiac recurrences in post-myocardial infarction patients,* American Heart Journal, **108**, *237.)*

'survival without cardiac recurrence' curves for these two treatment groups. Those subjects allocated at random to the experimental treatment had a significantly greater 'survival without recurrence' rate (94 per cent) after 3 years than subjects allocated to the control treatment (87 per cent) ($p <$ 0.01) (Friedman et al., 1984).

In summary, the RCPP treatment promoted a reduction in Type A behaviour after 1 year and a reduction in cardiac recurrences after 3 years, both of which were independent of reductions in any other CHD risk factor measured. These results suggest that alteration of Type A behaviour may be a viable target for the secondary prevention of CHD.

THE TYPE A CONCEPTUALIZATION

To understand how to treat Type A behaviour, one must first understand what it is. At its most basic level, Type A behaviour describes the overt behaviour and patterns of thought of individuals engaged in a chronic struggle against time and other people (Friedman et al., 1974). This struggle is said to have two major overt components—time urgency and hostility (Friedman et al., 1982). These emotional reactions are accompanied by arousal of the autonomic nervous system together with an excess discharge of the hormones noradrenaline (Friedman et al., 1960; Williams et al., 1982), adrenocorticotrophin (Friedman, Byers and Rosenman, 1972), cortisone (Williams et al., 1982) and testosterone (Zumoff et al., 1984), and a decreased plasma concentration of growth hormone (Friedman et al., 1971).

The psychological traits that motivate this overt struggle are not well understood (Matthews, 1982). Probably the most compelling hypothesis, based upon observation of Type A college students, is that Type As are motivated by an exaggerated need for control (Glass, 1977). Our observations of Type A coronary patients undergoing intensive long-term therapy have led us to hypothesize that a more basic psychological trait may lead to the

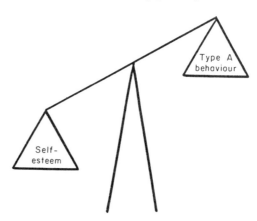

Figure 9.2   The relationship between self-esteem and Type A behaviour

exaggerated need for control observed in most Type A individuals. This trait is low self-esteem. To the extent that self-esteem is low, Type A manifestations are high. Figure 9.2 illustrates this relationship. When Type A behaviour is stripped of its glamour, it is synonymous with low self-esteem.

THE PROCESS OF TYPE A COUNSELLING

The aim of this treatment programme is to produce a sustained reduction in the emotional arousal associated with Type A behaviour. The desire to change is motivated by the observation of an association between Type A behaviour and low self-esteem. Once a philosophical commitment to change occurs, treatment becomes a process of exploring beliefs and attitudes associated with high self-esteem.

Treatment is organized around two major stages. The first emphasizes skills in identifying the Type A behaviour pattern. The patient is instructed in the behavioural, cognitive and physiological aspects of Type A behaviour. During the course of discussions about these more superficial characteristics, latent beliefs and attitudes emerge. These beliefs must be made consciously available to the patient. Seeing a possible connection between one's beliefs and attitudes and low self-esteem stimulates interest in alternatives. This signals the beginning of the second stage of treatment. Here the emphasis shifts to an exploration of the patterns of behaviour and thought associated with high self-esteem.

Treatment was developed following a behavioural model, where change is assumed to be a process of replacing undesired habits with more healthful alternatives (Bandura, 1977). However, the basic principles have been adapted by RCPP therapists to suit other theoretical orientations.

Identification of the Type A Behaviour Pattern

Each patient must become sensitive to his/her own personal Type A behaviour pattern so that he/she can replace these behaviours with healthier ones. What characterizes this phase more than others is the use of a variety of audiotaped and videotaped examples of behaviours of interest.

The first sessions are important because Type A patients tend to make snap judgements about the usefulness of counselling. If they judge it to be useless or irrelevant, the chance that they will drop out or attend sporadically is great. To keep early interest high, we discuss topics that are impersonal, easy to understand, easy to observe, and likely to result in an early sense of mastery. One topic well suited to this is Type A behaviour while driving a car. We might begin a discussion with this quote from a columnist for the *San Francisco Chronicle*.

Why do people drive the way they do? Not because they're in such a hurry to get from Point A to Point B, obviously. Even a dolt knows that in city driving, the tortoise beats the hare every time. No, it's rage, frustration and hate. You have seen their faces as you lumber along in your law-abiding fashion—the bulging eyes, the white-knuckled death grip on the wheel, the flipped finger. These are the choleric signs of the times and it's a wonder that more of these sad and highly dangerous people don't die of heart attacks while trying to pass a cable car on the wrong side. (Herb Caen, 23 September 1979)

We would then elicit from the group stories of their experiences on the road and instruct them systematically to observe Type A behaviour over the coming week.

Another good starting point is to provide lectures and discussion on the physiological implications of chronic Type A behaviour. This is of value for pragmatic Type A subjects who tend not to be very interested in psychology. Very simple lectures on the relationship between behaviour and physiology can provide subjects with an intellectual rationale for the need for Type A alteration. They can actually observe the relationship between behaviour and physiology by practising physical and cognitive relaxation using a biofeedback device.

It is wise to confine these early discussions to observation of Type A behaviour in *other people*, since defensiveness at this stage tends to be high. For example, we may ask subjects to read excerpts from Kearns's biography of President Lyndon B. Johnson (Kearns, 1976). Her description of this extreme Type A individual highlights the phenomenon of inadequate maternal love and the use of tremendous repression as a defence against it.

It was then that he began to talk more and more about his childhood. . . . A painful story of an unhappy boy trapped in a divided home, relentlessly tumbled among the impossible demands of an unyielding mother, love offered and then denied in seeming punishment; contempt for a father who had failed, admiration for a father who was a model for a Texas manhood; commanded to be what he could not be, forced to become what he was not. How different from his earlier public descriptions—the rags-to-riches rise from a happy childhood, guided by an adoring mother and the example of a manly, principled father. (p. 17)

To illustrate the connection between overt Type A manifestations and low self-esteem, we rely upon descriptions similar to that of Peter Sellers, written by David Niven at the time of Sellers' death, and reported in *The Times*.

Peter Sellers was expensive, difficult, ungracious, despotic; a man who would fire directors and turn scripts upside down; bitter, depressed, lonely, in a constant state of turmoil; vexatious, quarrelsome, distrustful, self-destructive, neurotic, and arrogant. . . . Even when he was right on top of the mountain, Peter's advisors were constantly trying to restrain him from leaping at the very next film presented to him because he was genuinely afraid that he would not be offered another. . . . Niven recalled that a few years ago he and Sellers attended a memorial service for Noël Coward. 'As we walked out into the sunshine, Peter said: "I do hope no one will ever arrange that sort of thing for me." I asked him why. He looked a little sad and said, "Because I don't think anyone will show up." ' (8 September 1980)

A description of track star, Mary Decker, makes the same point. Says a former coach, 'What you've got to understand about Mary is that she judges her worth as a person solely by what she accomplishes on the track. It's scary to contemplate, but the competitive nature that we so admire in this woman is actually a huge personality flaw' (*Newsweek*, 5 August 1983).

As an atmosphere of supportive trust evolves, patients begin to identify aspects of their own Type A behaviour. The therapist can promote progress in this direction by reinforcing and helping to clarify individual self-observations and asking other group members for reports of similar feelings.

Some of the techniques we have found to be useful in promoting self-observation of Type A behaviour include making it a habit to follow group discussions with the question, 'Have we observed any Type A behaviour just now in the group?' Table 9.1 presents a list of those Type A behaviours likely to occur during group discussions. It is helpful for a therapist to retain this list in memory to facilitate on-the-spot observations. We have also found it useful to ask group members to write their own obituaries and read them to the group. One therapist made a habit of instructing his group members to 'listen to others' angry comments. Instead of listening with regard to the *object*, listen to what it says about the person themselves. You think that every time you tear someone else down you build your own self-esteem. You will see, through careful observation, that in actuality you tear yourself down.'

Raising self-esteem

Perhaps the greatest challenge to the process of altering Type A behaviour is to help individuals improve their self-esteem. Self-esteem has two components. The first concerns feelings of control or efficacy (Glass, 1977; Bandura, 1982). While the Type A person can be depended upon to perform bravely, indeed superbly, in any present-day exigency, he still remains fearful of these contingencies. Admittedly, while the present myriad of technological changes do leave in their wake thousands of 'obsolescent individuals', the insecurity of most Type A persons stems not from the contemplation of these environmental changes but from a lack of confidence in their future capacity to deal with these changes. This lack of confidence manifests itself in pervasive insecurity. The second component of self-esteem is self-worth

TABLE 9.1   A selected list of common Type A behaviours, attitudes and environmental determinants likely to emerge in group members during group discussions

OVERT BEHAVIOUR	*Hostility* Relives anger about past incidents Hypersensitivity to criticism Argues tenaciously to win small points Annoyance at trivial errors of others Defensiveness/rationalizations Strong opinions Challenges validity of statements of others Short-tempered Edginess *Time urgency* Interrupts others Poor listener Polyphasic behaviour, thoughts Rapid, accelerated speech
ENVIRONMENTAL DETERMINANTS	*Trivial situations which are uncontrollable, unexpected* Driving a car Waiting for someone who is late Waiting in a queue Interpersonal challenge People who talk too much with nothing to say Incompetent telephone operators, shop assistants, waitresses/waiters, bank clerks Engaged tone on the phone *Ongoing struggle with family member, work associate*
SIGNS AND SYMPTOMS OF PHYSIOLOGICAL REACTIVITY	Tense body posture Fast, jerky movements Repetitive movements: knee jiggling, finger tapping Expiratory sighing Tic-like grimaces
COVERT ATTITUDES AND BELIEFS	Egocentrism: dominates conversations, interested in self only Suspiciousness: distrusts others' motives Competitive: belittles achievements of others, perceives other group members as adversaries Resentment: harbours feelings of ill-will Prejudice: stereotyped generalizations about groups Deterministic world view: believes self to be a pawn of the environment rather than active determiner of fate Short-term perspective: deals with problems from immediate consequences Belief in inherent injustice: acts like the policeman of the world

(Branden, 1969). This private estimate of one's worth is, in Type A persons, reliant upon criteria that are narrow and transitory. Thus, self-worth fluctuates with the nature of the feedback provided by these criteria (Price, 1982). To the extent that valued criteria provide negative or ambiguous feedback, self-worth remains low, but is raised upon receipt of positive feedback.

To enhance self-esteem by increasing feelings of control, we first ask patients to consider their notions about the meaning of being in control. One assumption is that being in control is synonymous with controlling the environment (i.e. other people, situations). The limitation of this assumption is that it promotes feelings of limited control when faced with an intransigent environment. An alternative assumption is that control has two components—control over others and control over one's *reaction* to others. This belief has more pragmatic value because, when the option of controlling others is not available (as is frequently the case), the option of controlling one's reaction to others always is available.

Type A patients can be helped to gain control by learning to exert control over others *and* their reaction to others. The latter skill is particularly important since it is used so infrequently. We will present descriptions of three skills that help Type A individuals to increase feelings of control. The first, assertiveness, helps patients to assume more control over others. The second and third, physical relaxation and cognitive restructuring, help patients to assume more control over their reactions to others.

Assertiveness is needed when it is necessary to stand up for one's rights, to make reasonable requests or demands of others, or to refuse to comply with unreasonable demands. Characteristically, Type As respond to such situations with anger and aggression and/or passive resentment and avoidance. Both reactions are counterproductive because they result in strong and/or sustained sympathetic nervous excitation and minimize chances for goal attainment.

Type A patients defend the use of anger and aggression because it 'gets results'. This assertion can be discussed from a variety of perspectives. Physiologically, anger and aggression are accompanied by sympathetic arousal which, over time, leads to the deterioration of the arterial walls. Patients spend '$5 worth of physiology on 5¢ worth of irritation'. Interpersonally, anger may not result in goal attainment. It may produce results in the form of short-term compliance, but these results tend not to endure. Intrapersonally, individuals who resort to anger and aggression are often perceived to be weak. This was observed by Ghandhi who stated, 'Violence of any kind, no matter how justified at times, is, in itself, demeaning'.

Assertive responses do not suffer from these limitations. To turn an aggressive response into an assertive one it is necessary to reduce the emotional intensity of the statement. In contrast to an explosive demand, assertiveness is a rational declaration. Folkman and Lazarus (1985) have observed that emotional reactivity is a function of time. The immediate response to a conflict tends to be emotional, but over time it is replaced by a more rational appraisal. To make this time trend work to Type A patients' advantage, they can be taught to 'buy time'; that is, to introduce some filler comments (e.g. 'Let me see if I understand what you are saying . . .'; 'Let me think about this for a day/hour/few minutes') that provide enough latency to permit a more rational appraisal and response.

The emotional intensity of a statement can also be reduced by accompanying it with psychomotor phenomena that are characteristic of assertive responses. This includes appropriate volume, degree of emphasis in speech, eye contact, and elaboration of the problems/feelings so that the request can be adequately understood. See Bower and Bower (1976) for an excellent discussion of these issues. Drilling in the psychomotor phenomena accompanying assertive responses is a central component of most assertiveness training programmes.

Group sessions can be used to practise assertive responses. It is sometimes effective to role-play patient's descriptions of conflict situations using assertive skills. Alternatively, hypothetical situations can be used to stimulate discussions about assertive skills. Table 9.2 presents two hypothetical situations in which assertive skills can be role-played in groups.

Physical relaxation is one way to change one's characteristic *response* to daily annoyances. It provides the cornerstone of most stress reduction programmes. Patients who learn to switch from sympathetic arousal to parasympathetic relaxation develop feelings of control based upon their ability voluntarily to bring about a relaxed state.

Physical relaxation is not easy for many Type A patients. They have become habituated to the feeling of arousal and preliminary attempts to switch from a familiar feeling of arousal to an unfamiliar feeling of relaxation

TABLE 9.2   Hypothetical situations with which to role-play assertive skills

---

SITUATION 1

Narrator: In this scene, picture yourself standing in a ticket queue outside a cinema. You've been in the queue now for at least 10 minutes, and it's getting pretty close to show time. You're still pretty far from the front of the queue, and you're starting to wonder whether there will be enough tickets left. There you are, waiting patiently, when two people walk up to someone in front of you, and begin talking. They're obviously all friends, and they're going to the same film. You look quickly at your watch and notice that the show starts in just 2 minutes. Just then, one of the newcomers says to his friend, 'Hey, the queue's a mile long—how about if we cut in here with you?'

Person in queue: 'Sure, come on, a couple more won't make any difference.'

Narrator: And as the two people squeeze into the queue between you and their friend, one of them looks at you and says: 'Excuse me. You don't mind if we cut in, do you?'

SITUATION 2

You have just come home from a hard day's work, dead tired. Your wife informs you that she has accepted an invitation for you both to visit some friends that evening. You are definitely not in the mood to go out.

Wife: 'I'm looking forward to seeing these folks tonight. Let's go right after we eat.'

are equated with loss of control and accompanied by fear or resistance. Practice at home between group sessions helps patients to become more familiar with the relaxed state. To sensitize patients to the difference between the relaxed and aroused states we use a biofeedback device called a 'biodot' (available from the Medical Device Corporation, 1555 Bellefontaine No. Drive, Indianapolis, Ind. 46202). This skin temperature responsive paper dot sticks to the skin and provides continual feedback about level of vasoconstriction.

Demonstration of skill at relaxation during the group sessions is not the final goal. More important, and much more difficult, is to learn to incorporate relaxation into one's daily schedule. Once a patient becomes sensitive to the feeling of relaxation, he can bring it about using any of a variety of relaxation strategies, including deep muscle relaxation at his desk, meditation, Valium, prayer, passing the time of day with a stranger, a brisk walk, or a humorous exchange with a coworker. Stroebel (1982) has written about 'quick relaxation', an accelerated relaxation strategy that takes less than a minute to perform in response to unexpected stressors.

Cognitive restructuring is another way to change one's *response* to daily annoyance. It is based upon the principle that an individual is an active construer of experience (Bandura, 1977). That is, an emotional reaction is produced by demands in the environment *and* one's perceptions of those demands. Since perceptions play a role in determining an emotional response, they can be used as a target for the purpose of altering that response. William James (1890) was among the first to make this observation. He stated, 'The greatest discovery of our generation is that human beings, by changing the inner attitudes of their minds, can change the outer aspects of their lives.'

An example can serve to illustrate how cognitive restructuring can be applied to daily life. A Type A individual arrives at a concert early to ensure that he gets a good seat. But just before it begins, his view is blocked by latecomers, who, because of the large crowds, have not been able to find seats. The Type A becomes irritated at the unfairness of the situation and the rudeness of the latecomers. He stews throughout the concert, or reduces his arousal by altering the situation (leaving the concert) or the behaviour of the latecomers (angrily insisting that they move).

The Type A's ability to achieve his goal (to enjoy the concert) is hampered by the environment (the latecomers blocking his way). If the environment is intransigent (the latecomers refuse to move), he is left with feelings of limited control and emotional arousal.

Alternatively, if his world view included a perceptual component, an additional target for intervention would be available. Cognitive restructuring in this situation might follow a chain of thought similar to this: 'Certainly this situation is unfair. But, in addition, it is a hook—just like the reckless driver on the highway, finding a parking space, the delay at the grocery store, and the parking ticket I received yesterday. They are unexpected, trivial annoyances that happen all of the time. I've waited a long time to enjoy this concert and I am not going to let myself get hooked today.' (Being 'hooked' is a useful concept: see p. 208.)

The point here is that the situation has a variety of descriptors. If the choice is made to perceive the situation as a hook, instead of a transgression, irritation is decreased and the perception of control (due to the enhanced ability to predict the event and the greater degree of self-control) is increased. Patients often report amusement at recognizing hooks. Amusement in the face of adversity may be a response to being freed from the tyranny of fixed perceptions. The following is a letter from one RCPP participant who was beginning to discover the freedom associated with identifying hooks.

A funny thing happened on the way home from the hospital yesterday.

At my garage I placed a dollar bill in my shirt pocket and two dimes and a nickel on the seat alongside so that I could pay my parking bill with ease. When I went to pay the attendant, I reached for the coins only to discover they had slithered away. God-da . . . HOOK! I felt just a wee bit smug when I handed the attendant an additional dollar bill and pocketed (smilingly) seventy-five cents change.

I had some important mail to register so a short while later I found myself in the post office. I placed my file folder on the work counter only to discover that someone had spilled water on the counter and my folder was now sopping wet. Son-of-a . . . HOOK! I took out a tissue, wiped off folder and counter, and felt pleased with myself. Two hooks in the first half-hour, both recognized and resisted, was a good score, I felt.

But there was more. When I finally got to the head of the post office line, the customer at the counter was passing the time of day with the checker, going on and on about everything from football to politics. By this time it was easy. That hook was so big and so reminiscent of our recent group that I was genuinely amused. But then I began feeling sorry for that poor fellow who obviously was not competent enough to keep tract of his mail. Thank goodness I didn't have to live inside of his skin.

The 'hook' analogy is only one way to restructure experience. Any of a variety of alternative perceptions can be developed. For example, we ask patients to practise a drill where they must 'substitute pity, understanding, and forgiveness for anger and irritation'. We also quote observations by famous people. For example, Winston Churchill might discuss the foregoing concert incident by observing, 'When a man cannot distinguish a great from a small event, he is of no use.'

Cognitive restructuring is not appropriate for all situations for this would encourage passivity in the face of clear personal, moral and ethical transgressions. The point here is not to replace but to expand one's response repertoire. By so doing, one expands choice and, at the same time, increases freedom.

The second component of self-esteem is self-worth—the private estimate of one's own worth. It is unalterable to the extent that the criteria used to judge it remain unaltered. In the case of the middle-aged Type A patient, these criteria tend to be narrow, transitory and conditional. The main criterion against which judgements of worth are made is individual achievement. Because achievement is tied to self-worth, the intensity of competition to achieve is great and the cost of failure is high.

In contrast, persons with high self-worth base their judgement on a variety of criteria. When setbacks occur in one area of life, other areas can be relied upon for affirmation. Thus, the perception of worth remains relatively stable. Persons with high self-worth often have a long-term perspective on life. This comes from having an overall sense of purpose such as commitment to the principles behind their work or to a spiritual dogma. Because this purpose is enduring, it helps them to weather the vicissitudes of daily life. Persons with high self-worth also have a broad perspective on life. They see themselves as one small unit within a larger context which provides them with a humility that counteracts egocentrism and the tendency to take themselves too seriously. Probably the most important quality associated with high self-worth is the ability to give and receive love (Powell, 1976). Intimate relationships can raise feelings of self-worth because they are unconditional. They provide support and perspective during shifts in transitory environmental circumstances, and provide a sense of being needed when that support and perspective is offered to another. The less personal version of this quality is a general attitude of altruism. Positive expectations of others generate good will and produce security in the knowledge that others wish one well.

We provide patients with examples of people with high self-worth. We then pursue a programme of general personality enhancement, which is based upon the idea that patients should be taught to expand the criteria upon which they base estimates of self-worth. They have many eggs, but they have put them into only one basket. The task in therapy is to help patients discover or rediscover their aesthetic sides. They are encouraged to bring hobbies to the group and are assigned readings from the classics. We announce aesthetic offerings in the community, and discuss quotes from famous people. Discovery of the importance of aesthetic appreciation is perhaps more delicate than it first appears. Type A patients tends to have a short-term perspective and to be highly pragmatic. When things are reduced to short-term cost-benefit ratios, the benefits of broadening interests are much less apparent than the costs of cutting down work time. Drilling (p. 207) can be particularly useful as a way to overcome resistance. Table 9.3 presents a list of drills and aphorisms that can promote this goal.

Another approach to increasing self-worth is aimed at self-acceptance. Friedman and Rosenman (1974) present a description of an individual who has achieved self-acceptance, despite past limitations and failures. 'When asked how a charming and relaxed doctor avoided Type A behaviour, he smiled and said, "A few years ago, I faced up to the truth that I always had

TABLE 9.3   Quotes, aphorisms and drills useful in the promotion of personality enhancement

---

QUOTES

Up to the age of thirty or beyond it, poetry of many kinds gave me great pleasure; and even as a schoolboy I took intense delight in Shakespeare, especially in the historical plays. I have also said that pictures formerly gave me considerable, and music very great delight. But now for many years I cannot endure to read a line of poetry. I have tried lately to read Shakespeare, and found it so intolerably dull that it nauseated me. I have also almost lost my taste for pictures or music. . . . My mind seems to have become a kind of machine for grinding general laws out of large collections of facts; but why this should have caused the atrophy of that part of the brain alone, on which the higher tastes depend, I cannot conceive. . . . If I had to live my life again, I would have made a rule to read some poetry and listen to some music at least once every week; for perhaps the parts of my brain now atrophied would thus have been kept alive through use. The loss of these tastes is a loss of happiness, and may possibly be injurious to the intellect, and more probably to the moral character, by enfeebling the emotional part of our nature.

Charles Darwin

It is only with the heart that one can see rightly. What is essential is invisible to the eye.

Saint-Exupéry

Culture is acquainting ourselves with the best that has ever been known and said in the world.

Matthew Arnold

To let friendship die away by negligence and silence is to voluntarily throw away one of the greatest comforts of this weary pilgrimage.

Samuel Johnson

The next thing most like living one's life over again seems to be a recollection of that life.

Benjamin Franklin

Human felicity is produced not so much by the great pieces of good fortune that seldom happen, as by the little advantages that occur every day.

Benjamin Franklin

APHORISMS

On the average, a man having no avocations on retiring receives only 13 Social Security cheques before he dies.

The chief ornament of a house is the friends who frequent it.

Success is getting what you want; happiness is wanting what you get.

DRILLS

Ask a member of the family about his/her day's activities
Verbalize your affection to spouse/children
Practise smiling and look at your face carefully to see if you detect hostility or tension

Recall memories for 10 minutes
Note carefully tree, plant, bush
Listen to music and do nothing else for 15 minutes
Visit an art gallery, aquarium or park
Invite someone to lunch and keep your friend talking about his/her interests, not yours
Take time off to plan a new hobby
Look at old photographs in albums. If they are in disorder, put them in order
Say 'good morning' or 'good afternoon' with a soft voice

---

been and always will be a second-rate physician. After I realized this, it was quite easy to begin to relax." ' (p. 175). At some point, most people quit life's struggle. The best resolution would be similar to the one achieved by this physician who quit by accepting what he is, despite his limitations, and enjoying what he has. However, others quit but deny any personal limitations, indulging instead in bitterness and resentment about what could have been. Still others quit by destroying themselves physically, financially, legally or socially (Friedman and Ulmer, 1985).

We would be greatly understating the complexity of the issue of self-acceptance if we proposed that therapy could produce a successful resolution to this important life passage. This is not to say it can't, but only to suggest that the issue is delicate and that preexisting beliefs are held tenaciously. At the very least, therapy can provide a setting wherein the issue can be examined.

We have had some success in discussing the issue of self-acceptance using William James's (1890) observation. He stated that self-esteem is the result of achievements divided by expectations, i.e.

$$\text{Self-esteem} = \frac{\text{Achievements}}{\text{Expectations}}$$

It follows that one way to raise self-esteem is to lower expectations (i.e. accept what is).

A different approach to this issue is to provide patients with the experience of unconditional positive regard from a respected other person. The therapist can serve this role, but it can come from other sources as well. For example, during the RCPP an unintended phenomenon occurred. Under the direction of a warm and caring field director, the office staff assumed a primary responsibility in giving care, concern and consideration to each of the 1000 participants. The field director herself assumed the critical role of mother surrogate to these patients, always making time to talk, provide information and offer support as needed. Programmes aimed at altering Type A behaviour often present rich and sophisticated content, but fail to mention the importance of caring. When treatment targets are delicate issues such as self-esteem and hostility, caring is the key. We believe that if this component is deemphasized, outcomes will suffer greatly.

DETERMINING WHEN TO END

Type A counselling is likely to result in diverse outcomes according to the individual patients. In the RCPP, considerable individual differences in response to treatment were observed. Some subjects failed to change at all. After 3 years of counselling, 34 per cent of those allocated at random to Type A counselling dropped out of treatment (Friedman *et al.*, 1984). Of those who remained in treatment, 20 per cent showed no evidence of change. Reasons for dropping out varied. Some felt that they had inadequate time; others felt that the principles taught in the programme were irrelevant. Those who were most likely to drop out were those who were most afflicted with Type A behaviour at entry (Powell, Thoresen and Friedman, 1985).

Other subjects changed but at different rates. After 3 years (44 sessions), 47 per cent provided some evidence of change; of these, 32 per cent markedly altered their Type A beliefs and attitudes (Friedman *et al.*, 1984). In a subsequent study of alteration of Type A behaviour in *healthy* middle-aged men, 42 per cent of the 62 subjects allocated at random to receive the same Type A counselling underwent marked change after only 20 sessions (Gill *et al.*, 1985).

Differences in the rate of change suggest that decisions about when to end counselling ideally should be made on a case-by-case basis. Patients who may not be ready to end counselling are those who appear fixed at rationalizing the importance or necessity of their own Type A behaviour, or those who appear fixed at talking and acting like Type Bs during group sessions, but continuing to think like Type As. Those who are ready to end counselling are those who present evidence of a shift in thought and in attitude.

Some patients may never get to this point, no matter how much counselling is provided. Therapists must acknowledge that this type of intransigent patient exists. We have observed therapists persist in the attempt to promote change in such patients long after it was clear that they were beyond help. This is particularly true if the therapist has considerable Type A behaviour him/herself.

Suiting length of treatment to individual needs may prove costly. Thus, if group treatment is to be offered, we suggest that a long-term approach be considered. Type A counselling is justifiable as a vehicle for reducing CHD only if it can produce *sustained* behaviour change. This is an ambitious undertaking. In the effort to keep costs at a minimum, short-term interventions may be attractive, but the possibility of erring on the side of producing short-lived change is great. Investigators and clinicians restricted to short-term treatment approaches may be well-advised to avoid conducting Type A interventions.

FOUR KEY ELEMENTS OF TYPE A COUNSELLING

Four elements of the RCPP Type A treatment programme deserve special mention because they were so useful in helping patients to reduce their Type A behaviour.

The small group

The RCPP treatment was conducted in groups of approximately 10 subjects although a group as small as 5 or as large as 15 does not appear to reduce treatment effectiveness. Small group counselling in the RCPP was done primarily for reasons of cost and convenience, but the group approach has actually provided much more. Other group members can be enlisted as aids in making observations about Type A—Type B behaviour. Messages that come from more than one source tend to be perceived as more credible. A small group can become a supportive laboratory for learning (Thoresen et al., 1982). Patients can learn about Type A behaviour vicariously by listening to others discuss problems and observing the similarities with their own struggles. The group can provide ongoing social support. Intimate interactions with other group members represent, for many, a relatively new experience. This experience can indirectly target hostility both in and out of the group.

These benefits associated with the small group are not automatic. An atmosphere of trust and support must be cultivated. When first assembled, group members tend to relate to each other as adversaries, in the same competitive and aggressive style that they relate to others in their lives. Patients triumphantly, rather than gently, point out Type A behaviours in other group members. When one patient begins to describe a personal situation, others may fail to listen and instead interrupt and give personal accounts of their own. The group leader can work towards the creation of an atmosphere of collaboration by giving consistent positive reinforcement for small steps in this direction. An attitude of trust, support and respect on the part of the therapist is likely to breed a similar attitude on the part of members. To remind members of their common goals and responsibilities, the RCPP groups ended each meeting with a benediction which began by stating, 'We are here because we all need more help than we can give ourselves. We need each other.'

Drills

In *The Principles of Psychology*, William James (1890) considered the topic of habit alteration. He stated, 'If we wish to conquer undersirable emotional tendencies in ourselves, we must assiduously, and in the first instance cold-bloodedly, go through the outward movements of those contrary dispositions which we prefer to cultivate.' We consider Type A behaviour to be a habit: alteration of this habit requires practising alternative habits until they are incorporated into the response repertoire. We call this habit replacement 'drilling'.

For use in the RCPP, we developed a Drill Book. This is a book composed of a series of daily drills designed to teach patients to act as a Type B individual acts. Drills filter through all phases of treatment. In the beginning,

TABLE 9.4   Typical group session format (time: 1½–2 hours)

---

(1) *Physiological information/relaxation practice (5–10 minutes)*
     Leader or participant led, using physical and cognitive methods (e.g. progressive
     muscle relaxation, deep breathing, autogenic suggestions, positive imagery)
(2) *Review of drills*
     Open Drill Book to appropriate page. Ask each participant if s/he has checked
     behaviours as they were practised. Inquire about problems, reactions and conse-
     quences of practising behaviour and reflections on weekly quotes.
(3) *Group discussion/problem solving*
     Focus on experience of participants. What is working well in reducing AIAI
     (anger, irritation, aggravation, impatience)? What are the current obstacles
     (spouse, coworker, personal ambitions?)
(4) *Assignments, reminders*
(5) *Closing benediction*

---

they are aimed at practising simple overt Type B behaviours. For example, patients may be asked to drive in the slow lane on the highway on purpose. To remind them to practise this drill, we ask them to stick a red dot on their steering wheel. To promote a relaxed driving attitude, we ask them to listen to classical music on the radio. As treatment progresses, drills shift to practising more subtle Type B attitudes. For example, to bring attention to the inflexibility of some of their opinions, we ask participants to practise saying 'Maybe I'm wrong' during conversation.

It takes considerable self-control to practise drilling regularly. The therapist can reinforce this habit by requiring that the Drill Book be brought to each session and restructuring group sessions so that time is always reserved for discussion of experiences while drilling. Table 9.4 presents a typical group session format.

Teaching tools

In the years since the RCPP began, a wealth of teaching tools have been collected. These tools are valuable because they illustrate complex ideas in simple ways. Some of the more successful tools are described here.

The acronym AIAI (anger, irritation, aggravation, impatience) is a synonym for Type A behaviour. It is useful because it strips Type A of any possible glamour due to its reputed association with 'getting ahead', and presents it in its most basic and unattractive form. The goal of Type A counselling is to switch from AIAI to ASAS (acceptance of the trivial errors of others, serenity, affection, self-esteem).

Being 'hooked' was a familiar metaphor among RCPP subjects. A trivial, unexpected situation which arouses irritation or impatience is a 'hook'. As 'fish', we begin our 'swim' for the day in clear water. Suddenly, a hook drops and we make the decision to bite (become irritated, annoyed) or to pass it by. Whatever one does with any particular hook is relatively unimportant because inevitably another one will follow and we must make another choice about whether or not to bite. As many as 30 hooks drop in front of us each day. Sometimes they come close together; at other times they are spaced widely apart. What is important is to consider the actual number of hooks we swallow as we go through each and every day and how many we have remaining in our mouths when we go to sleep.

Over the years, one of us (MF) has assembled a set of audiotapes and videotapes that convey rich information about a variety of topics associated with Type A behaviour. Audiotapes of various leaders of America, some of whom are Type A and others of whom are Type B, serve to stimulate discussions about the relationship between Type A behaviour and success. One powerful example is that of a famous Type B heart surgeon who, despite a very full schedule, appears calm, relaxed, confident, and in control. Audiotapes of widows describing the lifestyles of their dead husbands serve to teach patients about the personal and familial repercussions of Type A behaviour. Probably the most powerful audiotape we have is that of a severe Type A person describing his driving habits. It illustrates a variety of Type A psychomotor behaviours, and presents harried driving in both a humorous and a distasteful light. We have used this tape as 'punishment' whenever a group member reports having become irritated on the road. We put a tape recorder in front of the group member, play the tape through, and follow it up with a contrasting tape of soothing classical music.

RCPP therapists have devised a variety of graphic representations of complex concepts. Figure 9.2 is an example. We doubt if our success in modifying Type A behaviour would have been as clearcut if we had not had at our disposal chalk and a blackboard. Indeed, one crudely chalked diagram is more effective than quite a few paragraphs of didactic rhetoric!

As we have noted, a message is more convincing if it comes from more than one source. It is particularly convincing if it comes from a respected source. We have assembled a large number of quotes from famous people which are particularly relevant for Type A behaviour and can be used at appropriate times in the group meetings. Some of these quotes can be found throughout this chapter. A more complete list is in Friedman and Ulmer (1985).

Only a small portion of the richness of the Type A construct and Type B alternatives can possibly be transmitted during a group session. Thus, we assign books as outside reading to provide background. These books include Friedman *et al.* (1974), a detailed description of the nature of Type A behaviour and its association with CHD; Powell (1976), a profile of individuals with high self-esteem; Layden (1977), a discussion of ways to identify and alter hostility; Friedman and Ulmer (1985), a description of the RCPP treatment programme and ways to pursue a self-administered programme to alter Type A behaviour; Kearns (1976), a good example of the familial roots of Type A behaviour; and Stroebel (1982), presentation of a technique for incorporating quick physical and mental relaxation into one's daily life.

The Type A self-monitor

The formation of an internal 'Type A self-monitor' is one of the most important products of Type A counselling. The monitor is that part of the self which observes the *process* rather than the *content* of a reaction. That is, the monitor deemphasizes the *object* of the distress and observes instead the distress itself. For example, when impatiently waiting for a 'slow' lift, the self grumbles about 'archaic technology' in the building, but the monitor quietly makes the observation that the self is being impatient. *This perspective is valuable because it allows the patient to be inspected by a third-person entity who has first-person intimacy, including knowledge of the patient's foibles and rationalizations.*

When in a treatment group, the group leader and other group members serve the role of monitor. The self-monitor, in a sense, is the internalization of these messages so that they are present beyond the group context. Patients with effective monitors become aware of their Type A behaviour *at the time it occurs*. Some patients develop a restrospective monitor. These patients make a habit of reflecting back on 'Type A days' with regrets that they probably took things too seriously. Although this type of monitor is better than no monitor at all, it should be clearly labelled as a *step* in the process of development of a monitor. Retrospective monitors are ineffective in the long run; degeneration and rupture of atheroschlerotic plaques are not influenced by regrets.

THERAPIST CHARACTERISTICS

The role of the therapist is multidimensional (Thoresen *et al.*, 1982). He/she is a teacher, a facilitator, a respected professional and a friend. Therapists in the RCPP came from a variety of theoretical orientations, but they all had command of some basic principles. These included a basic understanding of the principles of behaviour change and self-management, the pathological and clinical aspects of CHD, and the spiritual wisdom and psychological insights found in the classics and humanities. Therapists in the RCPP were experienced clinicians. They looked and acted like mature, sensible, respectable and well-mannered adults. Thus, recommendations which at first glance appeared to be ridiculous were followed in good faith. They were effective communicators who often had the ability to inspire others. Recourse to psychological jargon spells disaster when counselling Type A patients because their difficulties in listening to simple English are multiplied when jargon is used. Successful therapists were sincere and believed in every statement they made. They had a good sense of humour and could laugh at their own foibles and silliness as easily as they could laugh at those of others.

The foregoing characteristics are desirable in a therapist treating Type A patients, but there are perhaps two that are keys to success. The first is a thorough understanding of the behavioural, cognitive and physiological aspects of the Type A behaviour pattern. The greatest advances in alteration of beliefs and attitudes come during the times when patients are struggling with their own personal problems. If the therapist is quick to recognize the underlying Type A attitude that creates and sustains the problem, he/she can help the patient to gain a similar perspective. This will attach great personal meaning to the principles of Type A alteration. Without a thorough understanding of the cognitive aspects of Type A behaviour, these unexpected opportunities may pass unnoticed.

One way to gain this in-depth understanding of Type A behaviour is to be actively involved in altering one's own Type A behaviour. It is possible that a coping Type A therapist may be more effective than a Type B therapist, as long as the current level at which the coping therapist is functioning is higher than that of the group members. This excerpt is from a letter sent to us by one of the RCPP therapists who, along with his group members, became actively involved in altering his own Type A behaviour.

Type A has become for me a living reality from the abstract concept of my first contact with you. It has become a metaphor which at times assumes transcendental proportion. In the process of getting to know my group members and helping them to transform their own Type A personalities, I have become profoundly influenced myself. My wife, the final arbiter of changes in my personality, has already given me an A minus (she grades easily) for changes in my approach. My former vesuvian temperament has mellowed considerably.

The second key therapist characteristic is the element of caring. Type A counselling is, at one level, helping individuals to gain or regain self-esteem. Perhaps more than anything else, a therapist can provide patients with that which many did not secure in childhood—unconditional love and affection from a respected parent figure.

FINAL COMMENTS

We are often asked about the feasibility of altering personality. We respond by stating that we do not attempt to alter personality: we alter behaviour. We examine the process associated with an emotional response, and teach patients alternatives at each stage of this process. We do not expect patients to make an abrupt shift from Type A to Type B behaviour. What we seek is insight into Type A behaviour and a philosophical commitment to attempt to reduce its frequency of occurrence in daily life.

This approach assumes that the problem is in the patient rather than in the demands of environment. This is admittedly one-sided. Certainly environments exist that would produce Type A behaviour in almost anyone. In these cases, the most pressing need may be to work for basic institutional or societal change. The programme described in this chapter would be complemented by a concurrent programme aimed at reducing stressors on the work site or in the community.

The true test of the effectiveness of this treatment is the extent to which patients have made a permanent lifestyle shift. The RCPP was a long-term intervention, lasting for 4.5 years. We do not know at this time the extent to which changes will be maintained after treatment is discontinued. Endurance of the effects of treatment is critical to CHD risk reduction. This may be the type of intervention that can be done once and result in a permanent philosophical shift. Alternatively, it may be a type of programme, like that of Alcoholics Anonymous, where the philosophy is kept alive through ongoing contact throughout one's life. We hope to answer this question in our future research.

Type A patients represent a tough clinical population. They are locked in a struggle, hoping that if they simply persist long enough they will win. The therapist presents a threat because he/she instils doubt—not only that the struggle may be futile but also that its process limits the quality and quantity of life. From this perspective, resistance directed towards the therapy and the therapist is to be expected. It is a challenge to break through this resistance and help patients gain the insight that what they are struggling for is not material or social rewards, but a more basic self-affirmation. Those who do gain this insight realize that basic self-affirmation not only eludes struggle but in fact is achieved by giving up the struggle. This realization constitutes the philosophical shift that is critical to the success of this treatment.

ACKNOWLEDGEMENTS

We gratefully acknowledge the contribution of the RCPP Type A therapists—Edward Bourg, PhD; Theodore Dixon, PhD; James J. Gill, MD; Gerald Piaget, PhD; Virginia A. Price, PhD; Donald L. Tasto, PhD; Leonti Thompson, MD; Carl E. Thoresen, PhD; Diane K. Ulmer, RN MS. Their skill, insight and knowledge led to the development of the treatment programme described in this chapter; their dedication led to its success.

The programme was aided by grants from the National Heart, Lung and Blood Institute (21427), the Bank of America, Standard Oil of California, the Kaiser Hospital Foundation and the Mary Potishman Lard Trust (Fort Worth, Texas).

REFERENCES

Bandura, A. (1977). *Social Learning Theory*. Englewood Cliffs, NJ: Prentice-Hall.
Bandura, A. (1982). Self-efficacy mechanism in human agency. *American Psychologist*, **37**, 122–147.
Bower, G., and Bower, S. (1976). *Asserting Yourself: A Practical Guide for Positive Change*. Boston: Addison-Wesley.
Branden, N. (1969). *The Psychology of Self-Esteem*. New York: Bantam.

Folkman, S., and Lazarus, R. S. (1985). If it changes it must be a process: a study of emotion and coping during three stages of a college examination. *Journal of Personality and Social Psychology*, **48**, 150–170.

Friedman, M., Byers, S. O., and Rosenman, R. H. (1972). Plasma ACTH and cortisol concentration of coronary-prone subjects. *Proceedings of the Society for Experimental Biology and Medicine*, **140**, 681–684.

Friedman, M., Byers, S. O., Rosenman, R. H., and Neuman, R. (1971). Coronary-prone individuals (Type A behavior pattern): growth hormone responses. *Journal of the American Medical Association*, **217**, 929–932.

Friedman, M., and Powell, L. H. (1984). The diagnosis and quantitative assessment of Type A behavior: introduction and description of the videotaped structured interview. *Integrative Psychiatry*, **2**, 123–136.

Friedman, M., and Rosenman, R. H. (1974). *Type A Behavior and Your Heart*. New York: Alfred A. Knopf.

Friedman, M., St George, S., Byers, S. O., and Rosenman, R. H. (1960). Excretion of catecholamines, 17-ketosteroids, 17-hydrocorticoids, and 5-hydroxyindole in men exhibiting a particular behavior pattern (A) associated with high incidence of clinical coronary artery disease. *Journal of Clinical Investigation*, **39**, 758–764.

Friedman, M., Thoresen, C. E., Gill, J. J., Powell, L. H., Ulmer, D., Thompson, L., Price, V. A., Rabin, D. D., Breall, W. S., Dixon, T., Levy, R., and Bourg, E. (1984). Alteration of Type A behavior and reduction in cardiac recurrences in post-myocardial infarction patients. *American Heart Journal*, **108**, 237–248.

Friedman, M., Thoresen, C. E., Gill, J. J., Ulmer, D., Thompson, L., Powell, L., Price, V., Elek, S. R., Rabin, D. D., Breall, W. S., Piaget, G., Dixon, T., Bourg, E., Levy, R. A., and Tasto, D. L. (1982). Feasibility of altering Type A behavior pattern after myocardial infarction. Recurrent Coronary Prevention Project study: methods, baseline results, and preliminary findings. *Circulation*, **66**, 83–92.

Friedman, M., and Ulmer, D. K. (1985). *Treating Type A Behavior and Your Heart*. New York: Alfred A. Knopf.

Gill, J. J., Price, V. A., Friedman, M., Thoresen, C. E., Powell, L. H., Ulmer, D., Brown, B. W., and Drews, F. R. (1985). Reduction in Type A behavior in healthy middle-aged American military officers. *American Heart Journal* **110**, 503–514.

Glass, D. C. (1977). *Behavior Patterns, Stress, and Coronary Disease*. Hillsdale, NJ: John Wiley & Sons.

Haynes, S. G., Feinleib, M., and Kannel, W. B. (1980). The relationship of psychosocial factors to coronary heart disease in the Framingham study. III. Eight-year incidence of coronary heart disease. *American Journal of Epidemiology*, **111**, 37.

James, W. (1980). *The Principles of Psychology*, vols I and II. London: Henry Holt.

Jenni, M. A., and Wollersheim, J. P. (1979). Cognitive therapy, stress management training, and the Type A behavior pattern. *Cognitive Therapy Research*, **3**, 61–74.

Kearns, D. (1976). *Lyndon Johnson and the American Dream*. New York: Harper & Row.

Layden, M. (1977). *Escaping the Hostility Trap*. Englewood Cliffs, NJ: Prentice-Hall.

Levenkron, J. C., Cohen, J. D., Mueller, H. S., and Fisher, E. B. (1983). Modifying the Type A coronary-prone behavior pattern. *Journal of Consulting and Clinical Psychology*, **51**, 192–204.

Matthews, K. A. (1982). Psychological perspectives on the Type A behavior pattern. *Psychological Bulletin*, **91**, 293–323.

Powell, J. (1976). *Fully Human, Fully Alive*. Niles, Ill.: Argus.

Powell, L. H., Friedman, M., Thoresen, C. E., Gill, J. J., and Ulmer, D. K. (1984). Can the Type A behavior pattern be altered after myocardial infarction? A second year report from the Recurrent Coronary Prevention Project. *Psychosomatic Medicine*, **46**, 293–313.

Powell, L. H., Thoresen, C. E., and Friedman, M. (1985). Modification of Type A behavior pattern after myocardial infarction. In H. Hofman (ed.), *Primary and Secondary Prevention of Coronary Heart Disease: New Trials.* Heidelberg: Springer-Verlag.

Price, V. A. (1982). *Type A Behavior Pattern: A Model for Research and Practice.* New York: Academic Press.

Review Panel on Coronary-prone Behavior and Coronary Heart Disease (1981). Coronary-prone behavior and coronary heart disease. A critical review. *Circulation,* **63**, 1199–1215.

Rosenman, R. H., Brand, R. J., Jenkins, C. D., Friedman, M., Straus, R., and Wurm, M. (1975). Coronary heart disease in the Western Collaborative Group Study: final follow-up experience of 8 years. *Journal of the American Medical Association,* **233**, 872–877.

Roskies, E., Kearney, H., Spevack, M., Surkis, A., Cohen, C., and Gilman, S. (1979). Generalizability and durability of treatment effects in an intervention program for coronary-prone (Type A) managers. *Journal of Behavioral Medicine,* **2**, 195–207.

Roskies, E., Spevack, M., Surkis, A., Cohen, C., and Gilman, S. (1978). Changing the coronary-prone (Type A) behavior pattern in a non-clinical population. *Journal of Behavioral Medicine,* **1**, 201–216.

Stroebel, C. F. (1982). *QR: The Quieting Reflex.* New York: G. P. Putnam's Sons.

Suinn, R. M. (1975). The cardiac stress management program for Type A patients. *Cardiac Rehabilitation,* **5**, 13–15.

Suinn, R. M., and Bloom, L. J. (1978). Anxiety management for Type A persons. *Journal of Behavioral Medicine,* **1**, 25–35.

Thoresen, C. E., Friedman, M., Gill, J. J., and Ulmer, D. K. (1982). The Recurrent Coronary Prevention Project. Some preliminary findings. *Acta Medica Scandinavica,* suppl., **660**, 172–192.

Williams, R. B., Jr, Lane, J. D., Kuhn, C. M., Meosk, W., White, A. D., and Schanberg, S. M. (1982). Type A behavior and elevated physiological and neuroendocrine response to cognitive tasks. *Science,* **218**, 483–486.

Zumoff, B., Rosenfeld, R. S., Friedman, M., Byers, S. O., Rosenman, R. H., and Hellman, L. (1984). Comparison of plasma and urinary steroids in men with Type A and Type B behavior patterns. Psychosomatic Medicine, **46**, 223–225.

SECTION 5

Pain and Anxiety

The Psychosomatic Approach: Contemporary Practice
of Whole-person Care
Edited by M. J. Christie and P. G. Mellett
© 1986 John Wiley & Sons Ltd

10

CHRONIC PAIN: A BIOBEHAVIOURAL PERSPECTIVE

SHIRLEY PEARCE

Department of Psychology, University College London, University of London, UK

INTRODUCTION

Chronic pain, usually defined as pain of 6 months duration, is a major economic as well as medical problem. Low back pain, for example, causes the loss of several million working days each year in the UK (Ward, Knowelden and Sharrard, 1968). The causes of chronic pain are various. Many patients have clearly identifiable organic disorders such as arthritis (600,000 new victims per annum in the USA) for which medical practitioners may be unable to offer treatment. Some patients with chronic pain may have no obvious disorder or disease, while others may have 'iatrogenic' pain developed as a result of medical or surgical interventions for some other, treatable problem.

To the concern of both physicians and patients the sophisticated developments in the understanding of the anatomical substrates and the physiological and biochemical processes of pain perception have not been matched by marked improvements in medical procedures for the control of chronic pain. The progress of surgical interventions for the reduction of chronic pain provides an example. Despite ambitious and technically successful surgical interventions at virtually all levels in the nervous system, ranging from sympathectomies to precutaneous cordotomies, no surgical intervention has been shown to guarantee reductions in chronic pain. This lack of success as far as physical (surgical and pharamacological) treatments of chronic pain are concerned may, at least in part, be due to the rather restricted model of pain that has dominated much medical practice and research. Pain has been largely viewed as a sensation occurring in response to input from the periphery. This view of pain assumes that pain receptors, stimulated by tissue damage, transmit impulses via pain pathways in the spinal cord to a specialized 'pain' area in the brain. There is now increasing evidence from anatomical, physiological and psychological research that such a model is inadequate.

The so-called 'direct transmission line' models of pain have been superseded by models of pain which attempt to account for the modulation (by both peripheral and central processes) of input from pain receptors. The most powerful theory to account for such input modulation is the Gate Control theory of pain proposed by Melzack and Wall (1965). Basically, the theory proposes that a neural mechanism in the dorsal horns of the spinal cord acts like a gate which can increase or decrease the flow of nerve impulses from peripheral nociceptors to the central nervous system. The degree to which the gate increases or decreases the nociceptive input is determined by the relative activity in the large and small diameter fibres as well as by descending influences from the brain. Hence an anatomical basis for the modulation of nociceptive input from the periphery by central processes such as attention or expectation is proposed.

Since 1965, when Melzack and Wall first outlined the Gate Control Theory of pain, considerable attention has been directed towards investigating and testing the existence of the neural mechanisms proposed at each spinal level to be acting as the 'gating mechanism'. A number of the pre- and post-synaptic inhibitory processes proposed in the model of the 'gate' have not been demonstrated experimentally and the theory has received considerable criticism from certain authors (e.g. Dykes, 1975). These criticisms are addressed by Melzack and Wall (1982) who accept that the particular physio-logical and anatomical substrate of their early theory has not been adequately demonstrated, but believe that the overall operation has now repeatedly been shown to exist. Although it is likely that further research may lead to alterations in particular details of the gating mechanisms, it is unlikely that the basic assumptions of the theory, namely the modulation of peripheral input by central cognitive processes, will be invalidated. For a detailed coverage of physiological processes in pain perception, the reader is referred to Wall (1984).

The development of theories of modulation of peripheral input by psycho-logical variables has been paralleled by the extension of the term 'pain' to include affective as well as sensory components of the experience. Melzack (1973) makes a further distinction between affective and evaluative components of pain. Fordyce (1976) extends the definition of pain to include those behaviours which are associated with the experience of pain. These may range from wincing or grimacing, to telling someone about the pain or taking the day off work and avoiding physical exertion. These different, broader, definitions of pain may be unified by conceptualizing pain as an experience made up of activity in three major systems, namely, physiological, subjective and behavioural. The subjective component may be further divided into sensory, affective and possibly 'evaluative' aspects of experience.

It is suggested that activity in the physiological system is perceived at a subjective level both as a sensation (e.g. burning, pricking) and as an unpleasant affect (e.g. distress, discomfort). This negative affective response stimulates pain behaviours (wincing, taking pills) which are aimed at communicating the pain experience to those around, and at reducing the intensity of the pain experience. Such a biobehavioural model allows the notion of a linear relationship between noxious stimulation and pain intensity to be discarded. The further away from the level of nociception, the more other factors besides the level of physiological activity are likely to become implicated in the pain experience. For example, social, cultural and personality variables, as discussed by Bond (1981) in the companion volume, may have as much influence on pain behaviours as does the activity in the nociceptive fibres. Hence the concordance between these three systems—physiological, subjective and behavioural—may vary. This model can be represented diagrammatically in the following way (Fordyce, 1978).

This broader view of pain in which psychological factors may influence the relationship between the physiological, subjective and behavioural components of pain provides a useful model for the understanding, assessment and treatment of all pain experience. Acute pain, chronic pain, so-called 'organic' and 'psychogenic' pain may be more easily understood within a broader biobehavioural framework. For some pain states the implications of the multidimensional model will be greater than for others. The management of acute pain may be least affected. Surgical and pharmaceutical methods will always be appropriate in the short-term management of, for example, fractures or serious injury. However, even in the management of acute pain consideration of psychological processes in recovery has led to the development of psychological interventions, such as those of preparing patients for surgery, which have produced reductions in pain intensity and medication requirements. Although it now seems that the early studies of psychological preparation for surgery (e.g. Egbert et al., 1964) may have led to rather overoptimistic claims about its value, it is clear that, at least for some people, psychological interventions can lead to reductions in acute post-surgical pain (Mathews and Ridgeway, 1981).

It is for chronic pain conditions, however, that the implications of a broader view of pain are particularly great. Fordyce (1976, 1982) has suggested that in chronic pain, whatever the original underlying pathology, the pain problem is unlikely to be solved if only the physiological component of pain is treated. This is because, in his view, behaviours occurring as part of the pain problem are, whatever their initial cause or purpose, very likely after several months to be maintained (reinforced) by environmental factors such as attention from a caring spouse or avoidance of undesired chores. Hence in chronic pain conditions the potential for desynchrony or discordance between the physiological, subjective and behavioural components of pain is possibly greater than it is for acute pain. It therefore follows that successful interventions for chronic pain patients must involve the consideration of pain behaviours (their assessment and management) as well as the consideration of physical pathology and its amelioration. This chapter will, therefore, outline the methods currently being developed by psychologists for the assessment and treatment of chronic pain.

THE ASSESSMENT OF CHRONIC PAIN

There are two main aims of pain assessment in the clinical setting: first, to guide the choice of treatment intervention, and second, to provide measures from which to evaluate change in the pain problem. For either purpose it might be argued that assessment should involve measurement of all three major components of the pain experience. If the term 'physiological component' is used in its broadest sense to refer to physical processes that might be contributing to the pain experience, it follows that assessment of this component will include a thorough medical examination. If pathology is observed, clearly the appropriate medical or surgical interventions should be administered. If this is the case, however, it does not obviate the formal assessment of the subjective and behavioural components of pain. The reasons for this are twofold. First, as indicated before, patients with chronic pain may not respond to apparently appropriate medical and surgical interventions and hence assessment of other aspects of the pain problem may suggest that an intervention at a behavioural level should be provided at the same time as the physical intervention. Second, the evaluation of outcome of a physical intervention cannot be assessed purely in terms of physical change. Changes in the subjective intensity and distress as well as changes in behavioural disturbance caused by the pain must also be considered in evaluating the efficacy of a physical treatment.

In most clinical settings this is done in an unsystematic way. Clinicians of both medical and psychological professions frequently evaluate their interventions by simply asking the patient at the next outpatient appointment whether or not he feels better. Such subjective and retrospective judgements of improvement are highly unreliable for a variety of reasons. These include such diverse factors as the patient's desire to please the clinician and the patient's unwillingness to notice and report change. Furthermore, the patient's present mood state may influence his perception of pain in either a positive or a negative direction, making his current report an invalid estimate of the pain experienced over the previous week.

The general problems involved in evaluating change in subjective states have been discussed at length in studies concerned with the evaluation of outcome in psychotherapy where similar problems emerge in the evaluation of changes in, for example, anxiety and depression (Bergin and Lambert, 1978). There is little reason to believe that the report of pain should be exempt from these influences. The remainder of this section will introduce some of the methods being developed to improve the reliability and validity of pain assessment methods. A more detailed discussion of the issues involved in the use of each method is provided by Pearce and Richardson (in press, a) and Melzack (1983).

The assessment of pain behaviour

Philips and Hunter (1981a) distinguish three categories of pain behaviour which they label as avoidance, complaint and help-seeking behaviours. Little is known about the relationship between these three, or about the relationship between pain behaviours and the subjective intensity of pain. A variety of methods has been used to assess all of these categories of pain behaviour, including those described below.

Direct observation

This is most easily conducted on an inpatient basis where staff make frequency counts of pain behaviours, e.g. wincing, complaining of pain, rubbing the painful area. Counts may be made either at particular times of the day (e.g. Richards *et al.*, 1982) or during a task, such as interacting with a member of staff (e.g. Rybstein-Blinchik, 1979). Other versions of staff observation methods involve staff making global ratings of their impression of the frequency of different pain behaviours on each shift rather than recording absolute numbers of behaviours (Swanson, Maruta and Swenson, 1979). A major problem with all such methods is that despite demonstrations of the reliability of such measures, the setting in which the measures are taken is a largely unnatural one for the patient and hence the generalizability of any of the measures to his more natural environment must be open to question. However, as a way of recording change in hospital, direct observation provides a reliable measure of pain behaviour.

Self-observation

Recordings of the nature or frequency of pain behaviour made by the patients themselves have the great advantage of not being situation-specific. Measures from a patient's natural environment can be easily obtained. Self-observation methods range from relatively simple tasks such as recording the number of specific exercises achieved each day (Cairns *et al.*, 1976) to more complicated recordings of pain behaviour taken as part of a behavioural analysis of the pain problem (Boudewyns, 1982). The latter do not usually measure pain behaviour alone. Records forming the basis of a behavioural or functional analysis of the pain problem will include records of situational variables (e.g. where I was, what I was doing), cognitive variables (e.g. what I was thinking and feeling), pain intensity and quality measures (e.g. where the pain was, how intense on a 0–10 scale), as well as details of what behaviours were engaged in as a response to the pain and what activities/behaviours were avoided because the pain had come again. By examining regular and detailed records such as these the therapist in conjunction with the patient is able to gain some picture of the pattern of the pain's impact on the patient's feelings and behaviour. Depending on the nature of the pattern emerging, appropriate methods of intervention can be considered. Such an analysis of pain involves similar processes and is accompanied by problems similar to those in the behavioural analysis of any other psychological or behavioural problem.

It should be noted that a number of studies have suggested that there may be a discrepancy between the frequency of pain behaviours as recorded by the patient in a self-observation procedure and the frequency of the same behaviour over the same time period as recorded by an observer (Kremer, Block and Gaylor, 1981; Sanders, 1983). The discrepancy itself does not invalidate either of the methods, and certainly when pain behaviours are being recorded as part of the patient's own behavioural analysis there is no alternative to self-observation. However, it does indicate that measures must be interpreted with some caution and that measures obtained from a number of sources may aid in understanding the overall problem. It also indicates the importance of devising self recording schedules that maximize patient compliance. Collins and Thompson (1979) have discussed the factors that contribute to the unreliability of patients' recording such as the frequency of the recordings and the amount of detail required in self observation methods.

There are surprisingly few self-report questionnaire methods for the assessment of pain behaviours. Philips and Hunter (1981a) have developed a checklist containing equal numbers of complaint, avoidance and help-seeking behaviours. Despite its ease of administration this checklist has only been used in research with headache (Philips and Hunter, 1981a) and low back pain patients (Zarkowska, 1981) but it should also prove to be useful with other patient groups.

The assessment of pain intensity

In view of the distinctions made earlier between the intensity and the quality of pain experience, methods used in the assessment of the subjective component of pain must make clear to the patient which aspect of their experience the rating scale or measuring device is trying to tap. Clearly, unreliability in recordings would emerge if the patient one day answered the question 'how bad is your pain today' by referring to the pain's intensity while on another day answered the same question by referring to how depressed the pain was making them feel today. Since there is no reason why pain intensity and how depressed the pain makes one feel should be linearly related, variability in the recordings would be introduced simply by failure to make the precise task clear to the patient.

Rating Scales are the most commonly used techniques for assessing pain intensity and are discussed in detail by Huskisson (1983) and Gracely (1979). The most commonly used forms are the Category Rating Scales (e.g. none, mild, moderate, severee, unbearable; or 1, 2, 3, 4, 5) and Visual Analogue Scales e.g. 10 cm line with anchor points at each end.

Although there are a number of studies showing a high correlation between these two forms of rating scales (e.g. Downie *et al.*, 1978), other studies have sugggested that the VAS (Visual Analogue Scale) is more sensitive to change and is therefore to be preferred if the scale is being used to evaluate outcome (Ohnhaus and Adler, 1975; Joyce *et al.*, 1975). Rating scales may also be incorporated into pain diaries as described in the previous section.

A very widely used questionnaire in the assessment of pain intensity and quality is the McGill Pain Questionnaire (MPQ) (Melzack, 1975). This questionnaire consists of 78 pain adjectives arranged in 20 groups, each reflecting slightly different aspects of the quality of pain. The 20 groups are further arranged into sets of words describing sensory aspects of pain (e.g. pricking, tingling, burning), affective descriptors (e.g. sickening, punishing, cruel) and evaluative words (e.g. annoying, miserable, troublesome). The questionnaire may be scored in a variety of ways to yield either an index reflecting the *intensity* of the words checked or more simply the *number* of words checked in each of the sensory, affective and evaluative categories. The MPQ has received considerable attention recently and a number of studies have investigated the validity of the adjective groupings using factor analytic methods (Prieto and Geisinger, 1983). Although most studies support the broad distinction between sensory and affective categories, the validity of its intensity measures within groups of adjectives has been questioned (Reading, Everitt and Sledmere, 1982). A collection of papers concerned with the structure and uses of the MPQ may be found in Melzack (1983).

The assessment of pain-related cognitions

Recent interest in cognitive behavioural treatments for chronic pain has led to greater attention being paid to the cognitive processes associated with both the onset of, and response, to pain episodes.

It is possible that cognitive processes may directly contribute to the onset of the pain episode. If situational variables are cognitively appraised as anxiety arousing or fearful, this may initiate physiological changes that make the onset of a pain episode more likely. Such a mechanism has been proposed in the case of tension headache where changes in muscle tension levels occurring as part of the body's response to stress might underly the head pain (Philips and Hunter, 1981b). The current interest in stress management techniques as a treatment for tension headache is a direct extension of this view of headache onset (Holroyd and Andrasik, 1978). Careful assessment of the situational variables as well as the cognitive events associated with the onset of headache should enable appropriate patients to be accurately selected for this form of intervention.

Cognitive processes which occur as a direct response to pain sensations may also be involved in the development of a pain episode. These include processes such as finding one's attention focused on the pain or imagining pleasant scenes in an attempt to divert one's attention away from the pain. In view of the influence of attentional factors in modulating the experience of pain, it seems likely that the nature of the cognitive responses to the pain experience might influence both the intensity and the duration of each episode of pain. In studies of experimentally induced pain it has been demonstrated that the nature of the cognitive strategy used by the subject can produce significant differences in pain tolerance measures (Turk, Meichenbaum and Genest, 1983). However, it is also clear that subjects differ according to the strategies which they find most helpful, as well as the nature of their existing 'home-grown' strategies for dealing with pain (Chaves and Barber, 1974). It therefore follows that in teaching pain patients cognitive strategies for coping with their clinical pain condition it will be necessary to discover their preexisting strategies, possibly by asking them to free associate while undergoing pain induced by an experimental pain stimulus (Karoly, 1982).

Assessment of the physiological component of pain

In addition to the medical assessment of the physiological aspects of pain, techniques derived from psychological methods may aid the choice of treatment intervention. For example, electromyographic (EMG) assessments in tension headache, or blood flow measures in migraine, may help to determine the appropriateness of biofeedback methods for these conditions. Individual assessment of these processes is being recognized as important since, despite the early enthusiasm about biofeedback techniques for headache (Budzynski et al., 1973), it is now clear that not all tension headache patients show abnormal EMG levels (Philips, 1977). Philips and Hunter (1981b) have therefore suggested that biofeedback might be maximally effective for those patients who are shown initially to have raised levels of tension in the muscles associated with the pain. Biofeedback may thus not be advised for patients who fail to show abnormalities in the physiological system thought to underly their pain complaint. Hence a thorough assessment of the physiological variables should be conducted in the initial assessment period to avoid inappropriate and potentially unsuccessful treatment interventions which are both discouraging to the patient and likely to reduce the credibility of the psychologist in the patient's eyes. Now that we have considered the processes by which a chronic pain problem might be assessed, the methods being developed by psychologists as intervention strategies in chronic pain will be outlined. It will be clear from the number of different approaches to pain treatment that for any one patient a variety of treatment methods, either sequentially or in tandem, is likely to be time consuming, confusing and even contradictory. For this reason it is hoped that what will become apparent is the importance of having comprehensively assessed the individual patient's problems in order to determine the most appropriate intervention for him.

PSYCHOLOGICAL METHODS IN THE MANAGEMENT OF CHRONIC PAIN

In response to the realization that traditional medical and surgical treatment approaches are not likely to provide all the answers to the problems involved in the management of chronic pain, there has been growing interest amongst physicians, surgeons and psychologists in the application of psychological methods of intervention for chronic pain. Most of the interventions so far applied to chronic pain fall broadly within the theoretical orientation of behavioural treatment methods. Despite interesting discussion of psychodynamic processes in the development of chronic pain (e.g. Engel, 1959), psychodynamic approaches to treatment have been neither widely used nor shown to have any demonstrable effect. This is not to say that some patients would not benefit from a psychodynamic intervention. For patients to become involved in psychodynamic psychotherapy, however, they must be prepared to accept that psychological processes play a causal role in the aetiology of the pain. For many chronic pain patients this assumption is quite unacceptable, particularly if the patient does indeed have some pathology which is not responding to traditional treatments. This discrepancy between the importance attached to psychological factors in pain experience by the therapist and by the patient is a problem for all types of psychological intervention for pain, but is most particularly a problem for psychodynamic interventions. This may help to explain the high dropout rates that have been observed in the few studies of psychotherapy for chronic pain (e.g. Henker, 1979).

The psychological treatment methods that have been used in the management of chronic pain include biofeedback, relaxation, cognitive behavioural techniques and operant/contingency management methods. In addition to these specific treatment strategies many inpatient treatment programmes (largely in the USA) take a strongly educational line and provide patients with lectures about, for example, theories of pain, the effects of analgesic and psychotropic medications, and the role of psychological factors in pain perception. These programmes have been called 'multimethod' treatment programmes. A more detailed review of psychological approaches to the management of chronic pain can be found in Pearce and Richardson (in press, b).

Biofeedback and relaxation

Biofeedback and relaxation procedures for pain have been reviewed in a number of other places (e.g. Turner and Chapman, 1982; Blanchard *et al.*, 1980) and will not be discussed in detail here. Biofeedback in the management of conditions other than pain is discussed in the companion volume by

McCroskery and Engel (1981). The assumption has been that both these treatment methods produce a reduction in pain by teaching the patient to control and thereby reduce disturbance in the physiological system thought to underlie the pain. It is now clear, however, that although some patients may show reductions in pain intensity during biofeedback this is not always paralleled by reductions in the physiological measure being recorded. Indeed, Andrasik and Holroyd (1980) showed that a tension headache group trained by biofeedback to produce increases in their frontalis muscle tension levels showed similarly significant decreases in headache activity as a group trained to decrease their frontalis EMG levels. This does not mean that procedures aimed at altering the physiological variables implicated in the pain experience (such as biofeedback) are not effective, but rather suggests that they exert their effect by processes other than a change in the physiological system itself.

Attention is now being directed to examining the so-called process factors (procedural variables) which may play a role in the overall outcome of treatment. Blanchard et al. (1983) showed that although therapist variables, such as the level of therapist training and whether the therapist is perceived as warm and friendly by the patients, did not affect treatment outcome during relaxation training and biofeedback for headache patients, the amount of home practice of relaxation was significantly related to the amount of head-ache reduction. Indeed, many of the early very successful biofeedback studies for tension headache instructed the patients to use home practice of relax-ation (Budzynski et al., 1973; Haynes et al., 1975). One explanation of this relation between home practice and treatment outcome is that patients who learn most effectively to reduce their frontalis EMG levels find home practice more rewarding and therefore they are more likely to increase the number of times they practise at home. In keeping with previous studies, however, Blanchard et al. (1983) found no relation between reductions in EMG level and treatment outcome. An alternative possibility is that those patients who feel that they are learning to gain some control over their headache (even if this is just a belief in control rather than absolute control per se) tend both to practise more and realize a greater reduction in head pain. There is certainly evidence from the research on experimentally induced pain that beliefs about control influence pain tolerance levels. The possibility that treatments which are apparently physiologically based may be effective because of cognitive changes is a theme that will be returned to later when considering the role of cognitive factors in all pain reduction methods.

The value of biofeedback training with patient groups other than headache patients has not been demonstrated. Despite some studies (reported by Keefe et al., 1982) suggesting that EMG biofeedback from spinal muscles may effect reductions in backache, recent studies have shown that although biofeedback of back muscles is effective in producing reductions in EMG levels of the muscles concerned this is associated with non-significant reductions in pain intensity.

Contingency management methods

The application of operant principles, including contingency management, to the problem of chronic pain is largely attributable to the work of Fordyce and his colleagues in the USA. Fordyce considers pain behaviours in many chronic pain patients to be maintained by their reinforcing consequences rather than by the physical changes that may, in the first instance, have initiated the pain problem. Pain behaviours may be either positively reinforced (for example, by attention from concerned family members) or negatively reinforced (for example, by being able to avoid some unpleasant task because of the pain). Fordyce's contingency management approach to pain treatment involves manipulating the consequences that are thought to be maintaining the pain problem. The aims of treatment within this framework are (1) to increase the frequency of 'well' behaviours (that is, those predetermined by the therapist and patient to be desired behaviours not associated with the pain problem), (2) to decrease pain behaviours and analgesic medication and (3) to increase activity levels.

The methods used to achieve these goals are described in detail by Fordyce (1976). In the inpatient setting that Fordyce and other proponents of the contingency management approach believe is necessary for the effective administration of an operant programme, nurses, physicians and family members are instructed to ignore all pain behaviours. Requests for analgesics are therefore ignored, as are complaints about distress or inactivity associated with wincing and grimacing. 'Well' behaviours such as physical activity will be rewarded, usually by attention from staff members (or family if they are present). This structure for the manipulation of the consequences of pain behaviour is accompanied by regular sessions in physical therapy where patients have daily exercise quotas that they are encouraged to achieve. Medication is provided on a time contingent basis, e.g. every 3 hours, rather than on a pain contingent basis, i.e. when the pain gets bad. In this way Fordyce hopes to reverse any reinforcing power of the analgesic medication. The concentration of the analgesic content of the medication provided at each occasion is gradually reduced during the inpatient stay so that by the time of discharge the patient should be weaned from medication.

A number of studies have now been published that attempt to evaluate the efficacy of this kind of treatment approach. Fordyce himself has published a number of single-case reports and a group outcome study (Fordyce, Fowler and Lehmann, 1968; Fordyce et al., 1973). Both the single-case studies and the group outcome data show that marked increases in activity can be produced by operant methods. However, these studies, along with those from other units (Roberts and Reinhardt, 1980; Anderson et al., 1977) have not included matched control groups receiving no treatment or alternative treatments. It is therefore far from clear whether the operant methods themselves have produced the increases in activity or whether the numerous non-specific factors associated with admission to hospital and learning to conceptualize the pain problem in behavioural rather than medical terms may have produced the change. This point is of particular importance in evaluating the bulk of American inpatient treatment programmes. Although many of them call themselves contingency management programmes they also incorporate a number of other ingredients that would not strictly be included in an operant treatment programme. For example, many include biofeedback as a matter of course for all patients, along with relaxation classes, lectures on pain-related topics and a variety of group psychotherapy sessions. In such multimethod treatment programmes the assessment of the active ingredients of treatment is extremely difficult. A detailed critique of the methodology and problems of interpretation of these studies can be found in Turk, Meichenbaum and Genest (1983).

A further criticism of the contingency management studies is that there is minimal evidence to date that patients who show such increases in activity also show reductions in pain intensity. Fordyce et al., (1973) asked all patients at the follow-up assessment to estimate the intensity of their pain at admission, at discharge and at follow-up, on a 0–10 scale. Although these are retrospective judgements and hence of questionable validity, it is interesting to note that although patients reported a reduction in pain intensity from admission to discharge they were still reporting at follow-up a mean pain rating of over 6 on the 0–10 scale. Hence, despite their increases in activity they are still reporting considerable subjective distress. Fordyce argues that this does not invalidate his treatment intervention since it is clear to the patient from the outset that the aim is to effect changes in activity levels, i.e. pain behaviour, rather than reductions in pain intensity. This defence of Fordyce's seems quite appropriate within the terms of the broader biobehavioural model of pain discussed earlier. Despite the lack of evidence concerning the specific effects of contingency management methods it is clear that changes in pain behaviour/activity levels can be produced. As a consequence of this, Fordyce's methods have had a major impact on clinical practice in American, and now increasingly in British, pain clinics.

Cognitive behavioural interventions

A range of treatment strategies for chronic pain have been subsumed under the term cognitive behavioural techniques. They can be divided into two broad categories (Pearce, 1983). First, there are those that are concerned directly with modifying cognitive responses to pain, and second, there are those which aim to alter cognitive responses to stress on the assumption that if stress is managed better then pain (usually tension headache or migraine) may be avoided. These will be considered in turn.

Modification of cognitive responses to pain

The methods involved in the assessment and modification of pain-related cognitions are discussed in detail by Turk, Meichenbaum and Genest (1983). In essence the process involves identifying the patient's internal construction and description of the pain experience and teaching him alternative, more adaptive cognitive responses to the pain. The nature of these alternative strategies is derived largely from studies with experimentally induced pain where pain tolerance levels have been shown to be increased by a range of different cognitive interventions. These are summarized in Table 10.1. To date, the clinical studies of the value of teaching patients such cognitive strategies for pain control have been largely anecdotal and uncontrolled. Although single-case reports show reductions in pain (e.g. Levendusky and Pankratz, 1975) the specific effects of the cognitive strategies per se are not demonstrated since a number of other treatment interventions were used at the same time. Larger studies have taught cognitive strategies within an educational or 'stress inoculation' framework. In this approach the description of cognitive strategies in pain control is preceded by an educational phase in which the patient is taught about models of pain (including the Gate Control theory) and the role of psychological factors in pain perception. After the strategies have been described the patients are able to practise the different strategies within sessions to determine which they find most effective. Early uncontrolled studies of such an approach to pain management produced encouraging results. For example, Rybstein-Blinchik (1979) reports reductions in McGill Pain Questionnaire scores as well as observer ratings of pain behaviour for headache patients following eight weekly sessions of stress inoculation training.

However, it must be acknowledged that the standard of treatment outcome research in this area, like that of operant methods, is as yet rather primitive.

TABLE 10.1 Cognitive strategies used in pain management

Strategy	Task	Example
Imaginative inattention	Imagine scenes incompatible with pain	Lying on a beach
Imaginative transformation	Relabel sensations as less distressing	Tingling, numbness, warmth, cold
Transformation of context	Imagine sensations occurring in a different, more appropriate context	Building a snowman, spy shot in the arm
Attention diversion		
(1) Internal	Attend to alternative thoughts	Mental arithmetic, recite poem
(2) External	Attend to alternative external event	Count ceiling tiles, focus on external object
Somatization	Focus on sensations in a detached way	Write a biology report about the sensations

One of the few controlled outcome studies of cognitive methods for chronic pain to date is that by Turner (1982). In this study the efficacy of group cognitive therapy was compared to that of group relaxation training and a waiting list control. Cognitive therapy was shown to be more effective than relaxation training on a number of outcome measures. Furthermore, this difference between treatment groups was still apparent at a 1½-year follow-up. Further studies of this kind are required to confirm the value of such cognitive interventions for chronic pain patients.

One rather different approach to the modification of pain-related cognitions has been the use of covert conditioning procedures. Cautela (1977) reported an uncontrolled single-case study of the use of covert reinforcement strategies in pain control. The successful treatment involved a patient, who suffered from arthritis, imagining performing target behaviours without pain and reinforcing this response by imagining a pleasant scene. However, a later group outcome study of covert reinforcement in the treatment of headache failed to demonstrate any difference between the effects of covert positive reinforcement and an equally credible placebo intervention (Turkat and Adams, 1982).

It must be concluded that although studies with experimentally induced pain have demonstrated that the use of certain cognitive strategies can significantly increase pain tolerance levels, it has not yet been demonstrated conclusively that they are of equal value in the management of clinical chronic pain. However, this conclusion is largely based on the poverty of the outcome literature rather than any demonstration of the inadequacy of cognitive techniques, and it is to be hoped that with the current interest in the area and the rapidly improving quality of the research the value of cognitive methods will be demonstrated.

Stress management in the treatment of pain

Most applications of stress management methods in the treatment of chronic pain have been conducted on headache patients. The basic components of stress management methods are (1) the monitoring of situations or stimuli which the patient finds stressful, (2) the identification of the patient's cognitive responses to those situations and (3) the development and practice of alternative, more constructive, ways of construing those situations and responding to them.

In a group outcome study Holroyd, Andrasik and Westbrook (1977) compared cognitive stress management with EMG biofeedback and a waiting list control condition. Cognitive stress management was found to be more effective than biofeedback in reducing headache frequency and duration. Since biofeedback is generally accepted as an effective method for tension headache, this might be considered powerful support for the effectiveness of cognitive stress management. However, Holroyd and Andrasik (1978) found no differences among groups receiving (1) cognitive stress management alone, (2) cognitive stress management and relaxation training, and (3) a control headache discussion group. All showed significant reductions in headaches whilst a symptom-monitoring group showed no such reduction. Holroyd and Andrasik (1978) explain the improvement in the headache discussion group by suggesting that similar cognitive changes occurred despite the lack of active cognitive training. Unfortunately, this conclusion can neither be confirmed nor disproved since cognitive responses to stressful events were not assessed. An alternative interpretation might be that all three groups were responding to a common non-specific component of the therapies.

An attempt to look more closely at the active ingredients of cognitive stress management training for chronic pain is provided by Mitchell and White (1977), who used a dismantling design with successive stages of treatment being available to a reduced proportion of the initial sample of migraine patients. Their results support the view that the main reduction in headache frequency occurred as a result of active treatment, namely relaxation and cognitive stress management, rather than from placebo components of the programme.

There are few studies that have looked at cognitive stress management methods for chronic pain states other than headache. Khatami and Rush (1978) provide a much cited exception. This was an uncontrolled study involving five back pain patients who each received (1) relaxation training, (2) cognitive stress management and (3) a form of family therapy. No consistent pattern emerged concerning the relative efficacy of any of the stages, but over a mean treatment period of 35 weeks all patients showed significant reductions in pain ratings, depression scores and analgesic consumption. In view of the absence of adequate control measures this study cannot provide much support for the effectiveness of cognitive stress management as a treatment for back pain.

In conclusion it is only for tension headache and migraine that there is any evidence that learning to identify cognitive responses to stress, and to develop alternative adaptive cognitive strategies, may effect a reduction in pain. The mechanism of this reduction is, however, still unclear. The lack of studies investigating cognitive stress management for other chronic pain conditions, such as low back pain, may be accounted for by the plausibility of the treatment rationale provided for the patient. There is a general acceptance that headache may in some way be related to stress, hence stress management has some apparent validity as a treatment strategy. For the majority of patients with low back pain, many of whom may be searching for organic causes for their distress, stress management may make little sense.

Similarities between different psychological treatments of pain

The interventions described above for the psychological management of chronic pain may, at first glance, appear to be of very different natures. Certainly, the underlying theory and methods involved in relaxation are very different from those involved in contingency management, for example. Furthermore, biofeedback would appear to have little in common with cognitive–behavioural stress management. However, it was frequently concluded in the preceding sections that the *specific* effect of any of these treatment methods has not yet been demonstrated. It remains a possibility that certain non-specific processes, possibly common to all the apparently diverse psychological methods for controlling chronic pain, may play a part in any beneficial effects of the interventions. Turk, Meichenbaum and Genest (1983) suggest that certain cognitive changes are common to all the treatment interventions. They identify three major areas of similarity across the different methods.

The first area of similarity concerns the implicit or explicit conceptualization of pain and therapy adopted by the patient. Although the methods differ in the amount of importance explicitly attached to the model of pain that the patient should adopt, implicit to all is the notion that psychological procedures (whether biofeedback, exercise programmes or family therapy) can play a role in pain reduction. The emphasis in all the methods is away from the all-powerful doctor having a magic potion which will cure the pain. Rather, pain is presented as an experience influenced by psychological processes as well as by pathological changes. In some psychological treatment interventions the acceptance of this model is considered central to any improvement. In the multimethod treatment programmes, for example, there are regular lectures on pain and stress and the limitations of traditional medical and surgical approaches to treatment. Cognitive methods aimed at teaching patients alternative responses to pain, especially those taught within a 'stress inoculation' framework, also explicitly teach a biobehavioural model of pain as a first stage of treatment. Other interventions do not attach central importance to the patient's reconceptualization of the pain problem. For example, relaxation training and biofeedback do not explicitly involve teaching the patient about any particular theory/model of pain perception. However, Turk, Meichenbaum and Genest (1983) suggest that implicitly, if not explicitly, in order to get a patient to find the treatment credible enough to cooperate, a model of pain in which psychological interventions are seen as potentially effective in reducing stress must be presented to him and accepted by him. Strict contingency management programmes are also an example of a treatment intervention which theoretically relies minimally on cognitive change to effect a reduction in pain. The aim of treatment is to produce changes in pain behaviour by the manipulation of reinforcing contingencies. However, it is clear from the detailed description of treatment that Fordyce (1976) provides for his patients that a great deal of attention is paid in the early stages of the programme to educating them about the role of conditioning processes in the development of pain behaviour and chronic pain problems. Although the focus of the explanation is concerned with pain behaviours rather than pain cognitions, nevertheless, the patient is required to reconceptualize his pain problem to incorporate the role of psychological influences on pain. Hence, although the exact nature of the explanations given to the patient may be very different from one psychological treatment method to another, Turk, Meichenbaum and Genest (1983) suggest that certain cognitive changes may be common to all of the interventions. They suggest that the nature of this cognitive change is such that the patients see themselves as having a role to play in the alleviation of their own distress. The responsibility for improvement is, therefore, shared between the patient and the professionals. This is very different from the expectations generated by treatment provided within the traditional 'sensation' model of pain in which the responsibility lies with the professional to identify and treat the underlying pathological changes.

Turk, Meichenbaum and Genest (1983) suggest that the treatment methods also have in common a stage in which new skills are learned and the practice of these new skills is encouraged. Certainly biofeedback, relaxation and cognitive relabelling techniques provide examples of treatment interventions in which new behaviours are developed and practised, hence providing for potential change in the patient's behavioural repertoire.

The third area of similarity between psychological treatment methods for pain involves the patient's cognitions concerning change as it occurs. Turk, Meichenbaum and Genest (1983) suggest that, whatever the nature of the psychological intervention for pain, there may be important similarities between the different methods in terms of the beliefs that the patients develop about the changes in their pain problems as improvement occurs. They do not, however, speculate at any length about the nature of these cognitions. The research on psychological factors in the perception of *experimental* pain suggests a number of cognitive processes that might be important in the modulation of clinical pain. In particular, the predictability of the pain (Bobey and Davidson, 1970) and the belief of control over the pain stimulus (Thompson, 1981) have been shown to affect pain tolerance in experimental situations. Indeed, it has been suggested that interventions preparing patients for acute clinical pain may be effective as a consequence of the sense of control and associated reductions in anxiety which result from information and advice being given to the patient prior to the painful procedure (Tan, 1982).

Since the psychological interventions for chronic pain described above involve, first, the patient reconceptualizing the problem as one for which he must take responsibility, and second, the patient learning new skills, it is possible that the associated cognitive changes in those cases where the treatment is effective involve changes in the perceived level of control over the pain sensations. In biofeedback and relaxation the patient is learning well-defined cognitive and behavioural strategies to use to combat the pain. Improvement may therefore occur as a function of the belief that he now has a means of control over the painful sensory input. In contingency management the patient is learning that increased exercise and physical activity does not necessarily result in increased pain and can even occur despite the pain. The patient, perhaps, then develops a feeling of control over the pain problem. In the cognitive treatments described in the previous sections, the emphasis on direct cognitive change is more explicit, and where the patient is able to use a newly taught cognitive strategy effectively it is likely that this is associated with more general feelings of control over the pain problem. It is possible that the concepts of self-efficacy discussed by Bandura (1977) in relation to other areas of problem behaviour and behaviour change may be relevant to the processes of pain control. According to Bandura (1977) 'self-efficacy' is the conviction that one can successfully execute the behaviour required to produce a suitable outcome. It is possible that psychological treatment methods for chronic pain bring about their effect by increasing the patient's 'self-efficacy'.

It would be unwise to speculate too widely at this early stage about the nature of general changes involved in psychological approaches to the management of chronic pain, but the view put forward by Turk, Meichenbaum and Genest (1983) that the apparently different interventions may have rather similar process factors which effect similar cognitive changes in those patients where the intervention is effective, is important and worthy of greater attention in future research.

ACKNOWLEDGEMENT

I should like to thank Professor P. D. Wall for his helpful comments on an earlier version of this manuscript.

REFERENCES

Anderson, T. P., Cole, T. M., Gullickson, G., Hudgens, A., and Roberts, A. H. (1977). Behaviour modification of chronic pain: a treatment program by a multidisciplinary team. *Journal of Clinical Orthopaedics*, **129**, 96–100.

Andrasik, F., and Holroyd, K. A. (1980). Physiologic and self-report comparisons between tension headache sufferers and non-headache controls. *Behaviour Assessment*, **2**, 135–141.

Bandura, A. (1977). Self-efficacy: toward a unifying theory of behavioural change. *Psychological Review*, **84**, 191–215.

Bergin, A. E., and Lambert, M. J. (1978). The evaluation of therapeutic outcomes. In S. L. Garfield and A. E. Bergin (eds). *Handbook of Psychotherapy and Behaviour Change*. Chichester: Wiley.

Blanchard, E. B., Andrasik, F., Ahles, T. A., Teders, S. J., and O'Keeffe, D. (1980). Migraine and tension headache: a meta-analytic review. *Behaviour Therapy*, **11**, 613–631.

Blanchard, E. B., Andrasik, F., Neff, O. F., Saunders, N. L., Arena, J. G., Pallmeyer, T. P., Teders, J. S., and Jurish, S. E. (1983). Four process studies in the behavioural treatment of chronic headache. *Behaviour Research and Therapy*, **21**, 209–222.

Bobey, M. J., and Davidson, P. O. (1970). Psychological factors affecting pain tolerance. *Journal of Psychosomatic Research*, **14**, 371–376.

Bond, M. R. (1981). Pain and personality. In M. J. Christie and P. G. Mellett (eds), *Foundations of Psychosomatics*. Chichester: Wiley.

Boudewyns, P. A. (1982). Assessment of headache. In F. J. Keefe and J. A. Blumenthal (eds), *Assessment Strategies in Behavioural Medicine*. New York: Grune & Stratton.

Budzynski, T. H., Stoyva, J. M., Adler, C. S., and Mullaney, D. T. (1973). EMG biofeedback and tension headache. A controlled study. *Psychosomatic Medicine*, **35**, 484–496.

Cairns, D., Thomas, L., Mooney, V., and Pace, J. B. (1976). A comprehensive treatment approach to chronic low back pain. *Pain*, **2**, 301–308.

Cautela, J. (1977). The use of covert conditioning in modifying pain behaviour. *Journal of Behavioural Therapy and Experimental Psychiatry*, **8**, 45.

Chaves, J. F., and Barber, T. X. (1974). Cognitive strategies, experimenter modelling and expectation in the attenuation of pain. *Journal of Abnormal Psychology*, **83**, 356–363.

Collins, F. L., and Thompson, J. K. (1979). Reliability and standardisation in the assessment of self-reported headache pain. *Journal of Behavioural Assessment*.

Downie, W. W., Leatham, P. A., Rhind, V. M., Wright, V., Branco, J. A., and Anderson, J. A. (1978). Studies with pain rating scales. *Annals of Rheumatic Disease*, **37**, 378–381.

Dykes, R. W. (1975). Nociception. *Brain Research*, **99**, 229–254.

Egbert, L. O., Battit, G. E., Welch, C. E., and Bartlett, M. D. (1964). Reduction of postoperative pain by encouragement and instruction of patients. *New England Journal of Medicine*, **270**, 825–827.

Engel, G. L. (1959). 'Psychogenic' pain and the pain prone patient. *American Journal of Medicine*, **26**, 899–918.

Fordyce, W. E. (1976). *Behavioural Methods for Chronic Pain and Illness*. St Louis, Mo.: Mosby.

Fordyce, W. E. (1978). Learning processes in pain. In R. A. Sternbach (ed.), *The Psychology of Pain*. New York: Raven Press.

Fordyce, W. E. (1982). A behavioural perspective on chronic pain. *British Journal of Clinical Psychology*, **21**, 313–320.

Fordyce, W. E., Fowler, R., and Lehmann, J. (1968). Some implications of learning in problems of chronic pain. *Journal for Chronic Disorders*, **21**, 170–190.

Fordyce, W. E., Fowler, R. S., Lehmann, J. F., Delateur, B. J., Sand, P. L., and Treischmann, R. B. (1973). Operant conditioning in the treatment of chronic pain. *Archives of Physical Medicine and Rehabilitation*, **54**, 399–408.

Gracely, R. H. (1979). Psychophysical assessment of human pain. *Advances in Pain Research and Therapy*, **3**, 805–824.

Haynes, S., Griffin, P., Mooney, D., and Parise, M. (1975). Electro-myographic biofeedback and relaxation instructions in the treatment of muscle contraction headaches. *Behaviour Therapy*, **6**, 672–678.

Henker, F. O. (1979). Diagnosis and treatment of non-organic pelvic pain. *Southern Medical Journal*, **72**, 1132–1134.

Holroyd, K. A., and Andrasik, F. (1978). Coping and the self-control of chronic tension headache. *Journal of Consulting and Clinical Psychology*, **46**, 1036–1045.

Holroyd, K. A., Andrasik, F., and Westbrook, T. (1977). Cognitive control of tension headache. *Cognitive Therapy and Research*, **1**, 121–133.

Huskisson, E. C. (1983). Visual analogue scales. In R. Melzack (ed.), *Pain Measurement and Assessment*. New York: Raven Press.

Joyce, C. B., Zutshi, D. W., Hrubes, V., and Mason, R. M. (1975). Comparison of fixed internal and visual analogue scales for rating chronic pain. *European Journal for Clinical Pharmacology*, **8**, 415–420.

Karoly, P. (1982). Cognitive assessment in behavioural medicine. *Clinical Psychology Review*, **2**, 421–434.

Keefe, F. J., Brown, C., Scott, D. S., and Ziesat, H. (1982). Behavioural assessment of chronic pain. In F. J. Keefe and J. A. Blumenthal (eds), *Assessment Strategies in Behavioural Medicine*. New York: Grune & Stratton.

Khatami, M., and Rush, A. J. (1978). A pilot study of the treatment of outpatients with chronic pain: symptom control, stimulus control and social system intervention. *Pain*, **5**, 163–172.

Kremer, E., Block, A., and Gaylor, M. (1981). Behavioural approaches to chronic pain: the inaccuracy of patient self-report measures. *Archives of Physical Medicine and Rehabilitation*, **62**, 188–191.

Levendusky, P., and Pankratz, L. (1975). Self control techniques as an alternative to pain medication. *Journal of Abnormal Psychology*, **84**, 165–169.

McCroskery, J. H., and Engel, B. T. (1981). Biofeedback and emotional behaviour. In M. J. Christie and P. G. Mellett (eds), *Foundations of Psychosomatics*. Chichester: Wiley.

Mathews, A., and Ridgeway, V. (1981). Personality and surgical recovery: a review. *British Journal of Clinical Psychology*, **20**, 243–260.

Melzack, R. (1973). *The Puzzle of Pain*. New York: Basic Books.

Melzack, R. (1975). The McGill Pain Questionnaire: major properties and scoring methods. *Pain*, **1**, 275–299.

Melzack, R. (1983). *Pain Measurement and Assessment*. New York: Raven Press.

Melzack, R., and Wall, P. O. (1965). Pain mechanisms: a new theory. *Science*, **150**, 971–979.

Melzack, R., and Wall, P. (1982). *The Challenge of Pain*. Harmondsworth, Middx: Penguin Books.

Mitchell, K. R., and White, R. G. (1977). Behavioural self-management: an application to the problem of migraine headaches. *Behaviour Therapy*, **8**, 213–222.

Ohnhaus, E. E., and Adler, R. (1975). Methodological problems in the measurement of pain: a comparison between the verbal rating scale and the visual analogue scale. *Pain*, **1**, 379–384.

Pearce, S. (1983). A review of cognitive–behavioural methods for the treatment of chronic pain. *Journal of Psychosomatic Research*, **27**, 431–440.

Pearce, S., and Richardson, P. H. (in press, a). Chronic pain: assessment. In S. J. E. Lindsay and G. E. Powell (eds), *Handbook of Clinical Psychology*. London: Gower.

Pearce, S., and Richardson, P. H. (in press, b). Chronic pain: psychological approaches to management. In S. J. E. Lindsay and G. E. Powell (eds), *Handbook of Clinical Psychology*. London: Gower.

Philips, C. (1977). A psychological analysis of tension headache. In S. Rachman (ed.), *Contributions to Medical Psychology*, vol. 1. Oxford: Pergamon Press.

Philips, C., and Hunter, M. (1981a). Pain behaviour in headache sufferers. *Behaviour Analysis and Modification*, **4**, 257–266.

Philips, C., and Hunter, M. (1981b). The treatment of tension headache: muscular abnormality and bio-feedback. *Behaviour Research and Therapy*, **19**, 485–498.

Prieto, E. J., and Geisinger, K. F. (1983). Factor analytic studies of the McGill Pain Questionnaire. In R. Melzack (ed.), *Pain Measurement and Assessment*. New York: Raven Press.

Reading, A. E., Everitt, B. S., and Sledmere, C. M. (1982). The McGill Pain Questionnaire: a replication of its construction. *British Journal of Clinical Psychology*, **21**, 339–351.

Richards, J. S., Nepomuceno, C., Riles, M., and Suer, Z. (1982). Assessing pain behaviour: the UAB Pain Behaviour Scale. *Pain*, **14**, 393–398.

Roberts, A. H., and Reinhardt, L. (1980). The behavioural management of chronic pain: long term follow-up with comparison groups. *Pain*, **8**, 151–162.

Rybstein-Blinchik, E. (1979). Effects of different cognitive strategies on chronic pain experience. *Journal of Behavioural Medicine*, **2**, 93–101.

Sanders, S. H. (1983). Automated versus self-monitoring of 'up-time' in chronic low-back pain patients: a comparative study. *Pain*, **15**, 399–407.

Swanson, D. W., Maruta, T., and Swenson, W. M. (1979). Results of behaviour modification in the treatment of chronic pain. *Psychosomatic Medicine*, **41**, 55–61.

Tan, S. (1982). Cognitive and cognitive–behavioural methods for pain control: a selective review. *Pain*, **12**, 201–208.

Thompson, S. C. (1981). Will it hurt less if I can control it? A complex answer to a simple question. *Psychological Bulletin*, **90**, 89–101.

Turk, D. C., Meichenbaum, D., and Genest, M. (1983). *Pain and Behavioural Medicine: A Cognitive Behavioural Prospective*. New York: Guilford.

Turkat, I. O., and Adams, H. E. (1982). Covert positive reinforcement and pain modification: a test of efficacy and theory. *Journal of Psychosomatic Research*, **26**, 191–201.

Turner, J. A. (1982). Comparison of group progressive relaxation training and cognitive–behavioural group therapy for chronic low back pain. *Journal of Consulting and Clinical Psychology*, **50**, 757–765.

Turner, J. A., and Chapman, C. R. (1982). Psychological interventions for chronic pain: a critical review. 1. Relaxation training and biofeedback. *Pain*, **12**, 1–21.

Wall, P. D. (1984). Dorsal horn. In P. D. Wall and R. Melzack (eds), *Textbook of Pain*, Edinburgh: Churchill Livingstone.

Ward, T., Knowelden, J., and Sharrard, W. J. W. (1968). Low back pain. *Journal of the Royal College of General Practitioners*, **15**, 128–136.

Zarkowska, E. A. (1981). The relationship between subjective and behavioural aspects of pain in people suffering from low back pain. MPhil dissertation, University of London.

The Psychosomatic Approach: Contemporary Practice
of Whole-person Care
Edited by M. J. Christie and P. G. Mellett
© 1986 John Wiley & Sons Ltd

11

BENZODIAZEPINES: THE SEARCH FOR TRANQUILLITY

ROBERT G. PRIEST

Academic Department of Psychiatry, St Mary's Hospital Medical School, University of London, UK

INTRODUCTION

The question is sometimes asked: 'Are benzodiazepines prescribed too freely?' In my view, it is still too early to answer this question. At the time of writing, the volume of prescription has begun to decrease in the UK because of a wider appreciation of the ill-effects of the drugs, an appreciation not only by physicians but also by the lay public. No doubt benzodiazepines have been misused, and for some patients have been prescribed too freely and for too long. Is this excessive prescription balanced by under-use of the drug? I suspect that there are quite a lot of people in the community who are suffering from excessive anxiety to a disabling degree who have never presented to a doctor. Among them, some would be better helped in other ways, anyway. However, I am sure that there are patients who could have been enormously relieved by benzodiazepines who never received them, and who had to endure their distress to its full degree. At present it is not possible to say whether this type of unnecessary suffering in any way matches the unnecessary problems induced by too free a prescribing hand (Priest, 1980).

MEANINGS OF THE TERM 'ANXIETY'

The benzodiazepines are a group of drugs used as tranquillizers for the relief of anxiety. When a doctor says that his patient suffers from 'anxiety' he may mean one of four things.

An emotion

Anxiety is a painful emotion that we experience when there is the possibility that something unpleasant will happen. It includes an element of uncertainty. This is in contrast to depression, which is the painful emotion we may experience when something unpleasant is certain to happen to us, or has already happened. According to the *Shorter Oxford English Dictionary*, the term *anxious* means 'troubled in mind about some uncertain event'. The emotion of anxiety can be quite normal, and is frequently experienced before examinations, important interviews or when waiting to hear the results of significant decisions.

A symptom

A patient may complain to a doctor about anxiety when it is excessive. It may be out of proportion either in duration or degree. That is to say, if the anxiety were experienced to a disabling degree, for instance, many years before an examination, this might be regarded by the patient as excessive, and this would be a legitimate concern to take to the doctor. A symptom is a distressing event that a patient reports to a physician.

A syndrome

A sign is an abnormality in the patient that the doctor observes, not necessarily complained of by the patient, e.g. perspiration or shaking. A collection of symptoms and signs that add up to a well-recognized clinical picture is called a syndrome. If a patient complains of a fear of an awful but unknown threat, of palpitations, tension pains, excessive perspiration and tremors, the doctor may well recognize the anxiety syndrome.

An illness

One form of mental illness is referred to as an 'anxiety state' (Priest and Woolfson, 1978). This takes various forms.

(1) The patient complains of anxiety, knows very well what the feared event is, but regards the degree or duration of anxiety as excessive.
(2) The patient complains of a fear that something unpleasant will happen, but does not know exactly what it will be. The emotion is present but its cause cannot be identified. In a sense this is by definition an excessive degree of anxiety.
(3) The patient complains of a constellation of physical symptoms normally associated with anxiety, such as shakiness, excessive perspiration, difficulty in getting off to sleep and dry mouth, *but denies experiencing the subjective component.*

Whichever of the three clinical pictures is presented, the casefolder diagnosis of 'anxiety state' cannot be made until certain other diagnoses have been excluded.

Some endocrine disorders, such as hyperthyroidism, can produce all of these symptoms. Many serious mental illnesses, such as depressive illness and schizophrenia, produce (in addition to their more characteristic symptoms) a crop of anxiety features, especially in the early stages. No matter how many anxiety symptoms the patient had, it would not make sense to refer to his illness as an 'anxiety state' if he also had the delusions and hallucinations of a psychotic mental illness.

The diagnosis of anxiety state as an illness in its own right, then, is made when the anxiety syndrome is present and when other causes of it have been excluded.

A similar situation exists with regard to phobias. Claustrophobia and agoraphobia do exist as diagnoses in their own right, but since they can sometimes be produced by more serious underlying mental illnesses the diagnosis has to be made not just by *including* the positive indications but also by *excluding* other conditions (Priest and Steinert, 1977).

COMMON FEATURES OF ANXIETY

Anxiety in general

Physical symptoms

Many of the physical features of anxiety may be regarded as resulting from overactivity of the sympathetic part of the autonomic nervous system (see Sartory and Lader, 1981). This applies to pallor, palpitations, excessive perspiration and difficulty in getting off to sleep—'initial insomnia'. Pains in various muscle groups, such as those at the back of the neck, probably result from excessive tension. For many patients, however, the 'tension' is metaphorical. In particular, some research has cast doubt on the notion that the headaches found in anxiety states are a result of excessive muscular contraction. For other symptoms, the mechanisms are obscure, such as the breathlessness at rest, or 'butterflies in the tummy'. Patients complaining that their knees are knocking together seem to be rare, but anxious patients commonly admit that their hands shake when they try to do something (Foulds, 1965). Some other common symptoms may be seen as *reactions* to anxiety, such as fainting and dizziness. These symptoms are akin to dissociation reactions of hysteria (Priest and Woolfson, 1978). The overbreathing may in turn result in altered blood chemistry which gives rise to numbness, tingling and cramps (particularly in the limbs).

Psychological symptoms

The main psychological symptom of anxiety has been referred to earlier as the key emotion experienced when there is the possibility that something unpleasant will happen. A useful and reasonably unambiguous term for this feeling is *apprehension*. It has also been described as 'fear spread out thin', and in its more acute forms becomes *panic*.

As was made clear earlier, the anxious person may know exactly what it is he is afraid of or he may have the emotion without knowing what the feared object or situation is, maybe having a general sense of foreboding or sensing a vague threat.

Anxiety is not synonymous with *distress*, since the latter term may include elements of depression. Neither is it the same as worry. *Worries* may include concerns about past events, about one's own future actions, one's present situation or about the fate of other people: it is a much broader concept.

Phobic anxiety

The concept of phobia is widely known and there is little difference between the use of the term claustrophobia, for instance, in everyday speech and its use in medical jargon. Phobic anxieties are experienced only when there is the presence of a specific object or situation or the possibility of it, and in between such episodes the patient may remain symptom-free.

Common subjects of phobias include storms, illness, enclosed spaces and animals. A distinction is sometimes made between fears, excessive fears and phobias. Some fears can be quite normal (e.g. fear of snakes). A fear of encountering snakes leading to a constant preoccupation with this possible threat when walking down a thronged street in the centre of London might be regarded as an excessive fear. An excessive fear becomes a phobia when it leads to disability. Thus many people are nervous in lifts, but if the fear leads to avoiding lifts and having one's work and leisure severely curtailed as a result, and having to walk seven floors up to one's own apartment, then this would qualify for the term phobia.

THE PREVALENCE OF ANXIETY SYMPTOMS

Anxiety symptoms are very common, both in the public at large and especially in psychiatric patients of almost all diagnoses.

Psychiatric patients

Foulds (a clinical psychologist) and his colleagues have clarified the frequency of symptoms of anxiety in patients presenting to psychiatrists (Foulds, 1965; Foulds and Bedford, 1975; Foulds and Hope, 1968). They collected a list of 80 questions (covering the commoner neuroses and psychoses) called the Symptom-Sign Inventory and determined whether these symptoms were present in a series of recently admitted psychiatric inpatients. There were ten questions on anxiety, ten on hysteria, ten on mania and so forth. They were attempting to find out if the patients with each diagnosis had the symptoms that they should have had according to the textbooks of psychiatry.

They found that *on the whole* the textbooks were not far from the truth. The patients with one of the four 'neurosis' diagnoses (anxiety state, hysteria, neurotic depression and obsessional state) had neurotic symptoms, and the patients with one of the psychotic diagnoses (psychotic depression, mania,

TABLE 11.1   Percentages of women admitting three illustrative anxiety symptoms in eight diagnostic categories. Adapted from Foulds and Hope (1968)

	Anxiety state	Neurotic depression	Hysteria	Obsessional state	Non-paranoid schizophrenia	Paranoid psychosis	Mania	Psychogenic depression
A2	47	56	52	46	33	22	13	62
A4	75	56	58	54	40	41	38	52
A8	68	69	73	31	47	43	13	75

A2 'Do you sweat very easily, even on cool days?'
A4 'Are there times when you feel anxious without knowing the reason?'
A8 'Have you any difficulty in getting off to sleep (without sleeping pills)?'

paranoid psychosis, non-paranoid schizophrenia) had psychotic symptoms. What emerged very clearly from their research, however, was that in addition to their psychotic symptoms patients with a psychosis also reported excessive numbers of neurotic symptoms. To put it another way, neurotics had neurotic symptoms alone, whereas psychotics had psychotic and neurotic symptoms.

This phenomenon had not received much attention in the literature previously, which Foulds attributed to the King Lear principle

Where the greater malady is fixed
The lesser is scarce felt.

The symptoms of anxiety and neurotic depression particularly were found to be distributed in great numbers throughout the diagnostic categories. The frequency of three symptoms listed in Foulds's 'anxiety' category is shown in Table 11.2. It can be seen that, for their sample of patients, although the frequency of A4 ('Are there times when you feel anxious . . .') was highest in anxiety states, for the remaining two questions the frequency was even higher in some other categories.

The general public

Foulds and his colleagues also administered the Symptom-Sign Inventory to a sample of normal controls. The frequency of positive responses to the ten anxiety questions is shown in Table 11.2. Since their sample was small too much weight should not be placed on the precise percentages. The questions were given in the order A1, A2 and so on to A10, so that this last question is a miscellaneous assortment of fears and problems. However, the figures give a general indication of which anxiety symptoms can be found fairly frequently in the general population, and in particular the frequencies for

TABLE 11.2   Frequency of ten anxiety symptoms in a sample of normal women
(Foulds and Hope, 1968)

	Symptom	Percentage
A4	'Are there times when you feel anxious without knowing the reason?'	25
A8	'Have you any difficulty in getting off to sleep (without sleeping pills)?'	17
A2	'Do you sweat very easily, even on cool days?'	13
A3	'Do you suffer from palpitations or breathlessness?'	9
A5	'Are you afraid of being in a wide-open space or in an enclosed space?'	9
A7	'Have you a pain, or feeling of tension, in the back of the neck?'	9
A10	'Have you any particular fear not mentioned above?'	9
A1	'Does your hand often shake when you try to do something?'	6
A6	'Are you afraid that you might be going insane?'	4
A9	'Are you afraid of going out alone?'	0

the symptoms A2, A4 and A8 can be compared with those found in psychiatric patients in Table 11.1.

Another approach to this question was that undertaken by Crisp and myself (Crisp and Priest, 1971; Priest and Crisp, 1972) using the Middlesex Hospital Questionnaire (MHQ). The MHQ was given to 778 persons in the general population. There are several scales relating to anxiety on this questionnaire. The same questionnaire was administered to patients in a psychiatric ward. Understandably, the patients in the psychiatric ward revealed the high levels of anxiety that one might expect from Foulds's work. To put this in perspective, however, it is noteworthy that roughly 10 per cent of the general population sample achieved scores typical of the psychiatric inpatients.

EFFECTS AND SIDE-EFFECTS OF BENZODIAZEPINES

The term *sedative* has more than one meaning. Two of its principal meanings are 'producing drowsiness' and 'producing a decrease in anxiety levels'. The two are not the same. It is possible to have a treatment that relieves anxiety without producing drowsiness, or to have (at least in theory) a treatment that produces drowsiness without reducing anxiety levels. The two meanings are not always carefully identified in ordinary speech and, while this confusion is regrettable, it is understandable how it has become widespread. For many decades the drugs which were used to treat insomnia (e.g. barbiturates) were from the same class as those used to treat anxiety, and sometimes were even identical compounds. Although the term 'sedative' might apply to their use in either context, when used to treat insomnia particularly they could be referred to as 'hypnotics'.

We now have two further classes of compounds available—the minor tranquillizers and the major tranquillizers. The epithets 'minor' and 'major' refer, curiously enough, to the type of psychiatric disorder for which they are prescribed. Minor tranquillizers, or anxiolytics, are used to treat minor disorders like anxiety states (neuroses). Major tranquillizers, or neuroleptics, are used to treat major disorders like schizophrenia (psychoses). The justification (or lack of it) for referring to psychoses and neuroses as major and minor respectively is discussed elsewhere (Priest and Steinert, 1977).

The following clinical effects of benzodiazepines are described: anxiety relief, sleep induction, anticonvulsant activity, muscle relaxation, disinhibition, amnesia, ataxia and dependence.

Anxiety relief

The benzodiazepines are effective anxiolytic drugs. The prescription of Valium and Librium for anxiety is so familiar to the layman that being 'on Valium' is almost a synonym for being under stress. In contrast to antidepressant medication, which may take days or even weeks to begin to show its effect, the benzodiazepines act immediately. Depending on the particular compound and its formulation, peak blood levels may not be reached until an hour or two after taking the benzodiazepine orally, but well within the first hour the patient begins to feel the benefit. Both diazepam (Valium) and chlordiazepoxide (Librium) have active metabolites. Taking the parent drug together with the metabolites, the elimination half-life may be as long as 48 hours, so that many patients will continue to experience relief of anxiety for a day or more after taking the single dose.

Patients do not always wish to take their tranquillizer as a single daily dose, however. Anxieties, tension and panic come and go during the day, and it is often more satisfying to take a small dose on several occasions at times of special distress, rather than to take a large dose once and then have to endure the fluctuations in anxiety impotently. I shall return to this point later in the chapter when the questions of duration of action of benzodiazepines is considered in more detail.

A wide variety of benzodiazepines are now available that are suitable for use as anxiolytics (see Table 11.3). In contrast to diazepam and chlordiazepoxide, the effective duration of action of some of the more recent drugs is relatively short. For instance, with temazepam and lorazepam, taking the combination of the parent compound and the active metabolites together, the elimination half-line is often under 12 hours (Priest, 1984).

The lowering of anxiety levels is shown both for the subjective symptoms (apprehension) and the physical symptoms (palpitations, etc.). The relief of phobic states is less predictable. In addition to the relief of anxiety, there is evidence that a recently introduced benzodiazepine, alprazolam, also has antidepressant properties (Feighner, 1982).

TABLE 11.3　Mean elimination half-lives of benzodiazepines and their active metabolites upon oral administration to healthy subjects (with variation or standard deviations)

Parent compound	Half-life (hours)	Active metabolite(s)	Half-life metabolite (hours)
Bromazepam (Lexotan)	12 (18–19)	—	—
Brotizolam	5.0 (3.1–6.1)	Active metabolites	Also short half-life
Chlordiazepoxide (Librium)	18 (10–29)	Desmethylchlordiazepoxide	10–18
		Demoxepam	37 (28–63)
		Desoxydemoxepam	44 (39–61)
Clonazepam (Rivotril)	34 (19–42)	—	—
Clorazepate (Tranxene)	2 ± 2	N-desmethyldiazepam	65 ± 36
Diazepam (Valium)	32 (14–61)	N-desmethyldiazepam	42–120
Flunitrazepam (Rohypnol)	15 (9–25)	7-aminoderivative	23
		N-desmethyl derivative	31
Flurazepam (Dalmane)	—	N-desalkylflurazepam	87 (40–144)
Ketazolam (Anxon)	2	Diazepam	32 (14–61)
		N-desmethyldiazepam	42–120
Loprazolam	6.2 (4–8)	?	?
Lorazepam (Almazine, Ativan)	14 (18–24)	—	—
Lormetazepam (Noctamid)	9.9 ± 2.4	—	—
Medazepam (Nobrium)	2	N-desmethyldiazepam	42–120
		Active metabolites	Also short half-life
Midazolam	2.5 (1–3)	—	—
Nitrazepam (Mogadon)	28 (20–34)	—	—
Oxazepam (Serenid-D)	12 (7–25)	—	—
Prazepam (Centrax)	1.3 ± 0.7	N-desmethyldiazepam	96 ± 34
Temazepam (Euhypnos, Normison)	12 (8–21)	—	—
Triazolam (Halcion)	2.3 (1.4–3.3)	Active metabolites	Also short half-life

Source:　Breimer (1984).

Sleep induction

Insomnia may take the form of

(1) difficulty in getting off to sleep in the first place—*initial insomnia*;
(2) broken sleep during the night—*middle insomnia*;
(3) *early morning wakening* in which the patient wakes up after a few hours' sleep and remains awake for the rest of the night.

It is initial insomnia that is most frequently seen with anxiety states. Subjects tend to complain of insomnia when it takes more than half an hour to get off to sleep after settling down for the night. Middle insomnia is also fairly common, and becomes more frequent in older age groups. Early morning wakening is typically found in depressive illnesses (Priest and Steinert, 1977).

Benzodiazepines are effective hypnotics and not only prolong the total duration of sleep but also reduce *sleep latency*, the period elapsing between settling down and falling asleep (Priest, Pletscher and Ward, 1979; Priest *et al.*, 1980).

In addition to causing a transient reduction of rapid eye movement (REM) sleep, benzodiazepines also reduce the deeper stages of sleep (stages 3 and 4, or slow-wave stages) sometimes by as much as 75 per cent (Priest, 1978).

Benzodiazepines that are marketed as hypnotics include nitrazepam and flurazepam. Like diazepam and chlordiazepoxide, these have long effective half-lives which may exceed 24 or even 30 hours. Temazepam and lormetazepam have effective elimination half-lives of 12 hours or less. Triazolam has a half-life of less than 6 hours.

The elimination half-life of a benzodiazepine is not always a good guide to its value as a hypnotic drug. Flunitrazepam, for instance, has a moderately long half-life, but produces an early peak in the blood levels that is of value in treating initial insomnia (Priest, Pletscher and Ward, 1979).

It has been known for many years that the intoxicating effect of alcohol depends not only on the absolute blood level but also on the rate of rise of that level. This partly accounts for the sometimes dramatic effect of drinking on an empty stomach. Similarly, a sleeping pill is much more effective if the drug is rapidly absorbed into the bloodstream, giving a rapid rise in levels. This does probably vary from one benzodiazepine molecule to another. It also depends on the *formulation* of the sleeping pill—the physical make-up of the tablet or capsule. Temazepam was effective as a hypnotic (Priest and Rizvi, 1976) even when the solid powder was enclosed in a hard capsule. It is even more useful now that it is available as a solution enclosed in a soft gelatine capsule shell.

In addition to their use for insomnia, the benzodiazepines can be used for other sleep disorders (Priest, 1978). The familiar nightmares of adults are particularly vivid and intense dreams and occur in REM sleep. *Night terrors* occur in children. In this condition the child sits up with a scream, stares into the distance, and eventually settles down again. The child is relatively inaccessible during the episode, and in the morning has no memory of it. In *sleepwalking* the child sometimes murmurs something unintelligible and usually shows the same two features—inaccessibility, and subsequent amnesia for the episode. These two disorders in fact occur in deep orthodox (slow-wave) sleep. In theory they can be treated with benzodiazepines which, as already noted, can cut down this deep sleep by 75 per cent. In most cases, however, it is more appropriate to manage the children in other ways, since long-term benzodiazepine administration has its own hazards (Tyrer, 1984).

Anticonvulsant effect

Benzodiazepines raise the seizure threshold in epilepsy and are particularly useful in treating convulsions when given intravenously. Diazepam has been used for this purpose for many years, but attempts have been made to produce compounds which have a greater effect on fits in comparison with their tendency to produce drowsiness, ataxia and so forth. Clonazepam and clobazam seem to be in this category.

Muscle relaxation

Since benzodiazepines relieve anxiety, it is understandable that they relieve the muscular tension that may be one of the symptoms of anxiety. However, they produce muscular relaxation over and above this effect. It is probable that this action is mediated through the spinal reflexes involving the gamma efferent nerves.

As a side-effect, patients on large doses of benzodiazepines sometimes complain of 'wobbly knees'. As a therapeutic action, benzodiazepines can be used to treat painful muscular spasms, for instance those arising after spinal injury.

Disinhibition

It is well known that, after a few alcoholic drinks, a person may behave in a way that is unusual for him. He will be less reserved, less inhibited, and lacking in the restraints that are usual in polite society.

Something very similar can happen with the benzodiazepines. Patients not otherwise appearing to be intoxicated with their medication can lack self-control. It has even been claimed that some cases of baby-battering are the result of the mother taking tranquillizers.

Amnesia

Patients undergoing endoscopy and other uncomfortable or frankly painful investigations are often given very large doses of benzodiazepines by the anaesthetist. The obvious beneficial effect is that the patient is relieved of his anxiety to a large extent, and the drowsiness may also be a help. A further effect can also be construed as a benefit—the patient has only a very hazy memory of the procedure subsequently. The benzodiazepine inhibits the registration of memory traces at the time. A cynic might say that this is more of benefit to the physician, because the patient, forgetting the discomfort that he went through, is more likely to agree to the procedure when he needs to go through it again.

Accepting that amnesia can be caused by the very large doses used by anaesthetists, is there any effect on memory from the lower doses used for treating insomnia and anxiety in ambulant patients? I would have found this difficult to answer from my own clinical practice but a research study that I carried out clarified the position in my own mind, at least.

The problem is that complaints of memory difficulties and absentmindedness are quite common in patients with psychiatric disorders. Difficulty in concentration and subjective impairment of memory are classified in the textbooks under the depressive syndrome, but sporadic depressive symptoms are in any case quite common among patients whose principal diagnosis is that of anxiety state. Thus it has happened that when my patients on benzodiazepines have complained of memory problems it has been difficult to know whether this was a side-effect of the medication or a symptom of the underlying psychological distress.

The fact that benzodiazepines can cause memory impairment in normal doses came out of a study that my colleagues and I did (McManus et al., 1983) using medical students as subjects. We were trying to investigate the effect of taking alcohol and benzodiazepines simultaneously. We tried four situations—drug alone, alcohol alone, drug plus alcohol, and control. We found that the memory performance of these healthy volunteers fell to about half their baseline values after taking a standard dose of a benzodiazepine in the 'drug alone' condition.

Ataxia

After large doses of barbiturates an ambulant patient may develop a staggering gait (ataxia), a slurred speech (dysarthria) and double vision (diplopia). Barbiturate addicts sometimes conceal and deny their intake of drugs. The bruises (resulting from the ataxia) are claimed to be spontaneous or mysterious in origin. The addict may develop a slow and deliberate manner of speech to disguise the dysarthria. Even if he does not admit to the diplopia, medical examination can reveal nystagmus—jerky movements of the eyes as they look from side to side, which tend to be associated with the diplopia.

These features are not common with benzodiazepines in ordinary doses. However, if patients take above average doses of the more cumulative compounds over long periods of time then these symptoms and signs may appear. This is a recognized hazard with elderly patients, particularly, who may fall over and break bones as a result of their ataxia.

Dependence

Dependence on drugs is divided into two categories: (1) psychological dependence (habituation, craving) and (2) physical dependence (addiction) (Priest and Woolfson, 1978).

Evidence for physical dependence on a drug usually takes the form of (1) tolerance after months of use, the capacity to take enormous quantities of the drug, and the need to take large amounts to get the same affect as was produced by small amounts originally, or (2) a physical withdrawal syndrome which varies from drug to drug, e.g. with opiates showing itself as lachrymation, salivation, diarrhoea, vomiting, gooseflesh, dilated pupils and abdominal pains.

It is accepted that taking benzodiazepines regularly can lead to psychological dependence. Patients often get fond of their tablets, and they are reluctant to give them up.

A more controversial question is whether physical dependance occurs. In my opinion it does occur, but it is uncommon. Patients vary widely in their response to a given dose of benzodiazepines, and some patients tolerate enormous doses right from the beginning, so evidence of tolerance is unreliable. To my mind the most convincing evidence of addiction is the demonstration of a distinct withdrawal syndrome. We have seen that many of the other effects of benzodiazepines resemble those of alcohol and the barbiturates. Do the benzodiazepines, like these other drugs, lead to delirium tremens (DTs) and fits on withdrawal of high doses?

Convulsions have been recorded on withdrawal. This is very unusual in clinical situations, but has been reported when high experimental doses in prisoners (volunteering for experiments) have been withdrawn. Since there is a high prevalence of abnormal EEGs in prisoners, this must be regarded as a special case (Hollister, Motzenbecker and Degan, 1961; Isbell and Chrusciel, 1970).

There have been some reports of delirium (possibly DTs) following use of high doses of benzodiazepines. For instance, in the treatment of the painful muscle spasms of tetanus high doses of benzodiazepines are used. It has been reported that after the (fairly sudden) withdrawal of the drugs, when the patients are over the spasmodic stage, delirium may occur within a few days. Here again the picture is complex, since tetanus itself can cause brain damage (Malatinsky, Prochazka and Kadlic, 1975).

Thus major withdrawal syndromes such as delirium and convulsions can occur after withdrawal of high doses of benzodiazepines, certainly in vulnerable patients, but probably in patients with a more normal premorbid status as well (Petursson and Lader, 1981; Owen and Tyrer, 1983; Schöpf, 1983).

The withdrawal syndromes resemble those found with addiction to barbiturates and to alcohol, but are much rarer.

It is claimed that a more subtle withdrawal syndrome occurs much more commonly (Petursson and Lader, 1981), affecting nearly 50 per cent of patients who have taken benzodiazepines for 6 months or more when they eventually stop their drugs (Schöpf, 1983). Many of the symptoms described are identical to those of anxiety state, so how can these be distinguished from a recurrence of the original anxiety (Ashton, 1984; Tyrer, 1984)?

Arguments in favour of their status as constituting a withdrawal syndrome rather then an unmasking of the original symptoms are:

(1) The time course is short, with spontaneous remission in a few weeks. It might be supposed that if the original anxiety state had already persisted for over 6 months, it would persist longer.
(2) Some patients were not receiving the benzodiazepines originally for anxiety symptoms but for muscle spasm, for instance, of physical origin.
(3) In addition to the anxiety symptoms certain other symptoms are present, such as pathologically heightened perceptions leading to distorted and painful sensations or illusions.

It remains to be seen whether the syndrome is sufficiently characteristic for it to be identified reliably. Most authorities would agree that, whether dependence on benzodiazepines is psychological or physical in nature, it can be persistent and powerful, and can make it extremely difficult for the patient to give up his drugs.

THE PHARMACOLOGICAL SPECTRUM: ALTERNATIVES TO THE BENZODIAZEPINES

The **major tranquillizers** are substantially different in their effect from traditional sedatives and hypnotics. This difference is not particularly apparent in small doses where both classes of compound, besides relieving anxiety, may also sometimes cause some drowsiness (e.g. 25 mg of sodium amylobarbitone or 25 mg of chlorpromazine). If the dose is multiplied fortyfold then the difference is dramatic. One gram of sodium amylobarbitone is likely to produce deep sleep, and the patient may be so unrousable as to be referred to as comatose or anaesthetized. An overdose of barbiturates can prove lethal. By way of contrast, many patients have taken one gram of chlorpromazine daily for months or years. On this dose they walk around, undertaking normal activities. Some will complain of drowsiness. Some appear quite alert and do not complain of feeling sleepy at all. The barbiturates, then, produce an increasing impairment of consciousness as the dose rises, an effect not seen consistently with neuroleptics.

As we have already seen, after a large dose of barbiturates, if the patient can be persuaded to remain awake, he may complain of a staggering gait, slurred speech or double vision. This triad of ataxia, dysarthria and diplopia is not likely to occur with neuroleptics (unless for some intervening reason, such as a sudden drop in blood pressure).

The barbiturates are addicting. That is to say, patients develop not only a psychological dependence on them but also a physical dependence. The latter may be demonstrated by a gradually increasing tolerance to their effects over the months. More convincingly in my view, if the patient suddenly stops his intake of excessive quantities, a physical withdrawal syndrome follows. The withdrawal syndrome associated with barbiturates and related compounds is quite different from the syndromes found after withdrawal of opiates or amphetamines, and takes one of two main forms (Ewart and Priest, 1967; Priest, 1978).

The first is that of seizures. These fits are similar to those seen in *grand mal* epilepsy. The second is that of delirium tremens. This type of delirium is associated in most people's minds more with alcoholism than with barbiturate addiction. In fact, we now know that though DTs can be linked with alcohol addiction, in those circumstances it is also a withdrawal syndrome and occurs when the alcohol intake has had to be stopped (e.g. admission to hospital for an operation) or at least drastically curtailed (Priest and Steinert, 1977).

What is delirium tremens? The word 'delirium', as used in the English language, corresponds to the diagnosis of 'acute organic brain syndrome' or 'confusional state' in the medical textbooks. The characteristic features of delirium in general are, first, partially impaired consciousness or awareness, and second, disorientation in time, place and person. The particular characteristics of DTs include not only 'the shakes'—a rapid irregular tremor affecting most of the body—but also visual hallucinations and extreme anxiety or fear. The fear and the hallucinations often come together in the form of visions of approaching rats or snakes (rather than pink elephants).

We can now see that many of the effects described earlier as typical of barbiturates are also found with alcohol. Alcohol in small doses is used as an anxiolytic—'This'll steady your nerves.' It is also used as a 'nightcap' to induce sleep. Sometimes very large quantities (e.g. two bottles of whisky) are taken at one time for a bet or a prank, and this can result in coma or even death.

If a fairly large dose of alcohol is taken and the subject manages to stay awake, he may demonstrate ataxia, dysarthria and diplopia (which can be seen as a common syndrome on Saturday evenings). Alcohol can be addicting if taken regularly, and abrupt withdrawal of a high regular dose can lead not only to DTs but also to convulsions. The resemblance to barbiturates is close. Other sedatives or hypnotics produce a similar pattern. They include chloral, paraldehyde, meprobamate and methaqualone.

The neuroleptic drugs are never associated with physical dependence in this way (a remarkable fact for a psychotropic drug, but also true of tricyclic antidepressants).

Effect of barbiturates on REM sleep

During the course of the night orthodox sleep is interrupted by bursts of rapid eye movement (REM) or paradoxical sleep lasting approximately 5–20 minutes. Altogether these episodes of REM sleep add up to about 20 per cent of the night or more. When woken from REM sleep subjects regularly report dreaming (Priest, 1978).

When a patient starts to take barbiturate sleeping tablets regularly each night the proportion of REM sleep at first falls. It then rises again and after about 10 days reaches the normal proportion once more. An increase in the daily dose of the barbiturate will cause a further temporary suppression of REM sleep.

If the barbiturates are suddenly stopped the proportion of REM sleep rises sharply over the next few days, and at this time the subjects may be woken by vivid, intense dreams, often frightening and nightmarish (Oswald and Priest, 1965).

Let us now look at the situation with the barbiturate addict. Over many weeks, months or even years he has repeatedly increased the dose of the barbiturate. Each time a temporary suppression of REM sleep has occurred. What happens if he suddenly stops all barbiturates? In these circumstances the proportion of REM sleep soars to 100 per cent of the night.

Percentages are sometimes misleading. One has to ask, A percentage of what? In this case it is a percentage of a rather small quantity. The addict who gives up his large quantities of sleeping pills is not going to sleep very well. He will have difficulty getting off in the first place. Eventually, he will go to sleep, passing directly from wakefulness into intense, vivid and frightening dreams. In a normal night's sleep we never pass straight into REM sleep—there is always a period of orthodox sleep first. Going straight from the waking state into nightmares for a short spell, and then waking up again, may well account for the clinical picture of complaints of visual hallucinations and disorientation that is seen in DTs.

Comparison of benzodiazepines with barbiturates, alcohol and major tranquillizers

We are now in a position to get a general view of the actions of benzodiazepines by comparison with other hypnotics and tranquillizers. We have seen that barbiturates produce, in increasing doses, ataxia, dysarthria, diplopia, nystagmus and coma (which may lead to death). In long-term use they may produce addiction, with true physical dependence. This characteristic pattern of effects is absent with the major tranquillizers (Priest, 1981a).

Qualitatively the benzodiazepines resemble the barbiturates, but their tendency to produce these unwanted effects is very much weaker. This is most clearly illustrated by the relative toxicity in overdose. Overdoses of barbiturates are dangerous and commonly lethal. Overdoses of benzodiazepines, when taken alone, are by comparison benign and are hardly ever lethal. Most of the deaths that occur after benzodiazepine overdose have been fatal because an overdose of other drugs (and commonly alcohol) was taken simultaneously.

Alcohol itself can produce most or all of the effects of barbiturates, but has some more specific actions of its own. It is a vasodilator drug, and may thus produce low blood pressure and (in cold ambient temperature) hypothermia because of heat loss from the skin. Prolonged use can lead to vitamin deficiencies (particularly of thiamin—vitamin B_1), cirrhosis of the liver and so forth. These problems are not encountered with benzodiazepines.

DURATION OF ACTION OF BENZODIAZEPINES

Many of the benzodiazepines are converted in the tissues to metabolites which are themselves active, though of half-lives that differ from those of the parent compounds. Quite often the half-life of the parent compound is relatively short, but that of the derivatives much longer (see Table 11.3).

Some components (e.g. temazepam, lormetazepam) produce active metabolites in such small quantities that they do not materially affect the clinical response.

Let us take the case of an imaginary benzodiazepine drug, used for sleep induction each night, which reaches peak blood concentrations 1 hour after administration, and falls to half this level 24 hours after administration. On the second night of administration the rise in concentration in the blood is superimposed on a blood level that is already half that of the previous peak. On the third night new record levels are set. At no time is the drug completely eliminated from the body. It is clear that in such circumstances the drug is cumulative.

Alcohol has a short half-life of only a few hours (with usual doses). A common experience is that, after an evening of heavy indulgence, sleep induction is very prompt, but waking occurs in the early hours of the morning. Part of the reason for this may be that as the soporific effect of the alcohol wears off an alerting effect is produced in the brain, although other factors may also play a part (e.g. a release of catecholamines into the bloodstream triggered off by the alcohol). Recent reports suggest that the very short-acting benzodiazepines may also run into the problem of early wakening. The current feeling is, then, that a half-life of about 8 to 10 hours is probably a suitable duration for a benzodiazepine intended for hypnotic use.

When a benzodiazepine is prescribed principally for anxiolytic use different considerations apply. There are two possible strategies for prescription. In the first it is the explicit aim to have the tissues constantly bathed in the drug. Here the long-acting compounds are ideal, and the fact that they are cumulative may even be a virtue. Certainly, when the time comes to stop them a more gradual and less disruptive withdrawal process is more likely. The other strategy takes note of the fact that some patients are not content to take their anxiety relieving pills at long intervals (e.g. once daily) but wish to obtain the psychological gratification of swallowing their potential solace several times a day. Here there is less requirement for a long-acting compound, and the desired abrupt rise in blood levels of benzodiazepines may be easier to achieve if the previous dose has largely worn off. In my opinion it is not a question of one strategy being the better of the two. Either is valid in differing circumstances.

INTERACTION WITH ALCOHOL

Patients taking tranquillizers are often advised not to take alcohol at the same time. Certainly, it would seem prudent advice to suggest that the patient monitors the effect of alcohol closely if he does drink. The similarity of many of the actions of benzodiazepines and alcohol would appear to make this advice merely an example of common sense.

However, recent research suggests that the question of additive effect is not a simple one. McManus and his colleagues (1983) found that alcohol actually mitigated the impairment of performance induced by the benzodiazepine loprazolam, particularly the effects on normal dexterity, memory and a computerized tracking task.

It is probable that patients dependent on alcohol are more likely than most other persons to become dependent on benzodiazepines. This does not necessarily mean that benzodiazepines should not be prescribed to alcoholics. Many physicians argue that, by comparison with the benzodiazepines, the consequences of excessive alcohol intake on the body are so horrendous that it would be much better if the patient would cut down his drinking even if the consequence were that he became dependent on benzodiazepines. At least the benzodiazepines would not produce, for instance, the serious physical damage of vitamin deficiency associated with alcoholism.

NON-PHARMACEUTICAL ALTERNATIVES

What other methods are there for anxiety relief that compete with the prescription of drugs? The most obvious solution is to deal with the source of the anxiety. This is difficult when the source is unknown. Even when the source is quite obvious, it may be immutable. However, sometimes with advice and manipulation of the environment the patient is enabled to avoid what seemed to be an inevitable threat.

Insight-oriented psychotherapy (based on Freudian or other psychoanalytic principles) aims to enable the patient to deal with his problems in a more realistic and creative way, and for some patients this will be a preferable alternative. Why only for some? The disadvantages of psychoanalytically oriented psychotherapy are

(1) It is expensive and not always available locally.
(2) It is not always successful.

(3) It can be anxiety *producing* in the short term.
(4) Either because they cannot endure the stress of the psychotherapy itself, or from other unsatisfactory personality features, not everybody is regarded by the psychotherapists as being a suitable case for treatment (Brown and Pedder, 1979).

Supportive psychotherapy is often given for anxiety states. This approach involves sympathy, reassurance, explanation, encouragement and sometimes suggestion. It does not aim at eradicating the roots of the anxiety, but since in many cases the anxiety state is essentially a transitory phase, it may be just what the patient requires to tide him over and make him feel better until the abnormal state resolves spontaneously (Priest, 1981b).

An alternative type of psychotherapy is *non-directive counselling*. Here one of the principal ingredients is ventilation. The therapist listens to the patient and, when the patient dries up, encourages him to talk some more about his problems (usually not a difficult task). The bulk of the time is spent with the therapist listening. When he does talk, his intervention may be of a supportive, or analytic, or neutral kind. It is not entirely clear why this method is so successful. It is possibly something to do with allowing the patient to get problems 'off his chest'. It may be that in talking about them, those fears and threats that seemed to be of gigantic, nightmarish proportions are cut down to a life-like and manageable size.

Yet another approach is that of *behaviour therapy* (or behavioural psychotherapy) (Mackay, 1975). Like supportive psychotherapy, this does not aim to ferret out deep unconscious conflicts as the cause of the patient's anxiety. Rather, it deals with the problems as the results of maladaptive learning in a very pragmatic way, using the learning theory of modern psychology. This approach is particularly successful in the treatment of phobias, but extentions of it are increasingly being used for other forms of distress.

WHEN TO STOP TAKING BENZODIAZEPINES

When a patient presents to a physician with pathological anxiety the doctor should whenever possible try to deal with its cause. Failing this, he should consider non-pharmaceutical methods of relieving the anxiety. However, most physicians will feel that there are at least some patients where neither of these alternatives is appropriate or possible, and benzodiazepines form the group of drugs most commonly prescribed for anxiety relief. Clearly it is desirable for them to be used for the shortest possible time. Some authorities recommend that they should not be given for longer than 2 weeks. But if alternative approaches are not possible, and the patient's underlying anxiety is still unabated, is the doctor arbitrarily to refuse to prescribe any further relief at the end of the fortnight? To do so does seem rather heartless, even if the purpose of acting this way is the laudable one of preventing the patient from becoming dependent on his medication.

One frequently hears criticism of overworked (or lazy?) general prac-titioners reaching for the prescription pad as soon as the patient mentions psychological distress. There may be some genuine cause for concern in this direction. Nevertheless, frequently the doctor is put in the situation of prescribing tranquillizers because the *patient* is unwilling to contemplate an alternative approach to his symptoms. After all, the non-drug methods for dealing with anxiety are likely to be time consuming for the patient as well as the doctor, and many of them involve a degree of impulse control and a tolerance of delay that is frustrating, to say the least. Tablets and capsules are so convenient, and their effects so prompt and reliable.

One way that the physician can ameliorate this situation is by emphasizing that the tablets merely provide temporary, symptomatic relief *before he agrees to prescribe them.* He may go on to say, 'I do not want you to go on taking the pills after 2 weeks if it is at all possible. If you are not over your tendency to anxiety by then we shall have to consider other remedies at that stage.' Warned in this way, the patient is more likely to accept an alternative therapeutic contract as part of an overall plan, and not suspect that the doctor has just lost patience and sympathy with him.

In fact, to me 2 weeks seems rather a short time, but it is obviously better to aim for a duration of weeks rather than months, in view of the high risk of dependence after 6 months' treatment that I alluded to earlier in the chapter.

HOW TO STOP TAKING BENZODIAZEPINES

The two most important considerations in being able to stop taking benzodi-azepines are motivation and a gradual reduction in dose.

Motivation

Withdrawal from benzodiazepines is possible even without a commitment from the patient (e.g. on admission on hospital or to jail) but in ordinary life it is more likely to succeed if the patient's active collaboration is achieved.

When the problem is merely a lingering psychological dependence on the drug, and the original anxiety symptoms have disappeared, withdrawal should be preceded by education. The nature of the withdrawal symptoms should be explained to the patient so that they are identified for what they are. The patient should be brought to the stage where he recognizes his state of dependence and agrees that he wishes to end it. The fact that the with-drawal symptoms may last for 2 or 3 weeks even after complete abstinence should also be explained to him.

Unless the patient understands what is likely to happen, and is prepared to accept the withdrawal symptoms for the sake of getting off the drug, then he will be tempted to start taking benzodiazepines again—either those left in the house, or others borrowed from friends, or even a fresh prescription from a different physician.

Gradual withdrawal

For moderate and low doses the drug intake should be gradually reduced and abandoned over 4 weeks. For higher doses a much longer period may be necessary. Shorter periods of withdrawal, or sudden complete cessation, run the risk of serious physical withdrawal syndromes (delirium, fits). Longer periods prolong the agony: the phase when the patient is gradually reducing the medication is an unpleasant one, even before the stage of complete cessation is reached, and patients frequently give up the process and resume taking higher doses. Too long a period of withdrawal increases this risk.

Other factors

Patients may become quite depressed when coming off benzodiazepines, and some require specific treatment for the depression (psychotherapy or antidepressants). Other patients who are particularly bothered by palpitations or tremor may be helped by β-adrenergic blocking drugs (e.g. propranolol). This class of drug, though limited in its range of action, does at least have the virtue that it is not habit-forming.

For those patients who still have their original anxiety symptoms the withdrawal of the drug may be combined with the other methods of anxiety relief described earlier in the chapter. All patients are likely to require considerable emotional support at this time.

CONCLUSIONS

Despite their drawbacks, there can be little doubt that benzodiazepines are safer than alcohol, both in terms of dependence potential and in terms of toxicity in overdose. Yet in most countries benzodiazepines are available only by physician's prescription whereas alcohol can be bought over the counter. It could be argued that if alcohol were introduced as a new drug today it would never be licensed for public consumption. The debate has similarities to that on the possibility of legalizing the use of cannabis.

The advantage that alcohol has over benzodiazepines is that man has been using alcohol for a lot longer. Over the centuries traditions have grown up around its use, many of which have the function of rationing it or curbing excessive intake. We grow up learning the hazards of being an alcoholic or the danger of getting drunk. The benzodiazepines have been introduced too recently to have the same degree of institutional sanctions and taboos. It is possible that as the years go by people will learn to use them easily and safely, so that they can be bought at a shop in the same way as aspirin tablets. In my view we are not yet at this point.

I am certainly very pleased that the benzodiazepines have largely replaced the barbiturates. The latter were both more addictive and more lethal in overdose. The difference between the two groups in this respect is enormous. The difference in toxicity is illustrated by the fact that even today deaths from barbiturate overdose are common while those from benzodiazepine overdose are rare. The difference in dependence potential is more difficult to quantify, but there is no doubt in my mind that whereas dependence followed by the major physical withdrawal syndromes (fits and DTs) was common with barbiturates and related drugs, it is very rare with benzodiazepines. I would not like to go back to the era before benzodiazepines were available.

REFERENCES

Ashton, H. (1984). Benzodiazepine withdrawal: an unfinished story. *British Medical Journal*, **288**, 1135–1136.

Breimer, D. D. (1984). Pharmacokinetics of benzodiazepines. In R. G. Priest (ed.), *Sleep—An International Monograph*. London: Update Publications.

Brown, D., and Pedder, J. (1979). *Introduction to Psychotherapy*. London: Tavistock Publications.

Crisp, A. H., and Priest, R. G. (1971). Psychoneurotic profiles in middle age: a study of persons aged 40–65 years registered with a general practitioner. *British Journal of Psychiatry*, **119**, 385–392.

Ewart, R. B. L., and Priest, R. G. (1967). Methaqualone addiction and delirium tremens. *British Medical Journal*, **3**, 92–93.

Feighner, J. P. (1982). Benzodiazepines as antidepressants. In T. A. Ban (ed.), *Modern Problems of Pharmacopsychiatry*. Basle: Karger, pp. 146–212.

Foulds, G. A. (1965). *Personality and Personal Illness*. London: Tavistock Publications.

Foulds, G. A., and Bedford, A. (1975). Hierarchy of classes of personal illness. *Psychological Medicine*, **5**, 181–192.

Foulds, G. A., and Hope, K. (1968). *Manual of the Symptom–Sign Inventory*. London: University of London Press.

Hollister, L. E., Motzenbecker, F. P., and Degan, R. O. (1961). Withdrawal reactions from chlordiazepoxide ('Librium'). *Psychopharmacologia*, **2**, 63–68.

Isbell, H., and Chrusciel, T. L. (1970). Dependence liability of 'non-narcotic' drugs. *Supplementary Bulletin of the World Health Organization*, **43**, Geneva.

Mackay, D. (1975). *Clinical Psychology: Theory and Therapy*. London: Methuen.

McManus, I. C., Ankier, S. I., Norfolk, J., Phillips, M., and Priest, R. G. (1983). Effects on psychological performance of the benzodiazepine, loprazolam, alone and with alcohol. *British Journal of Clinical Pharmacology*, **16**, 291–300.

Malatinsky, J., Prochazka, M., and Kadlic, T. (1975). Transient psychological syndrome following diazepam therapy for tetanus. *Postgraduate Medical Journal*, **51**, 860–863.

Oswald, I., and Priest, R. G. (1965). Five weeks to escape the sleeping pill habit. *British Medical Journal*, **2**, 1093–1099.

Owen, R. T., and Tyrer, P. J. (1983). Benzodiazepine dependence: a review of the evidence. *Drugs*, **25**, 385–398.

Petursson, H., and Lader, M. H. (1981). Withdrawal from long term benzodiazepine treatment. *British Medical Journal*, **283**, 643–645.

Priest, R. G. (1978). Sleep and its disorders. In R. G. Gaind and B. Hudson (eds), *Current Themes in Psychiatry*. London: Macmillan, pp. 83–93.

Priest, R. G. (1980). The benzodiazepines: a clinical review. In R. G. Priest, U. Vianna Filho, R. Amrein and M. Skreta (eds), *Benzodiazepines Today and Tomorrow*. Lancaster: MTP Press, pp. 77–83.

Priest, R. G. (1981a). Major tranquillizers. *Pharmaceutical Journal*, **226**, 117–119.

Priest, R. G. (1981b). The psychotherapeutic management of the patient in general practice. Alternatives to drug treatment. In G. Edwards (ed.), *Psychiatry in General Practice*. Southampton: University of Southampton.

Priest, R. G. (ed.). (1984) *Sleep: An International Monograph*. London: Update Publications.

Priest, R. G., and Crisp, A. H. (1972). The menopause and its relationship with reported somatic experience. In N. Morris (ed.), *Psychosomatic Medicine in Obstetrics and Gynaecology*. Basle: Karger, pp. 605–607.

Priest, R. G., Pletscher, A., and Ward, J. (eds) (1979). *Sleep Research*. Lancaster: MTP Press.

Priest, R. G., and Rizvi, Z. A. (1976). Nitrazepam and temazepam: a comparative trial of two hypnotics. *Journal of International Medical Research*, **4**, 145–151.

Priest, R. G., and Steinert, J. (1977). *Insanity: A Study of Major Psychiatric Disorders*. Plymouth: Macdonald & Evans.

Priest, R. G., Vianna Filho, U., Amrein, R., and Skreta, M. (eds) (1980). *Benzodiazepines Today and Tomorrow*. Lancaster: MTP Press.

Priest, R. G., and Woolfson, G. (1978). *Minski's Handbook of Psychiatry*. 7th edn. London: William Heinemann Medical Books.

Sartory, G., and Lader, M. (1981). Psychophysiology and drugs in anxiety and phobias. In M. J. Christie and P. G. Mellett (eds), *Foundations of Psychosomatics*. Chichester: Wiley, pp. 169–192.

Schöpf, J. (1983). Withdrawal phenomena after long-term administration of benzodiazepines: a review of recent investigations. *Pharmacopsychiatry*, **16**, 1–8.

Tyrer, P. J. (1984). Benzodiazepines on trial. Leader in *British Medical Journal*, **288**, 1101–1102.

SECTION 6

Wellbeing in Community Environments

The Psychosomatic Approach: Contemporary Practice of Whole-person Care
Edited by M. J. Christie and P. G. Mellett
© 1986 John Wiley & Sons Ltd

12

PUBLIC HEALTH—COMMUNITY MEDICINE OR MEDICINE IN THE COMMUNITY?

MARK R. BAKER

Bradford Health Authority, West Yorkshire, UK
and
Clinical Epidemiology Research Unit, University of Bradford, UK

INTRODUCTION

In Britain, of 1000 men who smoke cigarettes regularly, 1 will be murdered, 6 will die in road traffic accidents and 250 will die prematurely from the effects of their cigarette smoking.

Had the legislation, making the wearing of seat belts in the front seats of cars compulsory, been passed by the British Parliament at the first attempt, more than 10 000 deaths would have been avoided—equivalent to all the deaths from childhood leukaemia throughout the same period of time.

These two examples demonstrate the wide range of influences on human health—behavioural, environmental and political—in addition to the influence of those whose professional responsibility involves other people's health. In particular, they draw attention to the importance of the attitudes of the population in general and, consequently, of the legislators they choose to elect as their representatives in national decision making.

It is more than 30 years since the hazards of cigarette smoking became widely known; since then the prevalence of smoking has fallen by almost half, but one third of the population still smoke cigarettes regularly. Professional attitudes to smoking have generally been consistent with the evidence concerning its harmful effects. Nevertheless, in the UK, 20 000 doctors and almost ten times as many nurses still smoke. Public attitudes to smoking have changed extremely slowly and antagonism to smoking has been largely confined to the higher social classes. This is particularly regrettable since it is the manual workers and their families who suffer most from smoking-associated diseases (Doll and Peto, 1981). Governmental response to the health effects of smoking has been inconsistent and usually dominated by economic and political considerations rather than concern over the public's health. Perhaps the most effective disincentive to smoking is the fiscal regulator which the chancellor of the exchequer exercises in his annual budget. Yet the amount of increase in the excise duty on tobacco is determined by the needs of the Treasury rather than the health needs of the population.

Similarly, the siting of so many cigarette-producing factories in marginal constituencies is unfortunate for the opponents of smoking. Now that smoking is at last declining steadily in this country, the tobacco manufacturers are seeking new markets in developing countries; alongside the export of medicines and vaccines to the Third World we also export the source of much of the disease of the developed countries.

For many years, the British Medical Association, by no means the most unselfish or philanthropic organization, has been campaigning for compulsion by law for the wearing of seat belts in cars. As in many other public health measures, the UK lags behind most comparable countries in this matter. The experience of those countries where seat belts are worn has demonstrated both the feasibility of such legislation and the dramatic effects it has on survival from road traffic accidents. While the cause has been widely espoused by members of the health care professions, public opinion had not been swung before the legislation came into effect. Indeed, some remarkable reasons why seat belts should not be worn became part of the nation's folklore. It should be remembered that those who died because they were not wearing seat belts were not available for comment, while the few whose lives or limbs were spared through not wearing seat belts lived to deliver greatly embellished tales to all and sundry. Thus, it is fair to say that public opinion was not founded on objectivity in the seat belt saga. Politicians had numerous opportunities to enact the relevant legislation, but always managed to avoid doing so until 1982. Some of their number publicly championed the cause of freedom of choice even if that freedom resulted in severe injury or death. This difference of perspective between the rights of the individual and the benefits to a community reflects the very same difference between clinical medicine, where only the individual is considered, and community medicine, where the net benefit to a group of people is the criterion of success. In any event, if the individual exercising his freedom of choice just failed to kill himself in the process, the consequences would have to be paid for by the taxpayer who, as we all know, has no freedom of choice whatsoever!

There are a number of important lessons to be learnt from this brief analysis of two of the greatest public health issues of our time. First, it is clear that logical argument based on objective data is, on its own, insufficient to achieve the desired change in public attitudes and government policy. Second, to varying degrees, both the lobbies for change and the opponents to those lobbies were, and remain, guilty of profound hypocrisy. Third, on account of the above, it is usually necessary to resort to subterfuge to achieve the desired end; I am by no means sure whether it is easier to influence politicians through public pressure or whether it is better to influence public opinion through political will. Fourth, it is apparent that government inter-vention can have a profound influence on the health experience of the community. However, the pace of change is often funereally slow and the scale of intervention is so enormous that the range of modalities where government intervention is feasible is necessarily limited. Perhaps because of these constraints of time and scale, successive governments have tended to adopt a rather *laissez faire* approach to public health measures, a policy synonymous with an acceptance of no action. If a death is caused by the failure of a health care professional to take necessary intervention action in time, the relatives of the deceased may seek redress by demonstrating negligence. However, even though tens of thousands of lives may be lost by an unaccountable delay on the part of the government, there is no comeback.

It is neither a paradox nor an irony that the state, through government sponsorship, does more to support the tobacco industry than to tackle the problem of smoking-associated diseases. It constitutes no less than negligence.

COMMUNITY MEDICINE

The discipline of public health, now embraced by the specialty of community medicine, emerged during the aftermath of the Industrial Revolution and therefore constituted a central component of the scientific renaissance which has occupied the last quarter of this millennium. It was the first branch of medicine to be practised from a scientific basis; cynics might say that it remains the only such specialty.

The creation of the 'new' specialty of community medicine in 1972 encompassed three separate but related activities. These were:

(1) the study of the epidemiology of diseases and their consequences as carried out in university departments of public health, social medicine, preventive medicine, etc.;
(2) the delivery of public health and preventive services mainly through local authority public health departments;
(3) the organization of health services, especially hospital services, in central government departments and regional hospital boards.

Community medicine may be defined as that branch of medical practice which attempts to describe, explain and ultimately improve the health and sickness experience of human communities. Its scientific basis is epidemiology which is the study of the distribution and determinants of disease.

It would be fair to say that the major areas of work of the specialty have not changed as a result of the reorganization of the discipline (and of the National Health Service in 1974) but the balance between them probably has, and it would be wrong to assume that the process was merely a change of name. The two most important changes are the removal of the practising base from local government (comprising elected political members) to National Health Service authorities (comprised of appointed and mainly non-political members) and a substantial increase in the involvement with the management and organization of hospital services (DHSS, 1972). It is not the purpose of this chapter to debate the wisdom or value of these changes, but to assess the current role of the specialty in public health and to describe any gaps in public health concern which may have arisen from these changes.

In the early days of the specialty, practitioners of public health were usually clinicians who took a wider view of the health needs of the population. With increasing specialization throughout medicine, it is not normally possible for a doctor to practise at the highest level in more than one specialty. Not only, therefore, are community physicians wholly committed to their own discipline, but the much more numerous clinicians no longer share the work or even the ideals of their community physician colleagues. Indeed, the importance to public well-being of measures not immediately associated with health is now beyond the wit of most who work in, or are involved in the management of, the National Health Service.

One of the most common platitudes in both politics and health is 'prevention is better than cure'. However, platitudes are not enough to influence health and neither medical nor political practice actually reflect the active implementation of preventive measures in preference to those which are allegedly curative. For example, it is not regarded as ethical to implement preventive measures on a supposedly healthy population unless there is a sound scientific (epidemiological) base for doing so. Conversely, a wide range of so-called therapeutic measures have been introduced into clinical practice without evaluation of any kind. Indeed, the entire practice of some specialities such as neurology and rheumatology was, until recently, based on unproven remedies.

The implementation of an active policy of prevention requires either a population committed to protecting itself or a government committed to the protection of its population. In the USA, the general population has the necessary commitment; in Australia it is the government which has demonstrated its will to improve the health of its population through public health measures. In the UK, the commitment is lacking on both sides and the medical profession, despite its power and authority, has been unable to redress the balance. Indeed, the major hurdle which preventive intervention faces is that of reaching the population at risk. The unusually profound failure to do so in the UK is indicative of the *laissez faire* attitude on all sides—professional, individual and governmental. Instead, the government's response, with public support, is generally confined to shoring up the so-called curative services when demand overwhelms supply. Admittedly, it is easier to identify treatment need than prevention need but, essentially, this policy offers an easy way out for the government and the medical profession and ensures that neither has to make a difficult choice between competing demands. It also reflects the stable-door mentality which is the hallmark of our public policy and ensures that government policy in health care mimics the widespread victim blaming practised by the medical and other health care professions.

It is not disputed that the extended role of community physicians in the organization of hospital services at local level has been achieved at the ill-afforded expense of their role in preventive medicine. This is reflected not only in the current practice of the specialty but also in the training offered to those who espouse it. This has resulted, in the main, from two quite unrelated requirements. First, the community physician, in transferring from local government to the National Health Service, lost his political power base and the hospital service provided the ideal replacement. Second, the awareness, on the part of government agencies, that if doctors were ever going to be controlled it must be by other doctors, made the involvement of a managerially accountable medical practitioner of considerable seniority mandatory. Whatever the underlying explanation, and regardless of the wisdom or folly of these changes and the reasoning behind them, the role of the medical profession in locally based preventive initiatives appeared to decline and the more recent organizational changes have done little to alter the situation (BMA/FCM, 1980).

Despite this shift in personal responsibilities, community physicians in district health authorities remain the only relevant source of advice to their authorities on community and public health issues (Chaplin, 1982). They also retain some executive and advisory powers in respect of local government authorities. Their relative withdrawal from the front line of prevention has, however, inevitably created something of a vacuum and vacuums are always eventually filled. Let us now consider the different ways in which this particular vacuum might be filled bearing in mind that it is never more than a partial vacuum. First, the government has maintained its stance that health authorities should concentrate on preventive and community services in preference to hospital services. However, centrally issued lists of priority services make little or no mention of prevention. Instead, an occasional series of sporadic, ill-conceived and largely misdirected campaigns (e.g. rickets, whooping cough and rubella) have been launched without appropriate consultation, preparation or objective evaluation. Such activities serve merely to undermine the remaining preventive activity in the district rather than to supplement it.

An alternative approach is to delegate this function to a committed and supposedly expert quango (quasi autonomous non-government organization) such as the Health Education Council. Unfortunately, more often than not, the attitude of such bodies to health authorities is similar to that of government departments and they rarely serve to assist districts in preference to implementing central guidance, however irrelevant it may be in the local situation.

The third possibility is that the partial withdrawal of community physicians from the prevention battleground is followed by the entry or increased involvement of other locally based people or organizations. The personalities most involved in prevention, apart from community physicians, are general medical practitioners, health visitors, members of health education departments and community health doctors, together with organizations such as some local authority departments, the statutory consumer representatives on community health councils and non-statutory consumer groups such as the Campaign for Lead-Free Air (CLEAR) and the Spastics Society.

Generally speaking, although general practitioners, health visitors and health education staff have increased in number, their roles and responsibilities have not significantly changed and there has been no takeover of the former public health function of community medicine. Community health doctors have undergone some organizational change including a shift in management responsibility for delivery of services. But no change has occurred in the location of responsibility for the planning, provision and level of the relevant services which remains with the health authority on the advice of the community physician. Local authority involvement in health declined substantially in 1948 and further still in 1974 when community and preventive services were transferred to the National Health Service. Councillors do not usually strive to become members of health authorities and their interest in health matters continues to decline. Community health councils do occasionally raise important issues which demand a response from the health authority but, in general, they lack the expertise necessary to play a major role in organization which is, in any case, beyond their remit. Voluntary organizations, especially the two referred to above, have experienced rather more success but this, again, has usually been at national rather than local level.

It is also possible, of course, for the prevention vacuum to be filled by those involved in treatment services and it is certainly true that some secondary and tertiary preventive initiatives have originated from hospital consultants. However, it is probable that this was always the case and that the gap that requires filling is in primary prevention.

It follows, from the above discourse, that the vacuum in preventive medicine created by the partial withdrawal of community physicians has not yet been filled and that it is unlikely to be filled except by the return to the fold of community physicians. The way lies open, therefore, for the mantle of the protection of the public health to be grasped once again by those who have only recently loosened their grip on it.

Before the 1974 reorganization of the Health Service and local government, departments of public health in local authorities were headed by a community physician with the title of Medical Officer of Health. For 99 years, between 1875 and 1974, these appointments were statutory and the medical officer of health possessed a remarkable amount of employment protection including security of tenure so as to enable him openly to criticize his own employers without risking dismissal. In return, the medical officer of health was obliged to produce an annual report of his department's activities, including an overview of the health of the population he served and of the services available to meet the needs of that population. Although in the latter days of this period the production of the annual report became something of an industry in itself, the process did require some objectivity in the description of the health experience of the population and a well-argued case usually led to some remedial action being taken. This annual review process, recently reintroduced by central government for all health services as if it were an original thought, tended to militate against systematic initiatives and encouraged short-term responses to a wide range of problems. The present review procedures are, of course, concerned mainly with finance, manpower and hospital services and offer nothing to prevention. Indeed, not only is there still no systematic approach to prevention but there is no longer any objectivity or even any concern with health. It is in correcting this situation that community physicians have their major role in the future.

The advantageous position of community physicians in this venture, and the reason why their temporary abdication will prove not to be to their permanent disadvantage, is based on two tenets. First, as mentioned at the beginning of this section, their practice is based on the scientific objectivity which is so glaringly lacking in current policy formulation. Second, despite all the changes which have taken place in the relevant organizations and in their own status, community physicians remain closer to the political decision makers than any other group of doctors. Thus, despite all the arguments to the contrary, it is those who practise community medicine who are in the best position to describe, explain and improve the health of the population they serve.

Nevertheless, there remain a number of obstacles, inherent in the present system, which serve to obstruct the successful implementation of public health measures at this level. Health authorities, acting on behalf of the Secretary of State for Social Services, are concerned mainly with health services which are geared to the restoration of health rather than its maintenance. It is fair to say that most normal people are only concerned with their health when they lose it and share the political concern with services rather than outcome.

Furthermore, community physicians have a conflicting relationship, *vis-à-vis* their own role, with both the health and local authorities. In the Health Service, they represent the needs of the population expressed in advice to the health authority. However, as an officer of that authority to whom he is publicly accountable, it is not easy for the community physician to give public health advice which clearly conflicts with his other management responsibilities. As far as the relationship with local authorities is concerned, community physicians have both executive and advisory functions. However, in neither case are any resources made accountable to the community physician whose isolation in this respect is now almost complete. Together with this, while his role in service provision has been enhanced, the community physician has lost much of his status as a public figure and it is therefore much more difficult for him to influence public opinion against government inaction even if his accountability had allowed it.

With the changing power structure in our community and particularly the use of mass media for delivering messages, health behaviour at both individual and government level is influenced more by party political views on health and by specially orchestrated, blinkered, self-interested and usually hypocritical lobby groups than by objective analysis of health needs. Indeed, central action on health by recent governments of different shades appears to have been dominated solely by a desire to avoid politically embarrassing situations.

Mass media tend to be greatly overrated in terms of their ability to change public opinion. However, they can be used very successfully to reinforce views. All such media enterprises are governed directly or indirectly by either government or commercial interests. Generally speaking, therefore, they propound views which reflect either public opinion or governmental politics or both. There is no advantage whatsoever in presenting a viewpoint which is inimicable to both even if it is justified. This is, unfortunately, frequently the case with regard to public health measures.

Finally, amongst the most important agents in the delivery of public health and preventive medicine measures are general medical practitioners. However, they have retained their self-employed status throughout all the organizational changes in the Health Service and tend to see themselves as accountable only to the deity. It would be wrong to deny that most general practitioners serve the public well so far as treatment goes, but there is a great deal more that could be done in the field of prevention which their employment status inhibits.

STRUCTURE OF THE HEALTH CARE NETWORK

Ever since before the inception of the National Health Service there has been tremendous professional (especially medical) opposition to an increased role for government organizations in the organization of health services. This was largely responsible for the removal from local authorities of the responsibility for providing hospital services and their replacement by a two-tier (briefly three- tier) system of management. Thus, throughout the history of the Health Service, there have been two separate systems of quangos to manage hospital services and, after 1974, community services also. It is now proposed that a further group of quangos be established in 1985 to supervise primary care services including general practice. At the time of writing there are 14 regional health authorities and 192 district health authorities in England. When established in 1985, there will be 90 family practitioner committees in England and a further 8 in Wales.

One of the reasons for making these changes in the management arrangements was to attempt to increase the influence of elected representatives and decrease the influence of professional interests in the management of the service. The frequency with which these changes have occurred is testament to their failure in this respect (DHSS, 1979).

In addition, a number of national level quangos exist to emplement certain functions which the Department of Health feels it is unable to fulfil itself. Of particular importance are the Health Education Council, which has both educational and health promotion functions, and the Medical (MRC), Science (SRC) and Economic and Social (ESRC) Research Councils which, on occasion, carry out government sponsored research on health service delivery and organization.

Although not directly concerned with health services, professional quangos such as the General Medical Council and the English National Board of Nursing have an important part to play in fashioning the future pattern of health care in so far as they influence the training of students of medicine and nursing.

Returning to the health authorities concerned with the management of services, the role of professionals in influencing their decision making is substantial, both from within and without. The members of the health authority, appointed by region in the case of district and by the secretary of state in the case of region, include a consultant and a general practitioner working in the locality, a practising nurse and a representative—usually clinical—of the medical school in the region. These are minimum requirements; teaching districts have additional academics who are usually clinical, and many authorities have medically qualified members representing political or other interests. Indeed, it is not unusual for up to half the members of a health authority to have a personal professional interest (i.e. vested) in the Health Service.

These health authorities are advised by a team of chief officers; at regional level, the five chief officers include a community physician and a nurse; at district level, the management team of six includes an appointed community physician, a consultant and a general practitioner elected by their colleagues in the district, and a nursing officer.

In addition, the authorities must establish and recognize formal medical advisory committees representing all the branches of the profession. Furthermore, through a complex system of accreditation of training posts and intimate involvement with the appointment of consultants and the nature of their work, the medical royal colleges and faculties exercise a power greater than that of any quango and frequently greater than that of the government itself.

Let us turn now to the activites of central government in this health care network which is mainly of its own making. In most Western democracies, governments now play a much larger role in health care than hitherto. This role has two chief aspects: first, to attempt to control total expenditure on health care, and second, to provide those services which the private sector is unwilling or unable to provide. The extent to which governments dominate health care varies enormously but is probably as great in this country as in any other democracy. More than 90 per cent of expenditure on health care in the UK comes from the public purse or taxes, including charges. Politicians naturally argue that, with such a commitment, governments must be allowed to influence decision making to a great extent. However, such a large commitment is almost synonymous with a monopoly which is inevitably bad for the quality of the services provided. This establishes the basis of the paradox of nationalized health services. The state can provide and manage a health care system efficiently in economic terms or it can try to offer a high-quality service which meets the needs of the people comprehensively. From a government's point of view, it is not possible to do both because the demand will inexorably increase to beyond the supply. Indeed, it is unlikely that the public demand for health and social care can ever be satisfied.

A state-financed health service inevitably places financial matters in the forefront of its concern with health. We have already discussed the folly of it doing so to the exclusion of all else, but it is clear from recent debates that financial control is anything but far-sighted.

The major cost of health care, in any system, is the cost of what doctors do. Any attempt to limit expenditure, therefore, has to be achieved by limiting the freedom and/or the activities of doctors. Not only are doctors in a position of strength with regard to local management of the service but there is practically no effective way of persuading them to perform in a way they do not wish to perform. Thus, without control over the spenders, the government cannot control expenditure except in a sledgehammer fashion—which is the method usually adopted in consequence. The secretary of state has delegated (passed the buck) many of his powers in this connection to the health authorities but they are no more effective because of their inability to exercise any authority over the doctors. The system does allow the secretary of state to blame the health authorities, which is politically much more acceptable than blaming the doctors for overspending. However, in the majority of instances, the wrath-receiving authorities do not even employ the consultants responsible directly or indirectly for their financial plight. It is apparent, therefore, that any significant changes in the relationship between clinicians and the authorities responsible for financial control can only be achieved with the wholehearted consent of all the clinicians concerned or by a substantial, revolutionary and probably unjustified change in the employment regulations for doctors.

In Communist China, where the government attempted to exercise this level of control over the doctors by ordering their dispersal to rural areas, the medical establishment, less well developed than our own, countered by recommending the development of a system of 'barefoot doctors' thus enabling their own return to the cities. Thus, both dictatorial powers and greater ingenuity than that of the medical establishment will be necessary to change significantly the balance of power within the Health Service.

Without seeking fundamental changes, the government has attempted to influence decision making at local level by exerting a range of pressures on health authorities. It has to be remembered, in fairness to governments, that these authorities are the formal representatives of the Secretary of State for Social Services and that their members are charged with that representation only. For example, the consultant member of a health authority does not represent other consultants, at least not in the way that local authority councillors represent their electorate.

First of all, the chairmen of health authorities are appointed at the highest level and are mostly political appointments. Second, the annual review system seeks to ensure that government policies are being implemented, something which has rarely happened comprehensively in the past. Third, tight financial controls in the form of cash limits introduced by an earlier (Labour) government have been further strengthened by the need to account for certain avenues of expenditure. All this having largely failed, the government is seeking further organizational change, through the recommendations of the Griffiths Inquiry, to strengthen the role of chairmen and senior managers at the expense of the less easily controlled health authority members.

While the underlying strategy behind these moves might be political, health services are still being provided and the need for preventive medicine remains great. Within this seething quagmire of political intrigue, the already shaky foundations of preventive medicine are further weakened by the conflicting pressures exerted by external agencies. The level at which most preventive measures are coordinated and delivered is the district health authority which is the most compact epidemiological unit in health terms. Programmes of health promotion based on behaviour change are initiated by community medical and health education staff according to the identified needs of the district. In a number of regions, initiatives in health promotion have been taken at that higher level and in some cases these have been prescriptive, thus depriving the district of its individual approach to its unique health problems. This can only serve to weaken the prevention function at the district level where it has to operate most effectively. At least these various initiatives from within the health service tend to be based on the common tenet of encouraging behaviour consistent with improved health across a wide range of pathologies. Unfortunately, government intervention/interference extends into this area where its ignorance has no bounds. Worse still, its quango established for the purpose of furthering health promotion, the Health Education Council, is as prescriptive as the most culpable region and rather disjointed in the range of its approaches to health authorities and the public. Furthermore, lobby groups—mainly voluntary agencies—whose interests are disease oriented, have persuaded politicians to adopt their causes and thus prescribe disease-based health promotion activities across the nation regardless of the local relevance. While some of these moves are laudable, many are naïve, misleading and irrelevant and almost all are wholly ineffective. In a society where curative services are devoted to the 'disease' mentality, it is perhaps not surprising that prevention should adopt the same nomenclature but there is no logic to the notion that avoidance of one disease is synonymous with an improvement in health.

Thus, the government, the voluntary sector, the Health Education Council and some regional health authorities, while expressing an interest in and commitment to prevention through district departments, are operating in such a way as to weaken the resolve, freedom, capacity and independence of those deparrtments to provide the preventive services, education and political support for change which is most relevant to the population they are intended to serve. Once more, the only effective way to overcome this problem is a strengthening of the professional resolve in prevention at all the levels involved. Of particular importance is a strong and effective community medicine chain between districts, regions and central government together with a closer involvement between community physicians and relevant local and national politicians. This would not solve the problem of prescription from lobby groups or even the Health Education Council, but it would increase the ability and the willingness of district departments to withstand such pressure.

THE INTERFACE BETWEEN CLINICAL AND COMMUNITY MEDICINE

Epidemiology may be the principal scientific base for the practice of community medicine, but it is also a much used discipline in clinical medicine although in a rather different way. The science of epidemiology embraces all the behavioural, genetic, environmental and social factors which together fashion our health experience. It is the use of the methods applied to this study which is of interest to clinicians in that they are appropriate to studies of the immediate cause of ill-health and of the effectiveness of corrective measures, both medical and surgical. Indeed, as a research tool, epidemiological methods are used widely throughout the scientific world and misused extensively in the non-scientific arena too.

As in other areas, the cardinal difference between the clinical uses of epidemiology and its use in public health is that of the scale and range of study. That is to say that clinicians are concerned mainly with individual characteristics and, inevitably, disease states whereas community physicians are concerned with the definable features of a society and the interaction between the component individuals in that society. Some clinical specialties such as psychiatry and geriatrics do adopt an intermediate position where both individual and societal factors are important in individual care, and it is at the level and scale of intervention that community medicine retains a discrete function (McKeown, 1976).

Epidemiology, and the public health function arising from it, can be described in four ways. First, the oldest and best-known activity of clinical epidemiology which dates back to Hippocrates and is founded on the empiricism of clinical syndromes. This narrow empiricism has proved valuable not only in making possible the study of aetiology but in coordinating intervention in an effective way. Second, the association between health experience and temporal and meteorological factors which one might term ecological epidemiology and which arose out of Hippocratic writings but has moved away from the disease orientation of clinical epidemiology towards the role of environmental factors in health. Third, the post-renaissance development of demographic epidemiology which has contributed greatly to our knowledge of the importance of non-health variables in determining health experience. The work of William Farr in the nineteenth century and that of Thomas

McKeown in the twentieth have been particularly fruitful. Finally, the recent and more controversial discipline of social epidemiology, practised more by sociologists than by medical epidemiologists, and concerned with the role of social factors beyond the individual in determining thresholds for health and the response of society and the individual to each other.

It is clear that there are many groups of people, both within and outside health care, who are able and willing to use these techniques. However, such use tends to be confined to one of the four disciplines, whereas public health, and its practitioners, embraces them all in depth, if not necessarily equally.

In recent years, epidemiological data have been used in the formulae used to calculate the distribution of health service resources (DHSS, 1976). It has been said that the indicator of need selected, the Standardized Mortality Ratio, produced the politically desired result but it does signify some progress in the logic of distribution of state funds.

The most desirable use of epidemiology in the Health Service would be to fashion the extent and nature of service developments. Unfortunately, the epidemiological database at district level is frequently inadequate to provide the confidence necessary to pursue this course. In addition, like most public bodies providing care for individuals, the cornerstone of the service philosophy is crisis based—that is, meeting the immediate needs of the individual—and there has been little attempt to make long-term plans for other than emergency services.

Prevention, in the context of ill-health, extends far beyond the arena of health care or health services, is not the province of any one group and does not necessarily require professional involvement. However, as the major environmental hazards are brought under control or removed, then the role of the medical and other health care professions increases and the importance of prevention at individual level comes to the fore.

It is conventional to describe three levels of preventive activity. Primary prevention may be considered as the absolute prevention of a disease such as is achieved by immunization or the avoidance/cessation of cigarette smoking. Secondary prevention involves the diagnosis of disease states at a stage where cure is easily achievable or the significant consequences of the disease may be avoided. Classic examples include screening for cancer of the uterine cervix and the treatment of high blood pressure. Tertiary prevention may be regarded as the alleviation of the effects on the individual of incurable and sometimes lethal diseases. Sadly, the majority of health care is concentrated in this area.

It is clear that secondary prevention is entirely the province of health services. In addition, some primary and much tertiary prevention also falls within the range of health care. However, many of the greatest advances in human health have been achieved by factors beyond the control, or indeed the wit, of health care professionals.

The most significant change in the English people since the Norman Conquest has been the growth in their number—approximately 3000 per cent. Most of this increase has occurred during the last 300 years and has been associated with improvements in nutrition of sufficient quality and quantity to enable the population to withstand the major cause of death at the time, namely tuberculosis. This nutritional revolution engendered by horticulturalists, politicians and importing entrepreneurs, together with the public health revolution of the nineteenth century achieved by the great social reformers, has enabled infectious disease to be relegated to the second division of causes of death in developed countries. Except at the very end of this process when the earliest community physicians took a hand, this revolution in human health was achieved in the absence of medical knowledge and without the involvement of the medical profession. The medical-led advances of the twentieth century pale into insignificance compared with the improvement in health in earlier times.

This great advance in nutrition and infection control gave rise to healthier children and adults. Death in infancy declined rapidly around 1900; indeed, the great increase in the number of elderly today is due more to their unexpected survival at birth than to any improvement in their health since World War II. Similarly, healthy children grow up to be healthy parents and, in turn, have healthier children. Thus, much of the decline in childhood deaths, at least until 1975, was due simply to a progressive cohort effect. It is fair to say that technological advances have made a significant difference to survival in the last decade.

Although the scope for prevention by medical means at individual level is much greater than it has ever been, the opening paragraphs of this chapter suggest that more effective means can be adopted beyond the field of health care.

It is important to emphasize that prevention must be behaviour-based rather than disease-based if human life is to be improved in terms of both quality and longevity. It is necessary to be aware of the inevitable lethality of living and that the avoidance of one disease merely serves to increase the likelihood of dying from another.

While I take the view that medical technology and therapeutic aspects of health care have little effect on health relative to major social and environmental changes, that is not to denigrate the importance of health care services or, indeed, the crisis intervention which is its hallmark. Whether or not advantage is taken of preventive measures, human health will ultimately fail and it is for those occasions that the state provides comprehensive health care services. By and large, people are most concerned with their health when they no longer possess it, an attitude typical of a population which grossly under-insures itself. It is hardly surprising that such a population should elect legislators of like mind. Both the people and their leaders want expressed needs to be met. Unfortunately, is is usually the unexpressed need which most requires to be met and which is least likely to be.

It is in this area that health education has its most important role to play. It will probably be necessary to achieve a change of view amongst both the public and the politicians, but success with the former, if sustained, inevitably leads to change in the latter as public lobbies are espoused by political groups. The public requires educating in the following areas:

(1) Behaviour that will lead to the maintenance and/or restoration of health.
(2) Other factors which can influence the balance between health and its loss.
(3) The importance of certain symptoms and signs of disease which require early medical intervention.
(4) The most appropriate way to use the health services that are provided.
(5) The need to comply with preventive and treatment programmes in the long term as well as the immediate term.

It will be readily apparent that these tasks are practically impossible to achieve except in a small obsessional minority. Given the very limited resources available for health education, it is hardly surprising that the success rate is not impressive. Furthermore, the chronicity of most serious disorders results in a very long timescale for the effectiveness of health education programmes. It is difficult to persuade clinicians and politicians alike of the value of such an approach when their lives are spent seeking immediate solutions to often intractable problems.

A further problem of the intensive preventive approach to health care is that disease epidemiology exhibits a swings and roundabouts phenomenon. That is, epidemiologically based behaviour change to avoid one disease may lead to an increase in another. For example, cancer of the breast and ovary have similar epidemiological characteristics; cancer of the uterine cervix has an epidemiology almost reciprocally different. Attempts to reduce the death rate from ischaemic heart disease by lowering serum lipids have resulted in increases in non-cardiac deaths. In the sociopolitical arena, a major reduction in smoking will produce unemployment in the tobacco industry with all its attendant morbidity and, perhaps, mortality.

These multiple dimensions of the prevention equation do not mean that it cannot be solved. However, the conventional *laissez faire*, debate avoidance approach usually adopted in this country will have to be replaced by a more positive, perhaps didactic, attitude on the part of at least one of the relevant groups concerned.

CONCLUSIONS

With 'Prevention is Better than Cure' as their flagship, almost all governments have espoused preventive medicine at some time. Their reasons for doing so will vary but there are two main groups, neither of which, incidentally, has ever been proven to be efficacious.

There are governments who have no real policies other than an obsession with the economic state of the nation. In such cases, preventive measures are supported on the grounds that they are cheaper than alternative approaches. It is not at all clear where the rationale for this notion originates unless the principle of cash limits is combined with the definition of politics as the 'art of the possible'. For example, if a limited sum of money is available to tackle a certain health problem, the political mileage in spending that sum on a wholly ineffective pseudo-prevention campaign may be greater than that of a small and inadequate contribution towards the cost of the required intervention services. This is frequently described as 'commitment to prevention' but in fact it does the school of prevention nothing but harm, while depriving the public of the services it needs and wants. This, of course, is the blackest picture, but it is only fair to say that, with significant but rare exceptions, there is no financial justification for adopting a preventive approach instead of a treatment one. Ideally, of course, both approaches are used.

The more noble reason for adopting preventive methods is that they are better for the people concerned. In many cases this is undoubtedly true for those who would have developed a disease through lack of prevention, but does little for the majority who would not. Despite the wealth of knowledge about the causes of diseases, relatively little of relevance is known of how to convert that knowledge into effective prevention.

It is noteworthy that precisely the same reasons exist, and the same counter arguments may be made, for the adoption of community care in preference to institutional care for the elderly, mentally handicapped and mentally ill.

Despite the perennial presence of prevention amongst governments' stated initiatives and priorities, the field of prevention has failed to gain universal acceptance in this country amongst the public, professionals and politicians. The other major representative group in this country, the trade union movement, has also largely ignored the maintenance of the health of its members, preferring to seek recompense after the event instead of investment in avoidance. For example, if a fraction of the money paid in compensation to victims of asbestosis had been invested in preventive measures, both the employer and employee would have been better of.

It has to be admitted that most members of the health care professions—community physicians, health visitors and health education officers excepted—are not attracted to preventive medicine. The most important reasons are the absence of any significant private practice and the lack of rewarding feedback from grateful patients.

Given that it is easier to persuade a majority of the 650 members of Parliament than a majority of the 50 million population, I believe that if prevention is to be adopted and implemented effectively in the UK, the movement must be led by the government itself. The persuasion of the public to accede to the policy can be achieved by a combined professional and political campaign backed, if necessary and where appropriate, by legal compulsion. In addition, there are major industrial changes which must be achieved as part of the process. In particular, the evidence suggests that a further agricultural revolution will be necessary to improve our health significantly through dietary alteration away from fat towards unrefined carbohydrate (fibre). It is almost certain that the agricultural industries would prove to be at least as difficult nuts to crack as the tobacco manufacturers have proved to be. A government truly committed to prevention might be willing to 'buy' the farmers; unfortunately, membership of the EEC and the Common Agricultural Policy are inimicable to health.

Finally, the health care professions must change their attitudes to prevention in relation to other services, must be responsive to government initiatives and cognizant of the importance of measures not directly associated with health. Above all, perhaps, the government will want to be able to control the activities of members of the medical profession in such a way as to ensure that its policies are implemented.

REFERENCES

BMA/FCM (1980). *The State of Community Medicine*. Report of a Working Party chaired by Dr G. Duncan. London: BMA.

Chaplin, N. W. (1982). *Health Care in the United Kingdom*. London: Kluwer Medical (for IHSA).

DHSS (1972). *Management Arrangements for the Reorganised National Health Service*. London: HMSO.

DHSS (1976). *Sharing Resources for Health in England*. Report of the Resource Allocation Working Party. London: HMSO.

DHSS (1979). *A Service for Patients*. Report of the Royal Commission on the National Health Service. London: HMSO.

Doll, R., and Peto, R. (1981). *The Causes of Cancer*. London: Oxford University Press.

McKeown, T. (1976). *The Role of Medicine*. Rock Carling Fellowship. London: Nuffield Provincial Hospitals Trust.

The Psychosomatic Approach: Contemporary Practice
of Whole-person Care
Edited by M. J. Christie and P. G. Mellett
© 1986 John Wiley & Sons Ltd

13

TRAINING FOR PRIMARY HEALTH CARE

MICHAEL J. F. COURTENAY

Department of General Practice, St Thomas's Hospital Medical School,
University of London, UK

INTRODUCTION

In the National Health Service more than 90 per cent of illness brought to the attention of doctors is dealt with by general practitioners. They, with their practice team of nurses and health visitors, constitute the bulk of the front line, dealing with unselected problems. They share the acute load with colleagues in the Accident and Emergency Departments of hospitals and, on the preventive medicine side, with their colleagues working in community medicine, especially those concerned with gynaecology and paediatrics.

Wadsworth and Ingham (1981) reviewed the causes of the increase in demand for medical services in recent years. This seemed in part to be due to a more inclusive use of the term 'illness', and a move in attitudes to include many kinds of distress and deviance as the proper concern of doctors. The cause of illness has also undergone change from the old concept of host and environment towards one including personal behaviour, so that a patient is seen not merely reacting to external factors but rather as part of the process itself.

This change has also involved an appreciation of the fact that good doctoring depends not only on absorbing the necessary professional techniques, but also on being a certain kind of person. There is an aphorism that psychiatry is the other half of medicine, and today a general practitioner may consider that there are three 'halves' of medicine, the third being general practice.

Ingham and Miller (1976) found that in the context of the prevalence of psychiatric symptoms, only half of the population under study who had such symptoms came to the general practitioner; the other half dealt with them through their social support network. For those who do come, two dangers arise in the present climate of opinion; on the one hand the diagnosis of a somatized affective disorder can be missed even by experienced general practitioners, and on the other hand certain forms of distress may be medicalized in an inappropriate way. Sadness is not best treated with antidepressants, though the awareness that depression may arise in the context of, say, bereavement must always be borne in mind.

281

The situation is complicated further by the finding of Miller, Ingham and Davidson (1976) that stress contributed to the decision to consult, and was also strongly associated with the severity of psychological symptoms, though hardly at all with physical symptoms. The finding of Kessel and Shepherd (1965) that those people who seldom or never consult their doctors *do* appear to be healthy, completes the idea that there is a whole spectrum of individuals from those who have no need of a doctor, through those who have adequate reason to consult, but deal with the problem in other ways; those who seek advice for psychological reasons, either explicit or disguised by physical manifestations; to those who apparently suffer from physical illness.

Nevertheless, some patients who cannot be proved to be ill even in the light of exhaustive investigations continue to consume a large amount of doctors' time, and even those patients with conditions which a hospital-based physician would consider to be severely ill may develop such illnesses in the context of disturbed emotions.

Crisp, Queenan and D'Souza (1984) found that

within the general population, people destined for myocardial infarction are found to be more obsessional and greater worriers than others. Moreover, in the year before infarction they display high levels of sadness, anxiety-related symptoms, loss of libido, and fatigue, unrelated to angina and other physical discomforts. They also claim, more so than others, to have no fear of an incurable illness.

Preventive care in terms of reducing the incidence of myocardial infarction would therefore seem to require as much attention directed towards these psychological factors as towards the classical preconditions such as smoking, hypertension, hyperlipidaemia, excessive body mass and lack of exercise. Obviously some of the latter factors may interrelate closely with the psychological factors, so that a truly psychosomatic approach would seem necessary for doing effective general practice.

So the general practitioner must indeed be 'general' in the sense of being equally at home and competent in dealing with the psychological and physical aspects of illness even though in many cases the relationship between the two is poorly understood.

THE STRATEGY OF TRAINING FOR PRIMARY HEALTH CARE

The first problem here is that the choice of a career in general practice need not be taken until registration or later, so that at present all those who will eventually work in the primary health care field will begin training with those who will specialize in other ways. It might seem arrogant to suggest that undergraduate training should constantly bear in mind the importance of the special needs of the future general practitioner, were it not for the consideration that during the undergraduate phase those special needs apply equally to doctors who will practise secondary health care or community medicine. When it is also remembered that about half of all doctors who qualify become general practitioners, the requirements will seem even less unreasonable.

So the strategy will necessarily involve attention to what may be considered the psychosomatic aspects of medicine throughout the whole length of medical education. This begins with selection, a thorny topic (Crisp, 1984). The problem is that the student is being schooled to believe that a career in medicine depends solely on a facility to acquire and apply scientific information. It is true that most universities endeavour to broaden the educational base. In some there may be the opportunity to study such subjects as the philosophy of science, or anthropology, though this is a broadening of the scientific base rather than an attempt to seek personal qualities which may be necessary for producing the 'complete' doctor. It is true that most universities include behavioural sciences such as psychology and sociology, but in some instances this seems initially to be counterproductive in that many students reject the importance of these studies while at the same time being eager to meet patients in the flesh. It has been observed that students at this stage who, as part of the preclinical course, sit in a single surgery session with a general practitioner, report that this was the highlight of the course, yet at the same time may well pour scorn on the study of sociological principles. This is a serious situation, and while it points the way to changes in educational strategy within medical schools, it also implicates the process which started in the sixth form. Here, largely due to the requirements of medical schools, the emphasis is on the basic sciences, possibly including mathematics and biology. While it may be necessary for a medical student to be familiar with the language and methods of science, and knowledge in these fields is easier to assess, the choice at the age of 18 of people who are likely to be good doctors is not based on any clearly defined principles, scientific or otherwise. The significance of the social background of medical students is another factor which may reward study.

A changed role for the study of natural science has been suggested by Dornhorst and Hunter (1967), who felt that it might be more logical to learn the sciences associated with medicine together with, rather than before, clinical studies. This did not represent a 'soft' attitude towards scientific discipline, but a recognition that the intellectual challenges of a career in natural science might not be appropriate to the majority of medical students. Dornhorst and Hunter went on to attack the 'pastoral fallacy' in medicine, on the grounds that too much attention to the human relationship aspect of medical care would necessarily decrease technical competence. The logical basis of this opinion is hard to discern, and would seem to suggest that technical competence and humane competence are somehow mutually exclusive. Obviously the pastoral role must never be a substitute for technical care. Clinical competence must surely include technical competence and an effective doctor–patient relationship. Unless a patient feels understood, he will feel dissatisfied, and this is likely to lead to less than full cooperation with the doctor's attempts to restore the patient's health.

THE PRECLINICAL PHASE

Great changes have occurred in this phase of medical education in recent years. The time spent in studying anatomy has decreased and attention has been paid to studying human development and functioning, both in individuals and in societies. The problem for education is to make this more acceptable to students who are in danger of experiencing intellectual indigestion while being eager to apply their science to patient care.

One of the important ways this may be achieved is by teaching communication skills. Looking towards the future doctor, it is unlikely that the psychosomatic aspects of medicine will be understood unless the doctor and patient can meet in a way which will allow the patients to verbalize the whole range of their distress in the consultation, and the doctors to make use of all the symptoms and signs that are available to them. Too narrow an appreciation of what is a symptom or a sign may hinder the establishment of an accurate diagnosis. While it has long been observed that patients who have a myocardial infarct have previously complained of 'tiredness', only in 1984 have we published evidence of an analysis of the elements which might produce this (Crisp, Queenan and D'Souza, 1984).

So to include the study of communication skills in the preclinical phase may be a solution to the tension which students suffer, in that it can be seen as the first step towards talking to patients, while remaining an intellectually respectable activity. It is necessary first to promote the idea that interviewing is a skill. Some may be better at it than others but most people are able to improve their performance, if they understand something of the principles involved. Sanson-Fisher and Maguire (1980) suggest that the necessary skills include those required to put patients at ease, promote trust, obtain an accurate history, give information that is understood and remembered, give advice and prescribe treatment so that it is complied with, prepare patients for surgery and investigations, break bad news to patients and relatives, and talk with the dying and bereaved.

First, there is a 'grammar' of the process of communication, which will include beginning an interview, arranging the physical context of exchange in terms of seating arrangements and body posture, the appropriate use of eye contact and the avoidance of jargon. Interruption of the patient should be sparing, and facilitation used wherever possible to achieve clarification. The inclusion of the psychosocial area of inquiry should be considered, and empathy should be maximized, together with a sensitivity to any leads given, either verbally or non-verbally. Even silence should be seen as a useful technique just as a good style of questioning may be.

In addition to these 'grammatical' considerations, specific problems may have to be tackled when particularly sensitive subjects are discussed, whether it be sexual problems or dealing with the dying and their relatives.

On a practical level, actually conducting interviews, even in a role-play setting, can be an absorbing activity, and there is nothing so potentially educative with regard to interviewing skills as, after the event, watching one's own performance recorded on videotape. The problem here may be that it can be rather strong medicine to take. It can be mitigated in this phase when the student is not expected to know any pathology, so that there is no loss of face as a result of being ignorant in that sense. Their task can be to establish certain facts in the life situation of the person role-playing the 'patient', and the scenario can be agreed upon by the tutors at a preparatory session.

After the consultation, the video recording can be discussed safely by following a pattern of paying attention to the positive aspects before the negative.

The scenarios will begin with some which focus attention on the 'grammar' of interviewing skill, and later proceed to incorporate the specific problems for which particular sensitivity or techniques may be required.

The aim is on the one hand to make the human sciences a more practical pursuit in association with learning the theoretical concepts, and on the other hand to prepare the students for work with patients in the wards. At the moment most students are thrown into the deep end and have to swim for their lives. Unfortunately, their struggles may adversely affect the patients who are in the role of innocent bystanders in this educational process.

Experience of working with students at the time of their introductory clinical courses has shown that while they have, at that time, only a smattering of knowledge of pathology or of how to examine a patient, they are nevertheless able to identify the human problems of patients quickly and accurately. A year or two later they may have difficulty in distinguishing the human wood from the technical trees. It is hoped that acquiring skills in communication will equip them better for empathizing with the patients' distress when they meet this, and reduce the students' need to develop personal defences for coping with that distress.

THE CLINICAL PHASE

Crisp (1984) refers to the Recommendations of the Education Committee of the GMC in which are set out in broad outline the knowledge and understanding, the professional skills and the attitudes, to be acquired and consolidated before a primary medical qualification be granted. He goes on to say:

And then again, much of disease has a social element. In fact, half of the sections under the heading 'Knowledge and Understanding' are given over to these aspects, and inevitably these sections take up more space because such ideas cannot be expressed economically. The ideas of biological science are easier to express. Yet we would probably agree that the subject matter identified in these sections is important enough, for example: family planning, psychosexual counselling, health education, care of the dying, human relationships, personal and communal, economic, ethical and practical constraints in the provision of health care. Within this area of acquired knowledge, the 1980 Recommendations include encouragement to educators to get away from the cramming of facts and to help students develop powers of understanding and problem-solving skills. Yet the theory of practice as described by Hutte (1982) basic to the development of problem-solving skills is not in our curriculum, nor is part of the syllabus in many schools.

In fact, worldwide, only a few schools, following McMaster in Canada, have faced this challenge with a new approach: combining the biological, scientific aspects with a clinical approach in connection with a series of defined problem areas studied in turn.

Problem solving

Hutte (1982) suggests:

The Caring Professions can be defined in terms of role relationships between clients and practitioners, aiming at lessening complaints about the physical, social or mental well-being of clients. In many cases the degree of well-being of the client cannot be measured on quantitative scales, so that only an accepted degree of intersubjective agreement can determine if the role relationship is adequate and leading to expected results.

Strict application of distinct theories is seldom possible; the best description of what happens is often 'problem solving activity, shared by both practitioner and client'. That means in the caring professions there is not a direct relationship between theory and practice. Essentially, theory and practice operate on the same basic assumptions, but theory operates on a much higher level of abstraction and practice is closer to social values, has a shorter time span and is less stable.

If this is really the state of affairs, the question arises as to the best way to train students for these professions. If the core of professional activity is problem solving, theories of problem solving should be developed and taught—methods which can be exercised by students in simulated problem situations. Such theories should occupy themselves with the systemisation of the practical decision taking within the profession.

There is a great danger that this approach may be denigrated by some because it is apparently too woolly. Yet if it were necessary to understand and apply the physics of how a bicycle remains upright it is doubtful whether it would be commercially profitable to build them. In practice even children can learn to ride a bicycle quite easily. The physical principles involved were deduced *after* the feasibility of bicycle riding was firmly established.

Even in a medical school where the problem-solving based type of learning is not established, some regard can be paid to the theory of practice. In the month in which medical students are attached to the Department of General Practice at St Thomas's Hospital Medical School, four seminars are assigned to dealing with some aspects of problem solving relevant to the general practice setting. Problems are presented with the help of slides, using a similar format to the Modified Essay Questions posed in the examination for membership of the Royal College of General Practitioners. The first slide sets the scene with the presentation of the complaint, and when the students have responded to that, further information about the development of the illness and other factors of a psychological or social nature will be presented on a second slide for further comment and discussion. A series of slides is designed gradually to widen and deepen the considerations to which the students have to react, and their understanding of the problem develops a stage at a time. In addition to a wider appreciation of the problem presented, the steps in the decision-making process can also be reviewed in a manner which is closely analogous to actual practice, only drawing on theoretical considerations which follow from the practical issues, or which may be borrowed from other disciplines at the appropriate time.

Interview technique

Sanson-Fisher and Maguire (1980) make the point that doctors' skills in communication affect the adequacy of their clinical interviews; even so, traditional clinical courses do not usually include formal teaching of these skills. Yet obtaining a history, conveying information about diagnosis and treatment, achieving patient compliance, and monitoring how patients and their relatives adapt to illness and treatment, are all essential requirements for future doctors. In the past it has often been left to medical students to model themselves on the consultants and others on the 'firms' in which they have spent their clerkships working through the various specialist departments, and they in turn are likely to have been self-taught. The adequacy of such skill thus acquired has only, until recently, been judged as a result of students reporting their encounters with patients to the members of the 'firm', and this may bear little relationship to the actual communication with the patients. Neither the adequacy of the models nor the quality of the communication skill can therefore be guaranteed. Only direct observation of the process can establish beyond doubt the strengths and weaknesses of the students in interviewing patients, and this is the keystone of the bridge between doctor and patient.

Since much morbidity, both somatic and psychiatric, remains undetected in practice, it would seem that interviewing techniques in the past have been defective, the consultation beng the most crucial means of reaching a correct diagnosis and instituting appropriate management. Direct observation of the process with the help of video recordings is now essential: response to verbal and non-verbal clues can be monitored together with any evidence that patients' spontaneously reported facts are being ignored. Unnoticed problems may approach the 40 per cent mark, and students taught by traditional modelling systems are significantly less effective than those given a specific training programme in history taking (Maguire and Rutter, 1076). Unfortunately, as time goes on during the training, improvement does not necessarily occur; students may become more confident but less sensitive to emotional problems. Even if the ability to empathize was encouraged in the preclinical phase, it may have significantly decreased 3 years later, according to Sanson-Fisher and Poole (1981). Empathy is often considered to be an innate gift or an unteachable skill, but this view is challenged by Maguire and Rutter, who consider that medical students can learn to improve, and confirm that audio or video feedback is a very effective means. These authors suggest that the resistance to such training in communication stems from the view that physical intervention, aimed at correcting an underlying disease, is the most potent factor in medical care: a concept that permeates psychiatry as much as medicine and surgery.

As Kirsch, Grozzi and Francis (1968) express it:

This approach usually ignores patients' emotional responses to illness and tends to interpret any emotional problems as physical symptoms requiring medication, even when the cause is psychological. It encourages doctors to maintain a distance from patients so as to strengthen their image as authority figures and increase their power to reassure patients.

Sanson-Fisher and Maguire (1980) conclude: 'Among the specific skills which appear to warrant inclusion in a communication skills training programme are: how to interview, methods of giving information to patients, the use of interpersonal styles which enhance satisfaction and compliance, and some basic counselling skills.' It is difficult to believe that anyone would seriously disagree with these aims, essential for any doctor who is to engage in clinical practice. The assumption that such skills will automatically accrue during medical training can only arise from complacency, in the absence of direct feedback from patients.

At the undergraduate stage it is likely that role-play may substitute for patients: in the interests of the latter, roles can be assumed by actors, tutorial staff or fellow students—though the last is best avoided if possible, as hurtful personal interaction may be generated. (In the postgraduate phase, trainee general practitioners can be allowed access to real patients reasonably safely.) The methods outlined in the preclinical phase can be used with attention to the more complex 'grammar' of the interview, starting with the verbal and non-verbal interaction and proceeding eventually to considering whether or not the patient was finally understood by the doctor in personal and pathological terms, and even whether the patient understood this to be so.

Rating scales have been developed by several workers in the field such as Maguire and Rutter (1976). They may relate to areas which are relatively easy to observe, such as to how the interview was opened and closed, what pattern of body posture was adopted by doctor and patient, whether eye contact was used appropriately, whether jargon was used, whether facilitation was given, whether issues which arose were clarified, whether the reason for the interview was kept in focus, whether personal issues were avoided, or psychosocial areas ignored, and whether leads were followed and empathic statements pronounced.

Pendleton *et al.* (1982) have developed an even more sophisticated conceptual framework, which includes appraisal of how problems were dealt with in terms of definition, aetiology, effects, doctor's understanding and action. Also included are assessments of patients' ideas and expectations, their involvement in management decisions and a helpful relationship with the doctor. At-risk factors and the use of time and resources are also included in the rating. A course based on the conceptual framework should consolidate the understanding gained in the preclinical course on communication skills, and on the one hand apply it more specifically to the practice of medicine, while on the other paying attention to more sophisticated concepts in the 'grammar' of communication.

Specific problem areas

Dealing with psychosexual problems is a good example. This requires a base of adequate knowledge of human sexual physiology, the doctor's ability to be at ease with his or her own sexuality, and a facility for handling the patient's embarrassment which may arise when talking about intimate emotional states in an important area of living. The fact that a detailed account of the physiological changes during human sexual activity is only a generation old testifies to the problems which have beset progress in the treatment of sexual disorders. Certainly, a practical approach to such problems necessitated detailed observation of couples during copulation, and information about the physiology of women's internal genitalia during such activity was dependent on instrumentation which would have seemed totally unacceptable 50 years ago. But before this practical approach, the psychotherapeutic approach had not relied on such invasive methods, and many patients were helped by this approach to gain insight into the problem.

However, a combination of knowledge and skill is appropriate for a range of problems. Just as it was demonstrated by the women doctors working in family planning clinics with women having problems in consummating their marriages, that the combination of vaginal examination and talking was more effective than counselling alone (Dawkins and Taylor, 1964), so a behavioural approach to such problems often meets attitudes which need to be changed in order to carry through the treatment programme. If, for instance, in attempting to treat premature ejaculation with the 'squeeze' technique, the wife asks whether she can wear gloves while handling her husband's penis, this revulsion from handling his genitals may have to be resolved in counselling rather than behavioural terms.

Resistance appears to exist in this area as in that of learning communication skills. Many doctors seem to think that becoming sexually competent is merely instinctual and that no learning process is involved.

The amount of sexual experience and maturity in medical students will probably vary widely, but even the most experienced and mature are unlikely to have had much time to integrate knowledge and attitudes, unless they are entering medical school at an unusually late age.

In any case, it is essential that those who have not had the inclination or opportunity to form sexual relationships of a satisfactory nature should be able to respond to patient needs in an appropriate way. The theoretical knowledge may be comparatively easy to acquire, but the attitudes and skills are more challenging.

It is extremely difficult, if not impossible, to allow students to clerk real patients in this field, but role-played interviews, constructed on the basis of real patient problems, may be shown on video, and then the students can be encouraged to role-play diagnostic and treatment situations. This will enable them to gain some experience in talking about sexual matters, and to gain some sensitivity about the problems which may be encountered with those patients who have difficulty in talking about such matters.

In some medical schools, films of various forms of sexual activity are used to broaden the students' awareness and to confront them with their own reactions to seeing such activity. It is, of course, essential to deal in a safe group setting with the feelings engendered and it may be necessary to arrange for personal discussion if the experience has been upsetting.

In conclusion, it may be said that learning how to take a sexual history and to institute a treatment programme for a sexual disorder is extremely useful training for handling any patient problem. If the student is able to attempt a diagnosis and to give instructions without making himself (or herself) and the patient uncomfortable, then it is unlikely that a more demanding situation will be encountered, unless it involves terminal illness.

This is another good example of a specific problem area. Again, a role-play technique can be very effective in showing the students where difficulties may arise in talking to dying patients and their relatives. Questioning the appropriateness of either a direct approach or a retreat into euphemisms and deceit may be coupled with discussion of modern regimes of symptom control, such as those pioneered at St Christopher's Hospice (see Chapter 19), while visits to terminally ill patients in their homes or in a hospice may reveal the information and sensitive attitudes required to handle a dying patient.

THE POSTGRADUATE PHASE

Postgraduate training is essential in all branches of medicine, partly because the accumulated body of knowledge and skill is now too vast to be covered in the undergraduate phase, and partly because a fully trained doctor needs to acquire a degree of personal maturity in order to deliver health care effectively. This maturity must include an awareness that the population at large contains a wide spectrum of intelligence and emotional reaction patterns, and an ability to operate reasonably effectively over the whole spectrum.

The spectacle of an extremely intelligent senior registrar trying to communicate with the patients from the Clapham omnibus and reaching a state of frustration so great that he has to give up and leave the ward is unfortunately not apocryphal. The fact that most students are still selected mainly on their grades in advanced level examinations may suggest that academic ability alone is given undue weight in the selection process. Though the problem of assessing the future capacity to relate and communicate with patients is daunting, is it perhaps a fruitful field for research in itself?

Vocational training for general practice

The statutory provision for such training includes at least 2 years of post-registration hospital medicine in a limited number of specialities, but may include a short period in community medicine as equivalent experience, and a year's training in an approved general practice or practices.

During the general practice year, the main educational requirement of the training is to enable the doctor to move from working in the hospital setting into that of general practice. Understanding the difference is the essence of the problem. The first dimension of the difference is the patient population. As almost 100 per cent of the population is registered with a general practitioner, the usual portal of entry into the health care system, except in cases of serious accident or emergency, is via the general practitioner. Patients consulting the general practitioner come, therefore, from a limited and, to a greater or lesser extent, a changing population. The patients who come are self-selected and need no referral procedure. Access may be regulated through artificial means by such mechanisms as appointment systems, but is essentially open. Patients have frequent contact with their general practitioner as a rule; 70 per cent of the practice population see their doctor each year, and 90 per cent will do so within a 4-year period (Kessel and Shepherd, 1965).

Certain sectors of the population make high demands on medical care, notably the very young, pensioners and women during childbearing years. The last-named may usually appear healthy physically, and lest it be thought that their threshold for complaint is unduly low, we should note that Banks, Beresford and Morrell (1975) showed that these women consulted for only 1 of every 37 symptoms they had experienced and recorded in a special diary, though those who scored highly on an anxiety inventory consulted more often, on a level with those who experienced a high number of symptoms. This exemplifies the need for future general practitioners to be aware of and competent to deal with 'psychosomatic' complaints.

The spectrum of illness does indeed differ from that encountered in hospital. For example, Watkins's (1982) data show that of those patients who presented with chest pain, only 3 per cent was of cardiac origin, 12 per cent was due to pneumonia or pleurisy and 30 per cent was due to disorders of the musculo-skeletal system. This leaves no less than 55 per cent of chest pain which could not be assigned readily to any category that might be the concern of a hospital department. This means that the majority of such complaints will probably not have been seen by a hospital-based doctor unless working in the hospital component of primary health care—the Accident and Emergency Department.

The very nature of the illnesses with which the general practitioner is concerned makes them less easy to submit to scientific inquiry than the more clearly defined illnesses seen in hospital. Furthermore, the outcome measures that are important to those who receive the care may be at odds with the outcome which the profession may generally approve. For instance, as Watkins (1982) suggests, obstetricians are properly concerned with reducing perinatal mortality and morbidity to the lowest possible level by the application of technology. But many mothers-to-be see pregnancy and childbirth as important life experiences and resent what they feel is an intrusion of technology in a natural process; some of them are prepared to accept risks to enjoy childbirth in their own homes. Perinatal mortality is easy to measure but how is the value of an important life experience to be measured? The general practitioner is faced with many similar types of problem in the management of chronic disease and terminal illness, so that factors which may not be seen as important in the hospital setting have to be included in planning management of primary care. The other consideration is that hierarchical structures are weakened in general practice, and may become of little account in a close relationship between doctor and patient developed during an episode of illness.

There are two ways of helping the trainee general practitioner to adjust to the new setting: one is to use video-recording consultations as described for the preclinical and clinical phases of undergraduate training, but with real patients in the context of the surgery consultation. (Modern video-recording equipment has become so compact and inexpensive, that wide use is possible.) By this means the trainee may subsequently observe that much of the consultation time was spent writing notes rather than looking at the patient. This behaviour must then be assessed as either a habit which stems from the doctor's personality, or a special response to a particular patient, and this avoidance understood. Obviously the trainer must be sensitive to the possibility that the trainee may find recorded interviews rather strong medicine, though from the point of view of patient welfare, it is more dangerous if the trainee cannot see any deficiencies in consultation skill!

The limitation of this method is that it is concerned with the observation of behaviour and verbal exchange. These may be very valuable, but the doctor's thoughts and feelings may not be registered, although these form an important part of the doctor's functioning. This is not to denigrate the method, merely to point out the obvious: painting by numbers is not likely to produce a great work of art, though it may give a good likeness. Nevertheless, it is a necessary part of the checks and balances required to develop the skills of the trainee, in association with case presentation in a small group setting.

Group discussion produces another facet of the truth—though self-deception is possible. The fact that the doctor is reporting the contact with a patient gives him control of the material reported and this may differ from the impression that might be gained from a video recording of the consultation. I remember an occasion in which a doctor reported an interview to a group, showed a recording of the interview and maintained that the recording substantiated the verbal report, while the rest of the group considered that there were great differences. Nevertheless, the verbal report remains valuable on at least two counts. First, it is observable that the reporting doctor often role-plays the patient's affect and body posture, although being apparently unaware of the fact. Second, he is able to describe the feelings generated in him by the patient in the interview, whether they be bafflement, irritation, anger or extreme involvement with the patient's distress. The leader of the group has the role of focusing discussion, has responsibility for protecting every member from inappropriate criticism, and should constantly bring to the attention of the group the nature of the doctor–patient relationship exemplified during the contact described.

The concept that the doctor, who is the professional, is in charge of the interview and must remain in an active role wherever possible dies hard. It may be difficult for the trainees to understand that a different role may sometimes be appropriate. In the face of the insuperable problems which patients may bring to them, there may be a need for a sharing of power, a state of being with rather than acting on the patient. Trainees need, above all, to appreciate the fact that in any consultation the many forces which determined what the doctor said and did, were generated as much by the personalities of both patient and doctor as by the factual material discussed during it. If, rather than just judging the quality of the exchange, the trainees can come to see why they behaved as they did during a consultation, then a new dimension of understanding will be achieved. In the primary health care setting such breadth of understanding is essential, because the relationship may be a prolonged one. A specialist can easily discharge a patient from his care; a general practitioner can only take the extreme step of requesting that a patient be removed from his list. The reasons for that step might be an interesting study.

In-service training

There are two aims in this virtually lifelong commitment: one is to keep abreast of developments in medicine and the other is professional development. The former can be achieved by reading, attending updating courses, and discussion with specialist colleagues.

Professional development has two themes, the intellectual and the personal. The good general practitioner must aim to blend and balance thinking and feeling in his daily work, using the emotional responses in the interview as much as the intellectual process when making a diagnosis. It is necessary to be self-aware during the interaction with a patient, with the capacity to identify with the patient's distress and then to stand back: to observe not only the clinical facts, but also the nature of the communication process.

Academic initiatives

The Royal College of General Practitioners and the academic departments of general practice have been instrumental in encouraging general practitioners to look at what happens in their practices. It is all too easy to get so submerged in the day-to-day pressures of general practice that soon it is impossible to see the wood for the trees.

Some departments have originated a new field of inquiry: examination of the reasons why patients consult their general practitioners and the nature of the disorders they suffer from. Psychological factors have, time and again, emerged as important aspects of the reason for consulting and the nature of the pathology. The general practitioner will need to see diarrhoea as a symptom, the aetiology of which ranges from anxiety to infective agents, and all the possibilities in between.

Research into psychosomatic associations is as difficult to design and carry out in the general practice as in any other setting, but there is scope for a wealth of imaginative projects in the field.

The personal doctor

Following on from the consideration of in-service training, it would appear that while intellectual activity concerning facts is an essential part of the process of personal development, it is equally important for the doctor to refine the modalities of personal communication with patients to increase the effectiveness of the diagnostic process on the one hand, and the management aspect on the other. In recent years the respectability of certain procedures which are currently classed as 'fringe' medicine has come to be recognized, such as osteopathy in musculo-skeletal disorders, acupuncture in many types of painful conditions, and hypnosis. Interestingly, these techniques might be seen as being based on an authoritarian model, in which the practitioner knows what is best for the patient, were it not for the fact that they all depend on a special kind of history taking in which the interaction between doctor and patient remains crucial.

New concepts of 'holistic' medicine include an aspect of power sharing, in which the contribution of the patient in the transaction is seen to be important and the solving of problems is considered to be the product of a partnership, rather than something imposed by the professional.

Other techniques actively categorize the nature of the relationship. Thus transactional analysis has become a popular method of interpreting the doctor–patient relationship. This might be seen to have stemmed from a theory of practice, being an attempt to categorize patterns of interaction in terms of equality or subservience in given situations, couched in the everyday imagery of parent–child or equal adult relationships. The Royal College of General Practitioners arranges courses in this approach.

Perhaps the most open-ended method for professional development is that of the Balint groups. Although started by psychoanalysts, the method has always eschewed any theoretical model based on psychoanalysis. It depends on the quest for the widest and deepest understanding of what happens during doctor–patient interaction in which the doctor as a person and professional is intimately engaged. Although the emphasis in most groups is away from dwelling on the personality of the doctor in the interaction, change in the doctor will necessarily depend on an increased degree of self-understanding. It is probably this that makes it a minority activity which not more than 1 per cent of general practitioners seem to feel able to tolerate. Michael Balint (Balint et al. 1966) himself thought that not more than 50 per cent of doctors would find the method acceptable, though even this figure seems somewhat unrealistically high unless one includes the dilute form described in his section on vocational training for general practice. It is this problem which has prompted efforts to find equivalent methods of encouraging professional development of doctor–patient relationship techniques.

Nevertheless, it is important to use the experience gained by those doctors who have espoused the method as it illustrates certain important goals for dealing with patients in general practice. The method does encourage 'power sharing' in that it is freely recognized that the patients' needs are paramount, that meeting the patients' expectations is important, and that it must be ensured that patients feel truly understood; all this contributes to maximum compliance in the treatment schedule mutually agreed upon.

It does encourage 'self-gardening'—to borrow a term from holistic medicine—by increasing the understanding by the doctor of his own feelings and behaviour. Moreover, it allows the use of personal feelings in the doctor as yet another meter with which to measure part of the patient's condition. Negative feelings in the doctor may be reflecting negative feelings in the patient while positive feelings may alert the doctor to the dangers of overidentification with, or even seduction by, the patient, both being samples of the way in which the patient relates in his social setting.

After a time the doctor will be aware of a subtle but definite change in his approach to patients and their problems, becoming more ready to be used, though not abused, by patients. There will also be a shift towards more realistic goals, with the mature acceptance that all problems cannot be solved, and that perhaps some patients need to keep a problem as a way of coping with the rest of life: this may even include having a doctor who cannot solve their problem.

Altogether the aim of in-service training must be to set in motion a continuous learning process to realize the full potential of the doctor as far as time and circumstance allow.

CONCLUSION

Effective training for primary health care would seem to require a shift in approach from traditional medical education and training. Further, there is evidence that such a shift is required for *all* future doctors who are going to work in a clinical setting. This does not mean that the accumulated treasure of medical knowledge should be jettisoned: on the contrary it has to be used in practice. The most specific and effective remedy will be of no avail if the patient will not accept it, and this depends on the doctor striking a successful bargain with the patient which allows him to receive the necessary care.

While this problem is common to most clinical settings, the general practitioner has closer relationships with patients over longer periods of time, relative isolation, and the need to deal with a huge spectrum of problems. There is a danger that after a time, apparent ability to handle all these factors will generate in the doctor a false sense of competence and even of omnipotence.

Training for the general practice setting must, therefore, aim at encouraging a continuing attitude of inquiry and self-monitoring, and pay particular attention to developing the doctor's personal skills in relating to patients as part of the process of delivering effective medical care.

This process has several strands: the intellectual stimulus from the scientific foundations of training can be channelled into a disciplined approach to monitoring the process of practice, and development of insight into the interactive process of consultation. Both 'external' observation methods which can show behavioural characteristics, and 'internal' observation of feelings and perceived responses during interview of patients can be used.

The enormous advances in medical science in the last 150 years have tended to allow the atrophy of some human qualities necessary for good doctoring. There was perhaps a swing from visiting the pneumonia patient 3 times a day in order to support those whose nursing procedures were the front line in the battle for life, to the confident attitude that a course of an appropriate antibiotic would automatically deal with the pneumonia, leaving very little need for further personal attention by the doctor.

Now, however, there are an increasing number of problems such as those associated with an ageing population—itself due partly to more effective medicine—and problems of increasing social complexity produced by more stressful social settings. These range from the plight of decaying inner cities, to the more permissive sexual mores, and even the greater dependence on anodynes such as alcohol and other drugs. These problems are not amenable to straightforward medical procedures, but with these the general practitioner must necessarily cope. General practice is in the thick of life, and training for this setting has to recognize its unique characteristics.

REFERENCES

Balint, M., Balint, E., Gosling, R., and Hildebrand, P. (1966). *A Study of Doctors.* London: Tavistock Publications.

Banks, M. H., Beresford, S. A. A., Morrell, D. C., Waller, J. J., and Watkins, C. J. (1975). Factors influencing the demand for primary medical care in women aged 20–44 years. *International Journal of Epidemiology*, **4**, 189–195.

Crisp, A. H. (1984). Selection of medical students—is intelligence enough? *Journal of the Royal Society of Medicine*, **77**, 35–39.

Crisp, A. H., Queenan, M., and D'Souza, M. F. (1984). Myocardial infarction and the emotional climate. *Lancet*, **i**, 616–619.

Dawkins, S., and Taylor, R. (1964). Non-consummation of marriage. *Lancet*, **ii**, 1029–1033.

Dornhorst, A. C., and Hunter, A. (1967). Fallacies in medical education. *Lancet*, **ii**, 666–667.

Hutte, H. A. (1982). Caring professions and social science—is there a real relationship? The Fourth Curran Lecture, Wyeth.

Ingham, J., and Miller, P. McC. (1976). The context of prevalence of psychiatric disorders and symptoms. *Psychological Medicine*, **6**, 217–225.

Kessel, N., and Shepherd, M. (1965). The health and attitudes of people who seldom consult a doctor. *Medical Care*, **3**, 6–10.

Kirsch, B. N., Grozzi, E. K., and Francis, V. (1968). Gaps in doctor-patient communication. *Paediatrics*, **42**, 855–871.

Maguire, P., and Rutter, D. (1976). Training medical students to communicate. In A. E. Bennete (ed.), *Communications between Doctors and Patients*. London: Oxford University Press.

Miller, P. McC., Ingham, J. G., and Davidson, S. (1976). Life events, symptoms and social support. *Journal of Psychosomatic Research*, **20**, 515–522.

Pendleton, D. A., Schofield, T. P. C., Tate, P. H. L., and Havelock, P. B. (1982). *The Consultation: An Approach to Learning and Teaching*. London: Oxford University Press.

Sanson-Fisher, R., and Maguire, P. (1989). Should skills in communicating with patients be taught in medical schools? *Lancet*, **ii**, 523–526.

Sanson-Fisher, R., and Poole, A. D. (1981). An appraisal of the short term and long term benefits of training medical students in inter-personal skills. In D. Oborne, M. M. Gruneberg and R. Eiser (eds), *Psychology and Medicine*, vol. 11. London: Academic Press.

Wadsworth, M., and Ingham, J. (1981). How society defines sickness: illness behaviour and consultation. In M. J. Christie and P. G. Mellett (eds), *Foundations of Psychosomatics*. Chichester: Wiley.

Watkins, C. J. (1982). Workshop 'Erfahrungen und Konzepte Basisorientierter Gesundheitsversorgung'. Paper given at the Free University of Berlin.

*The Psychosomatic Approach: Contemporary Practice
of Whole-person Care*
Edited by M. J. Christie and P. G. Mellett
© 1986 John Wiley & Sons Ltd

14

CLINICAL PSYCHOLOGY IN GENERAL PRACTICE

RICHARD W. SHILLITOE

*Department of Clinical Psychology, Airedale Health Authority, West
Yorkshire, UK
and
Undergraduate School of Studies in Psychology, University of Bradford, UK*

M. RÖÖSHMIÈ BHAGAT

*Department of Clinical Psychology, Airedale Health Authority, West
Yorkshire, UK
and
Postgraduate School of Studies in Psychology, University of Bradford, UK*

ANTHONY P. LEWIS

The Health Centre, Bodriggy, Hayle, Cornwall, UK

INTRODUCTION

At the beginning of the 1970s, clinical psychologists and general practitioners knew little about each other. With only about 600 clinical psychologists then in post, the majority of whom were based in mental hospitals, most general practitioners would have been hard pressed to say much about the skills and methods of clinical psychologists, and even less about their background and training. Similarly, most clinical psychologists knew little about general practitioners, their training, organization, back-up services, or relationship with the National Health Service. Even had a general practitioner wished a clinical psychologist to see one of his patients, he would have been unlikely to know how to refer to him directly. Indeed, the conditions of employment of the clinical psychologist may well have made such an approach an impossibility.

Since then, all of that has changed profoundly. Today, although some departments of clinical psychology are still constrained in the application of their skills to particular patient groups—especially to those referred by consultant psychiatrists—most clinical psychologists are working directly with general practitioners, to a greater or lesser extent. Typically, this will involve the provision of a clinical service, organized as a sessional commitment at the health centre, or on the practice premises. Sometimes it will include involvement with the local vocational training scheme, sometimes research or other form of collaboration.

One of the most obvious characteristics of this new venture has been the willingness, shown by both parties, to become involved in exploring and defining the parameters of the endeavour. This enthusiasm has only recently been tempered by the sobriety of investigative research reports. One of the aims of this chapter is to draw together for the reader—psychologist or doctor—some of the themes which have begun to emerge. It will ask why clinical psychologists have felt drawn towards general practitioners and why, for their part, general practitioners have been keen to welcome them. A discussion of the clinical contribution a psychologist can make to the psychological disorders encountered in the surgery precedes an account of some alternative, or complementary, working relationships which have been proposed.

BACKGROUND

Recent developments in clinical psychology

Most professions have had their roles and duties clarified and refined by long usage. The expectations of those within and outside the profession are, therefore, both accurate and specific. Practitioners and recipients of the service alike know what to expect. This has never been the case with clinical psychology. For a profession so recent in origin and limited in numbers, clinical psychology has evolved rapidly and undergone fundamental changes. This is true in terms of professional orientation, organizational and career structure, and clinical services. Clinical psychologists' involvement with primary health care is one example—general medicine and paediatrics are others—of an area where these changes have been particularly evident.

Originally, clinical psychologists began as psychometricians, assessing skills and aptitudes, as well as cognitive and personality variables. The aim of this activity was, primarily, an attempt to help to refine the accuracy of psychiatric diagnosis, both in general and in regard to the problems presented by individual patients. Although clinical psychologists often felt uncomfortable in this role, offering what appeared to amount to a technical service to psychiatrists, there was at least a recognizable link between assessments of this sort and the psychologists' academic experimental background. The other main activity of clinical psychologists—psychotherapy—followed a tradition quite separate from this background. Many clinical psychologists probably shied away from becoming concerned with 'treatment': the clinical situation was felt to be so unlike the experimental laboratory situation that the objective, scientific status of the psychologist was, in some way, compromised.

However, changes in psychiatric treatments, advances in psychology and changes in society's perception of the disadvantaged, all contributed to the outgrowth of this role. One of the consequences of this has been the development, not only of new skills, but of fresh situations in which to practise those skills.

Behaviour therapy has undoubtedly been a great impetus for change; it gave to clinical psychologists identifiable and definable clinical procedures. Doubts have been expressed (e.g. by Marks, 1981) about the conditioning basis of neurosis and the relationship between clinical procedures and their supposed laboratory antecedents, but whatever the ultimate merits of the behavioural philosophy and technology, they have, in the short term, given to clinical psychology a sense of professional and clinical security. Without this, the development of the profession would undoubtedly have been quite different. A readiness to engage in research and quantify the effects of the new treatment methods made clinical psychologists distinguishable (in their own eyes at least) from the paramedical professions, and gave clinical psychology the hallmark of a profession, the basic stance of which was a critical appraisal of its own activities. In 1977 the report of the Trethowan Committee (Trethowan, 1977) gave recognition to the independent, professional status of clinical psychology, making the application of psychological skills in a variety of settings much more likely.

Other concurrent developments included an increasing awareness of the redundancy or futility of much of the psychologists' activity. The attempt, for example, to use psychometric methods to improve psychiatric diagnosis largely foundered on the realization that a test validated against the very diagnostic procedures the test was supposed to improve was unlikely to be of great practical value. Similarly, the concern with personality assessments waned as evidence accumulated in favour of a viewpoint which saw behaviour as a consequence of social learning processes rather than as a manifestation of underlying traits (Mischel, 1968).

The community psychology movement added its voice, criticizing clinical psychology for many things, including 'its inefficiency, its unrealism in terms of manpower and costs, its ignoring of familial and societal variables' (Bender, 1976, p. 27). There was, then, a feeling that hospital-based services and hospital-based outpatient clinics were relatively ineffectual because they minimized, or failed to deal with, the influence of environmental factors in the genesis and maintenance of psychological disorders, and the home circumstances to which the discharged patient returned.

This move to see people as part of their social context has been evident in many areas of medicine and for different reasons. Psychiatrists, aided by advances in drug treatment, together with economic and political pressures to keep people out of mental hospitals, adopted community care as a policy. It became a matter of common consent that many of the mentally handicapped were misplaced in hospital and were quite capable of existence, with varying degrees of support, in the community. That clinical psychologists should become part of this process seems, with hindsight, to have been inevitable. Yet in 1972, with the publication of the first paper outlining possible advantages of a closer working relationship between clinical psychologists and general practitioners, it was necessary for the author to state explicitly that 'disorders of behaviour are not confined to psychiatric patients, [they] are all around us' (Broadhurst, 1972).

The report of a DHSS subcommittee, entitled *The Role of Psychologists in the Health Services* (Trethowan, 1977), lent its support to this contention saying, 'We see the future role of psychologists in community-based work as an important one in which they may well be able to make a significant contribution to the prevention of some illnesses, and to primary care in the case of others.' The importance of pilot studies to evaluate the effectiveness of such a role was emphasized.

More recently, the British Psychological Society has submitted evidence to a DHSS joint working group on the primary health care team (British Psychological Society Professional Affairs Board, 1979). The report of the Royal Commission on the National Health Service (1979) noted the need to consider the place of psychologists in the primary care team, and discussions have been held between the British Psychological Society and the Royal College of General Practitioners concerning the establishment of a joint standing committee to deal with matters of mutual interest. The college has commented upon the potential value of clinical psychologist attachments to training practices (Royal College of General Practitioners, 1981).

At a national level, therefore, there are clear signs of activity, and considerable momentum has been created. Yet it remains true to say that most developments have been in response to local initiatives on the part of general practitioners and clinical psychologists. There is considerable variation in working methods as a consequence of this, although trends are emerging.

Psychological distress in general practice

None of this activity could have come about had there not been good evidence of the existence of large numbers of people in the community suffering from psychological disorders who might benefit from some form of psychological treatment. A number of authors have estimated the prevalence of psychological disorders in the community. The figures quoted vary widely: between, for example, 9.4 per cent (Kessel, 1960) and 42.8 per cent (Hopkins, 1956), although this latter figure includes 11.1 per cent suffering from formal psychiatric illness. Most studies relate to minor psychiatric disorders, and it cannot be assumed that these populations are necessarily the same as those which are of direct interest to clinical psychologists. Considerable overlap does, however, seem likely. A specifically psychological perspective was taken by Eastman and McPherson (1982) who surveyed a sample of 40 general practitioners, as part of a wider study, exploring their perception of the relevance of clinical psychology to their current methods of coping with psychological problems. On average, the doctors believed that 27.6 per cent of all their consultations involved patients with psychological problems. Nineteen per cent of all consultations were said to involve psychological disorders warranting treatment, whilst only 2.1 per cent of all consulting patients were judged to require the intervention of a specialist agency dealing with such problems. An earlier study by McPherson and Feldman (1977) used estimates made by clinical psychologists following a 6-month period of their 'sitting in' on GP surgeries. It was estimated that a useful contribution could be made to the treatment of 8.4 per cent of all cases.

A number of the general practitioners in the Eastman and McPherson survey were already referring patients to clinical psychologists. In view of possible effects a new treatment service might exert on practitioners in terms of attitudes and perceptions concerning psychological disorders, it would be interesting to compare incidence rates reported by doctors already referring patients to clinical psychologists with those not doing so.

It is clear, however, that the vast majority of psychological disorders presenting to general practitioners are managed by the general practitioners themselves, without recourse to specialist agencies. It has been suggested that general practitioners feel particularly ill-equipped to cope with patients with psychological problems, although they may feel it is an important part of their job to do so 'e.g. Cooper, 1964; *Journal of the Royal College of General Practitioners*, 1979; see Whitfield and Winter, 1980, for an alternative viewpoint). The large number of prescriptions for minor tranquillizers has been explained by this:

> The vast boom in prescribing of psychotropics, although universally criticised, can be interpreted equally as an appropriate recognition by primary medical care of the fundamental nature of many patients' problems. . . . Despite their lack of training, despite the relentless criticism from all sides, despite the pressure and lack of organisation, general practitioners voted with their pens and showed that they clearly understood that many of the problems presented to them were behavioural in origin by treating them with what was at that time the only behavioural treatment at their disposal—psychotropic drugs. (*Journal of the Royal College of General Practitioners*, 1979)

Although many psychologists will find it difficult to regard tranquillizers as a 'behavioural treatment', the point is made that a prescription is often a response to distress in the patient, which is recognized by the doctor, yet who feels unable to cope with the situation in any other way. A clinical service to general practitioners by a department of clinical psychology might offer an effective means of managing these sorts of problems. Many arguments have been proposed in favour of this proposition. They have been listed by Johnston (1978) and Burns (1982). Briefly stated they are as follows:

—Greater accessibility to psychological help
—Greater continuity of care for the patient
—Earlier appointments for the patient

—Earlier detection of psychological difficulties
—Reduced stigma attached to hospital attendance
—Increased opportunity for contact with the patient's family
—Facilitation of evaluation of therapeutic progress
—Reduced costs for the patient and NHS (e.g. transport, administration)
—Close liaison with all health centre staff
—Propagation of psychological models of illness
—Increased job satisfaction for clinical psychologists

Some of these arguments do have empirical support. Those relating to ease of access to treatment are known to increase the likelihood of attending for and complying with treatment (Di Matteo and Di Nicola, 1982). Others remain conjectural at present. There is a pressing need for a comparison study between a hospital-based treatment group and a community-based treatment group to substantiate the claim that community treatment is preferable. This requires to be done, not only in terms of symptomatic improvement, but also in terms of expense, effects on the patients' families, and the other variables which have been claimed to weigh in favour of a community-based service.

Taking the arguments as a whole, however, three main themes are discernible. First, clinical psychologists working within the community will be able to offer an improved, cheaper treatment service to a greater number of patients than would be the case if they remained hospital-based. Second, general practitioners and established members of the primary health care team will benefit from collaboration with clinical psychologists, not simply in terms of immediate patient care and a greater understanding of psychological dimensions to illness, but also from more fundamental contributions to education, prevention, research skills and general health care delivery. Third, clinical psychologists enjoy working with general practitioners away from the disputes and restrictions which have been associated with the more traditional areas of work, such as adult psychiatry.

This last point has received little formal recognition apart from the discussion of McPherson (1981), who suggests that 'psychologists are not motivated either by basic material rewards nor by altruism, but rather by job satisfaction in terms of operating an effective service within an interesting working environment' (p. 29). It is unlikely to be the sort of issue figuring prominently in the formal arguments put forward by a profession seeking development in times of economic stringency, but as a motivating force amongst psychologists its importance cannot be overlooked.

CLINICAL ISSUES

Patient selection

A number of authors (e.g. Kincey, 1974; Bhagat, Lewis and Shillitoe, 1979) have listed the sorts of clinical problems a psychologist might be expected to deal with. Kincey (1974) proposed a five-category framework within which most problems likely to be referred to psychologists might fall, together with the psychologists' possible contributions (Table 14.1).

If one were to prepare a similar list today, taking into account the developments in treatment which have occurred in the intervening years, it would be different in a number of respects. The relative importance of 'educational–occupational difficulties or decisions' has diminished. Treatment of 'problems of anxiety and stress' would require greater emphasis on cognitive methods of treatment with some reference to psychological treatment of depression (Williams, 1984). The greatest area of change, however, has probably been Kincey's category E: 'Psychological adjustments to problems stemming from physical illness'. The rapid growth of medical psychology now requires greater recognition in terms of the range of treatments offered and the variety of problems to which they are applicable.

One of the difficulties in establishing a new psychological treatment service is the very fact that, as Table 14.1 shows, the types of problem for potential referral are enormously diverse. So, too, are the treatment methods which may be employed although, in fact, the large majority of studies to be discussed have employed a behavioural framework. It cannot be assumed that general practitioners will have a clear idea of which patients are best referred unless there is prior discussion with the psychologist. Local needs and individual interests have caused a diversity of solutions. Some psychologists (e.g. Earll and Kincey, 1982) have circulated potential referrers with documentation stating the sorts of problems psychologists feel equipped to treat and the sorts of treatment methods practised. Others (e.g. Johnston, 1978) have 'sat in' on surgeries; alternatively, referrals have arisen out of personal contact and discussion (Liddell et al., 1981). It is likely that methods like these have been used by most psychologists at the commencement of a treatment service.

TABLE 14.1   Contributions of clinical psychology to clinical problems facing the general practitioner

Categories of problems	Functions of the clinical psychologist
Category A Problems of anxiety and stress These may involve patients with any of the following: High levels of 'free-floating' anxiety; 'panic-attacks'; phobic reactions; anxiety-reducing obsessional ideas or rituals; avoidance of stress situations; psychosomatic illnesses in which stress appears to play an important role, e.g. migraine, asthma, essential hypertension.	A detailed assessment of the behaviour and verbal report of the patient and of relevant signs and symptoms. After such assessment, treatment alternatives, if considered appropriate, could be selected from the following: Training in relaxation, with or without the use of physiological monitoring or 'biofeedback' information or hypnosis.

Specific behaviour therapy programmes such as systematic desensitization, 'flooding' or modelling.

Cateory B   Habit disorders
This category comprises those problems which can, to a useful degree, be construed as maladaptive habits, often endangering physical health and often resistive to change. These include:

Smoking; obesity and other inappropriate eating patterns; enuresis and encopresis; addiction to alcohol or other pharmacological agents; tics; stammering; children's behaviour disorders.

Analysis of the behaviour-maintaining reinforcement in the situation will usually be the first step in such problems. Behaviour change techniques based on a variety of procedures might then be introduced. Among others these include:

Classical conditioning procedures (positive or aversive) to alter the valencies of relevant stimuli.

Operant conditioning procedures differentially to reinforce (increase or eliminate) particular responses, with or without formal self-monitoring of behaviour or feedback of results.

Use of attitude change procedures and techniques to ensure adequate comprehension of information, alone or in group situations.

Category   C   Educational–occupational difficulties or decisions
Chronologically throughout the life-span a series of educational–occupational 'choice-points' or difficulties may occur. If inadequately resolved these may lead to physically or psychologically based presentations in the general practitioner's consulting room.

Psychological information concerning cognitive abilities, aptitudes, interests and values can be used to aid decision making at significant choice points in life. Training programmes based on the psychological principles of learning and skill acquisition can be used to reduce study problems, or help to train people for new occupations.

These procedures should help to reduce the frequency of medical consultation stemming from such origins.

*Category
D   Interpersonal–social–marital
problems*
This category comprises those problems in which a marked 'social' element is present, including:

Difficulties in social relationships stemming from lack of appropriate social skills, disruptive levels of anxiety or inappropriate patterns of dyadic communication. Sexual difficulties arising from anxiety, ignorance, or guilt.

Assessment of these problems would examine the effects of the relevant behaviour on both the individual patient and other key figures in the environment. Intervention, if considered appropriate, might concentrate on the individual alone or also use other, key, figures. Techniques used have included:

Teaching of social skills by use of role-playing or 'modelling', with or without video-feedback of behaviour and either alone or in group setting.

Masters and Johnson approaches to sexual dysfunction.

Investigation of self-concepts and of perception of roles.

The use of contracts between patient and therapist or between patient dyads designed to alter communication and behaviour patterns.

Category E Psychological adjustments to problems stemming from physical illness or other significant life events involving medical care
Problems in this category might merit either prophylactic or remedial intervention. Examples include psychological preparation of patients for hospital treatment or childbirth and the psychological problems of chronic ill-health, disablement following accident or illness, terminal illness, bereavement, abortion.

Preparation for medical care in patients with disabling levels of anxiety concerning hospitals, surgery or injections could involve any of the anxiety-reducing techniques discussed in category A.

Attempts to ensure adequate compliance with antenatal or postnatal care advice could involve the use of attitude and behaviour change procedures.

Remedial programmes can be established to maximize the potential of chronically ill or disabled patients such as those suffering from impairment of cognitive functioning after accident or illness. These will often involve readjustment to new roles with changes in 'self-identity' and relationships as well as retraining in cognitive skills.

Involvement in counselling at times of crisis (e.g. bereavement) could be useful, probably where inappropriate behaviour patterns are established.

Reproduced by permission of Update Publications Ltd from Kincey (1974)

Clinical effectiveness

A growing number of reports have been concerned with the evaluation of the effectiveness of clinical input at the primary care level. Many such reports have been largely anecdotal, describing the working practices of the author, from the clinical psychologists' point of view (e.g. Johnston, 1978; McAllister and Phillip, 1975; Wijesinghe, 1981), from the general practitioner's point of view (Update, 1980) or from a joint perspective (Bhagat, Lewis and Shillitoe, 1979). Some studies have used objective measures of outcome. The outcome measures most often employed are a comparison of consultation

rates and prescriptions for psychotropic medication before and after psychological treatment.

Some reports have been optimistic, others more cautious. A study by Earll
and Kincey (1982) found that during the period of psychological treatment,
patients received significantly fewer prescriptions for psychotropic drugs than
did a control group treated 'in whatever ways the general practitioner
considered appropriate' during an equivalent time period. At follow-up
(approximately 7 months), however, this difference had disappeared. The
treated sample continued to consult their doctor with the same frequency
during treatment as the control group. Ratings of subjective state at the time
of follow-up showed no differences in levels of distress between the two
groups. Unfortunately, subjective state was not rated immediately after the
treatment, so that any short-term improvement was impossible to assess. It
is not clear whether the reduced prescription rate, which was noted during
the treatment phase, reflected any change in the patient's state or a reluctance
on the part of the doctor to prescribe during active psychological treatment.

Such limited changes are particularly disappointing as the treatment offered
by the psychologist 'was largely based on a behavioural self-control model',
with emphasis being placed 'on the patient learning to cope more effectively
with inappropriate emotional or behavioural reactions to different situations'
(Earll and Kincey, 1982).

More encouraging findings were reported by Koch (1979) and Ives (1979),
who both obtained reductions in surgery attendance and psychotropic
prescriptions during treatment, which were maintained during follow-up.
Both these studies, however, are essentially retrospective analyses of each
respective author's own clinical practice and contain neither control groups
nor independent assessments of outcome; limitations of which the authors
are aware.

France and Robson (1982) report the preliminary findings from a larger
project. Rating scales, completed by patient and general practitioner, and
designed to reveal the severity of the problem, its effect upon the sufferer
and on the household, all showed significant improvement during treatment,
maintained at follow-up. There were also significant reductions, maintained
at follow-up, in the cost of prescriptions for psychotropic medication and the
number of consultations with the general practitioners.

Similar results have been reported by Jerrom et al., (1982). Self-ratings by
the patient improved significantly, and psychotropic prescriptions fell during
the course of treatment. Both were maintained at follow-up. A 43 per cent
drop in attendance rates during treatment was also maintained during follow-
up, but despite this large reduction, the consultation rate for treated patients
(and their spouses) remained high, at twice the national average.

The studies so far reported, apart from that by Earll and Kincey (1982),
have shown falls in prescription rates and frequency of consultation which
appear to be maintained during follow-up. Follow-up periods have, however,
been short and there is, as yet, no evaluation of the effectiveness of psycho-

logical treatments undertaken in primary care for periods longer than 12 months after discharge. Such evaluations would be extremely useful. For continued intervention at the primary care level to be justified and extended, stable long-term change will need to be demonstrated. In the meantime, the evidence concerning the long-term effectiveness of behaviour therapy in other settings (see Marks, 1981) suggests that similar findings may be expected when these techniques are applied to the surgery.

Of the outcome measures themselves, Jerrom et al. (1982) point out that it is not known whether or not consultation rates and prescription counts are valid indices of symptomatic improvement. Whilst reduced surgery attendance and medication intake may well be worthwhile goals in themselves, there is a need for caution when they are employed as measures of improvement. A recent review by Marks (1983) has shown that many of the patients for whom behaviour therapy is successful also exhibit a dysphoric mood which is not affected by behaviour therapy. Whilst behavioural treatment can remove or improve the behavioural component, such patients remain prone to episodes of dysphoria, for which they may well consult their general practitioner and receive medication. If surgery attendance and drug prescription rates are used as outcome measures, these patients will be rated as unimproved. The possibility that general practitioners are reluctant to prescribe during psychological treatment has already been mentioned. Presumably, many clinical psychologists will be encouraging their patients to reduce their reliance on medication during treatment. This, too, will contribute to difficulties in interpreting changes in prescription rates during or following psychological treatment.

Freeman and Button (1984) have commented upon the apparent sequence of 'crisis and remission' which is detectable in patients who attend surgery with complaints of a psychosocial nature. The changing consultation frequencies found by these authors make interpretation of reduced surgery attendance and drug prescription difficult.

The effective use of therapists' time

A number of additional factors need to be taken into account in the provision of a treatment service. Foremost amongst these is the need to identify patients for whom psychological treatment is both indicated and likely to be effective. Other considerations include how to make psychological help available to the large numbers of individuals identified as suffering from psychological distress in view of the relatively small numbers of clinical psychologists in post.

It is clearly important to be able to discriminate between those patients for whom psychological treatment may be effective and those for whom it may not. This has been most clearly expressed by Johnston (1978): 'It would be possible, in primary care, to occupy one's time with patients who, whilst they had definite psychological problems, would be unlikely to be helped by a psychologist's intervention and might receive more appropriate help from the continuing support of the general practitioner.'

Similar difficulties apply concerning disorders of recent onset. The problem here is to predict who, of new surgery attenders, with, for example, minor mood disorders, will be likely to require treatment and who will improve spontaneously without treatment. An attempt to clarify this issue has been reported by Catalan et al., (1984) although the authors did not consider their results to be of day-to-day value in the surgery of the general practitioner.

One answer to these difficulties of patient selection might be to limit those patients accepted for treatment to those groups with particular disorders—such as phobic, obsessional and sexual problems—which might reasonably be expected to respond to the behaviourally based treatments usually offered (Marks, 1981). This may not be a very realistic strategy, however, as the problems actually encountered in general practice tend to be far more diffuse than any simple classificatory system can account for, or for any single treatment style to be employed.

Other responses might include an attempt to develop therapeutic methods specifically for a general practice setting. For the most part, skills developed initially in the psychiatric setting have made a successful transition to other medical settings, but there has been little progress so far in the development of methods of intervention directly from the experience of working in general practice. Little is known about the ways in which general practitioners currently assess and manage psychological problems presenting in the surgery. It has been proposed that research into such areas would be a worthwhile pursuit of the clinical psychologist (Salmon, 1984; Freeman and Button, 1984).

There is certainly an opinion amongst clinical psychologists that the traditional 'one-to-one' type of consultation may be of limited value in the community setting. McPherson and Feldman (1977) and Hood (1979) have pointed out that only a small proportion of potential users of a clinical service can ever be reached by clinical psychologists working in a one-to-one capacity. McAllister and Phillip (1975), in describing their own method of work, wrote that 'the number of cases being referred will soon make it impractical to treat each patient on a one to one basis'. Ives (1979) reported having to reduce the length of sessions with patients due to pressure of referrals, and Jerrom et al. (1982) reported a growing tendency for urgent referrals to be made. Clarke (1979) is unusual in reporting that over 60 per cent of cases were discharged after only one or two sessions, it being the experience of most psychologists that, once a new service becomes established, the demand for a therapist's time rapidly exceeds supply.

In response to this pressure, a number of authors have reported the use of group methods, to use the therapist's time more effectively. The frequency with which some of the disorders present at the surgery makes endeavours of this sort particularly attractive. It is to be hoped, therefore, that more well-designed trials are to be reported.

Cormack and Sinnott (1983) and Skinner (1984) have described small-scale studies investigating group methods of anxiety management. In the former case the aim was to reduce benzodiazepine consumption, and in the latter case, to provide an alternative to minor tranquillizers. Coupar and Kennedy (1980) have described a course of group treatment of the obese, teaching weight control and dietary management, run jointly by a general practitioner and a clinical psychologist. This report is interesting in that the patients were largely self-selected, responding to a waiting room poster rather than being referred in the usual manner. Despite a substantial dropout rate, the project was felt to be successful. Cape (1981) has expressed reservations about the suitability for psychological treatment of the individuals that such a method of selection might attract. Medlik and Fursland (1984) have reported the use of relaxation classes organized in response to 'an overwhelming flood of referrals for stress and anxiety-based problems'. Some patients attended as a result of reading a waiting room notice, and referrals were accepted from all other members of the community-based team.

THE GENERAL PRACTITIONER'S VIEWPOINT

So far in this chapter, the discussion has been largely from the viewpoint of the clinical psychologist. The service offered by the psychologist must, however, be considered in the context of general practice as a whole. Issues which are particularly relevant include the general practitioner's perception of the role of the clinical psychologist in the management of psychological disorders, and other services which may be available to the general practitioner for helping psychologically troubled patients.

Some attempts have already been made to examine psychological services, not only in terms of benefit to the patient, but also in terms of the general practitioner's perception of the service. The principals concerned in a study by Butler and Davidson (1982) reported the advantages of an 'on site' clinical psychologist to be the opportunities for direct referral, professional liaison and the personal discussion of problem cases. Jerrom et al., (1983) conducted a more formal survey: they found a high level of satisfaction, with 98 per cent of participating doctors rating the service either 'useful' or 'very useful' in respect of clinical input, contact with the psychologist and communication. The clinical psychologist involved in this particular service is one of the few clinical psychologists in the country who is community based, holding clinics in a total of nine health centres, with a catchment population of 127,600 and a total of 78 general practitioners. In the first 2½ years of the service, 420 patients were referred. In view of the morbidity estimates referred to earlier, it is clear that here, as elsewhere, only a small proportion of patients with psychological problems were actually being referred to the psychologist. It is particularly interesting to note, therefore, that despite the high level of expressed satisfaction with the service, only 18 per cent of the doctors wished the service to be expanded. It would be valuable to know if those doctors wanting an expanded service were, in fact, those who used the service most, and why expansion was seen as desirable.

A further moderating note is sounded by Eastman and McPherson (1982). A sample of general practitioners, some of whom were already working with clinical psychologists, were asked which professions they wanted working from their premises, and to rank order the four professionals who were perceived to offer the most to general practice. Although just over half the sample wished to have a psychologist working with them, in terms of ranked importance, a psychologist was accorded only joint eighth position out of eleven, alongside a psychiatrist, and behind, in descending order of import- ance, a practice nurse, community nurse, health visitor, midwife, physio- therapist, community psychiatric nurse and social worker. Only family thera- pist and dietician received lower rankings. There were other important reser- vations. Over one third of sympathetically disposed doctors stated that they did not want psychologists working from their premises, and over half expressed concern about such issues as clinical responsibility, differences in working practices, confidentiality and general 'friction'. Only one fifth of sympathetic doctors felt that clinical psychologists had a role in prevention, or in health education, and only 12 per cent felt that the psychologist could have an advisory role on aspects of patient management. The authors feel that achieving credibility as therapists may hinder the establishment of credi- bility for any other role. They warn of the danger of being restricted to a purely clinical role by the creation of clinical expectations, and consequent pressure of referrals.

It is not surprising that general practitioners see those professions with an established history of being surgery-based as having most to offer them. There is, perhaps, a case for helping such professions enhance and refine their own psychological skills. Many clinical psychologists might wish to argue that this is a most effective way of using scarce clinical psychology resources. The notion of training other professions in psychological skills will be returned to later. In the meantime, let it be noted that the general prac- titioner's less than total commitment to a new profession of unknown poten- tial value is mirrored in relationships with a more established sister profession with a shared medical background: psychiatry. Given 'unlimited resources', over two thirds of a sample of general practitioners still said that they would refer less than 20 per cent of their patients with psychogenic problems to psychiatrists. Neither would they want consultant psychiatrists visiting their surgeries to discuss problem patients (Whitfield and Winter, 1980).

It seems clear that general practitioners jealously guard their indepen- dence. In fact, the primary care physician is encouraged to perceive himself as the cornerstone of community care. Whilst it is inconceivable that clinical psychologists will ever reach sufficient numbers to have a significant clinical effect on the burden of care shouldered by the general practitioner, any large increase in clinical load shouldered by clinical psychologists may be actively resisted.

OTHER PROFESSIONS

In this context of potential demand, it is of considerable interest to observe that several other professions are offering very similar clinical services to general practitioners. Like clinical psychologists, such groups are actively involved in promoting change and innovation. This appears to be due partly to administrative restructuring and partly to policies favouring a broader based training within these groups.

A number of professional groups can be identified, all of which are extending their roles in this fashion. In addition to clinical psychologists, psychotherapists (Brook and Temperley, 1976; Temperley, 1978), social workers (Cooper *et al.*, 1975); Corney and Briscoe, 1977), marriage guidance counsellors (Cohen, 1977; Cohen and Halpern, 1978b; Waydenfeld and Waydenfeld, 1980; Heisler, 1979) and other counsellors (Anderson and Hasler, 1979; Martin and Mitchell, 1983), health visitors (Perkins and Linke, 1984; Briscoe and Lindley, 1982), nurse therapists and community psychiatric nurses (Bird, Marks and Lindley, 1979; Marks, 1981; Paykel *et al.*, 1982) have published reports which are remarkably similar. This is true in terms of the skills offered, the types of problems for which these skills are held to be appropriate, and the overall success rates. Thus, the skills offered typically include relaxation training, behavioural management, support, counselling and vocational guidance (Anderson and Hasler, 1979). The disorders for which these various skills are requested typically include 'anxiety and stress, marital problems and relationship problems other than marital, sexual problems, abortion, bereavement, depression and psychosomatic problems' (Martin and Mitchell, 1983). Improvement has usually been assessed by changes in consultation and prescribing rates (Waydenfeld and Waydenfeld, 1980). The familiar arguments of increased accessibility, earlier referral, and ready availability of an expert opinion, make regular appearances. Some of the problems encountered will also be familiar to clinical psychologists. Heisler (1979), for example, reports that 20 per cent of marriage guidance counsellors felt that referrals were not always appropriate for counselling, and the clients were 'resistant' because they had been 'sent' by their general practitioner, sometimes without a referral question being clearly formulated.

It remains to be seen whether, when a clinical psychologist offers 'counselling' (e.g. Kincey, 1974; Ives, 1979) or a counsellor offers 'behaviour therapy' (e.g. Anderson and Hasler, 1979), each is performing something that the other would recognize and accept, but clearly there is considerable overlap of function (Wyld, 1981). To the 'consumers' of those services—patients and general practitioners—role boundaries and professional differences are likely to appear less real than they are to the providers of the services.

It is, perhaps, with mixed feelings that clinical psychologists will recognize amongst these professions an old familiar face—psychiatry. Having left psychiatric hospitals to practise his skills in the community, a clinical psychologist may well now find a consultant psychiatrist practising his skills in a community-based outpatient clinic in the same surgery. Issues of convenience, stigma, continuity of care and interdisciplinary communication have been raised, and answered, in a positive direction (Tyrer, 1984). The cost-effectiveness of such services has also been the focus of inquiry (Tyrer, Seivewright and Wollerton, 1984).

The psychologist's approach to patient care, then, overlaps with the approaches of many others. Already established members of the primary care team, such as health visitors or practice nurses, almost certainly employ psychological skills, although perhaps covertly. Such groups may justifiably claim that this type of role belongs more properly to them. King and Eiser (1981) suggest that their technique of counselling pregnant smokers might be effectively performed by general practitioners or maternity nurses in the patient's home. This could much more easily be accommodated by those professions than by clinical psychology. With the move towards, for example, a broader based training for nurses (Hall, 1979), there is an increasing probability that individuals from the nursing professions will become competent in skills more conventionally performed by clinical psychologists, and may be better placed for the execution of those skills. This carries implications for training and career structures in those nursing professions. Interdisciplinary relationships will need careful examination. If, as has been claimed, 'psychologists have been able to develop their approach . . . more systematically than other professional groups which eschew the need for systematic research', then, because of the relative scarcity of clinical psychologists, 'they may come to exert a greater influence by teaching other professions or non-professionals to use the treatment techniques which psychologists have so effectively developed in the hospital setting' (Goldberg and Huxley, 1980, pp. 152–153). These implications need analysis, without which any rational or concerted development in services is unlikely to occur.

In addition, possible disadvantages of proliferating treatment agencies have yet to be explored. It is not yet clear what effect referrals to clinical psychologists have on referrals to other professions with overlapping interests, although Ives (1979) reports that referral rates to psychiatric clinics did not change during the period of his study. There is a general feeling that psychologists in primary care are tapping a population which previously remained untreated, at least by referral to specialists. The effect of this on the perception of psychological distress, both by general practitioners and by patients themselves, is difficult to evaluate. Although psychologists have generally adopted a coping, problem-solving or self-management model, the very fact of referral to a specialist might tend to contradict or undermine this approach. The 'early referral' argument would be severely weakened were this shown to be the case, aided also by the difficulties in predicting at an early stage which patients are likely to require treatment and which are not.

WIDER ROLES

Non-clinical contributions

The approach so far discussed may be characterized as an attempt in general practice to apply and adopt existing clinical skills to a somewhat different area of work. Some of the difficulties associated with this approach have already been discussed. These have included the feasibility, or even desirability, of ever reaching more than a small minority of patients in general practice with psychological problems, and the fact that many other professional groups lay claim to similar therapeutic skills applicable to similar patient groups.

Arguments such as these have led psychologists to point out that, even were a direct treatment service shown to be cost-effective in primary care, clinical expertise is but one aspect of a psychologist's work and training. To concentrate endeavours on the clinical field would be to ignore large areas of psychological knowledge, the application of which may in the long run prove to be more fruitful.

One worthwhile enterprise might be to encourage the systematic application of existing knowledge regarding the process of the consultation itself. There is a considerable body of knowledge concerning the variables which affect such fundamental phenomena as doctor–patient communication, and compliance with recommendations. The application of this knowledge by the practitioner and other health centre based staff would be expected to show immediate pay-off in the health of the community—far greater than face-to-face contact between a psychologist and a limited number of patients ever could.

Ley and his colleagues (Ley, 1977, 1979) have produced a set of simple guidelines for use by the physician to increase the amount and content of a patient's recall. Such guidelines have been tested in general practice and other contexts and have been shown also to exert significant effects upon compliance and medication errors. In a similar vein, Sackett (1979) has prepared a hierarchy of simple interventions designed to be straightforward enough for use in regular clinical practice.

Other findings likely to help general practitioners improve their interactive skills have been reported. Analysis of videotaped consultations (Pendleton and Bochner, 1980) showed that general practitioners gave less information to patients of lower social class. As higher social class patients are better informed about medical matters, and as such knowledge is a known mediator of the uptake of medical advice (Becker, 1979), it would make good sense for doctors deliberately to offer more information to their lower class patients.

Attempts have been made to understand these issues within broad theoretical frameworks such as the health belief model (Becker and Maiman, 1975); the literature on compliance is currently proliferating (e.g. Haynes, Taylor and Sackett, 1979; Cohen, 1979; Di Matteo and Di Nicola, 1982).

The training of general practitioners

The application of research findings such as these offers an opportunity for psychological knowledge to achieve a much more widespread impact than could be achieved with clinical intervention by the psychologist working with individuals or groups of patients. General practitioners are undoubtedly willing to collaborate with clinical psychologists. In 1981 the Royal College of General Practitioners emphasize that 'discussion of the psychological consequences of physical illness should become a normal part of clinical case presentations' and recommended the experimental attachment of clinical psychologists to training practices (Royal College of General Practitioners, 1981).

Pendleton and Tate (1981) have described one way of disseminating psychological information through involvement with a general practitioner vocational training scheme. Short courses are run for trainers and trainees, during which the participants are exposed to the research findings and discuss videotaped and role-played consultations in the light of these findings. The trainees are required to achieve certain consultation-oriented goals following the course, and feedback is given either by the practice trainer or at regular day release follow-up sessions.

A number of such training methods have now been reported, reviewed by Schofield (1983). Verby, Davies and Holden (1980) achieved limited success: a group of trainees had videotaped interviews rated for interview skills at the start and end of a 4–month experimental period. All trainees attended lectures on interpersonal communication and were given relevant reading material. Half of the group made further videotapes during the experimental period, which were used as the basis for discussion and teaching in one-to-one tutorials. During the first 6 months of the project, little change occurred in either group, although during the next 6 months the trainees who had received the additional teaching showed some slight improvement, whilst the remainder showed a decrement in interviewing skills. A similar project involving experienced general practitioners showed a much quicker improvement, in this case following peer group discussions (Verby, Holden and Davies, 1979).

Verby explained the disappointing findings for the trainees in terms of a sudden role transition from hospital-based to community-based training, raising the question of the most appropriate timing for training in interviewing skills. On the other hand, early intervention appears justified as some of the data were interpreted as suggesting that a doctor's interviewing behaviour is established within a few years of entering practice, and persists unaltered in the absence of any opportunity for critical examination. It is possible, too, that doctors unused to having their interviewing methods analysed, find this and the use of video feedback threatening, in which case it might be more appropriate to make greater use of general practitioner trainers as providers of feedback rather than psychologists.

The need to evaluate such proposals remains paramount. Indeed, many clinical psychologists would argue that research is a prime function of the clinical psychologist in the surgery, as elsewhere. This would be not just in terms of evaluating clinical services, but also in more general terms—making use of the psychologist's training in experimental design and research methodology for all aspects of primary care. The measurement of subjective states, management of drug side-effects, and a greater understanding of attitudes to health problems among the population, are all fields where a clinical psychologist's training in applied research might prove fruitful; 'as the applications for psychology within medicine continue to increase, it is essential that efforts be sustained to document empirically the contribution that is being made as this will ensure that psychological factors are perceived as relevant concerns, rather than peripheral issues to be considered if time permits' (Reading, 1982). A large percentage of general practitioners express interest in research involvement with clinical psychologists (Eastman and McPherson, 1982). How best this is to be pursued is a matter for local discussion and priority, bearing in mind that general practitioners themselves are increasingly perceiving the importance of enhancing their own research skills. There remains plenty of scope for using existing knowledge in the sensitization of general practitioners to the presence of psychological distress in surgery attenders (e.g. Bhagat and Shillitoe, 1978).

Preventive work in the community

Cape (1981) has described some preventive education directly aimed at patients rather than their general practitioners. Talks on such topics as 'coping with stress', understanding yourself', and 'parent–child relationships' were delivered to people who responded to posters displayed in the surgery's reception area. A series of evening classes entitled 'learning for life', utilizing a 'humanistic' approach, but including practical exercises and assertive training, was also delivered. The author, however, expresses reservations as to whether a health centre is an appropriate location for this type of work. Additionally, although the classes were intended for primary prevention and early intervention, those who actually attended included 'some of the most chronic general practice cases' (Cape, 1981) and the classes could not, therefore, be described as preventive.

Also in this context, calls have been made to help change public attitudes to psychological distress (Farina and Fisher, 1982). The presence of a clinical psychologist in the surgery may have a significant effect on the ways in which psychological distress is perceived by the general public. This effect may be enhanced by the presence in the community of a body of treated individuals who have been advised how best to construe their troubles. It might be useful, for example, to teach patients to present themselves to families, friends and neighbours as having undergone stress, and having been unable to contend effectively with it. 'It would also appear helpful to have ex-patients indicate they are now relying upon themselves for problem solutions, and that they are able to exercise considerable self-control' (Farina and Fisher, 1982).

Others would extend this approach even further: the increasing awareness that social conditions figure largely in mental health problems (e.g. Brown and Harris, 1978) has been seen as an argument for psychologists working to change these social conditions. To date, clinical psychologists have mostly been involved with individuals or, if with groups, with a group composed of individuals having a shared problem (such as groups for smokers or the obese). There has been little involvement with social groups or organizational groups. Working in the community will be welcomed by some as an opportunity to examine social factors and, rather than treating the casualties of social systems, to try to influence those social factors with a view to reducing psychological morbidity. Without attention being paid to the variables which influence the wellbeing of an individual in society, adjustment in a treated individual is likely to be tenuous, due to lack of change in the environment.

> It is in this context that the general practice can become a useful strategic position for effecting entry into groups in the community. The general practitioner holds a central role in the community, and close liaison with him means that the clinical psychologist can either gain similar prestige or can utilise the general practitioner's prestige and the professional bond established to initiate invitations into target groups in the community. (Humphreys, 1981)

Such target groups might include housing groups, well-baby and well-woman clinics, day nurseries, self-help groups and so forth.

All of this moves clinical psychology further away from the hospital wards and outpatient clinics towards the high street. It raises issues about society and psychology's place and responsibility within that society. Of more immediate present concern, it also raises practical issues of the relation of clinical psychology to the NHS. For example, the Trethowan (1977) Report recommended that all referrals to clinical psychologists be channelled through a medical practitioner. Whilst this places clinical psychology firmly within the structure of the NHS, with consequent advantages to the patient in terms of clear channels of communication, and of responsibility, it also makes primary prevention unlikely.

Most clinical psychologists are employed in district departments. Only a handful have been appointed to work specifically in primary care, or are jointly funded with social services. District or unit managers are unlikely to look favourably upon clinical psychologists' diminishing input to priority groups, or well-established patients' groups, in favour of increasing commitment to primary care. This is especially likely to be the case if psychologists depart from normal working practices in favour of self-referrals, and change in emphasis away from direct clinical work towards other roles. The financial implications of providing services for general practitioners who are funded by family practitioner committees rather than district health authorities remain unclear.

All in all, however, the diversity of approaches in evidence so far, indicates a strong desire among clinical psychologists to contribute to primary care. Psychologists have felt drawn to primary care because of dissatisfaction with the limitations of traditional mental hospital roles and because of the attractiveness and potential of the setting, which appears to offer the opportunity to practise a wide variety of skills—treatment, education, research—with a wide range of client groups. General practitioners, for their part, appear to accept a clinical contribution because it is a well-understood role and fits into a well-established medical referral system. From the available evidence it would seem that general practitioners feel less comfortable with the wider or non-clinical roles that many psychologists have envisaged. Whether this is because of unfamiliarity with clinical psychology, or because general practitioners have a clear view of their own duties and responsibilities, or because clinical psychologists, alone among a GP's colleagues, do not simply desire a closer working relationship with the general practitioner, but wish to change his methods of work and approach to patients, is not clear. But at whatever level the interaction is pitched, the endeavour requires willingness and cooperation on both sides as well as demonstration of the effectiveness of the proposals which are being made. The former is undoubtedly present now; the latter is taking a little longer.

REFERENCES

Anderson, S. A., and Hasler, J. C. (1979). Counselling in general practice. *Journal of the Royal College of General Practitioners*, **29**, 352–356.

Becker, M. H. (1979). Understanding patient compliance: the contributions of attitudes and other psychosocial factors. In S. J. Cohen (ed.), *New Directions in Patient Compliance*. Lexington: Health, pp. 1–31.

Becker, M. H., and Maiman, L. A. (1975). Sociobehavioural determinants of compliance with health and medical care recommendations. *Medical Care*, **13**, 10–24.

Bender, M. P. (1976). *Community Psychology*. London: Methuen.

Bhagat, M. R., Lewis, A. P., and Shillitoe, R. W. (1979). Clinical psychologists and the primary health care team. *Update*, **18**, 479–488.

Bhagat, M. R., and Shillitoe, R. W. (1978). Attempted suicide and general practice. *Update*, **17**, 1479–1481.

Bird, J., Marks, I. M., and Lindley, P. (1979). Nurse therapists in psychiatry—developments, controversies and implications. *British Journal of Psychiatry*, **135**, 321–330.

Briscoe, M. E., and Lindley, P. (1982). Identification and management of psychosocial problems by health visitors. *Health Visitor*, **55**, 165–169.

British Psychological Society Professional Affairs Board (1979). Evidence to the DHSS Joint Working Group on the primary health care team. Leicester: British Psychological Society.

Broadhurst, A. (1972). Clinical psychology and the general practitioner. *British Medical Journal*, **1**, 793–795.

Brook, A., and Temperley, J. (1976). The contribution of a psychotherapist to general practice. *Journal of the Royal College of General Practitioners*, **26**, 86–94.

Brown, G., and Harris, T. (1978). *Social Origins of Depression*. London: Tavistock Publications.

Burns, L. E. (1982). The role of the clinical psychologist in primary care—an analysis of current practice. In C. J. Main (ed.), *Clinical Psychology and Medicine.* New York: Plenum, pp. 85–95.

Butler, R. J., and Davidson, R. J. (1982). A psychological service in general practice. *Update,* **25,** 497–503.

Cape, J. (1981). Educational approaches with patients in primary care. In A. Broome and R. Ball (eds), *Proceedings of the DCP West Midlands Branch Conference.* Dudley, West Midlands.

Catalan, J., Gath, D., Bond, A., and Martin, P. (1984). The effects of non-prescribing of anxiolytics in general practice. II. Factors associated with outcome. *British Journal of Psychiatry,* **144,** 603–610.

Clark, D. F. (1979). The clinical psychologist in primary care. *Social Science and Medicine,* **13a,** 707–713.

Cohen, J. S. H. (1977). Marital counselling in general practice. *Proceedings of the Royal Society of Medicine,* **70,** 495–496.

Cohen, J. S. H., and Halpern, A. (1978a). A practice counsellor. *Journal of the Royal College of General Practitioners,* **28,** 481–484.

Cohen, J. S. H., and Halpern, A. (1978b). Non-directive counselling in a general practice. *British Journal of Guidance and Counselling,* **6,** 229–234.

Cohen, S. J. (ed.) (1979). *New Directions in Patient Compliance.* Lexington: Heath.

Cooper, B. (1964). General practitioners' attitudes to psychiatry. *De Medicine Tuenda,* **1,** 43–48.

Cooper, B., Harwin, B. G., Depla, C., and Shepherd, M. (1975). Mental health care in the community: an evaluative study. *Psychological Medicine,* **5,** 372–380.

Cormack, M. A., and Sinnott, A. (1983). Psychological alternatives to long-term benzodiazepine use. *Journal of the Royal College of General Practitioners,* **33,** 279–281.

Corney, R. N., and Briscoe, M. E. (1977). Social workers and their clients: a comparison between primary health care and local authority settings. *Journal of the Royal College of General Practitioners,* **27,** 295–301.

Coupar, A. M., and Kennedy, T. (1980). Running a weight control group: experiences of a psychologist and general practitioner. *Journal of the Royal College of General Practitioners,* **30,** 41–48.

Di Matteo, M. R., and Di Nicola, D. D. (1982). *Achieving Patient Compliance.* New York: Pergamon Press.

Earll, L., and Kincey, J. (1982). Clinical psychology in general practice: a controlled trial evaluation. *Journal of the Royal College of General Practitioners,* **32,** 32–37.

Eastman, C., and McPherson, I. (1982). As others see us: general practitioners' perceptions of psychological problems and the relevance of clinical psychology. *British Journal of Clinical Psychology,* **21,** 85–92.

Farina, A., and Fisher, J. D. (1982). Beliefs about mental disorders: findings and implications. In G. Weary and H. L. Mirels (eds), *Integrations of Social and Clinical Psychology.* New York: Oxford University Press, pp. 48–71.

France, R., and Robson, M. (1982). Work of the clinical psychologist in general practice: preliminary communication. *Journal of the Royal Society of Medicine,* **75,** 185–189.

Freeman, G. K., and Button, E. J. (1984). The clinical psychologist in general practice: a six year study of consulting patterns for psychosocial problems. *Journal of the Royal College of General Practitioners,* **34,** 377–380.

Goldberg, D., and Huxley, P. (1980). *Mental Illness in the Community.* London: Tavistock.

Hall, J. (1979). Nurse therapy and role change in health care professions. *Bulletin of the British Psychological Society,* **32,** 71–73.

Haynes, R. B., Taylor, D. W., and Sackett, D. L. (eds) (1979). *Compliance in Health Care.* Baltimore: Johns Hopkins University Press.

Heisler, J. (1979). Marriage counsellors in medical settings. *Marriage Guidance Counselling Journal*, **18**, 153–162.

Hood, J. E. (1979). Clinical psychology and primary care: a plea for restraint. *Bulletin of the British Psychological Society*, **32**, 422–423.

Hopkins, P. (1956). Referrals in general practice. *British Medical Journal*, **2**, 873–877.

Humphreys, A. (1981). Has general practitioner–psychologist liaison any relevance for community psychology? *Bulletin of the British Psychological Society*, **32**, 235–237.

Ives, G. (1979). Psychological treatment in general practice. *Journal of the Royal College of General Practitioners*, **29**, 343–351.

Jerrom, D. W. A., Gerver, D., Simpson, R. J., and Pemberton, D. A. (1982). Clinical psychology in primary care—issues in the evaluation of services. In C. J. Main (ed.), *Clinical Psychology and Medicine*. New York: Plenum Press, pp. 97–111.

Jerrom, D. W. A., Simpson, R. J., Barber, J. H., and Pemberton, D. A. (1983). General practitioners' satisfaction with a primary care clinical psychology setting. *Journal of the Royal College of General Practitioners*, **33**, 29–31.

Johnston, M. (1978). The work of a clinical psychologist in primary care. *Journal of the Royal College of General Practitioners*, **28**, 661–667.

Journal of the Royal College of General Practitioners (1979). Editorial: Behavioural problems in general practice. *Journal of the Royal College of General Practitioners*, **29**, 323–327.

Kessel, W. I. N. (1960). Psychiatric morbidity in a London general practice. *British Journal of Preventive and Social Medicine*, **14**, 16–22.

Kincey, J. A. (1974). General practice and clinical psychology—some arguments for a closer liaison. *Journal of the Royal College of General Practitioners*, **24**, 882–888.

King, B., and Eiser, R. (1981). A strategy for counselling pregnant smokers. *Health Education Journal*, **40**, 66–68.

Koch, H. C. H. (1979). Evaluation of behaviour therapy intervention in general practice. *Journal of the Royal College of General Practitioners*, **29**, 337–340.

Ley, P. (1977). Psychological studies of doctor–patient communication. In S. Rachman (ed.), *Contributions to Medical Psychology*, vol. 1. Oxford: Pergamon, pp. 9–42.

Ley, P. (1979). Memory for medical information. *British Journal of Social and Clinical Psychology*, **18**, 245–255.

Liddell, A., May, B., Boyle, M., and Baker, M. (1981). How to stimulate general practitioner referrals to a clinical psychology unit. *Bulletin of the British Psychological Society*, **32**, 164–165.

McAllister, T. A., and Phillip, A. E. (1975). The clinical psychologist in a health centre: one year's work. *British Medical Journal*, **4**, 513–514.

McPherson, I. G. (1981). Clinical psychology in primary health care: development or diversion. In I. McPherson and A. Sutton (eds), *Reconstructing Psychological Practice*. London: Croom Helm, pp. 21–41.

McPherson, I. G., and Feldman, M. P. (1977). A preliminary investigation of the role of the clinical psychologist in the primary care setting. *Bulletin of the British Psychological Society*, **30**, 342–346.

Marks, I. (1981). *Cure and Care of Neurosis*. London: Wiley.

Marks, I. (1983). Are there anticompulsive or antiphobic drugs? Review of the evidence. *British Journal of Psychiatry*, **143**, 338–347.

Martin, E., and Mitchell, A. (1983). A counsellor in general in practice: a one year survey. *Journal of the Royal College of General Practitioners*, **33**, 366–367.

Mayou, R. (1980). Management of neurotic problems in general practice. *Journal of the Royal College of General Practitioners*, **30**, 678–681.

Medlik, L., and Fursland, A. (1984). Maximizing scarce resources: autogenic relaxation classes at a health centre. *British Journal of Medical Psychology*, **57**, 181–185.

Mischel, W. (1968). *Personality and Assessment.* New York: Wiley.

Paykel, E. S., Mangen, S. P., Griffith, J. H., and Burns, T. P. (1982). Community psychiatric nursing for neurotic patients: a controlled trial. *British Journal of Psychiatry*, **140**, 573–581.

Pendleton, D. A., and Bochner, S. (1980). The communication of medical information in general practice consultations as a function of patients' social class. *Soocial Science and Medicine*, **14a**, 669–673.

Pendleton, D. A., and Tate, P. (1981). The psychologist in primary care: the noncliniical alternativee. In A. Broome and R . Ball (eds), *Proceedings of the DCP West Midlands Branch Conference.* Dudley, West Midlands.

Perkins, T. S., and Linke, S. B. (1984). Management of behavioural disorders. *Health Visitor*, **57**, 108–109.

Reading, A. E. (1982). A Strategic and methodological aspects of behavioural medicine. *British Journal of Clinical Psychology*, **21**, 79–84.

Royal College of General Practitioners (1981). *Prevention of Psychiatric Disorder in General Practice.* Report of a Sub-Committee of the Royal College of General Practitioners. London.

Royal Commission on the National Healthh Service (1979). *Report.* London: HMSO.

Sackett, D. L. (1979). A compliance practicum for the busy practitioner. In R. B. Haynes, D. W. Taylor and D. L. Sackett (eds), *Compliance in Health Care.* Baltimore: Johns Hopkins University Press, pp. 286–294.

Salmon, P. (1984). The psychologists' contribution to primary care: a reappraisal. *Journal of the Royal College of General Practitioners*, **34**, 190–193.

Schofield, T. (1983). The application of the study of communication skills to training for general practice. In D. Pendleton and J. Hasler (eds), *Doctor–Patient Communication.* London: Academic Press, pp. 259–271.

Skinner, P. T. (1984). Skills not pills: learning to cope with anxiety symptoms. *Journal of the Royal College of General Practitioners*, **34**, 258–260.

Temperley, J. (1978). Psychotherapy in the setting of general medical practice. *British Journal of Medicine and Psychology*, **51**, 138–145.

Trethowan, W. H. (1977). *The Role of Psychologists in the Health Services.* London: HMSO.

Tyrer, P. (1984). Psychiatric clinics in general practice: an extension of community care. *British Journal of Psychiatry*, **145**, 9–14.

Tyrer, P., Seivewright, N., and Wollerton, S. (1984). General practice psychiatric clinics: report on psychiatric services. *British Journal of Psychiatry*, **145**, 15–19.

Update (1980). *Our Team: The Clinical Psychologist*, **21**, 483–487.

Verby, J. E., Davies, R. H., and Holden, P. (1980). A study of the interviewing skills of trainee assistants in general practice. *Patient Counselling and Health Education*, **2**, 68–71.

Verby, J. E., Holden, P., and Davies, R. H. (1979). Peer review of consultations in primary care: the use of audio-visual recordings. *British Medical Journal*, **1**, 1686–1688.

Waydenfeld, D., and Waydenfeld, S. W. (1980). Counselling in general practice. *Journal of the Royal College of General Practitioners*, **30**, 671–677.

Whitfield, M. J., and Winter, R. D. (1980). Psychiatry and general practice: results of a survey of Avon general practitioners. *Journal of the Royal College of General Practitioners*, **30**, 682–686.

Wijesinghe, B. (1981). The development of a district community psychology service. *Journal of the Royal College of General Practitioners*, **31**, 113–115.

Williams, J. M. (1984). *The Psychological Treatment of Depression.* London and Canberra: Croom Helm.

Wyld, K. L. (1981). Counselling in general practice: a review. *British Journal of Guidance and Counselling*, **9**, 129–141.

The Psychosomatic Approach: Contemporary Practice
of Whole-person Care
Edited by M. J. Christie and P. G. Mellett
© 1986 John Wiley & Sons Ltd

15

OCCUPATIONAL ASPECTS OF WHOLE-PERSON HEALTH CARE

COLIN MACKAY

Medical Division, Health and Safety Executive, Liverpool, UK
and
GRAHAM LUCAS

Medical Division, Health and Safety Executive, London, UK
and
Department of Psychological Medicine, King's College Hospital,
London, UK

INTRODUCTION

In terms of prevention of disease and promotion of health, the role of work and the associated working environment represent a double-edged sword. On the *negative* side, the toxicity of many industrial materials and processes has been well established for many years (see Hunter, 1978). The investigation and treatment of occupational ill-health is at the core of classical occupational medicine; the list of ailments brought about by specific workplace hazards is a long one ranging from the exotic, such as arc eye, at one end of the spectrum to the more mundane and prevalent ones, such as repetitive strain injuries, at the other. In the past, the traditional medical model has been largely adequate to cope with these ailments. On the *positive* side the correlations between work and positive mental health have been well known for many years and appear in the writings of early pioneers of psychological medicine such as Freud. Even though the links between mental health and job satisfaction have been recognized only comparatively recently, the use of work as a prophylactic aid in psychiatric rehabilitation goes back to the eighteenth century and before.

Thus, although there have been some notable exceptions, the disciplines concerned with psychological medicine have had a very small part to play in mainstream occupational medicine and particularly in occupational health care provision. In the past the psychiatrist's role has been confined to the identification of the mentally ill, referral and subsequent rehabilitation where appropriate. Likewise, the occupational psychologist's role in the organization has been confined largely to aspects of selection and training. Over the last quarter of a century, however, a number of changes have been taking place which have led to the uptake of expertise residing in these specialties.

In some areas this has been occurring gradually over many years; in others it is a much more recent phenomenon.

First, there have been quite fundamental changes in the nature and pattern of work, working practices and the structure of organizations, including the impact of the change process itself. Second, as a gradual development, but also as a reaction to the above, the provision of occupational health care (specifically the nature of the service) is changing. There is a move away from traditional problem areas (pre employment and statutory medical examinations; the provision of first aid and other emergency services; prevention of accidents and occupational disease) towards providing a much more diversified service aimed at promoting health within (and indeed the health of) the organization. Of course, the extent to which these developments are taking place is variable and, unfortunately, significant sections of the workforce still do not have access to any form of occupational health care, although this deficit is being slowly remedied. The most recent estimates (Health and Safety Commission, 1977) are illuminating: although some organizations had well-established occupational medical services, about nine out of every ten firms had no medical staff; many of these being small firms. Overall, however, some 44 per cent of the working population had no access to immediate medical advice at their place of work. Until recently this included Britain's largest employer, the NHS. The inequalities in health evidenced by differences in the current mortality statistics between social groupings and occupations, and highlighted in the Black Report (Townsend and Davidson, 1982), provide clear evidence of the impact that work and its ramifications continue to have on our health.

Third—and this is in part the impetus for volumes such as the present one—a change in both emphasis and attitude, and a consequent change in approach, to medical problem solving and management is currently under way. The rationale for this development has been the realization that a simplified medical model is inadequate for dealing with the health care problems of the last quarter of the twentieth century. Elaborate models of health and disease have become both necessary and acceptable, as evidenced by psychosomatic (Lipowski, 1977) and biopsychosocial (Engel, 1980) approaches. These are relevant in the occupational setting as much as, if not more than, in the general setting of health care delivery whether be this concerned with the effects of work on health or the converse—the effects of health on work. Part of this movement has been the willingness not only to consider the psychosocial problems surrounding traditional occupational diseases and accidents (including aetiology and prognosis) but also to take on board terms such as 'wellbeing' which are particularly relevant as explanatory concepts within current thinking in occupational health (World Health Organization, 1980; Commission of the European Communities, 1984).

It is not our intention in this chapter to review the current state of the art in occupational medicine (see, for example, Schilling, 1981; McDonald, 1981) nor to discuss specific concerns of occupational mental health, but rather to alert the reader to instances in some of the above where new problems have arisen, new techniques and methods have been developed and current practice has been improved. Although the psychosomatic/psychosocial approach is implicit rather than explicit we believe that it will have a growing part to play in identifying, preventing and treating future occupational health problems.

Scope

At a simple level of analysis, the role of the occupational physician can be seen in terms of evaluating and managing the impact of the organization on the individual or group and vice versa. Here the traditional concern with occupational disease is only part of a much wider and elaborate picture. Figure 15.1 sets out a framework in which the whole-person approach to health care within the work setting can be seen. Many of these problems can be envisaged as job-related rather than true occupational diseases. In contrast to the latter, the former cannot usually be defined by simple cause–effect relationships (and Figure 15.1 is not meant to indicate cause and effect models as such). They are usually multifactorial in origin, having risk factors that are not only work-related but also related to the individual person and his lifestyle. Some writers have used stress-related concepts to describe these phenomena. Thus, in describing problems encountered with night-work and shiftwork, Colquhoun and Rutenfranz (1980) have written: 'The objective

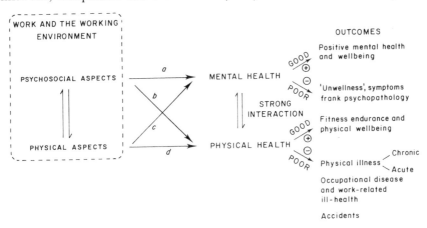

Figure 15.1 A highly simplified diagram to show some of the health outcomes, positive and negative, of work and working environments. The very powerful influences on health which feed back are not shown. Arrow *a* indicates the traditional occupational stress area but also emphasizes positive effects. Mental health aside, arrow *b* shows the link between the psychosocial environment and chronic physical ill health. The physical nature of work may influence mental health (arrow *c*) either by toxic effects or by stress mechanisms. Arrow *d* represents the traditional concerns of occupational health and safety

stress resulting from the disruptions of physiological rhythms by shiftwork, and from the slow rate of re-entertainment of these rhythms to the changed wake–sleep cycle, induce a state of subjective strain in the shiftworker that can potentially affect his working efficiency, his physical and psychological health and well being, and his family and social life.'

The likelihood, therefore, of a particular shiftworker suffering from a shiftwork-related health problem will depend upon a number of intervening variables acting alone or in combination. These include (1) particular characteristics of the shiftworker (age, sex, personality, rhythmic 'type', physiological adaptability, pre existing health problems), (2) factors relating to the actual job he is carrying out (physical and mental load, length of shift, type of shift system) and the environmental conditions of the workplace and (3) his non-work circumstances and activities (social, domestic, marital status, housing conditions, commuting time) (Rutenfranz, Haider and Koller, 1985).

The remainder of this section deals in more detail with a number of the salient occupational health issues, drawn from Figure 15.1, where whole-person approaches are relevant.

OCCUPATIONAL HEALTH PROBLEMS

Toxic effects: threats to well-being

The use in industry of substances that may be hazardous to man has become a subject of much concern in recent years and has given rise to the development of different methods of monitoring specific hazards. Potentially, exposure to toxic substances may adversely affect almost any organ system, but the hepatic, pulmonary, cardiac and central nervous systems (CNS) seem particularly at risk. Both structural integrity and functional capacity may be severely compromised, which may be manifested by both acute and chronic phases. In some instances the concomitant changes in behaviour associated with exposure may be unremarkable. In the case of asbestos, 25–30 years of exposure may elapse (usually asymptomatic, certainly as far as the CNS is concerned), following which asbestos-related disease appears and is invariably rapidly fatal. In contrast, other toxic chemicals increasingly widespread in industry, such as the heavy metals (lead, organic and inorganic mercury) and the chlorinated hydrocarbon solvents, may produce behavioural symptoms which are subtle and of rapid onset (certainly in the case of the solvents). It has long been recognized that occupational exposure to high concentrations of many materials leads to profound behavioural changes or to a toxic organic psychosis. The widespread use of mercury compounds in the hat-making industry often produced symptoms of psychotic illness known as erethism (the term 'mad as a hatter' is still common currency). Similarly, exposure to carbon disulphide used in the cold curing of rubber was often responsible for suicide, workers typically throwing themselves out of high windows. Nowadays such high concentrations for the most part are not found and the more dangerous substances have or are being replaced by less toxic ones. However, over the last 20 or so years there has been growing concern over more subtle but nevertheless significant effects of exposure to a wide range of substances encountered at the workplace (Weiss, 1983a, 1983b).

Typically these adversely affect CNS functioning and are manifested in changes in mood and behaviour. Both work-related behaviour (efficiency, ability to do the job safely) and non-work activities (sleep, general lifestyle) may be impaired. These may be seen as threats to wellbeing.

The concept of biological monitoring has been developed as one aspect of medical monitoring in industry, as ideas on health surveillance have been progressively refined. Here, physiological and biochemical tests are used to detect signs of early or incipient disease. There remain some grey areas, however; at one end of the spectrum such tests are able to show definite (though early) clinical evidence of disease; at the other a departure from 'normal' functioning may or may not indicate unacceptable harm. To fill this gap some progress has been made in developing tests of psychological functioning for use in assessing exposure to neurotoxic compounds. Two principal but related reasons have been advanced to justify the use and development of behavioural methods in toxicological studies. First, it has been suggested that behavioural techniques may be more sensitive in situations involving chronic low-dose exposure than the more traditional methods which rely primarily upon clinical, experimental or epidemiological studies. The second, related, reason is that behavioural measures may indicate early effects of irreversible functional disorders. In achieving the success of behavioural methods, the primary problem is not to devise a test which will characterize a transitory phenomenon, but rather to detect at an early stage the effect of an agent that may accumulate very slowly through time but which produces behavioural effects which are at present discernible only after it reaches a critical concentration. If the insidious onset of neurobehavioural effects can be readily demonstrated then exposure can be checked and irreversible functional and structural damage halted.

Clinical aspects

Individuals presenting with complaints apparently related to exposure to toxic chemicals typically report a constellation of symptoms, few of which are unique in the sense of being pathognomonic of exposure to a particular toxic chemical. Although clinical examination can go some way to elucidating the nature of the effects and possible causal factors, many of the symptoms shown in Table 15.1 are not amenable to quick or reliable quantification. However, many of the early manifestations of exposure (fatigue and lassitude, disturbance of memory, concentration and speed of decision) suggest it may be possible to detect objective changes in behaviour, and for this reason objective behavioural testing both for its own sake and as a check on the validity of subjective reports is now taking place (Baker *et al.*, 1983). As to more subjective changes in mood and emotion, these are influenced by a host of confounding variables and reporting biases but nevertheless accurate and reliable methods of quantification can be achieved (Mackay, 1980). Both from a practical and a scientific point of view the choice of tests and testing methods is a difficult one. A number of points need to be raised. First, it is most improbable that all behavioural functions are equally susceptible to toxic insult. Second, it is likely that different substances may affect different functions. Third, these functions are unlikely to be of equal practical significance or importance. Fourth, at the present time it is not clear which functions might be the best warning of later symptoms of clinical significance (i.e. which tests of specific functions have the greatest predictive validity). Medical monitoring programmes in industry include tests of individual system functioning (e.g. audiometry, liver function tests, spirometry). For assessing respiratory function, for example, a battery of tests is now routinely employed in many industries which relies upon both objective and subjective techniques (spirometry, symptom checklist—which in the UK uses the MRC questionnaire—and chest radiograph). As far as behavioural assessment is

TABLE 15.1   Some behavioural and neurological consequences of common industrial pollutants

	Carbon disulphide	Asbestos	Mercury	Lead	Carbon monoxide	Noise
Tremor			/			
Muscle weakness	/		/		*	
Headache			/		*	
Dizziness			/			
Seizures				/		
Sensory loss			/		*	/
Mental retardation				/	/	
Memory defects	/		/			
Severe insomnia	/					/
Fatigue, lassitude			/		*	/
Drowsiness			/		*	
Irritability	/		/	/		/
Uncontrolled anger	/		/	/		
Homicide attempts						
Sexual impotence	/					
Crying spells			/			
Depression	/					
Delusions	/					
Hallucinations	/					
Confusion	/				/	
Disorientation					/	
Autism					/	
Suicide	/					
Death—direct medical consequence		/				

* Effects of acute intoxication.
/ Chronic effects.

concerned, tests are not yet in routine use and for that reason are less well validated; test selection has, in the past, been astonishingly heterogeneous and unsystematic. However, the growing use, for routine purposes, of both specific tests of impairment and more general test batteries should lead to a better understanding of psychological deficits following industrial exposures.

ALCOHOL

Over the last decade or so there has been a growing concern about the problem of alcohol abuse, and, in the present context, particular concern about work-related alcohol problems. Some occupations have long been associated with drunkenness and alcoholism; literary stereotypes of the drunken doctor or judge spring to mind. There is a great deal of evidence supporting such long-established folklore and it is possible to draw some general conclusions about why this is so. As far as the size of the problem is concerned, only rough estimates are available but are nevertheless illuminating. Estimates in the UK suggest that problem drinkers account for about 1.2 per 100 individuals in the workforce and between 75 and 80 per cent of those with alcohol-related illness and receiving treatment are at, or will return to, work (Gardner, 1982).

Drinking becomes a problem when excessive alcohol consumption: (1) causes medical and social harm, (2) disrupts the work of the individual and his colleagues, (3) requires some form of treatment or help. The extent of the problem is illustrated by Edwards's work at the National Council of Alcoholism's information centres (Edwards et al., 1967). In Edwards's study, clients attending these centres (in other words, people who recognized that they had a problem) fall into a number of categories. First, 88 per cent of clients periodically engaged in drinking before work. Second, 62 per cent sometimes brought a bottle of alcohol to work. Third, 12 per cent brought a bottle to work every working day. Fourth, 91 per cent sometimes drank continually throughout the day. The prevalence of alcoholism has also been highlighted by recent statistics published by the Office of Population Censuses and Surveys in 1977. Their figures suggest that in England and Wales 500 000 people—in other words, one in every hundred—suffers from alcoholism. A common misconception is that the alcoholic is usually an elderly male or social derelict; however, this is not the case and most alcoholics are in full-time or part-time employment. Similar estimates are available from US sources. The Comptroller General of the United States (1970) estimated that the number of alcoholic federal civilian employees ranged from 4 to 8 per cent if problem drinkers were included. A study by Mannello (1979) of drinking among male workers employed by seven large railway companies found that 75 per cent drink alcohol regularly at consumption levels approximately equal to the national average. It was found that 44 000 of the 234 000 railway workers are problem drinkers. That is three of four workers drink and one of every four workers who drink has a serious problem. A study of

TABLE 15.2 Occupational risk factors for alcohol-related problems

Risk factors	Occupations
(1) Availability of alcohol	The drinks trade and catering are implicated, but many jobs require alcohol availability as part of the role performance, e.g. those of salesmen, executives
(2) Social pressures	Traditions of 'hard drinking' die hard in the occupations of, for example, coal miners, seamen, service personnel, medical students and, of course, publicans
(3) Freedom from supervision	High occupational status workers such as company directors and lawyers and those with travelling jobs are at risk here
(4) Income	Those with high income can easily afford high alcohol consumption. Those with low income may seek 'solace' in drinking
(5) Collusion by colleagues	Covering up may be a problem but so also may be exploitation and seeking to gain influence at the drinker's expense
(6) Strains, stresses and hazards	Many 'high-risk' jobs in terms of danger or job insecurity may lead people to drink a lot, e.g. coal mining, 'big business'
(7) Separation from normal social or sexual relationships	Examples are oil rig workers, commercial travellers
(8) Preselection of 'high-risk' people	Some occupations may recruit people from particular kinds of backgrounds or who are for some other reason predisposed to become excessive drinkers

Source: Plant (1979).

corporate perceptions of drinking problems found that more than 40 per cent of the 1300 firms surveyed believed that at least 3 per cent of their employees have drinking problems (Conference Board, 1980). Approximately 33 per cent of the firms believed that only 1 per cent of their employees have this problem.

Alcohol is related to occupational factors in two ways, which can be simply stated in terms of cause and effect. First, the extent of consumption may be influenced by factors inherent in the person's occupation, factors such as boredom, pressure from work demands (including social pressures to drink) or exposure or proximity to alcoholic drinks. The situation does, however, appear to be complex: a self-selection process is thought to operate such that those with a drinking problem eventually gravitate towards jobs in which alcohol is either manufactured or dispensed. From the data reviewed by Plant (1979) it is possible to identify eight 'risk factors' associated with alcohol-related problems at work. Some apply only to specific occupations but they do collectively explain why such disparate occupations have high alcoholism rates. These are shown in Table 15.2.

The second way in which alcohol is related to employment concerns the effect of consumption upon work performance and other job factors. Alcohol may affect work performance in at least four ways:

(1) Short-term impairment in information processing.
(2) Chronic neuropsychological impairment.
(3) Reduced capacity related to physical illness and pathology.
(4) Behavioural problems; drunkenness.

Work difficulties related to these factors, such as poor performance, prolonged absence and poor interpersonal relationships, may result in disciplinary action, demotion, suspension and consequent unemployment. They may also be related to subsequent difficulties in coping during rehabilitation and return to employment.

WORK STRESS

Up to the mid-1960s industry in Western Europe was largely positively regarded by the various interested parties as a forum for sociopolitical reform and for increased private and public consumption (Gardell, 1981). However, during the late 1960s and early 1970s an intense debate began to develop around the question of work and the demands associated with it. It was soon realized that there was only a poor correlation between objective standards of living, albeit rising ones, and measures of subjective satisfaction and happiness. This discrepancy upset the traditional view that the quality of working life would continue to improve with increasing material wellbeing. Other factors are obviously at work. 'Stress' came to be recognized as one of these factors and one of the major threats to the developing quality of life. At work it was seen to give rise to low job satisfaction, poor job performance and impaired health. These effects reflect the cost of work. They balance out its benefits, normally regarded as earnings, or personal and social development.

Understanding the processes involved in long-term work stress requires appreciation of its impact on an individual basis since work stress largely resides in its perceptual nature—'in the eye of the beholder'. Any event or situation within a working environment is a potential cause of stress experienced within the individual. The potency of the stimulus or stimuli leading to such experiences will depend upon the *meaning* attributable to it/them, on the appraisal of ability to meet demands and the effectiveness of coping mechanisms. These are the essential elements of the transactional approach to stress (Cox and Mackay, 1981). The timing, frequency, intensity and duration of the unpleasant effects evoked by conditions at work influence the potential harmfulness of work-related stress (Brodsky, 1984). Depending upon a range of factors, prolonged or severe symptomatology may impel the person to visit a physician. The prevalence of such conditions in the work-force has been the subject of a number of recent studies. Fletcher and Payne (1980) have estimated that at any one time some 8 to 10 per cent of the workforce are experiencing disabling emotional or physiological ill-health, while many more suffer from a fluctuating array of minor psychological discomforts and physical ailments. Data from Jenkins (1981) indicate a case rate of minor psychiatric morbidity of one in three in a chemist's company and one in six in an advertising agency in the age range 20–35 using the General Health Questionnaire (GHQ). One in three is the prevalence expected in surveys of primary care attenders while community surveys esti-mate prevalences ranging from 18 to 39 per cent. The steel industry study by Tinning and Spry (1981) indicated that about 10 per cent of the working population showed current distress levels, again using the GHQ. Distinguishing the role of work from non-work factors in these data is difficult. However, longitudinal studies of occupational stress using changes in naturally occurring work situations have provided evidence that over quite short periods of time the nature of the work situation to which the person is exposed has significant effects on mental health, quite apart from contri-butions from personality and preexisting psychological health (Parkes, 1982).

The reduction of stress

The transactional approach suggests several ways in which the experience of stress can be alleviated and has considerable implications for existing stress reduction techniques (see Table 15.3). Many traditional methods seek to reduce stress at source by reducing or eliminating the external environmental demand along one or more relevant dimensions (e.g. reducing noise level, increasing lighting level). This approach is a characteristic method employed by ergonomics practitioners. It is usual for any remedy to be applied to groups of workers. Often, this group approach works reasonably well with physical environmental demands and with man–machine systems design, if some flexibility is incorporated. Proponents of the various forms of job redesign argue that increased psychological wellbeing in the worker popu-lation will be produced by adopting these techniques.

The well-publicized job redesign programmes in Scandinavia and the USA have demonstrated the usefulness of such techniques in improving man–job fit. However, in some instances where those methods have been adopted the outcome has not been as successful as one might expect. Proponents of these schemes usually attribute this practical failure to poor design of the new job, but also to poor implementation or mismanagement of the improvement

TABLE 15.3 Management and alleviation of stress

Alteration of actual demand
  Physical environment
  Psychosocial environment
Alteration of actual ability to cope
  Learning new skills
  Allaying illness and effects of ageing
Supporting existing ability to cope
  Social support and parenting
  Formal and informal helping organizations
Alterations of cognitive appraisal
  Prevent disorganization of behaviour
  Retain logic (emotional) based reasoning
Alteration of the behavioural responses to stress
  Alter perceptions of demand, capability and importance of coping
    Drugs
    Psychotherapy
    Personal belief systems
Alteration of the physiological response to stress
  Genetic engineering
  Psychopharmacological agents
  Cognitive-behavioural methods
  Anomaly
    Enhance response when active behavioural coping is required
    Dampen response when more passive coping is appropriate
Patterning of treatments
  Appropriate combinations

---

scheme. However, it is suggested here that the assumption that all workers in a particular group will benefit from such a scheme is unjustified. Perceived demands, capabilities and needs, while similar in workers performing the same task, are not identical. The result is that job design methods as they are currently practised may improve the psychological (and physical) wellbeing of many of the workforce but may have no effect on or may even reduce the wellbeing of others. One approach which overcomes this problem has recently been provided by Van Harrison (1976). He advocates a method of stress reduction where the individual worker becomes responsible for achieving optimum fit for himself, given an appropriate work situation. The individual worker would be free to modify the structure and content of his job in order to obtain an optimum balance between the demands of his job, his skills and his needs. Although this would be difficult to achieve in practice, it might not be impossible for some jobs providing that the organization's goals and output were maintained (or enhanced).

The transactional model predicts that the experience of stress can also be reduced by the alteration of cognitive appraisal. Traditionally this has been achieved by the use of socially acceptable drugs such as alcohol and nicotine (and more recently cannabis) as well as the centrally acting minor tranquillizers. Continuous use of these substances can lead to partial or total dependence and they are not, therefore, entirely satisfactory as stress management tools. Counselling and other psychotherapeutic programmes may be potentially powerful agents for promoting the management of stress, and should be used as an adjunct to chemotherapy. Meichenbaum (1975), for example, has described a stress inoculation skills-training procedure in which the individual is involved in generating self-statements related to appraisal and coping. When used in conjunction with relaxation exercises during stressful experiences, this technique has been shown to be particularly successful in reducing the individual experience of stress. Relaxation alone may mimic some of the useful effects of the minor tranquillizers, such as a reduction in muscle tension.

Two traditional methods of ensuring man–job fit are selection and training. These methods are used primarily for middle and high level occupations (clerical, supervisory, professional, management), but not for simple, repetitive shop-floor jobs. However, there is increasing evidence that production-line jobs are subject to as much stress as occupations such as senior management. One possible area of future research, therefore, would be to examine the different skills needed for technically 'unskilled' work and subsequently to design appropriate selection and training methods. In the industrial context, our definition of 'skill' may need reexamining and extending; 'politically' recognized and specific motor skills obtained through training programmes (e.g. apprentice schemes) are only a part of the range of 'skills' and strategies developed to cope with work. As individuals are promoted or moved within organizations, the demands imposed by the new job increase both quantitatively and qualitatively. An individual's skills may often fail to match the demands imposed by a new job until he has had appropriate training or experience.

Reducing work stress

Recent attempts to reduce levels of stress experienced at work adopt two complementary approaches. One, the stress management approach, emphasizes the need for help at an individual level—in other words, treating the person. The complementary approach emphasizes the need for interventions at the organizational level by job and task redesign. Unfortunately, only a few studies have attempted critically to evaluate job stress reduction techniques. In their comprehensive and critical review of both personal and organizational strategies for handling job stress, Newman and Beehr (1979) conclude:

> Perhaps the most glaring impression we received from the review was the lack of evaluative research in this domain. Most of the strategies reviewed were based upon professional opinions and related research. Very few have been evaluated directly with any sort of scientific rigor. In spite of this weak empirical base, many personal and organisational strategies for handling stress have been espoused. Although some of these strategies seem to glow with an aura of face validity, there remains

the extremely difficult task of empirically validating their effectiveness. Until this is done practitioners have little more than their common sense and visceral instincts to rely on as they attempt to develop badly needed preventive and curative stress management programmes.

Since 1979, there have been a number of published and unpublished studies providing a more rigorous evaluation of the various stress management options: on the individual level, clinically based strategies include biofeedback, muscle relaxation and cognitive restructuring. In a critical review of such techniques, Murphy (1984) concludes that they may have significant benefits for individual wellbeing apart from other advantages, including the following. First, they can be quickly evaluated and established without major disruption to work routines. Second, they can encompass the need to take into account individual perceptions and reactions, and are thus tailored to individual needs. Third, they can combat non-work as well as work-based stress problems (which may interact synergistically). Fourth, they can be incorporated into existing employer assistance/health education packages.

The fundamental problem with such 'stress inoculation approaches' is that for the most part they are designed solely to help the person cope with poorly designed working environments. Ganster et al., (1982) have suggested that stress management training should only be used to supplement organizational change/job redesign programmes in order to deal with stressors which cannot be designed out of the job very easily (e.g. seasonal workloads). Thus management at the secondary level (help the person to cope) should be used to supplement attempts to identify and restructure sources of stress in the work environment—organizational, ergonomic or psychosocial (Murphy, 1984; Broadbent, 1985).

Individuals with stress-related problems can also be helped by counselling services. On both an individual and an organizational level stress can be envisaged as a 'problem' and thus attempts at 'problem solving' are appropriate. For many individuals part of the difficulty is in actually defining what the problem is. Most persons experiencing stress are unable to unravel the complex personal, work and non-work factors which contribute to their feelings of uneasiness or distress. It is the *meaning* of each of these for the individual which is important as is the coming to terms with those which are immutable and the changing of those which can be changed (Brodsky, 1984). Counsellors can help the worker to manage neurotic anxiety, take preventive and therapeutic measures to improve health and reduce health concerns, identify and reduce sources of family dissatisfaction and discover personality traits that might contribute to the maintenance of a stressful situation (Field and Olsen, 1980; Rosenman and Friedman, 1977). During this process, the worker may discover that part of the problem stems from either personality difficulties or inappropriateness of training or personal skills. Whereas the former may be difficult to alter, the latter may be more conducive to manipulation by retraining or job change. Suggesting, however, that the worker leave the place of work, either temporarily or permanently, is not always in the individual's best interest and this should be considered only as a last resort. The nature of the problem identified during the counselling process has a number of implications.

If a difficulty has clearly arisen from within the individual then the process needs to help to resolve the problem within the individual, whilst always recognizing that this may have organizational consequences. On the other hand, if the problem is one largely imposed on him by circumstances, whether organizational or otherwise, then the consultation probably needs to be more concerned with strategies for resolving the situation. There must be, therefore, some mechanism by which decisions affecting the organization can be fed back, issues of confidentiality notwithstanding.

ACCIDENTS

Although workplace accidents are usually the concern of safety specialists, the treatment and prognosis of accident victims (particularly rehabilitation) have implications for the occupational health specialist. Ongoing illness itself, and the presence of difficulties (life events), may predispose towards unreliability and human error. There are empirical links between the experience of stressful life events and accidents (Connolly, 1982; Sheehan et al., 1981; Levenson, Hirschfeld and Hirschfeld, 1980). There also exist theoretical links between demanding life events, human reliability and psychological illness, and although the empirical evidence supporting such links is at present somewhat tenuous, it is quite promising (Broadbent et al., 1982; Stuart and Brown, 1981).

Return to work after a workplace accident or after treatment for a work-related chronic condition frequently requires the victim to confront the situation responsible for the original health problem and the precise location in which it occurred. Implicit in the situation is the fear or threat that the condition may be exacerbated or a further accident may occur. Such a chance of recurrence requires much more active coping with an ever-present threat. Accidents may therefore act as stressors long after physical recovery has taken place.

There are a number of clinical reports which describe the possible consequences of industrial and other accidents (Smiley, 1955; Hirschfeld and Behan, 1966; Modlin, 1967; Culpan and Taylor, 1973; Ferguson, 1973). Anxiety and depression may occur, and there may be delay in return to work far beyond that predicted by the medical disability observed. Accident victims may suffer a drop in job status even though medically fully fit and may show increased absenteeism. The response to an industrial accident appears to depend upon a number of distinct factors which impinge upon recovery time, disability and psychological health following the incident (Shapiro, Parry and Brewin, 1979; Derebery and Tullis, 1983). These include the following.

Circumstances of the accident itself

Accident victims may be divided into two groups. First, there are those who are the passive victims of unforeseeable accidents; and second, there are those who were in some way responsible for or in some way played a part in the causation of the accident itself (Verhaegen *et al.*, 1976). Passive victims are apparently less likely to report themselves as being under stress at the time of the accident and are less likely to show subsequent absenteeism. Shapiro, Parry and Brewin (1979) suggest that other important factors in this group might include the existence of any threat to the victim's life, the duration of any such threat, or the presence of any 'prepared' phobic stimuli (Rachman and Seligman, 1976).

Work attitudes

Accidents may in some ways represent or enhance possibilities for withdrawal from work and it has been predicted that there may be longer delays in returning to work and greater absenteeism in those accident victims with the most negative (preexisting) attitudes towards their jobs (Shapiro, Parry and Brewin, 1979). Recent evidence seems to support these hypotheses (Derebery and Tullis, 1983).

Perception of control

The third group of factors from Shapiro, Parry and Brewin (1979) concerns personality determinants of generalized expectations, on the part of individuals, about what the future holds and about their ability to influence it. These are based upon the concepts of self-efficacy (Bandura, 1977) and locus of control (Rotter, 1966). These expectations include the belief that events will turn out satisfactorily irrespective of personal action, the belief that the individual can influence events which impinge upon him positively, and personal beliefs about individual responsibility for negative outcomes. These ideas have been developed within the context of rehabilitation from the viewpoint of maintaining self-esteem and motivation (Brewin and Shapiro, 1979).

Attribution of causation

The fourth group of factors comprises specific beliefs and attributions about the accident. Bulman and Wortman (1977) have reported a relationship between success at rehabilitation and the causal attributions made concerning a mixed group of accidents, all of which left their victims at least partially paralysed. They suggest that victims who do best in rehabilitation tend to blame themselves for the accident, but also see it as the logical outcome of freely chosen behaviour. Blaming other people and feeling that the accident was avoidable are associated with poor rehabilitation. There is an interesting parallel here with the situations which are said to create 'learned helplessness' (Seligman, 1975); this condition, characterized *inter alia* by motivational deficits, seems to depend on the causal attributions that are made about unpleasant or unsuccessful experiences (Abramson, Seligman and Teasdale, 1978).

Reinforcement

In certain circumstances patients who are receiving compensation for illness or injury, or are in the process of obtaining such compensation, may have a disproportionate disability and delayed recovery because of primary and secondary gains consequent on the accident (or health problem). These gains can be viewed as 'reinforcers' provided by the accident (Derebery and Tullis, 1983), and include factors such as income, sympathy, attention from the family and community, escape from responsibility, revenge against the company and possibilities for resolving internal conflicts. Often the misused term 'malingering' is used to classify such patients, but for the most part the processes involved are unconscious—they are rarely conscious decisions to obtain recompense. Occasionally, in severe instances, certain internal conflicts can lead an individual actually to cause the accident and to hold

TABLE 15.4   Some patient characteristics associated with delayed recovery from injury

Background to accident	Characteristics of patient
Prior to incident	Increase in medical visits High sickness absence rate Recent critical life events Reports feelings of impending doom
The incident itself	Patient is the cause of the accident, rather than victim Disability disproportionate to the injury Experiences nightmares about it
Doctor-patient relationship	Frequently cancels medical appointments Shops for doctor Treatment compliance poor Invokes anger or dislike in doctor
Patient's history	Likelihood of alcohol or drug abuse Family history of disability Early dependency needs thwarted
Compensation	Legal action pending In receipt of compensation Patient aged and concerned about ability to continue working

onto the injuries sustained as a way of ameliorating current life crises or problems (Hirschfeld and Behan, 1963; Behan and Hirschfeld, 1963). Such patients are extremely difficult to treat and to return to work.

The task faced by the physician or occupational health service in treating a patient with such problems is made more difficult by a number of factors which include the type of compensation system in operation, prevailing medical attitudes, conditions of employment and patient-related factors. Additional bed rest and inactivity, commonly prescribed for chronic musculo-skeletal injuries, also compounds that problem. Clearly, that the early recognition of such complaints is crucial goes without saying, if treatment and rehabilitation are to be successful. A comprehensive history covering the accident or injury itself, medical and family history, mental status and a detailed physical examination should be undertaken. A number of high-risk factors which predict delayed recovery have been elucidated. These are shown in Table 15.4. Successful treatment should include early return to work, as far as is reasonably practicable; maintenance of optimum levels of physical activity, again depending upon the degree and site of injury; and relaxation techniques including biofeedback to enhance feelings of control. In some cases patients may benefit from counselling and brief psychotherapy.

PSYCHOGENIC ILLNESS

For the epidemiologist a new problem often begins with an outbreak of disease or a 'clustering' of new cases either in space or in time. For the most part, certainly in occupational settings, the presence of physicochemical hazards is often sufficient to explain such clusters. For the workers concerned, the outbreak of illness represents a dramatic and distressing event and the immediate concern must be the treatment and recovery of the affected individuals and the speedy detection and elimination of the source of the illness. Anxiety surrounding the outbreak gradually lessens as the problem is understood and even residual fears concerning long-term effects can be lessened if a rational explanation is accepted and future surveillance proposed.

Unfortunately, not all incidents are amenable to explanation using toxicological concepts, particularly where a work-based cause is not obvious. A very profound problem arises in such cases because recurrent episodes may occur long after the ostensible initiating cause has been removed or where symptomatology is too diffuse to permit diagnosis. Where the nature of the illness is unclear and where its causal factors are not known there is often an understandable increase in anxiety and fear simply because of uncertainty but more probably because of concerns that the working environment remains inhospitable. The appearance of such illnesses may be confined to one or two individuals, or it may afflict many in the case of mass psychogenic illness (Colligan and Murphy, 1982) where there is an element of 'contagion'. Physical symptoms may occur in which case the syndrome is referred to as 'somatoform disease' (Brodsky, 1983). Here, the physical symptoms are indicative of an underlying physical pathology, but one for which there are no demonstrable organic findings or known physiological mechanisms. In some individuals acute symptoms follow a particular event which is frightening or dramatic (release of gas or spill of liquids). In others, the onset is more subtle, consisting of a gradual awareness of a strange new odour or a report of, say, a gas escape. Typically, symptoms revolve around respiratory difficulties, nausea and vomiting, headache, dizziness, lassitude and fatigue. Where organic causes (including subtle behavioural effects from low-level exposure) are eliminated, a number of social-psychological factors appear to account for the reported symptoms. These in some ways parallel the psychodynamic mechanisms referred to earlier in connection with delayed recovery from known physical injury at work, and include attributing exposure to unwanted physical and mental changes, appearance of post-traumatic stress disorders, avenue for conflict resolution, secondary gains of the sick role and vindication against a 'bad' employer.

In contrast, Brodsky's second group are those with a gradual and vague onset of inexplicable symptoms not immediately linked to workplace exposure. Following discussions with coworkers and sympathetic physicians these individuals become increasingly convinced of a work-based exposure as the cause. The premorbid histories of this group show recurring features: a long history of preoccupation and concern over personal health; recurring symptoms over many years and many visits to doctors. Typically, they ascribe their afflictions to externally located agents rather than internal (psychological) difficulties. Confirmation by peers and coworkers of a work-based cause effectively legitimizes their earlier attributions. Unfortunately, once intoxication has become a justifiable explanation many tend to focus upon their symptomatology, begin to fear they have been seriously harmed, and suffer from somatic anxiety levels consistent with severe autonomic disturbance. Although a subgroup of these individuals are allergic or chemically hypersensitive, many appear to suffer from preexisting anxiety complaints, and are highly suggestible or frankly psychotic or prepsychotic.

Psychogenic illness, whilst possessing some of the features of somatoform disease, differs in a number of respects, notable among which is the way in which it spreads rapidly within a working group. Colligan and Murphy (1982) have provided an operational definition of mass psychogenic illness: 'the collective occurrence of a set of physical symptoms and related beliefs among two or more individuals in the absence of an identifiable pathogen'. Although implied in this definition is the notion of anxiety-related or stress-induced illness, simply labelling the phenomenon 'psychosomatic' or 'anxiety-induced' does little to illuminate the aetiology or mechanisms of the outbreak. Symptomatology shows some remarkable similarities across different outbreaks (Colligan and Murphy, 1979; Colligan et al., 1979). Headache is the most frequent complaint, followed by lightheadedness, dizziness, tiredness and weakness. Frequently, the onset of symptoms is preceded by some form of trigger, e.g. the smell of a strange odour or gas, or the use of a new solvent in the workplace. Studies have also consistently identified certain conditions which appear to act as potential precipitating factors. These include sociodemographic characteristics (e.g. sex of affected worker), nature of the work activity (highly repetitive, paced routine work, monotony), uncomfortable physical environment (noise, temperature variations, airborne contaminants and pollutants) and psychological/organizational stressors (work load, poor industrial relations). The most powerful predictors are not individual/personality ones but negative attitudes and reactions to the physical and psychosocial working environment.

Apart from somatoform disease and mass psychogenic illness there remain some outbreaks of illness where none of the above appears completely to explain the reported symptoms. In particular, there have been reports of outbreaks of mild illness and discomfort in modern office buildings which do not entirely fit the pattern of psychogenic illness. Some commonly used building materials and equipment give off very low concentrations of well-known pollutants or irritants (carbon monoxide, ozone, formaldehyde) and it may be that these are responsible for some of the symptoms of eye irritation and mild respiratory disturbance commonly reported. But probably interacting with these are a number of psychological mechanisms which may play a part in precipitating symptoms. These include the following:

(1) The *context* in which the problems have occurred, i.e. a new office environment in which individuals expect to feel relatively safe and comfortable. To feel otherwise is in a sense 'paradoxical'.

(2) The possibility of a (classical) conditioning effect overlying any direct effect of the hazard, which may account for the rapid onset and disappearance of symptoms on entering and leaving the building reported by some people (but see (5)).

(3) Attribution processes. Occupants in the building become aware of a problem because of the appearance of symptoms. Some aspect of the working environment is blamed for the problem but the precise cause is unknown. For a variety of reasons such uncertainty can lead to mild anxiety and increased physiological arousal which may possibly contribute to the CNS symptoms which have been reported. Contagion and the reinforcement of symptoms in others probably also occurs.

(4) Although it is possible to distinguish toxicological properties from *aversive* ones, in many situations the (presumed) physical hazard has no odour, visibility or taste and so cannot be said to be aversive in the usual sense of the word. Nevertheless, there may be some perceptual activity without conscious awareness (preconscious processing—Dixon, 1981). Moreover, environments which are thought to be hazardous, and where the nature and form of the hazard is unknown, could also be construed as 'aversive'.

(5) This notion of aversion is an important one, bearing in mind the conclusions of experimental studies which have investigated the psycho-

logical impact of undesirable environmental stimuli. The magnitude of such effects seems to be very markedly influenced by the unpredictability, uncontrollability and uncertainty surrounding environmental agents. Much of this work has been carried out using noise, but there is evidence that the effects observed generalize to other factors present in the working environments. Changes in work performance, poor motivation, fatigue and depressed mood have been found, and often these are most pronounced following exposure. Such 'after-effects' are consistent with the reports of depressed mood and fatigue which may occur 1 hour or so after leaving work.

HEALTH EDUCATION

It has been suggested that the greatest impact of health education programmes will come from their widespread introduction in the curricula of both primary and secondary schools where individuals are most receptive or susceptible to new information and where preparedness for behavioural change is at its greatest. In the meantime, many have recognized that the workplace is an ideal setting which offers opportunities for health education. The considerable potential which this environment has is now acknowledged by many who are concerned with occupational health and safety, and with wider health issues (Randell, Wear and McEwan, 1984). Unfortunately, at the time of writing, whilst there is undoubtedly much scope for developing health education within UK organizations, the potential impact is still largely unrecognized, although some of the larger companies run very successful health education programmes specifically tailored to the needs of their own workforce. In contrast, the health promotion concept is being pursued very vigorously within organizations in the USA (O'Donnell and Ainsworth, 1984).

Health education in the workplace may be concerned with increasing awareness on the part of employers and employees of the importance of preventing occupational accidents and disease. This awareness can be increased by making use of methods in health education which are of practical value and appropriate to a given occupational setting. Where necessary, health education might aim to create attitudes and behaviour in keeping with safe practices, to improve communication on health and safety matters or simply to impart information. In the UK this role is increasingly taken by the Health and Safety Executive. Health education in the workplace also offers a number of advantages, notable among which is the possibility of promoting more general health education programmes. Many groups, particularly those highlighted in *Inequalities in Health* (Townsend and Davidson, 1900), may be easier to reach effectively by workplace-based health education. Topics which have been included in workplace health education programmes include specific occupational health and/or safety education, alcohol and alcohol problems, smoking cessation, nutrition, exercise and physical fitness, stress/relaxation, breast and cervical cancer screening, pregnancy, preretirement preparation. Disease-oriented prevention projects are increasingly common and include those which encourage individuals to attend for disease screening tests (uptake of NHS facilities), to comply with medication regimens, and to adopt other behavioural styles related to prevention and/or control of the disease. Coronary heart disease is one such example. Whilst the disease-oriented approach clearly has its advantages in terms of, for example, highly motivated clients participating in order to prevent the recurrence of the disease or illness, more recent strategies, perhaps following the American approach which emphasizes positive health and 'wellness', have stressed the need for programmes which deal with health and healthy behavioural styles. These are likely to become the rule rather than the exception in moderate sized and large companies in the latter part of the 1980s and in the 1990s.

WHOLE-PERSON HEALTH CARE: CLINICAL ASPECTS

In two ways, the workplace provides a unique opportunity for identifying health problems and facilitating timely intervention. The first is by reducing the development from minor to major physical and mental illness. In the case of physical illness the employee is more likely to present to the occupational physician; however, because of the stigma attached to mental health problems, particularly in the work setting, sufferers from these complaints often require active identification. The second is by reducing sickness absence which inevitably impairs the effectiveness of the organization and creates stress for the other employees who have to cope. The Health and Safety at Work Act involves a degree of responsibility on the part of employer *and* employee in both these respects.

There is a subtle interaction of constitutional, psychological, emotional and social factors in the genesis of illness. The timing of referral is relevant in the context of when the employee is transformed into the patient. In the occupational setting the individual is not a 'patient' and for this reason supportive help can be delivered in a 'non-clinical' context. This approach can be seen as a preventive measure against the development of such a degree of morbidity as to require prolonged sickness absence.

Various psychiatric conditions may occur *coincidentally* with chronic physical illness; more commonly, however, psychiatric problems are caused or affected by the preexisting condition. Adaptation to chronic illness depends on several factors including:

(1) personality,
(2) patient's life situation,
(3) perception of illness,

(4) the amount of change of lifestyle caused by the illness and the quality and availability of support systems such as counselling and a caring family/person,

(5) specific impairments/deficits due to the illness—in this context pain is relevant,

(6) compliance with the therapeutic regime.

In managing the patient an awareness of these factors is crucial, and in particular there is a need for awareness on the part of the patient of his psychiatric condition and the treatment requirements. 'Medical model' type approaches to chronic illness can actually predispose towards psychiatric morbidity. Thus certain sequelae are assumed—e.g. in an acute medical/surgical illness, responsibility, both occupational and domestic, is abrogated without feelings of guilt. The patient retires on sick benefits and the support of friends and relatives. In the clinical context, passive compliance is the rule after quite severe chronic physical illness, and is still compatible with continued employment. Thus consideration must be given to diabetics, epileptics, arthritics and those requiring renal dialysis twice or three times weekly.

Obviously, such chronic medical morbidity does predispose to psychological or even psychiatric problems not associated with more acute medical problems. In this context, GP, occupational health physician and nurse play a useful part. However, the basic personality determines the individual's response to chronic illness. Thus the ability of both the individual and his key relatives to comply with intricate treatment procedures varies. Psychiatric complications result from loss of physical status, dependence upon family/technology, clinical treatment including diet and medication, i.e. the treatment dictates a 'life apart' thus causing occupational problems. Thus for the management of chronic physical illness, as far as the patient is concerned, a number of points are important:

(1) The patient's ongoing acceptance of responsibility is expected from the family. Nevertheless there is often dependency.

(2) The patient is positively encouraged to continue at work, yet enforced part-time involvement and interruptions for hospital attendance can have a disruptive effect.

(3) It is assumed that the person will attend to his own illness regarding such matters as complicated diet, self-administered injections and acquiring knowledge about the condition in order to identify early symptoms and adopt the treatment regime accordingly.

The limitations of the treatment programme become apparent when an appreciation of the physician's own failings and limitations as regards technique and attitude develops. In a sense the chronically ill are given contradictory advice:

(1) Continue to maintain as much life responsibility as possible including having a detailed knowledge of the illness and its treatment.

(2) Follow the specific treatment regime, including all instructions, without question. Given the wide range of intelligence and personality differences, not only of patients but also of their key relatives and work colleagues, such a 'blanket' message causes inevitable conflicts.

The interplay between the patient, occupational health practitioner, general practitioner and clinical team making the evaluation of management regimen and prognosis presents a unique phenomenon. The more flexible the treatment strategy and the attitude of the employer the better. However, the needs of the organization must always be taken into account.

PREEMPLOYMENT MEDICAL EXAMINATIONS

There have always been strong arguments for and against preemployment medicals. For some occupations there are statutory requirements which necessitate a thorough medical examination prior to beginning work, and a good case can be made out for screening, if of a rather less stringent nature, in other occupational groups. On the other hand, the predictive validity for many of the methods used remains in doubt and the real arguments against preemployment medicals may be seen in terms of the individual whose health problems may be unnecessarily highlighted to his disadvantage and lead to possible unfair rejection on the grounds more of stigma than genuine unsuitability.

However, the fundamental effectiveness of the organization, its productivity and the interests of other employees may be aided by the appropriate use of job-oriented preemployment medicals. It is recognized that there is a correlation between self-esteem and the earning of a living. This is relevant in both physical and psychological aspects of whole-patient health. However, the psychiatric rehabilitee is more likely to be rejected following a preemployment medical than someone with a different label. The broad classification 'psychiatric' is as unreasonable as 'surgical'. Functional effectiveness varies widely within such all-embracing terms.

Until the 1975 Employment Protection Act it was feasible to recommend several years' health probation. Subsequently, the maximum became 1 year, which appeared to improve employee protection. However, increased rejection at selection inevitably followed. Schizophrenic rehabilitees suffered in particular in that the percentage rejected increased from 17 per cent prior to 1975 to 46 per cent subsequently (Sergeant, 1984).

Preemployment and subsequent routine examination have had a long history in groups such as the armed forces. The 'PULHEEMS' system is widely used and 'M' and 'S' are significant in the present context denoting 'mental state' and 'stability' respectively. This typifies the recognition of whole-person health in that particular organization. More generally, the realistic conclusion on this controversial subject is that medical and psychiatric screening must meet entirely with the needs of everybody in the organization. That means that policies jointly agreed between employers and unions are to be welcomed.

CONCLUSIONS

Unemployment apart, the last decade has witnessed several changes in the way in which work is organized and the nature of that work. These changes include the rapid introduction of new technology, increased use of chemicals in work processes, increased mechanization and widespread use of shiftwork practices (Mackay and Cox, 1984; Bolinder, Englund and Magnusson, 1976; Gardell, 1977; Rutenfranz, Haider and Koller, 1985). Such changes have brought benefits both to organizations and to individual workers; working conditions have improved and accident rates decreased. The relative and absolute decline in many of the traditional heavy industries has in some ways been responsible for the disappearance of many of the long-standing occupational health problems. In their place the rapid changes in the nature of work, and working practices, have generated a whole range of new occupational health problems. Undersea operations and 'offshore' medicine, dangerous pathogens and genetic manipulation, the introduction of computer-based new technology have all thrown up new problems requiring new or modified solutions.

The public in general and the workforce in particular have become more aware of the potential dangers from industrial operations both to themselves as employees and to society as a whole and are prepared to give estimates of the likelihood and impact of various risks (Cohen and Mackay, 1985). That organizations and organizational activities have an impact upon health goes without saying, and is clear from the concern that most industries give to accidents and physical illnesses conspicuously associated with particular occupations. Yet the wellbeing and general health of individuals has not been seen to be the (legitimate) concern of organizations. However, with the realization of the possibility that many physicochemical environments may have subtle but nevertheless important effects, and the acceptance that work and working practices may have widespread effects upon the individual's health and wellbeing, much more elaborate concepts of occupational health needs are being advanced (World Health Organization, 1980). Observed increases in mental and psychosomatic diseases, particularly the psychoneuroses and physical disorders resulting from breakdown in adaptation, such as cardiovascular and gastro-intestinal disorders, have been highlighted as evidence of altered disease patterns in response to fundamental changes in working practices (Commission of the European Communities, 1984). To cope with this shift in the nature of work and health it is likely that a much wider concept of occupational health will be required to encompass 'whole-person' management. Table 15.5 covers some of the areas which are relevant to securing occupational wellbeing and the responsibilities of the various disciplines involved.

TABLE 15.5 Mental health promotion and disease prevention in the workplace

Problem areas	Solutions	Expertise resides with
Organizational change Organizational climate	Organization development. Early notification of changes to workforce—communication and consultation. Involvement and participation of workforce in planning where appropriate. Personnel management policy. Leadership Style	Organizational and industrial psychologists, management and personnel specialists, joint committees
Organizational aims and performance	Personnel development. Communication and dissemination of information	
Work arrangements	Planning negotiation	
Special work demands Workload and hazards	Job design, selection and training	Ergonomist; occupational psychologists specializing in selection and training
Handicapped (psychiatric rehabilitation)	Placement resettlement and follow-up	
Alcohol problems	Company policies, early detection, counselling, referral	General medical expertise
Psychosomatic symptoms	Worklife stress management. Health education	Specialist in behavioural medicine. Health education
Mental symptoms and illnesses	Health monitoring and screening Referral to care services Preemployment screening Counselling	Epidemiologists. Specialists in psychiatry. Counsellors. Nurses

Adapted from WHO document, 'Health aspects of wellbeing in workplaces'.

The impetus will be towards prevention and treatment approaches which emphasize psychosocial risk factors in causation, but will also be more positively active in facilitating workplace management. The general direction which is being taken is towards the prevention of ill-health and threats to wellbeing in the workplace. In North America prevention is taking the form of early identification of problems, with rapid referral, and at the same time workplace programmes are facilitating healthy lifestyles and behaviour. In the European countries the approach appears (to us at least) to emphasize the need to treat the organization rather than the individual. The two approaches are, of course, complementary, but although the latter is harder to achieve it is the one which promises the longer-term benefits.

NOTE

The views expressed in this chapter are those of the authors and not necessarily of the Health and Safety Executive.

REFERENCES

Abramson, L. Y., Seligman, M. E. P., and Teasdale, J. D. (1978). Learned helplessness in humans. Critique and reformulation. *Journal of Abnormal Psychology*, **87**, 49–74.

Baker, E. L., Feldman, R. G., White, R. F., Preston-Harley, J., Dinse, G. E., and Berkey, C. S. (1983). Monitoring neurotoxins in industry. Development of a neurobehavioural test battery. *Journal of Occupational Medicine*, **25**, 125–130.

Bandura, A. (1977). Self-efficacy. Towards a unifying theory of behavioural change. *Psychological Review*, **84**, 191–215.

Behan, R. C., and Hirschfeld, A. H. (1963). The accident process. II. Toward more rational treatment of industrial injuries. *Journal of the American Medical Association*, **186**, 300–306.

Bolinder, E., Englund, A., and Magnusson, E. (1976). *Kemiska Halsorisker i Arbetsmiljon* (*Chemical Risk Factors in the Working Environment*) Stockholm: Prisma.

Brewin, C. R., and Shapiro, D. A. (1979). Beliefs about the self and their importance for motivation in rehabilitation. In D. J. Oborne, M. M. Grunberg and J. R. Eiser (eds), *Research in Psychology and Medicine*, vol. 1. London: Academic Press.

Broadbent, D. E. (in press). The clinical impact of job design. *British Journal of Clinical Psychology*.

Broadbent, D. E., Cooper, P. F., Fitzgerald, P., and Parkes, K. R. (1982). The cognitive failures questionnaire and its correlates. *British Journal of Clinical Psychology*, **21**, 1–16.

Brodsky, C. M. (1983). Psychological factors contributing to somatoform diseases attributed to the workplace. *Journal of Occupational Medicine*, **25**, 459–464.

Brodsky, C. (1984). Long-term work stress. *Psychosomatics*, **25**, 361–368.

Bulman, R. J., and Wortman, C. B. (1977). Attributions of blame and coping in the 'Real World'. Severe accident victims react to their lot. *Journal of Personality and Social Psychology*, **35**, 351–363.

Cohen, A. V., and Mackay, C. J. (1985). Work-related and other risks. Public attitudes, worries and concerns. *Department of Employment Gazette*, **February**. London: HMSO.

Colligan, M. J., and Murphy, L. R. (1979). Mass psychogenic illness in organisations. An overview. *Journal of Occupational Psychology*, **52**, 77–90.

Colligan, M. J., and Murphy, L. R. (1982). A review of mass psychogenic illness in the work settings. In M. J. Colligan, J. W. Pennebaker and L. R. Murphy (eds), *Mass Psychogenic Illness: A Social Psychological Analaysis*. Hillsdale, MJ: Lawrence Erlbaum.

Colligan, M. J., Urtes, M. A., Wisseman, C., Rosensted, R. E., Anania, T. L., and Hornung, R. W. (1979). An investigation of apparent mass psychogenic illness in an electronics plant. *Journal of Behavioural Medicine*, **2**, 297–399.

Colquhoun, P. J., and Rutenfranz, J. (1980). *Studies of Shift Work*. London: Taylor & Francis.

Commission of the European Communities (1984). *Breakdown in Human Adaptation to 'Stress'*, vol. 1, ed. by J. Cullen and J. Siegrist. Dordrecht: Martinus Nijhoff.

Comptroller General of the United States (1970). Substantial cost savings from establishment of an alcoholism program for federal employees. Washington DC.

Conference Board (1980). *Dealing with Alcoholism in the Workplace*. New York: Richard Weiss.

Connolly, J. (1982). Life stress before accidents. *Psychosomatic Medicine*.

Cox, T., and Mackay, C. J. (1981). A transactional approach to occupational stress. In J. Corlett and J. Richardson (eds), *Stress, Productivity and Work Design*. Chichester: Wiley.

Culpan, R., and Taylor, L. (1973). Psychiatric disorders following road traffic and industrial injuries. *Australian and New Zealand Journal of Psychiatry*, **7**, 32–39.

Derebery, V. J., and Tullis, W. H. (1983). Delayed recovery in patients with work compensable injury. *Journal of Occupational Medicine*, **25**, 829–835.

Dixon, N. F. (1981). Psychosomatic disorder. A special case of subliminal perception. In M. J. Christie and P. G. Mellet (eds), *Foundations of Psychosomatics*. Chichester: Wiley.

Edwards, G., Fisher, M. K., Hawker, A., and Hensman, C. (1967). Clients of alcoholism information centres. *British Medical Journal*, **4**, 346–348.

Engel, G. L. (1980). The clinical application of the biopsychosocial model. *American Journal of Psychiatry*, **37**, 535–544.

Ferguson, D. (1973). A study of neurosis and occupation. *British Journal of Industrial Medicine*, **30**, 187–198.

Field, J. R., and Olsen, J. (1980). Stress management. A multimodal approach. *Psychotherapy and Psychosomatics*, **34**, 233–240.

Fletcher, B. C., and Payne, R. L. (1980). Stress at work. A review and theoretical framework. Parts 1 and 2. *Personnel Review*, **9**(1), 19–29; (2), 5–8.

Ganster, D. C., Mayes, B. T., Sime, W. E., and Tharp, G. D. (1982). Managing occupational stress. A field experiment. *Journal of Applied Psychology*, **67**, 533–542.

Gardell, B. (1977). Psychological and social problems of industrial work in affluent societies. *International Journal of Psychology*, **12**, 125–134.

Gardell, B. (1981). Strategies for reform programmes on work organisation and work environment. In B. Gardell and G. Johansson (eds), *Working Life*. Chichester: Wiley.

Gardner, A. W. (1982). Identifying and helping problem drinkers at work. *Journal of Social and Occupational Medicine*, **32**, 171–179.

Health and Safety Commission (1977). *Prevention and Health. Occupational Health Services. The Way Ahead*. London: HMSO.

Hirschfeld, A. H., and Behan, R. C. (1963). The accident process: 1. Etiological considerations of industrial injuries. *Journal of the American Medical Association*, **186**, 193–199.

Hirschfeld, A. H., and Behan, R. C. (1966). The accident process. *Journal of the American Medical Association*, **197**, 85–89.

Hunter, D. (1978). *The Diseases of Occupations*, 6th edn. Sevenoakes: Hodder & Stoughton.

Jenkins, R. (1981). Minor psychiatric morbidity in employed men and women and its contribution to sickness absence. *Psychological Medicine*, **10**, 751–757.

Levenson, H., Hirschfeld, M. L., and Hirschfeld, A. H. (1980). Industrial accidents and recent life events. *Journal of Occupational Medicine*, **22**, 53–57.

Lipowski, Z. J. (1977). Psychosomatic medicine in the seventies. An overview. *American Journal of Psychiatry*, **134**, 233–244.

McDonald, J. C. (1981). *Recent Advances in Occupational Health*. London: Churchill Livingstone.

Mackay, C. J. (1980). The measurement of mood and psychophysiological activity using self-report techniques. In I. Martin and P. H. Venables (eds), *Techniques in Psychophysiology*. Chichester: Wiley.

Mackay, C. J., and Cox, T. (1984). Occupational stress associated with visual display unit operation. In B. G. Pearce (ed.), *Health Hazards of VDUs?* Chichester: Wiley.

Mannello, T. A. (1979). *Problem Drinking Among Railroad Workers: Extent, Impact and Solutions*. Washington DC: University Research Corporation.

Meichenbaum, D. (1975). A self-instructional approach to stress management: a proposal for stress inoculation training. In C. D. Speilberger and J. G. Saraston (eds), *Stress and Anxiety*, vol. 1. New York: Hemisphere.

Modlin, H. C. (1967). The post accident anxiety syndrome. *American Journal of Psychiatry*, **123**, 1008–1012.

Murphy, L. R. (1984). Occupational stress management: a review and appraisal. *Journal of Occupational Psychology*, **57**, 1–15.

Newman, J. D., and Beehr, T. (1979). Personal and organisational strategies for handling job stress: a review of research and opinion. *Personnel Psychology*, **32**, 1–43.

O'Donnell, M. P., and Ainsworth, T. (1984). *Health Promotion in the Workplace*. New York: Wiley.

Parkes, K. R. (1982). Occupational stress among student nurses: a natural experiment. *Journal of Applied Psychology*, **67**, 784–796.

Plant, M. (1979). *Drinking Careers*. London: Tavistock.

Rachman, S., and Seligman, M. E. P. (1976). Unprepared phobias: 'Be prepared'. *Behaviour, Research and Therapy*, **14**, 333–338.

Randell, J., Wear, G., and McEwan, J. (1984). *Health Education in the Workplace*. London: Health Education Council.

Rosenman, R. H., and Friedman, M. (1977). Modifying Type A behaviour pattern. *Journal of Psychosomatic Research*, **21**, 323–331.

Rotter, J. B. (1966). Generalized expectancies for internal versus external control of reinforcement. *Psychological Monographs*, **80** (1, whole no. 609).

Rutenfranz, J., Haider, M., and Koller, M. (1985). Occupational health masures for night and shift workers. In S. Folkard and T. Monk (eds), *Hours of Work*. Chichester: Wiley.

Schilling, R. F. (ed.) (1981). *Occupational Health Practice*, 2nd edn. London: Butterworths.

Seligman, M. E. P. (1975). *Helplessness*. San Fransisco: W. H. Freeman.

Sergeant, H. (1984). Pre-employment psychiatric examinations. *Lancet*, **ii**, 212–214.

Shapiro, D., Parry, G., and Brewin, C. (1979). Stress, coping and psychotherapy: the foundations of a clinical approach. In C. J. Mackay and T. Cox (eds), *Response to Stress: Occupational Aspects*. Guildford: International Publishing Corporation.

Sheehan, D. V., O'Donnell, J. O., Fitzgerald, A., Hervig, L., and Ward, H. (1981–1982). Psychosocial predictors of accident error rates in nursing students: a prospective study. *International Journal of Psychiatry in Medicine*, **11**, 1981–1982.

Smiley, J. A. (1955). A clinical study of a group of accident-rone workers. *British Journal of Industrial Medicine*, **12**, 263–278.

Stuart, J. C., and Brown, O. M. (1981). The relationship of stress and coping ability to incidence of disease and accidents. *Journal of Psychosomatic Research*, **25**, 255–260.

Tinning, R. J., and Spry, W. B. (1981). The extent and significance of stress symptoms in industry. In E. N. Corlett and J. Richardson (eds), *Stress, Work Design and Productivity*. Chichester: Wiley.

Townsend, P., and Davidson, N. (1982). *Inequalities in Health. The Black Report*. Harmondsworth, Middx: Penguin.

Van Harrison, R. (1976). Job stress as person environment misfit. A symposium presented at the 84th Annual Convention of the American Psychological Association, Michigan.

Verhaegen, P., Vanhalst, B., Derijcke, H., and Van Hoecke, M. (1976). The value of some psychological theories on industrial accidents. *Journal of Occupational Accidents*, **1**, 39–45.

Weiss, B. (1983a). Behavioural toxicology and environmental health science: opportunity and challenge for psychology. *American Psychologist*, **November**, 1174–1187.

Weiss, B. (1983b). Behavioural toxicology of heavy metals. In I. E. Droesti and R. M. Smith (eds), *Neurobiology of the Trace Elements*. Clifton, NJ: Humana Press.

World Health Organization (1980). Health aspects of well-being in working places: Report on a WHO working group, Prague, 18–20 September 1979. Copenhagen: WHO (Euroreports and Studies 31).

The Psychosomatic Approach: Contemporary Practice
of Whole-person Care
Edited by M. J. Christie and P. G. Mellett
© 1986 John Wiley & Sons Ltd

16

TREATING THE HOME ENVIRONMENT OF THE SCHIZOPHRENIC PATIENT

RUTH BERKOWITZ

and

JULIAN LEFF

MRC Social Psychiatry Unit, Friern Hospital, London, UK

INTRODUCTION

The relationship of family factors to schizophrenia is one that has been studied for several decades. Much of the work has been descriptive. There was the important notion of the double bind which was elaborated by Bateson *et al.*, (1956) at the Mental Research Institute, Palo Alto. Others attached more importance to the role of the parental relationship. Lidz and Lidz (1949) wrote about marital skew and Wynne *et al* (1958) about pseudomutuality in the parents of schizophrenics. Much of the early work in family therapy was done with families in which there was a schizophrenic member.

This early work remains extremely valuable as a source of understanding of the interaction in such families. However, the approach emphasized mainly the family psychopathology in the development of the illness, and one of the less fortunate and simplistic interpretations of the work was that families are harmful to schizophrenic patients.

More recently a series of studies at the MRC Social Psychiatry Unit has shown that family factors do indeed play a crucial part in the course of the patient's illness. The development of reliable ways of measuring these factors has been accompanied by other trends. One of these has been to combine the idea of psychosocial factors with the notion of schizophrenia as an illness, with recognized symptoms, aetiology and treatment. Another trend has been a worldwide recognition of the tremendous burden suffered by families who have a schizophrenic member. Together, the role of psychosocial factors, of schizophrenia as an illness and the burden of the family have informed the work of some of those who have attempted to make a positive impact on the course of the schizophrenic condition.

Within the context of these influences, there has been a shift in the direction of certain attitudes to the schizophrenic patient and his family. One is that the family factors which are seen as deleterious are both an effect of, and a reaction to, the illness. If schizophrenia is viewed as an illness there are implications for treatment within a medical model and also a repositioning of the family as only one of several factors in the development of the illness. Finally, the experience of many professionals has enabled them to see the suffering of the families and to have a sympathetic rather than a critical approach to them.

These new ideas have emerged at a time when there is an increasing movement away from institutionalization and towards community care of schizophrenics. In many cases this means the family, and although it has always been important, it has become increasingly urgent that the family environment should be a helpful rather than an unhelpful one for the patient to live in. How this can be accomplished or how attempts can be made to achieve this end, will be the subject of this chapter. Several studies will be described in which attempts have been made to help both patient and family deal more effectively with the problems which arise when someone has schizophrenia. The main aim of such studies is to prevent relapse or—to put it another way—to keep the patient well.

FAMILY ATTITUDES

Expressed emotion

It was mentioned in the introduction that research has shown that family attitudes play a crucial role in the course of the schizophrenic illness. This research is reviewed in the earlier complementary volume in the chapter by Leff and Tarrier (1981) entitled 'The home environment of schizophrenic patients and their response to treatment'. Briefly, this research provided evidence that there is a significant association between schizophrenic relapse and certain emotional attitudes shown by relatives of the patient. These attitudes are called expressed emotion (EE) (Brown et al., 1962; Brown, Birley and Wing, 1972; Vaughn and Leff, 1976). Patients living with relatives showing either critical or emotionally overinvolved attitudes towards them (high EE) are much more likely to relapse in the 9-month period following discharge from hospital than those living with relatives who do not show these attitudes (low EE).

In addition, Leff and Tarrier present evidence which indicates that schizophrenic patients are highly aroused in the presence of high EE relatives. Patients interviewed together with a high EE relative continued to show high levels of arousal on measures of skin conductance. Those who were interviewed with low EE relatives, habituated—that is, became less aroused—suggesting that low EE relatives may have a calming effect on patients (Tarrier et al., 1979).

Expressed emotion is, however, only one of the factors associated with relapse in schizophrenia. The studies described by Leff and Tarrier emphasized the importance of two other factors in reducing relapse rates: regular maintenance medication and low face-to-face contact between relative and patient. The way in which these three main factors are related to relapse is shown in Table 16.1.

TABLE 16.1   Relapse rates

Low EE (N = 73)		High EE (N = 57)	
On drugs	12%	Low contact:	
Not on drugs	15%	On drugs	15%
Total	13%	Not on drugs	42%
		Total	28%
		High contact:	
		On drugs	53%
		Not on drugs	92%
		Total	69%

Sources: Brown, Birley and Wing (1972); Vaughn and Leff (1976).

It was on the basis of this evidence, both social and psychophysiological, that Leff *et al.*, (1982) mounted a trail of social intervention. The aim of this trial was to attempt to alter relapse rates in the group at highest risk (those in high EE homes and in high face-to-face contact) by trying to change EE from high to low, by reducing face-to-face contact between the relative and the patient, and by ensuring that all patients were on regular maintenance medication. This study will be described in more detail in the following section along with there other studies which were made on the basis of a similar rationale.

The family burden

There is evidence which suggests that families where there is a member who develops schizophrenia suffer considerable distress themselves. This was well described in the study by Creer and Wing (1975). A study by Hatfield (1979) in which 89 families were given questionnaires, which were followed up with interviews in 30 of the families, gives graphic descriptions of life with a schizophrenic patient. Families were constantly on their guard and living in a state of great tension. Patients often upset the routine of the household and other members of the family were neglected. Marital relationships were also under stress. In addition, many relatives lived alone with the patient and had sole responsibility as caretakers. This heavy burden was compounded by social isolation and fears about the future. Hatfield (1979, p. 340) sums up the findings as follows: 'Despite the near-intolerable burden borne by these families they were electing to stick with the patient. Given their unshakeable commitment and basic understanding of the patient they have gained through total immersion, these families are an invaluable resource in treatment and rehabilitation.'

Therefore, although there are good empirical reasons for undertaking research into the efficacy of social intervention with families, there are also humanitarian reasons. These reasons suggest that there is a tremendous need to find effective ways of helping relatives to deal with their distress.

FOUR STUDIES OF SOCIAL INTERVENTION

Differences in design

All four studies discussed in this chapter differed in some respects in their design. In the Goldstein and Kopeikin (1981) study (hereafter referred to as Goldstein), patients and their families were assigned at random to one of the following four conditions: high drug dose/family therapy; high drug dose/ no family therapy; low drug dose/family therapy; low drug dose/no family therapy. Families were seen over a period of 6 weeks, and followed up at 6-month and 3–6-year periods.

In the Leff et al. (1982) study (hereafter referred to as Leff), families were randomly assigned to an experimental or a control group. The follow-up period was at 9 months with a further follow-up at 2 years.

Falloon et al., (1982) (hereafter referred to as Falloon) assigned patients randomly to receive either family therapy or clinic-based individual supportive therapy.

In the study by Anderson, Hogarty and Reiss (1981) (hereafter referred to as Anderson), patients were randomly assigned to one of two conditions, combined family therapy and social skills or supportive individual psychotherapy.

Thus it can be seen that all trials used control groups with random assignment of cases to conditions.

Assessment procedures

The first assessment to be considered is the diagnosis of the patient. Goldstein used the Brief Psychiatric Rating Scale; Leff used the Present State Examination (PSE), and Falloon used the PSE (Wing, Cooper and Sartorius, 1974).

The assessment of relatives was made by Leff, Falloon and Anderson, all using the Expressed Emotion measure initially. Only Leff used this as an outcome measure as well. Other outcome measures such as community tenure, social functioning of the patient and family members and cost-effectiveness were used by Falloon.

Assessment of how much information the relative had about schizophrenia was made by Leff before and after education, and at follow-up using an instrument called the Knowledge Interview. This is an open-ended questionnaire consisting of 21 questions. In the Falloon study, a two-part questionnaire was given to relatives before and after their education.

The role of medication

In all four studies, medication was an essential element of the treatment. In the Goldstein study, two fixed levels of drug dose were used, but in the other three studies patients were on variable doses of maintenance neuroleptics.

Educational programmes

In three of the studies a specific phase of the intervention was set aside for education. In the Goldstein study, there was no specific education input, but it is a component which is sometimes contained within the family therapy approach: 'The therapist emphasises the relationship between these stressful events and the schizophrenic episode to illustrate the importance of stress as a trigger of decompensation and to highlight the value of preventing and adequately coping with stress' (p. 8).

Falloon gave education in two sessions at the start of family treatment to both the family and the patient. In the first session the family and patient's participation was encouraged. The patient was asked to describe his symptoms and the family was asked to express their feelings, similar experiences and their views. In the second session, the family was given a 'cogent rationale for long term medication management combined with stress management' (p. 69). In the two sessions, diagnosis, aetiology, management and the course of schizophrenia were described. These authors emphasized the ongoing nature of education and that in the other phases of the treatment the therapist might return to issues already mentioned, to sort out misconceptions or to stress the need to comply with medication.

Anderson gave the education in a group setting, which was called a survival skills workshop. The aims of this 'day-long multiple-family workshop' were broader than simply providing information, and included an outline of the themes of the entire treatment programme. The information given in this approach was also broad, going beyond facts about the illness and medication to include details about management. The fact that families do not cause the illness was underlined, together with the more positive point that families play an important role in the course of the illness. More helpful ways in which the family should manage the patient were described. There was emphasis on not overstimulating the patient, but also on not having such low expectations that the patient is not asked to perform 'on any level' (p. 85). Small goals and tasks are important, as is clear communication. Families were also encouraged to maintain a normal routine, to attend to the needs of other family members apart from the patient, and to maintain a social network. In addition, the families were told about some of the behaviours which are unhelpful to the patient, such as criticism of the patient, and too much or too little involvement with the patient.

Leff's approach is much narrower than that of either Falloon or Anderson. There were four short lectures covering the diagnosis, symptoms, aetiology and course of the illness. While all three programmes began by dealing with the experience of the illness from the point of view of both patient and family, there was a more personal approach in Falloon's and Anderson's work than in that of Leff. This was, in fact, considered to be an omission, and subsequent work has included a more personal or related way of informing relatives. The coverage of management is much less detailed than that of

Anderson, although emphasis is laid on the adverse effects of criticism and overinvolvement, as well as stressing the important role the family plays in keeping the patient well (Berkowitz et al., 1984).

Family sessions

In all four of the studies, family therapy was used, although the orientations as well as the emphasis on this intervention differed from one study to another.

In Goldstein's study, the treatment programme was carefully worked out. This study differed from the others in that it was crisis-orientated and therefore brief, i.e. six sessions. Four clear objectives were to be achieved over a period of 6 weeks. Attention was also paid to trying to balance the difficult dilemma of helping relatives to lower their expectations and not put pressure on the patient, while at the same time to retain hope in the longer term.

After exploration of the psychotic experience the more specific objectives of this programme were as follows.

(1) *Stressor identification*, i.e. an attempt to find which difficulties in the family's life presented the greatest threat to the patient's recovery.
(2) *Stress avoidance and coping emphasis* where attention was paid to joint problem-solving efforts rather than only trying to help the relative to adapt to the patient.
(3) *Evaluating the attempts at using stress management strategies.* This may involve refinement of strategies or help for families either in carrying out the strategies or, when they have failed, in implementing a task. This latter would require a reevaluation of the reasons for the failure.
(4) *Anticipatory planning* in which attempts are made to provide a similar approach to that adopted earlier, identifying and learning to cope with problems but this time looking to the future. Problems such as future employment, education, social activities and becoming more independent are also considered.

These four objectives were followed in sequence, and the authors point out that although they detail their therapeutic approach they do not wish to deny the importance of 'warmth, empathy, respect, expectations' (p. 12).

Falloon had a problem-solving orientation, and also used other behavioural paradigms. The therapy lasted for 2 years, and there were 40 family sessions in all. The sessions were held weekly for the first 3 months and fortnightly for the next 6 months. These sessions were all home based. Subsequent meetings, held monthly, were either in the home or in multifamily groups in a community centre. These authors outline the advantages of having home meetings in terms of engagement and improvement.

The approach of the therapist in this study is active and direct, imparting information, being a family adviser, offering support, either emotional *or* more concretely by going with families to meetings in courts, schools, etc.

The behavioural paradigms mentioned earlier represented the underpinning of the more specific problem-solving approach. There was *positive reinforcement*, that is the use of praise, attention and interest by both therapist and family. When used selectively, positive reinforcement is called *shaping*, to shift expectations, for example. When inappropriate behaviour appeared, reinforcement was withdrawn so that there was *extinction* of this behaviour. Another characteristic was *modelling* of desirable behaviours by the therapist. Rehearsal or practice of newly learnt behaviours was also encouraged. At the end of each session, the families were given *homework* or tasks since this would facilitate generalization of learnt behaviours to other situations.

Attention was paid by Falloon to communication training. 'In families of schizophrenics, the baseline communication skills are frequently very poor' (p. 71). One purpose was to enable families to communicate in a more positive way more frequently. Another purpose was to help them to communicate negative feelings more effectively. Finally, the improvement of listening skills was an aim of the communication training.

The structured problem-solving approach used by Falloon was a way of using the family as a resource. They should then be better able to cope with crises as well as day-to-day living. Six steps are outlined by Falloon:

(1) Identify a specific problem
(2) List alternative solutions
(3) Discuss pros and cons
(4) Choose the best solutions
(5) Plan how to implement solutions
(6) Review efforts

In addition, the therapist provided instruction on practical management strategies such as drawing up contracts, setting firm limits, social skills training for extra familial situations, dealing with depressive episodes and handling medication. These authors compare their approach with the strategies used by psychiatric nurses.

Anderson's orientation derives more from the structural school of family therapy founded by Minuchin (1974). The families were seen once the illness was under some control and for a period of 6 months to 1 year. The notion of boundary, 'who participates and how' (Minuchin, 1974, p. 53), is fundamental to the approach. The aim is first to strengthen the boundaries between individual members so that they neither talk for each other nor engage in mind reading. This sharpening of boundaries creates more distance between members, and families were helped to see it as positive, i.e. related to survival, rather than negative, i.e. related to rejection. The generational boundaries were also strengthened so that the parental subsystem could function effectively and independently with the children doing the same. The other aim with regard to boundaries was to weaken the boundary between the family and the outside world so that there was a decreased sense of isolation. The sessions, while having this theoretical stance, were highly task-orientated.

This task orientation followed through into the next phase of treatment, called patient responsibility. The emphasis was on finding the right pace for moving the patient towards greater participation in family and social life. The families' experience of increased frustration when this was very slow was responded to with support and concern.

The final phase of the treatment included an option of increasing the intensity of family sessions or maintaining family sessions of a gradually decreasing frequency. The former involved dealing with more emotionally charged and difficult issues not dealt with before.

Leff's family sessions were more eclectic, the approach being based not on a method of intervention but on a theory of schizophrenic relapse. The number of sessions varied from family to family, as many as 25 for one family and as few as two for another. They were all home-based. The guiding principles were the lowering of expressed emotion and the attempt to reduce the time which the families spent together. The creation of tasks was sometimes central and enabled the family to begin to manage familiar situations in different ways. Taking the rubbish out was an example, with attention paid to how the request was made, whether any praise or reward was given for a completed task, or indeed whether or not the task was done at all.

In some families, efforts were made to deal with the reduction of contact and most of the session was focused on this. It was thought at the start of the study that this would be the less difficult of the two aims, but it turned out to be the more difficult objective to achieve. It was possible to learn from this experience that separation must be achieved in small, very slow stages.

An important aspect of the family sessions was the support given to family and patient. In isolated families the visit of the therapist was often a welcome relief from the strain of being together too much.

The relatives' group

The only study which included a relatives' group was the one by Leff. Both high and low EE relatives were invited to attend the group, with the hope that the low EE relatives would impart some of their coping strategies to the high EE relatives. They were asked to come in the first instance for 9 months, i.e. until follow-up. The group was run for the most part by two therapists. The meetings were held once a fortnight and lasted for about 1½ hours.

The group was offered to the relatives as a facility from which they themselves could learn, and therefore have help with difficult problems. In addition they could, as experts having lived with the problems of schizophrenia, offer help to others.

The aim of the group was problem solving, and relatives would bring either a longstanding problem or recent difficulties for discussion. In the course of these discussions therapists attempted to make the group a therapeutic experience for members. Obvious strategies were making the group a safe place where they 'let off steam' without being criticized or blamed. Another obvious strategy was to enable relatives to share and sympathize with the problems of others. This was helpful to relatives in reducing their sense of isolation. Active efforts were made to encourage relatives to listen to one another, to communicate clearly and to be specific, avoiding generalizations.

The group had an important educational function which derived partly from learning from the experience of others and partly from asking either for a recapitulation of what they had already learned, or new questions that they had formulated.

The kinds of problems which relatives brought related largely to management of the patient, although a considerable amount of time was devoted to helping relatives manage their relationships with professionals in the wider network. In relation to the patient the difficulties fell into three main categories: dealing with positive symptoms, with negative symptoms and with the relatives' own negative feelings. The questions relating to positive symptoms were about how to react, whether to ignore hallucinations or delusions or to deal with them in a more positive way. Negative symptoms, apathy and withdrawal, raised the issue of how far it was advisable to push the patient and when he should be left. Relatives had been told during education that being upset or angry with the patient was not helpful and, while many understood this, they found it hard to cope with their own negative feelings.

Outcome

In the study of Goldstein, the maximum effect of family therapy in combination with a low dose of medication was at 6 months after the intervention. None of the 28 patients had relapsed at 6 months. This was intended as a 6-weeks crisis intervention only and appeared to have a limited effect, with the authors stating that 'the effects of aftercare seem to dissipate over time' (p. 25); that is, at 3-year and at 6-year follow-up the combination that had been effective in the short term was no more effective in the long term than any of the other combinations. However, the long-term follow-up was incomplete.

The results of one study, that by Falloon, showed that in the family treatment condition, one out of eighteen patients relapsed, whereas in the individual treatment condition, eight out of eighteen relapsed. This difference was highly significant. The study also found significantly lower levels of schizophrenic symptomatology in the former group. The family treatment approach was also associated with improved social functioning of patients and a reduced burden on the family.

A similar outcome was shown in the work of Leff, with one out of twelve patients relapsing in the experimental condition and six out of twelve patients relapsing in the control condition. This difference was highly significant.

There was also a significant lowering of criticism in the experimental group as compared to the control group. Emotional overinvolvement showed some downward change, but this only approached statistical significance.

As yet, none of the results of the Anderson study have been published, but it is reported that the findings are promising.

Conclusions

While all the studies report that there was a successful outcome, there are many differences between them. The question we need to ask is whether they share common elements to account for the positive finding?

All but Goldstein, who gave education informally, placed considerable emphasis on supplying information to relatives. There were many reasons for doing this, one of which was to enable relatives to see that some of the behaviours of the patient were due to the illness rather than simply because they were being difficult. Vaughn and Leff (1976) found that low EE relatives believed that the patient suffered from a legitimate illness, whereas high EE relatives believed the patient was being deliberately difficult. Creer and Wing (1975) found that when relatives were told very little about the illness, or were told in a perfunctory way, this caused them great distress. Other reasons for telling relatives have been suggested by Berkowitz and Leff (1984):

(1) The information they are given may be less terrifying than the beliefs they may have about the illness.
(2) Relatives may believe that no one knows anything about the illness and that it is totally unpredictable and unmanageable.
(3) An understanding that they are not solely responsible for the illness may help relatives to feel less guilty.
(4) The information offers relatives a language in which to discuss problems and a foundation on which to base questions in the future.
(5) Relatives may begin to be able to tolerate uncertainty as they realize many questions cannot be answered precisely.
(6) They gain a better appreciation of the need for maintenance medication.

One of the interesting features of the education programmes is the attempt to involve all the family members in the problem; for example, how was it for the family when the patient was psychotic? How was it for the patient when he was ill? There was also emphasis on the role played by the family in the course of the illness, with the negative role being pointed out but the positive role being stressed more.

All programmes took a positive and sympathetic approach to both patient and family. Therapy was directed towards trying to relieve the guilt feelings of families and to direct their efforts towards positive outcomes, both in terms of emotion and achievement. This approach drew on the belief that it placed a heavy burden on the family to have someone with schizophrenia living with them. In all the studies importance is attached initially to expressing negative feelings, originally anger, guilt, sadness and loss, which offers relief to family members. Pacing is also essential. Working slowly, keeping expectations at an appropriate level and rewarding effort and achievement are all important aspects of working purposefully and with hope.

There was considerable detailed description of all phases of therapy in the studies by Goldstein, Falloon and Anderson. The notions of timing and appropriateness of interventions were common themes which were absent from the work of Leff. Such a phased and detailed approach is to be recommended because, in the morass of experience that occurs in a thera-peutic encounter with these troubled families, guidelines for the therapist offer support and structure and some protection against the problems (described below) of doing this work.

The most striking feature of all these programmes is the emphasis on problem solving or management of tasks. None of the programmes encour-ages discussion of feelings or their interpretation, but all are clearly directed towards solving the day-to-day problems which arise, either as crises or as more mundane events. It is only towards the end of therapy that the Anderson study offers—note only effers—such help, although Falloon states: 'It is also important to communicate negative feelings such as anger, hurt, disappointment, or sadness in an effective manner.' The focus is not on the expression of feelings within the session but on a problem-solving approach to effective expression with the patient. There is no clear evidence why this emphasis should recur in all the studies. It may be that those who have worked with these families have noted that interventions which focus on the negative feelings of family members increase distress with often deleterious effects on the patient.

The role of the relatives' group is not clear. Many of the problems and solutions raised in the family sessions of the other studies occurred in the relatives' group. What is difficult to establish is whether greater therapeutic leverage could have been obtained with either the patient present in the group or with more family sessions at which with the patient is present. Work is currently in progress to assess the affect of the relatives' group as compared to family therapy.

THE FUTURE

One of the purposes of the trials which have been described is to provide guidelines for improved care for patients and their families. It would be the hope of some researchers that the work they have done would be of value to clinicians who could incorporate some, or all, of the principles into their practice.

The work so far has been described mainly in research terms, but it should be mentioned that difficulties of a more clinical nature may arise in the course of the work. Some of these relate to the specific problem of having a family member suffer from schizophrenia, while other difficulties are more a function of the setting in which the clinician is working.

The clinical problem

While it is not true of *all* families with a member who has schizophrenia, it is often the case that they are extremely sensitive because of the stress under which they have been living, and/or they have had experiences with professionals which they have perceived as rejecting.

In either case, the effect is that the family may be difficult to engage. It was our experience that it was worthwhile to persevere with such families. It was important to sympathize with their experience, give the family or relative space, but it was equally important to maintain contact. We would say we understood that they may not wish to see us at the present time, but we would be in touch, say, within a week. One of the side-effects of doing clinical research is to make therapists very keen to engage families, since each outcome has significance. This persistence paid off and was perhaps in itself therapeutic for families, all of whom in the experimental group were engaged and remained so.

In the case of families who have felt rejected by professionals, there is a necessity to establish trust and for them to feel that they are not taking further risks of rejection. This can be achieved by the emphasis on the problems which exist for all of them, not only the patient.

The problem for clinicians

Families with schizophrenic patients may behave in ways which lead to professional splitting and blaming. The problem has been more fully described in a paper by Berkowitz and Leff (1984). The family may have problems, for example, with feelings of helplessness. The clinician or clinical team may start behaving in a helpless way and begin to blame one another for the lack of progress. The family may handle its distress by putting family members down. Such a reaction may be reflected in the clinical team and there may be criticism by a team member at the top of the hierarchy of those lower down.

Berkowitz and Leff (1984) pointed out in the paper that such reactions are commonplace and may usefully be seen as information about the family. That is, the behaviour in the team can be used to help clinicians understand the nature of the family interaction.

This kind of objective use of the emotional reaction of clinicians to the families is more likely to happen when the team functions as a support group to its members. The work can be stressful: therapists may experience burn-out, and this can be avoided or alleviated by sharing negative feelings and experiences with one another.

The support group can also serve the function of helping therapists to reassess their goals and expectations. Families themselves may have unrealistic expectations of the patient or of themselves. Clinicians may become caught up in this with the result that goals are not achieved and everyone experiences a sense of failure. This should be avoided and expectations lowered so that the patient, the family and the clinicians retain a sense of hope.

The problem for wider systems or agencies

It is also important to remember that while the approach represented in the four studies is promising and may be taken up eagerly by social workers, psychiatrists, psychiatric nurses and clinical psychologists, there may be professionals who have been working in their own way for a long time. They may not be entirely satisfied with their own approach, but equally may not wish to take on some 'newfangled ideas'.

These longstanding approaches, it is our belief, must be respected and handled with sensitivity. It may irk a young, forward-looking professional to do this, but in the long run the outcome is likely to be better than an imposition of ideas. We should try to explain our approach as best we can, but be prepared to modify our ideas to fit in with their agency.

Table 16.2 shows some of the implications which may be considered by professionals who wish to introduce new ideas into their agency.

Finally, it is important when the work is under way for there to be a clear assignment of a role to each person involved in the work. This should be

TABLE 16.2 Implications for consideration

Personal	*Agency*
(1) Does the *general* approach require you to shift some attitudes?	(1) If you work this way, will there be reverberations in your professional system?
(2) Attitude to key issue of *separation*	(2) If so, will you have to *educate* colleagues? What about those outside your system?
(3) Attitude to the *activity* of the patient (ideas of under/overstimulation).	(3) How will you deal with colleagues who hold different beliefs? What about those outside your system?
(4) Attitude to persevering with the difficult families and unrewarding patients.	(4) What about *support* groups to avoid professional splitting and blaming?
(5) Education programme—do you approve?	(5) Who, what, where, to whom and when?
(6) Group	(6) Who, what, where, with whom and when?
(7) Family meetings.	(7) Frequency, approach and content.
(8) Long-term contact with families.	(8) Is it necessary? Who should do it? (Volunteers?)

decided by the professional with clinical responsibility and should be stated in the clearest possible terms to all members of the team concerned. Blurring of boundaries and problems with hierarchy are inherent in many of the families with a schizophrenic member. Clinical teams which have not dealt with these issues may be even more vulnerable to the kinds of problems described above.

In conclusion, the attempts at social intervention, particularly that of Leff *et al.* (1982), rest firmly on evidence from the early naturalistic studies. Leff and Tarrier (1981) presented findings about the relationship between the social environment and the course of schizophrenia which provided a sound basis for the studies aimed at altering the social environment of patients suffering from schizophrenia and thus reducing the risk of relapse. This has been achieved in several different studies, as we have attempted to show in this chapter. Treating the home environment of the patient with schizophrenia makes a positive impact on the course of the illness as well as relieving the burden on the family. What is needed now is refinement of therapeutic techniques in order to establish which are most useful in helping schizophrenic patients and their families.

REFERENCES

Anderson, C. M., Hogarty, G., and Reiss, D. J. (1981). The psycho-educational family treatment of schizophrenia. In M. J. Goldstein (ed.), *New Developments in Interventions with Families of Schizophrenics*. London: Jossey-Bass.

Bateson, G., Jackson, D., Haley, J., and Weakland, J. (1956). Towards a theory of schizophrenia. *Behavioural Science*, **1**, 251–264.

Berkowitz, R., Eberlein-Fries, R., Kuipers, L., and Leff, J. (1984). Educating relatives about schizophrenia. *Schizophrenia Bulletin*, **10**, 418–430.

Berkowitz, R., and Leff, J. (1984). Clinical teams reflect family dysfunction. *Journal of Family Therapy*, **6**, 79–89.

Brown, G. W., Birley, J. L. T., and Wing, J. K. (1972). Influence of family life on the course of schizophrenic disorders: a replication. *British Journal of Psychiatry*, **121**, 241–258.

Brown, G. W., Monck, E. M., Carstairs, G. M., and Wing, J. K. (1962). Influence of family life on the course of schizophrenic illness. *British Journal of Preventive and Social Medicine*, **16**, 55–68.

Creer, C., and Wing, J. K. W. (1975). *Schizophrenia at Home*. London: National Schizophrenia Fellowship.

Falloon, I., Boyd, J., McGill, C., Razani, J., Moss, H., and Gilderman, A. (1982). Family management in the prevention of exacerbations of schizophrenia. *New England Journal of Medicine*, **306**, 1437–1440.

Falloon, I. R. H., Boyd, J., McGill, C. W., Strang, J. S., and Moss, H. B. (1981). Family management training in the community. In M. J. Goldstein (ed.), *New Directions for Mental Health Services. Developments in Interventions with Families of Schizophrenics*, no. 12. London: Jossey-Bass.

Goldstein, M. J., and Kopeikin, H. S. (1981). Short and long-term effects of combining drug and family therapy. In M. J. Goldstein (ed.), *New Developments in Interventions with Families of Schizophrenics*. London: Jossey-Bass.

Hatfield, A. B. (1979). The family as partner in the treatment of mental illness. *Hospital and Community Psychiatry*, **30**, 338–340.

Leff, J., Kuipers, L., Berkowitz, R., Eberlein-Fries, R., and Sturgeon, D. (1982). A controlled trial of social intervention in the families of schizophrenics. *British Journal of Psychiatry*, **141**, 121–134.

Leff, J., and Tarrier, N. (1981). The home environment of schizophrenic patients, and their response to treatment. In M. J. Christie and P. G. Mellett (eds), *Foundations of Psychosomatics*. Chichester: Wiley.

Lidz, R., and Lidz, T. (1949). The family environment of schizophrenic patients. *American Journal of Psychiatry*, **106**, 322–345.

Minuchin, S. (1974). *Families and Family Therapy*. London: Tavistock.

Tarrier, N., Vaughn, C., Lader, M. H., and Leff, J. P. (1979). Bodily reactions to people and events in schizophrenia. *Archives of General Psychiatry*, **36**, 311–315.

Vaughn, C., and Leff, J. P. (1976). The influence of family and social factors on the course of psychiatric illness: a comparison of schizophrenic and depressed neurotic patients. *British Journal of Psychiatry*, **129**, 125–137.

Wing, J. K., and Brown, G. W. (1970). *Institutionalism and Schizophrenia*. Cambridge: Cambridge University Press.

Wing, J. K., Cooper, J. E., and Sartorius, N. (1974). *The Description and Classification of Psychiatric Symptoms*. Cambridge: Cambridge University Press.

Wynne, L., Rykoff, I., Day, J., and Hirsch, S. (1958). Pseudomutuality in the family relations of schizophrenics. *Psychiatry*, **21**, 205–220.

SECTION 7

Surgery and Oncology

The Psychosomatic Approach: Contemporary Practice
of Whole-person Care
Edited by M. J. Christie and P. G. Mellett
© 1986 John Wiley & Sons Ltd

17

THE WHOLE-PERSON APPROACH TO SURGERY

ANNE T. STOTTER

and

HUGH DUDLEY

Academic Surgical Unit, St Mary's Hospital Medical School, University of London, UK

INTRODUCTION

From his surgical attendants a patient needs not only a response to the technical problem but also a reaction to the person that he is and an appreciation of his individual needs. Ideally the surgeon, like any doctor, becomes for the patient exactly what is required: a combination of kindness and consideration but with at the same time determination and authoritarianism (Balint, 1964). The relationship can then work well provided both speak the same literal and figurative language. Given this, some will need detailed explanations, some will be frightened and some will be overwhelmed and reject efforts to enlighten. Some will wish to share in decision making, some will be incapable of so doing. Some will gain confidence if treated in a paternal fashion, others will be insulted. Adaptation of the doctor to these disparate needs of patients is not special to surgery; however, surgery does present interesting if not unique problems (Ray, Fisher and Lindop, in press).

GENERAL MATTERS

The nature of the treatment

Surgical treatment is essentially technical and to the patient it appears intrusive and radical if also, in diseases such as cancer, effective. In even the most simple operation the body is invaded by the surgeon and may be significantly altered, so demanding great trust from the recipient and placing a serious responsibility on the giver. The depth of the accompanying invasion of the patient's persona varies with the operation but culminates in the ultimate—the neurosurgeon's incursion into the seat of the mind.

Of necessity the patient adopts a submissive stance, the antithesis of that of his all-powerful, paternal surgeon. Such is an almost inevitable consequence of the nature of surgery. Its technicality makes the patient more of an object and less of a person, and for success its invasiveness demands a submissive, passive response. Similarly, the traditional stereotype of the surgeon as a god-like figure or hero, who performs dramatic and courageous acts assisted by a supporting team who follow his decisions unquestioningly, is a consequence of the nature of the job, as influenced by the social norms of the time (see next section).

In any illness people tend to regress to a less mature or even childish mode of behaviour, a natural reaction to being incapacitated and one which reinforces the attitudinal difference between surgeon and patient. In the extreme case, the latter may accept unquestioningly the advice of his or her surgeon, divorced from its technical merit, behaving very much as a young child, and investing him with supreme authority. By the same token, in surgery the consequences of actions are so obviously and directly linked to the patient's condition that a special personal link develops between the operator and the recipient. Surgical interventions are precise and definite, and the outcome very obvious. This, together with the usually short time-scale of the relevant events, makes the surgeon immediately accountable to his patient, to his colleagues and to the relatives (Bosk, 1979).

The penumbra of real or imagined events surrounding a surgical procedure may promote a strong relationship between surgeon and patient, yet para-doxically, at the same time, interfere with communication. How often has one heard the patient say 'But you never told me this' or 'That came as a surprise to me' when indeed the matter had been thoroughly gone into. Before surgery what is in fact happening is that the patient is adopting a coping style which blanks out the acceptance of things that are at any distance from the need to 'screw . . . courage to the sticking place'. Less common in our experience is a rift between intellectual and emotional acceptance: for example, though the patient may recognize the need for explanation and planning about a colostomy, he can only accept it after experiencing the real thing. For these reasons elaborate preoperative discussion and explanations may not always succeed and can indeed be a waste of time.

The surgical mind and the surgical role

No account of the interaction between surgeon and patient can be complete without reference to the surgical mind. A number of field studies are avail-able, though there is little formal documentation (see particularly Bosk, 1979). The suggestion is that the surgeon is essentially an extravert, committed to the idea of personal excellence, intolerant of mistakes by himself and others and with an essentially, though not exclusively, mechan-istic approach to his work. This is not to deny that he can be passionate, considerate and humane. It is only to say that, on the whole, his personality drives him towards domination in patient/doctor relationships and isolation from personal involvement. His own need for authority in what is often a situation of risk, may contribute to this, and indeed failure to adopt the paterfamilias or avuncular role (albeit flavoured with a strong element of authority) can lead to confusion about decision making which does not necessarily contribute to good clinical judgement. In situations of uncertainty the lay person may well choose the surgeon who can be dogmatically wrong for the right reason rather than the more thoughtful but less emotive colleague who is right either for the right or wrong reason.

This authoritarian attitude of the surgeon has both good and bad effects. On the one hand it can crystallize decision making when, though there may be intellectual and emotional doubt about how exactly to proceed, there is nevertheless the necessity to act. On the other hand, the *deus ex chirurgica* may find it difficult himself, or his patients may themselves feel intimidated, when it comes to discussion of matters of life and death, of risk and of the physical and emotional burden to be borne as a consequence of surgical treatment. Many surgeons, equipped as they are with personalities which make them technically successful, are unable to respond to the patient's cry for help on non-physical matters.

Though this may be the general rule from surgical history, it is not an immutable law. Either intuitively or as a result of conditioning, surgeons are as educable as most other medical specialists to the needs of their patients. What has been lacking until now is any clear appreciation of the nature of the psychosomatic responses which accompany surgery and thus of the disturbances and demands generated.

Another factor which bears on the continuity of attention to other than physical needs of the patient is the increasing and in some ways inevitable fragmentation of clinical care which accompanies technical specialization. Particularly in circumstances of the seriously ill with multisystem disorders, undergoing a long sojourn in the intensive care unit, who 'owns' the patient and whose responsibility it is to communicate with him is often forgotten. Serious depression, with group confusion and despair involving both the patient and his relatives, may then follow.

Admission to hospital

Most surgical illness requires admission to hospital. The patient abruptly loses his normal role in life, and with it much of his privacy and day-to-day routines. The stresses generated vary but may be considerable. For example, an elderly lady may be acutely distressed to be robbed of her normal toilet habits which are often fixed, sacrosanct and of ritual significance (Johns, Dudley and Masterton, 1973). Indeed, many who have difficulty coping in normal life, support themselves with carefully followed routines and may be brought to the limits of their coping abilities by the disturbance associated with hospital admission.

A hospital patient is, to a variable extent, confined to bed. For an active, independent young man, such restriction may be humiliating and add to his sense of loss of role. He may become aggressive and uncooperative, and higher intelligence does not appear to be a guarantee of greater cooperation (Johns, Dudley and Masterton, 1973). At the other extreme, being encouraged to become more or less dependent may bring an important relief of symptoms to someone sufficiently stressed by his illness, or by the psychosocial environment immediately before admission, or both.

Open wards are noisy (Bentley, Murphy and Dudley, 1977) and strange. The nextdoor neighbour may be confused and difficult to control and is liable to shout bizarre and distressing things in the small hours. People in pain are obvious. Ugly sights are seen. Occasionally someone may die. In this exposed environment perfect strangers—both patients and medical staff—discuss matters of life and death. A doctor will ask questions about the most intimate details with nothing more than an incompletely drawn curtain to provide a poor semblance of privacy. Physical examination may be embarrassing and unpleasant, especially it seems for the young. As a contrast to these undesirable effects, an open ward can have a socializing influence with the development of camaraderie and an optimistic—or at least cooperative—spirit (Solzhenitsyn, 1969).

For those who are most sick and need intensive medical and nursing care, the stresses are greatest (Dudley, 1975). Fortunately, their subsequent recall of the most difficult periods is poor (Ellis *et al.*, 1979). Severe illness (especially if it has metabolic effects), pain and fear contribute to stress. The ability to cope is further compromised by sleep disturbance (Schroeder, 1971; Dudley, 1975) and disruption of circadian patterns generally. Coping may also be adversely affected by drugs, and anaesthetic agents. Sensory overload, commonly due to excessive noise, is debilitating; so also is isolation, which can equally affect the patient in the intensive care unit despite staff endlessly and impersonally milling around (Ellis *et al.*, 1979).

Even in ideal circumstances, adjustments must be made to cope with the role of illness and with the environment of the ward, and these take time. *All* coping takes time, which is longer for the elderly. Despite pressure on beds and the desire to do things quickly and efficiently, such matters as this must be remembered.

Anaesthesia

The main aim of anaesthesia in surgery is to render procedures painless. Thus, small operations can be done with the aid of local anaesthetic either infiltrated locally or instilled around the nerves supplying the area. It is not usually possible to adapt such methods to larger operations, e.g. on the abdominal contents, and hence general anaesthesia is often necessary. This has the additional advantage that it makes the patient unaware of what is being done. Many surgeons and patients prefer such a state of oblivion at the time of an operation and hence general anaesthesia may be chosen for minor procedures even though it is not, of course, without its risks. For a minor operation, such as a hernia repair or varicose veins surgery, these risks—in terms of threat to life—though present, are vanishingly small. Nevertheless, most individuals appear to be remarkably unconcerned about any hazard. Not unreasonably, a tiny risk of death is trivial compared to the clear prospect, established by the experience of themselves or others, of postoperative pain or the operation 'going wrong'.

As in any other situation, unpleasant or frightening past events may influence response and those who have a well-developed phobia, either in-built or acquired, about anaesthesia, or even about a minor component of anaesthetic technique such as an injection, may need careful management and sympathetic support. Occasionally a patient will say that they are afraid of giving themselves up to an anaesthetic because of what they might do while unconscious. It *should* be possible, but is not always so, to reassure them by describing modern anaesthesia.

Hospitalization, anaesthesia and surgery are all events that an individual has to cope with, and, as has already been mentioned, there is some evidence that the agents used in anaesthesia may have an adverse effect on coping ability. Nowadays consciousness is recovered relatively rapidly after an oper-ation. However, it takes many more hours for the body to get rid of the agents used to induce anaesthesia, and for up to 48 hours there is evidence of a deterioration in psychomotor skills (Epstein, 1975; Korttila, 1981). Disturbances of affect have not been adequately studied (Elsass *et al.*, 1982) and those caused by anaesthesia are difficult to separate from the effects of surgery; it is not hard to believe that cerebral function as a whole is tempor-arily disturbed. After operations with cardiopulmonary bypass there is definite evidence of such disturbance (Henriksen, 1984). Hence, at least in part, the indifference to details of procedure and outcome that is commonly observed for a few days after a major operation. The elderly are especially prone to become confused and disorientated, even to the extent of psychosis, in the immediate postoperative period, when the combination of strange surroundings, drugs, pain, and hormonal and metabolic changes has its greatest impact. Every surgeon should be aware of the strains on the indi-vidual at this time and know that he must be careful and supportive, not only of the patient but also of his relatives and friends. It is essential to tell the relatives of an elderly patient who has become disturbed at this time the probable reasons and the likely temporary nature of the problem; otherwise all are likely to think that the final mental breakdown they secretly dreaded has actually occurred.

One potentially very frightening aspect of general anaesthesia is the possi-bility of awareness during an operation. Relaxant anaesthesia paralyses all the muscles of the body, including those that are used in breathing, and ventilation is maintained by mechanical means. It then becomes difficult to decide by conventional tests that the patient is unconscious and pain-free. Occasionally after an operation a patient reports that at some time he was aware of what was happening. Rarely, he is not only aware but also able to feel pain. In the latter situation the experience is a shattering one and liable to have serious long-term psychological consequences. Prevention remains difficult, but the modern habit of administering 'light' anaesthesia must be tempered to the recognition of such an undesirable effect. On the rare occasions that there is recall, it is important to listen to the patient's account and assess it, and not automatically to dismiss the experience as a dream. Even further damage is done by disregard, with loss of confidence and the conviction that madness may be the reason for what is falsely regarded as a hallucination.

Pain

The fundamentals of pain are discussed elsewhere in this volume (Chapter 10); however, a few points are pertinent here. The first is that virtually all surgical procedures involve pain to some extent. The disease process which requires treatment may be painful of itself, and management is always more or less of an agony. The surgeon can usually warn the patient of what to expect (though he may rarely do so). Information is particularly important if the pattern of postoperative discomfort will be difficult for the patient to understand without prior explanation. There are, however, limits to what can be described and it is not uncommon for a patient to complain after an operation that he was not told how bad it would be: 'If I had known . . . I would never have agreed.' It is a very real, if ineluctable, difficulty that there is no useful, let alone accurate, way of expressing the quality or extent of someone else's future pain.

Much attention has been paid to techniques of relieving postoperative pain, and the range of possible approaches is now wide. The conventional intermittent oral or intramuscular analgesics may be replaced by continuous intravenous infusions (Rutter, Murphy and Dudley, 1980), regional nerve blocks (Rawal et al., 1982), spinal and epidural anaesthesia or opiates (Reiz et al., 1981; Gallon, 1982), transcutaneous stimulation (Taylor et al., 1983) and inhaled agents (Kripke, Justice and Hechtman, 1983). However, one of the major problems in postoperative pain relief remains the difficulty of translating the patient's needs into effective action. Nurses, as a careful but rather alarming study by Johnston (Johnston, 1976) has shown, consistently underestimate the patient's reports of pain severity as judged on linear analogue scales. If, as in this study and as is so often the case in clinical practice, the administration of analgesia is controlled by nurses, underprescription is inevitable. Either regular administration or an 'on demand' system controlled by the patient who can meter drugs into himself (with certain programmed restraints to avoid overdosage) are to be preferred. Having said that, many patients are resistant to taking 'unnecessary' drugs and many see the acceptance of analgesics as a sign of weakness; in consequence, on demand systems are not in our view the best answer.

In caring for adults, it is usually possible to explain to some extent why pain is occurring and what may be done about it; if relief cannot be completely achieved counsel and reassurance may help. With children, especially the very young, rapport is less easily established. For them explanations are useless. Not only must they cope with the pain but also their attendants and relatives must respond positively to their suffering. For all concerned the experience may be harrowing, and remembered for a long time. Bernstein (1976) describes this problem with particular vividness in one of its most unpleasant forms: the pain associated with changes of dressings in children with extensive burns. He has successfully used hypnosis to help such children through desperate and terrifying times and comments on the value of the 'magical' associations of hypnosis.

Complications

Risk taking is implicit in surgical action. Every surgeon has a notion of the odds in favour of his success in a particular procedure, which can be adjusted up or down depending on the patient's age and medical condition and the surgeon's physical and mental fitness. The latter is determined by many factors including when he last performed the procedure, what hour of the day or night it is, the quality of his support team and whether or not his wife is having a baby or an affair.

A surgeon must only operate on a patient in the expectation of cure or palliation of his condition. At the same time, however, he is always aware that he cannot guarantee the outcome—he can only estimate the probability of success. He knows that complications may occur. The extent to which he shares this knowledge with his patient varies, depending on his personality (p. 372), the time he makes available for such discussion, the nature of the operation which is planned and his patient's nature.

It is generally felt to be unfair to burden a patient with knowledge of uncommon complications, because this would unnecessarily increase the fear of an operation and may be counterproductive to gaining the patient's confidence. However, it is essential that important risks, even if relatively rare, are explained. Nerve damage during head and neck surgery for benign disease is a good example: it should not occur if the operation is properly conducted; it does not occur often; but when it does it is deforming or disabling or both, and so the patient should know about it. Establishing the correct balance for any particular patient is inevitably difficult at times, as witnessed by many legal cases and much literature on the problem of informed consent. Litigation aside, the importance of comprehensible explanation is considerable because it contributes significantly to the patient's short- and long-term wellbeing. Not only can good communication ease distress but it has also been shown to promote recovery (Reading, 1979; Pearson and Dudley, 1982). However, before surgery such communication has its limits as we have discussed above.

When a complication does occur a whiff of blame automatically arises because the surgeon's previous actions are so plainly connected to the current problem. Of course, the surgeon may know that such a connection is spurious but how can the patient? He and his relatives may have sensed a statistical risk prior to surgery but probabilities are not things most people can work with; in everyday life they mean little. Patients will not generally expect complications and will be surprised or even shocked by them, not to say disappointed.

If a patient decides to place blame on his surgeon an awkward situation may develop. The surgeon may feel confident that he did not make an error and that blame is inappropriate; it was 'just one of those things'. He may explain this or, perhaps more commonly, ignore the patient's reaction, particularly if it is unspoken. Mistrust may then be generated. If the surgeon or any of his colleagues feels that a genuine error has been made there is likely to be considerable debate, in which the patient is not usually directly included. Error, in this context, is an essentially contested concept. By this is meant that because there is often no universally accepted 'correct' treatment, the events must be discussed to decide whether treatment that subsequently proves to be wrong (on the basis that the outcome is unsatisfactory) was an error or an action that, in the circumstances, was reasonable and therefore acceptable. A patient can hear whispers of the debate and fragments of often quite divergent views may be transmitted to him. Again he is liable to lose trust. He may become confused and unhappy, making his recovery even more difficult than the complication itself has already done. The same arguments hold true for relatives in the case of unexpected postoperative death.

The contested concept view of error means, incidentally, that discussions about blame which do not lead to acceptance of responsibility are often taken as 'cover-ups'. The medical profession is commonly thought to close its ranks as a response to accusations of mistakes or negligence; though sometimes true, this may on other occasions be an unfair interpretation of an honest auditing process.

SPECIAL FEATURES

Disfigurement, mutilation and dysfunction

Mutilation results in loss of confidence and self-esteem, and change in self-image. The patient may be rejected by others or feel that this is so. Customary roles may be no longer possible and goals must be redefined. Dependency may ensue.

A scar, the almost inevitable hallmark of a surgical history, may be trivial or have considerable and disproportionate psychological sequelae. Facial scars and burns can be particularly disfiguring. In his monograph on the subject Bernstein (1976) analyses in great detail the various aspects of disfigurement. He points out the importance of physical appearance in all relationships from the most casual on-the-street reactions between strangers to the most intimate sexual contacts. Facial disfingurement at worst provokes reactions of horror and disgust, and at best those who are visibly deformed are avoided, socially downgraded and rarely considered as objects of sexual attraction. The distortion and immobility imposed by facial scars limits the important part of communication that is conveyed by facial expression. Close relatives of those with mask-like facial scars must attempt deliberate adjustments to avoid the instinctive reactions to a blank expression.

The person himself has to cope with the fact that he is simply not as he was. Even if his injuries do not cause physical restriction, he may never be able to behave as before because he feels others must see him as he sees himself. His body image is irrevocably damaged. Our reactions to others are so inextricably linked to how they look and how they react in terms of changing expression and changing posture that no amount of familiarity or good will can completely reverse the effect of disfigurement. In rare instances total rejection of the perceived state ensues with either suicidal impulses or an unending search for a way in which things can be put right.

Coping with an acquired deformity such as mastectomy involves a period of grief both on the part of the patient and her relatives, often long, at the loss of the person who was. Withdrawal from social contact is common, and may be extreme. Depression is almost inevitable, may be long-lived, and can lead to suicide. Denial is an important and valuable aspect of coping mechanisms. Litigation, guilt and financial stringencies may all contribute to an individual's difficulties. Generally, the more severe the deformity, the more disturbed is the individual's life and that of his family. There can be no pretending that what has happened has not, but the cry 'Why did this happen to me?' is often heard and frequently is associated with anger. Nevertheless, in most instances the usual course of a grief reaction, with gradual reemergence of the patient, follows, aided by support from both professionals and relatives. Most surgeons learn intuitively that this is the case and do not attempt to hurry matters. Lingering though minor griefs and anxieties may, of course, persist because any experience, be it medical or not, leaves its traces on our lives.

On occasions the surgeon is presented with a situation in which a treatment option involves the creation of severe deformity or disfigurement. The patient usually has a malignancy that cannot be treated by radiotherapy or drugs. The only therapy likely to be effective is removal of a large part of the body (for example, forequarter or hindquarter amputation) or substantially altering a particularly important and visible part such as the face. The choice may be between severe mutilation and letting the malignancy take its course unchecked; the difficulties in making such a choice are considerable. Inevitably, the surgeon is the dominant person in the decision-making process, though patient, relatives, nurses, psychiatrist and social worker may all be involved. If on the one hand the surgeon is not prepared to perform the operation, the discussion is ended; he will never be persuaded to undertake major mutilating surgery should he have no personal conviction that the potential gains justify it. On the other hand, if he does feel that the operation is worthwhile, he may in effect make the decision to go ahead virtually on his own because—as with pain—it is only possible to communicate in the most rudimentary terms the deforming effects of surgery. The surgeon could say: 'We would have to remove the lower half of the right side of your face including that part of the jawbone and much of your tongue, together with part of the right side of your neck. We would reconstruct your face on that side with skin and tissue taken from your shoulder and brought up and round to fill the gap. You would need skin grafting from your leg to heal your shoulder. You would not look normal even when all the healing was complete. But it's the best way of treating the growth you have, and we would hope to cure it by the operation.' Such would constitute a very full and frank account, but how much idea would it give the uninitiated of the reality of the situation? And how much value can one place on 'informed consent' in such circumstances? By contrast, how could one do better? To show a patient someone who has been successfully treated in this way would be likely to horrify him and prevent his cooperating with such a plan of treatment. This might well give him an inappropriate bias because the consequences of not having treatment would not have been presented, and would probably be more horrific. The transference of authority to the surgeon is almost inevitable in such a situation and must be accompanied by a suitable if dispassionate humility on his part about what he can achieve and what price the patient will have to pay.

Lesser forms of deformity have less dramatic effects, but are nevertheless important. Each person, with his individual lifestyle, relationships, work and domestic arrangements, and overall priorities, will react differently to a given procedure. The surgeon's task is to decide what would be the best form of treatment amongst the various options, and then to try to work out both on his own and in discussion with the patient what would be appropriate for the individual. On occasion the two modalities are very different. One example is limb amputation when there is disability and deformity as distinct from gangrene or threatened gangrene.

The prospect of limb amputation is usually very distressing. Loss of a limb, like facial disfigurement, has been shown to evoke reactions akin to bereavement (Parkes, 1972) and the mutilation is compounded by all the potential difficulties of future self-care. One quarter of the patients studied are still depressed and withdrawn a year after surgery (see also colostomy below). Often the indication for amputation is peripheral vascular disease. The patient may well be aware of the likely progression of the underlying process and he may know of those who needed progressively higher amputations, subsequently to become wheelchair-bound. Apart from those who, for complex reasons usually dating back many years, are going to be happier completely dependent on others, this prospect is very daunting. Indeed, some may choose to die rather than face life after a major amputation.

An important and feared form of induced dysfunction is incontinence, which brings with it far-reaching psychological and social implications. In infancy, when continence is learnt, its maintenance is a significant personal achievement; evacuation becomes one of the most intimate and personal of activities (Devlin, 1983). Mostly it is a strictly private affair, though social norms allow men to urinate in company. As to the effects of loss of control of evacuation, women are at a slight advantage because familiarity with menstruation—essentially an uncontrolled flow—accustoms them to coping successfully with such effluent. The constant fear of accident and its attendant embarrassment is thus likely to be less.

Urinary incontinence in men is both physiologically and psychologically linked with impotence, making it all the more difficult to accept. Such incontinence is an occasional consequence of prostatic or rectal surgery and the surgeon responsible needs to be prepared to muster all possible physical, psychological and social support. 'Wet women' are a good deal more numerous, and many are young. The techniques, surgical or otherwise, available for their help are difficult and the results often uncertain. This group, again, need much support.

It is fortunately uncommon for surgical intervention to give rise to faecal incontinence (except when the surgery creates a stoma—see below). In its severer forms the passage of faeces and odour occur uncontrollably, and all normal social interactions may be impossible. Because of the associated smells, even with pads and plastic pants a trip to the local shops can be a nightmare. Many such patients are housebound by their condition and rejected by society. Counselling the patient who has urine or faeces in the perineum is not usually very effective.

In both forms of incontinence the obvious management is to correct the cause if at all possible. Good and effective clinical practice in relation to incontinence is still very much in its infancy but is the essential technical horse to pull the management cart.

The considerable psychosocial consequences of a stoma have been carefully studied by Devlin (1983). Not only is control of both solid and gaseous effluent lost, but they now come from a hole in the abdominal wall into a bag. Excitement, anxiety or sexual arousal stimulate the bowel and are therefore likely to increase the activity of a stoma, just at the time that it is least wanted. As a patient said, 'How would you like to be talking to the prettiest girl in the room at a cocktail party while your bowels empty into your left-hand trouser pocket?' Physical exertion may dislodge the bag. An airtight seal, while containing the odorous gases, may be incompatible with keeping the bulk of the bag inconspicuous. Without a good deal of effort and courage, it would clearly be only too easy for a ostomist to withdraw from an active social life altogether. He or she must learn to manage the stoma and appliance and integrate them into everyday activities which, despite every effort, may be changed or restricted in important ways. A young person has to cope with explaining to friends where necessary, and to prospective lovers, a fact about themselves that may be very difficult to express. It must help to have a well-developed sense of humour.

The widespread dissatisfaction with early stomata (particularly the first ileostomies) led in the 1940s and 1950s to the development of self-help associations. These were valuable for the exchange of practical information and for catharsis of woes but had also the strange and undesirable effect of making the patient more and more stoma conscious or even obsessed. With better techniques and a better understanding of the psychological problems, these associations have become more advisory and less of a wailing wall. However, no surgeon who makes a stoma can afford to be unaware of the problems of adaptation he generates for his patient. Women are more affected than men and are slower to come to terms. There are interesting differences, too, between ileostomists and colostomists not all of which are explained by the fact that the latter are older.

Sexual problems go further than just the existence of the stoma and appliance (Dlin, Perlman and Ringold, 1969). In females the associated pelvic surgery may have left internal adhesions, or chronic sepsis, which lead to pain on intercourse. In the male, up to half of those over 50 years of age who have had a colostomy after rectal excision for carcinoma, are impotent because of nerve damage. Even with excellent, complication-free surgery the psychological effect of an orifice on the abdominal wall may be to weaken gender status: the stoma may feminize a man or masculinize a woman if it prolapses to become gruesomely like a penis.

Even in this liberalized age, sexual function is not easily discussed by most doctors with their patients. This is unfortunate since it is such an important aspect of everyday life. Briefly, impotence related to surgery can be considered under three headings: psychological causes, neurological causes, and genital surgery.

Psychological difficulties are by far the commonest causes of surgery-related impotence. This is not surprising in view of the complex personal interactions that are involved in sexual intercourse. Perhaps the most important way in which surgery can affect sexuality is by mutilation. Women in particular, most of whom need to feel lovely and lovable, are sensitive to the effects of scarring. Face or breast surgery may have especially traumatic consequences. The converse is also true, that surgical enhancement of appearance may augment sexuality; the vast and difficult field of cosmetic surgery is a tribute to this.

After surgery, particularly related to the genitalia, a man may fear impotence even though the erectile and ejaculatory mechanisms are intact. Such fear of failure may lead to failure, though usually only temporarily.

Fear of causing damage to self or partner is another cause of loss of performance. For example, a man may worry after a hernia repair that the exertion of intercourse might bring the hernia back (though it should not).

The partner of someone who has undergone surgery may similarly be afraid of inflicting pain or damage.

Surgical damage to the nerves involved in genital function and sensation can occur, e.g. after abdomino-perineal excision of the rectum (Devlin, 1983; Neal, 1984). Such neurological damage may be temporary or permanent. The consequences are more obvious in a man but it is debatable whether the psychological effects are greater. In general there is no satisfactory treatment, and sympathetic support is usually the best the surgeon can do.

Surgery to the genitalia, including the breasts, inevitably affects sexual function. Even invisible changes, such as removal of the uterus, can profoundly alter self-image. It is perhaps too often forgotten that many individuals continue to be sexually active in their sixties and seventies when operations with the potential of affecting sexual function—such as prostatectomy—become commoner. It is rightly humiliating to be berated by a man in his sixties who was not informed beforehand of the risk and who after prostate surgery has been unfortunate enough to lose sexual function. The subject of cosmetic genital surgery, and transexuality, is too large to be covered here, though needless to say those involved need far more than technical skill to be successful.

Cancer

Some surgeons have few patients with malignant disease, but for many cancer treatment is a major proportion of their work. The public have an irrational fear of cancer by comparison with other disorders. The man with extensive vascular disease is more likely to suffer ill-health or die of the complications of arterial atheroma than the man with prostatic carcinoma is to succumb to his disease, yet the latter is much more likely to be frightened by his diagnosis. It is the inexorability of a cancer that has not been wholly eliminated that forms the basis of fear.

Some malignant growths, e.g. basal cell carcinoma of the skin, have the potential for local spread only and can be readily cured by local treatment. In others, for example, the breast, the disease may be widely disseminated before there is any sign of the primary growth. Some tumours grow slowly and take many years to cause serious ill-health; others, though they grow at a similar low rate, are rapidly devastating; brain tumours are a good example. Despite the wide spectrum of actual behaviour of malignant disease, cancer to the layman is likely to mean a lethal illness very much to be dreaded. In consequence, the surgeon caring for a patient with malignancy must choose his words carefully.

Two decades and more ago it was usual not to tell a patient his diagnosis if he had malignant disease. Now the pendulum is swinging the other way. To tell all the patients all the truth is likely to be just as wrong, as the study by Spencer Jones (1981) has elegantly illustrated. Nearly all would agree that to tell a close relative one thing and the patient another is usually bad for interpersonal relations.

The detail and technicality of acceptable explanations must vary according to the psychological state, intelligence and educational background of the patient. It is worth remembering that most people have a poor knowledge of the locations and functions of the body organs and hence often even simple explanations are not understood (Pearson and Dudley, 1982). Even those fully versed in medical matters need a sensitive approach, as is exemplified by these words written by a doctor with a teratoma of the testis: 'Trust is established by the doctor's clinical competence and by his honesty with himself and his patient. *Honesty does not mean that unpleasant information must be brutally presented to the patient.* The doctor who actively listens to what the patient is saying by word and gesture will learn what information to give' (Moreland, 1982—our italics).

Not only what to say, but when, and whether a close relative or friend should be there at the time, whether to touch the patient while listening and talking, and when to come back and talk again (for it is impossible to absorb all the information given and ask all the questions necessary in the first session) need to be judged as sympathetically as possible. Rules are difficult to formulate and it is awareness and experience that counts for most.

When the truth is too much to bear, the patient will not accept it but will resort to the psychological safety-net of denial (Spencer Jones, 1981). This mechanism has real value in tiding over the person presented with intolerable information (Bernstein, 1976) until he or she is either, with the lapse of time, better able to cope, or the facts themselves are improved. Excessive denial, however, makes communication very difficult between medical staff and patient, and also between patient and relatives and friends. This may severely strain the latter group. It is therefore important to try to avoid overwhelmingly bad news.

All this is common ground for those caring for cancer patients anywhere. The surgeon's special place lies in his ability, or lack of it, to treat the disease. His operation has a high rating with patients—it is a modern form of exorcism—but it also has the special consequences in terms of scarring and sometimes mutilation to which we have already referred. Only a surgeon can discuss these with authority. He provides a plan of management, with all its ancillary risks and consequences, and with that plan he provides a hope of relief or even cure. If he must send the patient on to a colleague for radiotherapy or chemotherapy, it helps if he can predict what that colleague will be able to do, and if he can talk about the referral so that additional fear is avoided ('He told me I would have to have radiotherapy; it must be too far gone for an operation').

A positive plan of management is the surgeon's distinctive contribution to the cancer patient. As time goes by and the disease progresses (if it does) this becomes increasingly difficult.

Routine cancer follow-up is stressful to the patient, and not just because it usually involves long waits in a crowded outpatient department. At each visit, even if they have noticed no change, they fear the discovery of some subtle evidence of recurrence. The news '. . . all seems to be fine; can we see you again in six months?' is rarely received as casually as it is given. If recurrence is detected, or even suspected—requiring special tests or a further assessment in less than the usual interval of time—the news usually needs to be broken most gently. For very few is the certainty of death easier to cope with than the uncertainty of prolonged follow-up with no evidence of recurrence (Naysmith *et al.*, 1983).

Recurrent disease usually means that there is no longer any hope of ultimate cure, and though some form of therapy is often available, the surgeon's knowledge that this is only palliation affects what he says and how he says it. Unless he is careful the hopelessness of the situation may be the patient's overwhelming impression, leaving a bleak and empty prospect, unconducive to his making the best use of the remaining time and energy.

Ultimately the disease process itself becomes untreatable, and management is aimed simply at minimizing symptoms. Although terminal care in a hospice is available for a fortunate few (for here the techniques for relief of symptoms and psychological support are best developed) most patients continue to be the responsibility of their general practitioners and the hospital consultant who first treated the condition. Thus it is the surgeon who should take the dying patient into his hospital bed should this be needed. Dying patients generally know (Witzel, 1975), but it is up to the surgeon to support what hope his patient has and to treat his symptoms.

Much time and thought have been spent on the care of the dying. However, now that there are effective forms of curative treatment for some malignancies, the problems of those who survive are also emerging. There may be profound psychological consequences to having been near death, and those who have been under the threat of malignancy may have prolonged changes in affect and behaviour, especially in interpersonal relationships. Of the survivors, those who do so only after prolonged treatment may be more depressed than those for whom a short clinical course was effective (Cooper *et al.*, 1979; Naysmith *et al.*, 1983). The period of illness may result in a loss of status or income that can never be recovered. Life insurance and a mortgage may become unobtainable. The physical abnormalities that may be the consequence particularly of surgical treatment may lead to social rejection, even if they do not directly affect work capability and independence.

Death

For the surgeon, however compassionate he may be, the patient who dies of cancer is easier to manage than the one who dies soon after an operation for benign disease. The latter death may be seen by everyone as the effect of the surgery. As the patient's course goes inexorably downhill, despite everyone's best efforts, the full burden of his responsibility is impressed upon the surgeon. He can usually console the relatives of those who die of cancer; it is much more difficult to help when the relatives feel that the death is the direct consequence of the surgeon's actions, particularly if he also feels that this is so. The distress is at its greatest when the patient dies on the operating table, for example when blood loss becomes uncontrollable, or a heart operated on under bypass does not resume its function. Even the experienced surgeon is liable to feel guilt and inadequacy: if only he had been more skilled, the patient might still be alive. In few other situations is it easier to feel that one has perpetrated a murder. Rationalization occurs, but the horror, grief and guilt may persist.

OTHER PSYCHOSOCIAL INFLUENCES ON THE PRESENTING PROBLEM

Thus far we have considered the average, ordinary surgical patient (who, like the 'normal' man, does not exist) presenting in an ordinary situation. We have largely ignored the possible social, financial and psychiatric background influences which may have an important impact on events.

General

A fundamental point common to all diseases, but perhaps more starkly apparent in a surgical context, is that in circumstances where an uncorrected social factor is the cause of the problem, treatment is often ineffective or at best a stop-gap. It is one thing to stop bleeding from oesophageal varices or to save life in acute haemorrhagic pancreatitis but quite another to alter the drinking habits of the patient. This 'hand in the hole in the dyke' role of surgery can frustrate the thoughtful surgeon or drive the less reflective one still further down the open road of technical excellence rather than along the more tortuous path of 'whole-person' involvement. Nevertheless, social case conferences about surgical patients (Dudley and Masterton, 1967) are rewarding even if, as is so often the case, they expose or stress the limitations of what can be achieved by mere surgical skill.

Alcohol

The surgeon has to try to repair the damage done in accidents in the home, on the roads and at work. He cares for those with head injuries, broken bones, disrupted nerves, tendons and blood vessels, damage to internal organs, and burns. In all these, abuse of alcohol is an important aetiological factor and also complicates what has to be done (St Haxholdt and Johansson, 1982). Chronic alcohol abuse leads not only to 'accident proneness' but also to liver and pancreatic disease. These, too, result in a need for surgical admission and treatment.

Smoking

Cigarette smoking is a major aetiological factor in ischaemic heart disease, peripheral vascular disease, carcinoma of the bronchus, peptic ulcer disease and carcinoma of the pancreas and the bladder, among others. This constitutes a large segment of the surgical workload.

Promiscuity

Tertiary syphilis used to generate work for surgeons—with its facial and articular deformities and its predilection for causing abdominal pain. Then the gonococcus took the limelight with urethral strictures and periurethral abscess. Now it tends to be Chlamidia and viruses that cause most trouble, with less in the way of acute surgical problems but with serious long-term possible consequences such as cervical cancer and the aquired immune deficiency syndrome. Homosexuality is increasing, and with it anal fissure, proctitis and warts in the genito-perineal region.

Poor domestic environment

Poor homes are associated with child and spouse abuse, accidents and over-consumption of alcohol (*Lancet* editorial, 1979b). Even worse off are those with 'no fixed abode'. Some are mentally subnormal or disturbed, many are alcoholics. They suffer accidents and other violence. They are at high risk of catching tuberculosis. In winter they get frostbite. It must not be forgotten, however, that some such homeless people are well adapted to their particular, and to us peculiar, lifestyle. It may be the surgeon's best contribution to restore the vagabond to his chosen environment rather than to venture into 'do gooder' activities.

Psychiatric illness

This results in surgery in many, often bizarre, ways (Tsuang and Woolson, 1977; O'Shea *et al.*, 1984). Those who are disturbed may swallow knives and razor blades and bury needles in themselves. The depressed attempt suicide by jumping from a height. The schizophrenic directed by his voices is liable to try almost anything. Such disturbed people are difficult and challenging to look after, perhaps most of all when they incidentally develop a surgical condition such as appendicitis or intestinal obstruction. Then their complaints may be minimal, or difficult to interpret in the context of their other problems. Likewise physical signs can be misleadingly slight. Once a surgical condition is diagnosed, consent to treatment may not be forthcoming, and the surgeon is faced with the difficult decision as to whether surgery must be embarked upon without the patient's consent.

Conversely, the 'odd' patient who mimics surgical disease in the absence of physical disorder must be recognized as such, and extensive investigations and treatment—which have the effect of ever more focusing the patient's attention on the possibility of a physical problem—avoided (Dudley, 1973). The subject is a large, complicated and important one beyond the scope of this essay (Bayliss, 1984). In conditions in which psychologically based complaints (which are not, in the long term, improved by surgery) are difficult to distinguish from those caused by surgically treatable physical disease, e.g. low back pain, psychological testing may help to determine who is more likely to benefit from surgery (Oostdam and Duivenvoorden, 1983).

Occupation

The influence of occupation on the chance of needing surgical attention ranges from the obvious to the very subtle. Butchers cut their hands; dispatch riders break their legs; taxi drivers develop pilonidal sinuses; bus drivers get more coronary artery disease than conductors; cabinet makers develop nasopharyngeal carcinoma and rubber workers risk bladder cancer. The list is endless.

Less predictable, and as yet very ill-understood, are the more subtle apparent influences of personality itself on the development of disease, particularly malignant disease. It seems, for example, that breast cancer is correlated with habitual suppression of anger (*Lancet* editorial, 1979a); smokers who develop lung cancer tend to deny and repress emotions and are less self-assertive than other smokers. Thus, other things being equal, some character types may be more likely to develop cancer than others.

PSYCHOSOCIAL INFLUENCES ON MANAGEMENT

General

These are often concealed and they may be so inconspicuously woven into the pattern of ordinary management that one could carry on without being consciously aware of their importance. It is not, in our view, possible to function properly as a surgeon without taking notice of the domestic, work and psychological background of a patient (Dudley and Masterton, 1967). There is no point in instructing a young, breastfeeding mother to come into hospital to have a lump removed next week if she cannot bring her baby with her. It is impossible for an elderly man to have his hernia repaired as a day case if there is no one to collect him at the end of the day, take him home and keep an eye on him. If it is planned that someone should have elective surgery, they may be offered a bed on a particular day, but it may well only be a provisional offer, to be withdrawn if an emergency admission has occurred. It is remarkable how many patients can cope with such uncertainty; however, there is a minority which must be recognized, who need to organize child care, to make arrangements for older dependent relatives or secure locum cover at work. Financial difficulties, such as unemployment, or loss of earnings in the self-employed, will also demand individual solutions. Psychiatric patients and the elderly may need to be admitted well before the operation to give them time to acclimatize; also they commonly need more support throughout both operation and convalescence. Some drugs should be stopped if possible well in advance of an operation under general anaesthetic; the oral contraceptive pill and one type of antidepressant are common examples. All this must be anticipated for treatment to run smoothly.

Having said this, the surgeon must focus on his part of the presenting problem. He must have a clear idea in his own mind what the correct treatment for any given condition should be. It is not in his patient's interests for him to get too sidetracked. It is better to say: the patient has a condition for which a certain treatment—be it curative or palliative—is appropriate; how, if at all, do age, social circumstance or any of a multitude of factors modify our approach (Dudley, 1984)? Equally, the nervous old lady with breast cancer who abhors the idea of an operation should not have her opinion immediately dismissed by her surgeon. His duty is to present to her the management plan that he thinks is objectively preferable and then to open negotiations with her. In this context it is right for him to use, with discretion, his status and authority to help persuade a patient to accept the best option available, because these two characteristics are based on his special training and experience.

There is occasionally an opportunity to improve psychosocial outcome after surgery by modifying the planned surgical treatment. Such a case might be immediate surgical reconstruction of the breast after mastectomy. Dean, Chetty and Forrest (1983) have shown that although this did not alter the outcome (in terms of psychiatric morbidity) for stable women in happy relationships, it went some way to prevent further deterioration where there were preexisting marital or sexual problems.

Whether privately or publicly funded, there are always financial limits on health care. There are always finite numbers of hospital beds, operating theatres, surgeons, anaesthetists, and the large numbers of other staff required for surgery to take place (Whitehorn, 1983). When treatment is particularly expensive, or facilities particularly restricted, surgeons sometimes have to decide who will be treated and who will not. Currently those working on the British kidney transplant programme, and those who perform coronary artery bypass surgery for ischaemic heart disease, are in this unenviable situation. The problem is to choose who, of a group of people equally ill, will not be treated and perhaps die as a result. The decision is made chiefly on the basis of age, work potential, presence or absence of concomitant disease, and psychological stability.

The results of surgery

It is obvious that in the complex circumstances of surgery, the inability of a patient to cooperate with treatment, or his frank resistance to it, may cause failure. For example, in a small study of patients having heart surgery it was found that those who were most mentally disturbed nearly always died while those with a 'psychiatric diagnosis' suffered more postoperative complications, independent of their physical health (Rubinstein and Thomas, 1969). The same may, to a lesser degree, be true of patients with slighter mental problems.

Less clear, but still of significance, is the possibility of the patient's social or psychological position truly influencing outcome through a mind–body reaction. In the short term, Eisendrath (1969) reported that eight out of eleven patients who died following renal transplantation had been abandoned by an important family member or had expressed panic or extreme pessimism about the outcome. Others have shown that preoperative depression, previous poor coping and lack of family support adversely affect the mortality and morbidity of surgery (Kimball, 1969). In the long term (perhaps through an influence on the immune system—Greer, 1979), it is known that the 'negative stoic' and the depressed 'giving up–giving in' woman suffering from breast cancer does worse (irrespective of the clinical stage of the disease) than she who either denies strongly or exhibits a 'fighting spirit' (Greer, Morris and Pettingale, 1979). It is our increasing belief that psychological 'set' plays an important part in determining life and death. On the patient's side anger, depression and uncontrolled fear seem to us to increase mortality and morbidity, whereas calmness, ebullience short of mania, and faith in the surgical team are all associated with a good outcome. On the surgeon's part his ability to condition the latter attitudes in his patients by his own behaviour may well be an important factor. The healing environment so produced may on the one hand be enhanced by good physical circumstances which exclude the disadvantageous factors to which we have already referred, and may on the other hand include analogies of recovery such as growing plants and blooming flowers. Perhaps with our mechanistic, science-driven imperatives (Dudley, 1983) we have undervalued the contribution that can be made by such apparently immaterial things.

We should not underplay an individual's right to self-determination. Elderly people seem to be able to choose when to die, giving up when their spouse dies (Rees and Lutkins, 1967), or after a birthday or Christmas.

He first deceas'd; she for a little tri'd
To live without him; lik'd it not, and di'd.
(Sir Henry Wotton, 1568–1639)

In our own surgical profession, Lord Moynihan, previously in fair health, put his affairs in order and quitted this life less than a week after his wife's death (Franklin, 1967).

ENVOI

Let us end with Theodore Fox's description of a doctor (Fox, 1965) for this is central to the role of the surgeon in relation to the patient as a human being:

It is not true that the doctor is simply a man among men: when his patients turn to him in affliction he becomes something more. With all its faults the profession to which he belongs is not a body of technologists interested solely in the means by which physical or mental processes can be restored to normal: it is a body seeking to use these means to an end—to help patients to cope with their lives. To this end they must keep their heads and sense of proportion, when other people are losing theirs and hence must not let intelligence and technical skill be overthrown by emotion.

He went on to say: 'Knowledge, skill, empathy, equanimity, perspective—each can be futile without the other. Often technical excellence matters most; for unless a patient survives, he will himself gain nothing from the other qualities of his doctor.'

The surgeon is in the business of securing survival through technical excellence. Should he achieve this—and it must not be forgotten that he often does—then he has a further duty to recognize his wider functions which we have endeavoured to describe in this contribution.

REFERENCES

Balint, M. (1964). *The Doctor, his Patient and the Illness*. Tunbridge Wells: Pitman Medical.

Bayliss, R. I. S. (1984). The deceivers. *British Medical Journal*, 1, 583–584.

Bentley, S., Murphy, F., and Dudley, H. A. F. (1977). An objective analysis of the noise background to surgical care. S.R.S. abstract. *British Journal of Surgery*, 64, 822.

Bernstein, N. R. (1976). *Emotional Care of the Facially Burned and Disfigured*. Boston: Little, Brown & Co.

Bosk, C. L. (1979). *Forgive and Remember. Managing Medical Failure*. Chicago: Chicago University Press.

Cooper, A. F., McArdle, C. S., Russell, A. R., and Smith, D. C. (1979). Psychiatric morbidity associated with adjuvant chemotherapy following mastectomy for breast cancer. S.R.S. abstract. *British Journal of Surgery*, 66, 362.

Dean, C., Chetty, K., and Forrest, A. P. M. (1983). Effects of immediate breast reconstruction on psychosocial morbidity after mastectomy. *Lancet*, 1, 459–462.

Devlin, H. B. (1983). Psychological and social aspects of stoma care. In *Stoma Therapy Review*, Part 4. Huntingdon: Coloplast. pp. 29–36.

Dlin, B. M., Perlman, A., and Ringold, E. (1969). Psychosexual response to ileostomy and colostomy. *American Journal of Psychiatry*, 126, 374–381.

Dudley, H. A. F. (1973). Odd patients. *New Society*, 25, 330–332.

Dudley, H. A. F. (1975). Affective disturbances in patients in intensive care. In W. F. Walker and D. R. M. Taylor (eds), *Intensive Care* Edinburgh: Churchill Livingstone.

Dudley, H. A. F. (1983). The controlled clinical trial and the advance of reliable knowledge; an outsider looks in. *British Medical Journal*, **287**, 957–960.

Dudley, H. A. F. (1984). Surgery in the elderly: take every case as it comes. *Geriatric Medicine*, **14**, 9–10.

Dudley, H. A. F., and Masterton, J. P. (1967). Social case conference in general surgery. *British Journal of Medical Education*, **1**, 127–130.

Eisendrath, R. M. (1969). The role of grief and fear in the death of kidney transplant patients. *American Journal of Psychiatry*, **126**, 381–387.

Ellis, B. W., Hoggart, B., Withey, J., Donaghue, K., and Jones, J. (1979). What patients recall of an intensive care unit. S.R.S. abstract. *British Journal of Surgery*, **66**, 358–359.

Elsass, P., Stibolt, O., Klauber, P. V., Christensen, S.-E., and Lunding, M. (1982). A clinical neuropsychological study of the postoperative course after three types of anaesthesia. *Acta Anaesthesiologica Scandinavica*, **26**, 151–155.

Epstein, B. S. (1975). Recovery from anaesthesia. (Editorial.) *Anaesthetist*, **43**, 285–288.

Fox, T. (1965). Purposes of medicine. *Lancet*, **ii**, 801–805.

Franklin, A. W. (1967). Lord Moynihan: a short biography. In *Selected Writings of Lord Moynihan*. Tunbridge Wells: Pitman Medical.

Gallon, A. M. (1982). Epidural anaesthesia for thoracotomy patients. *Physiotherapy*, **68**, 193.

Greer, S. (1979). Psychological enquiry: a contribution to cancer research. *Psychological Medicine*, **9**, 81–89.

Greer, S., Morris, T., and Pettingale, K. W. (1979). Psychological response to breast cancer: effect on outcome. *Lancet*, **ii**, 785–787.

Henriksen, L. (1984). Evidence suggestive of diffuse brain damage following cardic operations. *Lancet*, **i**, 816–820.

Johns, M. W., Dudley, H. A. F., and Masterton, J. P. (1973). Psychosocial problems in surgery. *Journal of the Royal College of Surgeons of Edinburgh*, **18**, 91–102.

Johnston, M. (1976). Communication of patient's feelings in hospital. In A. E. Bennett (ed.), *Communication between Doctors and Patients*. Published for The Nuffield Provincial Hospitals Trust by Oxford University Press, pp. 29–43.

Kimball, C. P. (1969). Psychological responses to the experience of open heart surgery. *American Journal of Psychiatry*, **126**, 348–359.

Korttila, K. (1981). Recovery and driving after brief anaesthesia. *Anaesthetist*, **30**, 377–382.

Kripke, B. J., Justice, R. E., and Hechtman, H. B. (1983). Post-operative nitrous oxide analgesia and the functional residual capacity. *Critical Care Medicine*, **11**, 105–109.

Lancet editorial (1979a). Mind and cancer. *Lancet*, **i**, 706–707.

Lancet editorial (1979b). Does unemployment kill? *Lancet*, **i**, 708–709.

Moreland, C. (1982). Disabilities and how to live with them. Teratoma of the testis. *Lancet*, **ii**, 203–205.

Naysmith, A., Hinton, J. M., Meredith, R., Marks, M. D., and Terry, R. J. (1983). Surviving malignant disease. Psychological and family aspects. *British Journal of Hospital Medicine*, **30**, 22–27.

Neal, D. E. (1984). The effects on pelvic visceral function of anal sphincter ablating and sphincter preserving operations for cancer of the lower part of the rectum and for benign colo-rectal disease. *Annals of the Royal College of Surgeons of England*, **66**, 7–13.

Oostdam, E. M. M., and Duivenvoorden, H. J. (1983). Predictability of the result of surgical intervention in patients with low back pain. *Journal of Psychosomatic Research*, **27**, 273–281.

O'Shea, B., McGennis, A., Falvey, J., and Cahill, M. (1984). Munchausen's syndrome. *British Journal of Hospital Medicine*, **31**, 269–274.

Parkes, C. M. (1972). *Bereavement—Studies of Grief in Adult Life*. Harmondsworth, Middx: Pelican.

Pearson, J., and Dudley, H. A. F. (1982). Bodily perceptions in surgical patients. *British Medical Journal*, **284**, 1545–1546.

Rawal, N., Sjostrand, U. H., Dahlstrom, B., Nydahl, P.-A., and Ostelius, J. (1982). Epidural morphine for postoperative pain relief: a comparative study with intramuscular narcotic and intercostal nerve block. *Anesthesia and Analgesia*, **61**, 93–98.

Ray, C., Fisher, J., and Lindop, J. (in press). The surgeon–patient relationship in the context of breast cancer. *International Review of Applied Psychololgy: Psychology of Serious Illness*.

Reading, A. E. (1979). The short term effects of psychological preparation for surgery. *Social Science and Medicine*, **13A**, 641–654.

Rees, W. D., and Lutkins, S. G. (1967). Mortality of bereavement. *British Medical Journal*, **4**, 13–16.

Reiz, S., Ahlin, J., Ahrenfeldt, B., Andersson, M., and Andersson, S. (1981). Epidural morphine for postoperative pain relief. *Acta Anaesthesiologica Scandinavica*, **25**, 111–114.

Rubinstein, D., and Thomas, J. K. (1969). Psychiatric findings in cardiotomy patients. *American Journal of Psychiatry*, **126**, 360–369.

Rutter, P. C., Murphy, F., and Dudley, H. A. F. (1980). Morphine: controlled trial of different methods of administration for post-operative pain relief. *British Medical Journal*, **1**, 12–13.

St Haxholdt, O., and Johansson, G. (1982). The alcoholic patient and surgical stress. *Anaesthesia*, **37**, 797–801.

Schroeder, H. G. (1971). Psycho-reactive problems of intensive therapy. *Anaesthesia*, **26**, 28–35.

Solzhenitsyn, A. (1969). *Cancer Ward* (N. Bethell and D. Burg, trans.). London: The Bodley Head.

Spencer Jones, J. (1981). Telling the right patient. *British Medical Journal*, **283**, 291–292.

Taylor, A. G., West, B. A., Simon, B., Skelton, J., and Rowlingson, J. C. (1983). How effective is TENS for acute pain? *American Journal of Nursing*, **83**, 1171–1174.

Tsuang, M. T., and Woolson, R. F. (1977). Mortality in patients with schizophrenia, mania, depression and surgical conditions. *British Journal of Psychiatry*, **130**, 162–166.

Whitehorn, K. (1983). When the doctoring has to stop. *Observer*. **6 November**, 25–26.

Witzel, L. (1975). Behaviour of the dying patient. *British Medical Journal*, **2**, 81–82.

The Psychosomatic Approach: Contemporary Practice
  of Whole-person Care
Edited by M. J. Christie and P. G. Mellett
© 1986 John Wiley & Sons Ltd

18

PSYCHOSOMATIC ASPECTS OF CANCER

BASIL A. STOLL

St Thomas' Hospital and Royal Free Hospital, London, UK

INTRODUCTION

Can psychosomatic factors lead to differences between indiviuals in the physical course of cancer? In the past 30 years, some have suggested a possible influence of psychosocial factors on the growth of cancer, and even that the cancer patient can contribute to his or her physical rehabilitation. While no firm conclusions can be reached on these questions, this chapter will review the newly developing evidence that the body is able to modulate the growth of many cancers (Stoll, 1982). Based on this knowledge, we can discuss a possible role for psychosomatic influences in the modulation of cancer growth activity.

The usual format of a scientific presentation is not possible for this topic because our knowledge is too fragmentary; but we can examine the available evidence and then formulate questions, hypotheses and experimental approaches. The review will consider possible interactions between mind and cancer under the following headings:

—Psychosocial factors and the development of cancer
—Psychological profiles and cancer prognosis
—Cancer modulation by the host
—Postulated psychosomatic mechanisms

PSYCHOSOCIAL FACTORS AND THE DEVELOPMENT OF CANCER

Any attempt to review the possible effects of mental and emotional factors on the initiation and growth of cancer must be in the perspective of the biological mechanisms which are known to be involved in the majority of cancers. These include, in most cases, a complex interaction of multiple factors over many years. To postulate a 'cause' for a patient's cancer would therefore be grossly simplistic.

In infant malignancy, hereditary or familial factors are predominant, but in most adult tumours, hereditary factors merely increase susceptibility to environmental factors capable of exerting an *initiating* action on the genes of body cells. These changes may then lie latent for a period of between 10 and 30 years until further *promoting* action from environmental factors finally triggers off the change to clinical cancer.

In this context, the term 'environment' includes both external and internal factors. It applies not only to physical and chemical carcinogenic agents, but also to the influence of habits, diet and co-carcinogens (e.g. alcohol or tobacco) on various organs. Initiating or promoting action may result also from the hormonal changes of adolescence, sexual activity, childbearing, breastfeeding, etc. The clinical presentation of a cancer is, therefore, the culmination of a series of carcinogenic and co-carcinogenic factors over a period of many years, and it is now recognized that it is only in the very late stages that the changes become irreversible.

Hormonal influences are thought to be involved in a high proportion of common tumours, including cancers of the breast, uterus, ovary, testis, prostate, liver, thyroid, colon, pancreas, salivary glands and malignant melanoma (Berenblum, 1984). In their promoting action, hormones may either influence the activities or the metabolism of carcinogens, or else they may influence the activities of the cell nucleus which control cell growth and invasiveness.

The frequency of cancer rises with increasing age. This is presumed to be associated with increasing numbers of chromosomal changes due to extended exposure to environmental influences, and also with increasing premalignant and degenerative changes in the tissues. Increasing age is also accompanied by marked changes in most hormonal secretions and decreased activity of the immune system. Recognition of age-related changes of this type has led to false conclusions as to cause and effect. For example, an association has been noted between the presence of breast cancer and depressive illness in middle age, but one is not necessarily the cause of the other. They may both be triggered by age-related changes in brain catecholamine levels (Stoll, 1981).

To discuss the role of possible psychosomatic factors in the development of cancer we need to define the variables involved. Psychosocial or stress factors which may be important include the personality of the patient and life events with high emotional arousal. The degree of a person's emotional reaction to stress may be a genetically determined personality characteristic or it may be a learned attitude, and the distinction may or may not be relevant to this inquiry.

Personality may play a role in the development of cancer either by involving the individual in excessive exposure to a co-carcinogen (e.g. tobacco or alcohol) or by causing changes in the body's internal environment which might predispose to cancer (e.g. hormonal changes). In this connection, it should be stressed that a change in the circulating level of cortisol is only one of many possible stress-induced hormonal changes (see discussion later).

Cancer predisposition

The medical literature of the 1950s and 1960s contained many psychodynamic papers describing cancer almost as a psychosomatic disease, precipitated by psychological disturbance or emotional stress. They suggested that cancer patients might be responsible for causing their own illness, a suggestion which might add an intolerable sense of guilt to an already overburdened cancer patient. The psychodynamic literature further suggested that the site selected by cancer might be favoured by psychophysiological factors (Bahnson, 1969). Thus, for example, sexual or emotional conflicts might lead to cancers of the breast or uterus.

It is, however, possible that a patient's cancer and psychological disturbance have a common cause. For example, epidemiological evidence shows that cancer of the uterine cervix is relatively more common in women beginning sexual activity at an early age, while breast cancer is relatively more common in women who have not borne children or else have not lactated adequately. Psychoanalysis of such patients is claimed to have shown greater evidence of genital conflicts in patients with cervical cancer, and frustrated maternal feelings in breast cancer patients (Tarlou and Smallheiser, 1951; Booth, 1969). In this connection, Reznikoff (1955) reported that women with breast cancer showed an abnormally high proportion with disturbance of feminine identification, and suggested that such psychological disturbance might be associated with hormonal disturbance.

Apart from assuming a cause and effect relationship, these early studies were not carefully designed and most had either no control group or else inadequately matched controls. They were also retrospective and thus ignored the effect that having cancer might have on a patient's answer to questions, in assuming them to be the same answers that the patient would have given before the disease developed.

Another approach has been an inquiry into the relationship of traumatic life events to the subsequent appearance of cancer. Several authors have noted that loss of an emotionally close relationship might be related to the subsequent finding of cancer (Le Shan, 1959; Greene, 1966; Becker, 1979). However, Muslin, Gyanfas and Pieper (1966) could find no relationship between such losses and the onset of breast cancer, nor could Grissom, Wiener and Wiener (1975) in the case of lung cancer patients.

With regard to the correlation between other socially traumatic life events and the appearance of cancer, no significant findings have been reported for breast cancer (Snell and Graham, 1971; Schonfield, 1975). They have, however, been reported for lung cancer (Horne and Picard, 1979) and for childhood cancer (Jacobs and Charles, 1980).

The significance of life events in cancer induction is hard to assess. The initiation of most cancers occurs 10–30 years before diagnosis and thus a recent life event could be only one of multiple promotion factors involved in triggering the appearance of the tumour. However, every individual has his own stress threshold for a given life event. It is interesting that in the case of cancer, more significance has been attached to depression following loss of an emotionally close relationship, whereas in the case of cardiovascular disease, association is claimed with chronic anger and irritation due to frustration (e.g. a way of life associated with stress and insecurity).

Life events have also been implicated in the reactivation of cancer after many years of dormancy. There have been several such anecdotal reports (Ogilvie, 1957), but no statistical evaluation of their significance. Physicians would tend to remember those patients who reported reactivation of long dormant cancer shortly after a bereavement, while ignoring the very much larger number of cases where no such life event was mentioned.

Depression or anxiety have been suggested as possible antecedents of the appearance of cancer. Of 28 men suffering from depression, 5 died from cancer over the subsequent 4 years (Kerr, Shapira and Roth, 1969). Shekelle et al., (1981) assessed 2000 men by the Minnesota Multiphasic Personality Inventory (MMPI) and followed their medical records for 17 years. Deaths from cancer were twice as high in individuals assessed as depressed as they were in individuals who were not depressed. In a small series, Greenberg and Dattore (1981) compared baseline MMPI profiles of Veterans Hospital patients who subsequently developed cancer with those who did not. The former group showed a significantly greater degree of dependency in their baseline psychological assessment.

On the other hand, Watson and Schuld (1977) found no difference in MMPI profiles between a small group of neuropsychiatric patients who subsequently developed cancer and those who did not. Again, Keehn, Goldberg and Beebe (1974) followed up 10 000 men for 24 years after they had been diagnosed as psychoneurotic. No increased mortality from cancer was found when this group was compared to a control group.

It must be stressed that symptoms of depression are recognized to be an early manifestation of some types of cancer, and are found in as many as 76 per cent of patients with pancreatic cancer (Fras, Litin and Pearson, 1967). Depression may even be manifest before the local tumour. Its cause is uncertain, but Brown and Paraskevas (1982) recently suggested that cancer cells can stimulate production of an antibody which could block serotonin receptors in the brain and lead to the symptoms of depression.

Thus, depression and anxiety are unlikely to be triggering factors for cancer, especially if they precede the appearance of the tumour by only a few months. With regard to the role of psychosis, Freeman (1928) reported cancer to be relatively less common in patients with a history of schizophrenia. Bahnson and Bahnson (1964) suggested that this might result from the patients having withdrawn themselves from environmental stresses at an early age. Scurry and Levin (1978) have commented on the paradox of an apparently lower cancer mortality in schizophrenics but an apparently increased cancer mortality among depressives.

Several prospective studies have attempted to correlate personality with the risk of developing cancer. Coppen and Metcalfe (1963) compared a group of patients with breast cancer with another group suffering from benign gynaecological disease and found a higher incidence of extraversion (but not neuroticism) among the cancer patients. Hagnell (1966) examined personality characteristics in a Scandinavian community and found among those who subsequently developed cancer a higher proportion with substability and withdrawal tendencies when depressed. Kissen (1966) carried out a psychological study of patients with lung disease prior to diagnosis of cancer and suggested that the lower neuroticism scores he found in cancer patients were evidence of poor emotional outlets in childhood. Morris et al., (1981) have noted lower neuroticism scores among breast cancer patients also.

Greer and Morris (1975) reported studies of women prior to biopsy of a breast lump and found that those proving to have cancer showed a very significantly higher proportion who suppressed anger and other emotions. Thomas, Duszynski and Schaffer (1979) reported a 20–30-year follow-up of 1337 medical students at Johns Hopkins University and found that those who subsequently developed cancer had originally shown less closeness to their parents and more controlled emotions. Grossarth-Maticek (1980) has reported a prospective study on the population of a Yugoslav village and concluded that the subsequent development of cancer was significantly correlated with a finding of depression and helplessness at the baseline psychological examination.

Experimental evidence

In experimental animals, it has been reported that shielding mice from noise and other stress causes the incidence of cancer to fall significantly (Riley, 1975). Early separation of infant animals from their mothers increases their predisposition to chemically-induced cancer, as does also overcrowding, isolation and sex segregation in adult animals (Rasmussen, 1969). However, the effect of stress on cancer induction, as reported in a large literature, differs according to the type of tumour, the type of stress and the species of animal. In a review attempting to clarify the conflicting reports, Sklar and Anisman (1981) concluded that acute *physical* stress in animals tends to increase cancer growth, while chronic stress tends to decrease tumour growth rate. Visintainer, Seligman and Volpicelli (1983) suggest that *social* stress in animals, whether acute or chronic, tends to increase tumour growth.

There is, however, clear evidence that the administration of stress hormones (whether cortisone or adrenaline) also accelerates the development of secondary deposits in cancer-bearing animals (Van den Brenk et al., 1976; Peters and Kelly, 1977). Thus, tumour cells disseminated prior to, or at the time of, diagnosis and treatment will be stimulated to develop into established metastases (Peters and Mason, 1979).

PSYCHOLOGICAL PROFILES AND CANCER PROGNOSIS

The previous discussion suggests that the multiple promotion factors involved in triggering off cancer make it unlikely that we will find evidence which will clearly correlate personality or temperament with the *risk* of developing cancer. A more fruitful line of inquiry may be to relate psychological factors to the rate at which the disease progresses and to the duration of the patient's survival. In the case of late cancer, we can examine whether the 'will to live' or its absence can influence duration of survival, irrespective of whether it is by an effect on cancer growth or by other mechanisms. In the case of early cancer, we can inquire whether psychosomatic factors can influence the growth rate of the tumour and consequent duration of survival.

The will to live

The will to live is important in any patient with a serious disease. Practically all clinicians would agree that in the late stages of cancer the patient who 'gives up' will shorten life expectancy, sometimes dramatically. Most clinicians have noted also the converse—that some patients who 'fight back' seem to survive longer than would be expected. There might, however, be considerable differences of opinion as to whether this possible extension of life is a matter of days, weeks or months.

Most of the evidence is anecdotal because neither variable can be measured with confidence. The individual patient's expected duration of survival cannot be predicted with any accuracy, and it is even more difficult to measure a quality such as the will to live. Nevertheless, there is no doubt that emotional factors can affect the physical condition of the cancer patient at every stage in the disease.

Thus, at the time of primary treatment of even early cancer, anxiety or depression will delay return to normal activity and the patient will require considerable psychological support to speed recovery. In late cancer, absence of the will to live may shorten life expectation. It is not uncommon to see patients tire of fighting back, turn their faces to the wall and die within a few days, although death might not normally have been expected for months. Premature death of this type can, of course, apply to any serious disease, and it has been reported that apathetic, depressed patients are less likely to survive major surgery, strokes or heart attacks (Morgan, 1971).

How does one die of apathy? It is only partly related to the effect of loss of appetite, starvation and physical inanition, and it is widely believed, but not proven, that inhibition of the vagus nerve deals the final blow in such cases. Apprehensiveness, in addition to apathy, can affect recovery from illness, and most surgeons would think twice before operating on a patient who has expressed profound fears that he will not survive the operation. The will to recover is affected. This is especially common in elderly patients who may lose interest in life when confronted with a diagnosis of inoperable cancer.

It is also well recognized by life insurance companies that widows and widowers have a much increased risk of dying in the first 12 months after bereavement. Parkes, Benjamin and Fitzgerald (1969) reported that deaths from heart attacks or strokes were the most prominent in the bereaved group, but that, in addition, deaths certified as from cancer were increased, although to a lesser extent.

On the other hand, survival may be unexpectedly prolonged in the patient with advanced cancer. It is possible for new hopes of recovery to cause dramatic subjective improvement associated with increase in appetite and weight and increased physical strength. This is certainly the basis for many claims of recovery made for unproven remedies in cancer patients. In the absence of invasion of a vital structure, such a placebo effect could prolong the duration of life by days or weeks and this could extend to months in the case of a slowly growing tumour.

Psychological coping strategy and cancer prognosis

We have dealt up to this point with anecdotal observations on advanced cases, but in the vast majority of earlier cases, the inevitable progress of highly malignant tumours seems to be little affected by the patient's will to live or lack of it. There is, however, a widespread impression among clinicians expressed in the opinion that 'patients who are apprehensive about their disease usually do poorly' (Miller, 1977). It suggests that anxiety and depression may accelerate the rate of cancer growth.

Several retrospective and prospective studies in the last 30 years have reported attempts to correlate the psychological characteristics of cancer patients with their duration of survival. The general consensus is that cancer patients who are able to show their emotions, particularly anger or anxiety, are likely to survive longer. Thus, one of the earliest retrospective studies (Bacon, Ronneker and Cutler, 1952) reported that rapid progression of cancer was more common in the polite and outwardly acquiescent patient, while patients who expressed their feelings openly tended to have a better prognosis.

Blumberg, West and Ellis (1954) compared the personality characteristics of advanced cancer patients showing rapidly growing tumours, with those of patients whose period of survival was longer than expected in that it exceeded by more than 50 per cent the mean expected survival for that type of cancer. Using the MMPI, they found that the patients with rapidly growing disease differed significantly from the other group in showing higher defensiveness, a greater degree of unrelieved depression or anxiety and a lesser ability to relieve tension by positive action. Those patients with slower progression of the disease had either a normal MMPI profile or escaped stress by neurosis or regression. The investigators concluded that inability to resolve emotional problems by the expression of emotion might lead to a shorter expectation of life in cancer patients.

On the other hand, in a group of patients with malignant melanoma, Krasnoff (1959) was unable to confirm Blumberg's findings and showed no difference in personality tests (including MMPI) between those with rapid growth and those with slow progression. Shrite (1962) examined a group of patients who had been treated for cancer of the uterine cervix, and found that those patients with persistent disease 2 years after treatment showed less ability to 'communicate' than those who were free of disease.

Stavraky et al., (1968) studied a large group of patients with various types of cancer and, using the MMPI and other tests, compared patients with the highest survival times with stage-matched controls who had only an average length of survival. Patients in the long survival group more frequently exhibited aggressive drives and an ability to retain emotional control. Similar observations were subsequently made by Davies et al., (1973). In a group of patients with advanced cancer, assessment was made of the patients' mood, attitude, defence mechanisms, degree of distress and coping ability. It was found that those patients with an apathetic, depressed attitude were more likely to have a shorter survival time. Rogentine et al., (1979) noted in malignant melanoma patients that those who recognized the need for a coping reaction survived longer than those who did not.

The weakness of retrospective studies is that the patient's memory may help to accommodate an interviewer's suggestion. For example, in a study of psychological characteristics of patients with remarkably long survival after a diagnosis of advanced cancer (Kennedy et al., 1976), it was concluded that 'most of the patients . . . were confident from the beginning of recovery'. Again, Le Shan (1959) reported that 77 per cent of cancer patients had lost a major relationship between 6 months and 8 years before diagnosis compared to only 14 per cent of controls. Such a finding might result from prompting cancer patients to find an explanation for their disease.

Among the prospective studies, Weisman (1976) reported on 163 patients with various types of cancer followed up from the time of diagnosis by a series of psychological assessments. The long-term survivors were found to have coped better with their problems, maintained good personal relationships, regarded their doctors as helpful and complained less. Those patients showing depression, passivity and apathy survived for shorter periods. Derogatis, Abeloff and Meliseratos (1979) reported that in 35 women with advanced breast cancer, those patients who died earlier were distinctly less able to communicate feelings of anger or hostility. This study has been criticized on the basis that this latter group had patients with more aggressive disease and were given more aggressive chemotherapy.

Greer, Morris and Pettingale (1979) have reported the results of a prospective 5-year study of 69 patients with operable breast cancer. The patient's psychological response to the diagnosis of cancer was assessed 3 months postoperatively and this was then related to outcome 5 years later. Recurrence-free survival was found to be significantly more common among patients who had initially reacted to their cancer by denial or a fighting spirit, than among those who had responded by stoic acceptance or a feeling of helplessness or hopelessness. The 5-year survival rate was 75 per cent in the first group compared to 35 per cent in the second group ($p < 0.03$).

Critical review of apparent correlation

Several criticisms can, of course, be made of the conclusions in the studies referred to above. The independent variable is the psychological make-up of the patient and this has so many facets that it is difficult to measure in a valid manner. Psychological testing is highly subjective and prone to observer bias and error. Even standard methods of assessing personality (such as the MMPI) have the disadvantage common to all self-rating scales that socially acceptable answers tend to be provided by the subject. For example, a patient who considers himself a 'fighter' might be assessed as passive by a trained observer.

The dependent variable similarly presents problems in assessment. Most studies have used length of survival as the end-point to be measured in each group, but the groups are markedly heterogeneous. The physician can assess only overt and not occult spread of disease and the latter may affect mood. Moreover, the individual treatment given to each patient will influence length of survival and, in any case, some patients die with, and not of, their disease. If patient groups are to be compared in order to evaluate the effect of psychological factors, it is unacceptable to assume that the rate of growth and stage of the disease are uniform for all patients in a group. It is essential to match groups to be compared by age, sex, stage of disease, type of metastasis, rate of tumour growth, etc.

It is remarkable that most reports mentioned above agree on one consistent relationship—those cancer patients who are withdrawn, apathetic, depressed or hopeless have a shorter expectation of survival. Although most reports are of relatively small series of patients, a number of independent observers seem to have arrived at similar conclusions about the prognostic significance of the patient's psychological coping strategy.

This consensus of findings has been widely interpreted as suggesting that the personality of the patient and his coping strategy are factors which may influence tumour growth. But an alternative explanation is that the higher degree of apathy and depression evident in patients with poorer prognosis is a *result* of the more advanced physical disease at the time of testing. All clinicians agree that the presence of advanced cancer is often associated with these symptoms even in the absence of brain metastases. In the series mentioned above (Davies *et al.*, 1973) where apathetic, depressed cancer patients were found to have a shorter survival time, the writers comment that these patients also showed more advanced disease at the time of examination. They suggest that the patient's mental attitude may have resulted from that.

TABLE 18.1   Prognosis in 250 consecutive breast cancer patients in relation to
regular use of tranquillizers in the 10 years before mastectomy (Stoll, 1976a)

Of those cases who showed:	Percentage on tranquillizers	
Metastases at presentation or recurrence before 12 months	22	
Recurrence after 12 months	16	
Recurrence-free 1 to 5 years	15	$p < 0.03$
Recurrence-free over 5 years	8	

Such an influence may explain (at least in part) the results of the investigation of Weisman (1976) on coping strategies. It was found that patients
with advanced cancer who were able to maintain their personal relationships
had a significantly longer average survival than those who showed anxiety,
withdrawal or depression. This observation does not necessarily prove that
mood is a factor influencing growth of breast cancer in the individual. It is
possible that the emotional reaction may result from the presence of large
overt or unsuspected tumour deposits in the body, which would, of course,
be associated with a poorer prognosis.

This difficulty in interpretation led me to investigate 250 consecutive breast
cancer patients, using a different approach (Stoll, 1976a). The stage of the
tumour at presentation and its subsequent behaviour were related to the
record of the patient's mood disturbance over a period of 10 years prior to
the diagnosis of cancer. This retrospective survey inquired about the use of
psychotropic drugs for a prolonged period during that time. It was found
that patients with a history of regular use of tranquillizers during the 10 years
before mastectomy were significantly more prominent among those with early
recurrence of disease than among those remaining recurrence-free for 5 years
or more (see Table 18.1).

There are alternative explanations also for this observation: mood disturbance might stimulate tumour growth; tranquillizers might stimulate tumour
growth; mood disturbance might be evidence of more extensive occult cancer;
or an overanxious patient might delay seeking treatment for a breast lump.
A recent paper by Funch and Marshall (1983) noted that the emotional
stresses experienced by a group of patients in the 5 years prior to diagnosis
of breast cancer were related to their subsequent length of survival. However,
retrospective self-reports of this type may be influenced by mood change due
to the presence of more extensive occult disease.

To sum up this section, there is some evidence of a relationship between
personality, mood and prognosis in the cancer patient. A major problem in
confirming it is the difficulty of defining the two variables. Even when similar
types of assessment have been carried out (e.g. MMPI, Eysenck Personality

Inventory) results have varied, although some of these variations may be due to differences in the types of cancer included in relatively small series. Because of the increased number of biological influences on the tumour in older people, one might expect psychosocial factors to show a more obvious influence in *younger* patients, and this is indeed claimed in some series (Bacon, Ronneker and Cutler, 1952; Becker, 1979; Funch and Marshall, 1983).

CANCER MODULATION BY THE HOST

Before we speculate further on the role of psychosomatic influences on the growth of cancer, it is important to examine recent evidence that the body is not merely a passive host to cancer. The tissues react specifically to the threat of cancer growth and spread, and sometimes modulate its course. In the past, it was assumed that such reactions were mainly immunological, but recent research shows that local hormonal and enzymic growth factors are likely to be involved (Stoll, 1982). It has been shown that the relationship between malignant cells and their environment is an equilibrium which is readily disturbed, and that even reversion from a malignant to a non-malignant state is possible in certain circumstances (Brinster, 1974).

During the prolonged interval between the first genetic changes due to initiating factors and the final appearance of cancerous cells, the stages to a fully developed malignant state may be accelerated or slowed up. For example, there is clear evidence that precancerous changes in the uterine cervix may regress spontaneously. Similar regression may occur in precancerous changes in the bladder or lung, particularly following the administration of vitamin A analogues (Bollag, 1983).

The majority of established cancers show aggressive growth and therefore some clinicians disparage the importance of modulating effects by the host. Yet host influences are clearly evident in repeated clinical observations of fluctuation in growth rate, unexpectedly prolonged survival, prolonged dormancy or spontaneous regression in cancer. These host influences can be recognized only in a minority of patients but they occur in every type of cancer, including such highly aggressive tumours as cancers of the lung and stomach. Examples of growth modulation by the host are not necessarily confined to cancers showing an apparently less malignant or favourable pattern of growth under the microscope (Dawson, Ferguson and Harrison, 1982).

Dormancy and spontaneous regression of cancer

It is now recognized that a cancer does not advance irrevocably at the same rate (Devitt, 1979). At different periods in the natural history of a cancer, growth may be rapid or slow, and in practically all experimental and human cancers, there is a tendency for slowing up of the growth rate as the tumour gets larger. In a patient with multiple secondary deposits at different sites, they do not all grow at the same rate (Brennan, 1977), and Willis (1973) has shown different mitotic rates in different secondaries in the same patient.

The influence of host factors on cancer growth is most obviously seen in the spontaneous regression or slowing up of breast cancer activity at the time of the natural menopause. Similar regression, often of a dramatic nature, can be induced in several hormone-sensitive types of cancer by hormonal manipulation, e.g. castration in breast or prostatic cancer, anti-oestrogen therapy in breast cancer, progestational therapy in uterine cancer and anti-androgen therapy in prostatic cancer.

There are many cases where incompletely excised cancers never recur, or where secondary deposits lie dormant in the host tissues for up to 30 years before finally manifesting. Since dormant cancer may permit a very long life-span and normal health, it is likely that in many patients death occurs in the interim from so-called 'natural causes', and the patient is regarded as having been cured of the cancer. A prolonged dormant or recurrence-free period is seen most commonly in cancers of the breast and kidney, and in malignant melanoma and neuroblastoma, but can be seen in any tumour (Willis, 1973). When the tumour does eventually reactivate, it is often highly malignant in its behaviour and manifests a shower of secondary deposits at multiple sites (Stoll, 1976b). Dormant cancer is well recognized also in experimental animals and in these the equilibrium can be easily disturbed, either by immunosuppression (Eccles and Alexander, 1975) or by hormonal stimu-lation (Noble and Hoover, 1975).

The wide variation in the dormant period between the removal of the primary growth and the first clinical manifestation of a secondary growth is commonly ascribed to a greater or lesser proliferation rate in the tumour cells. But the rate of growth of a tumour does not merely reflect the rate of cell proliferation; it reflects also the rate of cell death (Steel, 1967). Since over 80 per cent of new cells in a cancer deposit may be lost by cell death, desquamation or metastasis, dormancy may result from increased rate of cell death or from decreased rate of proliferation. Thus on a biological basis, dormancy could be due either to lack of stimulatory growth factors or to restraint by growth inhibitory factors such as those described in the next section.

Spontaneous regression of cancer is real, even if uncommon. Clinicians question its existence if it is defined as complete and permanent disappear-ance of cancer in a patient. In fact, it means any measurable and confirmed shrinkage in the size of a tumour (primary or secondary) for a period of months or years, in the absence of treatment ordinarily regarded as being capable of inducing regression (Boyd, 1966).

In 1966, two Chicago surgeons (Everson and Cole, 1966) verified 176 examples from the world medical literature, including some of their own cases. In the same year, an eminent Toronto pathologist (Boyd, 1966) published a further series of cases mainly from his own experience. Neither series specified that tumour regression must be complete or permanent, but did require microscopic confirmation and absence of significant treatment. The 176 cases covered 18 sites of cancer although cancers of the kidney, neuroblastoma, malignant melanoma and choriocarcinoma accounted for about half the total number. Both primary and secondary tumours were represented. The recorded duration of spontaneous regression varied from a few months to over 10 years, and in over half the total it lasted over 2 years.

Every year, between 20 and 30 new cases of spontaneous regression are reported in the world literature, and this is said to represent about one in 100 000 cases of cancer. In fact, its true incidence is likely to be many hundred times as large. The medical literature tends to record only dramatic cases, under close scientific investigation, receiving no accepted orthodox treatment and under the observation of important medical centres. Numerous cases of partial regression for months or years, particularly those under the care of non-academic doctors or unorthodox practitioners, would not be reported in the medical literature.

The adjective 'spontaneous' merely means that the cause of tumour shrinkage could not be identified in a particular case. In some cases, Everson and Cole (1966) suggested, the apparent triggering factor could be either trauma by surgical or radiotherapeutic procedures incapable of curing the tumour, or else trauma by chemicals or an infective process. For the majority, immunological or hormonal mechanisms have been assumed mainly because these are the most common methods of regression noted in experimental animal cancers. Even if rare, the phenomenon of spontaneous regression offers proof of the reversibility of cancer growth, and enables us to study the phenomenon so that we might apply its mechanism to a larger proportion of cases.

Dormant cancer and spontaneous regression of cancer are qualitatively similar phenomena. Both are most obvious in large cancers of the kidney and malignant melanoma (where immunological factors are thought to be involved) and in breast cancer (where endocrine factors are thought to be involved). But restraints on cancer growth are probably much more effective in small than in large masses of tumour, and it is our inability to recognize the less dramatic examples in small deposits which has led us to underestimate the frequency of the phenomena. Another reason for failure to recognize growth restraint in cancer is the fact that 99 per cent of proliferating cells in a tumour can die without leading to an obvious change in the size of the tumour (Stoll, 1979).

Mechanisms of cancer modulation

The last few years have produced increasing evidence that growth-regulating factors of a polypeptide nature are of major importance in deciding whether a cell behaves in a malignant manner. Regulators of this type probably exist for every major type of body cell, although most evidence has been accumulated about epidermal growth factor, nerve growth factor, fibroblast growth factor, haemopoietic growth factor and angiogenic growth factor.

Growth-regulating factors are most active during the embryonic stage of development and again in the cancer cell, and Sporn and Todaro (1980) have therefore suggested that malignant transformation of a cell involves reactivation of those foetal genes which control the growth factors used by the cell in early embryonic development. Busch (1980) has even postulated that growth invasiveness and spread (typical features of cancer tissue) are merely aspects of embryonic growth which are repressed in normal adult tissue but reexpressed in cancer cells.

It is believed that both experimental and human cancers can produce growth factors which then act on their own cell receptors. This process maintains the growth of the cancer (Sporn and Todaro, 1980) and depriving the cells of these factors will cause growth inhibition. In addition, specific tumour growth inhibitory factors have recently been isolated (Todaro et al., 1982) and these appear to block the growth-stimulating effects of the other factors.

The concept of the reversibility of cancer into normal tissue is supported by experiments carried out by Brinster (1974) and confirmed by subsequent workers. They took tumour cells from an embryonal cancer of a rat and injected them into a rat embryo before placing it in the uterus of a rat foster mother. It was found to develop into a normal animal with the coat colour of the cancer strain, showing that the new environment of the embryo had reverted the cancer cell into a normal cell.

It therefore appears that cancer cells may still remain responsive to physiological growth-regulating mechanisms, and also that cancerous qualities in a cell need not necessarily be regarded as irreversible. The controlling mechanisms may still persist so that local factors responsible for embryonic tissue becoming nature can cause similar maturation in cancer cells (Busch, 1980). In fact, such changes are seen in both breast and uterine cancer in women as a result of changes in the hormonal environment of the tumour.

We noted above that spontaneous regression of breast cancer is not uncommon around the time of the menopause. The mechanism is presumably similar to that seen in experimental breast cancer where castration leads to tumour regression with evidence of individual cell death (apoptosis) (Gullino, 1981). The administration or a high dosage of oestrogen also leads to regression of both experimental and human breast cancer, but such cases show evidence of maturation of the cancer tissue into functional tissue (Hilf, 1977).

Similarly, it has been shown in the case of uterine cancer that treatment by progestational agents leads to evidence of individual cell death (apoptosis) and also to maturation of some areas of the tumour into functional tissue (Ferenczy and Gelfand, 1982). If hormonal changes can induce tumour regression by these two mechanisms, could the same mechanisms also be called into play by psychosomatic influences?

Individual cell death (apoptosis)

Increasing attention is being given to spontaneous death of cells in tumours by the process of apoptosis, as a result of local programming of growth. Physiologically it is seen in the uterine endometrial lining when it is shed at the onset of menstruation as a result of a sudden fall in the levels of the supporting hormones. It involves detachment of the cell from its neighbours, fragmentation of the nucleus, increased activity of the lysosomal enzymes in the cell and increased phagocytic activity.

The process of apoptosis in cancers is quite distinct from the large areas of necrosis resulting from failure of oxygen or nutritional supplies. The sensitivity of slowly growing tumours, such as those of the breast and prostate, to sudden changes in their hormonal environment, cannot be adequately explained by the normal mechanisms of cell kinetics observed in cancer. The form of cell death observed is reminiscent of the switch mechanisms seen in the normal hormonal control of target organs such as the lining of the uterus.

Apoptosis has been reported in untreated tumours including cancers of the lung, bowel and uterine cervix, but it is particularly prominent in basal cell carcinoma of the skin, a tumour which shows very slow increase in size in spite of high mitotic activity. The function of apoptosis is regulation of cell numbers in a tumour, but its mechanism of control is not yet clear. A rise in the level of intracellular cyclic AMP may play a central role, as this has been shown to induce apoptosis in some experimental tumours.

Maturation of cancer

In recent years it has been shown that some tumours can be induced to change from malignant to non-malignant behaviour by stimulating their capacity to mature into differentiated (specialized) functional tissue. Following therapy by agents specific for each tumour, change from malignant to non-malignant characteristics has been observed in neuroblastoma, teratocarcinoma and myeloid leukaemia (Tisdale, 1982). The same change can also occur spontaneously and is presumably responsible for many reported cases of spontaneous regression in cancer. It is most common in neuroblastoma in children and in testicular teratocarcinoma in adults, but similar changes with spontaneous regression have been seen in retinoblastoma, nephroblastoma and embryonal sarcoma in children (Willis, 1973).

Thus, while many tumours tend to progress and become more malignant and invasive with time, others may spontaneously become more differentiated and less active in their growth. Some degree of differentiation is going on in tumours all the time, and may come to dominate the tumour in certain circumstances. A recent triumph of cancer chemotherapy is the long-term cure of teratocarcinoma of the ovary or testis. The residual tumour after such treatment is often found to consist of well-differentiated teratomatous tissue, showing that following the death of malignant stem cells, a cancer has been converted into a benign tumour.

That differentiation occurs spontaneously even in rapidly growing tumours is shown in squamous cell carcinoma of epithelial tissues, where groups of differentiated cells lie adjacent to undifferentiated cells (Pierce and Cox, 1978). These observations question the traditional belief that cancer is an irreversible change leading always to increased malignancy. 'Spontaneous' regression of cancer could be due to factors which lead the tumour to differentiate and lose its malignant properties. We even know of factors which can trigger such changes.

Recent observations have shown that tumours can be made to regress by inducing maturation in malignant or premalignant tissues. Clinical studies have shown that administration of retinoids (analogues of vitamin A) can reduce premalignant changes in the bronchial lining of heavy smokers, and also inhibit hyperplastic changes in the skin or bladder epithelium in some patients. Preliminary studies have shown some degree of tumour regression following retinoid administration to patients with cancers of the lung, oropharyngeal region or breast, or with malignant melanoma (Bollag, 1983). The effect appears to be correlated with the presence of specific retinoid receptors in the tissues, and in the case of breast and pancreas such receptors are said to be more common in the cancer than in the normal parent tissue. The mechanism by which retinoids exert this effect is not clear, but it may again be through cyclic AMP which plays an important role in the differentiation and arrested growth of malignant cells in experimental tumours.

So far, spontaneous regression of cancer is the only one of these manifestations of host influence in which a possible psychosomatic influence has been entertained (Everson and Cole, 1966), on the assumption that it might trigger (or promote) an immunological or endocrine change. Although a similar influence may affect the growth of many cancers in a less dramatic fashion, it is almost impossible to identify its contribution because of the wide variation in the natural history of cancer between one patient and another, and the multiplicity of factors that determine prognosis (Stoll, 1979). For this reason, this chapter will make no attempt to discuss the various reported uncontrolled clinical trials claiming that psychological intervention can prolong life-span in cancer (for review, see Feinstein, 1983). To conclude, it must be emphasized that there are likely to be different promoting and modulating factors for different cancers (e.g. those of the lung, breast, bowel, etc.). For this reason, future scientific research on the role of psychosocial or stress factors needs to concentrate on cancers at specific sites, preferably in an accessible and measurable situation.

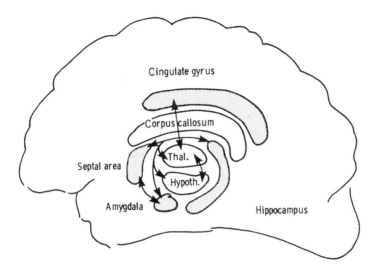

Figure 18.1   Interconnections of the limbic system in the human brain. *Reproduced by kind permission from* Hormonal Management of Endocrine-Related Cancer *(1981) edited by Dr Basil A. Stoll. London: Lloyd-Luke (Medical Books)*

POSTULATED PSYCHOSOMATIC MECHANISMS

The previous section suggests that both psychoendocrine and psychoimmunological promoting factors may be implicated in the triggering of spontaneous regression of cancer. Psychoendocrine factors are especially feasible in view of known hormonally induced remissions in breast and prostatic cancers, and of changes in hormone secretion under psychological stress. Thus, many would accept the possibility of psychoendocrine influences on hormone-sensitive cancers of breast, prostate and uterus.

If endocrine or immunological mechanisms modulate an effect by mental or emotional influences on the growth of cancer, one would expect it to be more evident in cancers developing in the middle years, between 40 and 60. It might be less likely in old age when endocrine and immunolological activity is weaker, and in childhood cancer where congenital factors play the greatest role.

The following discussion will concentrate on endocrine and immunological mechanisms which are modified through the agency of the hypothalamus. The median eminence of the anterior hypothalamus receives stimuli from the frontal lobes of the brain and also from the limbic system which is thought to control emotion of a more primitive type (Figure 18.1). As a result, the anterior hypothalamus may then release neurotransmitter agents (biogenic amines) which stimulate hormone-releasing factors acting on the anterior pituitary gland. In turn, this releases the various trophic hormones which

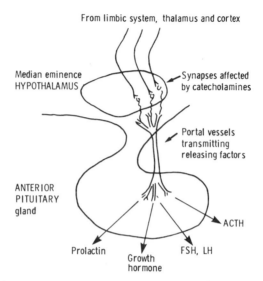

Figure 18.2   Pathways by which emotional stress may influence the release of anterior pituitary hormones. *Reproduced by kind permission from* Hormonal Management of Endocrine-Related Cancer *(1981) edited by Dr Basil A. Stoll. London: Lloyd-Luke (Medical Books)*

control the activity of the gonads, adrenal cortex, thyroid gland, etc. (Figure 18.2).

There are other pathways by which the hypothalamus may affect cancer growth. Emotional stimuli originating in the limbic system or frontal lobes can affect the posterior hypothalamus leading to the release of adrenaline or noradrenaline through the sympathetic nervous (Figure 18.3). These may

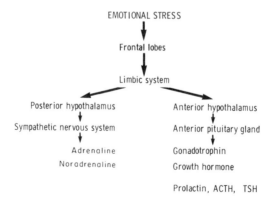

Figure 18.3   Possible mechanisms by which emotional stress may influence the growth of cancer. Effects may be mediated either by the anterior or by the posterior hypothalamus. *Reproduced by kind permission from* Hormonal Management of Endocrine-Related Cancer *(1981) edited by Dr Basil A. Stoll. London: Lloyd-Luke (Medical Books)*

affect tumour spread either directly or through the immune system. Apart from controlling hormone secretion and release, the hypothalamus has been shown to influence the automonic nervous system (including visceral regulation) and the general immune response. The hypothalamus is therefore key to the majority, if not all, of psychosomatic mechanisms which may influence cancer growth.

Postulated psychoendocrine mechanisms

Most of the classical reports on the response of the endocrine system to stress are concerned with secretion from the adrenal medulla and cortex. Acute stress stimulates the sympathetic nervous system with the consequent release of both adrenaline and noradrenaline. It has been suggested that noradrenaline may be more predominant in anger (with lower levels in submissive situations) (Taggart, Parkinson and Carruthers, 1972). It has been hypothesized that an abnormal balance between the two hormones may exist in emotionally inhibited individuals with psychosomatic symptoms.

More prolonged stressful situations affect the release of hormones from the anterior pituitary gland, and stimulation of ACTH release will lead to increased cortisol output from the adrenal cortex. Various emotional states are associated with increased output of cortisol, e.g. mourning, separation, clinical depression and breakdown of psychological defences. The subject is discussed extensively in other chapters but certain questions may be posed here in relation to cancer. Bahnson (1981) has suggested psychodynamic repression of emotion to be a feature of cancer patients, but the evidence in this chapter would suggest that *conscious* suppression of emotion is more likely to be associated with the development of cancer. Is suppression of emotion likely to be associated with greater elevation of cortisol levels than is repression of emotion? It is generally accepted that coping behaviour and anticipation of stress will decrease the adrenocortical response. Does an attitude of apathy and depression increase the response?

It must be taken into account also that cortisol is only one of the markers of the effect of stress on the psychoendocrine system. Stress stimulates also the secretion of growth hormone, prolactin and thyroid hormone, while the secretion of oestrogen, androgen and insulin tends to be suppressed. All of these hormones can exert an effect on cancer growth.

Growth hormone levels rise rapidly in response to exercise and emotion, but the response of growth hormone does not always run parallel to that of cortisol. Anticipation of a stressful experience may have a greater effect on growth hormone levels than the event itself (Kurokawa et al., 1977) while repetition of the stress does not diminish growth hormone response as it does for cortisol. Prolactin levels also have been observed to increase in response to emotion and exercise and, not surprisingly, a rise has been shown during sexual intercourse (Noel et al., 1972).

The pituitary/adrenal axis has been subjected to most study in patients with breast cancer. Increased corticosteroid production is commonly found in breast cancer patients (Bulbrook, Hayward and Thomas, 1964) and was originally suspected to be evidence of adrenal dysfunction related to the origin of the disease. However, the increased corticosteroid production probably results from the presence of cancer, as it is more marked with increasing spread of the tumour (Saez, 1974). Emotional stress will further increase the circulating cortisol level, and higher levels have indeed been found in breast cancer patients who appear apprehensive (Katz *et al.*, 1970). Increased excretion of corticosteroids has been shown also in patients with lung cancer (Rao and Hewit, 1970).

Peptide hormones secreted by the anterior pituitary gland could affect the growth of breast cancer by mechanisms other than by stimulation of corticosteroid secretion. For example, gonadotrophin, thyrotrophin, ACTH, growth hormone and prolactin have all been shown to affect the development and growth of experimental mammary cancer. In the human, the influence of these peptides on the growth of breast cancer is less certain, but it is clear that steroid hormones such as oestrogen, progesterone, androgen and cortisone may exert an effect through their respective protein receptors in the cancer cell (Allegra *et al.*, 1979).

It appears, then, that mechanisms exist whereby emotional stress and psychoendocrine factors acting through the hypothalamus may stimulate hormones which can affect the growth of hormone-sensitive cancer. The mere existence of such pathways, however, does not prove that psychogenic factors actively influence the development or growth of cancer. Clinical observations on the growth of the tumour in relation to emotional factors (together with parallel immunological and endocrinological studies) are required to establish such a relationship.

Role of hypothalamic dysfunction

In the last 20 years there has been considerable interest in the effects of both ageing and cancer on neurotransmitter chemical activity in the brain, particularly in the hypothalamus. The biogenic amines most actively studied are the catecholamines (dopamine and noradrenaline), the indolamine serotonin, and acetylcholine. The concentrations of dopamine and noradrenaline are particularly high in the hypothalamus where they act as neurotransmitters to stimulate specific releasing factors for each trophic hormone of the anterior pituitary gland.

Increasing age is said to be associated with increased resistance of the hypothalamo-pituitary axis to feedback suppression by steroids (Dilman, 1971: Adamopoulos, Lorraine and Dove, 1971). This hypothalamic dysfunction is thought to result from changes in neurotransmitter levels in the brain, and the resulting rise in the level of circulating hormones could affect the growth of cancer. It has, moreover, been reported that breast cancer patients show a greater likelihood of hypothalamic dysfunction than do normal subjects of the same age distribution (Schweppe, Jungman and Lewin, 1967; Bishop and Ross, 1970; Saez, 1971; Dilman, 1974). According to Saez (1974), hypothalamo-pituitary resistance to corticosteroid inhibition increases as breast cancer advances from Stage 1 to Stage 3, and those patients with an unfavourable course seem especially likely to show such abnormality.

There is evidence of hypothalamic dysfunction also in about half of patients diagnosed as suffering from endogenous depression (Butler and Besser, 1968; Carroll and Davies, 1970; Schlesser, Winskur and Sherman, 1979). Corticosteroid suppression of plasma cortisol levels, and growth hormone response to hypoglycaemia have been the two most commonly used tests of hypothalamic dysfunction in such patients. Remission of the state of depression is usually paralleled by return to normal in the tests of hypothalamic function (Sachar *et al.*, 1973; Carroll, Greden and Feinberg, 1980). A neurotransmitter disturbance in common (e.g. serotonin or noradrenaline depletion) has been suggested for the association of endogenous depression and hypothalamic dysfunction (Carroll, Greden and Feinberg, 1980; Christensen *et al.*, 1980). The former may represent neurotransmitter disturbance in the limbic system while the latter may be due to a similar change in the hypothalamus.

This association between endogenous depression and hypothalamic dysfunction suggests an alternative explanation for the association noted earlier in the chapter between depression and apathy in the cancer patient and a shorter expectation of life. *In cancer patients, neurotransmitter disturbance in the brain may result from the presence of more active tumour* (Stoll, 1981). This would account for the observation that hypothalamic dysfunction increases with increasing spread of cancer (Saez, 1974), and also for the observation that depression and apathy are associated with a poor prognosis. The mechanism by which cancer affects neurotransmitter activity is not clear but it has recently been proposed that cancer cells can stimulate production of an antibody which can block serotonin receptors in the brain. This could lead to the development of clinical evidence of depression and apathy (Brown and Paraskevas, 1982).

Opioid peptides such as endorphins and enkephalins also have an effect on mood and behaviour, presumed to be mediated by the limbic and extra-pyramidal systems of the midbrain. They may play a part in the growth of cancer because of their role as neurotransmitters and as neuronal and hormonal modulators in the brain. They are found mainly in the autonomic, limbic and neuroendocrine systems and become active only under conditions of stress.

In the neuroendocrine system, opioid peptides inhibit gonadotrophin release but stimulate the release of growth hormone, thyroid hormone or prolactin. With regard to ACTH, opioids may either inhibit or stimulate its release under different types of stress (Grossman and Rees, 1983). In this way, they may influence the development and growth of cancers (particularly those retaining hormone sensitivity) but our knowledge is still too fragmentary to speculate on this possibility.

With regard to the effect of stress on neurotransmitter levels in the brain, increased turnover in brain noradrenaline has been shown in experimental animals under stress conditions. In the human, levels of brain noradrenaline cannot, of course, be measured under stress, but a major metabolite of brain noradrenaline is 3-methoxy-4-hydroxy phenylglycol (MHPG). Its level in the urine reflects central nervous system adrenaline metabolism as opposed to peripheral noradrenaline metabolism which is reflected by 3-methoxy-4-hydroxy mandelic acid and normetanephrine levels (Ebert and Kopin, 1975). Increased MHPG excretion has been shown in humans under stress (Rubin et al., 1970).

Postulated psychoimmunological mechanisms

Experimental lesioning in the hypothalamus of animals can induce changes in the immune reaction—both in humoral and in cell-mediated responses (Stein, Schiari and Camarino, 1976). Corticosteroids are generally regarded as the major endocrine mediators of stress-induced changes in the immune system because of their well-known effects on B and T lymphocytes, antibodies, etc. (Solomon, Amkraut and Rubin, 1979). Thus, Kiecolt-Glaser et al. (1983) have reported that some groups of psychiatric patients have increased blood cortisol levels and also relatively low natural killer (NK) cell and lymphocyte stimulation levels. However, other pathways may be just as important. Lymphocytes have been shown to possess receptors for catecholamines, prostaglandins, somatotrophic hormone, histamine and insulin (Melmon et al., 1976) and normal macrophage activity is responsive to prostaglandins and catecholamines (Ignarro, 1977).

A variety of other hormones may also play a part in psychoendocrine effects on immune function (Stein, Keller and Schleifer, 1979). The growth hormone response to stress is, surprisingly, dissociated from the corticoid response, in that it may enhance the immune response (Gisler, 1974). Thyroid hormone also is involved in the modulation of immune function (Denckla, 1974) and its secretion responds to stress. Androgen levels in the male respond to stress and may have a suppressive effect on immune function (Wyle and Kent, 1977). Adrenaline and noradrenaline levels are increased in response to stress and will suppress various immune responses (Kram et al., 1975).

Psychoendocrine disturbance could therefore indirectly stimulate the growth of cancer by inhibiting immune reactivity. In animals, Laudenslager et al., (1983) have reported that the lymphocyte response to mitogens is suppressed by a condition of inescapable shock but not by escapable shock. In man, the peripheral blood T-lymphocyte response to mitogens is found to be significantly reduced after stress (Palmblad, 1981) and also after bereavement (Bartrop et al., 1977; Schleifer et al., 1983). Moreover, the level of circulating lymphocytes is reported to be reduced after stressful life events (Locke et al., 1978) and NK cell activity is known to be related to immune defence against cancer.

Observations on immunoglobulin levels in the blood have been reported in relation to personality (Pettingale, Greer and Tee, 1977). In patients subjected to biopsy for a breast lump, the mean serum level of immunoglobulin A was significantly higher in those patients who habitually suppressed emotion, whether the breast lump turned out to be benign or malignant. A subsequent report (Pettingale et al., 1981) showed that at 3 months after surgery, immunoglobulin M levels were higher in those patients who showed denial than in those who showed either a fighting spirit or stoic acceptance of the diagnosis of cancer. The significance of these immunoglobulin level changes to the defence against cancer is unknown.

SUMMARY AND CONCLUSIONS

In the terminal cancer patient, life may be prolonged or shortened according to the patient's will to live. The mechanism is unknown but the phenomenon is seen also in other types of serious disease. In the patient with less advanced cancer, psychoendocrine and psychoimmunological mechanisms exist through which psychological factors could affect the growth and spread of cancer, and thus the duration of survival. Mental stress can undoubtedly modulate the growth of cancer in experimental animals, but in the human it is impossible to identify its contribution because of the wide variation in the natural history of cancer between one patient and another.

Most of the reported attempts at scientific investigation suggest that a depressed or withdrawn attitude in the cancer patient is associated with a shorter survival period than is a more positive attitude to recovery. Alternative explanations have been put forward—either that depression and apathy lead to a more active tumour or that a more active tumour leads to depression and apathy. A third alternative is proposed—that the presence of a more active tumour may lead to abnormal neurotransmitter levels at receptor sites in the brain, and this can cause both endogenous depression and hypothalamic dysfunction with neuroendocrine disturbance.

To clarify the reported correlation between shorter survival and apathy, prospective, scientifically planned observations are being made on tumour growth and length of survival in relation to temperament, coping attitude and the effect (if any) of psychotherapeutic intervention. Associated immunological and endocrinological studies may help to explain any correlations observed. It is essential that each investigation should concentrate on one specific type of cancer—preferably in an accessible and measurable situation.

REFERENCES

Adamopoulos, D. A., Lorraine, J. A., and Dove, C. A. (1971). Endocrinological studies in women approaching the menopause. *Journal of Obstetrics and Gynaecology of the British Commonwealth*, **78**, 62–68.

Allegra, J. C., Lippman, M. C., Thompson, E. B., Simon, R., Banlock, A., Green, L., Huff, K. K., Do, H. M. T., and Aitken, S. C. (1979). Distribution, frequency, and quantitative analysis of oestrogen, progesterone, androgen and glucocorticoid receptors in human breast cancer. *Cancer Research*, **39**, 1447–1454.

Bacon, C. L., Ronneker, R., and Cutler, M. (1952). A psychosomatic survey of cancer of the breast. *Psychosomatic Medicine*, **14**, 453–460.

Bahnson, C. B. (1969). Psychophysiological complementarity in malignancies: past work and future vistas. *Annals of the New York Academy of Science*, **164**, 319–333.

Bahnson, C. B. (1981). Stress and cancer: the state of the apt. Part 2. *Psychosomatics*, **22**, 207–220.

Bahnson, C. B., and Bahnson, M. B. (1964). Cancer as an alternative to psychosis. In D. M. Kissen and L. Leshan (eds), *Psychosomatic Aspects of Neoplastic Disease*. London: Pitman Medical.

Bartrop, R. W., Lazarus, L., Luckhurst, E., and Kilch, L. G. (1977). Depressed lymphocyte function after bereavement. *Lancet*, **i**, 834–836.

Becker, H. (1979). Psychodynamic aspects of breast cancer. Differences in younger and older patients. *Psychotherapy and Psychosomatics*, **32**, 287–296.

Berenblum, I. (1984). Two stage carcinogenesis and multiple cancers. In B. A. Stoll (ed.), *Risk Factors and Multiple Cancer*. Chichester: John Wiley, pp. 3–12.

Bishop, M. C. Ross, E. J. (1970). Adrenocortical activity in disseminated malignant disease in relation to prognosis. *British Journal of Cancer*, **24**, 719–725.

Blumberg, E. M., West, P. M., and Ellis, P. W. (1954). A possible relationship between psychological factors and human cancer. *Psychosomatic Medicine*, **16**, 277–286.

Bollag, W. (1983). Vitamin A and retinoids. *Lancet*, **i**, 860–863.

Booth, G. (1969). General and organ-specific object relationships in cancer. *Annals of the New York Academy of Science*, **164**, 568–577.

Boyd, W. (1966). *Spontaneous Regression of Cancer*. Springfield: C. C. Thomas.

Brennan, M. J. (1977). Breast Cancer research. *UICC Technical Report Series*, vol. 27, Geneva: UICC, pp. 1–16.

Brinster, R. (1974). The effect of cells transferred into the mouse blastocyst on subsequent development. *Journal of Experimental Medicine*, **140**, 1049–1056.

Brown, J. H., and Paraskevas, F. (1982). Cancer and depression: an autoimmune disease? *British Journal of Psychiatry*, **141**, 227–232.

Bulbrook, R. D., Hayward, H. L., and Thomas, B. S. (1964). The relation between the urinary 17-hydroxycorticosteroids and 11-deoxy-17-oxosteroids and the fate of patients after mastectomy. *Lancet*, **i**, 945–949.

Busch, H. (1980). Molecular oncology. In T. Symington and R. L. Carter (eds), *Oncology Supplement: Scientific Foundations of Oncology*. London: Heinemann Medical, pp. 1–30.

Butler, P. U. P., and Besser, G. M. (1968). Pituitary adrenal function in severe depressive illness. *Lancet*, **i**, 1234–1236.

Carroll, B. J., and Davies, B. (1970). Clinical association of 11 OHCS suppression and non-suppression in severe depressive illness. *British Medical Journal*, **1**, 789–791.

Carroll, B. J., Greden, J. F., Feinberg, M. (1980). Neuroendocrine disturbance and the diagnosis and aetiology of endogenous depression. *Lancet*, **i**, 321–322.

Christensen, N. J., Vestegaard, P., Sorensen, T., Jarris, A. G., and Rafaelsen, O. J. (1980). Cerebrospinal fluid adrenaline in endogenous depression. *Lancet*, **i**, 722–725.

Coppen, A., and Metcalfe, M. (1963). Cancer and extraversion. *British Medical Journal*, **2**, 18–19.

Davies, R. K., Quinland, R. M., McKegney, F., and Kimball, C. P. (1973). Organic factors and psychological adjustment in advanced cancer patients. *Psychosomatic Medicine*, **35**, 464–471.

Dawson, P. J., Ferguson, D. J., and Harrison, T. (1982). Pathologic findings of breast cancer cases surviving 25 years after radical mastectomy. *Cancer*, **50**, 2131–2138.

Denckla, U. D. (1974). Role of the pituitary and thyroid glands in the decline of minimal oxygen consumption with age. *Journal of Clinical Investigation*, **53**, 572–576.

Derogatis, L. R., Abeloff, M. D., and Meliseratos, N. (1979). Psychological coping mechanisms and survival time in metastatic breast cancer. *Journal of the American Medical Association*, **242**, 1504–1507.

Devitt, J. E. (1979). Fluctuations in the growth rate of cancer. In B. A. Stoll (ed.), *Mind and Cancer Prognosis*. Chichester: John Wiley, pp. 9–18.

Dilman, V. M. (1971). Age-associated elevation of hypothalamic threshold to feedback control and its role in development, ageing and disease. *Lancet*, **i**, 1211–1219.

Dilman, V. (1974). Changes in hypothalamic sensitivity in ageing and cancer. In B. A. Stoll (ed.), *Mammary Cancer and Neuroendocrine Therapy*. London: Butterworths, pp. 197–228.

Ebert, M. H., and Kopin, I. J. (1975). Differential labelling of origins of urinary catecholamine metabolites by dopamine-C14. *Transactions of the American Association of Physicians*, **88**, 256–258.

Eccles, S. A., and Alexander, P. (1975). Immunologically-mediated restraint of latent tumour metastases. *Nature*, **257**, 52–56.

Everson, T. C., and Cole, W. H. (1966). *Spontaneous Regression of Cancer*. Philadelphia: W. B. Saunders.

Feinstein, A. D. (1983). Psychological intervention in the treatment of cancer. *Clinical Psychology Reviews*, **3**, 1–14.

Ferenczy, A., and Gelfand, M. M. (1982). Steroid-induced regression in endometrial cancer. In B. A. Stoll (ed.), *Prolonged Arrest of Cancer*. Chichester: John Wiley, pp. 369–386.

Fras, I., Litin, E. M., and Pearson, J. D. (1967). Comparison of psychiatric symptoms in carcinoma of the pancreas with those in some other intra-abdominal neoplasms. *American Journal of Psychiatry*, **123**, 1553–1562.

Freeman, W. (1928). Biometrical studies in psychiatry—the chances of death. *American Journal of Psychiatry*, **8**, 425–441.

Funch, D. P., and Marshall, J. (1983). The role of stress, social support and age in survival from breast cancer. *Journal of Psychosomatic Research*, **27**, 77–83.

Gisler, R. H. (1974). Stress and the hormone regulation of the immune response in mice. *Psychotherapy, Psychosomatic Medical Psychology*, **23**, 197–205.

Greenberg, R. P., and Dattore, P. J. (1981). The relationship between dependency and the development of cancer. *Psychosomatic Medicine*, **43**, 35–43.

Greene, W. H. (1966). The psychosocial setting of the development of leukemia and lymphoma. *Annals of the New York Academy of Science*, **125**, 794–801.

Greer, S., and Morris, T. (1975). Psychological attributes of women who develop breast cancer: a controlled study. *Journal of Psychosomatic Research*, **19**, 147–153.

Greer, S., Morris, T., and Pettingale, J. K. W. (1979). Psychological response to breast cancer: effect on outcome. *Lancet*, **ii**, 785–789.

Grissom, J. J., Weiner, B. J., and Weiner, E. A. (1975). Psychological correlates of cancer. *Journal of Consulting and Clinical Psychology*, **43**, 113–114.

Grossarth-Maticek, R. (1980). Psychosocial predictors of cancer and internal diseases. An overview. *Psychotherapy and Psychosomatics*, **33**, 129–138.

Grossman, A., and Rees, L. H. (1983). The endocrinology of opioid peptides. *British Medical Bulletin*, **39**, 83–88.

Gullino, P. M. (1981). Mechanisms of hormonally-induced tumour regression. In B. A. Stoll (ed.), *Hormonal Management of Endocrine Related Cancer*. London: Lloyd-Luke, pp. 20–29.

Hagnell, O. (1966). The premorbid personality of persons who develop cancer. *Annals of the New York Academy of Science*, **125**, 846–855.

Hilf, R. (1977). Biochemical mechanisms in tumour regression. In B. A. Stoll (ed.), *Secondary Spread in Breast Cancer*. London: Heinemann Medical, pp. 225–240.

Horne, R. L., and Picard, R. S. (1979). Psychosocial risk factors for lung cancer. *Psychosomatic Medicine*, **41**, 503–514.

Ignarro, J. L. (1977). Regulation of leucocytes, macrophages and platelets. Quoted by G. F. Solomon, A. A. Amkraut and R. T. Rubin. In B. A. Stoll (ed.), *Mind and Cancer Prognosis*. Chichester: John Wiley.

Jacobs, T. J., and Charles, E. (1980). Life events and the occurrence of cancer in children. *Psychosomatic Medicine*, **42**, 11–24.

Katz, J. L., Ackman, P., Rothwax, Y., Sachar, E. J., Weiner, H., Hellman, L., and Gallagher, T. F. (1970). Psychoendocrine aspects of cancer of the breast. *Psychosomatic Medicine*, **32**, 1–17.

Keehn, R. J., Goldberg, J. D., and Beebe, G. W. (1974). Twenty four year mortality follow up of army veterans with disability separations for psychoneurosis in 1944. *Psychosomatic Medicine*, **36**, 27–46.

Kennedy, B. J., Yellegen, A., Kennedy, S., and Havernick, N. (1976). Psychological response of patients cured of advanced cancer. *Cancer*, **38**, 2184–2195.

Kerr, T. A., Schapira, K., and Roth, M. (1969). The relationship between premature death and affective disorders. *British Journal of Psychiatry*, **115**, 1277–1285.

Kiecolt-Glaser, J. K., Ricker, D., George, J., Messick, G., Speicher, C. E., Garner, W., and Herman, M. V. (1983). Urinary cortisol levels, cellular immunocompetency and loneliness in psychiatric inpatients. *Psychosomatic Medicine*, **46**, 15–23.

Kissen, D. (1966). The significance of personality in lung cancer in men. *Annals of the New York Academy of Science*, **125**, 820–826.

Kram, T., Bourne, H., Naibach, H., and Melman, K. (1975). Cutaneous immediate hypersensitivity in man. *Journal of Allergy and Clinical Immunology*, **56**, 387–389.

Krasnoff, A. (1959). Psychological variables and human cancer. A cross-valuation study. *Psychosomatic Medicine*, **21**, 291–295.

Kurokawa, M., Suematsu, H., Tamai, H., Esaki, M., Aoki, H., and Ikemi, Y. (1977). Effect of emotional stress on human growth hormone secretion. *Journal of Psychosomatic Research*, **21**, 231–239.

Laudenslager, M. L., Ryan, S. M., Drugan, R. C., Hyson, R. L., and Maier, S. F. (1983). Coping and immunosuppression. Inescapable but not escapable shock suppresses lymphocyte proliferation. *Science*, **221**, 568–570.

Le Shan, L. (1959). Psychological states as factors in the development of malignant disease: a critical review. *Journal of the National Cancer Institute*, **22**, 1–18.

Locke, S., Hurst, M., Heisel, J., and Honnig-Rohan, M. (1978). The influence of stress on the immune response. *Annual Meeting Proceedings of the American Psychosomatic Society*.

Melmon, K. L., Weinsaein, Y., Bourne, H. R., Shearer, G., Poon, T., Kraany, L., and Segal, S. (1976). Quoted by G. F. Solomon, A. A. Amkraut and R. T. Robin. In B. A. Stoll (ed.), *Mind and Cancer Prognosis*. Chichester: John Wiley, pp. 73–84.

Miller, T. R. (1977). Psychophysiologic aspects of cancer. *Cancer*, **39**, 413–419.

Morgan, D. H. (1971). Neuropsychiatric problems of cardiac surgery. *Journal of Psychosomatic Research*, **15**, 41–52.

Morris, T., Greer, S., Pettingale, K. W., and Watson, M. (1981). Patterns of expression of anger and their psychological correlates in women with breast cancer. *Journal of Psychosomatic Research*, **25**, 111–117.

Muslin, H. L., Gyarfas, K., and Pieper, W. J. (1966). Separation experience and cancer of the breast. *Annals of the New York Academy of Science*, **125**, 802–806.

Noble, R. L., and Hoover, L. (1975). A classification of transplantable tumours in Nb rats controlled by oestrogen from dormancy to autonomy. *Cancer Research*, **35**, 2935–2944.

Noel, G. L., Suh, S. K., Stone, J. G., and Frantz, A. G. (1972). Human prolactin and growth hormone release during surgery and other conditions of stress. *Journal of Clinical Endocrinology*, **35**, 840–846.

Ogilvie, H. (1957). The human heritage. *Lancet*, **ii**, 42–49.

Palmblad, J. (1981). Stress and immunologica competence: studies in man. In R. Ader (ed.), *Psychoneuroimmunology*. New York: Academic Press, pp. 229–257.

Parkes, C. M., Benjamin, B., and Fitzgerald, R. G. (1969). Broken heart: a statistical survey of increased mortality among widowers. *British Medical Journal*, **1**, 740–748.

Peters, L. J., and Kelly, H. (1977). The influence of stress and stress hormones on the transplantability of a murine tumor. *Cancer*, **39**, 1482–1485.

Peters, L. J., and Mason, K. A. (1979). Influence of stress on experimental cancer. In B. A. Stoll (ed.), *Mind and Cancer Prognosis*. Chichester: John Wiley, pp. 103–126.

Pettingale, K. W., Greer, S., and Tee, D. E. H. (1977). Serum IgA and emotional expression in breast cancer patients. *Journal of Psychosomatic Research*, **21**, 395–404.

Pettingale, K. W., Philalithis, A., Tee, D. E. H., and Greer, S. (1981). Biological correlates of psychological responses to breast cancer. *Journal of Psychosomatic Research*, **25**, 453–458.

Pierce, G. B., and Cox, W. F., Jr (1978). Neoplasms as caricatures of tissue renewal. In G. F. Saunders (ed.), *Cell Differentiation and Neoplasia*. New York: Raven Press, pp. 57–66.

Rao, L. G. S., and Hewit, M. L. (1970). Prognostic significance of a steroid discriminant function in patients with inoperable lung cancer. *Lancet*, **ii**, 1063–1069.

Rasmussen, A. F. (1969). Emotions and immunity. *Annals of the New York Academy of Science*, **164**, 458–461.

Reznikoff, M. (1955). Psychological factors in breast cancer. *Psychosomatic Medicine*, **17**, 96–108.

Riley, V. (1975). Mouse mammary tumours. Alteration of incidence as apparent function of stress. *Science*, **189**, 465–467.

Rogentine, G. N., Van Kammen, D. P., Fox, B. H., Docherty, J. P., Rosenblatt, J. E., Boyd, S. C., and Bunney, W. E. (1979). Psychological factors in the prognosis of malignant melanoma: a prospective study. *Psychosomatic Medicine*, **41**, 647–655.

Rubin, R. Y., Miller, R. G., Clark, B. R., Poland, R. E., and Arthur, R. J. (1970). The stress of aircraft carrier landings. *Psychosomatic Medicine*, **32**, 589–597.

Sachar, E. J., Hellman, L., Roffwarg, H. P., Halpern, F. S., Fukushima, D. K., Gallagher, T. F. (1973). Disrupted 24 hour pattern of cortisol secretion in psychotic depression. *Archives of Psychiatry*, **28**, 19–24.

Saez, S. (1971). Adrenal function in cancer: relation to the evolution. *European Journal of Cancer*, **7**, 381–387.

Saez, S. (1974). Corticotrophin secretion in breast cancer. In B. A. Stoll (ed.), *Mammary Cancer and Neuroendocrine Therapy*. London: Butterworths, pp. 101–122.

Schleifer, S. J., Keller, S. E., Camerino, M., Thornton, J. C., and Stein, M. (1983). Suppression of lymphocyte stimulation following bereavement. *Journal of the American Medical Association*, **250**, 374–377.

Schlesser, M. A., Winskur, G., Sherman, B. M. (1979). Genetic subtypes of unipolar primary depressive illness distinguished by hypothalamic pituitary adrenal axis activity. *Lancet*, **i**, 739–741.

Schonfield, J. (1975). Psychological and life experience differences between Israeli women with benign and cancerous breast lesions. *Journal of Psychosomatic Research*, **19**, 229–234.

Schweppe, J. S., Jungman, R. A., Lewin, I. (1967). Urine steroid excretion in postmenopausal cancer of the breast. *Cancer*, **20**, 155–163.

Scurry, M. I., and Levin, E. M. (1978). Psychosocial factors related to the incidence of cancer. *International Journal of Psychiatry in Medicine*, **9**, 159–177.

Shekelle, R. B., Raynor, W. J., Ostfeld, A. M., Garron, D. C., Bieliauskas, L. A., Liu, S. C., Maliza, C., and Ogelsby, P. (1981). Psychological depression and 17 year risk of death from cancer. *Psychosomatic Medicine*, **43**, 117–125.

Shrite, M. L. (1962). Towards identification of a psychological variable in host resistance to cancer. *Psychosomatic Medicine*, **24**, 390–399.

Sklar, L. S., and Anisman, H. (1981). Stress and cancer. *Psychological Bulletin*, **89**, 269–406.

Snell, L., and Graham, S. (1971). Social trauma as related to cancer of the breast. *British Journal of Cancer*, **25**, 721–734.

Solomon, G. F., Amkraut, A. A., and Rubin, R. T. (1979). Stress and psycho-immunological response. In B. A. Stoll (ed.), *Mind and Cancer Prognosis*. Chichester: John Wiley, pp. 73–84.

Sporn, M. B., and Todaro, G. J. (1980). Autocrine secretion and malignant transformation of cells. *New England Journal of Medicine*, **303**, 878–880.

Stavraky, K. M., Buck, C. N., Lott, J. S., and Worklin, J. M. (1968). Psychological factors in the outcome of human cancer. *Journal of Psychosomatic Research*, **12**, 251–259.

Steel, G. G. (1967). Cell loss as a factor in the growth rate of human tumours. *European Journal of Cancer*, **3**, 381–388.

Stein, M., Keller, S., and Schleifer, S. (1979). Role of the hypothalamus in mediating stress effects on the immune system. In B. A. Stoll (ed.), *Mind and Cancer Prognosis*. Chichester: John Wiley, pp. 85–102.

Stein, M., Schiavi, R. C., and Camarino, M. S. (1976). Influence of brain and behaviour on the immune system. *Science*, **191**, 435–437.

Stoll, B. A. (1976a). Psychosomatic factors and tumour growth. In B. A. Stoll (ed.), *Risk Factors in Breast Cancer*. London: Heinemann Medical, pp. 193–206.

Stoll, B. A. (1976b). Effect of age on growth pattern. In B. A. Stoll (ed.), *Risk Factors in Breast Cancer*. London: Heinemann Medical, pp. 129–48.

Stoll, B. A. (1979). Restraint of growth and spontaneous regression of cancer. In B. A. Stoll (ed.), *Mind and Cancer Prognosis*. Chichester: John Wiley, pp. 19–30.

Stoll, B. A. (1981). Neuro- and psychoendocrine factors in cancer growth. In B. A. Stoll (ed.), *Hormonal Management of Endocrine-related Cancer*. London: Lloyd-Luke, pp. 194–204.

Stoll, B. A. (1982). Introductory discussion. In B. A. Stoll (ed.), *Prolonged Arrest of Cancer*. Chichester: John Wiley, pp. 1–8.

Taggart, P., Parkinson, P., and Carruthers, M. (1972). Cardiac responses to thermal physical and emotional stress. *British Medical Journal*, **3**, 71–76.

Tarlou, M., and Smallheiser, I. (1951). Personality patterns in patients with malignant tumours of breast and cervix. *Psychosomatic Medicine*, **13**, 117–121.

Thomas, C. B., Duszynski, K. R., and Schaffer, J. W. (1979). Family attitudes reported in youth as potential predictors of cancer. *Psychosomatic Medicine*, **41**, 287–302.

Tisdale, M. J. (1982). Prospects for cancer arrest by growth modulators. In B. A. Stoll (ed.), *Prolonged Arrest of Cancer*. Chichester: John Wiley, pp. 311–326.

Todaro, G. J., Marquardt, H., Twardzik, D. R., and Delanco, J. E. (1982). Transforming growth factors produced by tumour cells. In A. H. Owens, D. S. Coffey and S. B. Baylin (eds), *Tumor Cell Heterogeneity: Origins and Implications*. New York: Academic Press, pp. 205–223.

Van den Brenk, H. A. S., Stone, M. G., Kelly, H., and Sharpington, C. (1976). Lowering of innate resistance to the growth of blood-borne cancer cells in states of topical and systemic stress. *British Journal of Cancer*, **33**, 68–85.

Visintainer, M. A., Seligman, M. E. P., and Volpicelli, J. (1983). Helplessness, chronic stress and tumour development. *Psychosomatic Medicine*, **45**, 75–76.

Watson, C. G., and Schuld, D. (1977). Psychosomatic factors in the etiology of neoplasms. *Journal of Consulting and Clinical Psychology*, **45**, 455–461.

Weisman, A. D. (1976). Coping behaviour and suicide in cancer. In J. W. Cullen, B. H. Fox and R. N. Ison (eds), *Cancer, the Behavioural Dimensions*. New York: Raven Press, pp. 331–341.

Willis, R. A. (1973). *Spread of Tumours in the Human Body*. London: Butterworths.

Wyle, F. A., and Kent, J. R. (1977). Immunosuppression by sex steroid hormones. *Clinical Experimental Immunology*, **27**, 407–411.

SECTION 8

Terminal Care

The Psychosomatic Approach: Contemporary Practice
  of Whole-person Care
Edited by M. J. Christie and P. G. Mellett
© 1986 John Wiley & Sons Ltd

19

A PHILOSOPHY OF TERMINAL CARE

CICELY SAUNDERS
St Christopher's Hospice, London, UK

INTRODUCTION

To cure sometimes, to relieve often, to comfort always.

This quotation, known in Latin, French and English, is difficult to attribute as it appears to be 'one of those sayings which have, so to speak, evolved with the passage of time' (Payne, 1967). Fox referred to it in a Harveian oration as 'the classical summary of the doctor's vocation' (Fox, 1965) and it may certainly be used to summarize the demands of hospice medicine or terminal care. At first glance, perhaps, it may be thought that the commitment of hospice medicine refers to the last phase only, but a closer look at the treatment needed by patients whose disease has escaped cure or further palliation shows that this may not necessarily be so. Once terminal distress is carefully analysed, indeed 'diagnosed' as a disease of its own, there will be found elements that can be cured and others that can be relieved. There have been many advances in the past two decades that have moved this branch of medicine away from some kind of soft option labelled 'care' into the field of respected therapeutics, as deserving of the title 'treatment' as the earlier phases of the doctor's concern for his patient.

The aim of terminal care at this stage is no longer the abolition of the patient's disease but the opportunity for living to his fullest potential in physical ease and activity and in relationships with his family and others around him. The achievement will be the patient's own. The need for comfort for both him and his family and, indeed, the staff involved, will continue till his death and after.

With this in mind, we turn to definitions for a *philosophy* of terminal care, using two given in *The Shorter Oxford English Dictionary*: 'that department of knowledge or study which deals with ultimate reality' and 'the study of the general principles of some particular branch of knowledge, experience, or activity'. Both definitions have been used to cover the substance of this chapter in the belief that, as in any field of care, we will only respond fully to the second if we give heed to the first. Here we are concerned with the nature of man, with living and dying, and with the whole man—body, mind and spirit—part of some family unit, with emotional and social as well as

427

physical and practical needs: it is for us to tackle these with maximum competence.

WHEREVER PATIENTS HAPPEN TO BE DYING

Terminal care does not have to be carried out in a geographically separate unit, though there are some patients and families who need the expertise and the space they should find there. Some separate hospices will be needed for patients with intractable problems and for research and teaching in terminal care, but most patients will continue to die in general hospitals, cancer or geriatric centres or in their own homes; the staff they will find there should be learning how to meet their needs.

The following account of the essential components of terminal care is the fruit of years of working in different units and of many discussions of the principles underlying standards for such care (Wald, 1979). Above all, it is the outcome of the good fortune which gave me the opportunity of listening to patients and their families during the 35 years since a dying patient told me that he wanted 'what is in your mind and in your heart'.

Over the past two decades increasing attention has been given to the needs of dying patients and their families, and the hospice movement has developed in diverse ways (Saunders, Summers and Teller, 1981). When St Christopher's Hospice opened in 1967 as the first research and teaching hospice its main aim was that tested knowledge should flow back into all branches of the National Health Service, as well as to the older homes and hospices to which it owed so great a debt. That there should now be specialist wards in general hospitals, and home and hospital teams working in consultation with the patients' own doctors, are in many ways more important developments than the growth of special units. Most important of all has been the general change of attitude to a more analytical and positive approach to the needs of a dying patient and his family. Anecdotal evidence is replaced increasingly by objective data as the scientific foundations of this branch of medicine are laid. The essentials of good terminal management have been clarified and are now being widely discussed.

ESSENTIAL ELEMENTS IN THE MANAGEMENT OF TERMINAL MALIGNANT DISEASE

Maximizing potential

A patient should be enabled to live until he dies, at his own maximum potential, performing to the limits of his physical activity and mental capacity, with control and independence wherever possible. He should be recognized as the unique person he is and helped to live as part of his family and in other relationships with some awareness from those around of his own hopes and expectations and of what has deepest meaning for him.

This demands full consideration both of the nature of his suffering and of the appropriateness of various possible treatments and settings in his particular circumstances. Alertness to any remission of his disease should accompany the effective control of all the manifestations of an inexorable advance.

Even in the terminal stages of disease it can be true that there is potential for new achievements or the resolution of long-standing problems.

Place of choice

Patients should end their lives in the place most appropriate to them and their families and where possible have choices in the matter. This does not necessarily mean total 'open awareness' on the part of the patient, but some insight into the serious nature of the condition will help facilitate realistic decisions. Continuity of care can be maintained in the midst of change if there is effective communication and easy movement between different settings. Many will be cared for in their own homes, others in the hospital with staff who have carried out previous treatments, while some will need the smaller community of the separate hospice unit. These, increasingly used as 'tertiary referral centres', act as a *complementary* local service for particularly complex physical and social situations.

Alternatives need to be planned ahead and the patient and his family fully involved, visits arranged and flexibility maintained. A few days or even hours at home may alternate with time in institutional settings, or the primary health care team may manage all needs alone or with the support of a team or a specialist nurse.

The patient and family as the unit of care

When a person is dying his family find themselves in a state of crisis, with the joys and regrets of the past, the demands of the present and the fears of the future all brought into stark focus (Earnshaw-Smith, 1981). Help may be needed to deal with guilt, depression and family discord. Emotions are intensified, and although they may seem irrational there is also the possibility of resolving old problems and finding reconciliations that greatly strengthen the family group.

If this time is to be fully used there needs to be some degree of shared awareness of the true situation. Truth needs to be available (though not pressured) so that the family can travel together. Choices presuppose some degree of 'informed consent' and, in general, sharing is more creative than deception. The often surprising potential for personal and family growth at this stage is one of the strongest objections most hospice workers feel for the legalization of a deliberately hastened death.

Families should have every available option open to their choice and expect recognition of their cultural and individual needs. Once this has become part of the ethos of a ward it appears to be largely self-perpetuating and emphasizes the importance of including the family in the care of any seriously ill person. Not everyone will have the time or the understanding to embark on long family discussions, but everyone can recognize the family by name, appreciate something of their distress and recognize when they should refer the family to others, such as the social worker or the chaplain. They must be accepted as an integral part of the team caring for the patient and we should aim to give the maximum of privacy to those who need it for peace and for the expressions of tenderness which are inhibited in a general ward.

Bereavement follow-up

Many hospitals make special arrangements for bereaved families who come to collect certificates and property, but our work should not end there. The family has to recover. A bereavement follow-up service will identify and support those in special need, working in cooperation with the family doctor and any local services which can be involved. Many doctors give such support as part of their service to the families they have known over the years. Some of the bereaved are not so fortunate and some extra follow-up may be needed to ease the tragedy and long morbidity of some bereavements. Social workers and chaplains have initiated such work from general hospitals; some hospice groups work together with Cruse (the Organization for Widows and their Children), while others have set up their own team to meet with those in need, with a leader to train and support the visitors themselves. There is no doubt that many families suffer from the sudden break from the people who have cared for the patient and have perhaps for a long time been a great part of their lives. In a small unit families will be recognized as they enter the door and reception staff as well as ward nurses have a special role in this part of care for the bereaved. An informal welcome may be all that is needed and many families will return spontaneously. Much still needs to be learned and tested in this area of terminal care.

Competent symptom control

The patient and his family will not use the time left to them to the full unless there is good control of pain and all the other symptoms that may arise. All doctors and nurses should be aware of the developments in these skills and special units have a responsibility to initiate research and disseminate such knowledge. Terminal pain is so different in character and meaning from much of the pain met in a teaching hospital that the methods of giving relief and the standards of comfort and alertness which should be expected are sometimes difficult to establish in a general ward. Nevertheless, it is not impossible and this has been demonstrated through the initiative of both doctors and nurses. If patients are to have adequate treatment for the many symptoms that often accompany this usually generalized disease it must be seen as relevant and possible everywhere. Once good symptom control is achieved it is then easier to become aware of the mental and social aspects of suffering. If pain and other distress are not controlled, neither the patient nor the family will be able to use the time remaining effectively.

Constantly reviewed analysis and assessment are aimed no longer at the diagnosis and treatment of the underlying condition but at the details of the pathological processes of a now incurable disease. Once the 'why' of a symptom is understood the 'how' of relieving it becomes more rational and effective and relates better to the approach and training of acute medicine.

This does not end until concern for the process of dying itself helps to ease such problems as the confusion or restlessness that may arise during the last 48 hours or so. *How* a patient dies remains in the memories of the family and of the other patients around who may be facing their own deaths.

An experienced clinical team

The team or unit for terminal care must carry out its practice in such a way as to earn the respect and cooperation of the doctors who refer their patients. Both there and where the patient remains under his usual clinicians, a multidisciplinary medical approach is as important in the later stages of cancer management, for instance, as in the earlier phases of the disease. Consultation will often be needed between physician, surgeon, radiotherapist, chemotherapist and sometimes the psychiatrist or the clinician who runs the local pain clinic. It is no longer adequate medicine to try to cope alone with difficult decisions in terminal cancer management, even though the needs of many patients have been and still will be dealt with successfully by their own family doctors single-handed.

A group of consultants in a unit or team may act merely as a resource while the patient remains in the care of his family doctor or of the clinicians who were involved with his initial treatment. A team may, however, take over his treatment completely, particularly if there is some special need such as intractable physical distress or complex family problems. There need be no feeling of rejection if transfer to a special ward or hospice is carefully discussed and planned, but whenever the original doctor keeps in touch his visits are likely to have a special place in maintaining a patient's morale.

Supportive team nursing

Henderson and Nite (1978) describe the unique function of nurses as being 'to help people, sick or well, in the performance of those activities contributing to health or its recovery (or to a peaceful death) that they would perform unaided if they had the necessary strength, will or knowledge. It is likewise the function of nurses to help people gain independence as rapidly as possible'.

The particular character of the nursing of dying patients illustrates this definition. It includes the time given to do things at the patient's pace, to listen to the fears that are often revealed first to the helper in an intimate situation, to offer tenderness, understanding and humour alongside practical deftness and to greet and include the family both as cared for and as carers.

A nursing plan or nursing process helps to define appropriate goals, to give the patient a guiding voice and also to maintain excellence in symptom control to the end. Confident leadership by the ward sister or nursing officer in the community helps to support and integrate a team approach, which is the best way to sustain this demanding branch of nursing and to emphasize its rewards.

An interprofessional team

This is not the field for total individual involvement, which can be most unhelpful for both patient and staff member. It takes time to build a satisfactory way of working together but such interprofessional teams are to be found in many specialized units—for example, intensive care and renal dialysis. They are particularly needed by those who are grappling with emotional as well as with practical demands. Psychiatrists and social workers have frequently been involved as support. Volunteers may have an important role both within an institution and at home but they must be sensitively selected, and receive training and support.

Such a team, together with all its professional members, should be seen to include the ward orderlies, domestics and porters, often the people to whom hospital patients turn most easily. Their support should not be underestimated or ignored. It is important that as many different members as possible meet for frequent discussion; referral notes are not enough. Though the clinician does not abrogate his clinical responsibility, each member should be ready to assume a degree of leadership concerning an individual patient or family.

A home care programme

Any programme or plan for home care must be developed according to local circumstances and be integrated with the family practices of the area and any local beds that may be available. Patients can then be admitted at the moment of their choice and a time of accurately defined medical need; they will also be able to move easily to and from the hospital or hospice wards for periods varying from days to weeks or months as short-term improvements are fully exploited in the place most suited to them. Skilled support and confidence in their potential may enable a family to keep a patient at home, often confounding all predictions. Where patients have access to adequate nursing, a 24-hour call service and other support which may well include volunteers as well as good neighbours, home is likely to remain their choice. Even so, some people who have said they would like to die in their own homes need inpatient care, if only for the last few days. Some families find much greater relief and unity in a professional milieu in the last days and others realize that they cannot face the thought of death at home after all. Both possibilities should be open to them.

Methodical recording and analysis

Effective recording makes possible the evaluation and monitoring of clinical experience and the establishment of soundly based practice. Research into the common clinical syndromes, into pharmacology and therapeutics and in psychosocial studies is needed to define and refine our practice and our attitudes. Much can also be learned and passed on in carefully recorded case studies.

Considerable progress has been made, both in the direct hospice approach (Walsh, 1983) and in related fields (Wall and Melzack, 1984), but the scientific foundations of this particular field are only now being laid. Conferences for those who are active in the work further the exchange of views on practical problems at local, national and international levels and give encouragement to those who feel that they are battling against much inertia or opposition and who need to keep alert their spirit of inquiry. This is a challenge to those who feel that 'tender, loving care' is all that is needed. Nothing can take its place, but terminal care of the 1980s developed from, and should not be the same as that of, the 1890s or even the 1960s. 'Efficient loving care' is our aim and every resource of clinical and social medicine has to be exploited.

Teaching in all aspects of terminal care

Teaching in this field is much in demand by students and graduates of all the disciplines concerned as it has only a meagre place—if any—in general curricula. The subject is tackled in conferences and seminars, in workshops, lectures and ward rounds and as in-service experience, both within the special units and in outside visits made by members of staff. We find that any lectures and ward rounds of this kind are likely to be overcrowded. However (in spite of encouraging comeback, often years later, from those who have attended only one session), there should be reinforcement of such teaching for medical, nursing and other students in their own hospital wards. One of many groups of medical students who visited St Christopher's Hospice at their own request wrote afterwards: 'It was a relief to be able to discuss freely a subject which is usually actively avoided in a large teaching hospital.' Though much of the future development must be more closely integrated with general teaching centres, the special units are likely to maintain their role of stimulating initial interest and organizing courses for those who will in their turn be concentrating on this field. This is no longer a discipline in which no special past experience is required.

Imaginative use of the space availalbe

Dying patients may be nursed in a separate unit or in a ward or a section of a ward in a general hospital, but most patients will and should return to their own hospitals, to a general ward. Wherever it may be, there should be space for families and opportunities for patients to move around; room for staff to work easily and to relax and 'transition spaces' for the anxious to take time to relax or to brace themselves for a meeting. Emphasis should be given to the need for spaces for private talk; these must be found. Good public transport and a feeling of openness to the world outside are chief among the needs of any unit for terminal and long-term care. Some of us have been fortunate enough to plan for the purpose, others have learned to adapt whatever they could find, and successful practice has often arisen from the imaginative use of structural peculiarities.

The proportion of single rooms to bays or wards dictates the way a ward team handles the patient's last hours and the needs of his family at that time. Some feel strongly that no patient should be expected to witness the death of another person in the same room or bay. Others, mainly those with fairly generous space and windows, find that this can usually be managed so that the reaction of most patients and their families is almost entirely positive. The peaceful death of a patient who shows no distress in breathing or in any other way, who is not left alone and, above all, who is not hidden behind screens and curtains, enables other patients to feel more confident about their own end. A distressing death would, indeed, have the opposite effect but those who are expert in such care should not let this occur. Patients and families admitted within a very short time of death will usually require single rooms. Longer stay patients play a special role in the life of a ward as part of its hospitality and support although, like the staff, they will need a holiday from it at times.

Families in the bays talk with each other and with other patients, and most hospices find it is rare for them to return for the practical business on the day following bereavement without going to see those they have known to give thanks for the friendship that has comforted them all. This may happen, too, in a general ward.

Supportive administration

Efficiency is very comforting and competence in administrative detail gives security to patients, families and staff. It eases the liaison with outside contacts that is essential for the small, specialized unit and supports those who are managing such work among other pressures.

All members of staff will at times become drained by the work of the wards and in other contacts with the families of patients. Informal safety valves should arise spontaneously according to local personalities and surroundings, but care must be taken to see that not only regular off-duty but study leaves and extra time off are arranged before a crisis is reached. Staff members must be prevented from investing all their emotional commitment in their work and be given a chance to talk with those who are more detached from it, who can emphasize realistic goals and appropriate successes.

The search for meaning

The work will at times cause pain and bewilderment to all members of the staff. If they do not have the opportunity of sharing their strain and questions they are likely to leave this field or find a method of hiding behind a professional mask. Those who commit themselves to remaining near the suffering of dependence and parting find they are impelled to develop a basic philosophy, part individual and part corporate. This grows out of the work undertaken together as members find that they each have to search, often painfully, for some meaning in the most adverse circumstances and gain enough freedom from their own anxieties to listen to another's questions and distress.

Most of the early homes and hospices were Christian foundations, their members believing that if they continued faithfully with the work to which they felt called, help would reach their patients from God. Some of the traditional ways of expressing this faith are being interpreted afresh today, and there are also many people entering this field who have still to consider their own religious or philosophical commitment. This is not an optional extra; it has a fundamental bearing on the way the work is done and everyone meeting these patients and their families needs to have some awareness of this dimension. A search for truth as we continually endeavour to keep our minds open to our own testing experiences will help to sustain a climate in which others find hope and heart to do the same.

'Finally, the physician should bear in mind that he himself is not exempt from the common lot, but subject to the same laws of mortality and disease as others, and he will care for the sick with more diligence and tenderness if he remembers that he himself is their fellow sufferer' (Sydenham, 1666).

REFERENCES

Earnshaw-Smith, E. (1981). Dealing with dying patients and their relatives. *British Medical Journal*, **282**, 1779.

Fox, Sir Theodore (1965). Purposes of medicine. *Lancet*, **ii**, 801–805.

Henderson, V., and Nite, G. (1978). *Principles and Practice of Nursing*, 6th edn. New York: Macmillan.

Payne, L. M. (1967). An elusive quotation. 'Guérir quelquefois, soulager souvent, consoler toujours.' *British Medical Journal*, **4**, 47–48.

Saunders, C. M., Summers, D. H., and Teller, N. (eds) (1981). *Hospice: The Living Idea*. London: Edward Arnold.

Sydenham, T. (1666). *Methodus curandi febres*. London.

Wald, F. (1979). Report of international work groups in death, dying and bereavement: proposed standards for terminal care. *Nursing Times*, **75**, 69.

Wall, P. D., and Melzack, R. (eds) (1984). *Textbook of Pain*. London: Churchill Livingstone.

Walsh, T. D. (1983). Terminal care. Pain relief in cancer. *Medicine in Practice*, **1**(27), 684–691.

INDEX